GREAT GF

Glass 1 : 1.618 full

What are those blue remembered hills,
What spires, what farms are those?

That is the land of lost content
I see it shining plain
The happy highways where I went
And cannot come again

A. E. Housman, *A Shropshire Lad* (1896)

I know, I know,
To begin a memoir with these
- **lines** -
is like beginning a thriller with
It was a dark and stormy night...

but *A Shropshire Lad*
(Pete Postlethwaite's definitive 1996 recording)
contributes some of my favourite
- **tracks** -
for tormenting my family on car journeys

- **and** -
the quote explains the
- **happy highways** --
in the subtitle of this book,
for those to whom it suggests
some drug-fuelled confessional.

We might as well get it out of the way before we start,
I have never drunk a glass of alcohol, smoked a cigarette or
taken any drugs. So you won't find drug tales in this book.

But you will find sex, and you will find rock & roll.

GREAT GREAT GREAT

Lines, Tracks and Happy Highways
to
Knebworth House

First published in 2022
by The 39 Production Company Ltd.
www.the39.com
© The 39 Production Company Ltd. 2022

ISBN 978-0-9539649-7-0

Print Production by Jarrold Publishing
www.jarrold-publishing.co.uk

Printed by Cambrian Printers
www.cambrian-printers.co.uk

* * * * *

For more information on Knebworth House
visit www.knebworthhouse.com
Contact the Knebworth House Archivist
at info@knebworthhouse.com

This book is dedicated to my thumbs

out of which I've chewed
every idea I've ever had

and to Martha

who loves me
despite my thumbs

and the ideas

CONTENTS

Most of what follows is true
William Goldman, *Butch Cassidy and The Sundance Kid* (1969)

ACRONYMS

M.O.W.F.I.T.
William Goldman, *Butch Cassidy and The Sundance Kid* (1969)

Allowing for you being OK (au-fait) with UK, USA, EU, P (as in page), BBC, HBO, TV, MGM, VHS, VCR, DVD, DJ, LP, EP, BP (as in petrol), AKA...&, ie, eg, cf, etc.

P. I. O. A. T.	Put It On A Tripod!
S.A.T.T.	Sitting At Tables Talking
S.N.T.	Show Not Tell
N.I.E.	Not Interesting Enough
C.J.D.	Mad Cow Disease
C.C.D.	My A-Level Results
L.D.O.B.	Life-Defining Obituary Byline
M.O.W.L.	More Of Which Later (U.U.)
U.U.	Used Ubiquitously
T.B.E.	To Be Explained
M.O.R.	Middle Of The Road (no 'T'?)

N.I.E.
NOT INTERESTING ENOUGH

(a few for non-UK readers:)

M.P.	Member Of Parliament (no 'O'?)
B.N.P.	British National Party (just no)
U.K.I.P	UK Independence Party (ditto)
P.M.	Prime Minister
C.R.B.C.	Criminal Records Bureau Check
S.A.G.	Safety Advisory Group
B.F.F.	Best Friends Forever
LAX	Los Angeles Airport
K.I.S.	Keep It Simple

T.O.T.P.S.G.O.S.	Top of the Poppers Sing Gilbert O'Sullivan
A.D.R.	Additional Dialogue Recording
C.G.I.	Computer Generated Imagery
H.T.M.L.	Hypertext Markup Language (any the wiser?)
U.S.P.	Unique Selling Point
T.M.I.	Too Much Information
A.O.B.	Annals of Bizarrity
T.L.D.R.	Too Long, Didn't Read
C.B.O.C.	Circumstances Beyond Our Control
T.T.T.T.	Typo Torment Th(r)ough Time
F.F.F.	Flashily Financially Fecund
A.P.I.T.S	A Place In The Sun
F.O.I.T.E.	Fuck Off, It's The End

Film titles are followed by date of release (if blessed to have one), not of production

INT. BANQUETING HALL, KNEBWORTH HOUSE - EVENING

SWOOSH! Curtains are thrown aside. A floppy-haired YOUNG MAN
sweeps into a beautiful panelled Jacobean Hall arms outstretched,

                YOUNG MAN
        Read the rede of this old roof tree!
        Here be trust safe, opinion free..

He twirls in his long frock coat, his hand directing a lightly
startled AUDIENCE at fine lettering around the high frieze..

                YOUNG MAN
        Worth in all, wit in some
        Laughter open, slander dumb
        Hearth where rooted friendships grow
        Safe as altar e'en to foe..

He spins to a stop in front of a flickering fulsome hearth fire,
his hands still spread wide, towards his Audience.

                YOUNG MAN
        Home where chivalry and grace
        Cradle a high-hearted race
        If thy sap in these may be
        Fear no winter old roof tree!
          (warm grin, he's
           done this before)
        ..words of welcome to Knebworth House
        written by the 19th Century author and
        politician, Edward Bulwer Lytton.
        My name is Henry Lytton Cobbold. I am
        Edward Bulwer Lytton's great-great-
        great-grandson - and it is my great-
        great-great-pleasure to welcome you
        today to our home..
                (MORE)

FOREWORD

I don't see why anything shouldn't be told through a love story
William Wyler, quoted by David Lean in 1984 (*David Lean: Interviews* 2009)

Always start a screenplay a third of the way down the page. That way, before your reader knows it, she is turning the page. Your story is already a page-turner.

Landscaping is important. Every page turn is a pause. Make those pauses count. Consider where the page break falls on every page.

Only put in your screenplay what is important to the narrative. If it's important that he has floppy hair, put it in. If it's not, leave it out.

Do pander to your actors and performers. They may not be 'young' - it's unlikely they'll be the age of your character - but no harm playing to vanity

A page of screenplay should represent a minute of screen time. Your lovers - for all good stories are driven by romance, whether between a man and his home, a man and his past, etc. - should embrace around Page 30 (metaphorically if needs be), make love around Page 60 (certainly metaphorically if a house), fall out around Page 70, and be reconcilled around Page 90. If you go over 100 pages you better be winning an Oscar, because ads are needed in that two hour slot to pay for it all...

Screenplays are about rules. Knowing them. Subverting them if you can get away with it. But writing to form.

The hardest thing in screenwriting is to convince your reader in the important belief that you are writing from your heart, when usually you are writing from your head. Because whatever you write in a screenplay, you can be sure, will be either discarded or abused - and that can only happen to your heart so many times.

This is not a screenplay. I've already convinced you to buy it. Or I've gifted it to you because you've paid for it in other ways. Therefore, in the words of the German pop song by Leslie Clio, *I couldn't care less (that's all I care about) *explicit version**. I don't have to follow any rules.

You'll still find my screenwriter training in these pages. But I shall be making the most of this rare opportunity to write exactly what I want to write, exactly how I want to write it. Unabashedly with my heart as well as my head. I'm looking forward to not following rules. As Jim Carey says in *The Cable Guy* (1996) - "You might want to buckle up, I've been drinking..."

...my imagination to the lees

my (young man's) fancy turned lightly

- and not always politely -

to the birds and the bees

(with - warning - the occasional photograph of these)

Henry Lytton Cobbold - Knebworth House 2020

My two favourite images of Knebworth House - above, 6th July 1847 by Frederick Hulme; below, one I took c.2000 - I know it's a March morning, as that's when the sun rises in the perfect place to light up the restored northern end and shadow the unrestored southern end

Great Great Great

*And thou wilt say, "My brother, hast thou found
Our home at last?"... Whilst I, in answer, sweet,
Shall heap my life's last booty at thy feet...*

*The spoils of time! The trophies of the world!
The keys of conquer'd towns, and captive kings,
And many a broken sword, and banner furl'd*

(Robert Bulwer Lytton - *For Ella*)

The Bulwer Lytton Family of Knebworth House

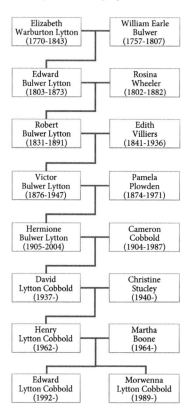

Left column: Custodial Line.   Right column: Spouse or Sibling

Great-Great-Great-Grandfather
Edward Bulwer Lytton

Great-Great-Grandfather
Robert Bulwer Lytton

I wonder. Did Edward Bulwer Lytton make a pact with the Devil?

By the time he was 50, my great-great-great-grandfather had achieved remarkable worldwide acclaim. For at least a decade - the 1830s, aged in his 30s - he was the best selling author in the English-speaking world. Beyond the English-speaking world, his books were translated into many languages. His novel *Pelham* became the very first paperback, his novel *Ernest Maltravers* was the very first Western novel to be translated into Japanese. As a politician his influence stretches from the Pacific coast in the west... to the Pacific coast in the east. He is responsible for the creation of both British Columbia in Canada and Queensland in Australia.

By the time he was 50, his son, Robert, my great-great-grandfather, attained the top job in the British Foreign Office, Viceroy of India. For Queen Victoria he administered a land of 250 million people, was made an Earl, and later, as Ambassador to France, was given the rare honour for an Englishman of a State Funeral in Paris.

By the time he was 50, his son, Victor, my great-grandfather, was Governor of Bengal and Acting Viceroy of India for a period. He went on to lead the Manchurian Commission for the newly formed United Nations, for which he earned the lasting thanks of the Chinese people.

By the time he was 50, his son-in-law, Cameron, my grandfather, attained the top job in the City of London, Governor of the Bank of England, a post he held for 12 years before being appointed Lord Chamberlain to Queen Elizabeth II and one of the last hereditary peers, Lord Cobbold.

I wonder. For Edward Bulwer Lytton's worldly success, and the worldly success of his progeny... Did the Devil seek something in return?

Well, consider this. Edward's eldest child died tragically aged 19 in mysterious

Great-Grandfather   Grandfather
Victor Bulwer Lytton   Cameron 'Kim' Cobbold

circumstances in a boarding house in London. His heir Robert's eldest child died tragically aged 6 of whooping cough in Vienna. His heir Victor's eldest child died tragically age 29 in an airplane accident in Hendon. His heir his daughter Hermione and her husband Cameron's eldest child died tragically aged 6 of peritonitis in 1937. Their heir David's eldest child is me.

I am the next heir in this line. The next eldest child. What chance for me?

Well, my father David's career was not, on the surface, the worldly success of his father's, grandfather's, great-grandfather's and great-great-grandfather's - but he too had success beyond the odds. He was British Petroleum's Treasurer during the North Sea oil boom of the 1980s, signing the largest UK cheque ever written, BP's quarterly tax return for 1984 of £684,149,248. He also secured the future of one of England's best loved historic houses. Without the energy and commitment that he and his wife Chryssie devoted to Knebworth House, this unique national treasure would likely have gone the way of the majority of England's historic houses in the 20th Century, a bitter time of their disassembly and destruction.

So will I die young? By today's terms it is possible. I am, as I write this, 55. For another 15 years or so, should it happen, it will be called 'young'. But it is not young. By any reckoning it is well over 'halfway to heaven'.

So is the Devil's account settled? Is a curse broken?

This summer my mother tells me a story that is not written in her memoir. Her delightful and candid 1985 *Board Meetings In The Bath* was written whilst her parents - and my father's parents - were still alive. When asked why the four-letter words are asterisked out in the opening chapters of the book, but not later in the book, she would say, "My mother will never get beyond the first few chapters".

Great Great Great Parents
David & Chryssie Lytton Cobbold

Great Great Great House
with Henry Lytton Cobbold

My mother tells me I was not my parents' eldest child. Also asterisked out of the beginning of her book was that she had conceived a child before me that did not live, and that she and my father had also had their measure of distress and grief over a lost first child. It turns out I was actually their second.

So maybe that's why the Devil's permitted me to make it to my mid 50s?

I now risk freaking out my eldest child. My daughter was pleased to make it through her 27th year, the year I write this - a year that is notorious for finishing off rock stars. She is a rock star. But not in the literal sense. Does she stand a better chance because she is not, literally, a rock star?

I have the following positive thoughts for her.

Firstly, unlike my father's fathers', my career has been decidedly undistinguished. Not uninteresting. The tales in this book are worth a Sunday afternoon of your time. But the Devil has been frustrating my career consistently, since its beginnings. So Bulwer Lytton's deal with the Devil, if there was one, should be off.

Morwenna Gray

August 16, 1989   6 pounds, 9½ ounces
Martha and Henry Lytton Cobbold

Then there was a touch of magic at my daughter's birth. She was born - at 8.48pm Pacific Coast Time, 16th August 1989 - in the few moments of a lunar eclipse. Just as the moon was hidden, and had lost its spell over the earth. When both sides of the moon were dark.

I trust the spell is broken. I trust the contract has expired. But as I wrote in my last book - the 1000-page life story of the first of the Bulwer Lytton family's lost eldest children, Emily - the measure of a life is not its length.

Nor is it "The trophies of a world! The keys of conquer'd towns, and captive kings, And many a broken sword, and banner furl'd", as Emily's brother Robert imagines laying at his lost sister's feet, when he finds her, wherever she has gone.

We are, in the end, all of us boiled down to a paragraph of obituary, a line in a history book or an entry in a census. Edward Bulwer Lytton is barely remembered today. There have been four other Earls of Lytton, and an hereditary peerage like 'Lord Cobbold', today, means no more than a fine tribute to a fine ancestor.

The best we can hope for, as far as posterity is concerned, is to be interesting. To be a tale worth telling to our great-great-great-grandchildren. To be an obituary byline that catches the eye over rye bread at breakfast. Whether our life has been a Comedy, a Tragedy, a Thriller, an

For Henry,

16th AUGUST 1989

THE MOON WAS HID BY MOTHER EARTH

I WATCHED IN AWE AND THOUGHT OF YOU

AT SUCH A TIME THE GODS GIVE BIRTH

I FELT THAT YOU WOULD KNOW THAT TOO.

AND SO IT WAS FAR FAR AWAY

FOR YOU A LIFE HAD JUST BEGUN

IN MARTHA'S ARMS YOUR BABY LAY

A GODDESS BORN TWIXT MOON AND SUN.

from his father

David

Adventure - whether an Epic, a Series, a Feature, or a Short - time dissolves, dries us all to dust like Osymandias. We survive only as long as the poets spin us in rhyme, or our legends enchant our great-great-greats at the fire grate.

My children and I have a collection of acronyms for judging movies. But the sentiments apply to most things, including life. I have a collection of these acronyms as ink stamps, given to me by my daughter for when I am being annoyingly judgemental. Stamps for the things that bug me in the films we watch, such as "P. I. O. A. T." - for "Put It On A Tripod!" - and "S. A. T. T." - for "Sitting At Tables Talking!"... but most damning of all, is "N. I. E." - for "Not Interesting Enough!"

With my "N.I.E." stamp at my side I have assembled the following stories. They are the life and work of Henry Lytton Cobbold before he turned 50. Unlike the tales of my grandfathers, these tales are not world-changing, nor for the history books. But they are, in turn, blessèdly light on tragedy. I'd rather it that way round.

My preferred measure of life is that when the tears are counted, no matter how many there've been - few or many - that more have been shed in joy than in grief. What collecting these stories tells me, is that by far the greater number of the tears of my life have been tears of love and tears of joy.

That's the lucky child I am.

CHAPTER ONE

Filmmaker

You are incredibly lucky if you know what you want to do in life. Incredibly lucky.
Andrew Lloyd Webber, *Live at The Other Palace: Andrew Lloyd Webber and Nile Rodgers (2019)*

I have known what I wanted to do since I was 8. I find it difficult to understand the many kids I meet who have no idea what they want to do when they leave school. Careers advice is easy. What would you do if you have a free Saturday afternoon? Figure that out, then look for a way to make a living doing it. If you like sitting on the sofa doing nothing, then figure out a way to make a living doing that.

I have known since I was 8 that I want to be a film maker. Since childhood I have been bewitched by the art that encompasses all arts. This life path was deter-

mined in the Palace & Broadway cinemas in Letchworth Garden City (above left) and the Regal cinema in Hitchin (above right). The same provincial dream temples that Michael Winner (L.D.O.B - "Irrepressible director of commercially successful films who had a notable second career as a writer, broadcaster and controversialist") formed a vision for his life 25 years earlier.

There were early promising signs that my career would mirror that of Michael Winner. As a schoolboy Michael Winner got an early journalist break from the future pre-eminent UK film critic Barry Norman at the *Kensington Times*. My first piece of journalism was interviewing Barry Norman for my school magazine. Michael Winner's first commercial film success was a 'nudie' picture, *Some Like it Cool* (1962), and he spent much of his early career challenging the British Board of Film Censors. My first commercial film success was writing a steamy US TV show, *Red Shoe Diaries* (1991), until I returned to the UK to spend five years challenging censorship in Britain. Michael Winner made a film (not a particularly good one) at Knebworth House - *The Big Sleep* (1978) with Robert Mitchum. I've made one or two films (not particularly good ones) at Knebworth House - *Harry The Horny Hypnotist* (1996) comes to mind... However, I accept, Michael Winner's childhood dreams at the Palace in Letchworth worked out better than mine. So far. So far. And does anyone under the age of 30 know who Michael Winner is?

To be a filmmaker continues, in my 50s, to be my career goal. I have done the training. Got the kit. Been out on the playing field earning a wage. Even been involved in some fancy assists. But the frank reality is that I haven't progressed from the lower leagues, and my score rate to date has not been notable. For most of the time I have had to have a second job. But thereagain... I've always had a second job.

I have also known since I was 8 that I would grow up with the responsibility of Knebworth House, a 500-year-old family home in Hertfordshire, England.

I was 8 in 1970. The year my parents accepted the challenge to fight to keep my family home a family home by making it a commercial enterprise. Knebworth House is not a typical family home. It's an Englishman's castle. One that actually looks like a castle. And nowadays castles-that-actually-look-like-castles are about welcoming people in, rather than keeping them out.

Wars had been good for castles for thousands of years, but in the 20th Century all that changed. Wars became bad for castles. Wars meant castles being trashed as training barracks or hospitals, eldest sons massacred at the front, their bereaved disabled by death duties. Most castles did not survive the 20th Century with either their roofs or their families intact.

Knebworth House could so easily have been lost to my family. My grandparents offered it as a campus for the University of Hertfordshire. My great-grandfather offered to give it to the National Trust. In both instances it was refused, its liabilities too great, its walls too crumbly, its roofs too porous.

My parents offered to make it their lives. To sell its stories in return for the chance to keep writing them. So, our extended throats were offered for the vampire bite of heritage preservation. Knebworth House would live on, but only if we devoted our lives and our children's lives to it. We pledged our Lytton blood to our Lytton home.

Consequently, when the call came - half way round the world, to Los Angeles, in 1993 - it didn't matter that the first feature film with my name as 'screenwriter' had just been produced, it didn't matter that I had been writing a successful American television series and my career had, at last, found its feet... I answered the call. I left balmy palmy Hollywood, and returned to the damp draughty Hertfordshire, where my coffin was waiting in the attic. I returned to that destiny.

And Knebworth has been a wonderful life. I would do it all again.

But, when I grow up, I still want to be a filmmaker.

My first produced feature film Lake Consequence was released in the U.K. in 1994. Martha and I went to see it at the old Empire Haymarket, in London, a cinema in which I had spent many Wednesday afternoons as a child

The decade of my birth, the 1960s, was a ripe time for children's movies. Disney discovered jazz. I loved *The Jungle Book* (1967). My grandmother Hermione had read us Rudyard Kipling. *The Just So Stories* and *The White Seal*. Kipling's parents had made the beautiful Lytton coat-of-arms banner that hung in our hall. Even my Dad, who was never especially enthused by the movies - although he liked *Monsieur Hulot's Holiday* (1953), and clearly had had a special moment once while watching *Hiroshima, Mon Amour* (1959) - adored Disney's *The Jungle Book*.

I must have seen it in the West End, as I have the movie brochure/program (in my collection of every single theatre program of every production I have ever seen. Ever. Yes, ever. I know. Obsession, you say. Archivism, I say. I live in a museum.) I own 'movie brochures' too for *The Jungle Book*, *Doctor Dolittle* (1967), *Chitty Chitty Bang Bang* (1968), *Bedknobs and Broomsticks* (1971)... I have a specific memory of the cinema where I first saw *Bedknobs and Broomsticks* - the massive Odeon Marble Arch. These enormous West End dream temples - the Odeon Leicester Square, The Leicester Square Theatre, the Empire Leicester Square - were places of pilgrimage.

But it was *Doctor Dolittle* that had the greatest impact. My father had read me the Hugh Lofting stories while taking his evening bath. My father's bathtime was our quality time. The smell of whisky reminds me of it today. He would have a nightly glass of whisky in the bath. It

When movies lived in palaces, they had printed programs

was the only time - except on holiday - his children had his undivided attention. It makes total sense to me that my parents later had their company director board meetings in the bath (the title my mother gave to her memoir). When we swapped houses, my father took his bathtub with him. I brought my bathtub back with me from California. It surprises me that this surprises people. I do some of my best work in my bath.

Doctor Dolittle remains in my top ten favourite films. And I have seen a lot of films. It is the root of much of my adult psyche. Its Victorianism, its Hippyism, its Vegetarianism, its Wanderlust, its Surrealism and Subversion... its beautiful songs, ingenious lyrics, its love songs to seals and all the fabulous faraway places I've yet to see. It tells me that you don't need to be able to sing to be a beautiful singer. That performing is just as valid as acting, and very often more fun to watch. And, perhaps most important of all, that one man's flop can be another man's masterpiece. I find it reassuring that critics don't like this film. It makes it all the more subversive. The only shame, in its lack of success, is that the soundtrack still remains in mono. You don't have to be able to sing to be a beautiful singer, but stereo does sound better than mono to creatures with two ears.

I became a vegetarian in 1993. For all the reasons. Ask me to name a few and I'll say, having not eaten much meat for the seven years I lived in California, I couldn't stomach the heavy Sunday roasts I returned to in England. I also came out in solidarity with my daughter, who at 3-years-old decided she did not want to eat animals. But all the other political, humanitarian and health reasons are pertinent too - like the fact that in the early 1990s diseased meat was turning people's brains to goo. My father made it into the House of Lords because a place amongst the 90 elected hereditary peers became available when a Baroness died of CJD. But, in retrospect, I believe the biggest influence has always been the subversive and animal-respecting message of *Doctor Dolittle*. Its message echoing G. B. Shaw's "Animals are my friends... and I don't eat my friends."

So it was not Godard or Truffaut, or Scorsese or Coppola, who made me want to be a filmmaker. It was, as a child, the magic of *Doctor Dolittle, The Jungle Book* and *Bedknobs and Broomsticks*. And, but for that one major Kantian diversion in 1993 (the call of duty, back to Knebworth House, not becoming a vegetarian) (although Immanuel Kant did say the poor treatment of animals degrades moral character) (enough Kant) an obsession with films and wanting to be a filmmaker has been at the root of pretty well all of my life decisions ever since.

Films determined the books I read at boarding school. I would read the novelisation of any film I was too young to be allowed to see. And I don't just mean *The Godfather, The Omen* and Harold Robbins - which every English Prep School boy in the early '70s read (specifically the 'horse in the bed' and the 'horsing in the bed' pages) - I mean every Hollywood movie. As a movie was released, and I was not allowed to go and see it, I would read it instead... *Westworld* (1973), *Freebie and The Bean* (1974), *Thunderbolt and Lightfoot* (1974), *S*P*Y*S* (1974), *The Taking of Pelham 123* (1974), *The Eiger Sanction* (1975)... if I couldn't see them, I would read them.

Films determined the tutor I chose at my senior school, Eton College - the maverick intellectual Christopher Dixon, who let you eat sweets in his 'O' Level classes and later committed suicide [his L.D.O.B.]. I chose Chris Dixon simply because he ran the school Film Society (okay & the sweets). He must have helped me organise my very first business

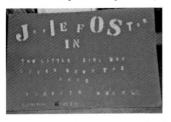

venture - an independent screening at school of *The Little Girl Who Lived Down The Lane* (1976) with Jodie Foster. I remember stencilling an announcement - yellow letters on a blue background, on a piece of plywood I sawed in the carpentry room. I can't remember if I made the money back. I was more interested in seeing the film. Whatever it took.

The only time I ever broke the rules at Eton College was to bunk off to the Granada cinema in Slough, which I did consistently. No pubs or smoking under the railway arches for me. Just films.

Films determined my choice of university. 1980 was the first year a British university offered a 'major' degree in Film Studies. My top three university choice was simple: Kent,

where I could do a 60% 'major' in Film; Warwick, where I could do 50% Film, with English; and East Anglia, where I could do a 40% 'minor' in Film. In that order. I didn't get the grades for Kent - they wanted BCC. I got CCD. Why, shall be discussed later. The D was History of Art. But Kent had just hired the high-profile Stephen Bayley (who went on to run the V&A) to up the profile of its under-subscribed History of Art Dept. Bizarrely, they asked if I would like to come and do History of Art instead of Film. I said, "yes" - and on my first day switched to Film. I did change my minor from Classical Civilisation to History of Art, by way of saying "thank you" to Kent's History of Art Dept., for reading my D, non-figuratively, as a B.

Films determined my first job. A dream first job. Production runner on a feature film called *The Shooting Party* (1985) - which, alleluia, had chosen to shoot almost exclusively at Knebworth House in the exact autumn of my departure from university in 1983. Films even started to determine my love life - an actress, another actress... until my subconscious reminded me that Knebworth House was more important, and my life partner would need to share that vocation. By the very greatest of good fortune I fell in love with someone who did. I made my one life decision that was not film related. The only decision in my life I absolutely had to get right. Life partner. Reader, I got it right.

But films determined our first married home. Los Angeles. Where I knew no one, but where I knew I had to be if I wanted to be a filmmaker. Films led to my apprenticeship with my self-adopted American parents, Patricia and Zalman King. Films lead to me learning a trade. Screenwriting. Screenwriting is now the one thing I can confidently say I do better than other people. I was trained in Hollywood by masters of the craft. Films led to about 30 Henry Cobbold screen and teleplays, a few produced episodes of a successful television series, a feature film... but, so far, I don't see the word 'filmmaker' making it into my L.D.O.B. Close, but no cigar.

This book gives the reasons why.

And when I've finished writing it, I shall return to pursuing the dream I have had since I was 8.

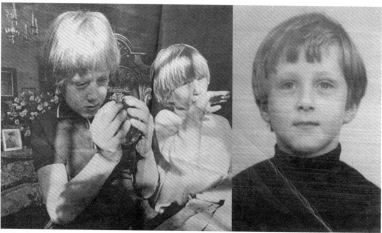

Peering into my great-great-great-grandfather's crystal ball (while my brother practices snogging)

CHAPTER TWO

Birth

FANNY
I've imagined you practically all over the world:
Paris, London, the Delaware Water Gap. Everyplace.
Everyplace except Henry Street. And here you are!

NICK
You've imagined me?

(Isobel Lennart - *Funny Girl,* 1968)

I was switched at birth with Emilio Estevez. He looks nothing like his father. And I look nothing like mine.

Emilio and I were both born in New York on 12th May 1962. Emilio, supposedly, in Queens and I, supposedly, in Brooklyn.

Thereagain, the baby said to be me did stand out in the Maternity Unit. The location - allegedly - on that hot early summer weekend, was Long Island College Hospital, Henry Street, Brooklyn. At 9lb 8oz, I was twice the size of the all the other babies and, unlike all the other babies, milky white.

"Everybody wanted me to go to Manhattan to have him, but I wouldn't" my Mum Chryssie tells in a 'Relative Values' feature she and I did for *The Sunday Times* magazine in 1986. "His birth was a nightmare. There were straps over my chest and my wrist and I couldn't move at all. They strapped my ankles up on two poles. I screamed and screamed and in the end they gave me an anaesthetic. I was covered in bruises and I didn't even know if I'd had a baby when I came to."

My grandfather Dennis Stucley sent a telegram from North Devon. The post boy announced it on the doorstep as a 'radiogram'. My grandmother Sheila (right) thought it was a record player and asked him to carry it upstairs. The telegram read, "Resist Disgusting Jewish Custom." No cause for alarm. My Dad had already come to blows with the doctor. "Just as well you are taking him back to England - with a name like Henry and uncircumcised, he stands no chance here."

Following other North Devon customs, I was immediately tightly swaddled in thick woollens. I cried and cried and went red in the face. My mother worried and took me back to the doctor. He asked if she was trying to cook me in the New York summer. I was stripped naked. Immediately, I was blissful. Ever since, I have been happier naked.

Alongside foreskins, breast feeding was also frowned on. My mother was determined. It wasn't easy. She boosted her strength and iron levels with pints of Guinness. To this day I have never drunk a glass of alcohol. I haven't needed to. Like Obelix, dipped in the cauldron as a baby, I have been slightly tipsy ever since.

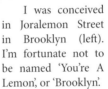

I was conceived in Joralemon Street in Brooklyn (left). I'm fortunate not to be named 'You're A Lemon', or 'Brooklyn'.

Henry has been fine. Although ubiquitous in my age group. There were three Henrys and a Harry in my immediate peer group at senior school. And l live with the reality that Henry is frequently prefixed with 'Hooray' - rather than suffixed with 'Hooray', which I prefer.

As their American child, my parents enjoyed calling me 'Hank'. They also called me 'Henry Higgins' - after Rex Harrison, I think, rather than the snooker champion. I'm happy to be associated with the man who was Dr Dolittle, although every show business biography says Harrison was not a particularly nice man. He is forgiven. For having my favourite singing voice of the 1960s.

I was only in the country of my birth for two months. We sailed for Europe on a German ship, the SS Bremen. My parents would put me to bed in the safety of the shower, before disappearing to drink to the horizon.

At least they had an escape on the boat. In Joralemon Street, I couldn't be left alone on the fire escape - where I was

taken to scream at night so my Dad could sleep. I picture my Mum in the moonlight singing "There's a place for us...." But in reality it was me putting my diaphragm through its paces. Just not as well as Rex Harrison.

In Europe, we settled in Zurich - where I learnt to kiss girls (that's me on the right with my first girlfriend Joanna Bircher)... oh, and talk.

The only thing I remember about Switzerland at this time is those little tubes of sweet condensed milk. They may have contributed to my first two words strung together. Proudly pointing back at my potty, I proclaimed, "'Nana Biggies!" I've been talking shit ever since.

Joanna's parents, Theresa (above) & Freddie (left) appropriately, bore a striking resemblance to Maria and Captain Von Trapp - Julie Andrews and Christopher Plummer

This pronouncement progressed to three words, "Might See Stag!" - indicative of the amount of time we spent driving through the forests, hills and mountains of Europe. I asked my Mum what a 'gypsy' was... "So does that mean we're gypsies?"

To this day, I love driving around Europe. A great number of my happiest childhood memories are being driven to, from, and on, holiday in Europe. Stopping for hot chocolate at the Swiss border in the middle of the night. Stopping for a 'knicker race' in a cold mountain stream - a brilliant way to turn a good wash and some emergency laundry into a fun adventure. My Mum wanting to spend the dregs of the holiday money on a motel, my Dad wanting to spend it on a Michelin Star meal (and a good bottle of wine) and then keep driving.... If I couldn't grow up to be a filmmaker, I wanted to grow up to be a long-distance lorry driver. That's still pretty much the case.

So who were these parents of mine if they weren't Martin and Janet Sheen? As it turns out, they were also rather special.

They were David Antony Fromanteel Lytton Cobbold, born 1937, and Christine Elizabeth Stucley, born 1940.

David was the son of Cameron 'Kim' Cobbold (left) 1904-1987, and Hermione Millicent Bulwer Lytton 1905-2004. They lived at Knebworth House in Hertfordshire, England, my grandmother's family home, which she had inherited on the death of her two brothers - Antony in a flying accident, and John at El-Alamein. David had studied at Cambridge and followed his

father into a career in banking. This began in Hamburg, then - on his marriage to Christine in January 1961 - moved to Paris, then New York. Himself a child of parents that loved to travel and enjoyed holidays in the sun, David banked the restlessness and energy of his desk job, and made the most of every vacation. Every free spell was turned into an adventure, whether a weekend jaunt, a winter trip to ski, or, most relished, a summer trip to the sunshine, usually the Mediterranean.

In Christine - who prefers 'Chryssie' - he found a kindred spirit in travel and love of the sunshine, and a match for his restless energy. She was a child of the wild Atlantic beaches, cliffs and moors of Hartland, North Devon. Her father, Dennis Frederic Bankes Stucley, 1907-1983, and mother Sheila Margaret Warwick Bampfylde, 1912-1996, (right) lived at Hartland Abbey, a 12th Century

Mum's 18th at Burwarton Hall was, I suspect, not as do what thou wilt' as a Francis Dashwood (left, in painting) party

Augustine monastery that had been given by Henry VIII to the Sergeant of his Wine Cellar. By the time of her 'coming out' as one of the last 'debutantes' in 1958, Chryssie had spent time studying in Florence, and lived with her grandparents on a farm in what was then called Southern Rhodesia in Africa.

David and Chryssie were married in the rain at the church of St Nectan on the cliffs above Hartland Abbey. David's parents had also married in the rain. Both of these marriages lasted a lifetime, making me concerned that it should rain at

my marriage. It was not raining when I got married, but it was dripping. Not only were <u>we</u> dripping, in 93°F heat in Tuscaloosa, Alabama, but all around us in the garden of the white-columned antebellum mansion large blocks of ice dripped on pedestals as industrial fans blew air across them to chill our guests. I hope that counts.

RUSH FROM CHURCH TO CAR DAVID HOLDING THE UMBRELLA FIRMLY OVER HIMSELF!

My parents fourth married home in four years took them from the Alps to the Mediterranean. We moved from Zurich to Barcelona in 1965. A fair shock for my parents, under Franco's austerity. As a family we were now four - my brother

Peter having joined the caravan in 1964. I was therefore less important. I was packed off to the 'English School' in Barcelona, which was not remotely English - in fact, I was the only English thing in it, and I was not very English. But the school was keen to have an 'English' student, so they accepted this screaming ball of misery. I had to be dragged down the hill to school. I clung to every lamp-post. I've been something of a lamppost-hugger ever since. I have a vague 'earliest memory' of being clasped to a teacher's large bosom and being given sweets. It is still the best way to make me stay anywhere.

Here I learnt Spanish. Apparently I was so proficient I could interpret between my mother and the incomprehensible local maid. This is extraordinary really, as I now cannot speak a word of Spanish. I tell a lie - 'yes' is 'si'... but I've got no idea what 'no' is. Probably my most used word then. I should probably relearn it.

"Buenas noches Tibidabo" - I would wave every night to the gleaming white church on top of the hill. Or to the amusement park next to it.

Christmas in Spain - or Twelfth Night - is my first 'fully-formed memory'. The Three Wise Men at my Dad's office party at BOLSA, the Bank of London and South America. I think sweets had something to do with this as well. Whenever in my adult life I see a Carambar ⦀ (which is French, not Spanish - but Barcelona doesn't think it's Spanish either), it triggers this distant memory. Amazing that all these years later some of my three-year-old brain is still present and flickering. Just a shame it's not the Spanish language bit.

Last summer walking the promenade at Sitges, just south of Barcelona, where my brother Peter now has a beautiful converted farmhouse (www.barcelonavilla.co.uk, sleeps 22) my mother tells us how she would come to Sitges for the flower festival, which was one of the few displays of beauty and abundance at a time when there was little to buy in the shops and poverty was the norm.

Apart from sunshine, whiskey was the only thing relatively easy to find, so it was used to sterilise the stomach against the limited local diet. Until my Dad caught hepatitis - then it just made his liver worse. It was time to come back to England.

CHAPTER THREE

Schoolboy

The romantic gypsy trail through Europe ended in 1966 outside the Paris Pullman cinema. Well, next door to it, Drayton Gardens, off the Fulham Road in London.

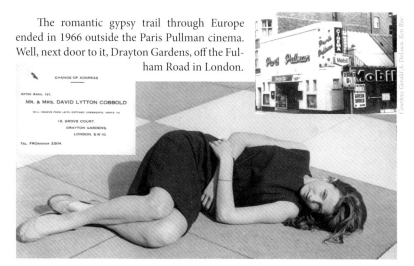

CHANGE OF ADDRESS

AFTER APRIL 1ST,

MR. & MRS. DAVID LYTTON COBBOLD

WILL REMOVE FROM LEITH COTTAGE, KNEBWORTH, HERTS TO

13, GROVE COURT,
DRAYTON GARDENS,
LONDON. S.W.10.

TEL. FROBISHER 2204.

Courtesy Gerald A. DeLuca, Ken Roe

I only recall two things about my new London school, The Vale. I got stars on the soles of my ballet shoes. So unlikely. And I learnt that green beans are poisonous. So unlikely.

The ballet came before my great-uncle Quasimodo's genes did their work on my feet. My monster feet have always been huge and pancake-flat. Hopeless for marching. That was good. For boys born with American passports, this is a decade of conscription and being napalmed in the Vietnam War. Flat feet meant I didn't have to be homosexual to avoid death. It could be optional.

The bunions and the crooked toes were to come. The first one, on my left foot, when I was twelve. My Mum blamed herself for not taking enough care fitting my football boots. You could pretty well watch my feet grow at that age. My shoes were too small a week after purchase. They were 12 (13 US), by the time I was.

The other bunion came later in life. My right side has always been less troublesome. If something is wrong, it will tend to be on on the left side of my body - an irritated mole in the armpit (removed at the request of my mother-in-law, whose friend had died from one), a teenage cyst on the neck (recently returned, and removed; without its Frankenstein bolt, my head did not fall off), a twitch in the eye (pretty constant nowadays), a veruca on the foot (Hitchin swimming pool, persistent bastard when I was a teenager, eventually removed), a cowlick in the profile (only answer to this, remove head)... name your irregularity, it'll be on my left side.

But the right side is beginning to catch up. Now, both my feet are shaped the way that (for reasons I've never understood) the end of shoes are actually shaped. Rounded to the centre. My toes make a perfect equilateral triangle.

But a glance at my grandfather Kim's feet and my Mum's off the hook. The progress of my bunions is deep in my Cobbold genes.

I can picture two things from this time at The Vale. I can picture the little gold and silver star stick-

On the lake at Knebworth with my grandfather

ers on the soles of my ballet shoes. Surely not for poise? Maybe enthusiasm? Plus I can picture the little boy across the dinner table who told me that green beans are poisonous. I know, I know - and knew - that green beans are not poisonous. But throughout my life, I've not been able to look at a long green bean and not remember this fake news.

Why do I remember this? There must have been so many formative moments at this school. Why is "green beans are poisonous" the only one that I remember? Disbelief at the barefaced lie? Maybe. But I also have a screenwriter's brain wired not to rest until I've found a rational explanation for all things... and finally, five decades

later, it occurs to me that maybe this little five-year-old's parents had told him that kidney beans, uncooked, are poisonous. There, finally, that throwaway comment in 1966 makes sense. I have rationalised it. Only took 50 years.

Leather seats in cars make me feel sick. This is a shame, because it is much easier to hoover Great Dane hairs off them. But I will never buy a car with leather seats. This, I'm sure, dates from this time, and the routine that most weekends - perhaps to give my parents a Friday night at the Paris Pullman - I would be driven up the Great North Road to Knebworth in the back of my grandfather's Bentley.

Nowadays, when I'm driving back and forth from Knebworth to London and the A1 motorway or trunk roads are blocked or being dug up (most of the time) and bollards force me onto the old A1 road, the landmarks that I pass take me back to these Friday evening car trips in the 1960s. Hatfield in particular resonates - maybe because it meant we were getting close to Knebworth - the distinctive 30s architecture, The

With Nanty at Rose Cottage

Comet motel and Waters garage - where Tim Rice, before he meets Andrew Lloyd Webber, was working as a pump attendant, and certainly will have filled up my grandfather's Bentley one Friday or Sunday evening.

Knebworth House, where my grandparents had been in residence since soon after the War, meant High Tea in the upstairs Day Nursery with my father's former nanny (a misnomer - nannys, like aunts, are never 'former'), 'Nanty'. Ribena with milk, and Rosehip cordial, are that memory. No wonder I felt sick in the back of the Bentley.

Returning to London, the Finchley Road is the particular resonance - again, probably because it meant we were getting close to home. I recall my grandfather remarking that the traffic lights in the Finchley Road are either all red or all green. Then, at the end of the road, on the left, just before Swiss Cottage, there was a Toy Shop called 'Toys Toys Toys'. The three words were each lit a different colour, and I convinced myself in my back seat dreams that I had to remember the order of the three colours, because if I was kidnapped that was the question I was going to be asked. For many years I committed the order of these three colours to memory... even when chasing through the green lights myself, as an adult. Now the Toy Shop is gone, and oddly I cannot remember the order of the three colours. So if I am kidnapped I will have to rely on some other form of escape. Fortunately my cousin, Jamie Blount, is a hostage negotiator. So maybe it doesn't matter.

After only a year or so, my parents took me and my little brother Peter to live in Knebworth village. To a lovely old park gate house, called Park Gate House (right). My parents bricked in a back courtyard, dug

a swimming pool, put French doors on the sitting room, laid a lot of bright red carpet, topped it with white Finnish igloo chairs and other white plastic furniture, acquired a brace of Swedish au pairs... and, most importantly, wired in a record player with speakers that turned out toward the swimming pool, and put on The Beatles. The joy that - ever since - I get from both music and swimming, I'm sure, derives from the enhanced pleasure of their combination in this thrilling time of the late '60s.

I also got another brother. A smiley one called Richard.

With another brother we also got our own nanny, much treasured Patti Razey from Hull, also never to be 'former'. Still looking after us 54 yrs on

Another home, another school. Knebworth Primary School. Again, I find it a little distressing that I only remember two things about my time at this school.

Parked in Knebworth High Street on my first day, my Mum promised me an Action Man (toy doll) if I was brave enough to go inside the school. Gilding the bribe, she promised an Action Man with 'real hair'. Or at least felt fuzz. On his head. Bucking the trend of his time, Action Man shaved his armpits... and went 'Hollywood' where he got no action.

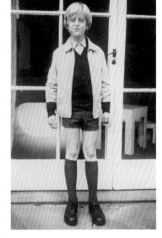

The second thing I recall, is being smacked on the bare thigh with a wooden ruler by my schoolmistress Mrs Desborough. Curiously, this has not become a fantasy that I like to revisit in adulthood, despite the slap resonating through the decades. But I do notice I have a lot of 12" rulers in my current desk drawer - wooden, plastic and rubber. I must have gone through a period when I could never find one, and my answer to that is always to buy half a dozen of the damn things.

My Mum remembers my relationship with Mrs Desborough differently. Apparently my rural peers were all Dickons to my Colin Craven (have you read *The Secret Garden?*) Unlike most of my direct contemporaries, I could read. My previous life in the big cities of London and Barcelona had me already amusing myself with Enid Blyton's *The Secret Seven* (any book that was 'secret') rather than patching up bird wings and fletching arrows from twigs.

When I arrived I was put into the year above. But when the year finished, Mrs Desborough wanted to keep me. Is that flattering? Not sure. My Mum didn't think so, and promptly moved me to another school, my fourth school in three years.

But I did go back to Knebworth Primary School. 40 years later. To be a school governor. I enjoyed those four years of Wednesday evenings. I was a rare governor who'd actually attended the school (the Dickons of my day having all long escaped Knebworth, their homes now the investments of London commuters) - but, sadly, volunteering to be something like a school governor has now become so perscriptive and thankless, requiring regular course-taking, that it is only done by saints.

During this time, however - C.R.B.C. in place - I was able to find my way through the mops and pony tails to the cavernous white room that once was the scene of my smarting bare thighs. The only thing that was familiar was the smell. You'd have thought that well-soaped and brushed 21st Century children would smell very different from their 1960s counterparts. But the smell wasn't the children. It was the 100 year old building. Whether it's Creme de Mould, Eau de Dry Rot, Chanel No Asbestos Dust, or the Powder of Human Skin... for me, old buildings carry their memories in their air. My eyes have seen much too much to recall. But my nose and my ears can release the most vivid of memories.

I could add taste to that. But whereas I have a good nose and a good ear, my sense of taste is dulled by too much ketchup and Coca-Cola when I was young. Like my insulin-levels, it's shot. Dissolved by sugar. But I can, to this day, taste the half-penny 'Fruit Salad' chews from Mrs Hall's sweet shop in Knebworth High Street, where we'd stop after school. And the Bazooka bubble gum, with the dusty little comic strip inside. Imagine that, a shop just for sweets on Knebworth High Street. Mind you, it was next to a shop just for vegetables.

I feel kudos today for having attended a school in my own community, the place I live today. Fewer and fewer people can say that. But I wear an even bigger badge for having attended my next school. Thanks to my fourth school, aged seven, I can say, "I went to school in Stevenage." My subsequent schools were so clearly and unfashionably schools of privilege. I rarely bring up Eton College unless asked. But if I meet you at a local civic dinner I will certainly have told you that I went to school in Stevenage before the second course.

Nowadays saying "I went to school in Stevenage" puts you in a league with Sir Lewis Hamilton and Ashley Young, but for most of my life it was a less glamorous boast and a pleasing deflection to those with pre-conceived ideas about my poshness. Stevenage, our local town, does not have private schools. For those that don't know it, it had a blinkered reputation as a concrete industrial warren of the white working class. The bulk of the town was created after the War, when bricks were in short supply, to re-house the homeless of the blitzed East End of London.

Stevenage is not, in fact, the concrete wasteland it is supposed. Hear this. The New Town of Stevenage was conceived to offer 8.5 hectares of open space for every 1000 inhabitants. The village of Knebworth, by contrast, has only one hectare of public green space for all 5000 of its inhabitants. I am inspired now to include here

a paen to Stevenage. I want to tell you that Stevenage was so finely designed that all its utilities run under its ubiquitous and health-promoting cycle paths rather than under its roads - so there is never a need to dig up a road in Stevenage... and that its main thoroughfares are designed so that you never have to turn across on-coming traffic... but I am guessing this is not the reason you bought this book. So for the purposes of my story, let's say - if you don't know my local town - it has, through my lifetime, been much maligned, but usually by those that don't know it.

Sum up Stevenage's image problem in one sentence? In its new district of Great Ashby the two hairdressing salons were named "Blades" (for men) and "Blonde Ambition" (for women). Until the 1980s, there was one restaurant for 80,000 people - a hamburger joint called Cody's. That's two sentences - sorry, it's an easy town to write about. Dickens would have been all over it. He knew its Old Town well. He did write about that. He said it was "drowsy in the dullest degree".

It's my home, and I love it - as Fanny Brice says of Henry Street in *Funny Girl*. I went to school there... Okay, so there was once a private school in Stevenage. Just the one. Before it was flattened in the early 1970s by a bright orange leisure centre. It was called The Chilterns - or, to us, Miss Woolley's - and that is where I went to school in Stevenage when I was seven (3rd from the left below). I remember a little bit more about Miss Woolley's than Knebworth Primary. It was the last time I was to be in the company of girls until I went to university.

I had my first crush. Arabella Dansie - I remember the name, not the girl. Except that she had dark hair. And her father was a local doctor. I wished she'd come

back to my house and play 'Doctors and Nurses'. This game of biological curiosity surely should have been called 'Doctors and Patients'? But I suppose it was the sexism of the time that if a female cousin was taking a look at your genitals it was because she was a 'nurse', and if you were inspecting her's, you must be a 'doctor'.

At Miss Woolley's I also found my first B.F.F. Johnny Pritchard. Johnny has since enjoyed a successful career making choc-
olate penises. He makes them in all different shapes and sizes... and colours, although dark of course proves most popular. He's been doing it for, can you believe, 30 years. His company - Spencer and Fleetwood - also do a nice line in candy (edible) g-strings, jockstraps, bras and nipple tassles. Our paths will cross again in the 1990s when I create an ideal place to show off a chocolate penis.... but more of that later.

In 1969, Johnny and I are at Miss Woolley's, eyeing up Arabella Dansie... and eating junket. Junket is a milk pudding that was served once a week at The Chilterns, and encountering it, was the first time in my life that a pudding had been disgusting. I still don't really know what junket is. But in a game of "Animal, Vegetable, Mineral" it's definitely "Animal".

At this school in Stevenage I encountered my first inspirational teacher. God bless the child who has inspirational teachers. A teacher who will not just put a brain in order, but will make it broader. A teacher who doesn't bore and preach, 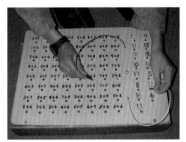but uses stories to teach. Miss Starling was not simply going to teach us maths, she was going to spend hours of her own time devising inspirational gadgets and games to win our attention. There was an 'adding machine' that used electric currents. And, most memorable for me, a series of stories and a board game about the Emerald Pirate, the Sapphire Pirate and the Ruby Pirate.

By one of those special miracles of life, I was to meet Miss Starling again 40 years later, living above a strip of shops on the Hitchin to Letchworth road. I invited her to tea, along with Johnny Pritchard, and whilst skirting delicately around what life paths her nurturing had inspired - "another chocolate finger, Miss Starling?" - I mentioned how the memory of the three pirates had stayed with me ever since.

Her eyes lit up - "I still have the game!" Extraordinarily, when I dropped her home, I saw it again. There it was. The Pirate Game. Still sitting with her in her little flat all those years later. A piece of schoolteacher creativity that completely captured my imagination as a seven-year-old.

My mother says that I had a boundless ability to entertain myself at that age. This was about to be beaten out of me by the structured routines of 'Prep' School. But, at seven, I was in a golden age of creativity. Thank you, Miss Starling.

Sadly I lost touch with Miss Starling soon after, having sent her a rock in the mail. I have a horrible feeling her relations might have thought this some kind of prank, or symbolic, gesture. It wasn't at all. It was simply that she told me that she now loved to paint pebbles, and I told her that the beach in Devon where my Mum grew up has the very best pebbles in the world for painting. I said I would find her one on my next visit.

I did not forget. Next time I was in North Devon I chose her a fine spherical little rock - but, as I was off to America, I mailed it to her, hurriedly, with no note, rather than deliver it. I never heard again from Miss Starling. She was elderly then, and is unlikely now to be with us. It's not the final gesture I would have chosen for this titan of my creative youth - a rock landing on her doormat - but I hope she knew it was sent to be made beautiful, by her, as I was.

But the bright colourful enamels of my seven-year-old self were about to be stripped and sandpapered by the old buffers of a 1970s English boarding school.

CHAPTER FOUR

Wellesley House

*Darling haven't you ever heard of a delightful little thing
called boarding school?*
(The Baroness, *The Sound of Music* 1965)

As my Mum tells it, my Dad swore to her when they were married that none of their children would ever be sent to boarding school. They had both had a share of boarding school traumas. But my Dad changed his mind. And my Mum wept and wept.

It was early September 1970 when - having driven for a good part of the day (this was pre-M25 and Dartford Crossing) to the far south east coastal town of Broadstairs - she watched her little 8-year-old shuffle off down the dormitory corridor of the Junior House of all-boy boarding school Wellesley House.

It was my father's old school. He had made lifetime friends there - two in particular, Oliver Rena and Alan Ponte, were also about to send their boys there. Both my brothers were to follow me. But I was the pathfinder. Tough being the eldest.

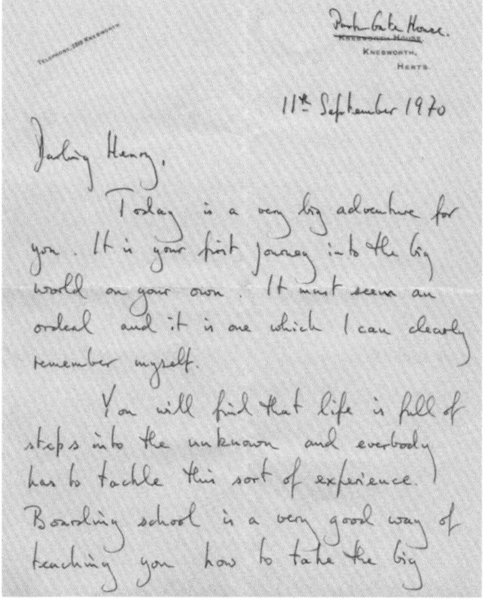

[Handwritten letter:]

Wellesley House.
KNEBWORTH,
HERTS.

11th September 1970

Darling Henry,

Today is a very big adventure for you. It is your first journey into the big world on your own. It must seem an ordeal and it is one which I can clearly remember myself.

You will find that life is full of steps into the unknown and everybody has to tackle this sort of experience. Boarding school is a very good way of teaching you how to take the big

steps in life and how to get on
by yourself & in the great world.
    Try to remember that it is
an adventure. Look around you
and learn from others. Always be
truthful to others and to yourself. Be
gentle and yet strong.
    You are a clever boy and
big for your age. There will be
others smaller than you and not so
clever — remember them.
        Good luck and lots and lots
of love from   Daddy   (am proud of you)

The contrast between my Dad's first letter (above)
and my Mum's (below) is revealing

Put Yes or No after
    each question.
Do you like School ?   yes and no
Have you lots of friends ?   two
What is the name of one ?   Evelereich yes may (cant put here!)
How many in your dormitory ?   5
How many in your class   11
Are your lessons easy ?   some are
Are your lessons difficult ?   some are
Which subject do you like best ?   HISTORY
Do you like football ?   yes
Are you a Dane, Roman
        Saxon or Viking ?   viking
Have you got the right clothes ?   yes
Is the food Good ?   yes
What do you like best ?   Film   (cant put yes or no!)

As I was separated from my mother to return to my dormitory and unpack my trunk, the matron suggested I hold hands with Hugh Fitzroy-Newdigate. This equally shell-shocked boy had his two favourite stuffed animals sewn together because school rules said you could only bring one. The two of us, hand in hand, set off back down the corridor to this new world.

Separated from all I loved, hand in hand with Hugh Fitzroy-Newdigate, off I went, as an 8-year-old child, to live with boys for 10 years. Off I went, to see puberty through in boys' dormitories. To learn about getting on in a boy's world. To learn how to survive the far reaches of Empire without getting maudlin and sentimental about Shropshire and rose-lipped maidens. To learn the myriad wonders of the arts and sciences. To learn about everything... Except being part of a family. Except how girls work. And preferably only picking up enough healthy Spartan man-love feelings not to trouble a future career in the Establishment or encourage spying for the Soviet Union.

I did not develop Spartan man-love for Hugh Fitzroy-Newdigate. Hugh was a lovely guy, who remained a peripheral friend, on and off, for 30 years. Until he was found dead in a hotel room in Rangoon. Heroin, I'm told.

I was soon beaten. The ruler on the thigh became the slipper on the buttocks. A slipper in the muscled right arm swing of Junior House Master, ex-Captain of the Great Britain Squash Team, Richard Boddington (L.D.O.B - Life Defining Obituary Byline - "International squash player who was hailed as a great tactician and went on to become an inspirational teacher"). An "accurate and dogged" squash ball thwacker, who could, accurately and doggedly, squash your balls.

It was my first test in the burden of responsibility. A dormitory brawl after lights out. Mr Boddington caught us. He declared that he considered me to be the most responsible of the half dozen boys, and therefore took my version of events.

I don't know what I said. I do hope it was responsible, and fair. But it certainly didn't include the fact that I had started the ruckus by petulantly pushing my neighbour's folded clothes off his bedside chair. Certainly I was hit less than the other Famous Five dormitory rioters, but I remember Mr Boddington saying that he felt that it was right that I should be punished too. So. Into Matron's Room. Up with the dressing gown. Bend over. Thwack! Thwack! Thwack! Thwack! Thwack! Thwack!... Ow.

Letter-writing was a formal weekly invigilated (censored) session. I livened up my Enid Blyton banalities, and the standard "The score in football was... The film this weekend was...", by drawing all over my letters (a bit like I'm doing now, distracting you from the text) and by adding a sellotaped comic of jokes & drawings about a fictional 'Donk Gang'. They don't show the same promise as this one (left) drawn for me a couple of years later by the now renowned cartoonist, Oliver Preston (with me in the centre above)

It takes a certain type of man to want to devote his working life to young boys. The masters at Wellesley House were a peculiar bunch. I suppose their life fantasies were formed at this formative age, in similar environments, and they welcomed the chance to regress to this. They tended to be either ex-Army or Lost Boys who never grew up. There were one or two gems. And, as everywhere, one or two germs.

I am not going to linger on the germs. I honestly don't remember much of the bad. I'll just mention the Assistant Head Master, who was notorious for bending boys over and taking a running penalty kick. He 'left' suddenly while I was there, in a mist of incriminating adult secrecy.

I'd rather focus on the gems. At the time I didn't especially like baby-faced Mr Bridges, who always wore the same maroon blazer. But thinking back on him, I think he was really quite extraordinary. My Mum says my creativity - or, more specifically, my ability to entertain myself - was eroded by the routines and rules of boarding school. But, in Mr Bridges, I had a schoolmaster who spent his leisure hours writing an elaborate fantasy story about the school being inter-connected by an underground railway. It was proper E. Nesbit. It was never going to be published, as it was very specifically about Wellesley House and its characters, but he must have spent a good part of his non-working life writing it. I suppose he didn't really have a working or a non-working life. He just had a life, and it was 100% a boys prep school. Although, to his credit, Mr Bridges' story did feature girls and, as I remember it, had the prescience to see the old Head Master's house at the bottom of the playing fields eventually being turned into a Girls' annex to the school. Although in his version, of course, connected by an underground railway.

I only remember one actual class at Wellesley House, and it was early on, in my first year. Mr Bridges brought in a record player, and announced that today's lesson would be listening to Beethoven's *Ninth Symphony*. I can see him lifting the needle onto the record. I have often thought how unlikely a lesson like that would be in years subsequent. It made a deep impression on me.

Another gem was pipe-smoking Mr Spencer. I don't think he was liked much by other boys, but I remember more of his aphorisms and brain teasers than of anything else I learnt at Wellesley House. He would set a quiz for the summer holidays. The questions were general knowledge, but I remember in particular 'Who said the following...?" I can reel off a number of the quotations, still, to this day - "Die, my dear doctor, that is the last thing I shall do" (Lord Palmerston), "So little time, so much to do" (Cecil Rhodes)... This must have been a section on the last words of England's Empiricists.

Question: How did the Post Office know how to deliver an envelope addressed:

Wood

John

Hants

Answer: John Underwood, Andover, Hants.

Having handed out the days task papers, Mr Spencer would ask, "Who'd like a clip?". He meant, of course, a clip around the ear.

But the line I think of most frequently, still, and which I very much want to believe is Mr Spencer's own, is - "Knowledge is knowing a fact, or knowing where to find it." I have been encouraged by this thought ever since. I love research. I have always been good at knowing where to find relevant facts and information. This line of Mr Spencer's has always made me feel 'knowledgeable'. That's a teacher.

Today we have Google, so everyone's a genius. What would Mr Spencer have thought of Alexa? It certainly would have made his Summer Quiz pretty pointless.

Much of what an English boarding school wants to teach, it thinks you'll find on its playing fields. I have never been particularly interested in sport. I'm with the Art Teacher, that endeavour is valid, but competition is vain. I tend to think victory and glory in competition is, at best, ephemeral and pointless, and at worst leads to conflict and war. And as for formalised exercise, well, I'm with Peter O'Toole - "The only exercise I take, is following the coffins of my friends who took exercise."

But I am vain enough to mention that I was better at sport than you think I was. I won medals for the Junior High Jump and the Junior 60 Metre Hurdles. My school record for the Junior 60 Metre Hurdles stood for seven years. I was good also

at swimming. But not as good as Angus Neish. He beat me into second place in every race, except the backstroke. I guess I was less bothered than him about bashing my head on the pool edge.

You're exercising only your finger and your focus, but I was also quite good at target shooting. My crowning glory was aceing one paper bullseye target by putting one bullet through the centre and the rest wide - thereby convincing the judge that all five shots had gone through the centre hole. Top score.

I liked football - a civilised and levelling game - my pace (not hindered by my flat feet) and left foot made me useful on the left wing. I disliked Rugby - a brutal, and brawn-rewarding, game. I thought it better named 'Bullyme'.

Cricket, however, I absolutely detested. Not only was it boring, it was lethal. Having a rock thrown at you at high speed, with only a thin piece of wood or your bare hands to defend yourself. I left the distant outfield on my last ever game of cricket at Wellesley House, vowing that that was the last time in my life I would ever play this horrid game. I have not played cricket since... although I have spent 20 years (and counting) supporting Knebworth Park Cricket Club in its quest to keep its volunteer, and floundering, village club alive in the 21st Century. In other countries, men dressing all in white, driving stakes into the ground and throwing stones at other men get arrested.

One of the oddest afternoons I recall at Wellesley House was when it was too wet for cricket. We were given the choice of either indoor P.E. (Physical Education) or an outdoor swim. Outdoor swim, right? No contest. There was a catch, however. The outdoor swim had to be naked. Now, since unleashed from my swaddling clothes as a babe, I have never had a problem with being naked in company. I have been self-conscious, yes, but not worried about running around with my willy flapping about. So why, I wonder, on this occasion, did I choose P.E., which I actively disliked, over swimming, which I loved? I have since ruminated over this strange day. I can only surmise that some kind of inner conscience told me that schoolmasters insisting that schoolboys could only go swimming if they were naked was not salubrious. Odd. But now lost in the mists of memory.

I can't speak for the schoolmasters, but certainly we boys were all fascinated by our penises. Penises were everywhere, popping out, flapping about, standing straight and stiff - especially when soaped up in the open sports shower, or in the rows of little bathtubs in the evening. I'd hang my towel on mine while I buttoned up my light blue airtek shirt. Very useful. You see, there were no vaginas around to be fascinated by - although Miss Quinn, the Under Matron, must have had one. It was probably quite close on occasions. Like when she was peering in your hair for nits. But if you've never seen one, it is hard to imagine.

We were eleven years old. *Star Wars* had not been invented yet, but in our hands we had our very own light sabre that buzzed. Why would you not have fun with it? For one term I was put in a dormitory for two - my proto-Jedi comrade and I would have light sabre clashes most nights before we went to sleep.

Penis fascination was also rife in the larger dormitories. If your penis is fun to play with, might it not also be fun to have someone else play with it? Or indeed to play with someone else's? This penis play was all fine and dandy - and I'm sure for centuries contributed to the success of the Empire, as ex-boarding school boys knew how to amuse themselves when marooned with Army or Navy colleagues in far-flung outposts of the World's pink bits.

The Seventies was a decade of sexual liberation, but I don't believe there was more of this in my time than there had been before. This is what happens when you ween boys from their home environment at a young age and expect them to find emotional bonds locked up with other boys just as their penises are starting to function in an adult way.

In ten years of boarding school, I only encountered one example of these penis games being non-consensual. I had a dormitory captain who insisted that each boy in the dormitory, in turn, over a course of time, became his bed mate. The worry of the unknown, as your turn approached, was the troubling bit. When my call finally came, I was fiddled with for a few minutes, but something about me didn't do it for the captain, so he moved on to the next sardine. What was wrong with me, I wonder? I suppose it was just power play. Physically, I was bigger than him.

So did this penis play at this formative time of my development have a lasting effect? If you are a psychiatrist, answers on a postcard please. From my perspective, I am not frightened of penises, as many people seem to be. I am quite content to be in their company, which I often am at the beach. I've been proud to stand up for them over the years, in anti-censorship campaigns. I don't subscribe to the view that they are ugly, or that they are less worth looking at than their female counterparts, as most filmmakers and censorship boards seem to think. But at the same time, I don't feel that they are any more interesting to play with than their female counterparts. And now I have the opportunity to live with the opposite sex, I find, sensorially, the female sex and its similarly fascinating erogenous bits are quite enough for me to be concerned with.

Much more of an influence on my sexual psyche is that my formative years of 8 to 18 spanned the exact length of the decade of the 1970s. I come from the age of *Emmanuelle* (1974), the cinema sex film, the age of permissive sex and *The Rocky Horror Show* (1973), the age of David Bowie and sexual androgyny. A brief fleeting moment in human history when making love was more fashionable than making war, when sex was more fashionable than violence. Respecting consensual harmfree pleasure in all its forms - eschewing taboo, dogma, labels - was where I stood then, and it is where I stand today. "Father. why do these words sound so nasty?" as the character Woof questions in the musical *Hair* (1967). "I know, Janet, but isn't it nice?" as Frank reasons in the musical *The Rocky Horror Show*. Your honour, I call the 1970s.

There are, I'm sure, less sex games today in boys' boarding schools. There are less boys-only boarding schools. And kids nowadays, well, now they <u>do</u> have *Star Wars* - sexless, and with actual light sabres, where the buzz is violence - and ubiquitous entertainment gadgets that are more fun to play with than even your penis.

The mores of the 1970s are so last century. We now live in an age where kids are criminalised for being interested in sex before they're told to be. An age where if I illustrated <u>these</u> two pages with photos from an old album, I'd be locked up. No, I don't have photographs of my prep school dormitories. We had a single teddy bear for comfort, not an iPhone. That world has moved on. The single-sex prep-school pashes of the 1970s are another country. But then there's no far-flung Empire to police any more. No need for a single-sex Army, Navy, etc... So maybe the English education system can do without these things now.

Single-sex boarding school may not have successfully turned me to homosexuality, but it did get me into musical theatre. The films I loved before I went to school were musicals, but now, at schools with music departments, I could actually be part of a musical. At both my junior and senior school there were productions of *Joseph and His Amazing Technicoloured Dreamcoat*. This musical was ubiquitous in my childhood. Thank the Lord (Lloyd Webber).

At the time I write, the ubiquitous musical is a Disney film called *Frozen*. It has 'comedy' songs, but overwhelmingly *Frozen* seems to be simply nasal Broadway M.O.R. psychotherapy belting. Musicals were more fun when they were written across musical styles by the Lord, and with the Python-Age wit of the petrol attendant of Waters garage in Hatfield.

I tended to be used backstage in these school productions. Too self-conscious? It would've been good for me to be out front. I only appeared on stage twice at school. An end-of-term revue at Wellesley House as a balloon-breasted version of *Star Trek*'s black female Lieutenant Uhura. Wrong in so many ways, and not a performance that has gone down in the annals of theatre history. Secondly, as a villager who survives the plague in *The Roses of Eyam* by Don Taylor, where I stood out for a particularly naturalistic turn, by interrupting the actor who had skipped over my one line. This production was more remarkable as the one where we all got kissed by the future Prime Minister, David Cameron, who was playing a saintly village lady ministering to plague victims.

Easy to spot, I'm the one who insisted on wearing his collar up and cuffs loose.
David Cameron is looking particularly fetching as the nearest one in a bonnet.

Here again, I think I was being infused and enthused by the early 1970s, beyond simply my school experiences. In the holidays my Mum & Dad took me to London to see the stage versions of *Hair, Jesus Christ Superstar, The Rocky Horror Show* - musicals more exciting and contrary even than *Doctor Dolittle*. Add *Cabaret* to this holy trinity and marvel at what a musical could be in the late Sixties, early Seventies. All the movie versions of these musicals remain in my top 20 favourite films. It's been downhill for original musicals ever since. However to feed my enthusiasm I went looking back in time - and discovered the musicals of the Fifties and, even better, the musicals of the Thirties. What kind of geeky kid was I, that knew more about Fred Astaire than Pelé?

I remember the looks of disapproval thrown at me and my brother (maybe 10 and 8) by adult theatregoers during the interval of the London production of *Hair*. What was the concern? That we were to be exposed to penises? I should have reassured them, "It's okay, I'm at boarding school." Or maybe, "It's okay, the penises are only in the play because of my Grandpa."

My grandfather Cameron 'Kim' Cobbold had been Lord Chamberlain - the Queen's formal secretary - throughout the 1960s and had worked with Roy Jenkins, the then Home Secretary, to remove censorship from the stage in the 1968 Theatres Act. It was plainly absurd for the Queen's secretary to be censoring plays in the 1960s, just because that was the way it had been done since Elizabethan times. Time spent insisting that "the balls of the Medici" be replaced with "the testicles of the Medici" was clearly not my grandfather's time well spent. His 'blue pencil' was being overtly tested and ridiculed by angry young playwrights, Osborne, Orton... O dear, there was even a Peter Cook & Dudley Moore sketch called *Lord Cobbold* (1964), which portrays my grandfather asking why he would want to see all that sex and violence at the theatre when he can get that at home.

Three generations back, my great-great-great-grandfather Edward Bulwer Lytton had tried to push this modernisation through Parliament in 1832 - alongside another absurd throwback to Elizabethan times, that only two London theatres (Drury Lane and Haymarket) were licensed to play drama. He succeeded in ending that monopoly, but not the Lord Chamberlain's powers of censorship. It took his great-granddaughter's husband to eventually see this anachronism off. And so - *Oh Calcutta!* - the penis was unleashed, and finally could be called by all the plethora of names the English have spent long and fruitful evenings across history making up for it - cock, dick, prick, knob... as you know, I could go on. The artifice of stage drama could at least look and sound a little more real, and adult themes could be expressed outside of metaphor and symbol, to a less demeaned audience.

Kim Cobbold became Lord Chamberlain after 12 years as Governor of the Bank of England. He was also a Governor of another repository of English promise. Eton College. He had attended the school, sent my father there, but I suspect this position had more to do with his friendship with the school's Provost Lord Charteris. His Governor portfolio was 'Steward of the Courts' - nowadays probably in charge of asbestos removal; back then, probably in charge of putting it in. Could this help in getting me into the school? Probably. But I still had to attain the required 13 points in 'Common Entrance', the exams 13-year-olds in English private schools take to progress to senior school.

I am not good at Exams. I am a slow writer. I am also not good at writing what I am expected to write. I usually knew as much as the next boy - except in science and languages, at which I was genuinely rubbish - but my teachers gen-

History	Total 100
1. Lytton Cobbold	92
2. Henderson	90
3. Eveleigh }	88
Dyson }	
5. Swift	80
6. Susie	78
7. Mason	72
8. Morlock	70
9. Reed	66
10. Lascelles	65
11. Wise	60
12. Kennedy	55
13. Hands	50
14. Fitzroy N	46
15. Preston	42

5A Music Test	Max 54
1. L. Cobbold	31
2. Henderson	28
3. Wise mi	27
4. Swore	26
5. Dyson	26
6. Eveleigh	25
7. Morlock	23
8. Mason	23
9. Swift	22
10. Lascelles	19
11. Reed	17
12. Kennedy	16
13. Fitzroy N	12
13. Preston	12

Mathematics Exam		100
V.A		
1. Lytton Cobbold	0	83
2. Wise	6	82
3. Henderson	6	81
4. Eveleigh	6	77
5. Hands	6	68
6. Dyson	6	65
Swift		63
8. Mason		62
9. Lascelles		
Swift		52
10. Kennedy		34

Geography Exam Va	Max 100
1. L. Cobbold	72
2. Lascelles	62
3. Hands Hi	57
Swift	57
5. Henderson	50
6. Eveleigh	59
7. Swore	47
8. Dyson	46
9. Wise	44
10. Mason	87
11. Kennedy	9

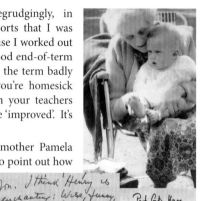

erally admitted, begrudgingly, in my end-of-term reports that I was bright. Maybe because I worked out early how to get a good end-of-term report. Always start the term badly (easy to do when you're homesick and miserable), then your teachers will always say you've 'improved'. It's a word they like.

My great-grandmother Pamela (right) was the first to point out how clever I am, when I was very small. I feel she was well qualified to make this observation, having been first love and lifelong friend to one of the 20th Century's great polymaths, Winston Churchill. I have fond memories of walking through the Wilderness Garden at Knebworth House to go and have tea with her at the Manor House. She always had a box of Black Magic chocolates by her bed with only the butterscotch ones (with the 'B' on them) left - too hard for her teeth, but also the only dark chocolates sweet enough to interest a child. She died when I was 9, and she was 97. My father wrote another wonderful letter to me at school (right), about how remarkable her life had been, to have gone to bed by candlelight as a child, but lived to see a man on the moon. But what resonates with me is that Pamela was born 15 months after the death of my great-great-great-grandfather, Edward Bulwer Lytton - and I knew her, and remember her well. What more could I need to be infused with a love and awe of history, and to feel connected to my Victorian ancestors?

But, like my great-great-great-grandfather - even if I was able to - I was not inclined to sum up the War of the Roses in half an hour. Why finish an exam question, if there's a novel in it?

But I am here to tell you that I passed every single one of my key school exams. With panache, I declare, over petty point scoring. In Chapter One I mentioned the two 'C's, and non-figurative 'D' that was key to Film Studies at Kent. Here I shall jump ahead and declare the fine poker hands that are my 'O Level results. The first year, aged 15, I got four 'B's. The second year, aged 16, I got seven 'C's ('C' being the pass grade.)

To sail the 7 'C's. How beautiful is that! How's that for being all-rounder? The perfect polymath. The right regular Renaissance man. I know a little bit about everything, and not much about anything.

My Common Entrance exam result for entrance into Eton was similarly pin-point perfect. 13 points. Exactly the pass mask. I'll have none of this 'feeder' school calumny that Wellesley House said to Eton, "You can have our scholars, but only if you take Henry Lytton Cobbold too." Nonsense! Nor that there was some intervention on his behalf by the Steward of the Courts. Poppycock! I passed every single school exam, and with beautiful results. None more beautiful, until the day my son graduated from Music College with A,C,D,C.

I was off to the boarding school of all boarding schools.

Buenas noches Kent. I'll be back in 5 years.

CHAPTER FIVE

Eton College - Part I

Pleased, as man, with men to dwell,
Jesus, our Emmanuel!
(*Hark! The Herald Angels Sing* - Charles Wesley,
with some 20th Century interference)

There are a lot of books and accounts of schooldays at Eton - one popular one from the 1930s about my great-uncle Antony. with a foreword by J. M. Barrie. The very best thing I can say about the school is that my account of my years there will be completely different from any other. Despite the obligatory posh boy black wool penguin suit, Eton College is not a cookie-cutter school.

I have met many who say they can tell an Etonian because, saint or shit, at least he'll be charming. This continues to prove truer than it

should, and currently to the detriment of the country. As I write, a bunch of Etonians in politics are taking the country to hell in a handbasket. With crocodile charm.

The school is unusual in that, despite its rules, traditions and ridiculous uniform, it encourages individuality. Etonians are by nature & nurture, diverse, independent, and different. If charm is a common denominator, the only other I detect is a shared sense of humour. You have to develop one of those pretty swiftly walking about a busy town dressed as a penguin.

I have never met an Etonian, however much we might abhor each other's company or politics, I can't have a laugh with.

Part of the diversity of the school comes from its size. It's flipping huge. 1250 teenage boys. And from the fact that it is spread across a town. Aren't most schools in a town? No. Most private schools are stuck away in a country house, often on a Yorkshire moor or on a barren Scottish hillside. Eton is under the Heathrow flight path, just off the M4, sandwiched between the busy industrial estates of Slough and the tourist treadmill of Windsor. However unreal the environment - and it is unreal - the school is surrounded by real life and the modern world.

Looking back at my time at Wellesley House, in the seaside town of Broadstairs, I am surprised at the freedom we were given when we became seniors, aged 12 or 13. We were allowed to walk down into the town centre on our own on a Sunday. I wonder if that was because it was the 1970s. I doubt this is the case now. But this freedom was important to my development. At home I didn't walk to town. The nearest town was a significant walk away, and there was never time to be off on one's own during the school holidays. There was always too much going on at Knebworth House, or we'd been whisked off for family time at a remote holiday destination.

So, exploring Broadstairs on my own, aged 12 or 13, was my first time to... go into a newsagent and buy an erotic book (which I have done since); steal a 5p postcard from a shop front (which I have not done since) [This was my first and last criminal theft. But I trust it means that I have the dark, troubled youth that is now required of the fully-rounded Hollywood hero, or the credible pop star]; while away hours browsing in magical bookshops (is the Albion Bookshop still there?); or, generally, have such thrilling adventures in the outside world.

I was determined my adventures in the outside world would continue at Eton. In my first term I read the school rules carefully. Etonians were not permitted to go to the neighbouring town of Slough, and were required to dress up in a shirt & tie to go to the neighbouring town of

Windsor... but there was nothing in the school rules about not going to the neighbouring hamlet of Eton Wick, on the third road out of town. Why would an Etonian want to go to Eton Wick? I don't recall there being a pub there, which for the person who wrote the School Rules was the only conceivable

destination of a Etonian outside of school. It was just a little community of council houses connected to the west of Slough by a footbridge over the M4.

I was not interested in going to the pub, or smoking under the railway arches. By the time I was 14, and throughout my schooldays, I was only interested in one thing. Girls. And dreaming about girls. I'd have been terrified to actually meet one. But I thrived on dreaming about them, and fantasising about romantic encounters with them in the fields and lanes around the school. Whenever I had spare time, or could get off 'games' (by pretending not to be any good at them), I went wandering to the west, to the fields alongside the Thames river, to Eton Wick, to the footbridge over the M4 motorway (the bridge you drive beneath thinking someone in the car has farted, because of the adjacent sewage works)... and eventually to

the west side of Slough, where, when I was old enough to look 18 (at 15), I would navigate the town's backstreets to the Granada cinema. Not to see mainstream films (I could wait till weekends at home or the holidays to see these) but to visit the third screen at the Granada, which showed sex films. To dream about girls.

This was the only time I broke the school rules. I committed the school rules to memory and, in all other respects, stuck firmly to what was written - taking advantage only of what was not written.   Slough was forbidden in the school rules, but the cinema, if I could make it there undetected, seemed to me 'safe as altar', a diplomatic free zone. Because, if I only went to see sex films, whoever caught me in there breaking this rule was also in there watching sex films - which no Eton schoolmaster was going to own up to, even in the 1970s.

Was I not seen in the street? "Achtung! Your papers please!" Not in the western backstreets of Slough I frequented. Plus, the only good thing about the English weather is that it is entirely normal to wander urban back streets completely concealed in a big cheap hooded anorak.

"What is a 'sex film'?" I hear you ask. And if you don't ask, I wonder if you know? It is a peculiar phenomenon that only really existed in the 1970s. Before the 1970s, there was the odd cinema club in London that showed 'art' films from Sweden. After the 1970s, there were VHS videos, that people took home to fast forward through. Only in the 1970s were there cinemas in towns like Slough that showed 'sex films'. These were generally British comedies-with-boobs-&-bums starring Robin Askwith, or Continental travelogues-with-boobs-&-bums-&-bushes about liberated women having sex whenever they felt like it. Despite my grandfather's unleashing of the penis in British theatre, there was never a penis to be seen in any of these films. Maybe once in a blue moon - once in a blue movie - one would glimpse a flash of flaccid white willy nestled in a thicket of pubes, but certainly nothing that had any blood in it. If there had been a penis in a 1970s sex film, it would instantly have been severed, and left on the floor of Mr John Trevelyan's British Board of Film Censors office in Soho Square. I'm afraid the mentality existed that intelligent people go to the theatre, those with the tools to process the sight of a penis. But films are the opium of common people, who can't be trusted to see a penis and not pass out... or, perhaps, spontaneously combust?

The result of this was that the liberated women in these films seemed to prefer having sex with each other. It was easier for the filmmakers, because it was easier on their budgets - not to have to cut out every close up of heterosexual sex for territories such as the United Kingdom. This was, of course, absurd, discriminatory, contrary to human rights... and a cause that I was to take up in the 1990s. But at the time it suited me. When you've spent all week amongst boys being beastly to each other, what better, on the weekend, than to spend a couple of hours watching girls being nice to each other?

Twenty years later when I found myself in Los Angeles making the 1990s equivalent of the 'sex film', I looked back on my British education to question how it had prepared me for this development in my career. Eton College, on reflection, ticked a number of boxes. Weekends spent in the Granada 3 cinema in Slough was personal time well used. Consider also my three 'A' level subjects. English, Ancient History and History of Art. In English we were reading Henry Fielding, about bawdy sex in 18th Century country inns; in Ancient History we were reading Suetonius, about Roman Emperors indulging in sex orgies in their palaces on Capri; and in History of Art we were reading Kenneth Clarke, about appreciating the Nude. It could be said that, at Eton, I had the perfect education for a future in sex films.

Surprisingly, on these dreamy adolescent wanderings out west, to Eton Wick and West Slough, I did eventually meet real girls. Even more surprisingly, I went on to discover there were actually girls living under the same roof as me. But it took a while longer to encounter these mythical denizens.

My five years living at Eton were spent in the care of two 'House Masters' - surrogate dads to 50 boys each. Both my House Masters had no sons of their own, but both did have daughters, who - in the first instance at least - were kept well out of view. I spent two years with Oliver Bull (O.R.S.B.), and three years with John Faulkner (J.F.). I was in three different physical houses, all in different corners of the town - two years in Wayneflete House (below), one year in Carter House (p.58) and two years in Warre House (right). All three

Above, with Mr Bull in the summer of 1976 at Waynefleet House. There I am under a side-parted hairstack at the left end of the middle rows. Below, with Mr Faulkner in the summer of 1980 at Warre House (in a more sun damaged image). There I am standing on the left again, under a centre-parted haystack. Only one future P.M. here, front row third from the right.

named after previous masters. There is no other good reason you would name a home for boys Warre House.

All three of these physical houses were no longer equipped to feed the 50 boys they contained, and so for all five years of my five years at the school I ate meals at the school cafeteria, named Bekynton. Meals at Bekynton were served by casually employed girls from the local area. Some of them no older than me. That doesn't mean that the average Etonian noticed them. The average Etonian was either terrified or disdainful (terrified) of girls that were not his sister or his cousin (and probably also terrified or disdainful of his sister and his cousin).

It surprises me that I was unusual in lingering after meals to chat up the 'Bekynton girls'. It astonishes me that I was almost alone in making friends with them. But I was. And would you believe it? They all lived in Eton Wick - and those that were still at school crossed the motorway footbridge to 'comprehensive' schools in West Slough.

I'd have to wait some time for the cafeteria room to clear before the girls were sent out to wipe down the tables. Remember I was 15, so my idea of how to start a conversation with a girl was to go around the tables putting two spoons either side of the salt and pepper pots to create long penis shadows in the afternoon sun. In my defence, the Victorian architect of Walpole House (below left) opposite Wayneflete

House (below right) had been similarly inspired - maybe by the house's name -

These photos were taken in January. As I compile the book it is now summer, so I could go back to Eton and get a photo of this perfect penis & balls shadow phenomenon on this front wall of Waynefleet... but that would be weird wouldn't it?

to do exactly the same. His chimneys and bonneted dormer windows, every afternoon in the high summer sun, threw huge penis & balls shadows on the flat wall at the front of our house opposite. And he didn't have the excuse of being a teenage boy.

Conversation started, I was soon making friends with Susan and Carol and Alison... and would meet up with them in the fields around Eton Wick, and occasionally go home to theirs for egg on toast with their parents. This is not what other errant Etonians were doing. They were smoking under the railway arches or sneaking into pubs. That said, I did on occasion allow curious school chums to accompany me, and this led to one momentous summer afternoon in the long grass alongside the Thames when I had recently turned 15. Picture a scene as pastoral as a Victorian narrative painting. Me, my friends Henry Pitman and James Althaus snogging with

Sue, Alison and Carol in the riverside grass - well, not James and Carol, they passed. But the two Henrys were going for it, tongues like pipe cleaners.

Sue, my first ever snog, was a nice girl - a little spotty, as we all were - mousey, sweet. But the story of my pre-married love life is that, somehow, the girl that I really fancied - the free spirit, with the long hair and the summer dress - always ended up with my best mate (or my brother). At that time this girl was called Alison. And she'd chosen the other Henry.

But this one time, there is a little miracle at the end of the tale. The Fourth of June is Eton's Sports Day, the day before the Summer Half Term when Mum and Dad come to visit with a picnic and to watch their expensive progeny throw rocks at each other (cricket) or, in my case, smile politely at the enamelled ashtrays and pipe bomb casings that we'd been required to make in pottery and metalwork. Eve-ryone, parents included, is dressed for the penguin migration and there is a general euphoria in the air. At the end of the afternoon, all boys must report to School Yard for Roll Call, before being driven home. I had managed to bunk off the boozy grown-up picnic half an hour before Roll Call and was on my own, kicking my heels in the street, when who should come floating round the corner, wearing a floppy hat and lovely blue cotton summer dress... but the unattainable one, Alison.

I don't remember what was said, but we were quickly in deserted South Meadow (right), lying in the long grass at the side of the field, me in my black woollen pinstripes, Alison in her blue cotton... It was the first time I had really felt the shape of a girl.

The fact that I had to report to School Yard in a matter of minutes - and then be off on Half Term - gave these few stolen minutes of snogging a girl I genu-inely fancied an intensity that kept me in dreams for months and years to come. Of course, when I came back from Half Term, it was as though it'd never happened. Alison had moved on.

But I did soon find another willing snogging partner. Also up the Eton Wick Road lived blonde and - if-you-had-a-elaborate-imagination, which I most certainly did - kind-of Jodie Foster looking, Stephanie, daughter of the man who looked after

the Physics Schools. Stephanie was the first girl I took home to Knebworth. She was allowed to come and stay for a few days in the holidays. This has since im-pressed me about her father and mother, as both she and I were 15. And I am also impressed that my parents put Stephanie in the bedroom opposite mine in Kneb-worth House.

Mrs Waldock, Knebworth House's elderly cleaning lady, on the other hand, was not impressed. She walked in on Stephanie and me in bed together on the first morning, and took her disapproval to my mother. To her credit, my Mum believed me when I said we had not had penetrative sex, and that I didn't intend to. You see, I was getting my Sex Ed now from the Granada 3 in Slough - from continental films with all the penises cut out, where lovemaking looked more fun if you did what the liberated lesbians did. It was only when lovers got round to 'penetrative sex' that the problems started. Ask John Trevelyan, the BBFC censor.

As long as I avoided '10' - I ranked the various sex acts from foreplay to penetrative sex from '0' to '10' - there were sex acts number '0.1' (holding hands?) to number '9.9' to experiment with. From the movies I had seen, 9.9 seemed more intimate and fun anyway. No need to worry about unwanted pregnancies, or cystitis, or all the symbolic associations of penetrative sex. I could be quite boring on the subject. I made it almost a campaign, and now wish I'd written that pamphlet to hand out at street corners, as I've forgotten the details. But I figured that if teenagers pledged to '0 - 9.9' and not to '10' then adults could relax, and we could all get on with experimenting and learning about sex. It was only '10' that adults were worried about. Free yourself from that stigma - convince adults that you are avoiding it - and you can have as much fun as Sylvia Kristel and her female tennis buddy in the changing room of the Bangkok Tennis Club.

I still think the '9.9' manifesto is a good idea for teenagers. I also think it's good for teaching about what adults call 'foreplay'. The problem's right there in the word itself. Foreplay. It should be called 'duringplay'. I did have worked out what all the various stages of 'duringplay' equated to on my 0 to 9.9 scale. I don't recall the chart any more. But I do remember that '7.8' was a favourite.

Sadly, my '9.9' manifesto - despite lectures I continue to give (including one on national Talk Radio in the 1990s) has never caught on. Your loss, teenagers.

My next adventure in the realms of girls led to the only time I met my Head Master. This might surprise you, but with 1250 boys at Eton College, the Head Master - a Mr McCrum - couldn't be expected to meet all of them.

I was always particular about which bedroom I was assigned - as a teenage prison cell, why wouldn't one care about its view, its neighbours, its secret storage space, its escape routes both physical and metaphysical?

In my 3rd year at Eton, when I was 15 going on 16, we moved for one year, with our new House Master Mr Faulkner, into centrally-located Carter House, whilst our future house on the edge of the town, Warre House, was re-furbished. In doing my research I discovered that tucked at the back of the house (right) two former maids' rooms were to be made available to boys since there was a shortage of rooms, and probably a shortage of maids. More senior boys than I - who got to choose first - were either unaware of these late additions, beyond Matron's quarters, or they preferred to be in the thick of things. So I managed to bag a particularly unusual room, tucked away under a back staircase. There were two of these 'maid's rooms'. The one above had been bagged by a more senior boy, Andy Morgan, a guitarist in the school's best rock band, The Syndromes.

Excuse a tangent here, because I consider myself fortunate to have been in the same House as the two guitarists of The Syndromes, a fine Clash/Jam-inspired indie band. The other, Justin Adams, is now Robert Plant's guitarist. Good fun therefore to read in an old school magazine clipping a review of a Syndromes concert in School Hall where, as an encore, the band teased the audience by playing the opening chords of *Stairway To Heaven*... before claiming they'd forgotten the chords and blasting into a punk number. I can picture Justin Adams, standing at Robert Plant's side today, performing exactly the same tease.

More of Led Zeppelin later, but now back to girls. My House Master Mr Faulkner had two daughters, maybe 11 and 14 (15? - I'm afraid I don't think so - but, remember, I was only 15) who would be allowed to play ping pong with us on a Sunday. One evening my friend Henry Pitman and I were standing together in a bathtub (clothed) peering out of a high window to see if we could see into Lucy Faulkner's bedroom window. Mr Faulkner appeared behind us and, reasonably enough, asked what we were doing... "Stargazing, sir" "Stargazing?" "Yes, sir. The stars look particularly beautiful tonight, sir." "If you wish to look at the stars, why don't you come and ask me, and I might give you permission to step outside to look at them?" "May we, sir?" "If you ask - yes." At which, Pitman and I went, very serious and

earnestly, to the House's front door, signed ourselves out as gone "Stargazing", and walked down to the middle of South Meadow... where we collapsed into giggles. For what it's worth, the stars above floodlit Windsor Castle were very beautiful that evening (unlike, right, in January 2020).

Whilst playing ping pong with Lucy, it was established, in a roundabout way, that her bedroom was not very far from mine, on the other side of Matron's quarters. I don't remember who first mentioned it, but it was playfully suggested that she should come visit. Maybe some form of challenge was proffered - "I don't believe you'd do it" - something that in the glare of hindsight would sound coercive, and dreadful. But, honest m'lud, I didn't for a minute think she would.

I was wrong. She did it. In the middle of the night, Lucy came creeping across the Matron's station and into my bedroom. What now?... Well, she lay on my bed and we cuddled... Come on! No, honest. I was 15, she was 14, for goodness sake. In my recollection is the shape of her breast under her nightie, but I don't remember any other touch or kiss. It was all really rather sweet and beautiful. In my memory it was Olivia Hussey and Leonard Whiting in Zefferelli's *Romeo and Juliet* (1968). Respect for them, kissing within 10 lines of meeting each other.

And then she went back to her own bedroom.

Who needs to stand in a bath?

And then she did it again. But this time, her father had heard her passage creeping... and stepped into the room behind her, as she was laying down beside me. Lucy was dismissed, sent immediately to her room. Mr Faulkner pulled up a chair. He was bright red in the face, lips pursed, and looked more anxious than we were. Having established that nothing had occurred beyond a cuddle, he went on to ask who I would tell about this?

I mumbled that I would probably tell my best mate of that time, Gordon Tait (also at the ping pong parties). "I would rather you didn't tell Gordon, Henry." "All right." "I would rather you didn't tell anybody." "All right." "You may want to tell your parents. I will tell the Head Master. But beyond that, let's keep this between ourselves?" "All right."

The next morning I went to a public phone box in the street (ironic that a 'public' phone box was where I could get some privacy) and called my Mum. "Were you in her room, or was she in yours?" "She was in mine." "Oh, that's all right then. Hopefully they won't throw you out." James Bond was expelled from Eton for being discovered in a House Maid's room. I was in a House Maid's room - but with the House Master's daughter.

I went to see the Head Master. A nice enough chap. He sat in a big leather chair and repeated what Mr Faulkner had said, that it would be better if I didn't talk about it with anyone, and asked what 'A' Levels was I planning to do? That was it.

And I didn't talk about it. Not until 30 years after I had left the school and I held a reunion weekend at Knebworth House with my Faulkner's House peers (below)... 12 out of 14 of my year in the House made it for the visit, from all around

A good turn out of my housemate contemporaries, 30 years on... and then 40 years on..

the world. But not Gordon Tait, who was in Denmark. So I still don't think I've told him.

Of the two House Masters I had at Eton, I am unusual amongst my housemates for having got on better with Mr Faulkner than our first House Master, Mr Bull. I understand why Mr Bull was popular - a genial bear of a man, who loved his music, humpfed about in loafers, scratching his chest. He generally had a more laissez-faire 1970s attitude to House Mastering. He also had daughters - even more of them - but we never saw them. Maybe because Wayneflete House was bigger. Or maybe because I was 13 & 14 whilst in his care, and hadn't yet discovered how to use two spoons and a pepper pot to engage with girls.

As part of fostering individuality, Eton is a rare school that offers boys a room of their own from their very first day at the school. On my very first day, my father helped me blu tack familiar and favourite posters on my new bedroom wall, to make me feel more at home. We placed around the room - in a row of matching rectangles, like the Tracy family's communication screens in Thunderbirds - my favourite film stars of the time. There was Robert Redford, Paul Newman, Clint

Eastwood, Charlton Heston, Charles Bronson, Omar Sharif... all men. My father suggested that I might get teased for having only men on my wall. I didn't know what he was talking about.

As it happened, I didn't get called 'gay'. I did get called 'wet'. I still don't quite know what being 'wet' means? I have just Googled it - "it generally means your genitals are lubricating." I don't think it does. Maybe Mr Spencer's summer quiz would not be invalidated by Google.

There was more serious gossip in the House on that front. One of the boys in my year was being stalked by a man from outside the school called Mr Andrews, who would hang around outside in the street, and I think at one point even made it into the house (no keypad locks in those days) and into the unfortunate boy's bedroom. This is shocking to consider now, but at the time it seemed acceptable that we should simply be on our guard for this sort of thing.

Hidden instead in my bedsheets, to traumatise me, I would find maggots. To be fair maggots were always going to get a bigger rise out of me. Not being a fisherman, I was unfamiliar with, and loathed, maggots. Little white wiggling penises flashed at me was not going to trouble me. Prep school had prepared me for those. There were other boys than me more fun to bully with a real penis.

My very straight Ugandan soon-to-be foster-brother Dan (left, see Chapter 8), was much more likely to have an erection waved at him from down the corridor, "What do you think of this, Bongo?!" Yes, the whole school called Dan 'Bongo'. This was the 1970s. An all boys' boarding school in the 1970s.

So did penis play continue at my senior school? Not so much at Eton, as we were all expected to be in our own rooms at bedtime. Plus, as a teenager, my fascination quickly zeroed in on girls. It was not long before Robert Redford and Paul Newman were joined on my bedroom wall by Brigitte Bardot in unbuttoned denim hot pants. And as my erotic fantasies and wall decorations evolved, the male/female ratio swung predominantly female.

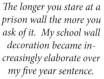

The longer you stare at a prison wall the more you ask of it. My school wall decoration became increasingly elaborate over my five year sentence.

In that first house, Waynefleet, my window looked out over the garden of Mr Nicholson's House opposite. Mr Nicholson was my first English teacher at Eton and I remember - in my very first ever lesson at the school - this tall grasshopper of a man getting no further than explaining the word 'corset' on the first page of C. S. Forester's The African Queen. M.A.N., as he was known, also had a daughter (it seems to have been a requirement of Eton housemasters), and I remember the talk of Waynefleet House was that, when the leaves fell off the trees, around the school saint St Andrew's Day, you could see straight into her bedroom window. I don't think that's why St Andrew was the school saint, but it would be a good reason.

I don't recall ever seeing Mary Nicholson - so this may have been a myth - but we would certainly enjoy stories of this mythical blonde told in the senior common room, where junior boys would congregate at certain times of the day to be sent on errands. 'Fagging' - junior boys 'slaving' for senior boys - was for centuries a throw up of a classical education... like pederasty. But, like pederasty, it became less fashionable post the 1970s. In fact, I am proud to say that it was my generation that abolished it in my House. Only shame being, that future Prime Minister David Cameron was a junior in my House when I was a senior, and I therefore never got to go to the tabloids with the headline "P. M. WAS MY FAG."

One boy in particular, who was in Mr Nicholson's House, I distinctly remember slouched on our senior common room sofas - and this is unusual, as I remember very few elder boys. I remember one or two for particular reasons - there was the one who had a spine condition (like contortionists have) that meant he could give himself a blow job, although I did not witness this personally; and everyone knew the notorious prefect Armitage who happily fined you for not wearing a tie when crossing Windsor Bridge. Alex married family friend Carolyn Allen and now I'd happily be fined by him for turning up inappropriately dressed at the delicious luncheons and parties he hosts at his lovely home. Otherwise, I recall only the two elder boys for whom I personally 'fagged', Richard Fife and Justin Frewen.

This personal 'fagging' was not as bad as it sounds. I'd have to take Fife and Frewen's suits to the cleaners, and tidy their rooms. But there were perks. I would get to read Fife's pile of Mayfair magazines (I say read, I mean stare at the big glossy photographs of women undressed) and Frewen would let me use his record player, to play Diana Ross's single Do You Know Where You're Going To? (which I liked because it was in a film - an 'AA' certified film which you had to be 14 to see, and I was only 13). I wonder if Frewen knew where he was going to? Jail, it turned out. A few years later. For defrauding old ladies, I was told. I liked him. Fife was all right too. Now a Yorkshire landowner. I owe them both. They gave me access to two main motivators in life - naked girls and music - at a key, formative age.

...oh, the boy from M.A.N. The one who sticks in my memory, because he must have exuded a natural charisma in excess of the other mouthy 18-year-olds lounging around the grubby sofas of the senior common room. Funny how some people just have it. Naturally. The only other senior boy I really remember from my time as a junior at Eton is Hugh Laurie.

CHAPTER SIX

Music

SubBread's the only thing in my head
Can't think of anything Bread hasn't said

(*SubBread*, 1978. The very first and the very worst lyric
I ever wrote. Embarrassingly, I was 16. Kate Bush wrote
The Man With The Child In His Eyes when she was 13.

Wellesley House suggested to my first House Master at Eton, Mr Bull, that I had a natural ear for music (part of its rich pitch to get me in?). In my first week Mr Bull sent me to see the Head of Music. A note was played on the piano and I was asked to sing it. I was clueless as to how to respond to a piano note. Laaaaaaaaaaa. A second note was played. Laaaaaaaaaaa. Why am I here? The thought was mutual.

I loved music, but its formal structures and science were beyond me. I regret now not persevering more with formal music training at school. The opportunities were there. A whole building full of instruments and instructors. But I preferred just to pick up a guitar in my bedroom, and learn the eight chords I needed to warble Smokie (Chinn/Chapman) tracks about wild angels and the girl next door.

I taught myself to strum well enough to attract the attention of my parents, siblings and girlfriends - by matching the finger chords for *Hush Little Baby* (traditional) and *All My Loving* (Lennon/McCartney) over and over and over and over - and then moving on to compose my own adolescent lullabies by singing different melodies to chord sequences by David Gates of the American band Bread. That was enough for me. Why?! It is still, to this day, where my instrument playing ability stands frozen in time. But you can play a lot of great songs with eight chords.

Photo: Nicky Evans

I must have been a disappointment to the very musical Mr Bull. But I did receive my House Master's praise for one thing. And this happy memory does suggest to me that we do all find our natural path, whether or not we are looking for it. Once a week we'd have to write a prose composition for Mr Bull. He'd give us a title or a theme, which I would resolutely ignore and subvert into something completely different. All of my offerings were provocatively surreal. To his great credit, and my great encouragement, Mr Bull praised these. Most of the time. Every so often he lost his patience and threw it back. But, overall, he said I had a talent for the surreal and, de facto, for writing. He said I had an original mind. Thank you Mr Bull.

Otherwise my memories of my two years - aged 13 & 14 - in his House, Waynefleet, are random... the round-bodied, round-headed, German ex-P.O.W. who cleaned our shoes - I don't understand why we couldn't clean our own shoes, but I'm pleased he got a job out of it; the distinct smell of the entrance hall (boys & boots & boot polish); and Tea Time. Tea Time was generally hot buttered toast in our bedrooms. No, not the Toast Game, where the last one to ejaculate on the toast has to eat it. I never played that. Each Term we were expected to choose some friends to share Tea Time with. I was unusual in that I preferred not to choose my friends. I knew my friends would not only be interested in me, but also in my food - and whether or not I turned up. I didn't want to be noticed if I wasn't there. If I was off dreaming in the long grass by the Thames, or off dreaming in the stained red velour of the Granada 3.

William Hobhouse was not interested in me, my food, or whether I turned up. I am not sure what he was interested in. I probably never asked. He is now a Liberal Democrat who sells industrial glue, with a brilliant wife who's M.P. for Bath. A liberal with a brilliant wife - so not so very different from me after all. At 14, he was my perfect Tea companion. If I turned up, it was just to eat - and listen to the D.J. Roger Scott on Capital Radio, and his 'Hitline', a daily Top 5 of the most requested songs on his phone-in line.

Photo: Anita Prinett - along with numerous others in this book - thanks Anita!

I've seen Hobhouse once since I leaving school. In Italy. How Merchant Ivory he and I look. I popped in for Tea

Every 5 o'clock, the point of interest to me was which single was today's Number 1 on the Hitline Top 5? For most of the summer of 1977 it was Rod Stewart's double A-side of *I Don't Want To Talk About It* and *The First Cut Is The Deepest*. This was the perfect late afternoon summer soundtrack for a drippy love-starved adolescent like me. As Hobhouse and I boiled our tins of soup/beans (tin can in the saucepan, so there was no washing up) the burning question for me was which side of the record would Roger Scott play? I always preferred *I Don't Want To Talk About It,* and was disappointed when he played *The First Cut Is The Deepest.* Nowadays, I get a greater thrill hearing the latter - but nowadays I prefer Lindt 70% Cocoa Dark to Cadbury's Dairy Milk. What do kids know?

Of course what everybody else wanted, was for those soppy girly ballads to be blasted off the Number 1 spot by the Sex Pistols' *God Save The Queen,* which the BBC and most other radio stations refused to play. Credit to Roger Scott and Capital Radio, who did play it, when of course the Hitline Top 5 was bombarded with phone votes for the Pistols. For me, however, June 1977 was all about Rod Stewart. Although I now have a healthy nostalgia for punk, at that time the best rebellion for a contrary teenager in my testosterone-filled environment was to like American love songs... West Coast love songs, especially David Gates; East Coast love songs, especially Janis Ian; Southern love songs, especially Crystal

No, never a convincing punk

You discovered 304 new artists this year. But you really vibed with Gallagher And Lyle.

Gayle; and Northern love songs, especially Lionel Ritchie - I know, the Commodores were from Alabama, but they were on Detroit's Motown... How about Northern love songs, as in Scottish? - Add to Rod Stewart the love songs of Benny Gallagher & Graham Lyle... and, even more confusing to my contemporaries, I especially liked the American love songs of the 1930s & 40s, in particular Bing Crosby and Fred Astaire (because I loved their movies). Although less so Frank Sinatra, because other people quite liked him.

I don't remember where I was when I heard that Elvis had died. But I do remember where I was, two months later, in October 1977, when I heard that Bing Crosby had died. I was in my 'Maid's Room' in Carter House and I was genuinely sad. The very first thing I ever recorded on a 'video cassette' was Bob Hope's moving tribute to Bing Crosby on his death. I listen to a lot of Bing Crosby. Even the later naff stuff. I get a warm glow from the familiarity of the later albums recorded in London by Ken Barnes (nerd alert - please do skip to the next chapter if you really couldn't give a toss). To this day, I make a point of playing Bing Crosby and Ken Barnes's jingly jangly and screamingly naff *On The Very First Day of the Year* (from Bing Crosby's final album *Seasons*) every 1st January. And I don't keep many traditions.

DOMINION THEATRE, Tottenham Court Rd.
DEREK BLOCK presents
BOB HOPE IN PERSON
plus Orchestra and Special Guest
WEDNESDAY **10** Evening 8.00
OCTOBER Doors open 7.30
STALLS
£10.00
ZZ 12

Bing Crosby died on a golf course in Spain, and although I have never seen the attraction of golf, I figure it must be an acceptable pastime if he did it. No rationale to this thinking. Apparently he wasn't very nice to his kids, and I won't be condoning that because he did it. But I've always been a big fan. And one of the more bizarre moments of my life was, many years later, when I stood before his granddaughter Denise, who looks very like him - facially, anyway - watching her have breathless, red-faced, simulated sex in a movie scene that I had written. But m.o.w.l. - more of which later.

The following year, 1978, came with another musical bullet to my teenage concentration. It is absurd, and a wretched indictment of early pop music, that Kate Bush's *Wuthering Heights* - written when she was a teenager - is the first ever UK No 1 single self-written by a woman. But it reminds of the sensation Kate Bush represented. The first proper concert I went to (apart from the ones in my own garden, m.o.w.l.) - on my 17th birthday in 1979 - was to see Kate Bush at the Hammersmith Odeon... and I haven't seen many concerts since that have sent me to bed with so many thoughts of possibility in my head. Kate Bush was soon moving Robert Redford even further down the pecking order on my school bedroom wall.

I remember Roger Scott playing Kate Bush's *Breathing*, and remarking that he couldn't see the postman whistling that one on his rounds. Kate Bush was beautiful. She wrote beautiful music. She was original. She was sexy. She was more or less my age. What was not to like?... Only that a lot of other people liked her. I remained a defiantly contrary teenager. I preferred the things my contemporaries disliked. And unlike them, I didn't dislike what I didn't love. I liked all music.

It was a good time for music. Alongside punk, new wave, disco, and the residuals of glam, some behemoth L.P.s appeared. *Hotel California*. *Rumours*. *Breakfast In America*. I am fortunate to have these albums as the soundtrack of my teenage years. But my special affection is reserved for my own particular like-what-nobody-else-likes soundtrack.

David Gates, formally of Bread, was the backbone to this contrariness. I've never met anyone apart from myself (and perhaps my sister) who likes the lyrically ridiculous *Took The Last Train* from David Gates's *Goodbye Girl* album - but also on this album are songs that I consider almost perfect. Compositionally, lyrically, consider if you will *Part Time Love*. I could be content not to write another thing if I had written this. And looking back over David Gates's catalogue, how perfect a lullaby is Bread's *The Other Side of Life*? These are songs that are apparently simple, beautifully poetic and composition-

ally rounded... perfect. I could listen to them over and over and over again. And nobody at Eton in the late 1970s was listening to David Gates.

I know, I know... that's the kind of paragraph that will make many want to toss this book out the window. Consider, if you are still reading, that this is exactly the same impulse my contemporaries had about my guitar and my radio at school... and later, when I was a senior, my record player. But I do love being annoyingly contrary.

"Seventeen, been a while since I was 17..."

American music, generally, was not listened to by my peers. Eton boys listened to English bands that came from American music: Zeppelin, the Stones, Clapton, etc., and English bands that seemed American: Fleetwood Mac, Supertramp, etc.... but otherwise it was British punk or British prog. That was it.

There were no such prejudices, however, in Roger Scott on Capital Radio. If my friend Nicky Horne (who compered a number of the early Knebworth Concerts) is reading this, I am sure Roger Scott wasn't the only one - but he was the DJ that was on when we were allowed to listen to the radio, in the late afternoon. Roger Scott championed American music. I remember he played The Beach Boys regularly. Again, American music that none of my contemporaries were interested in. And then, as the 1970s turned into the 1980s, he played even more Beach Boys... because Capital Radio was promoting a Beach Boys reunion at Knebworth Park on 21st June 1980.

Of all the things that remind me that I have had a privileged life, high up there is the fact that the green field outside my house has become Britain's largest concert venue, and recognised worldwide as England's 'home of classic rock'.

LIVE AT KNEBWORTH 1980

CHAPTER SEVEN

Knebworth Concerts

*Just had a McDs breakfast. Lord above.
Up there with Knebworth*

Liam Gallagher *Twitter* 10th July 2020
(punctuation added)

Almost all the greatest rock bands (especially the British ones) have played Knebworth Park, and many at key milestones in their careers. For many it has been a defining moment - Led Zeppelin's last ever UK shows with their original line up, The Beach Boys last ever UK show with their original line up, Queen's last ever show ever with their original line up, etc.

I am particularly fortunate as my life has intersected perfectly with this history. I was 12-years-old for the first concert in 1974 - and may expect to be 62-years-old for the 50th Anniversary in 2024. I have witnessed every one of them.

Except one. I was imprisoned at boarding school in 1975, when Pink Floyd played *Dark Side of the Moon* and *Wish You Were Here*. This, my father delighted in telling me, was the best Knebworth Concert. He has also been to every one, but one. I delight in telling him that, no, the only one that <u>he</u> missed was the best. He was booked on holiday on the Sunday night of Robbie Williams in 2003, which, in my book (the one in your hands) was the best ever Knebworth Concert. It was certainly the most fun and relaxed of the three nights of that breathtaking show-to-beat-all-shows. A show to beat all shows? Don't believe me? Watch the video.

Otherwise ask me what the best Knebworth Concert was, and I will say The Beach Boys in 1980. "The Beach Boys?! Not Led Zeppelin? Oasis?..." "No, The Beach Boys." Knebworth '80 was small for a Knebworth Concert. 40,000 people. Knebworth's unique single stage capacity is 125,000. But The Beach Boys was 40,000 people dancing in a field, which I don't believe had ever happened in Britain prior to this. Of course, thousands of people dancing in a field, since the 1990s, has been common. But this was 1980. The decades before had been about hippy swaying and head nodding. The Beach Boys at Knebworth was a festival of pure unabashed happiness and dancing.

The fact that I had almost completed my 'A' Levels, and was about to leave school for ever, may have contributed to my general euphoria. But I still say - except for Robbie Williams' Sunday night - it was the most tick-all-of-the-boxes Knebworth Concert. And the most fun. Therefore the best.

In the summer that my son Edward completed his 'A' Levels, and left school - 2010 - Alice Cooper (right) came to his garden and played *School's Out*.

We are, indeed, lucky kids.

The history of Knebworth Concerts is a subject for another book. Perhaps I'll write it for the 50th Anniversary in 2024. In the meantime, below is the cover photo I used on one I prepared earlier. in 2003 - available on Amazon for a few quid - a 48-page A4 scrapbook of the first 30 years. *Knebworth - 30 years of the greatest rock venue in the world!*

Nobody has yet challenged me on this title. Talk it up, my Hollywood training insists. And I don't let up in the book's preface: *Two million people share these memories. They were the summers of our youth. They were our escape from everyday worlds. They were early pilgrimages to the hillside of our heroes. They were lost moments with Ron-nie Van Zant (Lynyrd Skynyrd), John Bonham (Led Zeppelin), Dennis Wilson (The Beach Boys), Freddie Mercury (Queen), all of whom left this world soon after... and mass triumphal chants to 'Hey Jude', 'Roll With It' and 'Let Me Entertain You'. They were our music, our time... in Freddie's words, they were the days of our lives.*

Great photo by Sim Scott taken at the Deep Purple reunion concert in 1985. Even if, in retrospect - as my longtime & treasured book-keeper Jocelyn Rowe points out - it does look a bit like a BNP rally.

I've cropped the Confederate flag (celebrating Southern Rock) too, because here in the 2020s that's not helping either.

The very first Knebworth Festival on 20th July 1974, featuring The Allman Brothers, The Doobie

My kids are now the young teenagers that I was in 1974 when my parents host-ed the first 'Bucolic Frolic'. Another generation is set to make Knebworth its own. Here's to the next 30 years... may they have such memories as these!

Yes, I get heady talking about Knebworth Concerts. But they are heady days. For one weekend a year, the highs of my privileged life are lifted onto an even higher plane. Turned up to eleven. Like Christmas weekend. Or my Dad's Quatorze Juil-let birthday party - every second weekend in July - which always kicked off the summer-holidays. When people say, "How much fun to have grown up with all that rock and roll madness going on around you!" Yes. Yes. Yes. It was, indeed.

Particularly back in the years I personally did not have direct responsibility for it. Unlike the Eavis family at Glastonbury, my family has steered clear of promoting the concerts ourselves. We did used to have to be the event licence holders. This is because we were the ones still there on Monday morning, who could be held to account by the local authorities. My father ended up in court more than once for breaches of a concert licence over which he had no control. Still today, the licence - and our reputation - remains something we work hard to protect. We insist now on

working closely with promoters. We know how Knebworth Park works. We've done it before.

There is an audience bootleg of the audio of the first Knebworth concert in 1974. You can hear Van Morrison dedicating *Twilight Zone* to "Fred Bannister". The early days were not smooth sailing financially or organisationally, but Knebworth Park owes the beginnings of this world class brand to the legend that is the late Freddy Bannister [L.D.O.B "Rock promoter behind the first Knebworth festival who not only survived Hell's Angels but even Led Zeppelin's rapacious manager"]. Having inspired the Eavis family to start the Glastonbury Festival with his festivals at Bath, Freddy promoted all of our 1970s concerts. He was the one who saw the potential of Knebworth Park's natural bowl amphitheatre and motorway links. He was the one who persuaded my ini-

Brothers, Van Morrison, Mahavishnu Orchestra, Alex Harvey and Tim Buckley - all for £2.75

tially sceptical father and mother that they were sitting in the perfect location for a large scale rock concert - and could he bring Led Zeppelin?

He didn't actually bring Led Zeppelin until the end of the decade - and when he did, despite a triumphant event, it led to bankruptcy and the implosion of his promoting career. But in the years inbetween Freddy (right) built the basis for the legendary status that Knebworth Park enjoys today. All hail Freddy Bannister!

These were the early years of the commercial music festival. Very little of the licensing regulation, traffic regulation, health & safety regulation, etc. that is ubiquitous today existed in the 1970s. I have been told that the lessons learnt in crowd control at these early

concerts are now taught in universities around the country. Back in those days local Girl Guides would do the litter picking - without much thought to what they might pick up. The toilets, for years, were simply plyboard plinths, with

I had a reputation for listening to crap

egg-shaped holes cut in them, overhanging an earth pit. At the 1974 concert, one of the plinths couldn't take the weight of bottoms and collapsed, bottoms and all, into the shit pit. We've come a long way to the 'glamping' of festivals today.

Today crowds get the nannying they deserve for being less tolerant. When people complain at having to sit in traffic jams, I say you can't get 125,000 people into a field without a traffic jam - and it is being a part of 125,000 like-minded people that is what makes these events so awesome. We shouldn't not do them because they cause traffic jams. They happen on rare summer weekends. They give memories for a lifetime. What it takes to make them happen is worth it.

It is not a Knebworth story, but I have a favourite memory of the traffic jam after Wham's Final concert at Wembley Stadium in 1986. Everybody had their car windows down, still singing the earworm "Yeah, Yeah, Yeah... La, La, La, La, La, La" of *The Edge of Heaven*. A car park chorus. There was so much joy at the shared experience in the air. Long after the concert had finished... So I say, take a picnic. Turn up the stereo. Make the traffic jam part of the celebration. Don't just love the music. You can do that at home. Love the crowds. Love the queuing. Love the mud. Love the rubbish.

Love the communal urinating. Remember, your grandchildren will wish they'd been here. I read it on their Twitter feeds every day. You're the lucky one who is here.

'Peace & Love', of course, was in more abundance in the mid 1970s. The '74 concert - once Led Zeppelin had dropped out - was a mainly American affair, with the Allman & Doobie Brothers topping the bill. At 12 years old, I had a beautiful Custer jacket - brown suede, with tasselled arms and tasselled back - and in the euphoria of the

evening family friend Alan Ponte gave me a matching brown leather hat he'd just bought in Morocco. At 12, I was THE MAN. Ramblin' 'n' Runnin', 'n' Right On.

Two years later, at the Rolling Stones concert - with its spectacular red lips stage (designed by Bill Harkin, who also designed the Pyramid Stage at Glastonbury) - I was 14. I was no longer at the top of my junior school, but at the bottom of my senior school, fagging, spotty, gawky. Now I was clearly NOT THE MAN. I shook Mick Jagger's hand before the show, and what was my 14-year-old mind thinking? It was thinking, think where this hand has been! I was much more interested in the naked swimming pool parties than the music. *Star Trek* was more sexy to me than Mick Jagger (if you've not seen it recently, I promise you the Original Series is sexier than you remember. It was George Lucas who took the sex out of science fiction). There were many more girls in *Star Trek* than in the Rolling Stones. In the days before video cassettes and TiVo/Sky+, it was a big deal for a 14-year-old boy to miss a *Star Trek* episode. You wouldn't get to see it again. Whereas I would get to see the Rolling Stones again.

At the time, of course, that wasn't a given. Keith Richards was having fresh

blood flown in from Switzerland. Mick Jagger said he couldn't see himself "still doing this at 40." I have been harangued and ridiculed ever since for staying home to watch *Star Trek* when the Rolling Stones were playing in the garden. But I was popular for it at the time - for caretaking Knebworth House when no one else wanted to. And there was only me to answer the doorbell when Paul McCartney turned up for the afterparty. I think I told him to go away and come back later. I did pop out to the arena, quickly, for one song - maybe during a commercial break - and recall standing at the very back of the 120,000 crowd looking up at

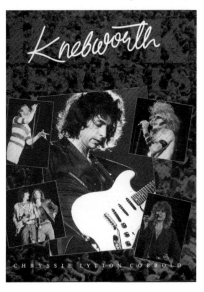

a large video screen. If this wasn't the first time video screens had been used in a concert crowd, it was one of the first. The song, I remember, was *Fool To Cry*. A love song. I liked that one.

So go read my Mum's two books - *The Knebworth Rock Festivals* and *Board Meetings In The Bath* - for stories of the wild house parties that went on during these early Knebworth Festivals. I was there - and loving every minute of the craziness - but I wasn't in the pool or in the sauna (a 1970s addition to Knebworth House), or down at the front of the show, or backstage (for backstage stories go to Freddy Bannister's book *There Must Be A Better Way*). I can tell you that, at the Rolling Stones show, Ronnie Wood's sister wanted to take a frog-shaped bamboo basket from our sauna room as a souvenir, and that 7-year-old Marlon Richards had a tantrum when Mick said he couldn't take one of my sister's pet rabbit's babies on tour... But I wasn't there when a family friend asked Jack Nicholson what he did for a living (he'd just won an Oscar for *One Flew Over The Cuckoo's Nest*), or when the band were all sat in a circle on the floor of the Queen Elizabeth Room bathroom being administered to by 'Dr Robert' or 'Groovy Bob', whichever one it was. What I noticed was that Keith Richards had the first domestic video camera I'd ever seen. Somewhere in the world are those video tapes. They would be worth watching.

Three years later, at the Led Zeppelin concerts, the party at Knebworth House was just as mad, but not as fun - as, no surprise, the Led Zeppelin bandwagon was not as much of a family affair. I remember showing Peter Grant, Led Zeppelin's manager, to the kitchen loo - and wondering if he would fit in the little room, as he was so enormous. Perhaps the fact that he was so sweaty would help lubricate him in. I will have assumed he wanted a pee. Peter Grant was not fun - like Ron Wood's sister had been three years before - and before the weekend was over he had strong-armed Freddy Bannister into liquidation and foreign exile. We didn't hear from Freddy again until after Peter Grant was dead, some twenty years later.

I do, however, remember the exact spot in the concert field where I was stand-

ing, on both weekends, for the eight minutes of *Stairway To Heaven*. Like *Fool To Cry* this was a track that resonated. Because it was beautiful.

But it was 1980 when I first really loved the music at a Knebworth concert. The Beach Boys was also a family affair. All the brothers and cousins were there (because they were all in the band) and, as it turned out, for the very last time (as Dennis Wilson drowned the following year). It was also the first time I was of interest to the band. I took Al Jardine to the very top tower of the roof and we spent most of the afternoon together. He gave me his address and said to look him up in Big Sur when we came to California later that summer. Brian Wilson was not in great mental shape, but perked up after woofing our entire chocolate cake. It was an emotional time for the band, and the footage is now a precious record. As @rossloco93 remarked recently on Twitter (01.05.20), Dennis is "banging them drums like he is in Sabbath."

Freddy tells the story that the only way they could get the band to stand together like this for publicity photos was to hire a stripper. In later versions, the photo has its top off too, and a Texas blue sky superimposed over Knebworth

I remember The Beach Boys all in our long Picture Gallery drawing room. At one end sat Paul Jones, whose band The Blues Band was opening the day's bill and who was dating a family friend, Carolyn Allen. The Beach Boys did not know who he was - and yet, throughout the 60s, if the Beach Boys were Number 1 in the States, Manfred Mann (of which Paul was the singer) would have been Number 1 in the U.K. This thought made an impression on me. The idea of having had fame, and then lost it or, like Paul Jones, set it aside. It became a romantic notion to me. One that would crop up in my screenplays in the

On the roof of Knebworth House with Al Jardine

future. The guy who nobody recognises, but whose song is playing as musak on the supermarket speakers. I dreamt of being a 'has been'. I still do. Thing is, you have to have been a 'been' first. And not - as my son says - a 'wasn't'.

There's still time. As the next set of concerts illustrated. Most of the headliners were much older than I am as I write this. When, in 1981, there were riots on Clapham Common, Capital Radio moved their Jazz Festi-

Day by day at Britain's greatest music festival
On two exciting weekends at Knebworth Park, Stevenage, Herts.

SATURDAY 17 JULY 12 noon to 10.30 pm	SATURDAY 24 JULY 12 noon to 10.30 pm
B.B. KING	**RAY CHARLES**
JIMMY CLIFF	**GERRY MULLIGAN**
	BIG BAND
BENNY GOLSON & ART FARMER JAZZTET	**M.J.Q.**
JAY McSHANN	CARMEN McRAE
RED NORVO/TAL FARLOW TRIO	FREDDIE HUBBARD/RON CARTER
BOBBY LAMB/RAY PREMRU BIG BAND	MIDNITE FOLLIES ● CLARK TERRY
RONNIE SCOTT QUINTET	PIZZA EXPRESS ALL STARS
JOHNNY GRIFFIN	DAVE BITELLI'S ONWARD
GB BLUES COMPANY	INTERNATIONALS
SUNDAY 18 JULY 12 noon to 10.30 pm	SUNDAY 25 JULY 12 noon to 10.30 pm
THE CRUSADERS	**BENNY GOODMAN**
DIZZY GILLESPIE	**LIONEL HAMPTON**
SPYRO GYRA	**BIG BAND**
ERIC GALE	**DAVE BRUBECK**
DICK HYMAN'S CLASSIC JAZZ BAND	GREAT GUITARS: BARNEY KESSEL, HERB
CHICO FREEMAN	ELLIS, CHARLIE BYRD ● STEPS: MIKE
NATIONAL YOUTH JAZZ ORCHESTRA	BRECKER, PETER ERSKINE, EDDIE GOMEZ,
GEORGIE FAME & MARIAN MONTGOMERY	DON GROLNICK, MIKE MAINIERI
IAN CARR'S NUCLEUS	WYNTON MARSALIS QUARTET
SHAKATAK	ART BLAKEY ● MORRISSEY MULLEN
	ZOOT MONEY ● BREAKFAST BAND

CAPITAL RADIO JAZZ FESTIVAL '82

PRESENTED BY CAPITAL RADIO
IN ASSOCIATION WITH CHILTERN RADIO

val to Knebworth Park for two years. In the early 1980s many of the original greats of Jazz and Blues were still alive. Ella Fitzgerald, Muddy Waters, Dizzy Gillespie, Dave Brubeck... were all in their 60s; Ray Charles, Chuck Berry, B.B.King, Sarah Vaughan, were youngsters in their 50s... Lionel Hampton and Benny Goodman were still going strong in their 70s. That is not usual now, but it was back then. Even Bing Crosby's brother Bob was there.... and a future hero of mine - as Julie London's guitarist - Barney Kessel. It was a breathtaking line up of heroes. Ella Fitzgerald (below, with my father,

THE OBSERVER, SUNDAY 4 MARCH 1984

PAUL GAMBACCINI offers his own theory for British success in the pop music field.

Two years ago, no one would have thought it could be chic to braid your hair and wear a smock.

Best..

Lurking in these two images is me having shed my 70s denims for 80s black trousers sewed to white trousers. In the foreground is Muddy Waters and Johnny de Falbe of Sandoe's Bookshop in Chelsea, which I trust therefore will stock this book.

EVENING STANDARD

Jolly Cobbold

I WAS intrigued at the weekend by the flamboyant dress of Henry Cobbold, 19-year-old grandson of Lord Cobbold, formerly Lord Chamberlain of the Royal Household and Governor of the Bank of England. At his second

cousin's wedding at the family estate of Knebworth, Herts, there was mild dismay at his New Romantic version of the 'tails' worn by other guests.

Henry donned a black-pointed poncho over his white ruffled shirt and evening trousers. His hair was plaited and beaded in a modest dreadlock style.

ISSUE DATED 27 JUL 1981

with his second engagement of the day, the ill-starred Capital Jazz Festival.

Henry, whose father, the Hon. David, manages the estate, said: "I normally dress like this but as a concession to the family I re-moved the beads from my cloak."

perhaps more in keeping

and his favourite album) caused the most excitement. She came for Tea. We kept the teacup with her red lipstick print on it, for many years, hanging on the dining room wall - until an untypically overzealous au pair washed it up after a party, thinking it was part of that night's decadence.

For decadence, the concert to beat became Queen's Knebworth appearance in 1986. By the mid-1980s, the bands were tending to helicopter in and out rather than stay the weekend, or for a Knebworth House afterparty. Queen, celebrating the end of their sell out world tour, chose to have their afterparty backstage. The band shipped in an entire fairground, complete with naked mud wrestling. The downside of everyone having so much fun, was that nobody remembered to press 'Record' on the video (for the video screens) of Freddie Mercury's last ever live performance.

Four years later, for the Nordoff Robbins charity concert - where everybody played (McCartney, Floyd, John, Clapton, Page & Plant, etc.) - the promoters brought in a Hard Rock Cafe for the backstage party. This was when it became clear that Knebworth had become a world brand. The concert was broadcast worldwide on MTV. Driving down Sunset Boulevard in Hollywood (where I was liv-

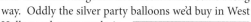

ing in 1990), up on a billboard, there was home - the album cover, and, in giant letters the word 'KNEBWORTH'. The little village in Hertfordshire had come a long way. Oddly the silver party balloons we'd buy in West Hollywood were made in Stevenage, but Stevenage has yet to make it onto a Sunset Boulevard billboard. Knebworth '90 even made it onto the front of KitKat chocolate bars.

Then in 1996, Oasis took a shot at trumping Queen for the most decadent Knebworth weekend. Melody Maker pointed out (17/08/96) that "if the audience from either show lay down in a row they would stretch from the Gallaghers' home in Burnage to Knebworth." And pass just south of Leicester. Again, no after party in Knebworth House - the brothers chose to remain backstage overnight between their two shows - but Noel made an attempt to sober up on Sunday morning by

turning up at the backdoor of Knebworth House asking if he could have a bath. A houseguest answering the door, thinking Noel was a straggling concert-goer from the night before, told him to "Fuck Off". The misunderstanding was cleared up - and Noel took a bath in Knebworth House's Queen Elizabeth Room four poster bath (left). We did not follow the Ella Fitzgerald tradition and keep the soap. But my father - described by Noel in subsequent interviews as 'a liveried servant' - brought him a bottle of champagne in the bath (not helping the sobering up). In the Visitor's Book on the way out Noel wrote, "Noel Gallagher. Clean." His minder wrote, "Rufus. Dirty."

After 30 years, Robbie Williams became the first 'solo' Knebworth headline. The three consecutive nights had sold out - 375,000 tickets - 10 months in advance. The whole show, everything - every single one of those millions of pounds and 375,000 travel plans made - rested on one man. He couldn't go on a bender and let his brother pick up the slack, or rely on Ron Wood to be there for any missed chords.

The week before the show Robbie did have a cold, and for the sound check on Thursday his voice was not 100%. I can only imagine the stress that caused him and the promoters. I was there when he arrived. I could have, would have, stepped forward with my hand outstretched and wished him "Welcome to Knebworth" - but I could see that in seconds I'd have been face-in-the-dirt with my arm twisted behind my back and his half dozen minders with their knees in me. His management, rightly, kept him fully cotton wooled and cling filmed. He could only drink from sealed containers. So he was not going to be leaving his lip print on our tea cup or woofing our chocolate cake. A new world order. And a shame. But the result was that Robbie Williams was back on

form - indeed top form - for the biggest weekend of his career.

That weekend was amazing in so many ways. As well as being - at 375,000 - the biggest music event in British history (the only close contender being the Isle of Wight Festival in 1970, where the ticketing went awry, and aerial photos show there were not as many as claimed), it was also probably the largest gathering of the fe-

male sex in a field in British history. A good 75% of the Robbie Williams audience was female. Most between the age of 18 and 50. The tickets sold out 10 months in advance. It stands to reason that a good percentage of these women would be pregnant by the day itself - and so pregnancy platforms (below) outnumbered disabled platforms.

Williams and Cobbold: five births at Knebworth Park extravaganza

Walking through the arena on the Sunday night during the climax performance of *Angels*, I have never witnessed such a universal state of euphoria, and find it hard to believe

there's ever been one. Not only was the entire record-breaking audience stretched and swaying in joy, but in every beer and falafel stand - where usually by this stage of the evening, the workers are knackered and packing up to go home - every single person had their hands in the air roaring "And through it all...!" Wow.

This is where I live.

Knebworth Concerts continue. Their history has become part of the social history that Knebworth House preserves, displays and interprets as its stories for future generations. Oasis posters hang on the walls alongside Victorian garden designs and art from

World War One. Our modern history is as fascinating to our visitors as our ancient history. I know that in 200 years the guides giving tours of Knebworth House will talk about the concerts of our time. That aerial image of the Robbie Williams crowd (p.65) will always be here, hanging on the wall. This book - and its stories of the 19th generation of the Lytton family - will still be for sale in the Gift Shop.

I'm getting heady again. But this chapter merits a heady end...

In recent years, there has been a return to bands and their families popping into Knebworth House. Nowadays the visits tend not to be after the show. Whereas in the 1970s my mother would be bustling between the kitchen and the drawing room, the liggers and the drug squad, getting clean glasses and tonic - my wife in our time will be out monitoring the traffic egress or at a midnight SAG (Safety Advisory Group) meeting in a police portacabin. Now the bands tend to pop in during the afternoon, like the Beach Boys, for a tour and cake. At Sonisphere - the metal shows we did between 2009 and 2014 - the 'backstage'/Artist area was positioned next to Knebworth House, just the other side of the balustrade. Curious - usually Ameri-

can - rock stars were frequently to be found hopping over the balustrade to see the 'castle'. My kids and I have enjoyed giving impromptu show rounds to Slipknot, Anthrax, Mastodon, Alice in Chains, Good Charlotte, Linkin Park, The Red Hot Chili Peppers, etc... and their kids, nannies, girlfriends and minders. But in this generation they are less likely to be found in the sauna, or leaving their underpants in the Queen Elizabeth bed, as Mick Jagger did in 1976.

In the next generation... who knows? The prognosis is good. My son (right, playing Sonisphere 2014) has been at Music College with many of the stars of tomorrow. There is more music madness to come at Knebworth Park.

CHAPTER EIGHT

Eton College - Part II

FORUM MAGAZINE
And have you ever been to a Fetish Nightclub?

HENRY LYTTON COBBOLD
No - apart from boarding school. That was not my
own choosing.. where you wear stiff collars and
get ordered around by older boys.

Forum Vol 38 No 6 2004

Despite my misdemeanours with his daughter, I got on better with my second House Master at Eton - Mr Faulkner, known as 'J.F.' I was unusual in this. To most of my contemporaries, he was petty and weasely and much more interested and much more interfering in what was going on in his House than Mr Bull had been. But I found that if I asked Mr Faulkner if I could do something, he would do his best to say 'yes'. This was because nobody else would dream of asking him. They would just do it. Sometimes they got caught. Sometimes they didn't. My communicating with him was held up as an example of how he wished his House to run. If you reasoned with Mr Faulkner, he would always try to say "yes".

"Sir, the sunsets are so lovely at the moment - it seems a shame to walk back from supper via the brick passageway, can I walk back through the fields instead?" "Because you asked, Henry, yes you can." I was building on the 'Stargazing' incident, when he'd said, "If you want to look at the stars, just ask. My inclination will be to say 'yes'. Do it without asking, and you'll be gated for the rest of the half." (Eton terms are called 'halves' even though there've long been three in a year.)

I made the most of this very reasonable dictate. Consequently I got away with much more than my contemporaries. Indeed I built it to heroic proportions. Admittedly the following example was after my 'A' level exams, but ask any Etonian the likelihood of a House Master saying yes to this... You won't find one. "Sir, there's a one-off showing of my favourite film 'The Rocky Horror Picture Show' at a midnight screening at the Windsor cinema this weekend. I would really like to go." "Because you asked, Henry - you can." Incredible. I went.

Of course, Mr Faulkner knew that films were my specialist subject. He had no scruples revealing that he had been snooping in my room - presumably in the wake

of the incident with his daughter - by questioning the pile of *Continental Film Review* magazines in my cupboard. This magazine, which I bought religiously every month, was dedicated to 'Foreign' Films - covering both what played at an 'art house' like London's Paris Pullman and what played at the Granada 3. 'Foreign' Films had to work harder to attract attention in the world market. There's always been one easy way to do that. *Continental Film Review*, consequently, was rich in images of nudity and sex.

"You can buy it at W.H.Smith, sir." "But do you <u>need</u> to buy it?" "Well, you see, sir, if you read the magazine-" "You <u>read</u> the magazine?" "Oh yes, sir, there are excellent articles on film theory - well, there's always one... every edition has one excellent article that I wouldn't be able to find anywhere else. Can I show you?" "No, no... Just keep them in the cupboard, Henry."

To my children today, it is extraordinary that erotic images were only available

My Eton view for my last two years at the school (impressively franken merged by Photoshop...

to the brave soul who had the courage (and height) to reach all the way to the top shelf of a newsagent, slip a copy of Mayfair or Penthouse under a copy of *Smash Hits* and, sashaying up to the till, gravel-voiced, ask for a bag with it. Or feign an interest in Art movies and proudly buy *Continental Film Review* from W.H.Smiths. Or do History of Art A-Level.

Were we the better for it? I don't believe so. My kids are much more relaxed about what they know, than we were about what we didn't know. Repression breads obsession. If you are old enough to be interested, you are old enough for the discussion.

For my senior two years at the school, we moved to the western edge of the town into a newly-appointed tall Victorian building called, as previously mentioned, Warre House. Here again my choice of bedroom best illustrates my character at the time. Choice of room was given in order of responsibility. Responsibility was in the hands of two levels of House prefect - 'Library' and 'Debate' - admission into which, as I recall, was voted for by the senior prefects. The second level, 'Debate' certainly was. When it came for some of my year to be elevated to the rank of 'Debate', Danny Matovu, my now foster-brother (m.o.w.l.), in the year above, was instrumental in voting me in as the first in my year. As a result, I got first choice of bedroom. I chose one of only four rooms at the very top floor of Warre House, looking west, over the fields towards the setting sun.

...with captions covering where the merge didn't work). I could Photoshop in a blue sky, but the 70s did look like this. Note the bursar's house top left.

I don't recall what the responsibilities of 'Debate' were. Maybe getting up early to ring the reveille bell? Whatever they were, they were well worth suffering for this first choice of room.

The next level of prefecture, Library, I wasn't remotely interested in. I didn't need my own common room and even more responsibility. My generation had already emancipated 'fags', so that cause no longer needed fighting for. I already had the only perk I wanted. Fortunately there were 14 boys in my year in the House, so I could politely decline promotion to Library and it wasn't really noticed.

I had secured my nest. A wonderful crow's nest looking west, towards the world. This top floor room made my final two years at school so much more bearable. Whatever its scholastic benefits, locking up 17/18-year-old boys every night at 6 o'clock to work or fraternise only with other teenage boys, is not healthy. In retrospect, this imprisonment is probably where my overdeveloped imagination - invaluable in my writing career - comes from. But, still, it is not healthy.

The view was spectacular in all weathers - blue sky, grey sky, clouds of every shape, rain, hail, storms, large setting suns... then after dark, the lights of civilisation beyond the fields - cars, trains, planes... Possibility.

It was the perfect perch for two years of literature and art study. The English system of specialising in three subjects from the age of 16 suited me. I was able to give up all the boring science and practical subjects. I could study only what I was interested in. Literature, Art, and a bit of History. Ancient History was mainly literature and art so I chose that over History. I had to actively scheme to get An-

cient History moved in the school schedules so that I could study it. It had been set up as a third subject for Latin and Greek scholars. But I saw that, in my year, none of that lot had chosen it. In fact, no one had chosen it. There was a danger of Ancient History not being taught at all... so I persuaded my friend Richard Wells and one other fairly disinterested boy that we should do it, and asked for the schedule to be altered so that we could. The schedule was changed. Victory. My foster brother Danny, a classicist, had done it the year before, so I could copy his essays. (Of course I didn't. Mr Roberts would have noticed.)

There was no influencing History of Art. Students were expected to learn all 3,000 years of it. Well, all the fashionable bits, anyway. English Art, for instance, stopped at Turner. So I made a point of choosing the Pre-Raphaelites and sentimental Victorian Narrative Painting for my projects.

Literature, however, I could influence. On the very first A-Level English Literature class, the lovely - D.H.Lawrence lookalike - professor Stephen Drew swept in and asked, "Right, what do you want to read?" Whilst everyone else was still taking their places and arranging their pencils, I thrust my hand in the air and replied, "Brontës, Eliot, Dickens and Tennyson... and maybe a little bit of Austen." "That'll do. How about one from the 18th Century? Fielding? Fine. That's settled then." At this point, the rest of the class looked up. A successful coup. Nothing mystifyingly medieval. Nothing tortuously 20th Century.

Although I did also take a class in American Literature, with the equally lovely - Dan Aykroyd lookalike -
visiting U.S. teacher, Cary Woodward. So I read a bit of
20th Century Hollywood literature - *The Last Tycoon,
The Day of the Locust*, Clifford Odets (again tailored for
me)... and, of course, before Hollywood, the Americans
had only managed 19th Century literature. So we did a
bit of Herman Melville and Mark Twain.

Thus I pretty much created my own A-levels.
Credit to Eton for allowing me that. Lots of romantic
19th Century literature, the history of beauty, and some
ancient Mediterranean melodrama... Perfect for a love-
struck teenager dreaming of his long summer holiday.

With all this romance in my over-active imagina-
tion, every evening I would take my 'extra' pint of milk - thought good for a teenager's bones (calcium), at the expense of his breasts (oestrogen) if he was male
and a packet of Abbey Crunch biscuits (for the sugar high - with no thought of
future insulin production deficiency), put something dreamy and beautiful on the
record player - e.g. a soundtrack by Francis Lai (*Un Homme Et Une Femme, Bilitis,
Emmanuelle 2*) - and sit at my top floor window, looking out at the real world in
the distance. I'd put my Platignum cartridge pen (made in Stevenage) down on an
essay about *The Lady of Shalott* - perhaps Tennyson's, perhaps Waterhouse's - and,
head lolled on my tie-dyed wall hanging, posters of Lizzie Siddal & Kate Bush,
I'd gaze out at the twinkling lights of civilisation and weave fantasies about being
free... and in the company of girls.

But, I have to tell you, mine is a charmed life. Because, also in my view, in the

middle distance, was the School Bursar's house. And the School Bursar had a teenage daughter. And the School Bursar had - very thoughtfully - chosen to put his teenage daughter in the one bedroom in his house facing a wall of 50 teenage boys.

Not that any of these boys noticed. Bizarrely they were all too busy talking Rugger or Bugger, or whatever... They all seemed to be looking inwards. I, on the other hand, was always looking out. And, every evening, I caught a glimpse of this pretty-girl-with-the-Kate-Bush-hair crossing her bedroom in her bathrobe.

I caught a glimpse because, at dusk every night, the Bursar's daughter would leave her curtains slightly open. I was an A-level student studying semiotics. These curtains were not firmly shut. Neither were they left wide open. They were always drawn part-way, leaving a thin strip of light... and a glimpse, every so often, of her.

She did not appear, like me, to be sitting there howling at the moon. But that gap in her curtains was not random. It was the same every night.

Or most nights. There was the odd night when the curtains were slammed shut. There was the odd night I even glimpsed her parents pop their heads into her room, probably to tell her to stop dreaming and get on with her homework. If anyone popped into <u>my</u> room, they tended to curse my music taste and leave.

The Bursar's daughter was my nightly companion. For over a year and a half.

And then I got bold. One evening, in my final half year at the school, I chose to close only my right curtain. The next night I closed only my left curtain. The next night only my right curtain...

Would you believe it? The Bursar's daughter started to do the same.

After a few nights of crude semaphore, this little window opposite was matching my curtain positions. There were fifty windows facing her single window, but it was my one - on the top floor, two along - that she was communicating with.

With the rest of my house oblivious - and the rest of her house oblivious - we had connected.

With the amino acids (tryptophan) in my milk, the sugar in my Abbey Crunch biscuits, the sweet spot harmonies on my stereo, the yearning of windswept Victorian romantic heroines in my homework essay - all, already, swirling serotonin into my romantically-addled teenage brain... Imagine this.

Did the Burser's daughter and I scale down our respective drainpipes and run, breathlessly, into each other's arms? No. God forbid we would ever meet. It might spoil this exquisite, unconnected, connection.

But we did continue to commune - via curtain - this unknown girl and I... until my room went dark for the Easter holidays.

Returning in the Summer Term, to A-level exams and a flurry of romantic letters from Hertfordshire girls I had met - finally - by working the holidays in Knebworth Park, litter picking, ticket selling, etc... I made the horrible mistake of bringing my friend, and top floor passage neighbour, Richard Wells, into my confidence about my curtain relationship. Richard Wells immediately produced binoculars. No! That's not the spirit of it! It's a beautiful thing! Not a pervy thing.

Increasingly the Bursar's daughter's curtains remained closed. She had seen boys in the background. She was becoming 'a thing'. Probably a boast. A challenge. A laugh. I don't know that she felt all this, but I felt it for her. The spell was broken.

Except the odd night. I could see her there. Wondering.

On my very last day at the school, I had finished writing my 'Leavers' - little photograph cards with messages to say goodbye to friends. I wrote one final 'Leaver' to the Bursar's daughter. Summoning courage, I walked across to the Bursar's house and rang the doorbell. She was called to the door. She knew ex-

actly who I was. I mumbled a few words. "This is for you." "Thank you." And backed away quickly.

The photo on the card was me on the staircase of Knebworth House wearing my "Don't dream it. Be it." t-shirt. Something I had resolutely not done. I know what I wrote on the card. Because I have a much re-written draft of it. It was sweet. Romantic. Grateful for the connection.

Hearing that I had done this, Richard Wells - much more brazenly - also made a trip to the Bursar's door. He issued an invitation to Tea at McDonalds in Slough. McDonalds, to be fair, was less ubiquitous and a more exciting date then than it is now.

With her parents' permission, she accepted. Graciously, Richard Wells included me. Richard is a lifetime friend. I love him dearly. So don't take too seriously how bitter and twisted I sound about his intrusion on my fantasies. Although this won't be the last time.

Across the polystyrene burger boxes, the Bursar's daughter and I stared at each other.

I had said all I had to say.

Richard, on the other hand, had lots to say. Would she like to come to the summer party at Henry's house the following weekend? (My Dad's Quartorze Juillet Birthday Party). She would.

Richard Wells had invited her to a party at my house. She was to be his date.

At the end of the Knebworth House summer party - which I probably spent alone with my records, DJing - all of my friends were in sleeping bags on the floor of my bedroom. I was alone in my bed. But my friend Richard Wells was in a sleeping bag on the floor of my bedroom... with the Bursar's daughter.

I lay there, listening... to him throwing up because he'd drunk too much; wondering... what is she thinking now.

The following year, I received some sweet letters from her - she had been sent for A-levels to the co-ed boarding school, Malborough College. Then I saw her once, many years later in London. Bizarrely she was living in a flat only a few blocks from mine, in Marylebone. A few blocks away, but too far to see from my window.

Since my first kiss with a girl, by the Thames, and my first encounter with a naked female body on the white carpet of the Knebworth House guest room, I had continued to actively seek out female company and balance my all-male school life and (of my own age) all-male home life. Because I had a split existence, half the year in one place, and half in another (or away on a family holiday) I was not in a position to have a proper 'relationship', a regular girlfriend. But by actively pursuing the company of girls, in the rare opportunities I had, I managed a fairly full teenage love life. Although only ever to 9.9. As with alcohol and cigarettes, I swore off Number 10 (see p.56). Coitus. "Father, why do these words sound so nasty?"

It was an invaluable time spent learning about the opposite sex, their pleasures, their pains, and their peculiarities. For instance, at 16, taking good fun 15/16 year-old girlfriend Jo (below right) to Paris for the weekend to the apartment of friends of my parents (the Birchers, yes, Julie Andrews & Christopher Plummer, parents of my very first girlfriend Joanna - see p.25), I remember breaking the shower rail, but I don't remember any 1 to 9.9. This, looking back on it, is most odd. In a Parisian apartment, on our own, at 16. But what memories there were, have been overshadowed by an incident of Jo, out-of-the-blue, becoming suddenly dismissive of me, strangely mean. And during such precious, hard won, time. My lack of memory is no doubt a clue. I am sure I could be frustrating. Peculiar, But I was never confrontational. I didn't understand mood swings. I didn't understand girls. Except the Victorian governesses I read about in books. And they were more like me. Not like any girl I encountered in the 20th Century.

My only other surviving memory of this weekend is it being the closest I've been to getting arrested in the U.K. Stepping back off the cross-Channel ferry, I was doing the gentlemanly thing and carrying the bag that contained both our allowances of tax-free cigarettes (both, as I recall, for Jo's parents) - and, at 16, we were not seen as a 'couple' by Her Majesty's Border Nazis.

A similar teenage bust up happened the first time I took a girl away on a long weekend in my first car - a little red Fiat 126 tin can, I must have been 17. Jane (above) was, I don't know, younger. I have a vivid memory of the two of us checking into a cheap terraced hotel in York. It was the first time I had done anything as grown up as checking into a hotel. It was thrillingly intimate. The freedom intoxicating. But again, I do not remember the night. Which is odd.

What I do remember is a dramatic argument in a blustering thunderstorm in the seaside town of Whitby. Jane, who I adored, stormed off, saying she was going to hitch a lift home with a lorry driver. This was a horrible horrible horrible thing. Those who've grown up in the age of mobile phones will find my feeling of helplessness and abandonment hard to relate to. I didn't feel I could go looking for her, in case she returned and found me gone, in which case she definitely would be off with a lorry driver. I paced in the torrential rain for an eternity, fearing the worst, and trying to come up with what I would say to her parents when I arrived home without her - or worse, imagining what could happen to her in the cab of a passing lorry driver. Dracula himself could give no worse Whitby nightmare. Drenched and weeping, I did not dare move from that desolate spot. I clung to a hope that she would not carry through her threat. But I knew she was crazy enough to do it.

After hours of horror and anguish, I finally saw her, in the distance - also drenched - sitting blankly on a bench.

Before we got to Whitby, we had stopped at Castle Howard. In later life I would have the privilege of staying here, when Simon Howard was in residence. In 1980, my only knowledge of Simon Howard was that Jane had a photograph of him, torn from a Sunday supplement, pinned to a corkboard in her bedroom. Simon was sitting on the edge of one of the fountains in front of the palace (it's more palace than castle), and the low angle of the photograph made his tennis shoe appear distortedly large.

Jane had thought this was funny. Either that, or she enjoyed goading me with an image on her wall of a young man who lived in a bigger house than I did. Of course visiting Castle Howard we had to recreate this photo, same fountain, same pose - but during the tussle in Whitby, my camera got knocked from my hand and the film part exposed. As a result, this image - the last of that trip that survived - has a wash of fiery red over it. A perfect summation of the weekend.

We had a more successful trip a second time. We set off again in my little Fiat 126, with Bruce Springsteen's *The River* on repeat on the cassette player. We visited Eyam in Derbyshire (scene of my school play). Liverpool (where the only entertainment we could find at our age was Ballet at the Empire Theatre) and - to a glorious burst of sunshine - the breathtaking Lake District. At last I was starting

to learn about this mysterious female of the species, whose company I had been denied since I was seven. I wrote about these trips in a song called Thank You. *For short steamy teared nights / And thunderstorm sea fights / You'll grab even barbed wire if you fall...* something like that. I was pleased with it. I requisitioned the chords of Janis Ian's *Jesse* for the verse.

Maybe I should not be using names in this chapter. These faraway figments of my memory no longer exist in reality. These 1970s teenagers should not be associated with the women they have become. But Jane is no longer called Jane. She left for Reading to become a croupier, and someone with a completely different name. I shed a lot of tears. I had not done that before. Not over a girl.

Evenings spent in Jane's streetlit bedroom in Burnham Green listening to Bowie, Lou Reed's *Berlin* and Nick Drake's *Bryter Layter* - specifically *Hazy Jane* - were the first time I felt like an ordinary kid. An ordinary bedroom in an ordinary house in an ordinary suburb. Two kids playing at hand ballet and wanting to have orange hair.

By this time, there were other girls I had met working in Knebworth Park. From two of these I received passionate letters during the final year I was locked up at boarding school. Re-reading these letters, they must have been sweet flower shoots of exquisite romance to me in my cell - but little materialised when I got home, I remember only one subsequent erotic encounter. On the sitting room floor of a parents' house. The only time in my life I have encountered breasts larger than my hands. I had little idea what to do with them. Whatever I did elicited a negative response. I have been slightly scared of big breasts ever since.

As I remember it, all of these girls in my teenage life finished with me, rather than the other way round. Letters from their bedrooms tell of them listening to David Gates, which clearly I'd recommended. That may have done it. Or maybe it was all the philosophising about sex rather than doing it? My almost missionary insistence on avoiding the missionary position. I was messianic on my Number 10 theory. Probably completely insufferable. Possibly these girls got fed up with me because they got fed up with what they saw simply as 'foreplay'? Very possibly. Sexually I was, basically, a lesbian. And they weren't.

Although one was. And, digging into my conscience, I have lied to you. There was one that didn't finish with me. There was one that I moved on from. One of blessèdly few moments in my youth that I'm not proud of, and I wish I'd finished the text of this chapter on the previous page. But I so want to include the happy photos below, of the very best of my teenage trips to Paris, with another lovely friend called Jo. My Paris weekend with Jo B was much more what I had dreamed of listening to *Un Homme et Une Femme* in my school cell. With Jo B it was nothing but fun. But one winter night at Knebworth, when Jo had gone up early to get into my bed - I stayed downstairs and, late into the night, watched the movie version of *Hair* for the umpteenth time with some girls from the same school, who my younger brother had moved on from... And I moved on.

Because I'd found someone who was a true soul mate.

And was up for doing my hair.

CHAPTER NINE

University of Kent

Up ahead the red and white ribbon tears itself in two
Seems to me it's the bright white side
That knows where it's going to
(*The Red and White Ribbon*, 1980,
lyric written on the A2 in Kent)

After junior school, I said "never again" to cricket. After senior school I said "never again" to haircuts. Well, school haircuts. Boring haircuts. The former vow I have kept. The latter, I have lapsed on, notably on my Wedding Day (m.o.w.l.)

But in the summer of 1980 I stopped going to the barber. I stopped having my hair cut. The back of my hair, that is. I still continued to ask girlfriends to cut the front & sides. Particularly the sides. To make my head thinner. Annoyingly that doesn't work. But the back of my hair, I unleashed - as now I could - to grow beyond the collar that had been its 'pale' at Eton.

I must have still looked reasonably square by Christmas 1980, because I got a holiday job in the Toy Department of Selfridges. I spent two weeks lining up little toy soldiers in a deep glass cabinet. Every kid, of course, wanted the one at the very front, which meant knocking every single one over with my sleeve cuff every time to reach it.

Pretty soon, however, my hair started to curl up at the sides. I looked like a girl. I didn't have a problem looking like a girl - but I was more interested in looking like Richard O'Brien (creator of *The Rocky Horror Show*) or David Bowie. David Bowie meant it had to be orange, so out came the henna. The same boxed henna that girlfriends had had the freedom to use when they were at school. I made sure to leave a blonde bit at the front, like Bowie in *The Man Who Fell To Earth* (1976).

But how to make the back stay straight? I wasn't going to pommade it. Oil in any form near my skin at that age was to be avoided like the plommague. My chest was already pitted for life from trapped sweat in polyester-rich school shirts under wool waistcoats and wool jackets.

For half of my life my skin has been too oily. For the other half it has been too dry. I have often considered that at some point - one glorious day, sometime around the age of 30 - my skin was absolutely perfect. One day. One perfect skin day. I wish I could have known that day. I would have spent it completely naked, pointing at myself, "Look! My skin is perfect. The one day in my life I am not a leopard or a lizard."

The solution to keep my hair straight at the back was braids. To plait the hair at the back of my head into little braids. It was not unheard of to see small braids in a man's hair at that time. Adam Ant comes to mind. But no one had a row of them at the back of the head. Bo Derek did. But she's had cornrows. I didn't need cornrows. I just wanted to keep my hair straight at the back.

How to seal the braids? Pipe cleaners. Fluff and wire pipe cleaners could be twisted round the ends, and through decorative punctuating beads. To begin with, I preferred coloured beads. I went with red, gold and green. Girlfriend Jo B had got

me into reggae beyond Bob Marley and Third World... all the way to Inner Circle and Aswad. Yes, that far. I was no Rastafarian. However I could claim to have

sat on the same loo as Emperor Haile Selassie. At my grandparents' home in Devon. My grandfather, as High Sheriff of Devon, was entertaining the Rastafarian god. My grandmother had walked in on him whilst he was on the throne. It was one of her favourite stories.

Soon the colour beads didn't feel right. In 1981 we were entering an age of black and white. In fact, for the first half of the 1980s I only ever wore black and white. I think grey crept into my wardrobe around 1985. I've not worn blue jeans since 1980.

So if not coloured beads, what now to wear at the end of my braids, to cover the twisted white pipe cleaners? I settled on little silver metal paper file separators. From the days when paper files were bound with string. The silver separators used to fit over the string to make turning the pages easier. I can't imagine this specialist stationery item is made any more.

From the time I left school - 1980 - until the time I got married - 1987 - I did not cut the back of my hair. It was, by then (when braided) 24 inches long. By 1982, the world had Kajagoogoo (bit fluffy on top for me). But, let's face it, the style did not catch on. So this look came very much to define me and only me. I was delighted to be different from everyone else.

I wouldn't have cut it when I got married. But my wife said she was not going to braid it for me. It is not something you can do yourself. Like nit grooming if you're a chimpanzee. The person who'd been braiding it for me for most of those seven years was my former girlfriend. My former girlfriend was not invited to come live with us in America. So I gave her the symbolic task of cutting it off in the summer of 1987, a month or so before I was married. Liz cut the braids at the base, with their pipe cleaners and silver separators still at the other end. The London wig maker Ray Marsden - who's made wigs for every

British movie ever - sewed up the ends. They were put in the Knebworth House safe, alongside my grandmother Hermione's hair, which was also cut in one piece when she was 19-year-old.

And there they have remained. But for one outing on my 50th birthday, when current 'head-thinner' Maree Dallaris sewed them into my hair for that party, They were a different colour from the rest of my hair. But at least I could say it was my real hair.

Back in 1980, I could wear my hair like this because I was no longer at Eton College. I was the only one of the 14 boys in my year in my House who was already at University. The rest of them had all pissed off around the world, doing a poncy thing called a 'Gap' year. I never understood a 'Gap' year. University is a 'Gap' three years. You have a three month summer holiday if you want to go travel the world. Why add another year of this painful penultimate step to being out - free - in the world?

I was in a hurry. And thank goodness. For it meant that I came out of University in September 1983 and straight into a job in the Film Industry. Straight into three jobs on three consecutive film sets. I hit the ground running. Whereas if I'd graduated the following summer - 1984 - there were no jobs to be had in British Film. The British Film In-

dustry had crashed with a soaring pound and a sinking company called Goldcrest (its laurelled goldenboy, that had invested in a disaster called *Revolution*). This, of course, was luck rather than me not taking a 'Gap' year. But it's given me an irrational dislike of 'Gap' years ever since. I am pleased to update you that - despite 'Gap' years being as popular as ever - neither of my two children took one either.

Photo: Åsa Brandt

My ageless university BFF Sherri steps in for remedial repairs at my 50th birthday - not for the first time. What are friends for?

I do have irrational dislikes. I have an irrational dislike of BMWs. I was convinced that I disliked all people who drove BMWs. But then my adopted California parents (m.o.w.l.) whom I adored, bought a BMW. Then my little brother, whom I also adore, bought a BMW. I was forced to confront my prejudice. Maybe not all BMW drivers are pillocks? Maybe.

Other irrational dislikes? Toto. The band not the dog. That bloody song about Africa is awful, isn't it?

Having to bend over after a meal to put things in the dishwasher. Why don't they make dishwashers at head height? Who wants to bend over after a meal? Actually, that's quite a rational dislike.

Magnolia? The paint colour, not the flower. Why do people (predominantly female) want to paint everything Magnolia? It's the colour of nothing.

Yellow opening titles in films. Always the sign of a bad film... But actually, as I get older, I am starting to waiver on this one. Films with yellow opening titles are often brilliant. Brilliantly bad, maybe. But still, brilliant.

The worst example of my irrational dislikes - one with which I now check myself whenever I find myself being irrational or judgemental - is David Gray (not David Gates, note). As a child of Bowie, and all the colour and glam of the 1960s, 70s & 80s, I didn't understand how, in the 90s, a bloke called Gray who appeared to make no effort at all, only ever in civvies to wail behind a guitar, could produce anything of worth. Totally irrational. It took my other self, Emilio Estevez, to slap me round. Emilio put David Gray's gorgeous *My Oh My* into his film, *The Way* (2010). As a result I actually listened to the *White Ladder* album, and discovered that it is, in fact, one of my top 10 favourite albums.

Prejudice. Don't do it. Look for the best in everything. The dull, the difficult, the different - the more so, the bigger the challenge. Challenge yourself to like - or understand - what you do not. I do try to live by this mantra.

And I add this photo below as an exercise.

But Toto are still awful.

At University I made a pact with myself. For three full years I would watch every single film that was shown in the campus cinema in the days I was on campus. I would practice no self-censorship whatsoever. Even if I knew I would detest the film, be bored senseless by it. I would still go. Three years of watching everything.

After I had done that - at that point, and for ever more - I <u>wouldn't</u> have to watch everything. After that three years, I could revert to being judgemental. I could walk out of films. (Although I've only ever done that once - *The Matrix* (1999) - ugly people spouting philosophy in a sewer). Now I could fast forward through films on VHS or DVD if they were only mildly interesting, and I didn't want to give them two hours of my life. I once asked the director Tim Burton if he ever did that. He was horrified. But then he's probably not done the 3 year challenge. I've done it. No self-censorship. See every single film. Three full years.

I say 'full' years. You may have spotted I included the caveat 'in the days I was on campus'. I'll say in a moment how many films that was. But first let me declare that I was only on campus for three days a week. Because I made another vow at university. That, for the first time in my life, I would live in one single place. So that I could have a regular girlfriend. A proper romantic relationship. That was the education I really needed from university after ten years at boarding school.

So I chose my courses based on when the classes fell in the week. I would only take a course if its classes were on a Tuesday, Wednesday or Thursday. This was so that I could return home to Kneb-worth on Thursday evening and not have to return to University until Monday evening. This meant that for the first time since I was seven, I was effectively living at home. The result was that I was able to keep the same girlfriend for two and a half years. It also meant I could help my Mum run Knebworth Park in the summer, during a particularly difficult time when we couldn't afford a manager.

Above: home for the weekend
Below: in charge of the Knebworth Park casual staff - Summer 1981

*My first cars: my red
Fiat 126, aptly licenced
'GROT', and my toilet-
cleaner blue Fiat Fiorino*

There was a price to pay. I would much rather have taken the course 'Women In Film' than 'Avant Garde Cinema'. But 'Women In Film' was on a Friday afternoon. 'Avant Garde Cinema' was on a Wednesday. My Friday afternoon was more important. Only two other students did 'Avant Garde Cinema'. Why would you? But one of them was Robert Wade (m.o.w.l.), a lifetime friend.

The other key to this arrangement was choosing a University that was in striking distance of Knebworth. I'd passed my driving test at 17. I'd had the benefit of Knebworth Park to practice driving in. Although previously I'd preferred to ride a motorbike or a moped. Presumably because I could ride a moped on the road at 16. My car driving instructor had asked, "Do you enjoy driving?" At the time I thought that was a very odd question. Surely driving is something you do to get from A to B?

Now I completely understand what he meant. As my long-suffering family will tell you, I love to drive. I love the freedom of it. I will not fly anywhere I can drive. I am not too bothered what car I'm in. As long as it doesn't have leather seats. But I prefer a modest car. I prefer a car that does not go over the speed limit when you put your foot on the accelerator. To me a holiday begins as I set off down the Knebworth House drive. Apart from the bath and beach, the car is where I best read (by which I mean listen to audiobooks), think, dream, compose...

When asked by my contemporaries for tips on passing my driving test, I'd say, "masturbation, chewing gum and looking over your shoulder. The first two to calm the nerves, the third what the instructor will be looking out for. Best not to let the instructor see the first two."

I needed a University that was an easy drive to and from Knebworth. Well, that's easy. Oxford is an hour and a half, and Cambridge forty-five minutes. Ha! It was not possible to takes Film Studies at Oxford or Cambridge. That was my excuse. My father had gone to Cambridge, his father had gone to Cambridge... But I had an even better 'Get Out of Tradition' card. It is time to tell you about my foster brothers, Danny and Harry.

In my House at Eton, there were two Ugandan brothers, one a year older than me, the other a year younger - but in my year because he was so bright. In fact, he was so bright that, after two years, they moved him out of my House and into 'College', with the scholarship students. The

boys were Daniel Mbusi Sagabi Matovu and Harold Nsamba Matovu. They had been sent to an English boarding school when they were seven and five (yes, five!). By the time they were teenagers, their father was working in Vienna for UNIDO - the United Nations Industrial Development Organisation - and their mother, from whom their father was separated, was either in Uganda, where her brother Godfrey Binaisa was president from 1979-1980, or in Kenya in long-term care.

Danny and Harry's father was an unusual man. His life revolved around a small apartment, a German mistress, a collection of lampshades, and his slippers - which he put on, with his pyjamas, whenever he was not at work... or used to beat his boys if their academic studies were not up to scratch.

I have said that all Eton boys have a developed sense of humour. The Matovu boys developed this early. More than any, they'd needed to. This sense of humour we certainly shared. But what tipped my friendship with them into brotherhood was that they were the only boys in the House (probably the school) who shared my music taste - specifically Hollywood music taste. As 14/15 years olds, they had a knowledge of the Great American Songbook of the 20s/30s/40s/50s that was unmatched. Except by me. For most of my teenage life in their company we were either singing, quoting or discussing Berlin, Gershwin, Porter, Kern, etc.

I had only one academic lesson with Harry. Maths was his worst subject. Maths was my best subject (bizarrely - my rational self popping up again). There were 8 'sets', graded to ability. For Maths we met in Set 4, my highest, his lowest. Harry and I would sit at the back, scribbling song lyrics to each other, challenging each other to complete couplets, etc. I have to say, this mental exercise has proven more useful to me over the years than trigonometry.

Unlike me, the Matovu brothers actu-

They did more often perform in black tie

ally made something out of this specialist knowledge. At Oxford University they formed a successful cabaret act called Black Tie. Black Tie performed professionally for a few years. It now has an almost legendary reputation. Helena Bonham Carter keeps pestering me for their phone numbers - but I know they won't revisit it, even for her. Their original pianist, a fellow Oxford student, was nicknamed 'Fingers'. Later on they changed their pianist to a chap surnamed 'Kok'. They had to change the nickname.

For Half-terms and Exeats (weekend breaks), Danny and Harry could not go back to Vienna (European flights were not as easy and inexpensive as they are at time of writing), so the Matovu boys would come home with me to Knebworth House. My parents - everybody at Knebworth - adored them. In those days they would - literally - sing for their supper. They were so much more fun than me and my brothers (Peter & Richard) and my sister (Rosina). But we refused to be traded in. Besides, my Mum had always wanted six children.

At the end of the school year came the long, eight week summer holiday. Danny and Harry returned to the small flat in Vienna, where they were expected to study. Their father was not interested in going out, or taking vacations. When he got home from work, he put on his slippers and went to bed. He spent money on only two things - his children's education and lampshades. Lampshades were all that remained in his apartment when he died some years later. The boys were to continue their studies all summer long, in this small urban apartment in Austria. This was not as much fun as Knebworth. At 15, Danny became bigger than his father. Plates of spaghetti began to fly.

One evening we got a call at Knebworth House. I remember exactly where I was, like the nights my other siblings were born. We were enjoying a family evening in the Oak Study. Danny was in a phone box at Vienna Airport, saying that his father had given him a one-way ticket to London. Could he come and stay?

Harry followed soon after. They were

never formally adopted, but they have been members of my family ever since. There is still a room at Knebworth House today called 'Harry's Room'. That night the Matovu brothers became part of the Lytton Cobbold family. My Mum got her six kids.

And as if that wasn't enough, Harry went on to marry my first cousin, Emma. I won't say that she looks Freudianly like my Mum... ah, I just said it. Nothing weird about that. But it was strange at the wedding to have one's family on both sides of the church. Bit like the old days.

So how was the arrival of the Matovu brothers for my natural siblings and I?

Well, it was bloody brilliant.

The Matovu boys were everything you would want in a child. Charming. Funny. Intelligent. Entertaining. They aced exams. They got shed loads of 'A's. They both went straight to Oxford, studied Classics and Law, and became very respectable, and respected, barristers. They satisfied every parental fantasy. The perfect kids.

Which massively took the pressure off me. And my natural siblings.

It left us free to go to provincial universities, and study the subjects that we actually wanted to study. Any call for me to follow my father to Trinity Cambridge and study Moral Sciences - as there had been for me to go to Wellesley House, and then to Eton, and to be a successful rower, etc. as my dear Dad had been - was off.

So I applied to the three universities where you could study Film. As discussed on p.21, there were only three in the UK in 1980. They were all within reasonable driving distance of Knebworth, so getting there and back did not become a factor. The factor was how <u>much</u> Film Studies you could do at each university.

The University of Kent was my first choice because it offered a Film Studies Major. 60% Film. I have already written about not getting the grades to be a Film Studies Major. How, having instead taken a place as a History of Art Major, I switched to Film Studies on my first day. In the same way that the University of Kent was pushing History of Art because it had recently hired a high profile staff member, it was also making sure that its brand new Film Studies Major (nothing like it had existed in the UK before 1980) was as academic and as serious as the University could make it. Remember, at this point in time, all undergraduate universities in England were free to attend. The government even gave you a grant to go. As a result the course was heavily intellectualised. The French nouvelle vague magazine *Cahiers Du Cinéma* was the bible. Marxism was the flavour. This was all probably quite good for me. Although I did struggle with the didacticism, the obfuscation. They were right to be suspicious of a 'D' in History of Art student.

The Film Studies course looked east to France and Italy and Germany, whereas I looked west to America. This is a generalisation, because we did study Hollywood. But the Hollywood directors that we focused on were predominantly European: Lang, Ophuls, Hitchcock... If there was an idol to bow down to, it was Roberto Rossellini. Neo-Realism was king. My reaction to this, was that Italian directors never paid any attention at all to the audio in their films, which meant they were not remotely realistic. Neo-Realism was a sham. Worse than that, it was boring. It can't be good politics if it is boring. It will not reach anyone. Unless it is authoritarian. As you can imagine, my professors loved this Etonian in their midst.

But I loved every minute of it. Even the two hours of reflections shot through a glass ashtray - Stan Brakhage's *The Text of Light* (1974) - or the 45-minute long zoom in on a window - Michael Snow's *Wavelength* (1967) - or the real popcorn popper, the three hour (yes, three hour) view of a mountain range shot on a single fixed camera with a robotic arm so that no one movement (of the exact same view) is the same - Michael Snow's *La Région Centrale* (1971)... I mean, what were they watching in 'Women In Film' on a Friday afternoon?! *All About Eve? Gilda?*... I'd look at an ashtray over Rita Hayworth if it meant a weekend with my girlfriend.

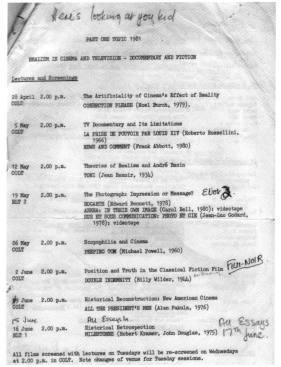

The lead Film Studies professor was a 5-foot spiky-haired intellectual called Ben Brewster. He would always sit at the very front and centre of the Corn-wallis Theatre on the

University of Kent campus. This was because he believed that one should always look up at a cinema screen. Like an altar. I love this idea, and still recall it every time I am looking down on a screen or a television. For, like most modern cinemas, the Cornwallis Theatre had seats that sloped down towards its screen. So you could only look up at it if you were in the front row. Looking down on the screen - and Mr Brewster's spiky hair - however, suited his students. The fact that we were behind him, in the dark, and - even better - that the theatre seats (which were behind a note-taking ledge) had no armrests. This meant that, once the film started, students could stretch out and go to sleep. When the lights came on at the end of the film there was always enough time to sit up before Mr Brewster turned around. At which point we could all look suitably dazed/dazzled by the film.

My long braided hair was never a drawback during this time. In retrospect I'm surprised I didn't get more abuse for the way I looked. Only once do I recall shouted abuse. Walking down the street in Thetford, Norfolk. But back then Thetford was the rat-run town in the sticks of red-neck East Anglia where the "Please Drive Safely Through This Town" sign was crumpled and mashed halfway up a tree. However there was one horrible moment where my hair got me into trouble. One day in the Cornwallis Theatre, when the lights came on after the end of a particularly gruelling film, during which I was indeed taking a (brief and, I'm sure, well earned) nap - I think it might have been *La Région Centrale* - my braids got caught between the seats. I was pinned horizontally. I could not sit up. I knew Mr Brewster was by now looking back from his front row seat. He might not have noticed had there been more than three of us in his class. I think I lost my separators - and possibly a large chunk of hair - as I jerked up, scrambling into view, clutching my pencil, mumbling that I had been retrieving it.

I do not begrudge Mr Brewster giving me the only 'Two Two' Degree of the six Film Major students. Only two of us went on to work in the Film Business. Me and Rob Wade. For many years Rob's career and my career followed a similar trajectory. We both became screenwriters. We both managed to carve the semblance of a living out of it through the second half of the 1980s. And we both, eventually, had feature film scripts go into production at about the same time - the early 1990s. His was called *Let Him Have It* (1991). Mine was called *Lake Consequence* (1992). Then, in the late 1990s, everything changed. For reasons that will

become clear in a later chapter, *Lake Consequence* was my first, and (currently) last, cinema release. Rob (left), on the other hand - with his writing partner Neal Purvis (right) - went on to write (amongst other films) *The World Is Not Enough*, *Die Another Day*, *Casino Royale*, *Quantum of Solace*, *Skyfall*, *Spectre* and *No Time To Die*. Which is presumably what Ben Brewster foresaw, when he gave Rob the only 'First' Degree amongst the six Film Majors. The other four students got 'Two One' Degrees. Blah. Who wants an average Degree? If you are not going to be top of the class, much more interesting to be bottom. No?

Certainly I was the only one who went to every single film - on a Tuesday, Wednesday and Thursday - for our entire time at university. That meant, usually, 10 films a week. On Tuesdays alone, we would have a film at 10, at 2, at 4, at 7.30 and at 10. That's five films on a Tuesday. I always knew when it was a Tuesday, because the sun would be shining. The English sun only comes out when you have to be indoors all day or you're abroad on a summer holiday.

Tuesday night was Film Club night. The Film Club was called 'Cinema 3'. If I had any expectations it was going to be like the 'Granada 3' in Slough, I was to be disappointed. It showcased contemporary Art Films. I was still to be regaled with boobs and bottoms - but they tended to be in black and white, in jump cuts, and in the wrong order. They were rarely on a beach with a volleyball, or in a Thai tennis club shower room, or running through a field of sunflowers in the Dordogne. I remember my very first Cinema 3 night vividly. The movie was the two-and-a-half-hour Polish socialist epic, *Man of Iron* (1981, though we were seeing it in 1980) by Andrzej Wajda. It was a life changing evening. But not because of Andrzej Wajda.

It was life changing because I made the only five friends I was to make at University - apart from Rob Wade. I knew I would be attending every one of these Cinema 3 screenings, so I thought I might as well get in for free by turning up early and volunteering as an 'usher'. An 'usher' had to hand out the A4 sheets that contained notes and a short essay on the film - and then had to pick them up, unread, off the floor, at the end of the show. The five would-be ushers that turned up that night, I still meet, to this day, once a year for Christmas dinner in London.

Well that's not quite true, because loathsome leukaemia took the nicest of them, Nicky Evans from Watford. And the not as nice, but endlessly inspiring and brilliant - my 'creative soulmate' - Rosemarie Jarski from Nantwich won't come to London, even at Christmas, because she channels Garbo and "vants to be alone"... to the extent that, as of the summer of 2019, she has completely disappeared. Despite calls, emails, notes through her letterbox, attempts to contact her sisters, I have heard nothing from her in, as I write, over a year. This is distressing. But because it is Rosemarie, it is not unlikely. I can believe she is still alive, and that she will be in touch when she wants to be. Sadly it will be too late for her to write the foreword to this book, so the quality of the gags herein will never be quite as intended.

The sort of anti-social misfits that go to university and want to sit in a room in the dark, in silence, watching other people's lives, are not, you might think, the best basis for a friend group. But I love them all. Well, enough to see them once a year. With Rosemarie (opposite, right of the left photo and left of the right photo) are monk-educated Maurice Hill from Walthamstow (top of the right), once-monk-apostate Stephen Rider from Pirton, Hertfordshire (right top of the right and left of the left), and mystery-monk Richard Sanford from Ilford (which is still the only thing I know about Richard, after 35 years - and much too mysterious to be in either of these pictures). Instead, also pictured, are (blonde) Nicky, who went to heaven; and (bottom right in both) Knebworth-raised Mark Mallard, who went to Australia. Then, the sparkly belt tying all this sackcloth together - the not-at-all-monkish, but then she wasn't so obsessed to tip up on the very first Cinema 3 night, but was introduced by Nicky in Week Two - "I've committed to sit in a dark room with five serial killers, you've got to come too!" - beautiful Barbados-bred, Sherri Gilkes from

Harlow. As I say, we meet still every Christmas, and Nicky's full joyous laughter echoes with ours at the table at Salieri's Italian Restaurant on the Strand.

These were my university friends. My only university friends. Because they were the only ones I saw. I only went to university to go to class and to go the cinema. I had had ten years of being social with schoolmates. I now wanted my social life to be at home. I didn't want to feel obliged to hang out with friends in Canterbury. When I was on campus I delighted in a new invention called a 'Sony Walkman'. This was a small black audio cassette player, not much bigger than the audio cassette itself, which slipped into your pocket and ran on AA batteries. It didn't have speakers. To listen to it you had to wear thin metal headphones that sat on the top of your head and covered your ears with circles of black foam.

For three years, whenever I was not in the Cornwallis Theatre, or in class, I wore my Walkman headphones. Nowadays this is common for most young adults. In 1980 I was a freak. Walkmans were becoming popular, but people wore them at home or whilst travelling. They didn't wear them walking around, in every day life. I loved it. My Walkman gave my life a soundtrack. Everywhere I walked I was in a movie, buoyed by soaring orchestral score.

I would walk between the theatre and classes and the library and the car park transported by lush romantic movie soundtracks, usually from French movies. This is probably a whippable offence in the county of Kent, which has forever been antagonistic to its continental neighbour. But being educated in French films, listening to French music, being free for the first time, and at university, I felt as chic as Belmondo or Delon, and as though it was 1968, and I was headed to a sit-in or a happening on the library roof. The continent was only a short seagull's flight away from this hill. The gulls could be there for lunch. It would be another ten years - and a tunnel - before us humans could be in Paris for lunch.

Instead lunch (if I wanted it - I was never that interested) was on offer in my college cafeteria. The University of Kent was, I think, one of only three non-Oxbridge universities that operated on a college system. In other words, students were attached to a college rather than to their subject faculty. This had the advantage that you socialised - if you socialised - with students of all types and persuasions rather than just those that shared the same interests as you. The other two non-Oxbridge universities that operated on this system were Durham and Bristol, which strangely were the two universities my two natural brothers, Peter and Richard went to.

At Kent I was attached to Rutherford College, which was a modern concrete building on the edge of the green hill overlooking Canterbury. Unlike its rival for my attendance, the University of East Anglia, which was concrete buildings separated by concrete walkways, Kent's campus had pleasant green spaces between its concrete buildings. Rutherford College, where I went only to eat, had a big wedge-shaped central dining area which, in a long window at the end, attractively framed the central tower of Canterbury Cathedral down below.

But every view - every thing - looked good to me. Because in my head - in my ears - everything was overlaid with film score. In my room on the top floor of Warre House at Eton, most Sunday mornings I'd lie in bed listening to the soundtrack of *Un Homme et Une Femme* imagining I'd woken up in a Parisian apartment with Anouk Aimée, and that all we had to do all day was to wander the cafés and riversides in black and white. This fantasy I had purloined from my Dad, and the 1960s. Then in the second half of the 1970s, along came my generation's version. Again courtesy of the French film composer Francis Lai. The fantasy moved into colour and into the French countryside and seaside, and was peopled with girls my own age (and younger, you will say, but remember I was still a teenager). *Bilitis* (1977).

The filmmaker, photographer David Hamilton, has now - by his 2016 suicide - been unmasked as a predatory paedophile. Damn him for trashing all his beautiful work. We'll talk more on that subject later - but for the moment let's stay with the composer Francis Lai. This mysterious moustachioed Frenchman, who has only just stopped working - due to death - in 2019. Francis Lai wrote the soundtrack of Henry Lytton Cobbold's late teenage years. Literally. Because the music on my Walkman - consistently in my head, and to which I lived - was almost always that of Francis Lai.

Un Homme et Une Femme, Bilitis and *Emmanuelle 2* were favourites, but my time at Kent University I associate with an unlikely Francis Lai score. I don't know that I ever saw the film *International Velvet* (1978). It was a quasi-sequel to *National Velvet* (1944) - Elizabeth Taylor and horses. *International Velvet* was Tatum O'Neal and horses. I was not particularly into either. I am bothered by things that are bigger than me that breathe.

Francis Lai's score for *International Velvet* became the soundtrack to my time at the University of Kent. I have tried to play it today, as I write this, to make the memories come flooding back. But it's not easy to find. There are little bits of it on YouTube. But the intermittent adverts of YouTube spoil its effect. I must dig out the old audio cassette. And something to play it on. My 1980 Walkman has long walked.

Supporting me at my last book launch in 2017 - or just along for the vol-au-vents - UKC BFFs:

Rosemarie Jarski, Sherri Gilkes, Maurice Hill, Anna Saverimuttu, Richard Sanford & Stephen Rider.

CHAPTER TEN

School's Out

Don't Dream It, Be It
(The Rocky Horror Show, 1973)

So what did I learn at university? Not much in History of Art, that I recall. Although at the time I remember thinking that it did turn out a better compliment to Film Studies than Ancient History (my intended 'Minor'). I think I mostly reused my A-level essays - most of my fellow students hadn't had the opportunity to study History of Art at A-level, so we went over a lot of ground that was familiar to me. I was delighted to revisit my unfashionable paeans to the Pre-Raphaelites. I also recall enjoying time spent with the subject's gospel, John Berger's *Ways of Seeing*.

At some point during the three years, I had to choose a one-off 'General Studies' course. I chose Philosophy. From this I gained a greater understanding of Monty Python's *The Philosopher's Song*. Philosophy also helped me to one important life conclusion. Or at least to put a name to it. It refined in me a basic Utilitarian belief that every single body movement I make - even the very smallest voluntary shift of a little finger - is my brain computing what will lead me to the most pleasure. Not necessarily that instant. Delayed pleasure is, usually, greater pleasure. Pain sometimes leads to greater pleasure (vaccinations come to mind). That is where wisdom comes in.

Wisdom is - best - the result of experience, but it is wise to know that it doesn't have to be. Wisdom can be learned. And, as such, I've always looked to acquire it. But I'm also very happy to take someone else's word for it. For instance, I do not need to go to the jungle. I've been told it is very beautiful, but also that it is dense, uncomfortable and dangerous. So I am delighted that somebody else has gone before me. And can show me the pictures.

You have seen me as an 18-year-old (p.85) wearing my *Rocky Horror Picture Show* Fan Club t-shirt urging, 'Don't Dream it, Be It' - but I have never fully subscribed to this mantra. I have wisdom enough to know that there are plenty of things that are better dreamt than done. That doesn't mean that I am not in the constant pursuit of 'pleasure' - it means I've looked over the fence (or read a book about it or seen a film about it) and the grass may <u>look</u> greener, but it still needs mowing, and the dogs still crap on it. So, computing all the formulas in my brain, I conclude there is more pleasure overall to be had by staying on this side of the fence.

I may be wrong - but that is my best judgment at this moment, and I shall move my little finger accordingly.

This philosophy is the very essence of me. It is therefore very possibly the most valuable thing I learnt - or defined about myself - at university. The root of it is to think both long-term and laterally. To put yourself in the minds of others. Consider the perspective of others. Consider every possible consequence. This is how to write a screenplay too. Then compute all of that to find your own path to personal pleasure. It'll make you as altruistic as Jesus.

And it should talk you out of martyrdom too. If you compute that there is more pleasure to be had in a final ecstatic self-believing moment of martyrdom than there's going to be from the whole of the rest of your life, then go right ahead. End it there. But wisdom tells me that Act Three happiness tends to be more satisfying than Act One happiness. The challenges of Act Two make it so.

So. Think long term. Think wide. Learn from - and move beyond - the mistakes of others, so you can make new mistakes for others to learn by. Look to spread happiness in others. See it as the best chance of achieving your own happiness... I've started using the word 'happiness' instead of 'pleasure', but it is the same thing. Pleasure is happiness measured in units. This is how my brain computes. Ones and Zeroes. Pleasure and Pain. Life makes sense to me if I look at it this way.

Having established at this point in my life that 'pleasure' should not be a pejorative word, I then moved on to 'vanity'. As part of this Philosophy course I was asked to write an essay entitled, "What is self-love?" I argued that self-love is a primary way to create pleasure for others. In simplistic terms, if you make yourself look

nice, you increase the pleasure of the people who have to look at you - which, in turn, increases your pleasure. In fact you are the one person who doesn't actually get to benefit directly from your own vanity, as you don't get to look at yourself all day. Unless you are Narcissus, in which case you turn into a daffodil. Again, better for everyone other than you. I submitted this essay on 'self love' to my philosophy professor handwritten on the back of a glossy A1 poster of myself.

Having determined that both 'pleasure' and 'vanity' lead to altruism, I moved on to reassess other unfashionable and pejorative words. 'Sentimentality', for instance. I wrote a number of essays on Victorian painting, praising sentimentality.

'Sentimentality', I argued, inspires empathy. 'Cynicism' is a quicker fix, but it leads, long-term, to bitterness & unhappiness. Like self-interest, 'sentimentality' leads indirectly to altruism. It did for the Victorians. As you enter your Third Act, the more sentimentality you have nurtured within yourself, the more you want to see good triumph in the

My version of J. W. Waterhouse's The Lady of Shalott

world. Your sentimentality bursts forth - caterpillar to butterfly - into 'nostalgia'. Another unjustly maligned word. Nostalgia is a powerful agent for your serotonin. Nostalgia wishes, for all the world, the good things that you have known... etc.

This was the way my head worked. And you can imagine how it sat with my brutalist modernist spiky-haired professors, in my brutalist modernist Kent classroom. But just to annoy them more, I loved them for it.

In Film Studies, and at the Cornwallis Theatre, I sat through three years of unfiltered movies from every corner of the world, and every year of the 20th Century (to 1983). It gave me extraordinary access to the varied perspectives of all humankind. It planted an extraordinary reference library in my head. A reference library that was not available anywhere else, pre-Internet, and one that I made doubly potent by absorbing unfiltered. It showed me the paths to pleasure and the paths to pain. It gave me empathy. It gave me wisdom. It was the perfect rock-bed for what I did not yet know would be my route to making movies. Screenwriting.

So those three-days-a-week at university were stuffed full of valuable life lessons. But even more valuable, after 10 years at boarding school, was what I learnt on the other four days. Not at university.

All my life I'd had a fantasy about living only in one place. From the day I asked my mother if we were gypsies. The fantasy was not to become a reality for another twenty years - when I moved back into Knebworth House, aged 38. Until that time it remained a dream to have all my life and worldly possessions collected together under one single roof. But in the autumn of 1980 at least I began, for the first time, to live at home. Mid-week, I commuted to spend a couple of nights with a landlady in Whitstable, just north of Canterbury, but my 'home' bedroom on the top floor of Knebworth House became my primary residence.

My landlady in Whitstable - for all three years I was at Kent University - was Mrs Smart of Borstal Avenue. I was inviting wude widicule to leave Eton College for Borstal Avenue. But Mrs Smart was no matron. Mrs Smart was an angel. I was spoilt nightly, on returning from late screenings at the Cornwallis Theatre, with tupperware tubs of crumbly sugar-dusted homemade shortbread. Unlimited short-

Then and now, any pretensions to dress style have never extended to my shoes. Not sure why this is. But budget & bunions are both relevant. Shoes have to be comfy

bread was included in the rent. A rent that I re-call one summer term Mrs Smart lowered to £13 a week as she felt I wasn't with her for long enough to charge more. I loved also that it was a real 'home'. Mrs Smart's daughter had recently departed to get married (I was in her room), but her son Bill was still living there, working for Mattel, safety testing Sindy doll's accessories, and her husband Terry worked for the council in Ashford. I was living amongst real life - so welcome for a boy who'd spent five years in cloisters in a penguin suit.

I was also finding real life now at Knebworth. Because for the first time I was able to nurture all-year-round relationships. The friends I was making working summers in Knebworth Park were now not simply disappearing for the winter, or relegated to pen friends for two thirds of the year.

Two of this these friends - again both girls - joined me in July of 1980 for a four-week 'Gap Year' Interrailing around Europe. Interrail is a European rail pass, designed for students to 'see (some of) the world'. This time, I got beyond Paris in the company of girls. Anita (below left), and Anne (below right - but you also may have wondered who the blonde is on p.61 & p.73) and I backpacked - via rail - through France, Italy, Austria, Switzerland and France again. Every third night we slept on the train. We would get on whatever overnight train was leaving that evening. Every third night we'd splash out on a cheap hotel (no AirBnB then) for, hopefully, a bath or a shower. And every third night we'd sleep in a campsite, in a tent that we shared the burden of carrying. Now I was sleeping with two girls.

Not like that. That would have been 9.99 (both figuratively and on my 0.1-10 scale). I have only once been in a sexual sandwich. And it wasn't 'Manhattan Club'. More 'British Rail white

bread'. Under a blanket watching the kids Saturday morning show *Tiswas*. Not exactly champagne in the hot tub. Just intimate with friends on either side of me. I can echo and embellish Betjeman reflecting on life, by saying I wish I'd had more group sex. But it wasn't to be.

I remember around this time watching the film *Here We Go Round The Mulberry Bush* (1968). This film had a special resonance for a number of reasons. It was set in my home town of Stevenage. It starred a bloke who looked like a cross between my local friends Nigel and Colin. It featured a local manor house where a boozy dad chases the Swedish au pair around bedroom passages. The hero (Barry Evans) does a grocery round, and all the housewives (this is the provinces, in the 1960s) want to shag him. I wondered why I'd never met any older women who wanted to shag me?

I don't think I was keeping a list of sexual experiences, but being very aware of the menu, from Seventies sex films (albeit a vegetarian, penis-free, carte), I was certainly intrigued. Where were all these sexually rapacious housewives collecting milkmen and young window cleaners in their upstairs bedrooms? Even if they had existed, I was not a good candidate for their advances, being so messianically celibate. And sure enough, when, one time, a infinitely classier and more seductive opportunity with an older woman did present itself, I disavowed my buoyant St John Thomas with hopeless excuses and quickly fled that cul-de-sac.

I guess the bored 18-year-old nanny who French-kissed me when I was 15 had been an 'older woman'. The one who gave me glandular fever just before my 'O' Levels. So if I <u>had</u> been keeping a list, I suppose I could have already crossed off 'older woman'. And 'STD' for that matter.

What I craved at 18 was the intimacy of female company. And the normality of female company. Travelling with Anne and Anita, as mates, rather than 'mates', was a perfect introduction to that. I slept in the middle - bee-dle-dee dee, dee dee

- but camping in a tent in Europe, as those familiar with the experience will tell you, is about staying warm & dry, not about getting hot & wet. As mentioned, we even stopped off in Italy to have Tea with Hobhouse.

There were a number of life lessons to be learnt on this trip. Don't arrive at Naples train station at nighttime with nowhere to go. The street looked like an Italian version of *Midnight Cowboy*. We got straight back onto a train. We woke up in Paestum (left) - a much better alternative. Do the south of Europe before you do the north of Europe. Because when you are squashed on a squalid floor outside an Italian train toilet with gigantic-bottomed Italian matrons stepping over you, you won't know that it doesn't have to be like this. Once you've been on a Northern European train - and on Interrail you can choose to go anywhere - you are not going to go back to Southern Europe. Having said that, also, don't arrive at Berne station at nighttime with nowhere to go.

Switzerland is the only place I have ever been confronted by a man with a knife. We arrived at Berne and there were no more trains leaving that night. It was too late to go traipsing about the city, and it was nearing the end of our trip so we needed to save our money for Paris. I don't know if we even had Swiss Francs or indeed if I had a credit card at that age. The only option was to lay out our sleeping bags in an underground concrete passageway. It was brightly lit, and I think there were one or two other sleeping bags further along the tunnel, so it wasn't quite the lunacy it sounds to me now. But there was no obvious security, and it was otherwise deserted.

No sooner were we settled, than Freddie Mercury, in tight shiny black leather and cap, came and sat on the end of our sleeping bags. I suspect it wasn't actually Freddie Mercury. Although Freddie Mercury did live in Switzerland. It could have been the cop from Village People. He was determined that we should come back to his flat. We could sleep there. It would be much more comfortable. Polite English children that we were, we gave him a friendly laugh and lied that we were quite comfy here on the concrete. Of course, he persisted. As I recall, he began fishing for a sexual dynamic between the three of us. Again, he was probably greeted with more friendly laughter and lies. Conversation was starting to dry up. Anita by now will have been pretending to be asleep, and Anne will have told him that we had an early train to catch and should be getting some sleep. He stretched himself across our sleeping bags. Gradually we became less polite. And so did he. And then he pulled a knife.

He toyed with the blade, saying we really should take him up on his kind offer.

Having been at boarding school for ten years, if I had learnt anything, it was not to rise to provocation. Time to play dead and let the grizzly bear pass. A sleeping bag is a falsely comforting womb in situations like this. But it's not easy - when confronted by a zipped sleeping bag - for Uncle Ernie to go down the bedclothes and up the nightshirt. The three of us hunkered down, fully covered, like molluscs, on the concrete, whilst the raven pecked and strutted around us.

Eventually he tired, muttered something about how he'd be back... and disappeared. I guess. I don't know. Because I wasn't looking. My eyes were firmly shut. I could feel Anita and Anne warm either side of me. So we appeared to have gotten away without being molested or stabbed.

Not that we slept much that night in Berne. First thing in the morning, we quickly rolled up our bags and headed back along the underground passage towards the station platforms. In the cafe at the end of the underground passage, bizarrely, there he was. Our nighttime tormenter. He was sitting at a table in a business suit, having his breakfast. Weird.

In Paris we slept in a 'Maid's Room', at the top of a bourgeoise apartment building. Much more my kind of sleeping arrangement. But now, in the final days of our excellent adventure, having shared nothing but bonhomie the whole journey, one of the two girls became incommunicative. She started to walk a few paces behind, and to be grumpy. What is it about Paris?!

I now understood a lot more about girls having spent these weeks with the lovely Anita and the lovely Anne. They weren't so very different from boys after all. But still, mysteries remained.

My Mum and Dad had a similar contretemps in the last few days of the other truly wonderful trip I took that summer of 1980. That same summer, my parents took my natural siblings and me on the last great family holiday of 'just us'. The family holiday to beat all family holidays. Four weeks in a 'Recreational Vehicle', exploring the American West. This was 'quality time'. For all my Father's absence in our youth - whilst he was at work in the City, or we were at work at Boarding School - he made up for it big time in his ability to switch off from work, and make family holidays as memorable and magnificent as any child could wish for,

Throughout my childhood, we were whisked away from Knebworth whenever we weren't at school or whenever there wasn't 120,000 people in the garden. I adored our family road trips. And this one was the last and the best. It was to the land of my dreams - Hollywood, and the Sunset Coast of The Beach Boys, then the Wild West of Utah and Nevada... and all in an RV, rolling to a great country rock soundtrack. The soundtrack was specific. It was from the movie *Urban Cowboy*. We'd bought the audio cassette halfway through the trip - but prior to that, songs from the film were all over the FM radio. Particularly *Looking For Love* by Johnny Lee.

We even stopped to see the film itself at a California Drive In. There was a spec-

California 1980
In the bosom of our father

tacular meteor shower in the sky behind the movie screen. We felt like we were, literally, travelling in Disneyland. Then we got to Las Vegas. Las Vegas, of course, is where the Devil lives. Mickey's neighbour. In Las Vegas my Dad decided it was time to take his 18-year-old son to a whore house. Brothels were legal in Nevada. It was a rite of passage. Suddenly my Dad was Lee Marvin in *Paint Your Wagon* (1969).

Thing is, I was Clint Eastwood in *Paint Your Wagon*. Too busy singing to the trees and mooning over Jean Seberg. That wasn't going to stop my Dad. I can still picture him, to this day, in a roadside phone box rifling through a directory trying to find a brothel he could take me to.

He couldn't find one that my Mum and siblings would have suffered the diversion for. But I have often wondered what would have happened if he had. As discussed, I was not ready to lose my virginity. It would have been like the time - many years later - when I was taken by my boss Harold Mollin (much m.o.w.l.) to a lap dancing club in London. I had to disappoint the lovely young hostess by insisting that - yes, my boss was straddled beneath her colleague next to me, but - all I wanted was a ginger ale.

It was not until the very last night of this very wonderful trip that my Mum and Dad fell out. It was the standard holiday disagreement, as I recall. He would rather eat, drive and sleep rough (less of a good idea around the back of LAX than on some Picardy farm). She would rather spend the money on a hotel room. In the end, money - or credit - was spent on an expensive airport hotel room. For my Mum. My Dad and us kids still slept in the RV in the hotel car park. Girls. Mysteries remain.

There were a few spare hours before the flight. I persuaded my parents to let me take a taxi back into town, to Hollywood Boulevard, which I think we'd only managed time to drive down in our RV. I wanted to buy movie posters. I think by the time the taxi got me to Hollywood (further away than you think), there was only time for me to talk the driver into waiting ten minutes whilst I rushed in and out of Larry Edmunds Bookshop. It was exquisite torture. I could have spent a week - a lifetime - in there, and I had ten minutes. I had to snap myself out of hypnotic wonder in minute nine. I grabbed a handful of posters which had been discounted by the side of the till, spent my last crumpled dollars, and jumped back into the taxi,

On the way back to the airport I glanced through the collection I had bought. The discounted pile had been old movie posters from adult cinemas that were closing down everywhere because of the rise of VHS (I should say 'Home Video', because at that time Sony had an alternate format, Betamax). These posters were not what I had gone to Hollywood Boulevard to buy. I can't remember if I had gone looking for specific posters. Certainly 1980 was not a classic year for movies. I didn't need a poster for *Xanadu*. But this collection turned out not only to be quite special - the artwork was unique, kitsch, very 'of its time' - but the purchase turned out to be quite prescient. The 1970s were finished and the cinema 'sex' film was dead. The genre would stay dead, until I returned to Los Angeles five years later - to witness, first hand, a rebirth... with the release of a film called 9½ Weeks, and the emergence of a filmmaker called Zalman King.

I did not appreciate the value of these posters at the time. I loved the artwork - the 70s naughtiness and humour of them - but I had no idea that today they would be valuable collectors' items. If I had, I might not have cut them up and blu tak-ed them, as collages, to my bedroom wall and headboard. The posters did not survive

Photo: Sherri Gilkes - plus the one at the top of page 116

The centre-piece of my headboard was The Pleasure Bed (1976) "Once you got in... it was impossible to get out."

this, but they looked brilliantly 'teenage bedroom' for a time. And maybe they did infuse themselves into my psyche, and - along with the Continental Film Reviews and Granada 3 before them - influence that future fork in my career. But I don't think so. It's just the way it turned out. The fork of Fate. Sounds like the title of one of them.

The other indelible mark left by this trip, was from a pair of tight blue denim shorts. It was a traumatic incident. Not only have I not worn blue denim below the waist since, but it wouldn't be until the 1990s that I wore shorts again. To this day I still think twice before wearing shorts. In the same way that my Mum brought us up without a fear of sugar, she also brought us up without a fear of the sun. Living in England we saw the sun as rarely as her generation during the War saw sugar. When we did see the sun, out came the ice cream, not the sun cream. If we did put suncream on, it was probably coconut tanning oil, and it was probably only above the waist.

Consequently, this trip, in my tight denim shorts, my legs got fiercely sunburnt. My legs were bright rhubarb to half way up my thigh. Above this they remained pale custard. For some months afterwards, when bare legged, it looked like I was wearing red stockings and suspenders. I've mistrusted shorts ever since. However hot (and I long to be hot) I would much rather sweat in pants/trousers. I like to sweat. It feels healthy. Or not wear pants at all.

CHAPTER ELEVEN

Disco Years

That's enough of that
Samaritan chit chat
This ain't no cause o'yours
If a man can't wobble
With 'is trouble & strife
What's 'e left in married life?
But night after night of
"'Ave a good day, dear"
"Mind what you say, dear"
"Don't let mother get in your
way, dear"
A man can take
Just so much, before 'e
Breaks! Breaks!
With conjugal 'eart ache.

Slap! Ow!
Stop That Row!
You grumpy old sod!
You moody old cow!
Stop it! Now!

"Having trouble
With a regular wobble?
Clashing every night?
Clash! Clash!
Well, wipe those tears
'Cos help is near
We're here to set your
wobbles right

Snap you out of that marital
fight, and put peace back in
your married life
Like it or not
This rot must stop
So take it! Take it!
Take it from the top!"

Slap! Ow!
Stop That Row!
You grumpy old sod!
You moody old cow!
Stop it! Now!
Stop That Row!

(*Stop That Row!* 1983)

During the three university years that followed this magical summer, I continued to find myself. "Are you there?" "Yes, I'm here". I progressed from the childish naughtiness of turning up the volume of Tom Robinson's *Glad To Be Gay* when Knebworth House was open to the public, to actually encountering a fellow student who called himself 'gay'. My children will struggle to believe this - and it's testament to how far the western world has travelled, even in my lifetime - but, until I went to university, I had never actually met anyone who would call themselves 'gay'.

In the 1970s, in the private schools of England, Kinsey's 10% were still in the closet. As they were amongst my parents' extended families and friends. Gay people on the telly didn't call themselves 'gay'. Larry Grayson. Frankie Howard. Danny La Rue. To be camp

As a 21st Birthday Card for Kim Wilde, my friend Jo B and I recreate her first album cover, with Jo as Kim's brother Ricky

was to be fun (Kenneth Williams). To be effeminate was to be fashionable (David Bowie). But to call oneself 'gay' was unusual, and brave. I enjoyed the rebellion of Tom Robinson's song, but I was not gay. Having been denied the company of girls, I was obsessed with girls. And this is where my new-found home life began to play its part in my formation.

Four days a week, every week, I was at home. I began to see my friends every weekend. The same friends every weekend. The whole year round. We worked all summer in Knebworth Park, and then we continued to be friends in the winter. This was not like friends I'd had before.

There was a group of them - including Jane, previously mentioned - who went to a girls school in the neighbouring town of Ware, called Presdales. These girls were mostly interested in my younger brother. First impressions, I was too scarily introspective. That's what I told myself. I wouldn't accept that Peter (right) was simply better looking.

Once they realised Peter was a dastardly Don Juan, they noticed me. All of the girls I hooked up with seemed to have been out with my younger brother first. Then, when they'd been baffled by me, they moved on to my reassuringly straightforward B.F.F. from school, Richard Wells. This happened again and again. Better for pulling the girls, at that age, to be pretty or predictable, than puzzling.

Please <u>do</u> think I was 'puzzling'... in fact, I was simply (what neither Peter nor Richard were)... shy.

The shy teenager hides behind his hair, his clothes... and, at parties, the record player.

As mentioned my Dad's summer parties were Something Special (Top 5 favourite album, by Kool & The Gang). Every second weekend of July. The weekend of his birthday, 14th July, Knebworth House burst into festivities. Increasingly, I'd found myself playing the music at these parties. I had a good understanding of the music my parents liked. I liked all music, and was happy to play to order. I remember only one time - as a younger teenager - being told I had the mood wrong. But it was too tempting not to play *Get Down, Make Love* (from Queen's album *News of The World*) to a heaving dance floor of my parents' friends. Apart from that one time, however, I spent many years as a popular party DJ.

This is quite surprising in one respect, because before the age of 18 I had never danced in company (except ballet lessons when I was six). I'd never had a reason or an opportunity to. I tell a lie. Once, when I was ten, I'd been pulled onto a dancefloor in a hotel in Obergurgl by my mother. I remember the Austrian DJ was playing *Get Down* by Gilbert O'Sullivan. Did my 10-year-old self, in my brown corduroys, 'get down'? I can't picture it.

The moment can't have been too traumatic because around that same time I bought my very first L.P. *Top of the Poppers Sing Gilbert O'Sullivan*. Note, not even *Gilbert O'Sullivan Sings Gilbert O'Sullivan*. I am quite proud of this. Okay,

T.O.T.P.S.G.O.S. is not *The White Album* or *Led Zeppelin IV*, but tell me *Alone Again (Naturally)* is not a good song, albeit one about wanting to throw yourself off a tower. Swindon, of course, is the cruelly forgotten Bethlehem of 1970s songwriters. Gilbert O'Sullivan's early collaborator Rick Davies went on to write Supertramp's *Downstream*, unquestionably in the Top 10 of most beautiful songs - and especially flowing with lyrical imagination, since you have to go some way downstream from Swindon to get "down by the sea".

I remain equally proud of the first single I ever bought. This was not David Bowie's *Rebel Rebel* or Marc Bolan's *Teenage Dream*. This was - from just up the road from Swindon, Banbury - Gary Glitter's *I'm The Leader Of The Gang*. This is also a great track, albeit one about the devil seducing you to join a gang, and I'm annoyed I'm not allowed to play it any more (loudly, when Knebworth House is open to the public). I find the randomness of whose art is acceptable and whose is not, based on the strength of tabloid/twitter storms absurd, hypocritical and dangerous. If we play Michael Jackson, we should play Gary Glitter. If we print Gauguin, we should print David Hamilton. "Art isn't for the artist," as Duncan says in Nick Hornby's *Juliet, Naked (2009 book, 2018 film)*, "any more that water is for the bloody plumber."

I began to DJ at my friends' 18th birthday parties. There was even money in this. I was paid to play records. For a moment I questioned my 8-year-old dream of a career making movies. I went to visit my Lloyds bank manager (look up 'bank manager' - a 20th Century phenomenon), Mr Peters, and asked if I could borrow

£5000 to buy a mobile disco. Extraordinarily, he said "yes". I went to the Squire Disco Equipment shop in Luton and purchased a Cloud Series 11 twin deck + amplifier, four giant black Squire speakers, nine par can lights and a controller. Mr Peters' confidence in me was well placed. Within a year I had paid Lloyds Bank back with money made from lugging this kit around Hertfordshire's village halls.

Remarkably, all these years later, those four Squire speakers still sit in the corner of my study, and still sound as good as that first day I stuck a jack in them. I use them today as my stereo. Mostly when the House isn't open. No need to open the window for Knebworth House visitors to *Get Down, Make Love* to these giant black woofers. I am also still surrounded in my study by the same par can lamps, on stands, working just fine, 40 years on. Amazing.

As a result, I have every dance record that was

released between 1980 and 1983. And not many from the years either side of that. But a fine collection from those years. Remember French club singer Ronny's version of Sly Stone's *If You Want Me To Stay*? A great record. Or Classix Nouveaux's *Is It A Dream*? Not such a great record. I saw Classix Nouveaux in Welwyn Garden City cinema, I think, round the back of John Lewis. The shiny skulled singer Sal Solo made his entrance by bursting through a plywood rectangle of rice paper - Da Da! Often I have questioned why I don't have a plywood rectangle of rice paper to burst through whenever I make an entrance. Da Da!

Now, in social situations, I had disco decks to hide behind. But it wasn't enough. I still needed eye make up, Sinbad trousers, a couple of waist scarfs and some fancy hair. My New Romantic look will be all over the photos in this chapter, but for those listening to the audio book, think Jeremy Healy of Haysi Fantaysie (who also looked a little like me). Now all I needed was a girlfriend. So I didn't have to talk to anybody else in social situations. I was thinking Kate Garner of Haysi Fantaysie. Surprisingly, I found her. She went to Presdales School, and she was called Liz.

I think we'd been to a Human League concert at the Rainbow Theatre in Finsbury Park the night intimacy was achieved. I was recognised by the bouncer, who'd worked for Don Murfet doing security at Knebworth Concerts, and we were pulled out of the queue and ushered straight to the front. "I love your love action."

I spent every extended weekend with Liz for 2½ years. Her home village, Great Hormead, was a twisted thread of lanes through Hertfordshire at least half an hour away from Knebworth, but I felt I could have driven it blindfolded. We were inseparable and I adored her. I was even ready to forgo family holidays abroad to be with her - so my parents, brilliantly, invited her too. She turned 17 on the floor of a chalet in Switzerland, with me alongside her. "It was long ago and far away. The world was younger than today."

We went beyond Whitby. We went beyond Paris. We went beyond Paestum. We went to America - four delicious weeks of adventure, driving from New York to a rented apartment in West Palm Beach... and then to Tuscaloosa, Alabama - home of the Boone family, hosts of an exchange trip I had made as a 13-year-old. More of that later. With our long braids and homemade black and white clothes, we were aliens in Alabama. But in the company of my childhood pal Buford, already a popular intern at the local police department and on his way to a career with the DEA and the FBI, we were protected from being given a hard time. We were curiosities to amuse.

We went as far as New Orleans, where Buford's sister Martha Boone was at Tulane University. Liz and I stayed in Martha's college dorm. She gave us her bed, and she slept in a neighbouring dorm. As a visiting gift we gave Martha some English music. In a pre-Internet age - and in a town like New Orleans - this was like taking clotted cream to the Incas. A 45-inch single of Ian Dury's *What A Waste* - "I

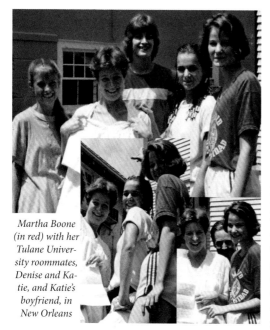

Martha Boone (in red) with her Tulane University roommates, Denise and Katie, and Katie's boyfriend, in New Orleans

could be the ticket man at Fulham Broadway Station" - seemed appropriately alien. And a debut album called *Fantastic* by a new band called Wham, which I felt lived up to its title. As well as being a great dance album, it featured rebellious teenage lyrics, even a quasi-rap before what we now know as 'rap' existed. I pompously announced that this teenage songwriter, George Michael, would one day be seen as the Paul McCartney of our generation. Martha was, of course, polite - but clearly hated both records.

Girls from Presdales school in Ware were meant to go out with boys from Richard Hale school in Hertford. Hanging out with Presdales girls I soon found myself with a new friend group of Ware and Hertford kids. The social hub of this crowd was a club night at a Ware discotheque called Beckets. The club night was called 'Club For Heroes', David Bowie being its lord high priest. It was Hertfordshire's version of Soho's Blitz Club, the birthplace of the 'New Romantics'. We had mascara to match London - and some pedigree, considering we were the country cousins. Bands I remember seeing at 'Club For Heroes' included The Marine Girls - one of whom was Tracey Thorn, later of Everything But The Girl - and whom Kurt Cobain later cited as one of his favourite bands and influences; The Palm Tree Club - whose singer Nathan Moore went on to be Brother Beyond... Am I convincing you how hip we Hertfordshire kids were?

We jerked our baggy trousered hips and tossed our teased tresses to Heaven 17's *(We Don't Need This) Fascist Groove Thang*, Simple Minds' *The American* and *Love Song*, Siouxsie and the Banshees' *Spellbound*, Bauhaus's *Bela Lugosi's Dead*... I recall my father questioning this 'scene' one evening as I was putting on my baggy blacks and dropping 'Eye Dew' into my eyes to make them 'dazzle'. I played him *Chant No. 1* by Spandau Ballet. My father was always pretty open to music - he'd instituted Knebworth Festivals - but, still, he didn't really get it. Phew.

The Richard Hale boys behind 'Club For Heroes' were Kev Saunders and Pete Moss. It was thanks to Kev that my mobile disco began to be used at every party and

gig (outside of Beckets) in the Hertford/Ware area for the next few years. Soon there weren't enough 18th birthday parties, so we held our own parties. 10 years later these would have been called 'raves'. Our venue was an old village hall in Knebworth Park called the Lytton Hall. There was no fee for these

parties. For that, they'd have to have been licensed. But there was a bruiser with a baseball bat at the door accepting 50p 'donations'. We were able to buy a lot of records. I still meet

people today with fond memories of these Lytton Hall nights. The elderly Mr and Mrs Waldock lived next door in the old Gardener's Cottage. I don't recall them ever complaining. Different times.

Kev (below) and I did cause more trouble, however, with an open air event. We promoted 'The Alternative Knebworth Festival' in Knebworth Park in the summer of 1981. We needed a space with

knebworth park, sat. 4th sept. 2pm to midnight adm. £2.40

23 skidoo design for living

portion control. tv personalities. wake up army! eternal scream. camping (tel. stevenage 812661) with this ad only £1.90 adm.

Knebworth Park is more used to visiting megastars like the Beach Boys and the Rolling Stones, but last week it was unknowns who got their chance to shine.

Welwyn and Hatfield Times June 11 81

local fan, Kim Wilde

ALTERNATIVE KNEBFEST RIDES AGAIN *Welwyn Times 27 August 82*
Punk chartbusters 23 Skidoo have been signed to headline the 2nd Alternative Music Festival at stately Knebworth Park...

The punks were there to hear 11 new wave bands and enjoy the Alternative Knebworth Festival...

a fence round it. Our Skateboard Park was perfect. My Mum and Dad had previously been heroes to Hertfordshire teenagers for - in a happy-go-lucky world before the Health & Safety and Liability Insurance Nazis took over - setting aside an area of Knebworth Park for a wide poppadom of ankle-smashing undulating concrete and a series of neck-breaking sunken half pipes to satisfy the skateboarding craze of the late 1970s. Sadly, the Skateboard Park was in the wrong place for a re-jigged operation of the park in the 1980s and was buried. And still, to this day, teenagers are the one age group that Knebworth Park struggles to entertain. It matters less now, of course, as teenagers get their exercise and fun killing things on palm-held screens in the back of the car.

Kev and I divided responsibilities for 'The Alternative Knebworth Festival'. He booked the bands. I worked on publicity. The bands Kev booked, I am told by my daughter's boyfriend, have since achieved legendary status. Particularly impressive, apparently, is that we booked The Television Personalities. I don't remember them, but I do remember having to find little cartons of grapefruit juice for the troublesome rider of our star headliners, 23 Skidoo. We were particularly proud to have booked these fire-extinguisher-banging Hare Krishnas.

I don't remember any of the music, but I do remember that Knebworth Park was hosting an English Civil War re-enactment that same weekend and the park was

full of Roundheads and Cavaliers. We succeeded, where Charles 1 had failed, in uniting the Roundheads and the Cavaliers, as open warfare broke out between them and the Punks attending our festival. One particular skirmish goes down in the annals of bizarrity, when the narrow gauge railway train, which ran past the Skateboard Park, was stormed by - I can't remember if it was the Roundheads, the Cavaliers or the Punks - like a scene out of *Butch Cassidy and The Sundance Kid*. Stuart, the train driver, barely spoke to me in 30 years after this incident.

Publicity was my responsibility. Knebworth Park at the time had a PR guy very much of his time. He was a bear of man called Dave Gordon who lived in a caravan somewhere in the Park. This may seem odd today, but these were lean times. Sunday shopping and increased leisure competition had lowered the promising visitor numbers of the 1970s. I played my part in the cut-backs, by becoming, in my pixie boots and ruffly shirts, 'Operations Manager'. There was hardly anybody in the Estate Office except part-time casual staff. Debts were mounting. Precious pieces of the estate were being sold off to pay bills. This decline was part-stabilised by the creation of the Knebworth House Charity, KHEPT (the Knebworth House Education and Preservation Trust) in 1984, m.o.w.l. But prior to this, it should not surprise you that our PR guy was a bear in a briar patch.

Dave knew that the quickest route to the English newspapers was bosoms. He wasn't the first, and he wasn't alone in this wisdom. Certainly during the 1970s, topless girls had been strapped to the wings of bi-planes to publicise the Knebworth Park Air Displays, which took place on the first Saturday of August. It always rains on the first Saturday of August. I know this because that's what eventually finished off the Knebworth Park Air Displays.

Dave's chef-d'oeuvre was a summer season opener of Lady Godiva riding through Knebworth Park. As I remember it, Lady Godiva was the big bubbly blonde girlfriend that lived with him in the caravan. She certainly made the local papers.

I think, under his guidance, I did one better. I managed to get 'The Alternative Knebworth Festival' into the national newspapers by posing a topless Dental Assistant from Welwyn Garden City in a large antique gold frame, and with Savlon antiseptic cream smeared on an artist's palette (it was a black and white photo) looking like I was painting 'Knebworth Festival's Back' down her spine. It made the popular 'Bizarre' column of *The Sun.* Not very 'Alternative'. But job done.

A lovely girl came up to me at a party recently and said, "You painted my Mum's back once." "Then I know your Mum was a lovely Dental Assistant from Welwyn Garden City." It makes me happy to have been involved in something worth telling your kids about.

The other two enjoyably silly black & white photographs of me at this time are my two album covers (right). Well, cassette tape covers. It was too expensive to cut an album, but you could go to a specialist shop by Highbury & Islington Tube Station and buy 46-minute blank audio cassettes in bulk and ask your friendly neighbourhood Australian hippy (Dave Brown, who turned up at the first Knebworth Concert in 1974 and never left) to print photo covers for you in your blacked-out bathroom. You did also need some original music.

My B.F.F. from school, Richard Wells, was all set to become an accountant. His father was an accountant, and he was expected to follow a geography degree from Exeter (sorry, I can't write 'geography degree from Exeter' without a parenthetical burst of amusement) with a job in the City, sailing the wide Accountant Sea. I thankfully put a stop to all that nonsense. His parents have never forgiven me. But Richard today still makes a good living out of music, as a composer for TV (*Being Human, 2008 - 2013*), films (*Mutant Chronicles,* 2009) and countless trailers and ads. More importantly, he's happy.

Throughout our schooldays I had loved Richard's untrained doodles on the common room piano. He had inherited a natural musical talent from a great-grandparent, I think, who wrote Victorian lullabies (one of which was to feature in my first film script). I lured Richard down into the cellars at Knebworth House, where I had assembled a collection of what-would-now-be-priceless 1980s musical effects boxes. With my eight chords on an acoustic guitar and his impressive piano dirges, we made two albums on a Tascam 4-Track Portastudio: *Another Reckless Libertine* and *Another Scopophilic Urge.*

Another Reckless Libertine channelled mainly the adolescent warblings of

my schooldays. The title references Laertes's father's request in Shakespeare's *Hamlet* that he not waste his college days. It was some sappy three chord love songs interspersed with Richard and I mucking about on early 1980s prototype synthesizers and noise boxes. I genuinely regret not keeping some of those music toys. I remember for instance, an analogue reverb tube, the length of a broomstick. Then there was a little pad box, purely to make that synthesized handclap noise that's all over early 1980s records. I owned a full finger-pad drum machine, and an original Roland TR-808... it is hurting me to write this, so I am going to stop. Suffice to say that I still have the Tascam Portastudio and the old cassette tapes - so the (much less valuable) music we made survives.

For the second album, *Another Scopophilic Urge* - its title showing me under the influence of a Film Studies degree - we co-opted a real musician. His name was John Martin, and he had briefly been in the 1970s band Guys 'n' Dolls, having co-penned their hit *A Whole Lot of Loving*. John was dating Gilly, a longtime mother's help

at Knebworth House, and living with her in the Old Estate Office across the back courtyard. John created the one truly special thing on this album, a beautiful four-minute guitar solo on a song of mine named *Unkind*. For many years the instrumental version of this has been the hold music on the Knebworth House telephone switchboard. Anybody ringing up with a complaint, after four minutes of this beautiful guitar solo, would have all their savagery soothed.

The one moment of mine on that album that I look back on with some pride is my screamed vocal performance on a punky garage-band thrash with a silly, but very Henry, lyric, *The Naked Noses*. The song questions why the nose, which has similar characteristic to the penis, is not considered obscene and routinely

covered up? I got through a carton of apple juice belting this song out. I don't believe my voice could ever have done that before or since, so it pleases me to have a recording of it. I am also quite proud of the ditty I composed and played all the instruments on, overdubbing one evening for a couple of hours, *Would You Like To Suck My Thumb?*. The plucked guitar sequence has an eerie circus/child-catcher feel to it, that I relished tormenting my children with when they were young.

The making of this masterpiece was interrupted one evening by the making of another masterpiece upstairs. In the Banqueting Hall of Knebworth House, 'the Welsh Elvis', Shakin' Stevens was filming a music video for his album *The Bop Won't Stop*, a bouncy version of Ricky Nelson's *It's Late*. Richard, John and I bounced upstairs from our cellar at a key moment and can be seen suppressing giggles at the back of the party scene (if you're quick enough with the pause button). It remains the only commercial music video I've appeared in to date. Although I did, many years later (1991), write a commercial music video. Not that they bothered much with the script. The video is for the song *Missing You Now* by Jesus-haired, Vegas-bound, white soul singer Michael Bolton, accompanied by elevator saxophonist Kenny G. Can you believe it? Even more naff than Shakin' Stevens. By comparison, back in that same year of 1983, my sister Rosina had a featured role in one of the all time great music videos, Tears For Fears' *Mad World*, filmed by Knebworth lake.

Unkind : LYTTON

In this bleary room of ours where I have heard it all
I can hear a silence like I've never heard before
And as I watch you emptying every cupboard drawer
A feeling of helplessness sinks me to the floor
Please believe me, when I say... "I tried"...

For still the tears that mark your face
Are like blood that's staining lace
Condemning me as guilty of a crime.

Damn that sword of Damocles hanging over head
That tells me to bar your way or change the things I've said
For that's the self same sword that caused the first lie
The lie that soured...until the love had died...
And now I can see...the last goodbye

In that blank stare of your eye...
And all the pain that it implies...
Oh how could any man have been so blind...and unkind.

As you go out silently and turn to close the door
I can see you pause and lift your head to look once more
A look to say...."Bless you, anyway...
I'll not forget...our love's yesterdays"
My heart quietly dies...

Wherever you go whatever you do I'll always love you
You know I never meant to be so...
Unkind.

The Scopophilic Urge : LYTTON

"Give me life
Look at me
Look at me
And I won't see
You're safe with me
Please let me be
Celluloid
Junkie"

Says the Temptress
Of the senses
"Take me body"
"But it's empty!"
"It's not empty
Can't you SEE it?"
"But it's empty!"
"Don't believe it!"

"You can taste me
But not touch me
All you have to do
Is watch me"

Play the beast at the Cine-Feast
Let yourself be lulled
Not afflicted yet addicted
Neither hot nor cold
But always warm.

The Naked Noses : LYTTON

Don't talk to me of legends
If it's not the greatest of them all
That tale of gallant snorters
Who'd sniff until they'd fall

The tale of how they suffered
Betrayed by fickle friend
The Evil Ears surrounded them
And picked them to their end

Since Adam ate the apple
Morality has told
The body has it's rude bits
To be hidden from young and old

To some this is a buttock
A breast, or little toes
But to our gallant heroes
Quite the rudest was the nose

To them the nose was private
Something rather personal
A sight for loved ones only
And not for one and all

They covered up their noses
With leather band or scarf
And never did they take it off
Except perhaps to take a bath

Without Goodbyes : LYTTON

Slipping through the tonal muse,
Dancing up the spiral,
Need no style, need no shoes,
Just reach out for the handle...

Warm air takes a hold of you,
Atmospheric angels
Catch you as you trip the light,
Flashing forth beside you.

You've seen that face a thousand times,
Loved those lips and cried those eyes,
But only now when it's hard to hear,
Can your heart step out without disguise.

Limbs out labelled "Line for Love",
Screws all out and screaming,
Strut right out, and slip full back,
Sink in Zano-tini.

White throat glistening, hair alight,
Fingers feel and cling tight
Breathing soft, caressing slow,
Love me now, then let me go...

You've seen that face a thousand times,
Loved those lips and cried those eyes,
But only now...it's the Midnight hour
And there is no love without goodbyes...

© 1983

True and upright folk were they
An example to you and me
Except of course for one or two
A rather liberal minority

These liked to look at nostrils
In naughty magazines
But then these lewd and greasy snorts
Were mostly in their teens

So come on all you snorters
Stop flashing to the world
Cover up your naked noses
Can't you see they're blue and cold

Learn from heroes of the past
Beware of what you hear
Nothing will lead you astray
Than the tricks of Evil Ears

They were the Naked Noses
Tougher than one supposes
They just didn't like their noses
To be seen in public...

It's probably a good thing that nobody beyond family and friends have a copy of *Another Reckless Libertine* and *Another Scopophilic Urge*. But that very nearly wasn't the case. Andrew Ridgeley of the *Fantastic* LP's Wham was close to taking one home from my 21st Birthday Party. Until I told him that I didn't think *Club Tropicana* was as good a single as *Wham Rap!*, *Young Guns* or *Bad Boys* - not appreciating that it was the first one that he'd co-written. That may not be the reason. But I prefer it to the other possibility, that my band mate Richard said Andrew Ridgeley couldn't have one without paying for it. Knowing Richard as well as I do, that does have a ring of awful possibility to it. He does have accountancy genes.

What was Andrew Ridgeley doing at my 21st Birthday Party? I'm not entirely sure. But half of Spandau Ballet turned up too. More than half. Martin Kemp, Steve Norman and John Keeble. I think they were friends of Mandy Wilde, Ricky Wilde's then-girlfriend-now-wife (Ricky had been at Richard Hale). Certainly Kim Wilde (former Presdales girl) was on the bouncy castle. I remember her splitting her lip. It is all a bit legend now, as very few photographs of this party exist. I've always thought that was because everyone was having too much fun to take photographs.

Thinking about it, it is weird that there are no photographs. Can you imagine that today? My 21st Birthday Party was the great climax of these wonderful New Romantic mobile disco years. And there is virtually no record of it. Everybody I knew - possibly ever - was there. Even Barry Norman. My party-loving parents pulled out all the stops. Beyond the tented, stage-lit back courtyard of Knebworth House, they set up a carnival fairground in the drive. Freddie Mercury would have approved. There wasn't naked mud wrestling, but there were naked bodies strewn around the swimming pool the following morning... when ceremoniously, Pink Floyd's *Dark Side of the Moon* was pumped out of loud speakers throughout the house. The Lytton Cobbold family's version of church on Sunday.

Mrs David Lytton Cobbold
at Home
Saturday 9th July, 1983,
for Henry (21) and Peter (18)

R.S.V.P.
Knebworth House
Knebworth
Hertfordshire.
Please bring this invitation with you
Black Tied Hop 9 pm
Dress: Hip for the Hop

So many of the people who came to that party I haven't seen since. For that was the end of this era. The end of my youth. All changed that September. I went to work in the Film Business.

The photo on the left - with Jane - has, until now, been the only one I have of my 21st birthday. However a second - with Liz - has turned up, and is a more fitting image of the end of this era.

CHAPTER TWELVE

The Shooting Year

You thought I loved Rebecca? You thought that?
Maxim de Winter, *Rebecca* (1940)

Autumn 1983. My career had the best possible start.

Straight outta Film Studies. Straight on to a Film Set.

One of my Mum's good friends and travelling companions, Ginny Fass, was in a relationship with a Film Producer called Jeremy Saunders. In 1983 Jeremy was Executive Producing a film with his friend and old National Service colleague, Geoffrey Reeve, called *The Shooting Party*, based on a novel by Isobel Colgate. The novel was about a shooting party weekend at an English country house on the eve of the First World War. Julian Fellowes, in a recent preface to the novel, acknowledges that both the novel and the film were inspirations for *Gosford Park* and *Downton Abbey*.

Jeremy brought Geoffrey and the director Alan Davies to look at Knebworth House, and the house got the job of playing Nettleby Hall. This meant the first and only film, to date, that Knebworth House has hosted where the whole house is featured, top to bottom, every room in its original use. Except for some initial exteriors of the characters being horse-and-carted to the shooting wood - filmed, I think, nearer to where the horse-and-cart was sourced - the whole production was to be based at Knebworth House for a six-week shoot. The Unit even took over our Estate Offices for its Production Office.

I had left university that summer, enjoyed a long summer holiday - including celebrating my 21st birthday - and that September/October went straight into the perfect job. A 'Production Runner' is a general assistant, for whatever needs doing on or off set. It was the best possible introduction to every aspect of the film production process. A dream job. But, better than that, I was a dream Production Runner for the Unit. Because I knew the location like it was my own home.

That was all I knew, of course. Film Theory teaches you semiotics in mise-en-scene, but it doesn't teach you to report to the Production Office on your first morning. Naively, I went straight to the set, Knebworth House's Queen Elizabeth bedroom, where the director was alone, pacing, planning his set ups. I waited there, awkwardly, not knowing if I should say something. After about 10 or 15 minutes of looming, one of the Assistant Directors found me and sent me off to where I was supposed to be. The Production Office. Embarrassing. But it got better.

The film had an awkward and embarrassing start too. Rather more seriously. On the morning of the first day of shooting, a few weeks earlier, at the film's other location, the horse of the horse-and-cart had bolted and tossed all the lead actors into a ditch. The lead, Paul Scofield, had broken his leg and the production had come to a grinding halt. Insurance picked up the tab - but the film lost its lead actor. After a few weeks, shooting resumed with a new lead actor - James Mason, in his last ever movie role. No disrespect to the very fine actor Paul Scofield, but I

Romantic leads: Judi Bowker and Rupert Fraser

Edward Fox

was now to be working with an actor who had worked with Max Ophuls, Nicholas Ray, George Cukor... the star of films I had studied and adored at university. I was to be making tea for James Mason.

A further upside of this drama - rather more drama, frankly, than was to be found in the actual screenplay of *The Shooting Party*; but, to be fair, that was the 'Merchant Ivory' fashion of the time - was that the insurance company paid for lovely female physiotherapists for the rest of the shoot to massage the remaining male actors' aches and pains from the accident. But the big downside for the production was that the delay had thrown the shoot - much of which was outside, and needed to match the same three weekend days in the story - further into the autumn, and further into the mercy of changeable weather. As a result, the film was still shooting exteriors the following January when there was snow on the ground and the leaves were all gone from the trees. This led to my most unusual role on the production. Ice breaker. It was my job to get up before everyone else and take a punt boat out onto the lake and, with long punt pole, break up the ice. By doing this, the ice would no longer look like ice. The camera would see it as water reeds. Rewatching the film, I can now admire this crucial contribution. The magic of cinema.

My other main contribution to the mise-en-scene was less successful. To boost the number of pheasants in the air during the main shooting sequence, live birds were brought in to the woods in large wicker baskets, like picnic hampers. I was positioned with a walkie-talkie alongside the actual Knebworth Woods gamekeeper, Doug Monger, a man born in his tweeds; and a collection of local 'beaters' who, in this case, were more 'releasers'. When the complex tracking shot around the guns was ready, I was to be given the signal on the walkie-talkie, instruct Doug Monger, and he was to shout to his cronies that the line of baskets were to be opened. I was not a vegetarian at this time, but I've never been a fan of pheasant shooting, and Mr

Monger was not my closest confidant amongst the Estate's staff. It was time for him to stitch me up, and fill his woods with fresh birds. A crackle on my walkie-talkie and he gave the command. The birds were released before the shot was ready - there

was much screaming and cursing over the airwaves as the cameras scrambled into action to catch what they could. I was back on dinner duty the next day.

But dinner duty had its upside. It gave me James Mason's attention for a brief moment. I can still in my head hear him say to me, as I apologised for his lunch in the woods arriving half way

Ginny Fass - who recommended Knebworth - with James Mason

through the afternoon, "Dear boy, I don't believe it is your fault." Whenever I have been dealt injustice since, I have wished for that line again, spoken by that man, in that most distinct, honey-throated voice.

The Shooting Party had the most remarkable cast. John Gielgud, Edward Fox, Robert Hardy, Gordon Jackson, Frank Windsor... and that was just the men. The ladies included Dorothy Tutin, Cheryl Campbell and every film-obsessed 1970s schoolboy's dream (after Jenny Agutter) Judi Bowker of Zeffirelli's *Brother Sun and Sister Moon*. As a teenager I had made what would now be called an 'internet meme'

but was then just called pervy. I had isolated a close up clip of a tearful Judi Bowker telling Diana Rigg in the film *In This House of Brede* (1975) "I love you" - and run it together again and again, "I love you" "I love you" "I love you"... ah, to sink into my single bed school linens listening to that over and over. And now I was working with

Ginny Fass - with Joris Stuyck and Edward Fox

Judi Bowker. I got to listen to that soft sweet voice every day. And get paid for it.

Dorothy Tutin, playing Lady Nettleby, was a splendid veteran actress (I know, I should be saying 'actor', but this was the early 80s, when toilets were still segregated). One day she asked if she could borrow one of the family's bicycles to take some exercise. I pulled out a rickety old-fashioned 'lady's' bike (yikes, even bikes were still segregated), one with a huge but tapered saddle, and puts some air in its tyres. As Dame Dorothy set off down the drive in her skirts, she called out, "What do I do over the cattle grid?!". Our whiskered 'Mellors' of a Deer Keeper, Wocko Watkins, who was in earshot, shouted back, "Enjoy it!"

The crew were a delight too. Over the course of my life I have run into most of them again in various guises. All hold a special place in their memory for *The Shooting Party*. The cast members that are still alive turn up occasionally at Knebworth House in other films and TV shows. Invariably their memories of *The Shooting Party* are of a happy company. Because the whole production was set in one house, it was a bit like being at a country house party, like the one the film depicted. One with the most interesting of guests. One that lasted the whole autumn. Overall credit for this 'theatrical company' feel on set must go to the film's Producer, the great Geoff Reeve, who fashioned himself as an 'old school' cigar-chomping paterfamilias.

Many years later I was involved in the making of the DVD Extras. Rupert Fraser, the romantic lead, and I tour Knebworth House recalling the various sets, and I appear in a 'Making-Of' documentary, staking a claim for the ice-breaking being just as important to the film as the leg breaking. This reconnection with Geoff Reeve led to a couple of tea parties at the St James's Hotel. Sadly by this point, Geoff was descending into some kind of senile brain-disorder that exaggerated his more imperious qualities. Rupert Fraser was amongst the group, along with Geoff's clock dealer, a couple of bemused young actors, and others I can't remember. We were sat at a large round table each with a cream scone in front of us, while Geoff ceremoniously unveiled a mood board for a new film based on Edward Bulwer Lytton's *Harold, Last of the Saxon Kings*. He was full of how we were all going to help him in this triumphant return to filmmaking. The speech was becoming increasingly unhinged and bizarre (not that making a film of *Harold* isn't a good idea), and all assembled were becoming increasingly uncomfortable. I think the scone was the only offer of a fee. Any resistance was greeted with great hurt, turning to anger as he pointed out that we all owed our careers to him. Gradually people began to make their excuses and leave. I was one of the last. Finally, he angrily tore the mood board to pieces, and like some abandoned Lear was led away by his anxious wife. It was a sad episode, and not the memory I would like to have of the last time I saw him. He gave me my first job. I would have always worked for Geoff. Probably for a scone. But this wasn't him.

A happier coda is that his son Tom Reeve brought a film to Knebworth House exactly 25 years to the month after *The Shooting Party*. Again, I gave over my part of the Estate Office as the Production Office. The film was *A Closed Book* (released in 2010), starring Tom Conti and Daryl Hannah, and it gave rise to one of my all time favourite Knebworth House memories. During a break from filming Daryl Hannah bounced out of her trailer, a guitar slung over her back, and asked me to take her to my "special places"... Now there's an invitation.

Amongst my all time favourite films is one that (premiere U.K. film critic) Barry Norman declared the worst movie of 1982. *Summer Lovers* is a glorious fantasy of being on summer holiday in Santorini with Daryl Hannah. And now here I was taking Daryl Hannah to my "special places". On the roof of Knebworth House, she hid behind the battlements and made spooky noises to freak out the crew down below. She snuggled Khan of the Aga, our Kitchen Great Dane. She listened to tracks I had recorded in my little recording studio. This was a gold-plated Knebworth afternoon.

Also from the A.O.B.s - the annals of bizarrity - I once made a film for Daryl Hannah's dad. Don Hannah. I don't think she's in contact with him. She certainly wasn't impressed when I told her. In the mid-1980s Mr Hannah from Chicago brought over an incentive travel group for a huge Indian Raj themed party in the gardens of Knebworth House. It was one of those rare no-expense-spared extravaganzas. A tent was erected over the whole garden, including the lime avenues and central pond, elephants were hired, etc. I committed the full Durbar to what was called 'ProVHS' tape - an antonym, but all that was available to me then. I did have a very nice 'ProVHS' editing suite. The machines were as big as flightcases. With a friend I had met on *The Shooting Party*, Rupert Dunn (in the transport dept., film trucks), I had, for a brief time in the early '80s, a little video production company.

We called the fledgling business "Soft or Sly?", because of the expression's symmetry, alliteration, and because my go-to doodle is a cartoon fox (below, and evolved). We had a few commissions - apart from the Durbar, I remember a Riding Stable somewhere in East Anglia wanting a faux Western starring all its members. It was a half-hearted venture - but prescient of what was to come the next time I could afford to buy a bit of kit, ten years later.

Kit buying was at the heart of it, and after my success with the mobile disco, I had been bitten by the dangerous bug of 'borrow, rent, own, use'. Urging me on, Weasel to my Toad, was an unlikely new friend. The actor

Warren Saire (left, and below left) was 15 when he played Lord Nettleby's grandson Marcus in *The Shooting Party*, but he'd already appeared in a number of television dramas and a film called *The Monster Club* (1981) with Vincent Price, which also shot at Knebworth. He was sparklingly precocious, with a developed sense of humour, and I enjoyed being persistently pestered by him, both during the shoot and afterwards in London.

Was it odd, at 21, hanging out with a 15-year-old? Warren was the same age as my younger brother and anyone of any age with a love of movies and a sense of humour

Soft or Sly?

PROFESSIONAL VHS
VIDEO PRODUCTION

Henry Cobbold
Warren Saire

39 Harewood Avenue
London NW1
Tel. (01) 724 0091/5

is a friend of mine. It was only awkward at lunch with my grandparents when my elderly grandfather suggested I should get my girlfriend some dessert. Warren was happy to get his own dessert. Better still he came with an-

other set of parents for me - not that I wasn't perfectly happy with my own parents, but Warren's parents were theatre-people, actors, comfortingly camp, and I wanted them as parents too. When I moved to London that year, they became my 'London parents'.

Pam Saire (right) was a chaper-one on *The Shooting Party* set, because Warren was under 16. There are few lovelier people in the world. Warren's dad Richard (left) would say that, actually, he is lovelier. But it is not true. Richard Saire's life's quest is to look younger than his children - indeed younger than everyone - but, like Dorian Gray's painting, the youthful curls conceal a dark heart. He rarely leaves his lair - then Barnes, now Eastbourne - but like the best gothic monsters, he is irresistibly entertaining. For a young man starting out in the business, he was a gusset-full of bitchy wisdom.

Better still. Warren had an elder sister. The 'perfectly perfectly lovely' (cf Hitchcock's *Rebecca*) Rebecca Saire (below) had been the BBC 'Juliet' aged 14. She was another young veteran of countless TV dramas. Now aged 20, she was playing James Mason's granddaughter Cecily in *The Shooting Party*. But of course, like all the desirable girls at that age, had a boyfriend inappropriately older than her.

And besides, I had a girlfriend. Liz was now at Middlesex Polytechnic and lived at my London house while I was at Knebworth that autumn. My Lon-don house (I sigh just typing it - if I still had it I'd be yabba-dabba-ering round the barn with Topol) was the great financial privilege of my gilded youth. Whilst they were selling corners of the Knebworth Estate to pay debts, my parents were also selling cottages to give each of their four Lytton Cobbold children a start on the property ladder in London. They themselves had a two-room flat at No 17 Harewood Avenue, alongside Marylebone Station. So they noticed when all four floors of No 39, a few doors down the terrace, came on the market for about £80,000. My 'cot-tage' was swapped. The ground floor

and the basement of No 39 were rented out to pay expenses and provide a small base income, and I moved into the top two floors. The ground floor was rented to a film editor called Joe Illing, and the basement rented to my friend, the musician, John Martin. I was especially pleased that John planned to turn this basement into a recording studio, fully sound-proofed, with a control booth window between the two rooms. He lived there as well. On the studio futon. But music was more important than domestic comfort.

I should have thought harder about the consequences of John investing his savings into this studio infrastructure without any written agreement. But I guess I thought most of his money was in his kit, which was movable. The studio carpentry had all been done at cost by his brother-in-law... This was naivety. And it was to bite me in the pocket book a few years later.

For the moment, however, it was the best possible fun having a bard in the basement, with a recording studio that hosted a procession of merry minstrels. Bonnie Tyler popped by. The session player Peter Oxendale was a regular. He played keyboards for Sparks, Dead or Alive and Frankie Goes To Hollywood, and is now a go-to forensic musicology witness in copyright cases (e.g. *Blurred Lines*). John reminds me of a story of Rafi Ravenscroft being down there - the guy who played the sax solo to Gerry Raffetty's *Baker Street*. He lived with that LDOB long before he died - so

HAREWOOD STUDIOS
39 Harewood Avenue
London NW1
Tel: 01-724 - 0095

when someone telephoned him at the studio and asked him where he was and he replied "Baker Street", it was assumed he was in the middle of some mad musical genius dream. But he was, actually, just round the corner from Baker Street.

Best of all about Harewood Studios, however, was that we got to make music down there. In particular, on John's pride and joy - his new Linn Drum, the state of the art in 80s drum machines. On that beautiful wooden box I wrote my answer to George Michael's *Bad Boys* rap, a cockney punch up called *Stop That Row!* (p.114)

Upstairs at No 39 I had some fun too. I went to Stevenage Glass and bought fitted mirrors for the walls and ceiling of the little toilet/bathroom, which instantly became Versailles. The two bedrooms I completely collaged, walls and ceiling. My one completely in black & white, and Gary (my lodger's) completely in colour. The ceiling of the colour room was the complete film of *The Rocky Horror Picture Show*, extracted from two copies of the full film picturebook (two copies because the book pages were two-sided). My black & white room was all old Hollywood movie stars - and, as my piece de resistance, I black-fabric-edged the wall opposite the bed to fit exactly the huge projected image of a Barco video projector hung from the ceiling. I could watch VHS movies - and *Tiswas* on Saturday mornings - in my own cinema. And, oh yes... the bed was a big double wood-framed water bed. This sounds appallingly 'Austin Powers' today, but water beds were not so unusual then. What I liked about it was that it was always warm. Above the bed,

I hung a giant black & white image of Knebworth House.

This was 39 Harewood Avenue. My very own house. And I loved it.

Above,
a taste of the 'Black & White Room'. The walls were
completely collaged except for the whole-wall white
screen opposite the harlequin double water bed

Above,
a taste of the 'Colour Room'.
The walls weren't actually wobbly - that's my Photoshop skills - this is another frankenmerge
of half a dozen old photograghs. I'll attach the opposite walls in the 4D version of the book.)

Finally, that winter, I got to live in it. The Production Manager of *The Shooting Party* was the brilliantly brilliant, switched on, fun, Tina Jamieson (right). She and I became great friends and she took me with her to her next job, which was editing the back-projection film for Roger Waters' *Pros and Cons of Hitchhiking* World Tour. The footage had been shot by an up-and-coming director called Bernard Rose. But what was really up-and-coming was the Production Company. They were called Working Title and they had just made their first feature film, called *My Beautiful Laundrette* (1985) with a buzzy young actor called Daniel Day Lewis. I was invited to the very first ever screening of

this film, in a little viewing theatre somewhere in Soho. I can still to this day picture the producer Tim Bevan slumped in an armchair outside the screening room, tortured as to whether the film was any good. He did not need to worry.

It was fun running film reels around Soho. That was my main responsibility. I felt very much at the heart of the business. Tim Bevan was actively involved, and I was often handing to or picking up from him personally. I met him again recently at the London Premiere of Working Title's *Victoria & Abdul* (2017), some of which was filmed at Knebworth House. I enjoyed hearing him nostalgic for those days of film reels and 'Runners' bustling them around Soho. It's all distant memories now, of course, with film long in the digital realm and Runners now restricted mainly to running to the kettle and back, as all the film 'running' is done on the internet.

I did also spend some time running to the kettle and back on that job. One memory makes me wince, handing a mug of piping hot tea to Roger Waters and burning the tips of his bass-playing fingers just before he was due on stage at Earl's Court. The job was all pretty 11th hour stuff - exciting as I remember it, more stressful I'm sure for Tim Bevan. The opening lead guitar of the title track of the album still sets the hairs up on the back of my neck. I was in Los Angeles a couple of years later, when the *Pros and Cons of Hitchhiking* World Tour finally made it to the Forum in Inglewood. I bought a single ticket at the back of the giant auditorium and enjoyed that I had played a part in the cutting and grading of those images projected for the 17,000 people in front of me.

This was my first time in a working editing room, and it was thrilling to see a Steenbeck flatbed film editing suite put to work. We'd had a couple of these grey monsters at university, as a way of studying films in class before videos were widely available, but here in Soho we were actually slicing up celluloid, seeing the scratches and the chalk marks flicker by on the film.

During *The Shooting Party* I had been invited to see 'rushes' only once. In those days Producers would book a screening room, velour seats, projector, cigar ashtrays, to check the raw footage from a day before. Today if they are not viewing it on video screens on set, they're checking it on their phones half way round the world. *The Shooting Party* rushes were screened at Elstree Studios, just down the road from Knebworth, and I was invited to see them on what just happened to be the day they were reviewing the one 'sex' scene (surely not a aforethought? God bless Geoff

Reeve and Jeremy Saunders if it was!). Consequently I marvelled through take after take of lovely blonde-curled Cheryl Campbell letting her dressing gown slip while her dark bedroom intruder Aharon Ipalé kisses her pale breasts. Of course the sound was unmixed - just the raw close up boom mike sound - which was therefore wonderfully wet and slurpy, and very much ruder than the very demure scene that appeared in the film. Film-making is fun.

I had done my Film Studies dissertation on sound - well, on the diegetic (real) and non-diegetic (not real) score of Samuel Fuller's *Underworld USA* (1961). But I was about to get the best practical lesson in Film Sound that I could ever hope for. My third job in the Film Industry - which followed straight on from the second - was as 'Third Man on Sound' with the sound department legends, Derek Ball and Ken Nightingale, the James Bond and Star Wars unit sound men. The film was a Cannon Picture, *Ordeal By Innocence*, based on the book by Agatha Christie. It was to shoot for six weeks in Dartmouth, Devon, in the Spring months of 1984.

I was recommended for the job by the lovely Prop Master Bert Gadsden (below). Film people are mostly lovely, but Bert took a particular interest in other people. He had been the Prop Master on *The Shooting Party* and was to be the Prop Master on this film. But I nearly fell at the first fence. I was pitched to Derek Ball as having my own van, which I did, but it was not

the van he was expecting. I turned up at his Berkshire home in my toilet-cleaner blue Fiat Fiorino (p.96), a humpbacked little two-seater, not in the Ford Transit the Bond team were expecting. I was about to be turned away. He was shaking his head, it's not big enough. The Sound Department needs to be self-sufficient. I reasoned that we should at least see if we couldn't fit all the gear in the back. The little van was practiced at shunting a large mobile disco around the lanes of Hertfordshire. I knew how to pack it like Jenga. I also offered that it would probably be easier to get around the little country lanes of South Devon, and into difficult locations. He humpfed. Alleluia, the gear did fit. Just. Reluctantly, he agreed to give it a try. There wasn't really time to change the plans. We were expected in Devon. But Derek was resigning himself to having to blow his budget the following week on renting a transit and, I could see, was not relishing six weeks with this neophyte.

Ordeal By Innocence was a fill-in job for Derek and Ken. Between big studio pictures. They'd become used to bigger budgets. Cannon was notoriously budget-shy, and liked to play hide-and-seek with the unions. Because the budget was declared to be a certain level, the production was permitted to do without a 'Third Man on Sound'. I had to declare myself a 'Runner' if the union turned up on set. Indeed, I'm not credited on the film itself, although I worked harder on this one than all the others of this time.

As it turned out, I was right about the difficult locations. My van was able to get much closer to remote rural sets than all the other crew vehicles. Derek was won round. I think, eventually, he and Ken quite enjoyed having this braided-haired spaceman in his blue bubble following them around. It amused them.

I had arranged to rent a room at a farm between Totnes and Dartmouth. Insurance insisted that I did not leave the expensive kit in the van overnight, so I spent much of the six weeks taking it all out of the van and putting it back in again. I was sure the kit would have been much safer in my van than in the basic farm shed into which I was off-loading every night. This added half an hour at each end of an already long day. But it was a dairy farm so I was still the last on the farm out of my eiderdowned bed. I can't believe I had any downtime before going to sleep, but I do have a memory that I read the whole of Catherine Cookson's *The Mallen Streak* on those evenings. And it was the perfect read. Although I was in the South West rather than the North East, this old farm was one of the most evocative places I could have found to read Catherine Cookson. I felt I was living with the characters.

Like *The Shooting Party, Ordeal By Innocence* had quite a cast. Donald Sutherland, Christopher Plummer, Sarah Miles, Faye Dunaway, Ian McShane, Annette Crosbie, Diana Quick and Phoebe Nicholls (both fresh from the success of *Brideshead Revisited*), and Michael Maloney. Michael Maloney became a friend-of-a-friend in later years and attended Knebworth parties. He is an excellent and regular reader of audio books, so I enjoy telling him he is coming on holiday with me. The poster of *Ordeal By Innocence* has hung on the toilet wall of Knebworth House since 1984, so I also enjoy telling him I think of him every morning.

No actresses to fall in love with on this set - apart from, obviously, my schoolboy crush on *Ryan's Daughter*, Sarah Miles. The love scene in *Ryan's Daughter* (1970), where Sarah Miles keeps her hands covering her naked breasts until Christopher Jones slides his hands under hers... remains one of my Top 10 sexiest moments on film. Although, by returning to Dartmouth for this film, she was reawakening the memory (certainly in me, surely in her too?) of her once notorious masturbation scene in the same seaside town in 1976's *The Sailor Who Fell From Grace With The Sea* - which I knew, not because I'd seen it (it was an X film, and I'd been 14 when it came out, plus it was too obscure to be on video yet) but as a dedicated schoolboy reader of *Continental Film Review*. During the shoot, she came up behind me and purred "What beautiful hair you have." I can't remember if she was stroking my braids as she said this, but the memory has been improved by this addition.

Then there was getting my bottom pinched by Annette Crosbie. This definitely happened. As in the actual murder mystery, Annette Crosby did it. This was welcome attention for a lowly runner like me, but it occurs that this impulsive act of mischief would not be acceptable now. I am all for the long-overdue redress of balance that #MeToo - the big Hollywood story as I write - has brought about, but I do also believe that different times deserve different judges. "The true censor of the age, is the spirit of the age", said my Great-Great-Great-Grandfather, Edward Bulwer Lytton (I think quoting Lord Chesterfield). Certainly revisit crimes decades later (Double Jeopardy is a very odd inalienable right of the American Constitution), but I say let misdemeanours be. Bullying is not okay, but the context needs to fit the crime - what's more, the century needs to fit the crime. Your true crimes should come back to haunt you, but not your impulsive mischief. More on this subject later.

Certainly on this set I was not going to get attention from younger actresses. Donald's Sutherland's romantic interest in the film was a grinning Betty Boop called Cassie Stuart. There was an obvious empty chair at her table one day as I approached with a lunch tray. She promptly got up and went to sit with the screenwriter. This makes me laugh now, as a screenwriter. In film set pecking order, if anything's as low as a runner, it's the screenwriter. There is a pre-#MeToo Hollywood joke about sleeping with the screenwriter.

I don't know what Cassie's relationship with this screenwriter was, but I do know a little about her relationship with the film's leading man. That is outside of the film's story. And that's because I was in the Sound Department. Donald Sutherland stayed radio mic-ed for the whole day, which meant that every so often a broad smile would spread across Derek's face, as he sat in the corner with his headphones on. It was said that the large Winnebago that Donald had in his contract - and which struggled to make it onto most of the remote Dartmouth sets (unlike my Fiat Fiorino) - was only used once a day, for 'parking his breakfast'. But this may not strictly have been the case.

Is that paragraph 'allegedly' enough? Of course I am only gossiping. And I've no business doing so, as I was not wearing the headphones. And Derek would not have betrayed an actor's confidence. I was purely reading the Sound Man's smile. But Donald did take the whole Sound Department, including the 'Third Man', out to dinner at Dartmouth's swanky restaurant of the time, The Carved Angel. Apparently he took a different department out every night, so this may not purely have been in return for keeping his confidences.

It was a memorable evening. I was sat at an intimate dinner table in a far corner of England with three veterans of the film business, including an actor I had grown up watching in *Kelly's Heroes* (1970), *M.A.S.H.* (1970), *S.P.Y.S.* (1974) and, from my Top Ten, *Don't Look Now* (1973). I felt very privileged to be in that company, and to be treated as part of a respected team. At the end of the evening, Derek, Ken and I were each given a silver tankard engraved, "Best wishes, Donald Sutherland". It sits in my study today, a treasured memento.

I loved working with Derek and Ken, although I was in at the deep end with these two old pros, and constantly having to live up to not being a real 'Third Man on Sound'. I was asked to splice up a Nagra ¼" audio tape, so we could play Donald Sutherland's side of a telephone call on set when the less important actor was being filmed on a separate day. I had no idea how to do that. Razors. Sticky tape. Shuffling the tape backwards and forwards. I learnt on the job, and got by. I also did some boom holding for Ken. Although he wasn't going to risk me on an actor. I was given the Hotel Reception desk bell's close up. Tough work holding a boom aloft for hours on end. Try it some time. I asked Ken if he did exercises between shoots to keep up his arm strength. His response was a rapid right wrist movement.

Most fun was being sent out with my own mic and recorder to pick up 'wild sound'. I wandered around Dartmouth looking like Inspector Clouseau. In my

London blacks, I got used to getting strange looks sitting in the corner of South Devon pubs. But having a microphone in my hand, strangely, I was more accepted - as though the locals wouldn't be surprised to see themselves on telly that Sunday evening, their natural habits being given narration by David Attenborough. I recorded cobbled street noises, ferry noises... but mostly a lot of seagulls. If you ever see *Ordeal By Innocence*, my seagull noises are right up in the very first scene, making a lot more sense in the scene-setting than the Dave Brubeck jazz score. And of course, later in the film, the Hotel Reception Desk Bell rings particularly finely.

You won't see me in the credits, as I've said. Because I wasn't union. But as a 'scab', I made good friends amongst my union colleagues. Including - and unusually for a runner - the most important crew member, the First Assistant Director, David Tringham. David, in his retirement, turns up at Knebworth occasionally with paints & easel and makes lovely paintings of my garden. I didn't know it at the time but almost twenty years before, he was also First Assistant Director on a film which will become important to my story later - *The Witches* (1966), starring Joan Fontaine, and directed by Cyril Frankel.

All of the above you may believe - but you won't believe that for the one day off we had a week - Sunday - every week, for six weeks, I drove five hours each way, up the M5 and along the M4, just to have a few hours in London with my girlfriend Liz. This was natural to me, a continuation of my drives home every weekend at university. But the sadness of this time is that Liz, my girlfriend of 2½ years was moving on. Not to Richard Wells. I think she was the only one. She needed the freedom to make the most of her time at Middlesex University... and she deserved a boyfriend who was a bit less predictable, and, who knows, perhaps not so hung up on retaining his virginity going on 22.

I look back on Liz as the other lover I loved the most. We remained good friends. I am so pleased she was at my wedding. After that we did not see each other for about 25 years, because I was in America, and then she went to live in Greece, then India, then China. But when she did pop by for Tea after all those years, with one of her three grown-up children, it was hard to get to sleep that night. Not because I would have done anything different, or that I wished for anything different. Just a mist of melancholy for a lost time... a blue remembered hill.

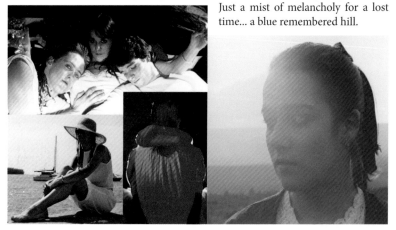

Extraordinarily there was a third film to go straight onto that summer of 1984. A year earlier I had been managing Knebworth Park for the summer when my favourite film ever to be shot at Knebworth turned up for a couple of days. It was a comedy financed by George Harrison's Handmade Films, called *Bullshot* (1983). It was a pastiche on the Bulldog Drummond films of the 1930s, Drummond being a 1920s James Bond prototype, who could save the world, win the London to Brighton (car rally), and still be home in time for Tea. I can quote most of the film, and unless you know its references, well I'm afraid you'll never quite be in my inner circle.

Knebworth House made a brief appearance in this largely ignored gem, as Bullshot's friend Binkie's house. Dick Clement was the director - of the Clement / La Frenais writing partnership - although this film had primarily been written by its lead cast for the theatre. Representing Knebworth House for the shoot, I got to know the Line Producer David Wimbury, and First Assistant Peter Kohn.

So when this same team, in the summer of 1984, made an original Clement / La Frenais script entitled *Water*, and the script required a few weeks in North Devon - miraculously - on the cliffs at Hartland, which was the estate of my mother's family the Stucleys, I was again, the perfect man for a job. I knew the location. I'd spent Christmases and Summer Holidays there since I was a small child. And I was building a decent film industry CV. I was hired as the Location Manager's assistant, and was sent to Devon some weeks before the Unit arrived.

Most of *Water* (1985) shot in St Lucia in the Caribbean (shame my uncle didn't own those locations), but for a number of scenes the story required an oil rig (in the story, for mineral water) and it would have been prohibitively expensive to construct one of those in St Lucia. So my job - and that of the Location Manager, Bob Jordan - was to make North Devon look like the 'wild Atlantic side' of the island of St Lucia. For this, we needed two things - well, three things, but more of the third later. The two main things we needed were plastic palm trees and bendy brush. By bendy brush I mean windswept bent trees and bushes. Plastic palm trees were relatively easy to source, but for bendy brush we had to do the rounds of all the local farmers asking if we could buy their bent roadside trees to replant them on our cliffside.

Devon farmers are wily folk.

It was as well I has just spent six weeks living on a Devon farm, reading *The Mallen Streak*. But my indispensable value was not so much as cultural diplomat, but as tee-total driver. Bob would thrash out deals in smugglers pubs, and in order to gain the farmer's confidence, would need to match the farmer's alcohol intake. By the end of the evening, the deal was done - but so was the Location Manager. To be fair to Bob, he did not particularly relish this routine, but it was the only way to do business with these characters. And our expansive cliffside location needed a lot of bendy trees.

I was there to drive Bob home... and re-mind everyone the following day what had been agreed.

It did help that I was a Stucley. My mother's family go back a long way in these parts - as forgers, wreckers, and general North Devon miscreants. And of course, respected squires of the county. I had a deep bond with my grand-mother (far right), who bought me up on stories of the local farming families where all the men had six toes on their left feet (the North Devon version of the Mallen Streak of white hair), and who had to advertise for wives as they never travelled far enough from home to meet a woman who wasn't a relation.

My mother's home, Hartland Abbey (above), in a beautiful valley leading to the tallest cliffs in England, had been pillaged off the monks by Henry VIII for the keeper of his wine cellar - so had been in her family for just marginally less time than Knebworth House had been in my father's. Although Hartland is one village away from the Cornish border, my grandmother crossed that border no more than a handful of times in the years I knew her, and one of those crossings was for my own daughter's christening - a story for later. Suffice to say, I am genuine Devon-stock and so was generally accepted by the locals that summer, which was useful for the production. It didn't protect our location signs though. Early every morning I would take wooden signs and a mallet round to every lane intersection to direct the

crew (this is long before SAT NAV) - it was the same route every day, but every morn-ing the signs would have been uprooted and tossed in the ditch or over the hedge.

Which brings me to the third thing needed to recreate St Lucia in Devon. Black people. There were scant black folk in North Devon in those days. On the first of two crowd scene days, coaches of extras were bussed in from Bristol, some two and a half hours away. The West Indies was brought to Westward Ho. Well, Hartland village... which is not where the buses

were meant to be. But of course my signs had been tossed in the ditch. The coaches proceeded to get stuck, lodged in the narrow streets. All the extras were asked to step out of the bus. The net curtains were twitching in the cottages of Hartland that morning. Eighty West Indians were wandering the deserted streets. The blackamoors had invaded. But then it was only a matter of time. After centuries of having had their trading ships lured onto the rocks.

Water had another impressive cast. Michael Caine, Billy Connolly, Leonard Rossiter, Valerie Perrine, Brenda Vaccaro... and of course the oil rig - a full size genuine oil rig. This, firstly, had to spurt an impressive amount of water into the sky, and then be blown up as part of the last scene. I know we think the summers of our youth were wall-to-wall, May-to-September, sunshine, when none of them actually were. Except perhaps 1976. But the summer of 1984 was, in fact, quite sunny. Perfect then, for recreating St Lucia. Yes - but not for finding water. The subject of our film. Because of the lack of rain, there was a hose pipe ban. The rivers were dry. And nothing was going to make the farmers give up their bowsers, not even sacrificing Bob to a night of heavy drinking at the Wreckers Arms... especially not to see all that precious water then simply tossed over the cliff into the sea. I think we got around the problem by pumping seawater up the cliff - but then there was an issue of spoiling the soil atop the cliff... It was not all going to be the brilliant wheeze it sounded, living with granny for a summer by the sea and getting paid for it.

Add to that the well-known North Devon fact that Hartland Point has its own micro-climate, that can be completely out of step with the rest of the country. So the whole of Great Britain may be bathed in golden sunlight, but Hartland Point will be under a cloud. This, of course, is what happened the day all the extras were scheduled for the big cliffside climax... indeed for the whole of that week. You could literally drive inland a couple of miles to the A39 and be in bright sunshine, but the Hartland cliffs remained under a permanent cloud. Fortunately, the filmmakers of *Water* were Britain's top comedy writers, therefore had a sense of humour.

It is sad, however, that Handmade soon ran out of George Harrison's money and this wonderful slate of British comedies, which had started with *The Life of Brian*, and included *Time Bandits*, *A Private Function*, *Withnail & I*, *Bullshot* and *Water* imploded. Like an oilrig full of sparkling water on an English cliffside.

Which is an appropriate thought with which to resume the tale of my love life. This is the losing my virginity bit. I'd skip these two pages if I was you - they're a bit maudlin - but do admire the lovely girl in the pictures on your way to the next chapter... I finally entered the doors of Number 10 on the night of my 22nd birthday in the Tudor bed of Knebworth House's Queen Elizabeth Room. 'Lost' is not a word that feels appropriate for virginity in the modern age, but I'm sorry to say that I do look back on my virginity as being 'lost'. I had been annoyingly protective of it for going on a decade. It had been a teenage 'cause' of mine - like not drinking, not smoking, not taking drugs... and all of those, I still, in my mid 50s, hold on to, with irritating self-satisfaction. Aged 22, I was Samson having a hair cut. Merlin caught in a bubble. Prey to the potions of a Circe, and turned into sensual swine. Or I had whatever everyone else just calls a 'shag'. And probably you'll say I needed one.

But then, having had one, and having followed it with a couple of weeks of having another one - on a Tuesday, Thursday and Saturday - I then didn't have one for another year and a half. And then only with the lover who was to become my wife. So this virginity 'losing' was kind of a momentous thing for me. However absurd that sounds.

The Baron to the Actress: "I have seen you, somewhere... I know..."

The Actress to the Baron: "The ending in the book is more believable"

The beautiful, talented, actor, writer, satirist, mimic, general all round wonderful person (enough?) Rebecca Saire remains to this day one of my very B.F.F.s. Therefore I have a couple of difficult paragraphs to write. Because, having become bewitched, bothered and besotted by this Burne-Jones beauty with whom I'd been the best of friends since *The Shooting Party*, I became bitter, twisted and tormented for some time when she dumped me a few weeks later for my best mate Richard Wells. The thing, fling, whatever it should be called, lasted only a matter of weeks. Rebecca had parted from her older

boyfriend, and turned up, en famille, at my 22nd birthday weekend at Knebworth. I was riding high. It had been a great year. *The Shooting Party*, *The Pros and Cons of Hitchhiking*, *Ordeal By Innocence*... going on to *Water*. I had my perfect London house, the beginnings of a promising career, guaranteed work through the summer. It was May. It

was my birthday. The sun was shining. Life was good. I fell into a magical bed with the magical daughter of my London parents. And it was all very fine. For a moment in time... And then it ended.

I remember my birthday. And I remember a fantasy few days when Rebecca visited me at Hartland Abbey during the making of *Water*. I don't remember much else. Maybe there wasn't much else. I suspect I have printed on the next page, a glamorous photo I took of Rebecca lit my by my car headlights in front of a couple of plastic palm trees

on a North Devon cliff. The Pre-Raphaelite in me entitles this *Circe*. It was probably a very wonderful time. But, by the time I returned to London at the end of the *Water* shoot, Rebecca had moved on, to Richard. I was a complicated kid, I know - much more complicated than my good friend Richard... but I must ask her one day why for the rest of that summer, she thought my best mate was the better option.

Richard is now married to a Great Dane (actually, that's me) - a lovely Dane, Malene. His adorable daughter Olivia is my only godchild (thank goodness the only one - the royalty cheques from *An-*  *other Scopophilic Urge* barely cover her fiver at Christmas). Rebecca, like Liz, came to my wedding in the U.S. It was perfect that she was there. Her fiction- al bedroom in *The Shooting Party* has long since been exorcised, sanctified and fortified as my marital bedroom at Knebworth House. In 2004, she mar- ried the exceptional actor, Roger Allam (Henry Graves in Samuel West's adap- tation of Bulwer Lytton's *Money* for BBC Radio, but you're probably more familiar with him as D.I. Thursday in the *Inspector Morse* prequel *Endeavour*) and is blessed with two beautiful boys. The Allams are coming to stay for the weekend next month.

Back in 1984, like all things, the back-to-back movie jobs could not go on for- ever... Although I did meet the producer Peter Heslop recently - an assistant with me on *The Shooting Party* - and despite what I'm about to say, he went on getting work on British movies. So disbelieve me if you will, when I tell you that movie produc- tion stopped in Britain in the second half of 1984... and didn't start up again until *Lock Stock and Two Smoking Barrels* in 1998. It's not altogether true. But it's the only plausible explanation for why, after such an auspicious start, I got no further work in the UK film business.

CHAPTER THIRTEEN

On The Road

Roses To You!
Joan Fontaine

With no movies to work on in the autumn of 1984, I went to work for a family friend, Les Eastaugh (below right), who ran an events company that was busy in the travel industry. The first gig was staging the Association of British Travel Agents annual conference in Toronto. My first time in Canada. I was instantly arrested. This is the only time in my life I've been arrested. To date.

On a mission for Les, I drove the wrong way up a one-way street. Quite reasonably, I was asked to produce my Drivers Licence. I said it was in England.

At the police station - as I remember it - the officiating constable got bored filling in my form. Probably before he got to the end of spelling my name. I was told to go away. Canada is a civilised country.

Dear Les, ever the very best of supporters, told me a couple of days before he died that he expected a copy of this book delivered to No.1 Pearly Gates. His will be the first copy. This is him asleep, not dead. I miss him.

I was thus not a particularly useful 'Runner' for Les. Brilliant, though, that to keep me off the roads he gave me the job of vision mixing the live conference video feed. In front of a packed conference hall of travel agents from around the world. I'd been to film school, hadn't I? This was my first directing job. Again, I was in at the deep end. No rehearsal. I had three cameras to direct, by radio mike, and was expected to keep the pictures on the main screen as interesting as you can make three people sitting in chairs talking about travel insurance. O, to unleash my inner Verhoeven. Close ups of legs uncrossing, beads of sweat on the brow, furtive glances... But I repaid Les's trust. And to this day, it's probably my most successful directing job. I loved it, and don't know why I haven't done more of it. "Come in close, Camera 3. Hold the long shot, Camera 2... When you've finished checking your camera focus on the breasts, Camera 1, can we pull back into a two shot... no, not that two shot - a two shot of the Presenters, please."

In the evening the crew went drinking. Less appeal in that to me. So I found my own entertainment hanging out playing guitar in the bedroom of the (lovely) 16-year-old daughter of a significant pre-marriage other of my Dad's, Miranda De Pencier, nowadays winning award-after-award for worthiness in Canadian film making. And I got to see Frankie Goes To Hollywood in a small theatre across town - because, although *Relax* was a massive hit in the UK, Canada hadn't completely caught on yet. So I turned up (by taxi, I was getting paid) and bought a ticket. I remember thinking, I alone in this audience know how big this band is going to be.

It reminded me of the time I'd been amongst less than a hundred people in the Kent Student Union Bar watching Duran Duran. Something to tell the kids. There you go, kids. What d'you mean you've heard it before?

Still no movies to work on. So I stayed with Les in the lead up to Christmas 1984 doing a road show of Christmas parties for employees of Thomson Holidays. This meant staging a corporate Christmas booze up in every major town in the UK, on consecutive nights, for about four weeks. I'd never travelled in the UK before, except to go to Devon, and to school. So I loved every minute of these 20 hour days. The parties would end at 11pm, then we'd have a two hour stage break down, before stealing a couple of hours sleep, and having to get up to drive to the next town to set up for the next evening.

I went to exotic places I've not been to since, like Aberdeen, Cardiff, Nottingham... I can now nod my head knowingly when these towns are mentioned, although I barely saw them for five minutes outside of a hotel. But I did get a feel for them because, after our corporate presentation and 'employee of the year' etc., there was usually a local DJ to keep the dancefloor buzzing to the local zeitgeist, and to prevent us from packing up and getting some sleep. This local DJ gave the best flavour of whatever town we were in. The great majority of Thomson's employees were female, and if we had a DJ who was determined that his audience preferred to play party games than to dance, my comrades and I - like Odysseus and crew - were dragged beneath the disco ball, into the midst of the drunken revels, to make up the male numbers. So, dear reader, picture me horizontal on the dancefloor doing press ups on top of some giggling Glaswegian lass, considering that I'm getting paid for this, and that the fine English education my parents sweated to buy for me was, up to this moment in time, successfully forging me a financially-secure career.

Apparently we got stuck in a lift in Newcastle. I have no recollection of this.

The climax of the Thomson Road Show was a final tour date for continental employees, in Berlin. Berlin - how soon we forget - was at this time surrounded by Communist East Germany. Thus an even bigger adventure than Cardiff.

Again, we saw very little of Berlin - but I'm pleased that I did see it, because it looked lightyears different from what Berlin looks like today. Borders are overrated. Walls too. All to be avoided. Alas, my misguided country, as I write, wants

Screen grabs from a ropey old VHS of the last night of 1984 Thomson UK Christmas Party Tour.

The crew join the dance floor, and frankly, rule over the Thomson travel agents, notably our leaders Simon and Liz Bagnall's blistering turn to Brown Sugar (bottom left)

borders back. (I hope this paragraph will date. I suspect it won't.)

The fun of Berlin for a bunch of English video technicians on tour, after a long day slogging in the conference hall, was not to trawl the nightclubs for a taste of Weimar, but to head to bed with a BNC cable, to bypass the pay box on the hotel porn channel. That'll seem odd to today's reader. But remember, 'porn' in England at this time was genital-less sex comedies. Germans were a bit more enlightened. The hotel porn channel was as culturally enriching to us as any visit to the kunst museum.

Eating cherry pancakes in an Amsterdam cafe, killing time before the ferry back to England, I contemplated my next move. I was determined to get back into movies. What was my best way back in? It wasn't so much, 'what aspect of filmmaking do I want to pursue?'. It was, 'where's the open door?' I contemplated the equivalent of being able to fart *La Marseillaise* to get an equity card (finding something no other union member can do).

I considered the three feature films I had worked on. What could I do as well as anyone on those?... I was by now a pretty good bendy tree purveyor and seagull recordist. But that wasn't going to get me to Hollywood.

Then I considered the three screenplays. I'd of course avidly dissected and inwardly digested all three of them. Yes, I genuinely believed I could have done a better job on all of them.

That's not to say that I thought I was a better comedy writer than Dick Clement & Ian Le Frenais - or even half of them. I just thought that I could have written all three of those screenplays. But the first two in particular - the adaptations - I thought I could have, at least, made more interesting.

I should write a screenplay. Using these three screenplays as a guide, I would write one of my own. That would be my ticket. That is what my literary education and college brain-banking of movies qualified me to do better than the other man.

As for getting to Hollywood, well, all I really needed was an airplane. So, with a year and a half of wages in my pocket (which I'd not spent, because on movies they give you cash 'per diems' on top of your food and lodgings, so you have no expenses), I did an apartment swap with Tom Reeve, son of *The Shooting Party* producer Geoffrey Reeve. My flat in Marylebone for his flat in Beverley Hills. If that doesn't sound like a fair swap, do consider that my flat did have a fully mirrored bathroom.

In the opening months of 1985 I went to Los Angeles for 9½ weeks to write a screenplay. It was exactly 9½ weeks... and, yes, that is prescient. Wait for it.

For I knew literally no one. All I had was a phone number on a scrap of paper. That was it. I rang the number.

"Hello, I was given your number by Jeremy Saunders-"

"Jeremy who?"

"Jeremy Saunders, a producer of *The Shooting Party*."

"Never heard of him."

"um... He said to give you a call."

"Well I don't know who he is."

"He said he met you with Geoff Reeve."

"Geoff Reeve?... That name sounds vaguely familiar... Well, look, I'm very busy, but if you want to come to a Drinks I am having before the Opera tomorrow, I'll give you my address... [sighs]... I've never heard of Jeremy Saunders, though."

The lady with whom I had this exchange said no more than a sentence to me at her cod Georgian mansion the following day. But a couple on their way to the Opera with her politely asked who I was. As though I'd unwittingly said some magic password, it was declared, "You must meet Jill Spalding."

Jill Spalding was the West Coast Editor of Australian *Vogue*. But that didn't appear to be relevant. What was relevant was that she would know what to do with this acquaintanceless alien. It appeared Jill had been briefed, because when a few days later I went round to her house - apparently Greta Garbo's former home - she 'vas not alone'. Sitting opposite her, side by side, on a high sofa, were my new 'L.A.' parents. Pat and Zalman King.

Photo: Gillian Lefkowitz

Pretty well everyone I met in Los Angeles over the next eight years spider-webbed out from this one moment of pure serendipity. Thank you Jill. And thank you Jeremy (who?) for that phone number on a scrap of paper. I saw Jill again once or twice, but she moved to New York when I moved to Los Angeles and I am sorry to have lost touch. Pat and Zalman, however (above) - to, and beyond, their deaths in 2012 and 2019 - have been a consistent, irreplaceable and beautiful part of my life.

Pat was a sculptress, painter, writer... artist in every atom. Zalman, an actor, hero, writer... an inspiration and teacher to me, and countless others. They met on a tall sail ship in the Caribbean when they were teenagers. Their love story is of the kind that Hollywood tells, but does not exist in the town itself. Except, that is, at Pat and Zalman's house - then on Rose Avenue in Venice, and as far as I was concerned the most beautiful 'home' west of Knebworth. This home then moved to Alta Avenue in Santa Monica (below), and if ever there was a western El Dorado this was it, with its gold being a richness of remarkable art - countless colourful and captivating curiosities collected, created and curated over a lifetime by Pat's consummate eye.

Photos: Ace Mintunas

Photo: Chloe King

Jill, I think, was thinking that the potential playmate for the acquaintanceless alien would be Pat and Zal's lovely 18-year-old daughter Chloe (above) - and, sure enough, for those 9½ weeks Chloe became a blessèd lifeline to the world beyond Tom Reeve's Beverly Hills basement, which otherwise I barely stepped out of. I did not have a car. This was Los Angeles. Chloe would come by at the weekend in her splendid giant bright-red Cadillac convertible and take me out for parties and outings with her school friend group, Jeff Martin (later of the band Idaho), Kip Koenig (later producer and writer of *Grey's Anatomy*), Mark Norris (who, in one of those there-are-only-300-million-people-in-the-U.S. moments, met at university, and dated, a schoolfriend of my wife's from Tuscaloosa Alabama, Virginia Cravens)... I loved this completely alien and detached sabbatical of being an emo Angeleno kid.

Photo: Chloe King

But the point was to write a screenplay. And in this I was given endless encouragement and guidance by Pat. She and Zalman at that time were working on a screenplay adaptation of the memoir *9½ Weeks* by an Austrian émigrée Ingeborg Day, writing as Elizabeth McNeill. It meant having to deal with an English producer, Antony Rufus-Isaacs, and an English director, Adrian Lyne. So they deserve even more credit for suffering yet another Englishman in their lives. Zalman had been a successful actor for 20 years, but was looking to move to writing, producing and directing. Pat had stepped aside from her sculpting and paintings to write various screenplays before *9½ Weeks*, notably *Lady Oscar* (1979) for Jacques Demy. They knew everybody. Their home was the water cooler of Hollywood. They were the only people I needed to know.

Tom Reeve's apartment in Beverly Hills was below ground, a basement - behind what used to be the Hamburger Hamlet at the western end of the Sunset Strip - so I literally holed myself up, and wrote. Apart from my weekend outings with Chloe, the only time I left the apartment was once a week to take a bus up Sunset to Ralphs supermarket for groceries, and once a week to walk down Doheny to the Academy Film Library, which at that time was on Wilshire just east of Doheny. I am known now for preferring a simple repetitive diet when I am on my own - but even I marvel at the memory of my shopping list in those weeks. I recall it consisted purely of pastrami and cabbage and ranch dressing, to make sandwiches. The cabbage was only because I mistook it for lettuce. It seemed to work fine as lettuce, so I didn't notice. Now and forever a food philistine.

The walks to the Academy Library were my back up plan. A Plan B, if the screenplay didn't lead to work. I'd make a documentary about the actress Joan Fontaine.

Why Joan Fontaine? Well, for all his Marxist, neo-realist, nouvelle vague, avant-garde, whatever, tastes, my Film Studies professor at Kent university, Ben Brewster, was a sap for an old-fashioned melodrama. On a 'Melodrama' course, we were shown the 1947 film *Letter From An Unknown Woman*, made in Hollywood by another Austrian émigré Max Ophuls. Ophuls directed it. But the film was actually made by the independent production company Rampart Pictures, the production company of actress Joan Fontaine and her husband William Dozier (later producer of 'dinner-dinner-dinner-dinner *Batman*!'). The film was based on a short story by Stefan Zweig, scripted by John Houseman, co-starred Louis Jourdan... but it was Joan Fontaine's film. It was, and remains, my absolute favourite film of all time.

The most seductive and beautiful thing in the film is Joan Fontaine's voice over. At university I had completely fallen in love with that voice, and then the actress. Fanatically I began collecting copies of every one of her 70 films and TV dramas. Even in today's world of online film libraries and international Amazon stores, this is not easy. Then, in the early days of home video, it was a particular challenge, even in Hollywood. I persuaded Jeff Martin's mom to let me use their family VHS recorder in the middle of the day to capture a rare TV broadcast of - I think it was - *Gunga Din* (1939) and over-excitedly snapped off the machine's tracking button, thinking it was the eject button. That was embarrassing. There's no way to make up for snapping off someone's tracking button. Thank goodness tracking buttons are no more.

At the Academy Library, I photocopied every newspaper article I could find about Joan Fontaine for a prospective television documentary. I began piecing her life together. Clarkson Woodward, the daughter of my American Literature professor from Eton, Cary Woodward, who lived in Baltimore, went to the lovely lengths of sending a copy of Joan's autobiography *No Bed of Roses* to Joan's home in Carmel for her to sign for me. Of course I already had a copy - probably several - but this is a special one.

When over the coming years I had a car in Los Angeles, the book *No Bed of Roses* became a way of getting to know the city. Joan was a regular house (and husband) changer as a young actress in Hollywood, so by visiting her previous residences (to photograph them for my documentary) I came to know a number of obscure corners of the city. The one I particularly remember was the one in the Brentwood hills that burnt down in the 1960s, and caused Joan to uproot what was left of her life to New York. This place was particularly evocative, as the building plot had not been redeveloped - and the foundations of the house and swimming pool, etc, were still there. In trawling the backstreet shops of Hollywood (pre-eBay, when such shops existed), I had collected every original 8x10, poster and lobby card I could find featuring Joan. Some of these black & white photos were publicity shots of her at this Brentwood home - which I was now standing in, amongst its forgotten remains, like her dream of Manderlay in her second greatest movie, Alfred Hitchcock - and Daphne Du Maurier's - *Rebecca* (1940).

At the end of my 9½ weeks in Beverly Hills, my friend Tina Jamieson (the Production Manager on *The Shooting Party*) arrived in L.A. and we arranged to hire a car and make a trip up the Pacific Coast Highway to San Francisco. Our guide, again, would be Joan Fontaine's *No Bed of Roses*. All the way up the coast it gave us places to visit - and to photograph with a new 'Olympus 10' 35mm camera. All

places associated with Joan's life. For instance, in Santa Barbara there was the theatre where she was first on stage... all to way to San Francisco, and the Franklin Hotel where she spent one of her honeymoon nights. I'm sure this sounds ridiculous to you. But I have found there is no better way to sightsee a place than to have a mission, however random. In fact the more random, the more interesting the corners it tends to take you. It's not the destination, it's the journey. Or maybe you think it is just plain perverse, documentary or no documentary. Stalkerish. In which case,

skip the next paragraph.

A highlight of this trip was Los Gatos High School (left). This is where Joan Fontaine and her sister Olivia De Havilland went to school. Tina and I arrived early in the morning, when only the janitor was on site. Our English accents and London looks were enough to convince him that we had come a long way on this quest. So he asked us if we would like to see Olivia and Joan's grade cards? Er... Yes. He took us down into the basement of the school and, asking me what year they would have graduated, pulled out long drawers of report cards. There they were. Joan de Bouvoir de Havilland and Olivia Mary de Havilland. Olivia's grades I remember were consistent and high. Joan's, on the other hand, were erratic - that familiar tussle between the left brain and right brain that I know well. This made sense to me. Olivia may have been the higher achiever. But Joan will always be the more interesting of the two.

I still have all these photographs of Joan's homes and haunts, but I've still not made the documentary. I should do. But I didn't, because, as it turned out, Plan B wasn't necessary. The screenplay I wrote in that basement apartment in Beverly Hills over 9½ weeks in the early months of 1985 was sent to Joan Fontaine. You may need to read this next sentence twice. Joan Fontaine responded that it was the best screenplay she had read since *Letter From An Unknown Woman*, and agreed to come out of 20 years of retirement from the film business to turn it into a movie. Wow.

Some of the posters and lobby cards from my extensive 'Joan Fontaine Collection' now hang in a guest room at Knebworth House. The 8x10s filed away could probably paper every bedroom.

CHAPTER FOURTEEN

Green For A Season

LADY SILVERTON (interrupts)
You know what I mean by eleven o'clock -
two indolent 'ones', standing to attention
next to each other, parallel, and prepared
to give witness to their witlessness.

(Green For A Season, 1985)

What screenplay should I write? Write what you know. Keep it simple. In those days, it still made sense to write to a budget. Nowadays budget matters less, unless you are writing for your own production. The middle budget film doesn't exist anymore, except in national subsidies. If you have the confidence to write on spec nowadays, you might as well write with money as no object. The film is only going to be made if money is no object. In the early 1980s, there was still a class of film in the low to mid budget range that could find a limited cinema release and some worldwide distribution, particularly if it was culturally specific. Hence a spate of very English period pieces, *Chariots of Fire* (1981), *Local Hero* (1983), *A Room With A View* (1985)... and of course *The Shooting Party* (1985).

It would make sense to pitch into that genre. It also made sense to collect together the elements I had around me that would contribute to an interesting film.

Knebworth House was the obvious one. So I'll set my screenplay at Knebworth House.

What period is best represented at Knebworth House? *The Shooting Party* had just proved this to be the Edwardian period. This was the last time any money had been spent on any major re-decoration of the house. So my screenplay will be set at Knebworth House in the Edwardian period.

I want to write it for Joan Fontaine. Joan Fontaine is in her 60s... so she will be the matriarch of the house. An anti-social widow who rules her private queendom, but rarely leaves it, preferring to live in the past, in an old century that is gone. This is an image I had of Edward Bulwer Lytton's mother, Elizabeth, in the early 1800s.

Did I have any other actor friends who might agree to be in it? Yes. Rebecca Saire. And another actress I'd met through Rebecca's brother Warren, when he was doing a C. S. Lewis play in Newcastle. Lucy Durham Matthews. They don't look similar. Rebecca has fair straight hair, and Lucy has curly brown hair. So they can't be sisters. So they must be step-sisters. There, immediately, is a dynamic.

So, a grandmother is living in her country house with a granddaughter and the granddaughter's step-sister. Why? Well, as was the case with many families - including mine - because the girl's parents are away in India. And they're not able to come back from India any time soon. But the girls are getting to an age where, their reclusive grandmother feels, reluctantly, that they should be introduced to society.

How does she do this? Well, again reluctantly, she accepts her best option is to re-introduce into their lives her daughter's first husband, her granddaughter's estranged father - of course, a roué aristocrat - to organise a 'coming out' for the two girls. This distant father is, naturally, a hero figure for the granddaughter. But of course the father only has eyes for the prettier, older, step-sister...

And so the story writes itself.

But how to give it some style? Here, I reached for my contrary History of Art essays. You'll recall that because I was supposed to like the Impressionists, I liked the Pre-Raphaelites. So my story will have a Pre-Raphaelite sensibility. The girls, imprisoned in their lush overgrown secret garden, will have long thick Julia Margaret Cameron tresses that stretch to their ankles. Their lives will reflect the Pre-Raphaelites' obsession with nature, sex and death. Every Edwardian adolescence, no?

I'd recently bought a beautiful set of the complete works of Algernon Charles Swinburne - decadent poet-in-residence of the Pre-Raphaelites - for more money than I would ever have previously contemplated spending on a non-essential item. In amongst the volumes, I found this verse, in *Hymn to Proserpine* (1866):

> *Laurel is green for a season*
> *And love is sweet for a day*
> *But love grows bitter with treason*
> *And laurel outlives not May*

I had my title. *Green For A Season*. I think I was aware of the verse first. But it may have been that, first, I was intrigued by a wooden bas-relief that my artist neighbour in Harewood Avenue, Phyllis Dimond, had in her studio. It depicted a young girl in profile holding a sprig of laurel, and the girl's name carved below, 'Laureta'. It was designed to be aesthetic, not sensual - but there was an odd dichotomy to it. Although the model looked young, like a teenage daughter, the girl's breast is clearly defined through her classical cambric dress. Who would have commissioned this? Surely not a father for his daughter?

This, along with Christina Rossetti's poem *Goblin Market*, provided all the inspiration I needed for the story of *Green For A Season*. I know it's irritating to hear a writer say a story writes it-

GREEN · FOR · A · SEASON

self. But it is a truth that all drama derives from only seven basic stories. The ingredients change. The author is simply someone with some knowledge or experience to come up with a decent recipe. And the desire and discipline to sit down and cook it.

GREEN FOR A SEASON

Imprisoned in a crumbling gothic mansion, bound in ivy vine and guarded by grotesque gargoyles, two repressed stepsisters battle jealousy, lust and madness to break free of their childhood and their dictatorial, dowager grandmother in a unique Pre-Raphaelite melodrama.

It is early summer, amidst the ashes of the Victorian era. Two stepsisters live cut off from the outside world with their reclusive, eccentric grandmother in a dark, dusty old English mansion, Silverton Hall. Laureta Montclair is the 16-year-old abandoned daughter of an army wife in India - repressed, tormented, the awkward outward appearance of a Victorian child, but the inner fire of a passionate, virtuoso pianist. Emily Barratt is the 18-year-old daughter of Laureta's army stepfather - beautiful, romantic, a fantasist who lives in her own imaginary world amongst the decadent novels hidden in Silverton's forgotten library.

The stepsisters see no one other than their grandmother and the three servants deemed sufficient for their simple needs. Worse still, they have little time for each other. Laureta is a quiet, incommunicative, child, who prefers to sit alone at the piano and express her anger in her fiery, violent compositions. Emily, meanwhile, prefers the solitude of Silverton's unkempt gothic garden, where she expresses her secret desires in a little commonplace book to a beloved lost governess.

Lady Silverton, Laureta's maternal grandmother, is the girls' guardian - iron-willed, bitter, disdainful of the outside world, a Victorian relic. But she can't keep the girls locked up forever. So, against her better judgment, she agrees to reintroduce into their lives their one available parent, Laureta's estranged father, Sir Edward Montclair. Laureta's mother's divorce from Sir Edward Montclair ten years before was a major scandal. His reputation is as a roué, a drinker, a gambler - but he's also an extremely wealthy well-bred aristocrat who, in company, is never anything less than charming. There is no one more qualified to organise - and pay for - a social season than Sir Edward Montclair, and no one Lady Silverton would not prefer for the task.

Sir Edward immediately lives up to the girls' expectations by defying all their guardian's wishes, but Lady Silverton is a formidable adversary, and sparks fly. Also sparked is a vicious jealousy between the girls. Sir Edward is immediately more interested in his daughter's beautiful elder stepsister. Laureta cautions Emily to remember that Sir Edward is *her* father

In the weeks that follow Laureta and Emily are fitted for ballgowns, taught to waltz, given lessons in etiquette. Against the odds they are transformed into eligible debutants. Laureta competes in everything to outshine Emily. But it's no good. On the night of the Silverton Ball – during a powerful thunderstorm - a drunken Sir Edward ignores his daughter, and stumbling upon Emily's commonplace book uses its secrets to seduce her. Despite herself, Emily resists him, escaping into the night. But Laureta's heart is broken.

Amidst the recriminations of the morning, fate deals the family a cruel blow. A letter arrives from India telling of Colonel and Mrs. Barrett's death from cholera. In an attempt to make amends, Sir Edward goes in search of Emily's lost governess. Instead of a governess, he finds a mother - Madeleine, one-time mistress to the Colonel. Sir Edward returns to Silverton with Madeleine. They confront Lady Silverton and request custody of the two girls. After a heated exchange, Lady Silverton agrees to let the girls decide for themselves.

Both girls are in their bedrooms, Emily locked in hers, and Laureta by choice. Emily falls into Madeleine's arms, and although hurt by the deception, readily accepts the chance to build a new life with her mother. Laureta, on the other hand, refuses to acknowledge her father. When Sir Edward breaks into her room, he finds her in a nightdress surrounded by her music manuscripts. Apparently deranged, she suggests he make love to her like he did to Emily, maybe this will persuade him to love her. Sir Edward cannot believe he has brought his daughter to this. With true remorse, he takes his first tentative steps towards being a true father...

A year or so later Lady Silverton receives a letter from Laureta, who is living with her father in New York. She appears happy, looking forward to an upcoming visit from Emily and Madeleine. Enclosed in the letter is a piano manuscript entitled "For my Grandmother". Lady Silverton plays it... It is exquisitely beautiful.

The one-page story summary for Green For A Season - a simple gothic tale, but 35 years after it was written its themes of teenage sexuality and incest seem almost untouchable in this century. Odd, in retrospect, that this early 80s The Shooting Party / Merchant Ivory inspired period piece should now have evolved into, perhaps, my most controversial original screenplay.

My neighbour's image of 'Laureta' became the artwork for *Green For A Season*. I had studio portraits taken of Rebecca Saire dressed as 'Laureta', and Lucy Durham-Matthews as 'Emily'. I wonder where that bas-relief (p.155) is today. It's out there somewhere. I regret not asking my lovely neighbour Phyllis to keep it for me. Her daughter Frances told me later that Phyllis sold it before she died, Frances thought to Liberty's the London Department store. Every time I pass Liberty's I think of it, and wonder where it is.

I wrote the screenplay *Green For A Season* in those 9½ weeks I was in Los Angeles, and Pat King loved it. That was all I needed. But then her friend Theodora Van Runkle - costume designer on *Bonnie and Clyde* and *The Godfather: Part II* - wrote to me saying she also loved it. It must be decent. So, I sent it out.

I sent it to three people. Joan Fontaine. A director called Cyril Frankel. And a Malaysian financier called Chin Yap. All three got in touch with me within a week saying they loved it. All three of them. And Joan Fontaine!

Joan. Fontaine.

Of course I still wallow, grinning, like a Zambezi hippopotamus in the fact that Joan Fontaine liked my very first screenplay. But I knew the screenplay alone would not be enough to commit her to *Green For A Season*.

However I'd done my research. A whole documentary's worth of research. I knew that the last film Joan had made, in 1966, was in England, for an English director called Cyril Frankel. I had also spotted that the only time that Joan had left America to work since 1966, was to do a production of *The Lion In Winter* in 1979 at the English Theatre in Vienna... for an English director called Cyril Frankel. If I could get Cyril Frankel to direct my film, then maybe, just maybe, Joan would consider coming out of retirement for my project.

I looked up 'Cyril Frankel' in Halliwell's Film Guide.

Ah. 'Cyril Frankel, Director, 1921-1974'. Cyril Frankel died in 1974.

But then, how come - also listed in Halliwell's - Cyril Frankel made a film called *Permission To Kill* with Dirk Bogarde and Ava Gardner in 1977... and a play with Joan Fontaine in 1979?

I rang up the Director's Guild. "Cyril Frankel?" They hadn't heard from him in some time, but there was an address in Harley Street. Harley Street? I pictured a director who was technically dead - maybe in an amniotic fluid tank - but could still direct by the reflex of raising a finger.

It turned out that, despite Leslie Halliwell's attempt to kill him off, Cyril (left) was alive and well. After spending most of the 1970s creating and directing TV shows for Lew Grade's ATV - *Randal and Hopkirk*, *The Baron*, *The Champions*, etc - he had settled into a string of BBC documentaries on some of his other passions - music, painting, ballet and contemporary ceramics. In contemporary ceramics he'd become one of the country's foremost experts, and was increasingly finding his time taken up consulting for auction houses. But he was delighted to have been sent *Green For A Season*. He liked the script, and would love to work with Joan again.

Which left the third piece of the puzzle. The money. I had teamed up with my friends from *The Shooting Party*, Tina Jamieson and Rupert Dunn, and created a production company named after my house on Harewood Avenue in Marylebone, The 39 Production Company Ltd. Rupert knew a Malaysian investor - the above mentioned Chin Yap - who apparently could handle our full budget. He too said "yes". At this point it was clearly all going much too swimmingly.

The investor wanted a 'completion bond', so we went to the company Film Finances, who had insured *The Shooting Party*, They were happy with Tina's budget and schedule. Tina, brilliantly, started going out with a high profile entertainment lawyer, Mark Devereux of Olswangs, whom she later married. This meant that we had excellent access to good advice, but it also meant I was going to have to start spending some money. Then Joan's agent, Martin Gage, in Los Angeles, said he wanted to meet us before he'd sign off on the contract.

"Planes to catch, contracts to sign" - I use this expression whenever I'm busy, but this is the one time in my life I've actually lived up to it. Tina and I flew to Los Angeles - for the day - to meet Martin Gage. His office was on the Sunset Strip, where a few weeks earlier I had been getting the bus to Ralphs supermarket to get pastrami and cabbage. His exclamation as we walked into his office was, "You're babies!" He didn't believe we could pull the film off - but Joan wanted to do a deal, and so the contract was ours. Joan was preparing to close up her house for the summer and looking forward to coming over to England. But he hoped we had deep pockets for when we defaulted.

I stepped back off the plane in London holding a contract with Joan Fontaine, star of *Letter From An Unknown Woman*, to make her first film in twenty years.

Wow. Even my Film Studies professor Ben Brewster might have been impressed.

I was turning 23-years-old. I'd been a runner in the business for a year and a half... But I did have the support of most of the creative team behind *The Shooting Party*. Maybe, just maybe, this could happen.

If the foregoing terms are acceptable to the Escrow Agent, please indicate such acceptance by signing where indicated below.

Very truly yours,

THE 39 PRODUCTION COMPANY, LTD.

By: *M. Jamieson*
Name:
Title: DIRECTOR

JOAN FONTAINE

Accepted and Agreed:

Date: *SEPTEMBER 17, 1985*

Noises from Chin Yap continued positive, so Tina, Rupert and I started the process of Pre-Production. We needed to, if we were going to meet the schedule we'd agreed with Joan. I can't remember if we'd suggested this schedule, or whether it was one that suited Joan? Certainly the film needed to shoot when we could give the impression of summer. So Tom Rand (*The Shooting Party*'s costume designer) started to sketch costumes. We told him Joan did not want brocade. Ray Marsden (wig maker on *The Shooting Party*) started to make a wig for our 'Laureta'. I remember when we signed up the sound man from *The Shooting Party*, Bob Allen, we offered him £750 a week - he said, "Tina, make it £700". Everybody was amazing. Willing it to work.

I'd settled on an exaggerated Pre-Raphaelite style for the look of the film. Next I turned to the sound of the film. It is a truth of cinema not universally acknowledged that it is music that makes a good film a great film. Knebworth House has a fine Bechstein in its downstairs drawing room, so in my screenplay I'd made the piano an instrument of expression for my troubled teenager, Laureta. I envisaged a rich vein of beautiful solo piano running through the film. For this I turned to Peter Martin, a veteran BBC arranger and father of my friend John Martin who'd played guitar on my early recordings and built the recording studio in my basement. Peter wrote two very special piano pieces for *Green For A Season*, to express the two conflicting sides of Laureta's character - beauty and torment.

After Joan Fontaine, these two pieces of music were the thing I was most excited to put on screen. I knew that whatever else we achieved it would be these two piano themes that would make my film truly beautiful. Ah, the twists and turns of the world! What these two pieces of music did do was lead to a BAFTA-nomination for Peter. Sadly not for *Green For A Season*. But Peter was giving piano lessons to Katrine Boorman, daughter of film director John Boorman, and I was invited to a dinner with Katrine and her father in Peter's basement flat in Chelsea. After dinner I insisted that Peter play these two themes. John Boorman - not knowing Peter composed - was so impressed that he asked Peter to create the music for his film *Hope and Glory* (1987). Here, again, Peter excelled, producing one of the most beautiful of English film scores. A song written on the main theme, with lyrics by Peter's partner Helen Sava, was offered to Vera Lynn. Vera Lynn made a mistake not recording it, as it was a classic worthy of her repertoire. Helen herself sang it for the film, and I cannot listen to it now without tears. But the most beautiful memory I have of Peter - who died in 2015 - is the last time I was with him. I visited him in

a Nursing Home, shortly before his death, and took him a copy of his *Nocturne* for *Green For A Season*. He hadn't seen it in decades and insisted on going to the piano and playing it. As I walked away, along the long disinfectant-smelling corridor of waiting rooms for the reaper, he was still playing it - filling that dry, dead space with its exquisite beauty - exclaiming as he played, "How lovely! How lovely!"

Back in 1985, casting for *Green For A Season* was going well. Veteran actor Charles Gray - the narrator in *The Rocky Horror Picture Show*, and Blofeld in *Diamonds Are Forever* - agreed to play the butler. He'd worked with Cyril before.

Brilliantly, another hero, Adam Ant agreed to be in it. An Adam Ant concert at the London's Dominion Theatre in 1981 is the only time I've witnessed the mania

that has teenage girls standing on their seats and screaming hysterically for two hours. Perfect. There was a part for a Dickon-type gardener (albeit older) who is an object of fantasy for the girls. This suited Adam, whose stage name derives from working in his youth in his neighbourhood Garden of Eden, Regent's Park.

Tina and I had a memorable Afternoon Tea with Adam in Fortnum & Mason, at which he enthused about the project. He sent us a kind note when the project was delayed, "I still feel the same about the project, would love to do it - if Spring comes off, I'll try + be there with you all. Relax - it will be O.K. - write me a few more lines ha! ha!"

I did the opposite. I'd have absolutely loved to have had Adam in my film - but rewrites showed that the script worked better replacing the gardener with a fantasy goblin (from *Goblin Market*) writhing in an ornamental pond of ripe fruit (a nightmare sequence, in case you think that's a regular occurrence round here). The part now had no lines. So was no longer for Adam. I saw him in concert again recently - less rabid screaming in the audience, but no less energy in the man. I remain in awe, particularly of his menisci cartilage, with all that bouncing up and down in boots. There is a man in his sixties with better knees than I, Gunga Din.

In polishing the script, I also came to the realisation that Rebecca Saire was too old - and too pretty (I've added that, for when she reads this) - to play my troubled teenager, Laureta. Laureta needed to be younger, physically smaller, and in the shade of her more traditionally pretty step-sister. But I'd found just the actress. She had done a couple of movies but they hadn't been released yet. She was just turning 19, but she looked younger. And she looked appropriately troubled. Her name was Helena Bonham Carter (left).

Again, I had been introduced by Warren Saire, Rebecca's brother. Warren had been playing Edward

VI to Helena's Lady Jane Grey in Trevor Nunn's feature film debut *Lady Jane* (1986), and bought his co-star round to Harewood Avenue as a kindred soul. Helena was exactly how I saw my Laureta Montclair.

King Edward VI   *Lady Jane Grey*

After two auspicious lead roles - the other, made second, but released first, was *A Room With A View* (1985) - Helena was meant to be off to Oxford University to study English Literature. My tuppence worth of advice was that she should follow her heart - and these great casting breaks - and stick to acting. Better to be living E. M. Forster in a Florence window sill, than reading E. M. Forster in an Oxford window sill. We can study anytime. She told me later that only two people in her life at that time took this view - me and her father. It was advice she followed, to even greater acting success.

It turned out that her parents were friends of my parents. Helena's father Raymond (above) had toured America after school with a party of friends that included my aunt Susan, and my parents had visited Helena's parents in Washington when they were living in New York. Indeed there existed

a photograph of me as a baby sitting on Helena's mother Elena's lap. It is a photograph that Elena (left) and I have restaged twice since - and indeed, is a position that I could be forever happy in. I loved them both. I wanted them as my parents too.

Helena started workshops with Cyril Frankel. But we still had the final piece of the casting jigsaw, the roué father. As a devotee of *The Rocky Horror Picture Show* (1974), I wanted the camp menace of Tim Curry. But I didn't know Tim Curry then. I did meet Tim Curry later, at a party given by *Minder*'s George Cole, to which I was taken by family friend Carolyn Allen. Carol had appeared with Tim in a West End production of *The Pirates of Penzance*. "When you say 'orfern'... do you mean 'orfern', a child bear-reft of its parents... or do you mean 'orfern', free-quent-lee?". We talked Tim into returning to Knebworth with us in my two-seater Fiat Fiorino humpback van. He must have thought he'd stumbled into some 'hunting lodge for rich weirdos', as my family were all obsessed by Rocky Horror and turned wide-eyed and giggly in his company.

Tim was given Knebworth House's Queen Elizabeth Room four-poster bed, and apparently did not sleep at all. This was a problem because he was due to debut as Mack the Knife in *The Beggar's Opera* that evening at the National Theatre. He said he was kept awake by visions, which he thought were the result of the wood treatment my sister had told him the room had just been given for woodworm. It seemed more likely to us that he was terrified he was going to be

As Rocky Horror obsessed teenagers we had broken into derelict Oakley Court before it was turned into a posh hotel

visited during the night by various members of the family insisting, "yes, Tim, but isn't it <u>nice</u>?!". I met him once more, years later, backstage at the Pantages Theatre in Hollywood after a performance of *Me And My Gal* - Helena was with us - but he had a previous, and more interesting, dinner date with him, David Hockney. Ding! Name drop quota exceeded. But my chance to say, all hail Tim Curry.

In fact Tim would not have been right for the role. The part of Sir Edward Montclair needed more creepy menace than camp menace. More Oliver Reed. In fact our initial approach was to another Tim, Tim Piggot-Smith, who'd been very successfully menacing in *The Jewel In The Crown* (1984). Tim Piggot-Smith, I recall, said "yes", and was - naturally - upset when we then turned him down because Cyril didn't think he was tall, dark and handsome enough. Cyril wanted yet another Tim. Another Tim who was also not right for the role. Timothy Dalton.

Cyril had worked with Timothy Dalton on his film *Permission To Kill* (1975). Timothy was certainly tall, dark and handsome. He could likely summon up some menace. But I wasn't sure he was sexy? Cyril assured me he was. Cyril had made no other casting requests. I felt I owed him this one. As it turned out, it was a mistake. But not because of Timothy's sex appeal. We never got the chance to test that.

Joan Fontaine. Timothy Dalton. Helena Bonham Carter. Charles Gray... This was a fine cast. We had the location. We had the wigs. Time for the money.

And this is when we discovered, what we should have spotted earlier, that 'Chin Yap' - if you think about it - sounds very much like 'all talk', or - in Spanish - 'bullshit'. Chin told us that circumstances had changed for him, but that it didn't matter because he had found us another financier. There was a man called David Dawkins in an office somewhere near Tower Bridge - I think the World Trade Centre, I don't recall exactly... but what I do remember is that there were marks in the wood stain under the door plaque, where all the previous door plaques had been. This should have been warning enough. But we were by this stage, dangerously, desperate.

David Dawkins wanted an upfront finders fee of £1,000 from us, then he would pull the rabbit out of the hat. You can be sure we asked all of our advisors about this snakeoil offer, Mark Devereux, Jeremy Saunders... but they didn't have an alternative in the timescale that was left to us. So I paid the £1,000 - and, for it, got a very nice dinner in a Mayfair Hotel, with large American gentleman who was what Central Casting would send you if you asked for a gangster called 'Tiny'. It went nowhere, and David Dawkins disappeared.

I was now in the hole for a lot of money. Plus I had a contract with Joan Fontaine that I was not going to be able to honour. There are low points in a career and there are high points. This, reader, was a low point. It was not to be the last.

The project was slipping through my fingers. So, again, I grabbed at the first chance of a solution. Cyril Frankel called his friend the producer Hank Moonjean in Los Angeles. Hank had produced most of Burt Reynolds' films and, would you believe it, had even made a film at Knebworth House, 1976's *Beauty and the Beast* with George C. Scott. He agreed to help, and found a New York production company, Co*Star, who would take on the film. The principal of Co*Star, Norman I Cohen had been a Production Manager on *The Great Gatsby* (1974) on which Hank had been Associate Producer. Norman had just completed a film called *The Gig* (1985), with Cleavon Little (the sheriff in *Blazing Saddles,* 1974).

But simultaneous to this, Timothy Dalton was offered the role of James Bond. This got Co*Star over-excited, because Timothy said he would do *Green For A Season* after he'd done Bond. So Co*Star determined to wait for Timothy. Hank Moonjean was put on damage control, and managed to persuade Joan Fontaine's agent that she should wait a year. Although disappointed, most of the rest of the team said they would, if they could, reassemble the same time next year. We'd put together a great team, so they were, perhaps not surprisingly, inordinately decent about the broken promises.

Co*Star thought the year could usefully be spent doing some re-writes. The company gave me $2,500 as an 'option' payment and I went to live in New York.

The following year Timothy came out of Bond having changed his mind. He did not want to go back to making period dramas. He wanted to play against type. He wanted to play a terminal cancer patient having a final fling in Amsterdam in *Hawks* - David Tringham, 1st Assistant Director; Peter Heslop, 3rd Assistant Director... Henry Cobbold disconsolate, and out of a job. The momentum had left *Green For A Season*. It withered, and died.

But of course Swinburne was being poetically bitter and desolate in *Hymn to Proserpine*, and laurel is not green for a season. Laurel is an evergreen. And Helena Bonham Carter says she'll do the film when she's old enough to play the Joan Fontaine part.

So, not too long to go now.

And Joan Fontaine forgave me. We kept in touch, and she visited me at Knebworth in May 1994 on her way to the Czech Republic to make what was to become her last film *Good King Wenceslas*. It was a television production, and not bad apparently. A quote from the film picked out on IMDB I find particularly fitting and bittersweet,

LEO McKERN
You might even try to smile a little.

JOAN FONTAINE
It's enough that I'm here.

As it turned out, Joan was not to make another feature film. Cyril's *The Witches* in 1966 was to remain her last. *Green For A Season* would have been a better swansong.

This book's dedicatees, my chewed thumbs, were keen to make an appearance

Jan is the lovely Oscar-winning hair stylist Jan Archibald, who would have styled GFAS

As part of writing this chapter I took the **Green For A Season** wig box down from my study shelf. I have not opened it since 1985. I expected to find the wigs crawling with creatures. Instead I found Laureta and Emily's hair immaculate .

CHAPTER FIFTEEN

The Light

Where the Cornish folk meet the Devonshire folk
And the West Wind blows from the Severn Sea
There's a little ol' ham named Nectanstow
That's the hoary ol' home of you and me.

Now e'er a place where the heart is broke
And the best men break in the toil of the yoke
There once live a man with a heart of gold
Whose God-fearin' soul could ne'er be sold.

Where St Nectan came from o'er the sea
Is a misty ol' myst'ry to you and to me
But the blessing remains that the pilgrim came
To lead us all in the Good Lord's name.

(Nectanstow - from *The Light*, 1986)

Before I moved to New York, encouraged by the reception of my debut screenplay, I began work on that 'difficult second album'. I applied the same thinking I had given to *Green For A Season*. What production value did I have access to? Who did I want to work with? My second home, growing up, was my mother's childhood home in North Devon. Beautiful Hartland Abbey on the wild North Atlantic cliffs was still the home of my adored grandmother, Sheila Stucley, and I'd spent much of 1985 living with her, soaking up her wonderful stories of this romantic place... and writing a new original screenplay called *The Light*.

My friendship with kindred spirit Helena Bonham Carter had evolved. We had broken into Highgate Cemetery together to visit the graves of Lizzie Siddal and Gabriel Rossetti. A blood pact by any other name. I had even taken the dangerous step of taking her to stay at Hartland. The last girl I had taken to this sacred place was Rebecca in the summer of 1984, and after the trauma of being tossed aside for my best mate, I had foresworn intimate relationships for going on a year and a half, whilst I rebuilt my virginity. But messing about, posing on a blustery beach at Hartland with Helena, I of course saw a new screenplay. The simplest way to write a screenplay is to start with the love scene. The first half of the movie is how did they get in to this. The second half of the movie is how do they get out of this? Naturally with an ending that resolves one way or another whether the lovemaking was a good idea or not. On the beach at Hartland with me was a mysterious young girl with exotic eyebrows and wild red hair. In my imagination was a mysterious girl with exotic eyebrows and wild red hair, in the surf, making love to the sea... tossed in the pulsing power of white foam waves, in bliss, surrendering to its enveloping strength.

What would a teenager who looked like Helena Bonham Carter be doing in North Devon? Well, with those exotic eyebrows clearly she is the daughter of a shipwrecked Spanish girl. For centuries 'wreckers' operated on this coast, luring merchant ships onto the treacherous rocks by tieing lanterns onto donkeys and leading

them inland, disorientating foreign navigators. If there were no survivors the locals got to keep all 'flotsam and jetsam' - anything that washed up from the stricken ship - including runaway Spanish girls, who, by chance, had escaped The Wreckers' Blade.

That was a good title. But, over time, the piece became more about a force for good in a dark land; more about a lighthouse on a dark and dangerous seacoast. So it evolved into *The Light*.

I wrote it both as a two part miniseries or, unusual for that time (though popular now), six half hour parts. All the locations were vivid and real to me, places around Hartland and Morwenstow, on the north Devon and Cornwall coast, where I had spent the holidays of my youth.

Cecil Woolf (Virginia's nephew) gave me permission to use this perfect Brigid Peppin illustration from his 1975 edition of **Robert Stephen Hawker: Selected Poems** *to create a cover to promote the new script*

Much of the screenplay I wrote at my grandfather's old desk (he had died two years earlier) whilst staying with my grandmother at Hartland Abbey (below).

Ship wrecks at Hartland Point; below, my grandmother, on a rare visit to Cornwall, at Morwenstow

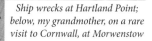

Again, Peter Martin and Helen Sava (below) helped me with music. This time Peter wrote me a folk tune, to which I wrote the words, *Nectanstow* (p.166). For the rest we drew pieces from a book of West Country folk songs as collected by the Victorian vicar, Sabine Baring Gould (lyricist of the hymn *Onward, Christian Soldiers*). These beautiful airs and melodies - I recall in particular *Furze Bloom,* "When the furze is out of flower, Then love is out of tune" (as laurel is an ever-

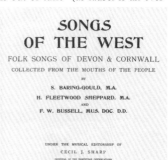

green, so furze heather is never without its yellow flower) - these, combined with this magnificent landscape was 180 minutes of beauty that barely needed a story. But, of course, a story too came easily - much of it inspired by Sabine Baring Gould's friend, the real life eccentric parson, Stephen Hawker (1803–1875), vicar of Morwenstow.

What casting beyond Helena? Again, I needed a roué father. A villainous Squire, this time based on the scoundrels that were my own Devon ancestors. Again, I wrote with Tim Curry in mind - although, again, probably more menace was needed, as in Oliver Reed. This time I also wrote a Riff Raff - an Iago, an Igor, for my villain - and Richard O'Brien (creator of, and Riff Raff in, *The Rocky Horror Show*) was absolutely in my mind for Sir John Penhenna's skeletal sidekick, Bone.

'Penhenna' is Cornish for 'the lair of the raven', which seemed the perfect name for a family of Wreckers. 'Nectanstow' was a version of Morwenstow, using St Morwenna's brother St Nectan, the parish saint of Hartland and beautiful Stoke church on the valley ridge above Hartland Abbey (right), where my parents were married. The heroine, of course, had to be named Morwenna, a name my wife and I chose a few years later for our daughter. At the time, I assumed a shortened, familiar version of Morwenna would be 'Wenn' or 'Wenny'. My daughter is now in her thirties, and no one has every called her 'Wenn' or 'Wenny'. To her family she is known as 'Mo'. I have always thought I should go back and correct that. But recently I met another Morwenna, who said she did used to be know as 'Wenny' and 'Wenn', and never as 'Mo'... so, now I'm not sure. I suppose 'Wenn' sounds more early 19th Century than 'Mo'.

THE LIGHT

Sweeping 18th Century romance blending the landscape, folk songs & legends of the wild coast of north Cornwall.
A Spanish girl shipwrecked into a dark world of cutthroat wreckers becomes the catalyst for its first lighthouse

Pulled from his nursery at dawn, Johnny Penhenna is ridden across high cliffs by his father to see the spoils of the ocean, the wreckage of a Spanish merchant brig spilt across the family's rock-toothed beach. Sir John Penhenna of Nectanstow Abbey is the dissolute squire of a remote village of wreckers that lure ships onto the rocks & slit the throats of survivors so unclaimed flotsam becomes theirs by law. A law that as local magistrate it is Sir John's duty to uphold.

This time, however, there is a survivor. A beautiful Spanish runaway whom the skeletal evil pirate Bone would take advantage of before he murders. The one force for good in the village, the elderly academic Parson - young Johnny's tutor - intervenes and takes the girl into his care. But she is not safe after an evening of drunken revelry in the village, and the knowledge that there must be no survivors. The girl is abducted from the parsonage, and is to be murdered in the church lych-house alongside the corpses of the Spanish sailors, when the Parson disturbs the unidentified assailant. The Parson's simple houseboy Rodney is made a scapegoat for the crime, and allowed to run away to sea.

Knowing he must hide the foreign girl to save her, the Parson conceals her in the crypt of the church. With the help and confidence of Johnny and his salt-o'-the-earth Nurse, the Parson tends the girl back to health. But he is not equipped to deal with the fact that she is pregnant. Tragically out of his depth during the childbirth, only the child is saved, and the concealment revealed. The Parson is accused by the villagers of fathering the child and hounded out of the church. Johnny is saved his father wrath by being whisked away from Nectanstow by his unhappy socialite mother to the Americas.

Sir John Penhenna settles on a compromise with the King's Preventative Men – the only policing in this remote place – of a lighthouse being built out of shipwrecked timbers on the headland. Man of charity that he is, he insists the lighthouse keeper will be the disgraced Parson and the illegitimate child. The broken old man, besotted by the little girl, will continue to be an easy workaround for the continuation of the village's wrecking and piracy.

15 years later, a young man, Johnny returns to find his father and village of Nectanstow even more dissolute & wicked. Sir John, a mind to his legacy, is pleased to see some healthy arrogance in his grown-up & disillusioned-with-the-world son. Perhaps the village's evil livelihood can continue into the next generation. But Johnny becomes bewitched by the wild orphan girl, Morwenna, brought up on the windswept cliffs and beaches by the eccentric Parson. He first encounters her making love to the sea, and his intrusion into her solitary world makes him her enemy. But Johnny's renewed relationship with the now very old & doddery Parson softens both his own world-weariness and, over time, Morwenna. Their combative encounters dissolve into something different, something that distresses Morwenna because the sea is witness to it. Johnny learns that Morwenna believes the sea is her father, and that her duty to her father comes before all anything else. And so should his.

On the eve of the village's Feast Day, a much-changed Rodney turns up during revelries at the local inn. He explains that he has jumped ship down coast of a laden cargo boat on its way to Bristol. He claims to have been abused by the captain of the ship, a madman who is intent on sailing up the coast despite a dangerous storm that is brewing. Rodney is quickly dispensed with, but the wreckers cannot resist the promise of a catch the night before their Feast Day.

Morwenna is with Johnny sheltering in a cave when they see the lighthouse extinguished. Morwenna is unconcerned. The Parson will be asleep and Morwenna has long learnt that his safety is reliant on him being oblivious and the villagers being left to their ways. But Johnny is uneasy, and rightly so, because they encounter a garrison of Preventative Men lying in wait for the wreckers, who assume that they are part of the treachery. They escape using Morwenna's knowledge of the beach, but the surprised wreckers are rounded up after a battle on the beach. Bone, who has extinguished the light on the headland, see the end and is able to escape, looting the Abbey before disappearing. Sir John meanwhile breaks cover and turns the tables on the Preventative Men, tying the constables up in the approaching tide. But Johnny will not let his father do this and challenges him. Single combat is going Sir John's way, but Johnny prevails just as Morwenna frees the Preventative Men and the wreckers once again are overwhelmed.

Johnny and Morwenna are celebrating their wedding with the Parson and Nurse at the Lighthouse, when a travelling monk passes seeking alms – it is Bone, who, to save Johnny's life, Morwenna dispatches over the cliff. But not before Bone has had the pleasure of telling them that Sir John is Morwenna's father and that their union is incest. Morwenna reassures Johnny that this is not true. Her father is the sea.

I have been told that *The Light* is one of my good ones, that I defied 2nd Album syndrome. Again, it's not yet been made. But for those precious days alone with my grandmother, I would happily sit back down with a blank sheet of paper and write every single word of it all over again.

So if it was such a good yarn, why no interest this time? Because the mid 1980s home video market had done away with the epic. David Lean had been buried finally with *A Passage To India* (1984), his first film in 14 years. And although the very best epic of all - unless you are a boy film critic and think that boy films like *Laurence of Arabia* (1962) are best - *Out of Africa* (1985) had just come out and won lots of Oscars, it was to become the last true epic of the 20th century... with one oasis of an exception, *The English Patient* (1996). Not that *The Light* was an epic on the scale of these films, but its landscape, its music and its romance were woven into it, intrinsic to it. Romance became of less interest to 1980s adults. Cinema became of less interest to 1980s adults. This was the age of the teen comedy and the (quasi-) erotic thriller. Films that suited the video rental market. *The Light* was not the sort of film or television series that was being made in the 1980s. *Poldark* was too 1970s.

So it was time for me to try something contemporary. Something for teenagers, rather than just about teenagers. I picked up on a newspaper story about the daughter of the French Ambassador going missing in London. It turned out to be an act of teenage rebellion, rather than a kidnapping. I made my piece about the tabloid journalism surrounding this misunderstanding. I called it *Kiss My Teddybears For Me*. I liked that title, but accepted that it sounded like - what it was not - an erotic thriller. It was a teen-romance-come-London-travelogue, so I changed the title to the more 'on the tin', *London By Daylight* - a play on the song title *London By Night* and the tabloid newspaper *The Sun*.

Liz - with her new London haircut - helped me create artwork for it

It was a K.I.S (Keep It Simple) tale of the American Ambassador's runaway daughter being befriended by a good-looking floppy-haired young Englishman whom she does not know is a tabloid journalist (yes, shades of *Roman Holiday*, 1953). He lends her his flat which, on the surface, is charmingly filled with the trappings of his childhood. In fact, his old teddybears are all teched-up with cameras in their eyes, and he is building up a sensational tabloid scoop. Except of course that he is also falling in love with her...

BOBBIE (antagonistic again)
The English figure they're all so smart, don't they?..
I mean everyone's a 'bloody' Sherlock Holmes-

EDWARD (butts in)
No, no. You overestimate the English, old girl...

He picks up a triangle of cucumber sandwich,

EDWARD
You know why we started cutting the crusts
off cucumber sandwiches?

BOBBIE
To feed your bird brains?

EDWARD
Losing our teeth.

> BOBBIE
> 'Hurrah'. So you could stuff more plums in.

> EDWARD (chewing)
> Boxing. You are not an Englishman until you've
> squared up over the love of a rose-lipped maiden.

> He's onto his second triangle of sandwich..

> BOBBIE
> Englishmen are Mad Dogs.

> EDWARD
> Certainly, there is madness. Explanation for that too.
> Lead water pipes.

> BOBBIE
> You're toothless Lions, brainless Scarecrows and heartless
> Tin Men. All flouncing about like Friends of Dorothy.

> EDWARD
> It's our lovely old country houses. The first in the
> world to have plumbing. All have lead water pipes.

> BOBBIE
> For battering Professor Plum in the Conservatory?

> Sandwich demolished, EDWARD licks his fingers,

> EDWARD
> Lead poisoning. Attacks the brain.

> BOBBIE
> And the British Empire collapses.

> EDWARD
> Precisely!.. Pudding?

Richard Curtis and Hugh Grant had not been invented yet. At that time, the bandwagon was John Hughes and the Brat Pack. And this piece seemed an acceptable offering in a world that had found the money to make *Oxford Blues* (1984) with Rob Lowe. But *London By Daylight* never got made either. Three screenplays down. And none of them picked up.

The lesson I had not learned from the three screenplays I had studied - the three British films I'd worked on in 1983/84 - was a simple one. Original screenplays don't get made in Britain. Britain only makes screenplays based on books or plays. Unless you are an established television writer - like Clement / La Frenais - you don't stand a chance in snooty literary England unless the material comes pre-approved as a published work.

I could either stay in England and try my hand as a novelist or a playwright, or I needed to go to a place where screenwriters were appreciated. Or if not appreciated, at least employed. America.

Initially it wasn't a foregone conclusion I would go. At this key fork in the road, a mighty temptation arose. Rev Stephen Hawker's vicarage in Morwenstow - one of the most romantically-positioned houses in the country, alone on a high lush green valley overlooking the North Atlantic - came up for sale. It was languishing on the market for something like £160,000. This beautiful grey stone building - with four chimneys modelled on the church towers of Hawker's previous church livings - desperately Du Maurier and romantic, was a key location in *The Light*. I had been living in this house in my imagination for the last year. My Marylebone house, bought for £80,000, had certainly doubled in value. I went to visit the vicarage.

Standing at the front attic window (you can see the window, and its view, above), where Hawker had his writing desk, the valley sides seemed like soft thighs leading to origin of the world. I saw myself sitting in this chair, growing a beard, and writing historical novels.

I put in an offer. I have often thought how different my life would have been had that offer been accepted. An alternative life. One that would have suited me in many ways.

But it was not to be.

The offer was used to chivvy along a preferred buyer, and declined. Searching on the internet today I find a beautiful glossy Savills brochure for Morwenstow's Old Vicarage, which must be back up for sale again. It looks truly amazing photographed in its beautiful valley with a 21st Century drone. Wow. There it is. 'Alternative Henry life'.

Instead I went to the American Embassy - not letting on what I'd just put the American Ambassador's daughter through in *London by Daylight* - and asked for a 'fiancé visa' (T.B.E. - To Be Explained in the upcoming chapter). A very nice lady with a West Country accent said she couldn't give me a visa, but she could give me my American passport back.

My American passport? I'd had one, because I was born in Brooklyn. But I thought it had lapsed, when I was 18. No - as I was to experience, uncomfortably, two decades later - to forgo American citizenship you have to go through a rigorous process of swearing disallegiance to the United States. It is not as simple as not renewing your passport.

Okay then. "Thanks."

The nice Cornish lady gave me an American passport.

And then asked for my tax returns for the last six years.

CHAPTER SIXTEEN

Martha

I love you now as I've always loved you. My life can be measured
by the moments I have spent with you and our child.
(Letter From An Unknown Woman, 1947)

"Welcome Home, sir." Before I went to live in New York in January 1986, I had been back to that city three times. All of these visits were on the American passport I had qualified for by being born in Brooklyn 24 years before. Each time, I was welcomed 'home' by a friendly Immigration Officer.

The first return to the place of my birth was aged 13. It was the summer hol-idays between my Prep School, Welles-ley House, and my Senior School, Eton College. My parents had enjoyed hav-ing an American son. They thought they should encourage the connection. They had given me the sweetest Ameri-can godmother, Marion Exter. Marion and John Exter (below) were my par-

Back in Brooklyn - April 2019

ents' 'parents away from home' when they lived in New York as a young married couple in 1961/62. John and Marion were friends of my grandparents. John had

worked in international banking when my grand-father was Governor of the Bank of England. They had a lovely lakeside house outside of New York, which had been a weekend retreat for my parents.

It was to Marion I was sent, aged 13, to dis-cover my American heritage. It was my first air-plane flight, aside from a brief ride in my Dad's Tiger Moth above Hertfordshire. Pan Am, as I remember. If I was scared and homesick, these were emotions I was familiar with, as a boarding school boy. Marion and John met me at JFK, and they could not have been more adorable; nor their home more idyllic. It was in New Jersey, in a rural suburb of Boonton, called Mountain Lakes. It was

a big glass-windowed villa on
a wooded lake - no mountains,
and no real need to spin the
name of the place either, as it was
quite lovely enough.

But I was a 13-year-old
brought up on 1970s American
movies, and novelisations of
1970s American movies that I
was too young to see. So it was
the city and Manhattan that held the excitement to me. Marion and John had an
apartment on the northern edge of midtown, and I was taken to all the sights. But
movies were my obsession and Marion was happy to indulge me. She loved movies
too, and John had never had much patience for them. She took me to my first Drive
In. The film was a Western called *Little Big Man* (1970), with Dustin Hoffman and
Faye Dunaway. My Godmother was fearful she had taken me to something very
inappropriate when Faye Dunaway started giving Dustin Hoffman a bath. I remember Faye Dunaway's southern-accented, sing-songy, "I shall avert my eyes!" And
that's all I remember, because my Godmother then drove me out of the Drive In.

The great thing about America - for a 13-year-old English boy - was that anyone under the age of 17 could go see an adult-themed 'R' (Restricted) movie with
an accompanying parent or adult guardian. This was not the case in England, In
England, no one under the age of 18 could see an adult-themed film, which was certified 'X'. Mild adult themes were given an 'AA' certificate, 'Adult Accompaniment
Required for Children Under 14'. It was only later in life that I saw the negative effect of the American 'R' rating. Violence was generally acceptable in an 'R' film, but
sex was not. So when filmmakers made adult-themed movies with sexual content,
the sex was either cut, or the film was given an American 'X' certificate - which did
restrict it to 18-year-olds, and meant that it couldn't be advertised in newspapers.
Thus in America the 'X' certificate had been purloined by the loin-purveyors, almost
exclusively for pornography.

The result. Lots of violence in American movies, and no sex. This was eventually challenged by some filmmakers with clout - Philip Kaufman's *Henry and June*
(1990) comes to mind - and the Motion Picture Association of America's response
was to create a new classification 'NC17' (no children under 17), for films with sexual content that were not sex films. But then the newspapers refused to advertise
'NC17' films, and if nobody knew about the film, nobody was going to go see it So
only a handful of NC17 movies have ever been made. And American movies are
still full of violence, and still contain no sex. Or at least no sex that isn't either glossy
or gross-out, the latter being acceptable because it's 'comedy'. It is the big weakness
of American cinema, and because of American cinema's reach and ubiquitous popularity, the world suffers as a result.

But I am veering into territory more relevant to later in this book. For the moment we are in New York in the summer of 1975, and I am being taken to lots of
movies by my movie-loving Godmother - movies that won't be released in England
for months, because in the 1970s piracy is not yet a big problem for the studios.

There are no domestic video recorders, and 'digital' only means having a watch that shows numbers not arms and hands. Marion also took me to Broadway shows - I remember *The Wiz*, a rock musical based on *The Wizard of Oz* (1939) - but I was less interested in those. What I could never understand about the theatre was why you would only want one angle on the drama for the whole length of the show, often at some distance. You might as well watch the TV in the corner of your living room.

But there was more to this American trip, aged 13, than movies in Manhattan. I didn't know it at the time, but my parents had also cleverly arranged my marriage.

Of course my parents insist my marriage was not pre-arranged. They'd met a dynamic, American publisher, Gray Boone (right), scouting for stories amongst the historic houses of England for her journal *Antiques Monthly*. They had discovered they had sons the same age. Two boys an ocean apart, but only a month apart in age. And what hindrance an ocean, for a child sent to school south of London before the M25? They would dispatch son number one immediately to the land of his birth on a cultural exchange. They insisted there was no aforethought to whether this American publisher may also have a daughter... Well, if they did know, why would it have been given a second thought? The daughter was only 10-years-old. No. The cultural exchange was about... well, what are teenage cultural exchanges usually about? Learning a language? Mum and Dad, you're busted. And I shall be grateful till my dying day.

Marion and John had been the very best soft landing in this mythical land of my birth. Some movies later, they took me back to the airport, and put me on a plane much deeper into the United States. My destination was Birmingham, Alabama. This time I <u>was</u> terrified. An ankle-socked schoolboy chicken, I was met at

Birmingham airport by Colonel Sanders, all ready to batter me and put me in a bucket. Yes, Colonel Sanders was actually there at the airport, sitting in a departure lounge in his white suit and hat; but, no, it was the dynamic and gushing Mrs Boone who swept me up into her arms. She was there with (almost) the whole family. Her husband, Jim Boone (left), also a publisher - of newspapers - was serious and quite scary. He spoke, when necessary, in short, considered, copy. He belied any theory of an 'arranged marriage'. To this day, the English boy, I'm sure, remains a puzzling proposition. But 'supportive' was - and is - Jim Boone's middle name where family is concerned, and he has more slack to cut for the eccentricities of his kin than can be imagined.

Dear Henry,

Hi. I am your soon to be friend (I hope), Buford. I am writing to tell you to bring clothes like levis (Blue Jeans), and T shirts and some dress shirts, and tennis shoes.

We are going to a lot of fun places while you are here. I work at my Dad's newspaper. If you like you might be able to work there a few days. We have a log cabin on a lake and we might go fishing, swimming, or ride small motors.

See you soon,
Buford Boone

'Buford' is Jim's actual middle name. His son shares his whole name. James Buford Boone. But the son is known as Buford. My intended exchange partner could not have been more different from me. Dark haired, stocky, outdoorsy. I don't believe he owned a pair of short trousers. I was an English schoolboy. I only wore long trousers after September. I was all ankle socks and striped pyjamas. Buford slept in his Levis. He was all pocket knives and gun cupboards. I was all comics and candy. Sorry to bring up Dickon again, but in this instance I was definitely Colin to his Dickon. I'd be reading *The Secret Garden*. He'd be skinning snakes... To allow us both a more flattering analogy, I was Spock to his Kirk. I like that analogy. But it's not really true. Increasingly I'm the one led by my emotions and he's the one spouting the systematic logic of an FBI investigator. But, like Kirk and Spock we've been close friends since Season One.

Also in the family station wagon - part wooden chassis as I remember it - was Martha Frances Boone. Buford's painfully skinny 10-year-old sister only had eyes for two large Great Danes, who had come along for the ride. There's a Rolf Harris song about a young suitor being confronted by a giant slobbering panting Great Dane, which you probably haven't heard unless you are my age, because you're not allowed to listen to Rolf Harris anymore (see p.116). Rolf Harris spends the whole song heavy breathing and panting, as Tiddles the Great Dane. This was how I remember the sound from the back of the car. Was the little English boy intimidated by this strange wooden car load? As Martha remembers it, I spent most of the ride back to Tuscaloosa in tears, of homesickness.

I had no problem with Great Danes - we had big dogs at home - but I <u>was</u> intimidated by the giant multi-tentacled sea anemone whose tank I was put to sleep next to. This was in the bedroom of Mrs Boone's eldest son. Kenneth Boone was off diving in Florida, perhaps collecting more of these terrifying aliens for his bedroom.

The Collier-Boone House in Tuscaloosa, and Martha's Great Danes, Gilda & B.G., painted by Beau Redmond

I stayed with the Boone family in Tuscaloosa for four weeks. And I got on just fine. Primarily because somebody had just invented HBO. Movies on TV! Buford could be off making gunpowder cartridges and I could be stretched out on the shagpile watching films. I loved Mrs Boone. Gray was determined that I was going to have a good time in the American South, so I was allowed to watch as much TV as I liked while she was at work. What is more, the Boone kids had TVs in their own bedrooms. That was the ultimate reason why it was better to be a kid in America. Whoo-Hoo!

When Gray was not at work, I was taken to the amusement park Six Flags Over Georgia, where I was chatted up for the very first time by a girl, a candystriper who wanted me to stay and talk to her because she loved my accent. I can count on one ring-fingered hand the times that has happened since. Alongside the wooden car, Buford's Dad also had a plane. His plane was less wooden, and unlike my Dad's not a rickety flapping cloth one. The Boone plane had magazines in the seat pockets and little cans of CocaCola, like Pan Am. And its own pilot. The cabin pressure did hurt your ears though. The pilot flew the whole family (except the Great Danes) to Washington DC to stay at the Watergate Hotel and attend the inauguration by

Henry, Martha and Buford at the Lincoln Memorial in Washington in the summer of 1975

President Gerald Ford of family friend David Matthews as United States Secretary of Health, Education, and Welfare. David Matthews had a daughter, Lucy, who was Martha's best friend. Lucy was lovely. She had dazzling long golden blonde hair. Are you sure I'm not meant to marry her?... No, because one day she'll cut that off, and there's more to eternal compatibility than liking someone's hair.

And so it was Martha Frances Boone that I pinned passionately to the hallway wall of a New York apartment one morning around Epiphany, early January 1986. She was 21. I had just stepped off one of the very first Virgin Atlantic flights (£99, launch price). I had come because I'd just sold my screenplay *Green For A Season* to a New York company... No, that was simply the gold, frankincense and myrrh that the mischievous wise men of destiny offered. I'd come because I'd had an early Epiphany. At Knebworth. Over Christmas. I'd realised that my true soulmate I'd known all along. My life soulmate. She'd been there since my childhood. All through those teenage years. All through those fumbling forays of female fascination and puppy love. This was big Great Dane dog love. I was following my star... to the place of my birth, to find my number one, top of the list, head of the heap, queen of the hill.

Our families had remained in touch, continued to visit each other. Buford had completed his half of the exchange in the summer of 1976. A good year to be at Knebworth. He'd cooked breakfast for Mick Jagger. Gray had visited me at Eton, been impressed that I'd happily changed out of my uniform trousers in front of her. She was, to me, another mum in a growing coterie of informally adopted parents. However good your real ones, why stop at two? In 1977 my family had done the first of its two U.S. road trip vacations. I was 15. My Dad drove us in a big triangle down the East Coast from New York to Florida, and across to Alabama. We have home cine film of Martha, then 12, showing off well practiced trampoline flips. Then Martha did a summer in England when she was 15. We were not her main hosts, but she spent time at Knebworth, where all were too busy to have much time for her. I was

home, but managing Knebworth Park. Imagine that. Martha sitting around while I managed Knebworth Park.

I had returned once more to New York. In 1985. Martha had transferred from Tulane University in New Orleans to New York University and was living in her mother's apartment on 24th & 9th. She had written a business plan to her fa-

ther, on why he should allow her to transfer. She wanted to do courses she could only do in New York. Journalism and History of Art. Her father had originally said he only wanted her attending a university that was east of the Mississippi river and south of the Mason-Dixon Line. In fact, Tulane is on the west bank of the Mississippi - so she side-stepped that target. However she did hit all her academic targets, and those looked good on the business plan. When I briefly saw her in New York, she was going out with an American Express exec and had cut her hair short in a ta-pered French bob. Not immediately auspicious.

But then there was a long phone call, made to New York that same year, whilst on my explor-atory visit to Los Angeles. I was in a faraway unfamiliar city where I knew no one. But I had a genuine friend in this foreign land, with whom I could share a laugh, with whom I had a natural affinity, a history. We'd already known each other for ten years. I hung up the phone with a buzz. Here was a lifetime friendship.

So when, a year and half later, Martha turned up at Knebworth for Christmas with her mom and without a boyfriend, I fought off cousins and foster brothers for her attention at a string of Christmas parties. That was not easy, as I was expected to play the records at these parties. She was off on the dance floor with everyone else, plenty of admirers wanting to drink champagne from her slippers.

Somehow I did manage to attract her attention. I think it was my long blonde wavy hair. By the mid 80s my braids were right down my back. She said she liked them. I said, that's how you tell eternal compatibility, by liking someone's hair. Also, I had a holster full of 12 inch slow numbers. And I knew when to play them. When the others were off re-filling her shoes. My brother Richard tells me it was the 12 inch mix of Spandau Ballet's *True*, when Martha and I first tongue-touched. That's why we have little brothers, isn't it? To notice things like that. I don't remember that detail, and it surprises me because that song had comic undertones to us, as we liked to pull up our trousers and flatten our balls for the fourth high 'ah' of "ah ah-ah ahhh!",,, No, I remember it being the early hours of the morning, and me playing Julie London's *Your Number Please* LP. A foggy little fella and a drowsy little dame... and my trousers being pulled up from the inside. If you get my meaning. Our pheromones covalently bonding. We retired to a corner of the Knebworth House's Oak Study - my bedroom probably had Richard Wells in a sleeping bag on the floor - and hid ourselves inside a giant fluffy jumper with Mickey Mouse on the front.

And a few hours later she left for New York. So, a few days later, so did I. I had fallen spiky head over pixie boot heels in love.

CHAPTER SEVENTEEN

New York

May I get excited tomorrow?
(Magnificent Obsession, 1954)

Green For A Season may not have gone to the ball, but the reaction the screen-play got from people like Pat King, Joan Fontaine, Cyril Frankel, etc. suggested to me that the screenwriting slipper fit. Screenwriting was to be my way back into the Film Industry. I'd lost a lot of money on the project. Desperately chasing a way to see through my contract with Joan Fontaine, I had effectively put the film into Pre-Production. I had purchased wigs that still sit on my shelf today. I was not so much Cinderella, as the traditional gambling wastrel of an elder son, throwing his money after bad, then escaping his debts in the United States... But I prefer to look at the money I spent on *Green For A Season* as what it would have cost for a Masters Degree in Film Production.

One of the purchases that makes me wince today for its many zeros is the £5,000 I paid for a Sony Word Processor. It was, to be fair, a splendid thing. Recommended by a writer friend, John Dyson, it was a state-of-the-art writing machine. It had a full A4 portrait shaped screen, so you could see a full page of screenplay. Page layout is important, I told myself. The natural pause is a page-turn. That's why I need an A4 screen.

Worse. When I moved to America, I couldn't take my Sony Word Processor with me. It was huge, heavy, and would have to be expensively shipped. So I spent $5,000 on an American one. With a full legal-sized portrait screen, I reasoned I didn't need a car in New York. And I was as fond of my big Sonys as anything else I could have spent 5,000 on. They were certainly better than a typewriter. Screenwriting is re-writing, and for

re-writing typewriters are no more useful than a waste-paper basket. I had become a professional writer in the most expensive few years in history to be a professional writer, inbetween the typewriter and the personal computer.

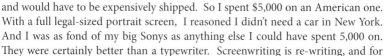

I don't recall asking Martha if I could come to live with her. But it was her mother's apartment I arrived at, and I'd always been welcome under Gray's roof. Martha and I had not even had a date. I moved in. #19A, 410 W. 24th Street.

Martha seemed warm to the idea. She even went out and spent a few hundred hard-earned dollars on a special table for my huge word processor. The table was gold brass, with round edges and a glass top, very chic, very mid-80s. I was not as immediately enamoured of it as I was of its purchaser. I was more of a wood table kind of guy. The first hiccup in our beautiful relationship. But one born of honesty. If honesty was our only problem, we'd be fine. I was still cursing the thing 18 months later, as I manoeuvred its non-dismantlable brass legs into the back of my brand new Toyota passenger van to drive it to L.A., and it ripped a hole in the ceiling lining. Its shiny metal looked even more out of place in our breezy California apartment, but there it stood, reminding us of our first upset. It has even followed us to England, and now stands in the corner of our office conference room, smiling with its rounded brass corners to see us still arguing (which we now only do at work). I've grown fond of it.

New York in the mid-80s was an Emerald City of high-rise romance and street-level grime. I was high in the clouds, in a 19th floor Chelsea apartment, embarking on a beautiful life relationship and a new career chapter full of possibility. On the streets, there was a beggar on every block, and the party was winding down for the Studio 54 generation, as a killer disease stole confidence and lives, and Gordon Gekko stole all the money. Martha lost her lovely neighbours, Tim & Alberto, to AIDS.

Martha inherited Tim & Alberto's ice cream maker. Ice cream became my New York decadence. Unlike where I came from, New York had an ice cream shop on every corner. And not just any ice cream. The hard stuff. Häagen-Dazs. My New York tales of sex & drugs are not of clubbing into the early hours to Prince's *Kiss*. They are of candlelit bubblebaths to George Winston albums. Dreamy-eyed lovers in a porcelain tub feeding each other out of a cardboard tub. Vanilla Chocolate Chip was my hit. I can taste it on my tongue now. I shudder at the sugar I consumed.

Martha had an exotic friend group. Mostly from overseas. Many from her NYU History of Art class. Beautiful, exotic, Italians, Nuti and Marina (left, now), and Ecuadorian, Bernardo (left, now & then). My university friend group were from Harlow and Ilford. I was now going to Jazz Clubs in the Village, seeing Stan Getz, and Astrid Gilberto. If we did go to a nightclub, it was to Little Nell's - yes, *Rocky Horror*'s Lit-

Avocado and Swiss - 2019 version - still delicious

tle Nell. We ate avocado and swiss omelettes at the Greek Diner on the corner of 9th & 23rd. Where I came from, if you'd seen an avocado, it would only have been at a la-di-da dinner party, sliced in half under unfrozen prawns.

Friends of mine also passed through New York. Just round the corner my friend from Los Angeles, Chloe King, was lodging at the Chelsea Hotel, which still smelt of Sid Vicious and Nancy Spungeon. My friend from England, Helena Bonham Carter, invited us to the premiere of her film, *A Room With A View*. Damn, there was Ismail Merchant -

he'd have made *Green For A Season* if I'd been gay and Edwardian. Such a shame for my career that I am only a bit gay, and Victorian.

Martha's lovely mother Gray, of course, was also to be found in her apartment. She was now publishing a visual & performing arts

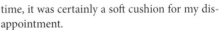

magazine, *Horizon*. So you couldn't go to the theatre with her without ending up backstage with Terrance McNally, F. Murray Abraham, Geoffrey Holder... There was inspiration and new contacts everywhere. The thrill of the city of my birth, a beautiful love affair, affirmation as a writer... if this was not *Green For A Season*'s

time, it was certainly a soft cushion for my disappointment.

To take a little pressure off Martha - a full-time live-in boyfriend for the first time, whilst aceing an NYU double Major, then a full-time position at advertising agency McCaffrey & McCall - most midweeks I'd take the bus out to New Jersey to spend a few nights with my adored godmother Marion Exter. Waking up in Mountain Lakes to adagios on the stereo in the huge-windowed living room looking out over the lake was the perfect perspective to take stock of this tumultuous time. It could see Act One resolving. I'd found my heroine. I'd had my page 30 embrace. I was ready to move on to Act Two.

The Manhattan view out of the window - on the 19th floor of 24th & 9th - was a wall of windows. At night, it was like watching 50 TV channels. In one window, there was an elderly couple. Every evening he'd be doing the washing up, and she would pass by and run her hand over his bottom. Was that going to be us in 50 years time? We hoped so.

Of course, we still had one test to pass. We had to survive a holiday together. Martha, you won't be surprised to hear, had also not taken a 'gap year'. I am not sure she'd ever taken a holiday. Not in the European sense anyway. She'd worked every vacation through university. Before she started work at McCaffrey & McCall, she was determined to have her own walkabout. She wanted the European Interrail experience. I'd done this. Martha wanted her own memories. She wanted to start this adventure alone. But we agreed that three weeks in, we would rendez-vous in Geneva, and she would join my brothers and I on a VW Kombi adventure into Italy.

Martha was New York streetwise, but if you recall my experiences in the railway stations of central Europe, you'll not be surprised at my apprehension. It is hard now to remember that time before we were all permanently connected by cell phones. Our relationship, I was sure, would survive the attentions of Gunther from Essen and the prosthetic limb salesman in Venice, but after that would come the real test. Would it survive a couple of weeks in a campervan with me and my two brothers, Peter (21) and Richard (17)?... Oh, and Peter's beautiful new girlfriend, a fiery Greek named Ginette was going to squeeze into the minibus too.

Our reunion in Switzerland was a happy one. A good start. I'd missed her like crazy. Then...

Italia! Avanti!

In the close quarters of the family holiday van we went through the full farting orchestral gamut of holiday emotions. There were blazing rows.

Voices raised. Van doors slammed. We lost one passenger for a few days. But the rows were all Peter and Ginette. Love-play, I think. They're now over 30 years into a beautiful marriage.

Martha and I had survived the final challenge. The family holiday. We'd had only one contretemps. An honesty bomb about the bright yellow shorts she chose to wear in Florence. Yellow shorts in Florence? I mean yellow shorts anywhere, but yellow shorts in Florence? My previous girlfriend had been Helena Bonham Carter, for flips sake. Even I was wearing a floaty white dress in Florence.

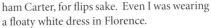

It was a magical time. We were different, but in so many ways the same. Where we were similar we fused. Where we were different we complimented. My head in the clouds. Martha's feet on the ground. We made for a tall partnership. We could see far into the distance. The prospect was good.

We were never going to agree whether to paint a room magnolia or brilliant white. We were never going to agree - both with History of Art degrees - who knew more about Titian. We were never going to agree how, when, or why, to take a holiday... No matter. It may not have been pre-arranged, but our match was clearly made in celestial realms. Destiny. It was time we got married.

To ask her father's permission, my first thought was to write Jim Boone a letter. I made a stab at it in my best A-level Victorian English. Martha's older brother Kenneth, on hand to advise, laughed. Did I know his father? If a sentence is more than three words it is too long. He's a journalist, not the Archbishop of Canterbury. So,

I'm supposed to express eternal love for his daughter in three word sentences?

Of course this needed to be done face-to-face. I had a traumatic flashback. Being met at the airport in Birmingham Alabama when I was 13, a chicken in ankle socks. So we took the train. New York to Tuscaloosa.

"I have something to ask you, Mr Boone." Picking up a foolscap pad, Mr Boone calls me into a room alone. Clearly I need to make notes too. I grab the closest thing to hand. My address book, Why was I sitting with my address book on my knee? It was a wind up. It wasn't the last. In America you have to have a venereal test to get a marriage licence. I was to get the results of my blood test from the Boone family doctor. Dr Burnham called me into his surgery, looking grave, "Do you have something you need to tell me, Mr Cobbold?"... "Just kidding."

All that remained was for our parents to have the fun of the Pre-Nup. He keeps his deer park, and she keeps her newspapers. We were happy to leave them to it, and go on an early honeymoon back to Italy. To Positano. But first... cramped in the train couchette on the way back to New York, I got down on my knees by the lower bunk and proposed. Just as we crossed the Mason-Dixon line.

I spent the $2,500 option fee I had received from Co*Star Entertainment for *Green For A Season* on an engagement ring.

CHAPTER EIGHTEEN

The Wedding

```
EXT.  FLOWER GARDEN, WHITE MANSION - EARLY AFTERNOON

The distinguished congregation is now sweltering in the
midday heat.. perspiring, red-faced, uncomfortable.  They
hear the siren, turn back to see..

The police car swerves to a halt before the foot of the
aisle.  Mr White greets the embarrassed SERGEANT, who jumps
out.

                     SERGEANT
          Mr White, if we'd known it was your
          daughter-in-law-

He turns, to let Sylvie out of the backseat.. but she has
already sprung out, indignant, still wrapped in the police
blanket.  She heads straight for the aisle.

                     MR WHITE
               (calls)
          Wait!.. Silly!  Celly!  Whatever
          your name is!

Nicholas stands at the other end of the aisle with the red-
faced Reverend, now purple-faced in the heat.  Seeing her,
with much relief, he signals to the orchestra-

The Wedding march strikes up.. the congregation stands.

CLOSE ON:  Sylvie grins, pumped up in defiance.

Lifting a clump of flowers from the side of the aisle, she
flicks back the police blanket-

Stark naked, she marches down the aisle.. brazen,
beautiful.. towards Nicholas.

Like a wave of dominos, the wedding guests pull back in
horror.. there are screams, upturned chairs.. pandemonium.

Grandpere beams at his granddaughter, belly laughs.
```

(*Wearing A Smile*, 1996)

An engagement party at Knebworth House, shared with my Dad's 50th birthday party, on the 'Quatorze Juillet' weekend of 1987, was a milestone of Knebworth Parties. It was another big, back courtyard extravaganza. Everyone from my youth was there. Literally everyone. Lifelong friends of my parents, friends from school, friends from working in Knebworth Park, friends from working my mobile disco, university friends (more than five even), film friends, even foreign friends from New York and beyond. My stunner of a fiancée had to remind me that she was there too.

I struggled to say more than a few words to good friends who had travelled long distances to get to Knebworth that evening. My childhood passed before my eyes across those few hours - I reached out... but it had passed on. I was 25. Half-way to my Dad's 50. I was moving abroad indefinitely. It was goodbye to all of this. My foster brother Dan and I put scarves on our heads and, as old ladies, sang *I Will Miss You* to each other from Sandy Wilson's *Valmouth*. I'd been an incurable nostalgic since I was 12, so this night was always going to be bittersweet.

I'm told this was actually a different party, around the same time - but never let the truth get in the way of a good story.

Goodbye everyone. It's been fun.

And then I did see them all again. Because they all tipped up at my wedding too.

Well not all of them. But a good many. We had an impressive turn out of Brits in Alabama. About 60, if I recall. We rented three buses to pick them up at Atlanta airport. A rest stop was required halfway to Tuscaloosa, and all 60 English people piled into a small rural diner, with one short order waitress and a couple of cops in the corner munching doughnuts. The Redcoats were back. That sort of thing doesn't happen every day in Alabama. I think it was Blount County, and with a contingent of my cousins bearing that name they naturally assumed sovereignty.

As had been the case in 1975, Tuscaloosa could not have been more gracious to this cultural exchange. The Governor's Mansion on the University of Alabama campus was procured for the bulk of the groom's party. But good people all over Tuscaloosa took in alien lodgers - and lifetime friendships were formed. Pam and Richard Saire (my London parents) would have regular telephone chats with the Boone family dentist, Mr Hughey and his wife, till this lovely couple died many years later.

Most impressive, was the turnout of old girlfriends. Liz, Rebecca, Jo... They weren't exactly weeping in the pews. But I was touched that they'd made the long and expensive journey to cheer me on - or rather cheer Martha on. I believe myself friends with every one of my former girlchums. I believe that speaks well of the teenage me. I think I'd like him if I met him.

Particularly special was that both Martha's Boone grandmother, Frances (below, front row, pink dress on the left), and my Cobbold grandfather, Kim (black bow tie on the right), were both with us. As both no longer were a couple of months later.

It was hot. Or so they tell me. I didn't notice. Evening weddings are not allowed in the U.K., because it is assumed the vicar, or the witnesses, will have had a drink by then and not be of sound mind. In the South, in the summer, it is essential. The midday sun is only for Englishmen. As mentioned earlier (p.27) we had out-

door air conditioning - and good luck rain - provided by large blocks of ice on pedestals in front of giant fans.

My ushers - my four brothers, Martha's two brothers, my best man John Martin (the musician from my basement, p.132) and representing my future home California, Hal Christensen, another adored dad-away-from-home (who'd been site manager at early Knebworth concerts) - were, I am sure, cursing me for insisting on white tie and tails. But I was only going to do this once. And we'd brought the Astaire songbook with us to America, in the form of Dan and Harry, who sang *Cheek To Cheek* into the early hours. Until the Americans got their own back, and stuck The Clash on the turntable.

I muffled one honesty bomb that I was less keen on the bridesmaid outfits, which were shiny blue. I couldn't picture Ginger

Rogers wearing shiny blue. But looking back now I love how bonkersly '80s they were. Plus, from the day I met her, I've always loved my wonderful sister-in-law Mary Lyman, maid of honor, who amazingly made every one of them. The dresses needed shunting up occasionally, as they were strapless and shelf-hung. During the Reception one bridesmaid lifted her arms above her head and her bare breasts joined the party. I'd been married for all of two hours.

The ceremony took place at Tuscaloosa's Christ Episcopal Church. Martha questioned whether my vow shouldn't have been spoken (like Dustin Hoffman) to her rather than projected (like Laurence Olivier) to the back of the hall. But I wanted the whole world to hear it. Even those in the cheap seats. I should have remembered, however, to lift the veil before I went in for the kiss.

At that time I was uneasy about wearing a ring. I hadn't worn a watch since I was 12, and still don't today. No earrings. No medallions. No nipple piercings. No Prince Albert. I am not really a jewelry kind of guy. My father had never worn a wedding ring. It was pointed out to me that, as a symbol, it should not be that a wife is bound to a husband, but that a husband and wife are bound together. So ever since, I've been pleased to do what I never thought I would, and wear a piece of gold jewelry. I wear it loose, because I've never forgotten trivia from my teenage fandom that Robert Redford's was so tight that he couldn't get it off. That creeps me out, in a sheep-castrating kind of way. My wedding ring has been crushed behind a fridge, reshaped, twiddled endlessly, but I have only once ever taken it off. To go swimming in rough waves on the beach in L.A. I was instantly chatted up by a beautiful blonde surfer babe. So I quickly put it back on.

Forever happy to wear the gold ring I was given on that beautiful day, I'll never, forever, understand why I chose it as the only day in my adult life to wear a side parting. A good number of my previous hairdressers were at the wedding. What was I thinking?! If I was to be Fred Astaire, I could have at least pomaded it down. Grandchildren, if you take one piece of advice from your grandfather's book be it that your wedding day haircut is going to stare at you from your mantelpiece forever. My fluffy, side-parted, so round - and yet so square - haircut, perhaps, was some subconscious throwback to when I first came to Alabama as a schoolboy. The ankle-socked chicken is back, to steal away your daughter.

Of course I was pulled over, driving Martha away. Buford had arranged that with his friends at the Police Department. But we didn't want to leave. We returned to the party. Our first dance was to a Dixieland jazz quartet playing *Quiet Night of Quiet Stars*, referencing a perfect romantic - and international - moment on our pre-wedding honeymoon in Sorrento, where we had danced to this Brazilian tune with the glittering lights of Naples across the bay, and a big moon hanging over - not Corcovado, but - Vesuvius. One day - maybe our 50th anniversary - I want to dance under the stars to *Tourna A Surriento* with Sugar Loaf mountain in view.

Continuing the wonderfully incongruous, international flavour of this very special event, the following day the very merry English contingent saw us off from the platform of Tuscaloosa Railway Station with a loud chorus of Vera Lynn's *We'll Meet Again*. The train guard that pulled Martha, me & the trousseau up onto the carriage must have thought the train had been tornadoed somewhere out of Kansas.

As we kissed for the crowd, high on the train steps, the mistake of putting on a shirt with no buttons meant my bare breasts joined the party... or at least my belly did. Take a look at that. That's 170 pounds. I'll never be that again.

Three days on the train to Los Angeles was the perfect (post-wedding) honeymoon. We'd splashed out on a couche rather than a couchette. The Sunset Express, as the train is named, is not really an express, but you can't argue with the sunset. Martha and I were heading off into the sunset. Perfect.

CHAPTER NINETEEN

California

California was the perfect place for us to begin our married life. We were both from places where our families were woven into the fabric. To build a new life - that was ours alone - we needed clean sheets, neutral territory. Of course it was comforting to have been out ahead, and made the bed. It was not like my first visit, when I knew no one. Now we had L.A. parents in Pat and Zalman King. We even had weekend-getaway parents in Hal and Sally Christensen up the coast in the idyllic Eldorado of Santa Barbara.

Before the wedding, I'd driven out to Los Angeles, with my mother and sister, in a brand new silver Toyota passenger van. I'd bought it in Vermont (minimal sales tax), driven it to New York to pick up our New York possessions (fine brass table, $5,000 word processor), then down to Alabama to pick up a U-Haul trailer of Boone possessions (and wedding presents, useful apartment essentials like silver trays and candlesticks - we'd been given 17 candlesticks). Then Pat and Zalman gave us real essentials, their old yellow fridge and an old flowery brown sofa suite (the fridge came all the way back to England with us).

We also owed our perfect starter apartment to Pat and Zalman. Zalman's cousin Howie Worth knew a lady called Jane Norsell who had a rental on Mentone Avenue in Culver City. It was identical in layout to the apartment Ryan Gosling and Emma Stone move into in *La La Land* (2016). But what was special about it was that you could see the MGM sign - above what was then MGM studios - out of the living room window. If you're going to move to 'Hollywood', it's good to know that you're there when you get there. We were a stone's throw from the stages where *High Society* and *Gigi* were filmed. I was as good as Louis Jourdan's neighbour.

In 1987 many of the legends of the movies of my childhood were still alive. I was now in their town, across the street from 'more stars than there are in heaven'. What miracle had <u>me</u> carrying over the threshold the girl I'd been friends with since we were kids, the 'sparkle turned to fire', the 'warmth become desire'... what miracle had given me this perfect movie ending, in the streets of my childhood dreams?

Louis Jourdan, of course, was in reality living up the coast. But I did pop in to see him. In a theatre production of *Gigi* in Santa Barbara, playing the Maurice Chevalier role. I'd not met Joan Fontaine by this time, but 8000 miles of separation was now much closer to six degrees.

But to meet our new neighbours, we just needed to hang out in Pat and Zalman's kitchen. Their home on Rose Avenue in Venice - a magic toyshop of giant bronze sculptures, carousel horses, ethereal angels, beautiful stained glass and mosaics of bright patterned tiles (see p.149) - was a Mecca for all the most interesting people in town. I got my first job almost immediately - through the English producer Anthony Rufus Isaacs, one of the producers on *9½ Weeks*. It was to write coverage on a screenplay.

MGM Studios sign
← behind this tree

Our apartment

'Coverage' is a specific term, a breakdown of a screenplay to help a Producer assess it - often so he/she doesn't have to read it themselves. As well as a filter, it's also used as an opinion to hide behind, so producers don't have to make their own judgement. There's inbuilt fear in Hollywood of having an opinion, as you'll likely be wrong. And you don't get to be wrong too many times.

I had no idea how to write coverage, and I had much too much of my own opinion. I didn't like the screenplay I was given to read. It was set during the slave trade, and it seemed to me that all the pleasure points in the narrative were based

on violence and abuse. In hindsight I would very much like to re-read it, because I later discovered that it had been written by the Dutch writer Gerard Soeteman, who had written one of my favourite films - one that in London we'd go see in 70mm in the Scala Cinema Club, King's Cross - Paul Verhoeven's *Flesh+Blood*. I have the poster for *Flesh+Blood* in my study toilet at Knebworth House, and everytime I am in there now I see Soeteman's name and regret my simplistic response - as I probably would have had the same initial reaction to the *Flesh+Blood* screenplay before I saw how it was to be interpreted. It was an important lesson to me. And one I am very aware of when I am writing my own screenplays that I know will be going out for coverage to neophytes like me. You've got to win on the first impression of someone who knows nothing.

I was never asked to write coverage again. The script I don't believe was ever made, but I suspect I was not the reason for that.

My second job also came from Pat and Zalman's kitchen. This also led nowhere, but again was an important early lesson. Because it was one of those jobs that young writers fall into with the best intentions, but which isn't actually a job. It is to collaborate with someone who has no money, but a good idea, and can't themselves write. Zalman's cousin Howie was also behind this introduction - to a similar middle-aged lady to the one who'd offered us the Culver City apartment, but this lady's good idea was less advantageous. I spent much too long working on a project that was going nowhere, just because it was a good idea. Screenwriting 101, Lesson Two. Good ideas mean nothing. There's hundreds of them. Pedigree and luck are what matter.

It was a good idea though. And, funnily enough, over 30 years later, now is probably a good time for it. It was a positive story of Americans in Communist China. The heart of the story at least was positive. It was the story of the 'Dixie Mission'. During the 2nd World War a diplomat from the State Department, John Service, and an Army Colonel, David D. Barrett, were sent to the mountains of Yan'an to explore relations with Mao and the People's Liberation Army. They got on well with the Chinese Communists, who they thought less corrupt than Chiang Kai-shek and the Nationalists. They sent positive dispatches back to Washington that Mao and his comrades should be engaged with, as positive allies. These reports were ignored, and the mission subsequently backfired on Service and Barrett, and their careers, in the McCarthyism that followed the War. The episode soured Mao and his comrades towards America, and the possibility of a turning point in history was lost.

The lady was called Irina Somerton. She had access to John Service, then still living in Northern California, and his unpublished papers. It felt like an important project, and I enjoyed, in the early flush of it, working creatively with someone else, something I'd not done before. I dream of successful collaborations, and am forever envious of successful writing partnerships like that of my college mates Rob Wade and Neal Purvis. But for some reason - and please tell me it's fate, and not my aluminium-free deodorant - I am still looking for my perfect writing collaborator.

Martha, meanwhile, went straight into a proper job. Knapp Publishing was delighted to have her journalism degree - and New York experience (working vacations) on *Women's Wear Daily* - at KCET magazine, the Public TV station magazine and part of the Hearst Group. Her office was up the solo white tower block opposite the Museum of Natural History on Wilshire, at La Brea tar pits. It made me nervous to have her up a tower block in Los Angeles, but this one was built on rollers, so that it swayed during earthquakes - and in the wind.

We were conscious of earthquakes, because within a couple of weeks of our arrival in Los Angeles in September 1987 there was a large one. It was around 7 o'clock in the morning. Martha and I were in bed watching the morning news show (yes, a TV in the bedroom - I was living the American dream). As we were feeling our new home shake violently, we were watching the news anchor - a preppy blond guy with the appropriate name of Kent Shocknek - dive under his desk, saying that he had not felt one like this before, and that if it was out in the ocean we should now all prepare for a tidal wave. Remind me why we moved here? A couple of weeks later there was a hurricane in England. So we reasoned we needed to be prepared for natural disaster wherever we were. We might as well be here.

Third time lucky on jobs from Pat and Zalman's kitchen. Italy introduced a tax break for first time female directors, and an enterprising Roman company called Ellepi Film, and a producer called Leo Pescarolo, signed the costume designer Milena Canonero, who has recently won an Oscar for *Out of Africa* (top 5 for me, a fan of all Pollack/Redford movies; the actress was good too) to direct her first feature. She chose an Italian novel about the Spanish Civil War, called *Madrid '37*. Her American husband, actor Marshall Hall, had worked with Zalman, and Milena asked Pat if she would write the screenplay. Pat was busy on another project, but said she would oversee it if I was taken on as screenwriter. My first proper Hollywood job - ironically, for a European company - and a great one.

Milena didn't have much interest in the novel she'd chosen. She liked the central idea of a wounded Republican soldier, hospitalised in a Madrid mansion, falling in love with an aristocrat hidden in the building, and leaving his cause to help her escape to France. I have long forgotten how much of the original novel remained in the story we came up with - but I did do, what Milena thought unnecessary, and used some of my budget to get the novel translated. It was translated for me by a friend of my father's, part-Scottish, part-Italian, Kirsten Anderson, who recorded herself translating the novel as she read it. Not only that, but the budget allowed for a paid researcher on the project. That has never happened to me since, and even today I stare wistfully at the two beautiful bound volumes of research on the Spanish Civil War that sit on my shelf.

But the most remarkable memory about this project is that the research led me actually to visiting and interviewing veterans of the Lincoln Brigade, the American volunteers who had gone to Spain in 1937 to join the Republican cause. That generation did not have many years left, and it's one of the great privileges of my life to have had that experience. What it told me, of course, is that real life stories are much more interesting than any fiction could ever be. But Milena was committed to her vision, and the story that we came up with I thought was good.

So not only was I working on a great piece - a period piece even - I was working with a genuine creative talent and with the safety cushion of a mentor, Pat, watching my back. This was the Hollywood I was looking for. We had script meetings in Milena's hillside apartment above Sunset, and occasionally at a mid-town bungalow near Franklin that her friend screenwriter Leonard Schrader was house sitting. This was also an aviary, internally netted, so exotic birds could fly freely about the house. I recall being distracted one meeting when some brightly coloured bird landed on Milena's white t-shirt as she was reclined on a sofa. It paced her breast, determined to throw my concentration as its prehistoric claws found a perch on her nipple.

The hardest thing about working for the industry's top costume designer is what to wear each morning. Perhaps the finest compliment she paid me was when she was decrying the appalling dress-sense of a prospective collaborator, and how it coloured her opinion of the guy's taste - "not like Henry, who always looks good". I did work hard to look the part. Martha and I spent weekends exploring the garment district downtown looking for snappy tapered trousers to wear with the collarless business shirts I'd inherited from my granddad's wardrobe.

As I remember it, Milena was also happy with my script. I only recall one scene that Milena - and Pat - did not like. It involved a Martha Gellhorn (American war correspondent) type character on her knees fellating the protagonist. In retrospect this image was not likely to stand with Milena. But to me the scene was not about the fellatio, it was about the look that passed between the protagonist and his love interest who had appeared, standing in the doorway. It was a key moment. A self-destructive moment of betrayal... No banana. The scene had to go.

I was particularly pleased with my ending. After having risked everything to help the Spanish Aristocrat escape to Biarritz, the American soldier sees her slip straight back into the decadent superficiality of her previous life, and realises he has no future with her... so quietly determines to return to the front. I invented a tattered tourism poster for him to pass in the last scene:

> *Au clair de la lune*
> *Nous irons s'il faut*
> *Jusqu'en Espagne*
> *Batir des chateaux*

Surely this film was going to be made?

No. It doesn't work like that. However good the project is. However promising the talent attached to it. Nothing in the film business is certain.

I don't know why *Madrid '37* did not progress. I think Milena got distracted by her day job. I know that problem. It was hard for her not to accept Costume Designer roles on movies that were being offered to her by top directors. Then something else happened - we shall call it a 'Timothy Dalton'. Manuel Puig, much heralded Argentinian author of the novel and subsequent play *Kiss of the Spider Woman* (adapted by Leonard Schrader into an Oscar-winning 1985 film) offered to rewrite the script. That was pedigree. That was worth pursuing, worth waiting for... killing off the project for. Manuel Puig actually died while he doing it, I think. And the producer Leo Pescarolo, is now long dead too. I don't think Milena has ever directed a film, but she is still deservedly winning Oscars for costume design.

I, meanwhile, can say I've been rewritten by Manuel Puig. I'd love to know if anything of mine hung around in that draft. Certainly if he had thought a blow job was good for the narrative, I suspect it would have stayed in.

                              YURI
         Mmm, fuck it - I did it too good - see, the incision scar
       follows lines of cleavage exactly.. it'll get fainter and fainter
        over the years until it's virtually impossible to see - so have
                      your grandchildren quick, okay?

                            MICHAEL
                 Have kids? - I can't even breathe!

                              YURI
         Breathe? - You've been breathing? - I told you not to
         breathe! - Nina, tighter with the adhesive strapping.

                       (*Madrid '37*, 1988)

CHAPTER TWENTY

Morwenna

PARSON
(in trauma)
I didn't know what to do... I couldn't do anything... What
could I do?... I didn't know what to do...

*The boy reappears, out of breath, clutching a salver of
overspilling water,*

YOUNG JOHNNY
I took it from the font -

NURSE
Bring it close, John! This side 'o the lass's leg... Keep yer
eyes that way... Little-un's goin' t'be alright..

(The Light, 1986)

By now, I was ready to work on another original screenplay. And this one did get picked up. This time the connection was not Pat and Zalman. Gray, Martha's mother, in inimitable networking mode, had dined in New York with a couple who had a daughter living and working in L.A., in marketing for Orion Pictures. Her name was Tina Tanen. She'd been brought up in Europe where her father was a diplomat, but had a connection to Hollywood in that her uncle, Ned Tanen, was the king. By which I mean he was head of Paramount Pictures. The Paramount Pictures that delivered *Top Gun* (1986), *Fatal Attraction* (1987) and trounced the mid-80s competition. So for four years, '84 to '88, Ned Tanen was the king.

Martha and I arranged to meet Tina, and she quickly became as close a friend as we were to have. We spent most weekends with her, usually at the beach, some-

times in Santa Barbara, Palm Springs... and when Martha became pregnant we did our entire series of Lamaze classes with her. The three of us on a rubber mat together doing breathing exercises was looked on as very modern by other couples in the class.

It made sense to me. I'm all for spreading the load in the challenges of parenting, Tina went on to become a godmother, and will be crossing the Atlantic to attend the child's wedding in 2022. In

1989 there was a chance I wouldn't be able to be present for the birth, so Tina would be able to stand in as breathing regulator. This possibility arose because Tina had found a producer who wanted to work with me on my new project.

The screenplay was set in Italy. Thinking back, it was probably set in Italy because I'd just been working for Italians, and I saw an opportunity to pitch an Italian project. There had been an intermediary producer on *Madrid '37* called Stefano Rolla, whose encouragement I recall. Tragically, echoing the plot of my new piece, Stefano was killed by a terrorist bomb in Iraq in 2003. The Italians didn't pick it up, but a producer that Tina knew called Beverly J Camhe, who had just produced a film with Gene Hackman called *The Package* (1989), wanted it. Not only that, but she had the promise of financing from a company called Odyssey Entertainment.

Odyssey was an appropriate name, as the piece was called *Sirens* - until somebody else made a film, much less appropriately called *Sirens,* in 1994, and my screenplay became *The White Siren.* It was about a nightclub in Sorrento, based on the cliffside terrace where Martha and I had danced on our honeymoon to *Quiet Night of Quiet Stars.* In my story the club is run by Sofia Loren and is a hotbed of spying on the American 5th Fleet. That's the same Sofia Loren who as I write, over 30 years later, could still play the part. It was a thriller. Smart. Sexy. Spectacular. That was my coverage anyway. I was very proud of it. Even my Dad liked it.

(The 1980s - when 'erotic' was a positive adjective for a thriller)

And again, nothing came of it. But other things came instead. It was during a *Sirens* lunch with Beverly and Tina on Melrose Avenue, that the waiter was asked to look for a blonde husband, because his wife was having a baby. Of course, both finely trained Lamaze practitioners, either Tina or I could have attended - but it was the flustered father who sprang for the bat pole, sped home, and promptly smacked his Toyota van into the garage wall. It was a 45-minute drive to San-

THE WHITE SIREN

Original Screenplay by Henry Cobbold

THE WHITE SIREN is a colourful, erotic, adventure that blends the fantasies of traditional folklore with modern political intrigue. It is set amidst the contrasts of exquisite beauty and industrial ugliness that are to be found in Italy's Bay of Naples. Using all the richness of Neapolitan landscape, song, and myth, it tells a story of two very different Americans seduced into a world of superstition, sex, and international terrorism.

* * *

Campania is in the grips of deathlike summer stagnation, caused by the dry winds known locally as 'scirocco chiaro' - from the murderous back alleys of the City of Naples, to the sinister black volcano Vesuvius, to the tragic ruins of Classical Pompeii, to the fluttering mandolins of Sorrento, to the azure caves of Capri, to the perched terraces of Positano, to the breathtaking cliffs of Amalfi…

A beautiful young blond New Yorker, with her canvas backpack and Eurorail pass, is afraid of nothing as her train approaches Naples' Stazione Centrale - she is headed for the San Carlo Opera House, to hear the heroine of her childhood, the ex-prima donna, give a special performance of Neapolitan song

A seasoned U.S. Navy Commander is airlifted off his Aircraft Carrier to the Island Of Capri to investigate the drowning of a fellow Officer whose naked body has been found entwined with that of a young Swedish girl, in the Blue Grotto.

* * *

THE WHITE SIREN is a modern day story about the Sirens, the female temptresses who have been associated with the Bay of Naples for three thousand years. In Homer's epic poem *The Odyssey*, the ancient world's aural sea manual to the Mediterranean, the beautiful Italian goddess Circe was the first to warn against the dangers of sailing too close to this seductive Southern Italian coast:-

"First of all, you will come to the Sirens, they who bewitch all men. Whoever sails near them unaware shall never see his wife and children once he has heard the Siren voices. They enchant him with their clear song, as they sit in a meadow that is heaped with the bones of dead men."

Today, Circe's warning is not heeded - Naples is the home port for the American Navy's Sixth Fleet…

ta Monica hospital. By the time Tina got there a few hours later, the moment was almost upon us and all those Lamaze classes were beside the point. The baby was twisted around the umbilical cord and was yo-yo-ing up and down the canal. I was up the top end being strangled, and Tina was down the other end with our coolly reassuring Japanese American doctor Jan Miyakawa. At one point, Jan was more concerned about me being strangled than the baby. This child was to grow up a notorious duvet twister, so looking back we might have expected she would wrap her-

self up. Brilliantly, but to the lasting detriment of the nerves in Martha's lower back, Jan managed to twist the baby around, and finally out she slid, fist first, like Supergirl.

It was around 9pm on 16th August 1989, at the exact moment California was experiencing a lunar eclipse. We named the miracle Morwenna Gray. 'Morwenna' after the patron saint of my mother's home in Devon. Well, the patron saint of the neighbouring parish. The sister of that patron saint Nectan. The baby looked more like a 'Morwenna' than a 'Nectan'. And 'Gray', after her beloved grandmother, the catalyst of the blessèd union that had created her.

'Morwenna' means 'sea wave' where St. Morwenna comes from. In the dialect of the native people where our Morwenna came from, the word for 'sea wave' is 'Malibu'. I suppose we could have called her Malibu, but in England this is more readily associated with a cheap drink. I am happy my daughter is not a cheap drink. I promised Martha that 'Morwenna' was a well known English name. I've not been allowed to forget that. Until *Poldark* was revived in 2015, our daughter's name was persistently mispronounced anywhere outside of the West Country - Mo-arn-er, Mo-weena, etc. As mentioned, in *The Light* I had assumed the shortened, familiar,

version would be 'Wenn' or 'Wenny'. To us it has always been Mo.

I think of her all the time, but particularly at the end of watching movies. As the Negative Cutter in the credits of every movie ever made is called Mo Henry.

The very first thing a father is expected to do with his precious baby is to take her off to have gunge

squirted in its eyes. Welcome to the world. I'm your father. Splat! Splat!... I hope in the years since I've made up for this a little.

Now I am about to write that our rented flat in Culver City wasn't big enough for a larger family, so we had to buy a new home in West Hollywood. But however much I kid myself, that's not true. In fact the place we went on to buy in West Hollywood wasn't much bigger than the apartment in Culver City. The thing is, I would dearly love to give you a good reason for why I made the worst business decision of my life. The worst by a long stretch. In fact, the only one I really regret... however much I tell myself je ne regrette rien - because every finger movement is measured, every decision reasoned as the right thing to do at that time, for a balance of short and long term satisfaction... But what in blue blazes was I doing, selling my London house?!

How I wish I had that house today. Aside from the fact that it would now be worth millions, it would be so very useful. Somewhere for my son to stay while he can't afford one. Somewhere for Martha to stay to save late nights on the chilly platform of Finsbury Park railway station having missed the Knebworth train. Something to borrow against. Goodness, something to keep me long into my retirement and senility... How come I didn't borrow against the house in 1989 to buy a place in West Hollywood? Because reader... interest rates were a lot higher then than they are now (I feel safe writing 'now' as it's hard to imagine them ever that high again)... I am sure there were lots of good reasons. I just can't think of them now.

It was complicated too. My best man - my musician in the basement - John Martin, as mentioned, had spent money on building a bespoke recording studio, that I was now asking him to dismantle. His new young wife was not going to let that happen without a battle. There were no written agreements. Had we considered an exit strategy, an end game, when it was being built? All I can remember is how much fun we were having writing Linn Drum patterns for *Stop That Row!* (p.114).

John is now long divorced. One happy result of that long ago union is the lovely Lucy Martin who reads the weather on BBC Look East, distinctive for her lack of a hand on one arm. I still love John, and have laughed with him since, at his 60th birthday; and wept with him since, at the funeral of his dear Dad, Peter... but I don't see him much now. He lives in a bedsit in Brighton, teaching guitar, no longer with any of the many women with whom he has hundreds of lovely children. Members of my family have still not forgiven him for holding me to ransom over the sale of my house in 1989. I've not forgiven him for not being successful in persuading me not to sell it. So ebbs the tide. One day he and I will make beautiful music again.

Having bought 39 Harewood Avenue for £80,000 in the early 80s, I sold it for £200,000 in the late 80s. I gave £20,000 of this to John for the dismantling of his stu-

dio. The rest I converted to dollars and - the exchange rate being reasonable - spent $275,000 on a condominium in West Hollywood.

I did love our West Hollywood home. It was brand new. It was brilliant white. It was four storeys (two small rooms a storey) of curved-edge, Adobe-finished, palm and bougainvillaea gated-terraced condo. Each unit had a private underground garage opening into the apartment. Number 9 of 12. 8562 West Knoll Drive. It looked west towards the skyscrapers of Century City. It looked to the sunset. It looked over the endlessly entertain-

ing outdoor swimming pool of the Ramada (Ram-harder) Hotel on Santa Monica Boulevard. Again, it was a view that said, 'you're living in Hollywood'.

My English agent, Linda Seifert, and her husband John Goldstone (producer of *The Rocky Horror Picture Show* and Monty Python movies) had an apartment on the same street. I've not mentioned my literary agent (found for me by Jeremy Saunders - "Jeremy who?" - *The Shooting Party* producer), because, although she was very nice, she never once got me any work. In fact I ended up sending her money for work that I'd sourced. I also had an American agent who never got me any work. Zalman set me up with a young gun at his agency, Triad, called Joe Rosenberg. I only ever met him once. He said I would be handled on a day-to-day basis by his junior associate, Charlotte. That sounded fun. But throwing cold water over

that novelty - what I absolutely did not expect - was that Charlotte was an Etonian! Bloody Etonians get everywhere. Charlotte Safavi had done her A-levels at Eton on secondment from a neighbouring posh school. She was very nice too. But Triad never got me any work either.

West Hollywood was a gay city. By which I mean that it had a City Council that was pre-dominantly gay. That meant that all the verges were neatly clipped, and there were little white dogs everywhere being walked on them. Specific to West Hollywood, every new building had to have a meaningful piece of art on display for the benefit of all before it was signed off by building control. Our building had copper cut-outs of a bird, a bull's head and an anteater next to a phallic faux bell tower.

There was a lesbian cafe at the end of the street where you could buy fresh bread in the morning. This was on Santa Monica Boulevard, one block west of La Cienega. Every Halloween there was a spectacular costume parade. Notable in our time was the year when ZaZa Gabor had slapped a traffic cop,

and there were male couples up and down the boulevard having slapping matches, dressed as the pair, but with no seat in the pants of the cop costume. As a couple of 'breeders' moving in with a brand new baby, if we were looking for baby sitters, all the girls next door were boys. I remember stopping for a burger (I know, yuk, before my Damascene moment) along Santa Monica boulevard, with Morwenna in her pram, and four guys squeezing onto one side of a picnic table to watch me eat.

Around the corner, on Holloway, one way was world bookshop, Book Soup, and world record shop, Tower Records, where much money was spent on $15 (sometimes $20) plastic-wrapped, and boxed, and plastic-wrapped again CDs, and the Sunset Strip, where big hair was being tossed and *Rock of Ages* was being lived; and the other way was the Sunset Marquis hotel, where top producers were holding court around the pool, and the Holloway Pre-school where I was dropping Morwenna off to sing "The wheels on the bus go round and round"... Maybe that's what the producers were doing too.

Some extraordinary monster-vehicles descended from the hills to drop kids off at the Holloway Pre-school. Chanel sunglasses hid Lyin' Eyes, but not the smiles that were no disguise. We took Morwenna to some memorable birthday parties. One was at the house of *West Side Story* dancer, and choreographer, David Winters. Instead of a piece of cake in the party bag for 3-year-olds, there were videos, CDs, probably tickets to the Hollywood Bowl.

To the east of La Cienega, West Hollywood became less gay and more Russian mafia. We had a number of friends who lived in rented apartments there. Mostly they were square characterless buildings, with fluffy fitted carpets and street views. If we'd stayed renting, we'd likely have ended up in one of these. It would not have

been the same. It would have been fine. But it would not have been the same.

The piece de resistance in our beautiful first family home was a private Mexican-tiled roof terrace under the Californian sunshine. We planted bougainvillaea, but it was it too wonderfully hot up there even for bougainvillaea. So instead I drove my van to northern California to an antique bathroom store in a mountain community called Angels Camp, and bought a large claw-foot porcelain tub. This I plumbed in to the roof terrace, against city ordinances, and spent a lot of time in over the next three years, waving at helicopter pilots.

In the next door unit was a young director called Michael Bay. He had a little white dog, but said it was his mother's. Aural evidence suggested that he was not gay, as many nights we lay in bed listening to him clearly thrilling young ladies... and me, ever the Englishman not wanting a fuss, worrying that he could hear our little girl screaming for a different reason. Colic. Michael's living room floor was a carpet of black & white 10x8s of female actresses and models. He was making Donny Osmond videos at the time, something that I enjoyed reminding him when he passed through Knebworth three decades later making *Transformers 5* (2017). When he started making blockbusters, not long afterwards, I noticed that in every film a little white dog comes to a

nasty end. I guess the little white dog must have been his mother's.

But, as mentioned, by far the most entertaining neighbour was the Ramada Hotel swimming pool. In those more enlightened times, very little was worn, and most guests were in L.A. to party. Airline stewards and stewardesses were regulars. And there was overspill from the gym opposite, The Sports Connection - known to us as The Sports Erection. Particularly entertaining were the gay weddings (then legal in California, but not in many other places around the world), merry lesbian couples in flouncy white wedding dresses ending up tussling in the swimming pool, like amorous frogs on waterlilies.

Little Morwenna found this all very entertaining. She was, as today, a child on the move. Even as a babe, she was happiest being swayed in the air in front of well-worn VHSes of favourite music videos. When I was in charge, this was *Greatest Hits* of the Blow Monkeys and Everything But The Girl. When she took control, it was Paula Abdul, and more Paula Abdul. We inherited an old orange-brown arm

chair from an elderly neighbour in Mentone Avenue, that's still in our kitchen at Knebworth House today. Little Morwenna would bounce & bounce & bounce on it all day long.

I am asked today, how much fun was it to live on the Sunset Strip during this time of Guns N' Roses, and Motley Crue, and the Viper Room? I'm abashed to reply that despite having a partner who knows every word of *Sweet Child O' Mine*, not only were babysitter nights usually spent at the movies (my reason, after all, for being in L.A.), but musically my tastes whilst in America had become resolutely un-American. Like Denys Finch Hatton and Reginald Berkeley Cole clinging to A. E. Housman in Africa, my wallowing in my roots was to the very British nostalgia of Everything But The Girl's *Idlewild* and the very British pop politics of the Blow Monkeys' *She Was Only A Grocer's Daughter* and *There Goes The Neighbourhood*. For me this time was all Dr Robert N' Paul Weller, not Tommy Lee N' Slash - which would, I accept, have given this chapter more interesting stories of life just off the Sunset Strip in 1990.

And if it wasn't British music I was trawling for in Tower Records, it was project-related music - and therefore, at this time, world music. I have always used music as a writing tool. I will play the same music relentlessly, over and over again, when writing a screenplay. So that, if I take a break, when I come back to the piece, the music instantly puts me back in it. So for *Sirens* I was listening to Neapolitan music - indigenous Campanian sirens like Lina Sastri and Giulietta Sacco. For *Madrid '37* I was listening to flamenco and the (not really Spanish, but Gitanos French) Gypsy Kings and the (not Spanish at all, but German) Ottmar Liebert... and of course the Blow Monkeys' tribute to *La Passionaria* and her rallying cry *¡No Pasarán!*.

Nothing, however, was to send my love of world music into overdrive more than my next job, and my next employer. For the time has come for me to go work in an office again. For my L.A. dad. Zalman King.

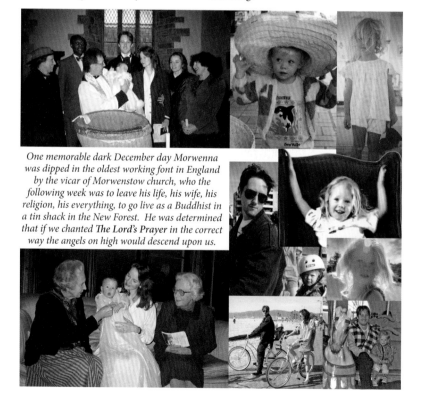

One memorable dark December day Morwenna was dipped in the oldest working font in England by the vicar of Morwenstow church, who the following week was to leave his life, his wife, his religion, his everything, to go live as a Buddhist in a tin shack in the New Forest. He was determined that if we chanted The Lord's Prayer in the correct way the angels on high would descend upon us.

CHAPTER TWENTY-ONE

Zalman

You can believe me, or you can believe your eyes!
(Zalman King - *Red Shoe Diaries: Talk To Me Baby,* 1992)

Music makes a good movie a great movie. And a bad movie worth the price. If I reel off a random list of my all time favourite movies, excluding musicals - *Now Voyager* (1942), *Brief Encounter* (1945), *Letter From An Unknown Woman* (1947), *Dr Zhivago* (1965), *Un Homme et Une Femme* (1966), *Walkabout* (1971), *Don't Look Now* (1973), *Out Of Africa* (1985), *Cinema Paradiso* (1988) *The Unbearable Lightness of Being* (1988), *La Teta Y La Luna* (1994), *The English Patient* (1996), *Lucía Y El Sexo* (2001), *The Notebook* (2004)... every single one of them has a beautiful score.

One filmmaker who absolutely understood this was my L.A. dad - not my 'real' dad, Martin Sheen, but Zalman King. Zalman King's movies all showcase brilliant and beautiful music. Whether the movie is good, or not so good - there was the occasional one that didn't turn out as planned - the music will always be beautiful.

When Zalman's movies are less good, the screenplay, you can be sure, will have been bettter. Take *Wild Orchid* (1989). Defying its critics, *9 1/2 Weeks* (1986) - aided by the VCR revolution, particularly in foreign territories - had now made so much money that Zalman was asked to follow up our wedding video (*Two Moon Junction,* 1988 - note the film's mention of Tuscaloosa) by reuniting with Mickey Rourke for a Brazil-based version of *9 1/2 Weeks.* He and Pat had written a great script, exotic, full of passion, great set-ups, great dialogue... but none of that matters if you arrive on set and it rains every day, and your lead actor won't come out of his trailer because he's botoxed his face into hamster cheeks.

Zalman did not shoot his and Pat's script. He and his beleaguered crew shot what they could, in adverse circumstances. This is a reality Film Critics neither consider, nor make allowance for. It didn't matter in this case. The film was going to make most of its fortune in dubbed, and rubbed, versions. It had sex, Brazil and music, Three words that sit close in the thesaurus. It made money. It led to Zalman being asked to make *Wild Orchid 2, 3, 4, 5*... (although they were not called that). Does that make it a good film? It makes it a good film for Henry Cobbold.

Wild Orchid 2 was called *Blue Movie Blue* - to us, later to the world it became *Wild Orchid II: Two Shades of Blue*. The film was in post-production in 1990, and Zalman's personal assistant Steven Kaminsky was being given a producer role. Zalman needed a new personal assistant. Should I go work for a friend? It could end in tears... Ultimately there were tears. And all the other emotions you look for in a good narrative. But at the end of two and a half epic years working with Zalman, I had, at last, fulfilled the dream I'd had since I was eight.

Zalman's office at the time was a little further down Wilshire from Martha's rolling skyscraper. It too stood on its own, a beautiful Art Deco island called the Omaha building, next to the old Carnation Milk factory. Sweetened canned condensed milk. How Los Angeles is that? Even after we left the Omaha building, I continued to enjoy visiting the building to get my hair cut by a mysterious English girl called Amanda B (for Benzaken). As much as I was assimilated into America culture, I was only ever going to have an English haircut.

View downtown from Zalman's office in the Omaha building on Wilshire - doesn't quite stitch together, seemingly because the air is clearer toward towards the hills, mountains & snow

Zalman's office was on the east side of the building, looking downtown (see above). The cafe/bar on the west side of the building was, we were told, a haunt of Leonard Cohen - I remember it for lunchtime discussions about whether all the carrot juice Zalman was drinking was turning his skin orange.

Working at Zalman's side would have been fun if we'd been carving the holes in the end of toothbrushes. As it was, we were making movies. Post-production was Zalman at his most relaxed, and much of the time at the Omaha building was working on the editing, ADR, and - most fun - the music for *Blue Movie Blue*.

The film was about the daughter of a jazz trumpeter and - like most of Zalman's work - wall-to-wall music. We were working with one of Hollywood's great not-as-appreciated-as-he-should-be composers George S. Clinton. The S. was to keep him out of Parliament-Funkadelic. Although, but for the hair, I'm sure he could have pulled that off. He pulled off the *Austin Powers* soundtracks subsequently.

Films are cut to guide tracks. A composer's nightmare, as guide tracks tend to be the director's favourite music, that the composer then has to better. And few directors have as fine and eclectic a music taste as Zalman King. I recall a good deal of Miles Davis in the *Blue Movie Blue* guide track. Zalman had been a producer on the film *Siesta*, written by his wife Pat, which had featured Miles Davis's music, and *Sketches of Spain* had been on the CD player pretty constantly since. It was awesome watching George pull off a truly beautiful score to replace a Miles Davis guide track. I recall only one piece of music on the guide track that became so ingrained in the edit that it wouldn't have made sense not to go get the rights of the original, The Neville Brothers' perfect Cadillac-in-the-dust lament *Sons and Daughters (Reprise)*.

Listening to *Sons and Daughters (Reprise)* now puts only one image in my head. The distinctly worn and pitted face of actor Robert Davi in Raybans and a Stetson. It was fun to be working with actors again. I'd been sitting in front of a computer in the spare bedroom for five years. In that time Robert Davi had been trying to kill Timothy Dalton. Can't argue with that. He'd been the prime villain in Dalton's Bond film *Licence To Kill (1989)*. Although by this time, I was beginning to forgive Timothy Dalton. I'd met him at a party at Jonathan Lynne's house with my friends Tom and Maureen Reed. He told me he'd just found the screenplay for *Green For A Season* on his shelf. Indeed. That's where he'd left it. He had also turned up that summer at Knebworth '90, the giant charity concert that featured every British music megastar. I was on the roof of Knebworth House with Rob Wade as Paul McCartney played *Live and Let Die*. Rob and I imagined Timothy, at that moment, was rolling around doorways backstage with gun fingers in the air. Nowadays, seven Bond scripts later, that's the way Rob Wade enters a room.

What you learn in Post-Production is how malleable film is to be both augmented and fixed. A change of inflection in ADR, a re-written line, a mood-changing musical cue, the surgical extraction or implant in editing of a sigh, a glance, a pause... can turn a film on a sixpence. It is dangerous knowledge. Because although such magic is possible, there aren't usually many sixpences left at this stage in a movie. But I was soaking up this evil knowledge, learning, learning, learning, from Zalman... but in nothing was I learning more from Zalman than in the trade of screenwriting.

My time with Zalman was an old-fashioned apprenticeship. I wrote good screenplays before. But doing time at Zalman's side I became a better screenwriter than other screenwriters. Unless you are lucky enough to work with your peers in a Writers' Room or actively work with a mentor like this, you are at a disadvantage. Most young screenwriters don't have this opportunity. You can read Robert McKee, Syd Field, John Truby... You can learn the rules. But there is no substitute for working alongside someone who is living by what he is writing. Day on day. These pages of written words were earning money. They were attracting talent. They were the life-raft that everyone was clinging to on turbulent studio and location sets.

My job was to sit with Zalman as he scribbled over countless re-writes. I needed to be at his side not least to be able to read and re-type the scrawl I'd seen expressed as he wrote it. I was to be a sounding board, to laugh when it was funny, not to laugh when it was not funny, to be a thesaurus, an eye-line, a response. Zalman had for many years been an actor, and his greatest talent was dialogue, wonderful

Photo: Chloe King

stream-of-consciousness lines - usually a character's cock-eyed defence as to why he should be forgiven for having fallen in love with you, why he may look like a punk, a hustler, but actually he's as sweet as your grandma's fruit pie made with those cherries you used to hitch up your dress to collect for her from her orchard when you were in bobby socks...

Seductions, in other words. Sweet seductions. And we were about to embark on the perfect project to suit this supreme talent of Zalman's. A far-sighted exec (every blue moon blue, one comes along) from the cable channel Showtime, Steve Hewitt, was looking to up his channel's original content. Big rival, HBO, was having increasing success with original content. The cable channels needed projects that the networks and their conservative advertisers could not contemplate. HBO was making the horror series *Tales From The Crypt* (filming one episode *Fatal Caper* with Natasha Richardson at Knebworth House) and taboo-challenging comedy shows with Larry Sanders and Tracey Ullman. If HBO were doing horror and comedy, it made sense for Showtime to do sex.

Red Shoe Diaries was to be a feature film, followed by a spin-off series. In the pilot film, a successful L.A. architect discovers his adored wife's diary after her suicide, and learns of a whole alternative life he knew nothing about. To help him understand how he could have been blind to this, he posts a classified ad for women to send him their stories of betrayal and passion... and 66 half hour shows ensue. *Red Shoe Diaries* became Showtime highest-rated original show, and popular across the world. Particularly, for some reason, in Canada and South Korea.

I was keeper of the script. Sometimes more than one version of the script. There would be a version for Showtime. A slightly hotter version for the foreign video market financiers like Mark Damon (another former actor whose company

Vision continued to co-finance Zalman after *9½ Weeks)*. And, hardest for me to reconcile, a slightly different version for his co-writer, his wife, Pat. This deception sounds worse than it was in reality. Usually it was a version with the odd line left in that Pat felt passionate about, but which Zalman did not wish to argue at this point. And here it gives me great pleasure to chip in that, brilliantly, in all my time at his side, in charge of his diary and his address book - and through all the passion, and all the erotica - I never saw Pat and Zalman's relationship threatened by physical indiscretion. Not a single instance. And I certainly saw opportunities that would have taken up by others. Pat and Zalman's marriage was a rare thing of beauty. I have seen it once or twice in my life, and nothing awes me more. There was no hidden Red Shoe diary in Zalman & Pat's house.

When Zalman's films are praised, it tends to be for being the first films to give mainstream erotica a female perspective. Certainly Red Shoes - or indeed any of Zalman's films of this period - would not have had the success they enjoyed if they hadn't reached a female audience. Behind this, fundamentally, was Zalman's greatest strength. His co-life. His wife. Pat.

Pat co-wrote the script for *Red Shoes Diaries*. She brought the wonder and the magic to Zalman's films. She brought out Zalman's sweetness amongst all the bad behaviour, passion and rage that make the drama. Zalman had the sweetness in him, but Pat brought it out. Together they created lovers that the audience wanted to share trauma with; wanted to overcome misunderstandings with; wanted, actually, to have sex with under a broken drainpipe in a city underpass...

Pat's influence is all over Zalman's films. Not only in the scripts, but also in the mis-en-scene (sorry - Film Studies word - 'stuff that fills the frame'). The architect's apartment in *Red Shoe Diaries* is not the apartment you will see in any other director's movie. It is rich with beautiful, esoteric

Self-portrait. Patricia Louisianna Knop

works of art that could only have been collected by Patricia Louisianna Knop. There is reason for the line of mad brilliant artists wanting to work with Pat - Jacques Demy, Agnes Varda, Jim Steinman, Andrew Lloyd Webber, Barbra Streisand...

As long as money and credits are not being discussed, filmmakers will tell you that the most important element of a movie is the script. Although, as a paid up member of the Writers Guild of America West, I'd truly like to believe that, I'm afraid, I don't. I know plenty of people - and see more on Twitter - who would quite happily pay to watch David Duchovny (star of *Red Shoe Diaries,* right) read his gas bills. Or for that matter listen to his music albums. Casting is the most important element of filmmaking.

If you get the casting wrong, it makes no difference if you've written the funniest joke in the world. It makes no difference if you are the Poet Laureate. People don't care. They want to spend Friday night with Tom Cruise.

Casting *Red Shoe Diaries* was even more fun than watching it being written. I accompanied Zalman on countless casting calls. This process is like Fantasy Celebrity *Blind Date*. Spending time with naturally appealing people trying to impress you, and up for playing party games. How much fun is that? But there is a price to pay. If you choose No. 1 fella from Woking, when you should have chosen No.2 fella from South Shields, your film will suck.

When we got to the Red Shoes series, we were interviewing every up-and-coming actor there was in Hollywood in the early 1990s. Some of those who ended up in the show went on to become household names - eg David Duchovny, Matt Le Blanc - and others, household faces - Arnold Vosloo (*The Mummy*, 1999), Robert Knepper (*Prison Break*, 2005), Tcheky Karyo (*Baptiste*, 2019), etc. But two meetings that didn't result in casting left the biggest impression on me.

It was probably on Robert Davi's advice that we went to meet his co-cast-member from *Licence To Kill* (1989) a young Benicio del Toro in his apartment in Fairfax Towers. I don't remember the reasons for not casting him - possibly his command of English at that time (Zalman's dialogue needed rapid-fire nuanced delivery) - but the image in my head of a gracious and genuine young foreign actor in a character-less rental apartment looking for his Hollywood break has stuck with me. When he not only got his break, but got an Oscar for it (*Traffic* in 2000), I had one of those rare warm feelings for Hollywood and its sweetened milk and dream factories.

The other meeting to leave an impression was just plain bizarre. For me. Not for anybody else. Interviewing Renée Soutendijk seemed absurd. Here was the star of two of my very favourite films - Paul Verhoeven's *Spetters* (1980) and *The Fourth Man* (1983) - both of which we had watched endlessly at college. We needed to interview her? We needed Renée Soutendijk to read lines?... Even if Zalman and the other producers had been familiar with her work, it was, of course, perfectly appropriate for her to read for the part. It just seemed very odd to me. She was not cast. Instead all Hollywood could come up with for Renée Soutendijk were a couple of cookie-cutter B pictures, so - who would blame her - she retreated back to Holland. At least 25 years later she is back being cast in interesting films, e.g. the *Suspiria* remake by Luca Guadagnino. Ironically her co-star in *Spetters* and *The Fourth Man*, Jeroen Krabbé, did get cast in a Zalman film a couple of years later, *Business For Pleasure*, directed by Rafael Eisenman and co-written by Laline Paull (m.o.w.l.).

Who we did cast, was David GoDownOnMe- sorry, Duchovny (the former was a name adopted for him by an office paramour). And this was great casting. David was smart, sexy, funny, very watchable, very like Zalman. A great alter ego for Zalman. And about to become very famous worldwide in an even longer running series, *The X-Files* (1993). He became so famous and sought after that it's to his credit that he had sufficient respect for Zalman to come back and film the wrap-arounds for all five season of *Red Shoe Diaries*. I enjoyed working with David, and am disappointed he hasn't lived up to his promise of turning up at a Knebworth concert one day. My disappointment will be slightly greater if he turns up to sing at one.

I don't recall a casting meeting for our tragic heroine, Canadian actress, Brigitte Bako - but there must have been one. I do recall a hiccup when the insurance company questioned an element of her health check at that time. Probably something perfect for her role as a tragic heroine. It's an exposing and personal business being an actor. Which is why it seemed absurd that Brigitte, or her agent, insisted on a body double for a planned close up of her naked backside. This is a dangerous

request for an actress to make, for the temptation is to give her a much bigger one. As it was, I was given the job of matching Brigitte Bako's ass. I was tasked with auditioning naked butts to find a match. As Ben Elton used to say, "my mother thinks I work in a bank".

Brigitte, of course, was given approval of the chosen butt. I am not sure why. She's the one person who's never seen her own butt. Certainly not from the angle that it was going to be shot. As it was, she did end up choosing a bigger one. If I may venture an opinion on this very subjective subject, I thought Brigitte's own was finer. But, again, we have probably stumbled on another reason why Brigitte was good casting for the self-tortured, troubled heroine of *Red Shoe Diaries*.

Billy Wirth & Brigitte Bako on set

For her illicit lover, Zalman chose Billy Wirth, an absurdly good looking actor with Native American blood, brimming with faux-innocent charm. Again this was great casting. Stir David Duchovny and Billy Wirth together in a big pot and what would come out would be pretty damn close to Zalman King. They were the perfect sparring pair. And both good basketball players, which made for the great, gritty basketball showdown at the end of the movie to the heavy funk of James Brown's *The Payback*.

Billy Wirth was my first experience of a Hollywood entourage. Billy did not show up as just Billy Worth. Billy showed up as Billy Wirth & Adrian Vitoria. Adrian was an English actor also blessed with more good looks and charm than is quite decent. Billy & Adrian were inseparable, and the two of them were the mischievous George (Michael) & Andrew (Ridgeley) of the set, having certainly more fun than was decent.

Adrian remained a good friend, and when he returned to England became a fine director of commercials, documentaries and feature films starring Sean Bean. He talked me into appearing in a documentary for U.K. Cable TV about posh people doing unusual jobs (*A Bit of Posh* 1998) - something I would only have done for him, but now am grateful to have in my possession as a record of an unusual time that will feature later in this story. He married actor & producer Rosie Fellner, niece of Tim Bevan's partner at Working Title, Eric Fellner. Adrian was the first to tell me, early this century, that there was a way to watch only television you want to watch - in England it was called Sky+ - which has since been somewhat of a revelation to me, meaning I haven't watched random television since. I think of him every time I watch Sky+. The last time I saw him was at my 50th birthday party, a neck-tie round his head, partying like there was no tomorrow. He died of a brain cancer aged 48 in 2016. I miss Adrian.

Billy Wirth was a pall bearer at Adrian's funeral in rural Suffolk. It was the first time I'd seen Billy since *Red Shoe Diaries*. Amongst the many sad images of that day, there's one image that is gradually erasing the others, and continues to make me smile. I can picture Adrian grinning too. Crossing the village from the church to the graveyard, Billy excused himself from our conversation about Zalman and Los Angeles 25 years ago, and jumped purposefully up on to a farm gate... to take a photograph of a sheep. It was a thing of great excitement to Billy Wirth to see a sheep.

I have rewatched *Red Shoe Diaries: The Movie* (1992) recently. I loved it. It holds up well. The only thing that really dates it - apart from its mainstream sensuality, which you don't see in today's romance recession - is David's baggy suit. Nowadays he'd be in tight fitted pants. Which would be a lot harder to get off.

Part of the reason *Red Shoes* hasn't dated as much as other movies of the period is, again, Zalman's eclectic taste in music. The opening funeral scene, for instance, is played beneath an exquisitely beautiful Ugandan lament by Geoffrey Oryama. It was one of my favourite jobs working for Zalman to be sent to trawl through Tower Records to find great music - usually World music. How great a job is that? To get paid to go find great music. For me that beats even casting bottoms.

Red Shoes' Music Supervisor, Toni Ellis, had her work cut out for her clearing the rights to some of the music we fell in love with. *Mujer* by old-school Mexican composer Augustin Lara was a challenge, as I don't think anyone at that record company spoke English. But what a beautiful track.

It wasn't all World Music. Richie Sambora was commissioned to write a blues track, and I remember the excitement when a tape arrived and we first heard *Never Really Know*. We spoke to up-and-coming Scottish band Texas about their music featuring in the film, and our sound man Stephen Halbert insisted that we listen to the Louisiana band The Subdudes - neither of these bands made it into the movie, but I still today buy every record put out by The Subdudes, and Texas's exquisite

Say What You Want features regularly in my playlists... I enjoy its Italian version too, *Fai Che Ci Sei* by Paola Turci - another lifetime favourite artist from this time, introduced to me by Steven Kaminsky's partner, another great Music Supervisor, Dawn Solér. As you can tell, a happy alternative career for me would have been as a Music Supervisor.

For *Red Shoe Diaries*, Zalman King's company 10dB moved from Wilshire Boulevard to a large group of warehouses in Canoga Park in the Valley. More of a commute, but a thrill to be working in a studio environment together with the whole team - pre-production, production and post-production. I got on well with the talented, eclectic and international group that Zalman and his business partner David Saunders had assembled. I even got on with pit bull producers Rafael Eisenman and Butch Kaplan, whose job was to be ruthless and unpleasant to everyone, so Zalman and David could play Good Cops. Not that, at work, Zalman was always his sweet self.

I wish now that I'd spoken more to Zalman about his acting days. The series that made him a household name in the US, *The Young Lawyers*, has recently been released on DVD in the US. He is great in the show. Watching it, I wonder if he was given the hard time that he occasionally gave to his actors. For Zalman would have no qualms emotionally torturing actors to get a performance out of them. I blame Lee Strasberg. Zalman was of the generation that believed that a performance needed to be real, that emotions needed to be felt, not acted. He could turn into Mr Hyde on set if he was not getting what he wanted from an actor... or indeed a crew member. I remain unconvinced that screaming and shouting is the best way to create results. But there are many directors who do work this way. Our West Hollywood neighbour, Michael Bay, comes to mind. It tends to be more of a Hollywood thing.

Then it came time to do the *Red Shoe Diaries* series. 63 episodes, That's a lot of television to write. Who's going to do that?

CHAPTER TWENTY-TWO

Writers' Dept

"Be here tomorrow night when two strangers use a fax machine to send scorchingly erotic commands."

"Yesterday it was just a fax machine. Tonight it becomes an instrument of erotic commands from a sexy stranger."

(Showtime trails for *Red Shoes Diaries: Double Dare* (1992)

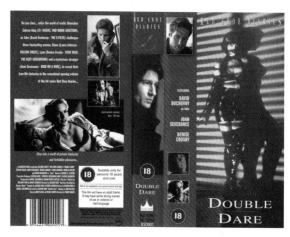

The first episode of the series *Red Shoe Diaries* to be made was called *Double Dare*. It was about a relationship between two people whose windows faced each other. Been there. See p.84. Although the script was not mine, I began to take some ownership over it. I contributed not only that tale from my Eton days, of me and the bursar's daughter window talking - which is told in the voice over of the episode - but also a fair bit of the writing. Zalman encouraged this. It was a busy time.

I inserted a scene where the first time a fax is sent by the sexy stranger in the window opposite, the heroine's secretary picks it up and assumes it's copy for an ad campaign. It became the first scene I wrote to be included in a commercial film.

The first dialogue of mine included in a commercial film became:

> SECRETARY
> I'm late. I'm late... Wish me luck.
>
> DIANA
> Hey, who is it tonight? Charlie, that gynaecologist from Tarzana?
>
> SECRETARY
> His name is Charles. And he's very nice.

Clearly brilliant. But even this was a rewrite. Zalman had rightly rejected 'Charlie, the toothbrush maker with the convertible Falcon'. But I was not going to get a credit for this script. That would go to another friend of Zalman's, whom I'm sure deserved it for something he wrote previously. I'd learnt from my early days in movies that credits do not directly equate with work done - as previously mentioned, in England in 1984, I had worked hardest on the film *Ordeal By Innocence*, which was the only job of that time I did not get a credit on.

During ADR for *Double Dare* I got one of Zalman's Spock eyebrows as I became increasingly vocal about how certain lines should be delivered. Time to give me my own episode. I was sent across the old MGM studio lot (then Columbia Studios, part of the Sony Corporation, whose sound studios we were using) to the studios' old Writers' Rooms (cf the ones in *Barton Fink*, 1991, or the Paramount ones in *Sunset Boulevard*, 1950), to write what was to become the second *Red Shoe Diaries* episode, *You Have The Right To Remain Silent*.

Time to pause again, and consider this. I was working in the Writers Rooms on the old MGM lot. The view from our first L.A. apartment had been the outside wall of this studio. This place was home to *Meet Me In St Louis*, *An American In Paris*, *Singing In The Rain*, *Gigi*, almost every musical I had spent my teenage years mooning over. Gina Davis passed by on the walkway outside the window, and smiled at me. I imagined Ginger Rogers doing the same. Judy Garland. Cyd Charisse. Eleanor Powell... I was now a Hollywood screenwriter.

Almost. I needed work produced. Stop daydreaming and write!

My inspiration for this little teleplay was not Eleanor Powell or Cyd Charisse, but a Brazilian friend, Monica Latvenas (right). As well as collecting World Music, Martha and I spent much of our time in Los Angeles collecting World Friends. Most of the friends we made in L.A. were not from L.A. Most of the people in L.A. were not from L.A. Where we were in L.A. anyway.

We'd held a dinner party in our apartment in Culver City for four of our early friends, none of whom knew each other. There was aforementioned French-Africa-raised Tina Tanen (below left, in the background); John Bruylant, a Belgian, eh (he told me Belgians always end a remark, 'eh'); Veronique Heim, a French Film Sales Agent introduced to us

by Jill Spalding as also 'new in L.A.'; and Daniel Nyiri (left), an Englishman whose French was so good he was clearly Hungarian, a London Film School graduate my Mum had brought to Knebworth as someone she thought I should meet. I think we'd kind of thought John was a good match for Tina and Veronique and Daniel would click. More fool us. Tina and Daniel ended up married. My first 'Best Man' speech in a hotel in South London. Two beautiful children later their marriage imploded, and to this day they still live in the difficult drama that this introduction sparked.

John Bruylant moved back to Europe and married an English girl from Suffolk, Christine - but before he did, he introduced us to Monica and Ivan, a Brazilian foreign exchange dealer living with a French lawyer from Nice, in a very grown-up suburban house with a swimming pool in Northridge in the Valley. Monica was as close to a Zalman King character as I had ever met. In real life, she was a mixture of all his post-*9½ Weeks* heroines. Smart. Successful. Looking for Perfect. Drawn to Imperfect. A wild orchid in Kenneth Cole red shoes. She is in the *Red Shoes Diaries* movie. She appears briefly in the birthday party scene. Not by any aforethought, but in the curious way that things turn out, Monica became either the source or the inspiration for almost all of the fiction of mine that was produced in the 1990s.

First up, *You Have The Right To Remain Silent*. Monica told me of a beautiful guy she saw every morning at the Gym. Unlike everyone else, this guy was not there to preen, or to check out - he was simply there to work out, and leave. Every day. Exactly the same routine. He never appeared to notice her, or any of the other beautiful women - or men - working up a sweat around him... It was driving her crazy.

And so in my script, Monica became a policewoman, who smashes this guy's car tail-light and pulls him over on the way home. She ties him up in an abandoned warehouse and - now she has his undivided attention - enters into a battle of the wits attempting to seduce him. Even in this state, he maintains a control over her, exposing her insecurities, messing with her mind... etc.

To play the woman Zalman hired Denise Crosby. Bing Crosby's granddaughter. Bing Crosby's granddaughter. Sorry, I had to write that twice. And for the guy - all credit to him - Zalman saw not a muscled gym bunny, but an intense and chisel-faced young actor from Ohio called Robert Knepper (right), who'd been in a handful of indies and the Brat Pack movie *Young Guns II* (1990). Robert has gone on to become the best male actor friend I have. He came to London subsequently to do a Tennessee Williams play at the National Theatre. He may be one of the world's finest actors, but nothing he can do in his career will ever impress me more than the nightly athleticism of stepping on the back of a wooden chair to bring yourself to the ground. Few have seen it in him, but Robert is a hoofer at heart - and I have been trying to get him in a musical ever since. Instead he became a worldwide star playing a paedophilic psychopath. T-Bag in the series *Prison Break*.

Punting with T-Bag, as you do

One thing that we noticed at the Red Shoes studio at the time that needed redressing was that this series about women's inner feelings and fantasies was being dreamt up by, mostly, men. Pat was still writing for the show, but from home - clearly we needed some female writers on staff, in the writers room, telling us that we knew nothing.

At that time a friend of Martha's from New York University, Melanie Finn (right), had moved to L.A., where she was seeing a musician from the band Blues Traveller. If our friend Monica had the aura of a Zalman King heroine, Melanie at that time, to my eyes, had the aura of an Emmanuelle Arsan - the novelist and eponymous heroine of the *Emmanuelle* films - a free-spirited, globetrotting photo-journalist chasing adventures. English, brought up in Africa, Melanie was an inveterate traveller to every exotic outpost of the earth, collecting stories that will soon make her a popular screenwriter and author. Melanie took offence at this comparison, but I meant it as a compliment. Where I had grown up, in the 1970s, the Emmanuelle Arsan character's independence and free spirit (reflecting that of contemporaries Nancy Friday and Erica Jong) was a positive and politically-sound result of the 1960s. The exotic globe-trotting I had done in my imagination as a teenager was through Emmanuelle adventures, and those of James Bond. The comparison was not specifically a reference to Melanie's sex life, any more than if I'd compared her to James Bond I'd have been referencing a tendency to violence. She forgave me. I think? I did get her a job as the first staff writer on *Red Shoe Diaries: The Series*. She went on to write 16 episodes - more than anyone apart from Zalman.

On the roof with Melanie in Manhattan

The first episode that Melanie wrote became the first episode of the series to be broadcast, *Safe Sex*, starring Joan Severence, who'd been in a Mel Gibson film, *Bird On The Wire* (1990), and Steven Bauer, who starred alongside Al Pacino in *Scarface* (1983). Melanie wrote the greater part of the episode, but as was the custom with credits, 'pass it along', and 'seniority rules' - so I shared equal billing. It was about a couple attempting to have a commitment-free relationship, one purely based on regular no-strings sex.

For Showtime to have chosen this episode to kick off the series, it must have been pretty good. But I remember my father visiting the editing rooms as it was finished. It was the first produced work of mine he had ever seen. At the end of it, the only thing he had to say was that he didn't understand why girls shaved their pubes into a landing strip. Not sure why this bothered him. Especially as an ex-RAF man.

Meanwhile, I was still Zalman's assistant and helping him with the fourth of the opening episodes of the *Red Shoe Diaries* series, *Talk To Me Baby*. This episode was vintage Zalman. A 20-minute monologue in a moving fast car by his star of *Two*

Moon Junction, Richard Tyson, as he tries to talk his way out of an indiscretion. It is not what people pick up on about Zalman, but episodes that he wrote himself tend to be the comic ones. These episodes remain my favourites of the series. Another good example is *Love At First Sight*, perhaps my favourite *Red Shoe Diaries* episode, because of its comedy, and because it is so 'Zalman'.

Zalman was much less interested in writing the incidentals that surrounded his magnificent marathon monologue in *Talk To Me Baby*. So I wrote the opening scene of the wet t-shirt contest that gets our hero into trouble. I looked to make it as kitch as possible. Richard Tyson is from the South. I named the girl that catches his eye, Regina, from North Carolina. Now, to me, that can only be said by a sleazy Southern compere, as "Re-gina [as in vagina] from North Carol-ina" - and so I meant it to be said. But that did not happen. As filmed, the compere repeats again and again "Regina [as in weiner] from North Carol-ina". It sounds so odd to me. And it has puzzled me since that the director missed this. But it's a good lesson for scriptwriters. Spell out every joke. Because more than likely you won't be there when it's told.

Zalman was also, at this point, too busy to direct everything. Of these first four episodes, he directed *You Have The Right To Remain Silent* and *Safe Sex*, but *Talk To Me Baby* was directed by our Israeli producer, Rafael Eisenman. Rafi, to me, had the air of a Mossad hitman retired to where he couldn't cause too much trouble. National Service in Israeli when Rafi was doing it was, I'm sure, all about teaching you how to despatch screenwriters with your bare hands. I recall few conversations with Rafi. Silence was his preferred weapon of both attack and defence. In defence it meant avoiding expressing an opinion. The one conversation I do recall 30 years later was his interest in the laundry advantages of a foreskin, for catching semen - funny what sticks in the head. It usually concerns the bed. Rafi was also given the job of directing a new feature film to be made whilst the Red Shoes series was on going. This was to be written by Zalman and his new 'Writers Dept.', Henry Cobbold & Melanie Finn. At last I was writing a feature film that was going to be made.

What's the difference between a TV episode and a feature film? It's a reasonable question to ask in our current golden age of television. In days gone by, television was a lower caste to film. Television was mostly free. Film actors did not wish to be seen as television actors. If an actor could be seen for free on television, why pay to go see them at the movies? Of course cable and, eventually, subscription television put paid to this, but even Cable TV in the early 1990s was a risk for a film actor. All credit to David Duchovny, therefore, for being one step ahead in this game. Indeed, David should be seen as one of the pioneers in breaking down this prejudice.

But cinema was always going to be special to me. After a childhood of trips to the Letchworth Broadway and the Letchworth Palace, and then London's

Melanie Finn

Odeon Leicester Square, the Odeon Marble Arch - there was always going to be a special thrill at seeing something up on a big screen in a cinema rather than in the corner of a living room on a box. Of course now the box in the corner is a giant centrepiece on the wall. Whereas screens at the old picture palaces, like the Letchworth Broadway, are now split into multiplexes and not much bigger than TVs.

I was now writing something that I would see in a cinema. Not only that, but I would get to see it in a cinema where I had spent and dreamt much of my youth. The Empire Cinema in Haymarket. The one that used to have particularly steep au-ditorium. Don't tell anyone, but by the time my film made it there, in 1994, this beautiful old cinema had also been carved up into a multiplex, and we were on in Screen 3 - which had a screen not much larger than a television. But that title in lights outside the Haymarket Empire was mine. A big life moment for this cinema-obsessed kid (see p.18).

The film followed the same theme as all the stories we were writing. A woman torn between two men. A woman torn between respectability and passion. A woman torn between a husband and a 'hod' (mixture of 'Homme' and 'God' - although also an acronym for 'Hand On Dick'). For this one, our woman was a suburban housewife (Joan Severance again), and our 'hod' a tree surgeon (Billy Zane, about to be the villain in the biggest film ever, *Titanic*, 1997). Having taken him a glass of lemonade, our

Foreign distributors preferred to see the film not as A Woman and Two Men, but A Man and Two Women

housewife gets trapped in the back of the hod's trailer and ends up down the rabbit hole of a beautiful deserted lake somewhere in the country. The white rabbit is a blonde free-spirit (May Karasun) who emerges naked from the lake and wonders why our suburban housewife is so pent up and buttoned up... and unhappy. I gave the lake its name. The name that became the English language title of the film, and would be made up in big black marquee letters outside the Empire Haymarket. *Lake Consequence*.

In simplistic terms, Melanie wrote the First Act of *Lake Consequence* (1992), I wrote the Second Act, and Zalman wrote the Third Act. Zalman's Act was again a long monologue from the hod, charming, sweet and absurd, trying to persuade the woman to go back to her husband and child. Melanie's Act was the set up, the troubled housewife, loving her husband and child but wanting some-

Collecting credits. Thank you Zalman King.

Lake Consequence got a Cable TV release in the United States on the Showtime Channel - and a good review from The Hollywood Reporter

Cable TV review

'Lake Consequence'

By Rick Sherwood

It has all the right elements to fail — a familiar story, familiar fantasies, familiar concepts. But thanks to great acting, a great look, its intimate style and a score that fits like a glove, "Lake Consequence" manages to rush together in a way that sweeps the viewer up and away with its tale of sexual desire, sexual shame and sexual healing.

Indeed, this Showtime original is a true erotic thriller. It's sensual, suspenseful, and surprisingly intriguing, a carefully told story that's both exciting and frightening. It definitely carries that unique stamp of filmmaker Zalman King, who is able to turn his production into the kind of offbeat R-rated erotica in the tradition of such efforts as "Wild Orchid" and "9½

LAKE CONSEQUENCE
Showtime
Showtime Networks Inc.

Executive producer	Zalman King
Producer	Avram Butch Kaplan
Director	Rafael Eisenman
Director of photography	Harris Savides
Screenplay	Zalman King, Melanie Finn, Henry Cobbold
Story	MacGregor Douglas
Associate producer	Steven Kaminsky
Production designer	Dominic Watkins
Editors	James Gavin Bedford, Curtis Edge
Music	George S. Clinton
Cast: Billy Zane, Joan Severance, May Karasun, Whip Hubley, Courtland Mead, Dan Reed
Airdates: Sunday, Feb. 28, 9-11 p.m.; also March 5, 11, 16, 22

Weeks."

Like those films, this one works on many levels. It's not quite as deep, broad or far-out, but it does well to add an intellectual layer that helps in its exploration of good and evil, right and wrong, pleasure *See* **"CONSEQUENCES"** *on page 88*

The Hollywood Reporter   Friday, February 26, 1993

'Consequences'

Continued from page 12—

and emotional pain.

This story finds a young woman literally swept up from her suburban tract home and plunked down in a place of fantasy and excitement — a place that allows her to live out her dreams and sometimes relive her nightmares. There, she's haunted by desire and action, and crippled by flashbacks that ultimately provide the punctuated answer to the riddles of this story.

It's a dark and very moody tale and has a look characterized by a starkness that heightens the feel of this film. The fine cast is led by a wonderfully strong performance from Joan Severance, a former Playboy cover model, who provides her character with dimension and complexity as she searches for sexual satisfaction and sexual healing. Billy Zane, as the strong, silent and slightly scary stranger, does well to contribute to this film's gritty, dark and engrossing feel as well.

May Karasun, another woman thrown into the unusual mix, does well in her supporting role.   □

thing more. And my Act was the middle. The sex. This time someone else was writing 'how did they get to this', and then 'how do they get out of it'.

Now, if you see this film - and there is no reason why you should, it's no longer playing at the Empire Haymarket, and is quite hard to find - you will say, what was there to write in the middle? There is barely any dialogue. Well, there you would be wrong. Only English screenwriters think that a script is all about dialogue. Zalman, in particular, insisted that every image the camera sees, every movement, be written in the script. Especially the sex. No dot-dot-dots in a Zalman King script sex scene. It was, in his words, the 'bread and butter'. He wanted every brushed fingertip, every breath, every swallowed gasp, every bead of sweat - on the page.

Scripts not having this relevant detail is one of the reasons we now have 'Intimacy Coordinators' expected on movie sets. To do the writer and director's job for them. And to prevent a male director from being blacklisted 30 years later for contributing on the day any of his own suggestions as to what he thinks is sexy. I expect there soon to be 'Soul-baring Coordinators'. And eventually 'Acting Coordinators', so the director doesn't have to appear at all from his hiding place behind the monitor

Please don't think I am making light of #MeToo. It's been a vital revolution and has fingernailed out much canker in the industry. But, as with all revolutions, there comes a point where you need to be careful not to flush out the flesh with the worm.

The injustices, bullying and coercion #MeToo has redressed needed to be exposed. But, as Arthur Miller warns us, we need to be wary of witchhunts. In particular in the case of actors. To bring a career to a grinding halt for an incident of inappropriate familiarity on a film set many decades ago smacks of McCarthyism. Especially when we lionise 'method' actors. Especially when we expect our actors to 'live' their roles. When we fete them for putting on weight, taking off weight, staying in character before and during filming, on set and off set. We shower these 'method' actors with awards. In the name of Lee Strasberg, Directors work actors up into an emotional fervour on set - I saw

Zalman do it many times - until they 'are' the troubled hero that you have written. For all heroes must have a troubled past in order to be interesting. Turn your actor into your character, expect him to live and breathe the truth, the passion, the violence - cherish him for it... but then don't be surprised if one time he's over-fresh and inappropriate with the make-up assistant.

What we see as respect in the workplace in the 2010s is not compatible with 'method' Acting. We're going to have to make up our mind which one we want. Personally I'm happy to bin 'method' acting. But I don't see others decrying it. I've already referenced the Laurence Olivier / Dustin Hoffman distinction. Did I mention where it came from? It was an exchange on the set of *Marathon Man* (1976). Hoffman told Olivier that in order to play a scene where his character has been up for three days, he'd prepared by not sleeping for three nights. Olivier's response was, "Why don't you just try acting?"

You'll read Zalman confirming in interviews that his insistence on the 'bread and butter' being in the script is for his actors. Remember he was one. Complete clarity of what is to be seen on screen enabled actors to trust him. He is absolutely right on this. '...' - dot-dot-dot - is lazy screenwriting, that will interrupt a shoot day. But for all the long months we spent writing his screenplays, making sure every comma was in place - and in the process writing some really great scripts - Zalman did have a tendency to turn up on set and shoot something different from what was on the page. Naturally the conditions of the day affect what is shot on the day, but I did get the sense sometimes that - having spent so much time with a script - Zalman was changing things because he'd become bored with it and the way it was written. He seemed to forget that we'd put that comma in there for a reason. I see this as another reason why - occasionally - Zalman's films are not as good as his scripts.

The prime rule of Zalman's Writers' Room was that everything had to come from the heart. And yet his writers could not afford to write from their hearts. Because they could be sure that the work they'd put their heart into would be torn, shredded, masticated, spat out and stamped on in the development process. There was much crumpling up of hard-wrought pages, and watching them fly across the room into full trash cans, accompanied by much shouting. Writers are naturally sensitive folk. Empathy, after all, is the root of all stories. I found this constant criticism tough, but I look back on it now as an important lesson.

"I hated it" is the second best response you can get to your work. Nowadays I feel I have to say to Producers that I've had this Hollywood training. It's okay, tell me that you hated it. Tell me it is the worst piece of shit you've ever read. I am Hollywood-trained. I am inoculated against criticism.

Sadly, you almost never get this. What you do get, in response to months, sometimes years, of work, is... silence. Silence is by far the worst response. Yet the most common.

Worst of all, I've had so much silence over the years that the inoculation is beginning to wear off. I am starting to get sensitive again.

If you hate this book, please tell me you hated it. It's good for me.

Mind you, it's even better for me to be told that you like it. Especially if you told me you hated the last one.

By challenging your passion, beating back against it, Zalman's intent was to grow it, make it more real. Make it 'Method'. But this didn't work for me. I simply learnt how to write-with-my-head whilst making it look like I was writing-with-my-heart. Just to survive. To keep my heart intact. It has been a lesson that has served me well over years of rejection. But, it's possible also, that it's contributed to that rejection. My work will always be born of passion, but I've perhaps been too ready to give that passion a coat of bitumen for the outside world. Too happy to be a hack. Not prepared to be driven crazy for art. I don't know. We'll see...

Meanwhile the pressure in the Red Shoes Studio passion-cooker was increasing. The first four episodes had been a success. Showtime committed to the rest of the series. Time to bring in more writers. Melanie and I were now the 'Writers Dept.', so Zalman needed a new assistant. Clearly this should be another female writer. And why alter a successful pattern? Let's add a third English writer. Zalman's daughter Chloe introduced another English girl, Oxford-educated and of Indian descent, Laline Paull (right).

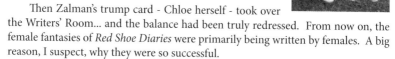

Laline soon moved into the Writers' Room too, and Zalman got a more permanent assistant in Linda Clark.

Then Zalman's trump card - Chloe herself - took over the Writers' Room... and the balance had been truly redressed. From now on, the female fantasies of *Red Shoe Diaries* were primarily being written by females. A big reason, I suspect, why they were so successful.

I'd been doing what I do best. Getting work for other people. And talking myself out of a job. I brought another Oxford-educated Brit into the Red Shoes Studio in the form of a friend of a friend of my younger brother who'd just arrived in Hollywood, George Waud. George was living on a shoe string, and I recall had bought the most clapped-out wreck of a car - the only essential in L.A. - on the basis that its overhead light worked. I got him his first job, in the Red Shoes Art Department. He's gone on to become a producer, scoring well with 2006's *Snakes On A Plane*.

I had one more episode, however, to write. It was another idea inspired by our Brazilian friend Monica Latvenas. Spending one New Year's Eve in California (unusual, as we often went back to England for Christmas & New Year) we had been taken to the beach at midnight by Monica and another half-Brazilian friend, Debbie McCoy (left), to do what coastal Brazilians all do New Year's Eve, make an offering to the sea goddess Iemanja. Dressed in white (we did everything but dress in white), you send your offering out to the sea goddess in a little raft, with a lit candle on it. If the goddess accepts your offering your wishes for the year come true, but if it is rejected and returned to the shore... well, less good. We did this on the beach in California that New Year's Eve of 1991... and it was all rather magical. Also magical were stories of Monica's Brazilian grandmother - her 'Vovo' - who we met around this time.

I had my characters. I wrote an episode of Red Shoe Diaries entitled *Iemanja*. It was set in California, where pages of a diary are picked up off a little raft floating

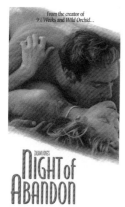

in the Pacific Ocean, etc... I liked it. It was never made. What was made, was a much later draft, renamed *Night of Abandon* - very little of which is recognisable in what was actually filmed by French director René Manzor (who I never met) in Brazil. In fact my two drafts are so different that I list them both in my writing credits, as separate episodes. I had stopped working at the Red Shoes Studio, and it was my turn to be re-written, but still to pick up the screen credit.

A key reason for the Brazilian version was that Zalman had reams of great footage of the Rio Carnival left over from *Wild Orchid*, which were shoehorned into the story. To be frank, *Night of Abandon* makes for a very lovely travelogue, but makes very little sense. It does have, however, my favourite all time image from any movie ever, which I screen grab (from a preview VHS) for you here (it looks even better in digital and without a timecode). I've never been to South America, but in this shot of the skyline of Rio de Janiero - with Corcovado in view - overlaid with 'Written by Henry Cobbold', you would think I was personally responsible for designing the whole glorious city. I must go one day.

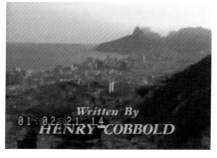

So to write about sex, do you need to have a colourful sex life? My response is that you don't have to commit murder to write about it. In fact it's better for your writing, generally, if you do not commit murder. I learnt as a teenager locked up in a boy's boarding school that nothing is better for the imagination than abstinence. So no, I don't need to have a passionate and illicit affair with a tree surgeon and his girlfriend in a Chinese bath house to be able to write about it.

Having said that - and having once heard a radio phone in where callers were asked to confess to the most unusual place they'd had sex, and the best that most of them could come up with was the beach, the kitchen... I realise I have been fortunate to have had above-average variety in exotic locations for sexual congress.

I have not had sex in South America. But I have had sex in at least one of the following locations (multiple choice in respect of the other party):

1) A cable car suspended high above the Interlarken Valley

2) A Ford Escort whilst driving in the slow lane of the M40 in Oxfordshire

3) The top of a gothic tower whilst below Pink Floyd plays Comfortably Numb...

You don't believe any of these? Then maybe it is all just in my imagination.

There is proof, however, that I have had sex more than once.

That is my second child. My son, Edward.

CHAPTER TWENTY-THREE

Edward

NICK
If you know anything at all about men, Mona Lynn
McCabe, you know that my temporary physical condition
doesn't necessarily mean I want to make love to you.

LYNN
You want me Nick. On the scale of one to ten...
(she looks down)
I'd say you were about nine and a half.

NICK
My cleaning lady, my bank teller, my aunt Louise, give me
hard-ons... that doesn't mean I want to make love to them.

She approaches him. Kissing him gently, she swings a leg
over his lap, straddling him, teasing him.

LYNN
Tell me about your cleaning lady. Tell me about your bank
teller. Tell me about your aunt Louise... You can't tell me
they were ever this close to you.

(*You Have The Right To Remain Silent,* 1992)

I have also never had an affair. At no time have I had sexual relations outside of my marriage. Has that blown Act Two for you? Not enough of a story arc? I know enough about narrative to know that this book would be more interesting if I had. So I've knocked a quid off the price to make up for it.

Of course I have run through the possibility in my head. I am a screenwriter. I have run though the possibility of all sorts of dreadful and dastardly things in my head. But unlike the majority of the human race, I am more interested in the long term than the short term. With the possible exception of chocolate after lunch, I have never knowingly done anything for short term pleasure at the expense of long term pleasure. Plus I am deeply and eternally committed to my consummate wife.

The summer of 1991, however, if my marriage had been a Zalman King screenplay, would have been the time to write in an affair. I'd been married for four years. The seven year itch in my generation had been adjusted for inflation to four. I had a small child in the house taking attention away from me. I wasn't staring out the window at the tree surgeon, but I was working in a highly-charged all hours environment with lots of gorgeous people gorging on emotions and the possibilities of sex.

And then something unusual happened. Unusual enough, that if it had been in a screenplay, no one who knows my wife and I would've believed it. Martha took Morwenna and went on a Mediterranean summer holiday with the whole Lytton Cobbold family without me. I was working. I couldn't go. I stayed behind in L.A.,

For a few weeks, I had a break from the surface elements of my marriage and fatherhood. I reminded myself of a few things that I hadn't done since I was a teenager. I got on the back of a motorbike and went downtown with new friend, Jeremy Parkin (left) - a Yorkshireman by birth, who'd grown up in a neighbouring village in England (but who I'd not met at the time because he was four, considerable, years older than me) and discovered that, still in my 20s, I had enough energy to work all day and go out clubbing with friends all night.

This was fun. I told Martha so on the phone. I said we ought to do more of this. There's another world out there for 20-somethings in Los Angeles. While we are young, and we are here, we should do more of this 'going out to nightclubs' thing. Rightly - as, half a world away, she simultaneously dealt with the tantrums of a two-year-old and the gossipy humour of her inlaws - Martha was disconcerted.

And here - in all seven stories on which all fiction is based - is where relationships can slip. Here is a slippery snake to slide down. He thinks to himself, "well, if she is going to be like that..." He notices the scent of others... I've written this so many times in my career. So I don't need to actually do it. I've read Act Three. And it belies all that high-octane, short-term fun in Act Two.

Did I start speaking Angeleno? I certainly started to preface my sentences with the word "boy" - "boy, the Santa Anas are as hot n' dry today as a bleached Bighorn bone in a Bakersfield's lizard butt"

When Martha got home I felt in the doghouse. Of course, that's a very proverbial doghouse, as any doghouse of Martha's still has fluffy sofas and dogtreats. So I took her out to dinner to a local restaurant that she and I had not been to before. The Maitre D' said, "Your usual table, sir?"

I had some making up to do. I could have sped her up Sunset, imploring her to "Talk To Me, Baby". But I don't have Zalman's charm.

Instead - when we finally got our toddler to sleep - there was some soul-searching, life questions, and tears. There'd increasingly been those over the pressure of my work at this time. I was finally doing what I'd dreamed doing of since I was 8-years-old, for a man I adored, who was both fierce firebrand and father-figure. But flipping between the harsh heat of Zalman's workplace kitchen and the gentle warmth of his home kitchen was conflicting and confusing, and my emotions were being boiled to soup. Soup that, at home, I was serving cold to a distracted and exhausted young wife, cutting coupons to save pennies, whilst bum wiping, snot wiping, plastic piss sheet wiping, sticky crumb wiping, marching ant wiping - cold soup wiping - wondering why she had bothered with a double degree and left New York.

I don't remember too much of this time. But I do remember one make-up session soon after Martha's return from Europe, on the big brown flower-patterned sofa given to us by Pat and Zalman. We were absolutely not tussling in tears saying that what this situation needs is more babies. But, of course, that's what happened.

Martha's second pregnancy was harder than the first. For the first, I remember the main challenge was nighttime trips to Marie Callendars in Culver City to satisfy a craving for cheese and potato soup. For much of this second pregnancy Martha was sick. This got particularly bad over a trip to England at Christmas & New Year 1991/92. There was high fever and a constant, lung-flapping cough. Then early contractions started. The doctors were concerned. They wanted full-time bed-rest. We made it back to L.A. Things settled a bit, but it was a worrying time.

The drama did not stop there. It then became April 1992 in Los Angeles. Drama spilt out onto the streets. "Why can't we all just get along?" pleaded Rodney King. The Police had nightsticked him into the tarmac. Someone videoed it. Riots broke out. South L.A. burst into flames. Looting. Curfew.

It was the curfew that was most bizarre. I'd lived in a city disrupted by riots (Thatcher's London), but I'd never before been confined to my home. Well, not since boarding school. This curfew was city-wide. Being on the streets anywhere in L.A. after dark was an arrestable offence. You Have The Right To Remain Silent.

Into this living movie, arrives my intrepid mother. For the birth of her third

grandchild (my brother Peter and his wife Ginette had given birth to a son, Freddie, two months earlier). In daylight hours it was permitted to drive through South L.A. to the airport. Permitted. Not advisable. It was like driving my Mum through some apocalyptic sound stage set on the Universal Studios tour. But it was La Cienega Boulevard (left). Burnt out, looted shops lined both sides of the street like smoking toast.

We'd booked my Mum into Le Dufy Hotel (now the Chamberlain), which was just up the rise of the hill from our townhouse in West Hollywood. She had a room looking out over the city. Fires burnt all across the skyline. What is this world we were bringing a new life into?

The anger was everywhere. Post-natal Martha, carrying her newborn, was threatened in the convenience store at the bottom of our street. The guy behind the counter had to intervene. A brave thing to do.

With our two small children we were stuck on one side of the street. And my Mum, who had flown 8,000 miles to see us for a few precious days, was stuck in a hotel room on the other side of the street. This was ridiculous. There was no one on the street. Who was going to see us if we crossed the road? We broke curfew.

We bundled up the baby, took hold of Morwenna's little hand, and set off across the street. We were the Von Trapp family. We were climbing every hill. We made it to the hotel. We had not been arrested. But the hotel door was locked. We had no choice but to descend the hill back into Austria.

We got away with this civil disobedience. But we would not have got away with driving to the hospital to give birth. The hospital, as before, was in Santa Monica, a 45 minute drive away. Had Martha gone into labour on one of those curfew nights, I don't know how we would have done that.

As it turned out we got lucky in this respect. It was all about Thursdays. The baby was due on a Thursday, but was born two Thursdays before. It was the Thursday inbetween these two Thursdays that curfew was imposed. I still contemplate what we would have done if Martha had gone into labour only one week early instead of two. I suppose we would have had a police escort to Santa Monica. A police escort through completely empty L.A. streets. How surreal that would have been.

I was pretty sure we were going to be blessed with another girl. The old wives' tale of the way the stomach sits suggested we were. The men I was working for - Zalman King and David Saunders - both had two daughters. They were going the distance to get me into the Writer's Guild union in time for the medical insurance to cover the birth. I am very grateful to them. We made that by the skin of the credits.

In the same hospital, on exactly the same evening - 23rd April 1992 - our G.P. Jan Miyakawa (who had delivered Morwenna) was herself giving birth to twins. She'd had to pass on delivering this one. In fact, as a G.P., she had now had to give up delivering babies altogether. Dictate of the mighty evil rulers of all things. Insurance companies. Our replacement paediatrician, Susan Moyer, was heading off on honeymoon, so it looked as though Martha would have to face - bum face - a locum. As it was, the baby had been wanting to join the party since Christmas, so called our paediatrician back just as she'd hung her white coat in her locker and started to put her sunglasses on.

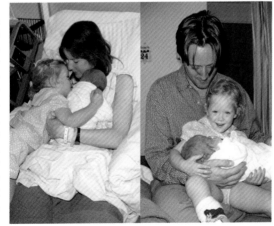

And he was a he. Purple but bonny. We called him 'Edward', after his great-great-great-great-grandfather. I was all ready with 'Lovisalya', middle name 'Need'. And, 'Louisianna' - after Patricia Louisianna Knop. But despite a happy two years at Tulane University, Louisianna wasn't going to wash with a girl from Alabama.

So just as well he was a boy. Although there were vetoes here too. I suggested Bear. That's an Alabama name. Bear Bryant. Alabama football legend. No. Then the name that means 'bear'? The bosom of every Victorian poet. Arthur. After King Arthur. Turns out, in America, this name is more readily associated - as Art - with a suburban accountant. Veto is important in cross-cultural naming. I recall the giggles that greeted the smiley all-American waiter who announced to the table of English children in 1980, "Hi, I'm Randy. What can I do for y'all today?"

But just to make sure his name was still quite silly, we extended it from Edward to Edward Stucley Fromanteel Lytton Cobbold. 'Stucley' for my mother's Devon family. 'Fromanteel' to continue a tradition for all male Cobbolds, in honour of a fertile Dutch ancestor. All credit to Edward's schoolchums, 15 years later, for emblazoning the back of his football shirt: Edward SillyLongName.

Then, if you thought the anxiety of the pregnancy was bad, that was just the thumbscrews. Morwenna had had colic as a baby. Distressing enough. Edward had croup. Croup went beyond distressing to terrifying. When you're taking your newborn out onto the balcony to help the poor little thing breath, it is not a good feeling. Then came the high temperature. Consistent high temperature. Does he have a rash? I can't see a rash. Are you sure he doesn't have a rash?... Back to the hospital. Your paediatrician is on vacation.

The ward doctor wants to give your newborn a spinal tap. Here's the form to sign. A maze of 6-point font. The procedure could result in paralysis. There is a good chance it won't. But we will be sticking a needle into your baby's spine. At this point - with the city burning around you - you wonder if you are actually in Hell.

Edward survives. His temperature eventually subsides. As soon as he is relatively stable, we escape up the coast to Santa Barbara.

And, you know what... in a parallel universe, we'd still be there.

If there was no Knebworth House, I suspect we would be living in Santa Barbara today. Maybe we would have an apartment in Los Angeles. I hope I would be part of some great Writers' Room on a Netflix or Amazon show, or maybe with a first look deal at a studio to direct my own features. Or perhaps I'd be in a Montecito study looking out over the Pacific at those Spanish galleon oil rigs on the horizon writing romantic historical novels...

But that was not to be.

There was pressure for me to come back to England. My father was starting to get nervous, I think, that I would not come back. He and my mother were looking to retire to a house in France. I was now 30, which was the age at which he took over the running of Knebworth House. A beautiful big house on the edge of Knebworth Park was available to us to get settled back in England. We'd be given a few years to learn the ropes. But was I ready to fulfil my destiny?

It was a mad time to come back. My screenwriting career was just starting to take off. After eight years of struggling to get my work made, that was now beginning to happen. My work was at last being produced.

In my head I have the argument that our townhouse in West Hollywood was going to be too small for a family of four, so either we move back to England now or we upgrade to a larger house in L.A. But looking back, I know we could have managed in that house for another few years. The kids were happy sharing a room. Morwenna only tried to pillow-suffocate her little brother once. We had a guest sofa bed in the living room. What's more, the housing market was in a slump. We were going to lose money selling our house now.

It's odd. The convincing reason to move back to England escapes me now. We arrived on 19th April 1993, just in time for Edward's first birthday. There was an au pair to meet us. Maybe that had something to do with it? She wouldn't have been happy on the sofa bed in the living room.

So was it about work? Did Martha want to get back out to work? I can't believe this. Did I need an 'out' from a Writing Team that I had filled with more suitable writers, so it didn't need me anymore? My fellow *Red Shoe Diaries* writers - Melanie, Laline, Chloe... were, let's face it, more female than me, and thus, possibly, better for writing female fantasies. They were also all at a different time of life. They were not leaving the screaming and raging of the work day to go home to a run-ragged partner, shit, vomit and more screaming and raging from a two-year-old and a newborn.

I'm sure your heart is bleeding for me. Plenty of people manage perfectly well in these circumstances, and much much - very much - worse. Martha and I would have made it through this patch. We would have thrived. It's just that I am searching for a reason... because - looking back - going back to England at this point of our lives doesn't really make sense.

It may have oiled the decision that a string of screenplay commissions looked like they were coming my way. From a producer who was actively making movies. Even if I left the Red Shoes Studio I could be confident of still of getting my work made. This producer had a more international wings. He was from Europe, had production and financial relationships across Europe. Maybe it would even be an advantage - now I had my Hollywood training, contacts and credits - to be back in Europe? Maybe? Je ne regrette rien, but - No No No.

We started to prepare. To import our belongings back to England without paying duty, everything had to be at least six months old. It was certainly worth buying white goods in the U.S. for our large house in England. We rented a lock up and - over six months before we were to leave - bought and stored a brand new giant double-doored American fridge, a top-loading washing machine, a top-loading tumble drier... all these things were four times the size of anything you could buy in England, and I knew Martha was not going to enjoy only being able to wash one sheet at a time, as in an English washing machine. No point buying a dish washer, we were told, as the water pressure is different in Europe.

I was certainly going to take my trusted Toyota passenger van back to England, but why not also take a future replacement for it? Cars were so much cheaper in the U.S. We should take back a European car. It would be easier to get parts in Europe. So I bought a Volkswagen Caravelle. A 90s version of the Volkswagen Kombi. All I had to do was to put 7,500 miles on it to escape import duties. I drove it for six months and managed just over 7,000. So a couple of days before it was to be shipped, we drove to San Diego for supper. That just tipped it over 7,500 miles.

The fridge was a great buy. It is still working almost 30 years later. The van not so. It had engine problems from the start, and not only was it not easier to get parts in Europe, it was almost impossible. All spare parts for this supposedly German car had to be purchased in America. When it broke down just north of the Paris Périphérique on a family holiday, it was the final straw. I sold it soon after at a loss. My old Toyota van, however, just kept on going. I had no problem getting parts for this Japanese car in Europe. It survived another couple of decades, became my work van, and made countless family trips the length and breadth of Europe, never giving me any trouble. I have only ever bought Toyotas since.

Already over six months old was my 6ft bath tub. This we unplumbed from the roof terrace and slid down our Adobe wall. Together with our 17 candlesticks and 6 silver trays, we piled it into a 40ft container to be sailed through the Panama Canal.

Before the container was sealed, I asked the movers to give me 30 minutes more. In my van I sped up to Sunset Boulevard to the framing shop where, for my whole life in California, I had admired a giant 1940s poster of Hitchcock - and Joan Fontaine's - *Rebecca*. "It's not for sale." I pleaded. I had a 40ft container. I was never going to have a 40ft container again. This was the only time in my life this opportunity was going to arise. He could have asked for my first born. Maybe not my first born. But I did start laying $100 bills on the table... I think it was on four, he said, "Take it! Get outta here! Before I change my mind!.

CHAPTER TWENTY-FOUR

England

ROSEMARY
What will Heaven be like?

HUGH
England.. on a June afternoon.

(Ron House, Alan Shearman & Diz White - *Bullshot* 1983)

My prized Rebecca poster - at two metres high, 6ft 6, well over a foot taller than Joan Fontaine

This treasured piece of Hollywood has hung on the walls of Knebworth House ever since. Not quite true. To begin with, this beautiful poster - and all my other beautiful Joan Fontaine artwork - hung on the walls of the Old Estate Office across the courtyard from Knebworth House. A corner was set aside as a new office for me. At one end of an old stable block that now contained our current Estate Office. At the other end, my parents and an Estate Manager John Hoy ran Knebworth Estates, Lytton Enterprises Ltd., and managed the charity the Knebworth House Education and Preservation Trust. But there was time to learn all that. And unlike for the heroine of *Rebecca*, there was no scary housekeeper intimidating me, and showing me how you could see her hand through the previous chatelaine's underwear.

There was a honeymoon thrill to being back in England. We'd managed to completely miss out on Kylie Minogue and Jason Donovan. We'd skipped the Stock Aitken Waterman years. Hooray. We'd bypassed the worst period of English music since the Second World War. All the interesting 80s bands had imploded - The Style Council, The Blow Monkeys, Spandau Ballet... Apparently there were some interesting bands around - I was told about The Smiths, The Cure - but they sounded pretty miserable to me and my Californian sensibilities. I was content to have missed out on them too. As for Knebworth Concerts, after the big legends extravaganza in 1990, in the first six years of the 1990s all that could be mustered was Genesis (bless them) in 1992. Their third Knebworth.

I had every intention of continuing to work in movies until Knebworth House was fully upon us. I had screenplay commissions, but I was conscious I needed some kind of a cash cow. The second most stupid thing I did at this time was not to re-invest the money from our West Hollywood home sale back into property. I put much of the sale money into our new home, Park Gate House, which was, on paper, mine - but that value was never going to be realisable. In fact, the value of that house was going to languish for many years in an interest-only mortgage to clear the family company debts when we were handed the reins.

What was left of the money, the precious gain from my Marylebone house, paid for our move back to England and fancy fridges and fancy vans, etc. Home improvements included adding the radiators to all bedrooms and bathrooms, something that Martha had in her contract for living in England. I was quickly with her on

Room for an au pair in this one. Back to my childhood home, Park Gate House. Plus VW Caravelle.

this. Before I went to California I didn't feel the cold in England. After California, I've only ever felt cold in England. My weather innocence was shattered. There are places in the world where you don't have to be permanently cold. Places in the world where you can live at the temperature of your summer holiday all year round. Places like the one we'd just left.

Where else did the money go? I suspect my company, The 39 Production Company, also had some historic debts from the aborted production of *Green For A Season*. I was certainly not returning from Eldorado having made my fortune. I told myself that Laurence Olivier's first spell in Hollywood ended the same.

After all was said and done there was about £50,000 left from the house sale. And this, I had the brilliant idea of spending on a computer.

That's not quite as stupid as it sounds. It's quite stupid. But not as stupid as it sounds. I was to make a much more stupid version of this mistake a couple of years later. This version actually turned out okay.

In Canoga Park, in the early 90s, Zalman was still cutting his films on big metal Steenbeck reel-to-reel desks, with physical 35mm film. Just before we left West Hollywood, an English commercials director, Nick Jones, was sitting in the orange armchair in our living room, telling me about a thing called Avid. This was a computer on which commercials were starting to be edited. Digitally.

Production Companies were all interested in this new technology, but not convinced yet to invest. There were only a handful of editors who were trained to use it. Nick's suggestion was to buy one and rent it out to Production Companies, so they could try it out before committing to buying it. By the time they'd figured that out, you'd have paid for your the machine and you'd own something that would make your films much less expensive to make. Better still, go into league with one of Avid's in-house training editors and your prospective clients would all show up, showing interest, without you having to go out looking for them.

Remarkably this idea worked. I went to a Broadcast & Technology trade show in Olympia London in 1993 and there, in purple triangles, was the Avid stand. It was along the row from another stand, much smaller, that I noticed, but didn't think too much about, announcing the 'World Wide Web'. World Wide Web? Is that something I should I be investing in? No, I was starting at the top of the alphabet.

Photo: F. P. Urschitz

Whopping 27" screens, as deep as they were wide, in '90s grey

I spent my last £50,000 on an Avid (left). It wasn't a regular Avid Media Composer - those were already being picked up by commercials companies for editing ads. I bought the very first Avid Film Composer sold in the U.K. (Avid was an U.S. company). The Film Composer was designed for creating an EDL, an Edit Decision List - something familiar to Film Editors as a list of reference numbers for Mo Henry to cut your film negative to. But the Avid would create this list using timecoded digital film clips, which was much simpler that faffing around with the short and curly bits of film.

This sophisticated new software was bespoke to its machine. The machine consisted of two monster 27 inch screens - that's 27 inches in every direction, including deep. They were the size of Disco speakers - something I was familiar with lugging around in my van. But these screens always seemed heavier. They were certainly more delicate. Then there was a big grey metal box, similar to the base of my Sony Word Processor. This was called a 'Mac'. There were a couple of desk speakers, a multi-coloured keyboard with hyroglifics on it, a little grey rollerball mouse (apparently easier for some functions than a keyboard)... oh yes, and then there were more gray boxes. These were called 'memory', where the film clips were stored. Computer memory is measured in bytes - and these were Mega. 400 Megabytes I think. For something like £10 a byte. So £4,000 for 400 Megabytes. I had a few of them. Film clips, even heavily compressed, still take up some space.

I am embarrassed to write that I never learnt to edit on my Avid. I did learn editing software later, but by then preferred to stick with my trusted word editing software supplier, Sony, and its software Vegas. I was spoilt. I didn't need to learn Avid, because I went into partnership with the best of only a handful of trained Avid editors in the UK, Renée Edwards (above). Out the machine went to work, with me lugging it around London in my Toyota van and Renée setting it up and offering support. Within a

"Qualifications?"
"I've got a hat."

year, the Avid Film Composer, and all its add-on Megabytes, had recouped its cost.

This year of rentals had also been an introduction to production companies all across town. I'd been away for eight years. This was the perfect networking tool to get me back into film industry offices. Amongst the projects my Avid Film Composer worked on in that year was Mike Figgis's *Leaving Las Vegas* (1995) with Nicholas Cage. I certainly thought I was on to something with this niche rental market. After the success of the first year, I decided to expand on the same principle. Buy brand new technology that the Production Companies want to test before they invest in. And at that time there was a lot of new broadcast technology being introduced because there was a new kid on the block. Digital.

Audio had started to go Digital almost a decade earlier, but now Video was catching up. In 1994 Sony released the first digital broadcast video camera that was affordable if you weren't running a television network. The format was

called Digital Betacam. I bought the first one sold in the U.K., straight from IBC (the International Broadcasting Convention) in Amsterdam.

With my brother Richard I started a new company in the Old Estate Office, called All Digital Ltd. The aim was to put together a fully digital broadcast production kit - from Pre-production to Post - something that was only now just about possible. Richard had been the founding partner in the '80s of a company that sold screens, Signos. It's unique selling point was an interface that allowed digital screens to be used in analogue set ups. For instance in submarines, or motorway toll booths - places the infrastructure was difficult or expensive to replace. The parts were made in China, via Hong Kong, and Richard sold them worldwide.

The best of my cash cows - for over 10 years, paid for itself many times over

We began to assemble a state of the art broadcast production set up. For rental. But also with the end game that we would be able to produce our own broadcast productions in house. To go with our digital editing machine and our digital camera, we added a digital mastering deck (left), and some film production kit like lights, blue screen cloths, a jib (see-saw arm for lifting your camera high) and a Steadicam Rig. Steadicam - a rig that turned your cameraman into a walking dolly... I'll pause there. I say cameraman because our preferred cameraman Graeme Towner (below) - who we sent to train up on the Steadicam rig - was male... and as for whether he looked like a dolly when he was all strapped up... well, that's for you to decide.

Steadicams were not new, but they hadn't been around long, and what appealed to us about them was the do-it-yourself element of not needing a whole camera crew to lug around tracking and all the other paraphernalia of a film camera if you want to move it off a tripod.

Now, we had digital post-production; we had digital production (as far as that went - digital lights were still a little way off); and we had digital pre-production. For pre-production our brand new Windows 95 PC laptop was loaded not only with screenwriting software, but also with film scheduling and film budgeting software. This software, again, was not new, but it had been developing over my years in Los Angeles. *The Shooting Party* in 1983 was scheduled on a black leather fold-out board with coloured cardboard strips. It's screenplay was written on a typewriter.

My £5,000 Sony Word Processor (and my $5,000 one) had been replaced while I was working with Zalman with a software called Word Perfect that ran on any PC (which you could get for around £1,000). For writing screenplays a software called Scriptor had been developed that also ran on any PC. The U.S. company that made it, Movie Magic, had also created software for Scheduling and Budgeting movies. I was fairly unique in the U.K. at this time for having experience on these softwares.

This kit was all bought with loan financing - and again we were making a reasonable return from rentals that was paying these loans off. We were even starting to collect some staff - and if not staff, certainly a young enthusiastic team of free-

lancers to work with. A local vicar's son called Jeremy Shaw (left, behind Graeme) kept writing to me for a job - any job - whatever we posted an ad for, he answered "I can do that." I was looking for folk with at least some experience, but eventually I relented and told Jeremy I'd give him £10 a day if he wanted to come in and help around the office (there wasn't a national minimum wage until 1998). He

could hang pictures. I had Joan Fontaine memorabilia I wanted on the wall. From the day Jeremy arrived he made it his mission to learn Avid. Having access to one of the few in the country, he quickly became one of the country's most experienced Avid editors. His career was off and running.

I was also working with writers, trying to keep the writing plates spinning whilst I was doing all this other stuff. Cally Phillips had written a play about the Brontë sisters. She came to assist me for a brief period, when I was looking to write a quasi-sequel to *Letter From An Unknown Woman*, called *Vienna*. Her partner at the time was a theatre/film fencing and stunt instructor called Mike Loades (right). Mike was a Military Historian. He went on to become a regular on the History Channel. He persuaded me

that we should use all this production kit to make a programme for sell-through video on the history of archery. He would provide all the content and I would make it, and we would split the return. The programme should go on selling indefinitely as there was always a new generation interested in archery.

Archery - Its History and Forms became the first programme in the U.K. to be made on Digital Beta-cam. It put the digital video through its paces too, as much of it was shot in the Knebworth Woods. The more detail in a frame - i.e. leaves - the more digital information required. The film still looks great today - although archery enthusiasts have clearly moved on to other programmes on the subject, as its Vimeo page is not creating the occasional cheque that I used to receive from California (where Mike went on to live). What lets the film down today is not the look of it - or the content, which was also first rate - it's the much more important element previously discussed. The music. The dreadful tinky-tinky score is virtually unlistenable to today. I was not involved in that element. I hadn't got to music yet in our production set up. I was still concentrating on the excitements and possibilities of the quality and the look we could get from digital video.

Like CDs which you were meant to be able to spread with jam to no injurious effect, the wonders of digital video were also, looking back on it, overplayed. Yes, the ghosting that came with analogue video - particularly from light sources like candles - was now gone. But what you got instead was pixilation, when the camera became overwhelmed with large amounts of detail. However in order to promote the low light quality and the lack of ghosting on our new camera, we resolved to make a little promo video for All Digital Ltd.

What should we shoot by candlelight? We had an old gothic house. Lots of candelabras. So, someone walking through that house in the dark with a candelabra? Perfect. Something spooky. Something sexy. Footage to catch attention within production companies, that I could use in a music video one day.

We advertised for actresses with Pre-Raphaelite sensibilities and looks, who were at ease with nudity. A surprising number replied. One of them was Michael Winner's partner at that time. But they were all very actressy... all very... English. I was not finding the creative free spirit I was looking for... until a Spanish performance artist walked through our Hertfordshire door. Marta Casas. She was working in London at the ICA with the mime and performance artist Albert Vidal. She was 'Shameless Innocence' in his piece *The Monk of Chaos Worships The Bull.*

There was a line about Performance Artists at this time, that Performance Art (not widespread in the UK, but fairly common in California) was almost exclusively about getting naked and eating fish. We didn't see a role for fish-eating in this promo, but getting naked would, I knew from experience, attract attention for our new camera. Marta had a mass of long wavy waist-length blonde hair. That, in combination with a complete lack of self-consciousness about her body, its skin, hair, sweat, and everything else... was exactly what I wanted not to have to concern myself with

as we concentrated on testing our digital pixels.

So, we had our Performance Artist awake, startled, in Knebworth House, as though she's heard a mysterious call. Taking a white sheet - trailing behind her, rather than wrapped round her (looks better) - she picks up a lit candelabra and walks, with mysterious hypnotised eyes, through the silent house... to the large empty hall, where, unexplained, there is a roaring fire in the grate (but if you want an explanation, it was to show how firelight, like candlelight, also doesn't ghost using digital video). Looking around for the sound, our nightwalker is drawn to the fire. She puts down the candelabra, and steps into the fire... (not literally, of course - here we are testing our 'blue screen'). Raising her arms like an Indian princess, she dissolves up the chimney... Happens to guests at Knebworth House all the time. We were getting good at this. Someone should let us make a film.

They were about to. But first, what had I been writing? Not much for this promo. But plenty of screenplays. And plenty of TV series pitches. Looking back, it was the most productive writing period of my life. With *Red Shoe Diaries* - Showtime Networks' "Highest Rated Series Ever!" (see image p.210) - under my belt, surely, now in England, I could pitch a similar show to a U.K. network?

Red Shoe Diaries was half hour fantasies/seductions. The perfect scheduling for after the *News At Ten*. After half an hour with your head in your hands over the world's problems, what better than half an hour of fantasy to cheer you up and release the valves before lights out? So, why not stick to that basic idea of half hour fantasies/seductions, but instead of dreaming the stories up, why not use real stories? In *Red Shoe Diaries* David Duchovny puts an ad in the paper asking women to send him their stories. We were in London, where the listings magazine *Time Out* had, in the 1980s, had the mystique of its Classified Ads section magnified by the book *Castaway*. The author Lucy Irvine has answered an ad placed by Gerald Kingsland to spend a year on an uninhabited island off Papua New Guinea. Nicholas Roeg made a fine film of their story in 1986, starring Amanda Donohoe and Oliver Reed (perfect casting of a man-not-called-Tim).

Tangent. Bless you. I was privileged to be present at the brilliantly disastrous Derek Malcolm interview with Donohoe and Reed at the London Film Festival screening of *Castaway*, when Reed lurched about the stage, off his head mid-afternoon, answering any serious question by complimenting Donohoe on her beautiful breasts. You could tell Donohoe had been on a desert island with Reed for some time, and knew exactly how to deal with him, but the perplexed Malcolm struggled, in what was as compulsive and appropriate a coda to this particular film as you could imagine.

So, we put a Classified Ad in *Time Out*.

And got 40 letters back. Yes, 40 letters.

We chose 'Travel Tales' as the theme of the first series of *(in complete confidence)*. The thinking being, that we could then spin it out into Series 2, 'Business and Pleasure'; Series 3, 'Friends and Neighbours'; Series 4, 'On Holiday'... etc. But travel was a theme I knew would work. Everyone has had the 'stuck in a lift' fantasy... No? You mean you haven't contemplated being stuck in a lift with that work colleague you've always fancied? You mean you haven't judged the aura and scent of the passenger who sits next to you at the beginning of a long haul red eye? You mean you haven't tried to get into the tube seat, or (my well-heeled readers) onto the ski lift... with the person you wouldn't mind being stuck with, should the electricity fail and you are stranded in a dark tunnel, or left swinging over a mountain precipice?... At least until the reality of no toilet dawns?... No?

Well, clearly plenty have. Because from one ad in *Time Out* offering £200 for a successful submission, we received 40 letters.

The 10:35 to Lights Out

Working people want to be asleep by 11 o'clock.

The 10 o'clock News scrambles your brain with the horrors and anxieties of the world... then you go to sleep?

The alternative? A 2-hour movie? You won't be asleep till after midnight. Another current affairs programme? Another documentary about A&E, the police...? Another expose on domestic abuse, serial killers...

At 10:35 you want half an hour to untangle your brain. You want to watch something short, beautiful & romantic. You want a head full of happy, sexy, sweet, seductive television...

You want a quality half-hour drama, that's intelligent, plot-driven... with beautiful images, contemporary music, actors you love... where nobody dies.

A SERIES OF 30-MINUTE ROMANTIC DRAMAS
FOR ALL INTERNATIONAL TELEVISION MARKETS

(in complete confidence)

TRAVEL... the unique state where strangers are given licence to be alone together, where they can cast off the rest of the world, their lives, their inhibitions, their commitments... and share intimate secrets with people they will never meet again...

(series one)

Travel Tales

"...I thought I would die. I closed my eyes. I dared not look. Just in case this was really happening... But it was. When I opened my eyes, the carriage was spinning round. I was anchored only by his piercing green eyes. I didn't know where I was or what I was doing. I didn't care. It seemed so natural. The most natural moment of my adult life..."

STRANGERS... shut off from the rest of the world, for a moment in time, thrown together by nothing more than a common destination, given licence to stare at each other, sit interlocked with each other, be pressed against each other, share the tensions and thrills of travel, and the real world passing by...

"...he was leaning over me. I looked up into his eyes and he kissed me and said... 'Thank you, you're beautiful, and I'll never forget you.' And with that he turned and walked out. I never saw him when I got off the train, but it seemed right that way. I don't regret it and I'll never forget him. He changed my life, and I never even knew his name..."

THE FOLLOWING STORIES ARE TRUE, TAKEN FROM REPLIES TO
AN ADVERTISEMENT PLACED IN THE LONDON WEEKLY MAGAZINE "TIME OUT"

(in complete confidence)

WHERE REALITY BECOMES FANTASY

I bought two of them - a train one, and a bus one - and wrote scripts for three episodes. The airplane one, I felt, was such a universal tale, it could write itself. Before you ask, no it was not something that happened to me. Although I do have a few innocent and beautiful travel tales (from deep within the safety of my marriage), that I'll be pleased to recount to you some evening. If you want to tell me yours.

We got a "keen to pursue" from producer Robert Page and his company Lifetime, which was riding high on the success of a sell-through home video called *The Lover's Guide* (1991), that had pulled off the admirable coup (pre-2000, m.o.w.l.) of being granted a U.K. certificate despite featuring real sex, in the name of sex education. *The Lover's Guide* sold well over a million copies in the UK, and more beyond in over a dozen languages. But somehow *The Traveller's Companion* (our original working title) got lost in development. I don't recall why, but I suspect it was a nervousness at the broadcasters. It took the UK broadcasters until 1997 before they even considered broadcasting *Red Shoe Diaries*. Shame.

So, if network television's not yet evolved enough, should we look downmarket? I went to see Richard Desmond, at time of writing more commonly known as the owner of the *Daily Express*, but then sitting atop his shiny blue knobbly tower in Canary Wharf - in which every object (except, I think, the staff) was monogrammed 'R.D.' - as the publisher of *Penthouse UK*, and its spin-off, bedside-table-size, *Forum*. Northern & Shell was, at this time, investing in adult satellite channels that were to become *Television X*. *Forum* ran a regular prose feature called *Erotic Stories*. I pitched to R.D. a TV series version of *Erotic Stories*. But clearly he saw straight through me. I had artistic aspiration written all over my thumping heart. No banana.

I did not give up. I developed two other pitches for short-form television series be-

TRUE STORIES OF ROMANTIC ENCOUNTERS

(in complete confidence)

EPISODE ONE: HONEYSUCKLE
A NIGHT TRAIN FROM NUREMBERG TO PARIS
Armin cannot believe his luck when a beautiful German woman chooses to share his empty compartment. Gradually seducing each other, everything is set for a night of passion... until an elderly Portuguese couple burst in, and start making salami sandwiches... With Paris rocketing towards them, Armin desperately considers his options... he could pull the emergency cord, force the Portuguese couple out at knifepoint, requisition a sleeping car... or wait, pray, that the couple fall into a deep sleep...

"...When I opened my eyes, I saw I was alone in the compartment... She was standing outside on the platform, looking at me through the window. She smiled at me. But it was a sad and vulnerable smile. While I struggled to open the train window, she picked up her bag and walked away. I couldn't open the window. I couldn't shout to make her halt. I rushed to pick up my belongings, but the corridors were still full of people, blocking my way. When I stepped out onto the platform, the town had already swallowed her..."

EPISODE TWO: PERFECT STRANGERS
AN AIRPLANE FROM NEW YORK TO LONDON.

EPISODE THREE: SWEET PEACH
A RURAL BUS ACROSS THE ISLAND OF SANTORINI
Fiona is fed up. She's cutting short her Greek holiday having become a third wheel to her girlfriend's romance with a local fisherman. But on the crowded bus to the port, her luck changes when an irrepressible American archaeologist challenges her to answer an ad in a magazine soliciting true travel romance stories... Together they search their own fantasies to come up with an erotic story... a story that quickly starts to become a reality...

"...He talked on, his words caressing my body, his breath touching me, stroking me... Letting his words wash over me, letting my mind drift away, letting the movement of the bus rock me back and forth... I felt the sweat down my back, the wet warmth between my thighs..."

EPISODE FOUR: ICICLE
AN CHAIRLIFT IN THE ITALIAN ALPS

EPISODE FIVE: MIND THE GAP...
AN UNDERGROUND FROM GOODGE STREET TO HENDON CENTRAL
Tim has travelled the same tube train every morning for over a year. And every morning, without fall, the same girl sits across from him. In true British fashion they have never spoken a word to each other. Tim, however, has created in his mind an elaborate fantasy world in which he's already naming their children... And so they would go on, for many years... but for one night, when, after working late, Tim finds himself on the last train home, alone in a carriage... The girl steps aboard. He must be dreaming... he must be dreaming...

"...clattering into Hendon Central... the young woman stood up to leave. Walking past me she smiled, took my hand and, without a word, led me off the train. We held hands in the lift and out onto the street. We'd managed without words so far and I was terrified to break the spell..."

THE DECADENTS

**A TELEVISION SERIES OF EROTIC
SHORT STORIES TOLD BY THE
MOST FAMOUS ARTISTS, POETS,
NOVELISTS, MUSICIANS & ACTORS
OF LA BELLE EPOQUE**

MOST OF WHAT FOLLOWS IS TRUE...

Bohemian Paris. Late 19th Century. The City of Pleasure. A Mecca for artists and celebrities, who flock to its opulent salons for culture, creativity, and sex. The most notorious of these salons is at No.2, Rue Laffitte. Europe's most famous and infamous characters make pilgrimages here. The address is known as 'The Clitoris of Paris'.

An Englishman, Captain Frederick Hankey, is their host. Once royal page to Queen Victoria, now Europe's foremost connoisseur of Erotica. A disciple of De Sade, so dissolute, so debauched, that an invitation to his salon is entirely irresistible. The Captain makes it his business to entertain all the leading men and women of La Belle Epoque.

Gabriele D'Annuncio, Charles Baudelaire, Aubrey Beardsley, Sarah Bernhardt, Sidonie Colette, Sergei Diaghilev, Sigmund Freud, Paul Gaugin, Pablo Picasso, George Sand, Egon Schiele, August Strindberg, Henri de Toulouse-Lautrec, Richard Wagner, Oscar Wilde, Emile Zola...

All the Captain asks, for his lavish and licentious hospitality, is a story. An erotic story, drawn either from their experiences or from the genius of their imaginations. The dramatization of these stories is our series...

EPISODE: BAUDELAIRE. Baudelaire tells how in his longing for exotic journeys, he explores the world, the tastes, and cultures of foreign lands without ever leaving Paris... through the bodies of its women.

EPISODE: GEORGE SAND. Sand, the celebrated romantic novelist & transvestite, tells of the night she spent between the two heartthrobs of her generation, Chopin and Liszt .. "sand-wiched" as Hankey puts it.

EPISODE: PICASSO. Picasso tells of the foolish landlord who keeps sending his beautiful daughter to collect the rent off him and his roommate Guillaume Apollinaire.

EPISODE: RICHARD WAGNER. Wagner squares off against his countryman Leopold von Sacher-Masoch, the father of masochism, on the joy of sex. To Wagner it is domination. To Sacher-Masoch it is to be dominated.   ...etc

fore the end of the century. One was a response to the fin-de-siècle, that blended the centenary of the La Belle Époque with the eroticism of *Red Shoe Diaries*, and of course my current location, Europe. *The Decadents*.

The other dialled down the eroticism, but made use of my other asset-at-hand, Knebworth House. I envisaged a series where the location was the consistent link. Each episode would tell a story from a successive generation of residents of the same house. Ideas similar to this have been done since, but mine worked well because Knebworth House actually has an interesting true story from each generation. For instance, it was the home of White Russians in 1913 when it was the honeymoon bolthole of Grand Duke Michael Romanov and his divorcée wife Natasha; then during the Second World War it was home to the Froebel Institute a teacher training college for young women evacuated from London; then, of course, in the '70s it became a weekend hub of rock & roll excess for bands like Pink Floyd, the Rolling Stones and Led Zeppelin... etc. Good stories like these are to be found in every generation of Knebworth House's history. And Knebworth House works well as a location for period stories, because all of these different periods remain represented somewhere in the house and gardens. Because, having only been in single family ownership, the house has never been completely renovated, each generation wanting to keep of little of the style of the generation before.

Again, I'd start with the best story-teller of all. The truth. Each episode would be a romantic drama, so I'd introduce a single conceit in the pilot that a exotic character similar to my great-great-great-grandfather Edward Bulwer Lytton - but more of a Sir Richard Burton type explorer - brings a stolen Tibetan princess back to Victorian England. Her demise in the unnatural gloom of the dark gothic mansion infuses her essence and magic into the building's walls as an aphrodisiac to future generations. Shall we call it *The Walls of Love*? No. Not unless Hallmark's paying. How about *An Englishman's Castle*? Better. But we haven't had to settle on a title yet, as the project is still languishing on a shelf on that building's walls. But it does come up (or down) every so often. We'll get there one day.

CHAPTER TWENTY-FIVE

Mr Sarlui sir

MADAME SNOW
You're not going to give out on me now.

.

Madame Snow approaches.. wrapped in her silk robe, full of
energy, resplendent, vibrant. She stirs the cocktail with a
table spoon, lifts a mouthful to William's lips.

MADAME SNOW
It's a special recipe.. Mexican bullfighters use it to keep
their strength up.

William swallows.. winces, gasps..

WILLIAM
What the hell is it?

Madame Snow scoops another spoonful, presses it between
his lips..

MADAME SNOW
Bull's semen..

William splutters.. the cocktail spills across his naked chest.

MADAME SNOW
..with a touch of brandy.

(*Strange Relations* 1993)

But what of feature film screenplays? In the wake of my sparkling credit on
Lake Consequence? Here I had more success. Rewind to Zalman King's office in Canoga Park in 1991/1992. One of the foreign distributors who had made good money
from *Wild Orchid* was a Dutch ex-pat producer called Eduardo Sarlui (below, with
his wife Etka). Amongst his business interests he owned a chain of cinemas in Guatemala, which guaran-
teed a cushion return
on film investments.
He wanted to work
with Zalman again.

I think Mr Sar-
lui - I only ever called
him Mr Sarlui. In fact
I only ever called him
'Mr Sarlui, sir'. Which
amused him. As did
my insistence that I'd

named my son after him. I think Mr Sarlui, sir, might have had financing available in Russia, or in Eastern Europe, because the project that evolved out of our genial meetings was a Russia-based story of mine called *The Governess*. I wrote a script. Zalman loved it. He thought it was my best work. It kicks off in France, with a convent girl having sex with a Priest in a confessional. All the best European movies do.

Period pieces are boring! They've become either dainty drawing-room dramas supposed for a female audience or bloody beast & battle epics supposed for a male audience. Somewhere in the middle, the old-fashioned romantic adventure has become the reserve of children's entertainment. So let 's pretend this story's for children. After all, of what possible interest to adults is...

THE FRENCH GOVERNESS

- A ROMANTIC ADVENTURE -

Rural France. 1912. In a confessional, a convent school girl, Sofie, confesses to her Priest her desires for him. She reasons that God gave man lust, and therefore how can satisfying this God-given appetite be considered a sin? Already bewitched by this beautiful, brilliant student, the Priest succumbs to temptation. They are discovered. Sofie's pompous, bourgeois Father angrily escorts his disgraced daughter from the convent. To avoid a scandal, he sends her away with Nebrasov, a Russian wine merchant visiting France to stock the cellars of Imperial Russia.

The wily Nebrasov knows that his client Count Vasiliy Meller-Zakomelsky is looking for a French governess. On the road to Russia, fiery and independent, Sofie exploits Monsieur Nebrasov's fascination with bullfighting by challenging him to a duel to draw blood, by which she might win her freedom. Nebrasov plays along, only to rebuff and humiliate her. Amused, he compliments her that such spirit will get her far in Russia. All she needs are beauty, charm and cunning and her opportunities are boundless. Untouched by the ravages of democracy and socialism, Russia, he declares, is the last civilized country in Europe.

A horse-drawn sleigh delivers Sofie at a spectacular castle at the foot of the Ural mountains - the home of Count Vasiliy Meller-Zakomelsky. Still bitter and resiliant, Sofie is greeted by the Count's silent, brooding private secretary, Tikhonov, a good-looking young man, who does not appear to care for anybody very much. The Count is away with his regiment in St. Petersburg, so Sofie is presented to the Countess, a harsh, dictatorial woman, who is never without her Mongolian fortune-teller and mystic, the monk Hasagal. The icy Countess informs Sofie that her predecessor had worked for the family for 70 years and knew her place, and that nothing less is expected of her. She will instruct their only daughter Katerina every morning except Sunday, and supervise her exercise in the afternoon, which will be taken within the walls of the castle. She is to teach the child only what is suitable for a young lady of court, French and religious studies.

Shown to large sparse quarters, Sofie asks her new maid Kiska if the Countess is always that cold. Kiska replies that all the staff, except Tikhonov and Olga her maid, live in fear of her. Sofie, to Kiska's astonishment, burns the few convent clothes she's travelled with, including the dress she is wearing, and asks to be shown to the Countess's boudoir. Choosing two of the least ostentatious dresses, she asks Kiska to help fit them for her. The maid protests that Olga will know. Sofie confesses she only intends to stay at the castle a few weeks, just long enough to earn a little money to begin her escape back to France. Disappointed, Kiska says she hopes Sofie will change her mind.

If anything is to persuade Sofie to stay longer it is her pupil Katerina, a sweet, timid, 15-year-old. Sofie sees in Katerina much of the abuse of her own childhood. She immediately sets about breaking all the Countess's rules. The repressed Katerina is instantly enamored of her rebellious governess. Sofie sneaks Katerina outside the castle gates. They explore the beautiful snowbound wilderness, joining a band of gypsies dancing and drinking by a frozen river. Sofie assures her that love is God's foremost gift to man, and its expression should not be suppressed. On their way back to the castle they pass three drunken peasant women, who proposition Sofie and Katerina with obscenities. One is Olga, the Countess's maid. Realising who she is addressing, Olga and the other two women tumble quickly away. Sneaking back into the castle, they encounter a surreptious Tikhonov, a Bolshevik newspaper in his jacket. Fierce, cryptic, Tikhonov warns Sofie that by staying at the castle she is putting her life in danger.

The following day, Sofie is called before the Countess. Olga stands beside her mistress with Kiska, who weeps miserably. Fiery, outraged, the Countess accuses Sofie of stealing her clothes. Sofie confesses readily and seeks dismissal, asking only that the Countess supply her transport to the nearest town. A little surprised, the Countess accepts. But they are interrupted by Tikhonov, who announces the unexpected arrival of the Count. Count Vasiliy Meller-Zakomelsky is sadistic, lecherous, arrogant and obstinate. Taking one look at the new governess, he rebuffs his wife's charges. The governess should be provided clothes worthy of her position. He will have even finer dresses made for her, since she is to accompanythe family on a trip. They will visit Russia' s foremost Military Academy where Anton, their son, is receiving special honours for excellence. The Countess consults her fortune-teller. Hasagal warns her that if she takes the trip she risks unbearable grief. She decides not to travel.

Zalman talked Eduardo into purchasing an option on this screenplay. I remember he went to his safe and gave me the money in cash. $5,000. I'd never seen that much money in cash. I said to Eduardo that I did need to declare it. He said, do what you like with it. I took it home, and want to tell you we tossed it in the air and danced in it. We didn't. But we did sit and stare at it for a while.

The Count departs with Katerina, Sofie and their maids. They travel in gilded sleighs, chauffeured by liveried drivers, and with an armed escort of four officers . Throughout the trip the Count presses his designs on his new governess. He compliments his wine merchant's taste. He confides that he pays Hasagal to tell his wife what he wants her to hear. Sofie's resilience to him only inspires him more. Meanwhile, Katerina, now desperately in love with her governess, and on her way to see her adored brother, could not be happier.

Anton, the Count' s 19-year-old son, is a dashing, beautiful boy, but brow-beaten by his cruel father. As the family take tea in fashionable town tea rooms, the Count humiliates his son by revealing that his honours were purchased. Katerina leaves the table with her brother. Left alone with the Count, Sofie asks to be let go. The Count accepts, suggesting a way whereby she can earn the money for a trip back to France. There is a competition to be held at his Officer' s club on the night of the Grand Ball.

In the lead up to the Grand Ball, Sofie accompanies Katerina and Anton amongst the festivities, skating, playing in the snow - she is comforted by how happy they are together, away from their parents. Anton joins the rest of his family by falling in love with Sofie. At the Grand Ball, Anton and Katerina dance the Mazurka, both wishing that Sofie was with them. Sofie, however, is with the Count, winning a lascivious club contest where she must melt a 16-inch icicle without using her hands. Dropping Katerina back at her boarding house, Anton discovers that Sofie is with his father. Assuming she is at his club against her will, he goes to 'rescue' her, causing much embarrassment to all, and losing Sofie her winnings.

Back in the street, Sofie confesses to Anton that she is going back to France. She says Katerina doesn't need a governess, she needs a family - and that's him. She makes him promise to steal Katerina away, and to go and live somewhere away from their mother and father. Anton agrees. Together they go back to his barracks to collect his belongings. They are interrupted and detained there by a gang of drunken Cossack cadets looking for trouble. Using her wits, and her wile, Sofie engineers an escape from the Cossacks. However, pursued across the rooftops by the leader of the gang, Andreich, Anton is drawn into a duel. Silhouetted against the dawn, he and the Cossack fight a brutal duel, despite Sofie's pleas. Anton is badly wounded, but he and Sofie escape down bell tower ropes. Carrying him back to the boarding house, Sofie discovers to her dismay that the Count has left already with Katerina.

The nosy, prim landlady, Madame Petrov is able to tell them everything about the urgent note that had arrvied from Tikhonov. It has expressed concern for the Countess's safety - militant Bolshevik revolutionaries were known to be in the area of the castle. Sofie assumes it's a plot, and instantly fears for Katerina's safety. Anxious, she bids farewell to a dying Anton.

The Count arrives back at the castle in a howling snow storm. He leaves Katerina and the maids in the sleigh, and enters the castle with two of his armed escort. Immediately the gate is bolted, and silently anyone faithful to the Count is surprised, and their throat cut. The Count discovers his wife involved in a sexual ritual with Hasegal - pulling him out of her bedroom, he compliments the monk for exceeding his brief. Giving him money, he requests that Hasegal elope with his wife... to safety.

Sofie reaches the castle shortly afterwards. Stealthily and heroically, she frees the maids and Katerina, then catches up with the Count just as he is ambushed in the chapel by Tikhonov and his fellow revolutionaries. The Count's escort is shot. He is left alone - one sword against ten guns. Appealing to Tikhonov' s better nature, Sofie manages to talk Tikhonov out of killing the Count. As they walk free out into the swirling snow, the Count wraps the governess in his arms, kissing her fervently. But Sofie's concern is now back with Anton. Together the family races back to the Academy town, where to great relief they find Anton alive... in bed with Madame Petrov.

Sofie asks the Count if she has earnt her fare back to France. He replies not only that, but he personally will escort her. Leaving Katerina, happy, in the care of her brother, Sofie travels with the Count towards Europe. As they approach the border, the Count tells her his plans for them to visit castles in Austria, opera in Milan, palaces in Venice. At the border, Sofie slips out of his carriage, into another, headed towards France. As the Count frantically searches for her at the busy border post, Sofie disappears into the sunset. Her companion in the new carriage is a Priest - her first question to him mirrors her question at the very start of the story: "Father, how can there be salvation without sin?..."

The property of and presented by The 39 Production Company ~ www.the39.com

Credit to the Bank of America for not batting an eyelid when I came in to deposit it. I suppose that sort of thing was not unusual on the Sunset Strip. It certainly would have ruffled the bank manager in Stevenage. Together Zalman's 10dB and Mr Sarlui's Beverley Hills Producers Group were going to make *The Governess*.

A film called *The Governess* did get made a few years later. With Minnie Driver. But it wasn't my film. It also wasn't anywhere near as interesting as my film would have been. I don't know why my film didn't get made. Probably something as simple as the Russian money falling through. I do remember that script notes came back from Russia, or Eastern Europe, or wherever it was, asking for the film to be rewritten 100 years earlier. I'd set my story at the time of the Russian Revolution. For some reason the Russians financiers didn't want to deal with the Russian Revolution. Not that that period had done *Dr Zhivago* any harm. They wanted the world of *War and Peace*. This change would have completely trashed the Third Act of my story. Made much of my plot not make sense.

I'm sure I would have done the rewrite if I'd thought it meant the film would be made. I was a writer for hire. But I liked my script. Zalman liked my script. And I don't remember there being any money for such a fundamental reworking of the story. I got the sense it would be a lot of work for nothing. Eduardo didn't seem too bothered. He was enjoying working with me. Was I interested in writing other screenplays for him? Er... Yes.

Eduardo Sarlui was actively making movies at this time. It was 1992. Eduardo Exec-Produced six movies in 1988, six movies in 1989, six movies in 1990, and three movies in 1991. This, I am sure, had a lot to do with me feeling comfortable to leave the Red Shoes Studio, where I was getting my first work produced and where work was abundant. Eduardo and his lovely Peruvian wife Etka lived in one of those white mansions on a palm-lined avenue in Beverley Hills. In many ways he was the archetype of an old school Hollywood film producer - larger than life, cigars, bonhomie... and a study lined with antique typewriters. My young family and I were regular visitors for Sunday lunch at his home, at which he loved pumping me for stories and possible projects.

Before I knew it, I was being asked to write not one screenplay, but five. Two were Mr Sarlui sir's idea - modern updates of the two German Expressionist films, *Dr Mabuse* and *Dr Caligari*. Two were my idea, a Louisiana comedy *Louis Louis* and an Ancient Greek drama *Sappho*. And one was a story taken from Mr Sarlui's remarkable life, *Strange Relations*. Well, not straight from his life - I wrote a contemporary teen comedy - but inspired by a bizarre episode in Eduardo's life during the Second World War that he let slip one Sunday lunch.

He was living in occupied Paris, concealing his Jewish routes - which I thought was story enough, but not what he was enjoying recalling - when he was seduced into an affair by a much older woman. This widow lived on the very top floor of a tall apartment block. By the time he'd climbed the countless stairs, he was already exhausted - but this woman wasn't having any of it. She was insatiable for sex. She would feed him raw eggs to keep his energy up... *Strange Relations*.

"Do you want me to seduce you? Is that what you're trying to tell me?" Inappropriate relationships. Inappropriate women. Mrs Robinson. Lolita. Men continue to be their victims. But none more so than artists. For artists it is a duty to be tortured. No true art comes from domestic bliss. True art comes from...

STRANGE RELATIONS

- A ROMANTIC COMEDY ABOUT INAPPROPRIATE WOMEN -

A dusty garret overlooking the rooftops of Paris. A dream-come-true for Art School graduate William (early 20s). He's left fiancee, Stacy, in California for one last stab at Bohemia. But this is it. He's to be married on his return. So he'd better make the most of it. This is his last chance to prove himself as a serious artist. In the apartment below, also hiding in the anonymity of an obscure Parisian backstreet, lives an American romancewriter, Madame Snow (40s? 50s? 60s? - we'll never know). Some years ago she abandoned husband and family to elope with a bullfighter. A bullfighter and a bullshitter. Now a complete recluse, she leaves her apartment only once a day, at dawn, to go to the market. By day, she struggles to write, but can't. She no longer believes in romance. Finally, way below, at the foot of the tall winding staircase, bored out of her head, lives the concierge's daughter, Juliette (17? 16? 15? - we'll never know). Living alone with an abusive sloth of a father, she has all the time in the world for mischief. The tatty old apartment block is her kingdom, and it's only a matter of time before ...

William returns to his garret to find Juliette posed naked on his floor mattress, demanding he paint her. William's better nature asks her to leave. The teenager has never taken "no" for an answer. William accepts there can be no harm in a sketch. But William's fascination is for the mysterious older woman in the apartment below. His attempts to engage her in conversation are rebuffed. The only time she will talk to him is to complain at the noise he's making. But in reality, the good-looking young man has sparked Madame Snow's interest. Much more so than the Doctor (40s/ 50s) from the local hospital who tries to chat her up every dawn as she passes the cafe on her way to the market. Or indeed the market traders, who's day is made by flirting with the most regular of their regular customers.

The following day Juliette is again naked on William's floor mattress. She has thrown the framed photo of his fiancee Stacy out of the window. William demands that she leave. Juliette asks if he's gay - she's heard many artists are. Again William is persuaded to use her as his model. In the name of Art. Long-distance on the public telephone in the street, William reassures Stacy that his mind is on his work. The call exacerbates his loneliness. He takes a bottle of wine to bed. Asleep, clutching the empty bottle, he is startled awake by Juliette. It's the middle of the night. She's brought her girlfriend Lou-Lou to be painted too. They want to be immortalised by this future famous artist. They make an intriguing tableau, decadent, bohemian. Against his better judgement, William picks up his brush and palette and starts to paint. The two girls tease him, make it as difficult as possible for him to concentrate. Surely he wants to make love to them? In desperation, he is about to throw them out, when the garret door swings open - in storms the brash, hulking Concierge, streaming expletives. He grabs his naked daughter. When Juliette struggles, he slaps her hard across the face. Gallantly, William springs to her defence, but for his trouble is sent smashing violently into his easel and all his canvasses. Groaning in a puddle of paint, William regains consciousness to see Madame Snow peering down at him. She has heard the commotion and, on her way out to the dawn market, has checked in on him. William looks down at a large gash in his leg, where he's fallen against his easel, oozing thick red blood. He passes out.

William wakes up, in fresh clothes, in a strange bed. The room around him is white, bright, luxurious. It is Madame Snow's apartment. Madame Snow appears with a hot plate of hash browns. He must be dreaming. But Madame Snow is as cold and dismissive as ever. She's got better things to do than pick up after some sweaty liaison with a teenage tart. And worse still, William's infected leg has meant she's had to invite her admirer the Doctor into her apartment. The Doctor has recommended resting the leg for a few days, and a course of antibiotics - he is only too happy to check on the patient on his way to and from work. William is only too happy to stay right where he is, in clean sheets, being served cooked food. Rightly, Madame Snow distrusts the will of these two men for a quick recovery. But nursing William brings a change about Madame Snow. Her verbal quips remain, sour and sharp, but she softens.

I made him a young American, present day, in Paris to paint. And I gave him two inappropriate women to deal with.

Again, this was a good screenplay. Not expensive to make. But atmospheric in a *Delicatessen* (1991) kind of way. It also is still to be made.

When the market traders marvel at her broken routine - double orders of everything - she shares the joke. And most importantly, Madame Snow begins to write again. Juliette, meanwhile, is gated. A prisoner in her father's ground floor rooms. Building inside her, a dangerous mix of angry rebellion and confused curiosity about how, and where, William is.

Shut away with Madame Snow, William becomes increasingly seduced. And increasingly anxious. The physical intimacy with this mysterious, beautiful woman is unsettling him. He does his best to tell her about his fiancee, but Madame Snow couldn't be less interested. The thaw in Madame Snow is not lost on the Doctor. He strikes with a dinner invitation. To his astonishment, she accepts. Across the table, he watches, bewitched, as the seafood, wine, music, cause her guard to slip. She explains her grudge against romance; she explains she is still married - her husband wouldn't divorce her; she explains that the grass is never greener on the other side of the fence - it still needs mowing and dogs still crap on it; she explains that she can't invite him up for a coffee - because, on his recommendation, she has company.

Kicking off her shoes, unzipping her dress, the lightheaded Madame Snow makes straight for the beautiful, barechested William, asleep in the moonlight on her daybed. Before he can stir, Madame Snow is astride him, her open lips pressed against his. Their lovemaking is intense. Madame Snow has been saving up. And, well... so has William. William wakes in a cloud of guilt. Madame Snow wakes in the clear light of lust. She cracks eggs, stirring in Tabasco and brandy, to make a cocktail to keep his strength up. He really must speak to her about his fiancee. He splutters at the taste of the thick creamy concoction. It spills across his chest. Madame Snow laughs, licks it off.

Morning finds the Concierge, as usual, slumped, snoring, in front of a blaring T.V. Juliette knows an opportunity when she sees one. She also knows exactly where to find her father's set of master keys. William and Madame Snow are a tussle of sheets, torn lingerie and egg cocktail. They do not hear the key in the lock. Juliette shrieks in horror. William IS gay! He can only do it with OLD women! She begins throwing things, smashing everything in the sight. William, dripping with cocktail, manages to catch hold of her. She struggles, hitting out at him, cursing his cheap American ass. William marches her to the door... and into the arms of the Doctor, who has arrived to visit his patient. Stunned, the Doctor, in calm dignity, escorts the girl downstairs... and thinks better of returning.

William turns back towards the bed. Madame Snow looks at him from twisted sheets. "I guess you're better". William looks down at his legs. Madame Snow grins, "Come here. Show me how much better." But William doesn't come. He can't go on. He has to come clean with her. "I've not been straight with you, Mrs Snow. I'm engaged to marry your daughter." Madame Snow stares at him. "The date is set. At the Wayfarer's Chapel in Palos Verdes. I know the best wedding present I could give Stacy is to persuade her estranged mother to come to her wedding. Stacy doesn't know I'm staying here. I've been waiting for the right moment to ask. I knew you wouldn't go for the idea instantly." Madame Snow is silent. Then she begins to shake. Her smeared lip quivering, she manages, "Get out!"

Dressed for travel, carrying his suitcase and portfolio, William passes Madame Snow's closed door. It is silent within. He continues down the stairs. On his way out, he passes the concierge's desk. Juliette can be heard screaming blue murder within. The Concierge, laughing, slaps William on the back, congratulates him warmly, for defrosting the Snow Queen.

The Wayfarer's Chapel, Palos Verdes. A beautiful wedding overlooking the Pacific Ocean. William and Stacy stand before the preacher saying their vows. Stacy glances at her father, a gentle-looking man, who stands alone. He shoots her a look of encouragement. Then her eye catches... her mother, demure, beautiful, slipping in at the back. Stacy looks at William, in shock. The Preacher concludes. "You may kiss the bride." William kisses his wife.

William and Stacy catch up with Mrs Snow on the beach after the ceremony. Mrs Snow gives the couple a wedding present - a romance she has just finished writing, 'Strange Relations'. She urges William to read every word to Stacy... because the flower of romance thrives only under the rain of truth.

It got close this one, with continued interest over the years - later from an Italian producer called Silvio Muraglia, who is now head of a company called Paradox Studios and busy making all sorts of movies - so why isn't he revisiting this one?

I started writing all five of these screenplays at the same time. There was no great hurry, but I was bursting with ideas for movies, and wanted to be planting as many acorns as I could. So I looked for help in writing the screenplays. I had recently found writers for Red Shoes. Who would help me write these new stories up? Again, I was giving away work - and some of my small advance - to be able to take on more. Looking back on this now, it was not necessary.

I have a particularly fond memory of Eduardo standing on a kitchen chair in his Beverley Hills home playing the King of France, as we discussed *Louis Louis*. Passing through Louisiana on a driving trip back to Alabama, I had picked up a local book by a political journalist, John Maginnis, called *The Last Hayride* about the Louisiana Governor Edwin Edwards. This was in the days when populist demagogue politicians only got elected in places like Louisiana. Edwin Edwards was elected Governor four times. Twice as many terms as any other Louisiana chief executive. Ten years after I wrote this story Edwards spent eight years in jail for racketeering. He is quoted as saying before an election that the only way he was not going to win this election is if he was found in bed "with a dead girl, or a live boy".

My story was about a wayward Governor of Louisiana doing a deal with the would-be heir to the throne of France (in reality there's a couple of contenders, mine was called Louis) for the State of Louisiana to secede from the Union and restore him as King. The comedy was built around a hate/love/hate romance between the young King and the Governor's daughter, Evangeline - which was part of the deal. Aside from the extraordinary stories of the political machinations of Edwin Edwards there had been a newspaper story about one pretender to the French throne being caught shop-lifting, and being something of a lost soul. There had also been talk through the 1980s of Quebec seceding from Canada. So the satire wasn't so far fetched. It seems even less far fetched now in the age of Trump and Brexit.

Eduardo and I had a lot of fun over a number of Sunday lunches laughing over this tale. I wrote the beginning, but in my craving to be able to take on more work, I gave this story to my friendly Dutch neighbour in West Hollywood, Marc Susan (right), to write up. I had good laughs with Marc also. But although a fine artist and journal editor, Marc had not been through the Zalman King ringer, and his screenwriting did not reflect my style enough for me to feel happy to give his work to Eduardo. *Louis Louis* was a good, and original, comedy, and I always intended to write it up myself one day. But I never have.

Dr Mabuse also did not get fully written up. Here I worked with my brother Richard. We came up with a solid three-act thriller set in Moscow about a criminal mastermind and master of disguises running rings around both the CIA and the KGB. The director of the three original *Dr Mabuse* films, Fritz Lang, had been the subject of a module in my Film Studies course at university, so I knew these original films well.

Richard and I had previously written a spec comedy - very broad comedy - called *Everybody Say "Yeah!"* based on his experience as a driver for the Capital Radio Jazz Festival, when he had driven a Memphis Soul band from the airport to their hotel. This one van ride had provided enough comedy material for a full screenplay - and, as far as I know, is still the only script to feature a timpani player as its heroine. Listen to the track *Jesus Will Fix It* by Al Green and you'll get the nub of this picture.

The Russian thriller, although it had all the feel of a number of the films that Eduardo had been making in the 80s, also got left behind by other screenplays that, at the time, were more 'me'. Horror is not me, but I felt I could do something camp and interesting with *Dr Caligari*. I wrote a small town American teen movie, about a mysterious gypsy reeking havoc on the town burghers in revenge for when, as teen-

agers, they had run his parents out of town. When I returned to England, I wrote a second version, set in England. *Hot Fuzz* (2007) was over 10 years away, but my *Dr Caligari* had shades of that.

Then, 20 years later, I reworked this idea again with the plan of shooting it around a Knebworth Rock Festival, which from 2009 were happening yearly as the Sonisphere heavy metal shows. My friend Robert Knepper was making a horror film in London called *The Hoarder* (2015) and was told that if there were any other horror films he'd like to make to let the producers know and they'd finance it. Robert asked if I had any horror stories. I said I had one. And that it could not be more relevant. The animosity felt towards Eastern Europeans in small town England at the time was an evil canker spreading about the land, weaponising the political forces of Brexit.

In the 90s I'd seen my Dr Caligari as an Alice Cooper type figure. In 2010 Alice Cooper came to Knebworth to play Sonisphere. The film suddenly seemed very possible. And, if the yearly Sonisphere event at Knebworth was the background, this was a film that only I could make.

So I went full tilt on that angle with a new script, about a Romanian heavy metal star called *Pricolici* (Romanian for werewolf, if you are not up on your lycarian folklore). Such a great title for a camp horror movie. I can't believe the film wasn't made on the strength of this title alone. But - looking back on the pitch - it probably did look a little ambitious for producers who has just made a film set in a mini-storage lock up.

The multi-day Sonisphere festival at Kneb-worth would have made this film easier to make than most imaginations could possibly picture. However Sonisphere came to an end as an annual event in 2014. And then Brexit became a real horror story. So *Pricolici* will have to wait until its time is right again to howl at the moon. I don't doubt that time will come. All of these scripts lining my shelf wrapped in manila hemp are like the undead. Some alignment of the stars will bring them crawling out again. Meanwhile I torture myself with the thought of them lying there in all their beauty on the cold shelf, their promise unrecognised, their potential unfulfilled.

The fifth of the five screenplays written for Mr Sarlui, sir, was the one I cared for the most. *Sappho*. Again, this is a story that I can't believe has not yet been made into a film. I recall Helena Bonham Carter telling me once of a conversation with Emma Thompson, about how they should make films of all the great feminist icons of history. When, in the year 2000, I got word from our cafe at the Knebworth Barns that Emma Thompson was having tea with her children, and Jim Carter & Imelda Staunton, having visited our garden, I sped over to hijack- I mean, say hello. I recalled paparazzi photos of her on holiday on the island of Lesbos. She was the only actor I'd ever seen pictures of on holiday in Lesbos. She was the only household name I was ever aware of that had any connection at all to Lesbos except Michael Dukakis - the 1988 U.S. Presidential candidate, who offered the tantalising prospect of America getting a Lesbian President before it had a female one. Emma Thompson, must, therefore be interested in story of Sappho. As I babbled this out to her, she looked at me like I was completely barking bonkers. She'd only come for a scone.

She did give me her telephone number and said she would be pleased to come to tea again. I did invite her. The scones are still in the freezer. She did, however, give me the nicest of greetings when I ran into her again a few years later in the Banqueting Hall of Knebworth House during a recce for *Nanny McPhee* - for which she brought to Knebworth an even more awesome icon of mine, "Eglantine! Eglantine!", *Bedknobs and Broomsticks'* Angela Lansbury.

But back to Sappho. Sappho was the first woman in Western History to achieve worldwide fame not because of who she was born or who she married. She is Western History's first independent woman, its first internationally-known female singer/songwriter, and the reason we use the word 'lesbian' every day (I use it every day, don't you?)... yet her story has never ever been told.

This may be because no one knows it. There is no written history of this woman or this island in the Aegean Sea in the 600BCs. But that is not a good enough excuse. In the London Library I found a novelisation of Sappho's life written in the 1930s by Margaret Goldsmith. I am not sure I got much further than the first scene of this lovely old book, but just from Margaret Goldsmith's first scene of Sappho as a child missing out on a party in her father's house, I instantly knew that whatever there was known about Sappho and her love songs needed to be pulled together, dramatised, and turned into a movie.

Now I understood why I had studied Ancient History O Level, A Level and - for a week - undergraduate degree. This subject was for me. A couple of problems. I'd not studied Ancient Greek, so I commissioned my friend Daniel Nyiri to do new English translations of Sappho's poems. I did not, strictly speaking, satisfy any of the definitions of a 'lesbian' - but, unquestionably, I was not a woman. A film about the Western World's first feminist couldn't, with any seriousness, be written only

She is the reason we use the word 'lesbian'. She invented the love song. She is the first woman in our history to become famous for what she achieved, not who she was born or who she married. Her story has never been told on film...

SAPPHO THE LESBIAN

The Greek island of Lesbos has not changed much in three thousand years. The same volcanic rock, rough grass cliffs, wild violets, olive groves, white-washed houses and silvery blue Mediterranean sea. This is the setting for a story that changed western history. In 600 BC beauty was born. It was not that there was not beauty in the world before. But it was not until a girl called Sappho, that beauty was written about, sung about... became embedded in our culture. But Sappho paid a price. She taught love, but in her own life it was cruelly snatched from her. Those she loved were lost to the bloodlust of her age. Her success, won without a father, or a husband, was ridiculed. She was a woman who didn't need a man. She was a woman who sung of the beauty of young girls. She was Sappho the Lesbian...

Greece. 600BC. Over the cliff-edge... the goddess of love, Aphrodite, tumbles down the rock face, smashing to pieces on the wave-lashed beach below. The statue has been destroyed by Sappho, who collapses in the grass at the cliff edge, the most famous, successful woman of her time... the first famous, successful woman of all time.

Eleven years earlier, a girl of 15, Sappho is a prisoner in her step-father's house. Her father has been killed in a war initiated by her step-father, Myrsilos, the tyrant of the island state of Lesbos. Myrsilos has married Sappho's mother then sacrificed her to a breech child, ripped from her belly in the hope of a son and heir. The baby girl is Sappho's only companion.

Disgusted by one of her step-father's drunken council dinners, Sappho rescues a beautiful foreign dancer, 'Aphrodite'. Swept away by the grateful affection she receives from this mysterious exotic woman, Sappho plans to escape with her. But while Sappho returns to collect her little half-sister, the dancer is captured and taken from the island. Contemplating suicide at the cliff-edge, Sappho is interrupted by Alcaeus, a soldier from her father's battalion, returning from the war to ask her to marry him. He has fallen in love with her from her father's stories of her and her love songs.

But with the war over, Sappho is resolved to marry General Cercolas, her father's best friend, whom she believes will stand up to her step-father. Cercolas marries her, but only out of a fantasy for her mother and a guilt that he could have prevented her father's death. Battle-scarred and impotent, he restores Sappho to her father's house, before running himself through with his sword in a brothel on their wedding night. It is Alcaeus, now Lesbos's favorite singer of war and heroism, who encourages Sappho to exploit her talent for love songs and turn her father's house into a school. She will teach the orphan daughters of war... music, love and the cult of Aphrodite.

"Qualifications?"
"I've got a hat."

by a man. So I requisitioned my friend Rosemarie Jarski (below) to come in on a co-credit. I can't remember how much exactly Rosemarie contributed. No actual writing, that I recall. But she has edited and annotated my entire creative life since university - until her unexplained disappearance in 2019 - so her name should be inserted somewhere within the 27 letters of my name whenever it appears in a creative context.

I wrote a screenplay that I loved. It is *A Star Is Born* all over the eastern Mediterranean in the early 600BCs.

I even had a sequel mapped out that moved the characters into the world of the *Old Testament's Book of Daniel*. I wonder if Eduardo would have eventually got

Five years later, Sappho's school has grown in renown and is home to the most accomplished girls of the eastern Mediterranean. But Sappho, for all her teaching of love, has not found it in her own life. She has been unable to shake free from the spell of her youthful tryst with the dancer 'Aphrodite'. She determines to try and return Alcaeus's love - but it's too late. Alcaeus and his war veteran companions are now deeply embroiled in a secret plot to overthrow the tyrant Myrsilos. Against Alcaeus's wishes the coup is planned for a festival at Sappho's school. Myrsilos is murdered, but the coup backfires when the rebels' chosen replacement, the war hero General Pittacus refuses to stand on the shoulders of treason. He sentences the rebels to death and Sappho, whom he believes complicit in the plan, he banishes from the island. Sappho has lost everything. Her school. Her girls. Her one true friend and potential lover. She sails to the end of the known world... and into oblivion.

Six years later, a drunken woman in a sailor's tavern in Egypt claims to be Sappho of Lesbos. Sappho is now a legend, presumed dead, her songs famous across the known world. Many of her former students have married influencial princes and politicians and carried her words and music to new lands, new audiences, people disaffected with the bloodlust and heroic traditions of war that plague their world. One former student, Abanthis, is married to an Egyptian prince. She discovers Sappho, a wreck of her former self, and nurses her back to health. They visit the Pyramids. Here, a bearded travelling singer, working for small change, is made reluctantly to sing the songs of Sappho by young female tourists. Sappho recognises Alcaeus. Thanks to the sacrifice of one of Sappho's girls, some of the rebels had escaped. Now Alcaeus regrets not going to his death, for every day he is asked to sing the songs of Sappho and suffer the guilt of betraying her. Sappho gladly forgives him, but again, it's too late. Laying down his instrument, a broken man, he disappears into the desert.

Another former student, Atthis, is married to Minos, the king of Crete. This peaceful, cultured king is a huge fan. He pursuades Sappho, who like Alcaeus would rather drift into oblivion, to come to Crete to perform her songs. She arrives to pandemonium. She is a huge star. A celebrity. Like never seen before. At the sell-out concert, Minos announces that word has come from Lesbos that General Pittacus has stepped down, and that Sappho is welcome to return home. In contrast to her departure six years before, Sappho is greeted as a national hero, reunited with her little half-sister and restored to her school.

But still, to Sappho, there is a feeling of emptiness. Then, in the cheering crowd, she believes she sees the dancer 'Aphrodite'. After a celebratory banquet in her honour, she hurries to the cliff-top scene of their tryst all those years before, where she has since erected a statue of Aphrodite. But no one is there. Just the cold, stone statue. After spreading the goddess's message of love around the world, why has she been treated like this? In drunken self-pity, she topples the statue over the cliff. As she clings to the grass at the cliff-edge, she hears a voice behind her speak her name ... a woman's voice.

round to making *Sappho*? The early 1990s was a dry period for so-called, 'sword and sandal' pictures. *Gladiator* wasn't due until the next century. Since *Star Wars*, the future had ruled. *Robocop. Terminator.* There were period love stories in those 20 years, but they tended to be about English people having tea in Italy, or Africa. They'd even stopped making versions of my great-great-great-grandfather's story, *The Last Days of Pompeii* in the early '80s. I remember taking the script to David Aukin when he was Head of Film at Channel 4 - his words were "I will consider anything... as long as it is not set in World War 2 or a bio-pic." I guess *Sappho* counted as a bio-pic. And I guess he'd also have passed on *Saving Private Ryan* too, which went on to win the Oscar that year.

But a more serious obstacle was about to emerge. I've had bad luck in my career, but what was about to happen ranks right up there. But first Eduardo made a trip to England. He brought to Knebworth with him a mythical icon of my youth, Aristide Massaccesi. Joe D'Amato, as he was known professionally, had directed every single movie I watched at the Granada 3 in Slough as a teenage schoolboy. Not absolutely every one, but *Emanuelle in Bangkok* (1976), *Emanuelle in America* (1977), *Confessions of Emanuelle* (1977), *Emanuelle and the Last Cannibals* (1978), *Emanuelle and* the Erotic Nights (1978)... and, having studied him at Eton College, maybe I should be writing his new film The Two Emanuelles? I did some work on a treatment, but I don't think the film was ever made. Aristide died a few years later, aged only 62, but having made 197 films. And here was I, at 32, trying to make one.

THE TWO EMANUELLES

In the distant mountains of Tibet, in an old stone monastery, Emmanuelle has discovered an ancient text hidden by the monks for centuries. It is a book of love, more beautiful, more erotic, more comprehensive, than the Kama Sutra. Her translation will be the crowning achievement of her career, But the monks have agreed only to give her access to the book if she is willing to leave her life behind and enter the monastery. She is not allowed to leave until they are satisfied that she has completed a study of every last sacred word. Emmanuelle is entering her fourth year at the monastery and still the manuscript is turning up new ways and acts of love, so beautiful, so mystical, so far beyond the bounds of human imagination.. ...*etc.*

This sort of film I knew so well from my schooldays I could write standing on my head... or, I'm sure, in any one of the 64 positions described in the Kama Sutra

But this visit to Knebworth - and talk of Italian sex films - gave Mr Sarlui sir an excellent idea. Why not make a quick little sex comedy using Knebworth House, while the money was coming together for the other projects?

Sure. I was getting nervous in England not being in production yet, whilst my Red Shoes colleagues were continuing to rattle off shows, one after the other. A little sex comedy all set at Knebworth House? Easy. I'd lived there during the 1970, which was pretty much a permanent sex comedy.

It was time to return the favour to director Nick Jones, for the Avid advice. He and I dreamt up a little tale, and I wrote a screenplay. In four days. I have never written anything in four days. Before or since. Even letters take me longer than that. Particularly Thank You letters. It was The Governess Lite. I called it *The Maid*.

The Maid was about the family living in Knebworth House finding a supine woman in satin and high heels on the lawn in the moonlight. Once inside the house, she uses her influence to bewitch every member of the family, becoming their Maid, Mary Poppins, Mary Millington, etc... until they see her as the answer to all their problems. She is, of course, a Trojan Horse - a grifter laying the groundwork for her evil

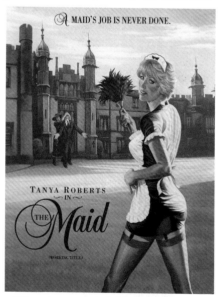

This mock up made in California as a sales pitch for the film still makes me laugh. It is not remotely representative of the screenplay, but in those days may well have been all that was needed to raise the money. As I write this caption Tanya Roberts has just died. A day later she hasn't died. Then a day later she has died. What a bizarre world.

boyfriend to turn the place over. But - can you believe it? - she begins to feel genuine affection for the family and the house, and - can you believe it? - sides with the family to see off her former partner. Lots of good gags. Sexy. Sweet. The best screenplay I'll ever write in four days.

Mr Sarlui, sir, loved it. Well, I don't know whether he loved it. But it made him laugh. With that high English production value, a good looking blonde and some laughs, he knew he could get his money back. In Guatamala at least. He decided to put it into production. He went 'pay or play' with Tanya Roberts, Bond girl from 1985's *A View To A Kill*. This means he guaranteed to pay Tanya Roberts $80,000 and $5,000 make up money - even if the film was cancelled. Surely <u>now</u> we were making a movie?

No. We were not. Tanya Roberts got her $85,000. But we did not get a movie.

I console myself that once or twice in my career, timing has worked for me. I have been lucky. Once or twice. But, on the whole, timing in my career has been working on some kind of 11 hour clock. At the 11th hour, there is no 12th.

Let me tell you about the Italian waiter Giancarlo Parretti (of course he was many other things than a former waiter, but allow me a little tabloid embroidery- I'm a bitter wronged filmmaker) who bought MGM studios in 1990 for $1.2 billion, using money borrowed from a Dutch subsidiary of the taxpayer-supported French bank Credit Lyonnais. Wikipedia picks up the story: *"Under Paretti's control, MGM released almost no films (one victim being the James Bond franchise), while Parretti enjoyed a Hollywood mogul lifestyle. He fired most of the accounting staff and appointed his 21-year-old daughter to a senior financial post. He used company money for presents to several girlfriends, including a former runner-up for Miss Universe..."* Wow, Wikipedia seems bitter too.

Suffice to say, the Parretti/MGM deal imploded, splattering French tax payer's money. Lawsuits flurried in the gales of outrage and recriminations that followed, and - just as *The Maid* was about to go into production - they gusted Mr Sarlui's way. He - who had once or twice mentioned Pasolini-esque tales of lavish orgiastic Riviera lunches with bankers and donkeys eating from the same table - had some kind of involvement in the securing of Credit Lyonnaise film finance... and Credit Lyonnaise was blowing though everyone's keyhole.

All of my Sarlui projects came to a grinding halt.

Phew, at least I had a little rental business.

Trips to Los Angeles always include a visit to see my dear friend Etka Sarlui. Eduardo died in 2010, and Etka now lives in an apartment in Century City. But she still has in her kitchen the same large painting that used to hang in her Beverly Hills home of a riotous Riviera lunch, reminiscent of the ones Eduardo used to tell of as film finance meetings. The happy memory it stirs in me, however, is of the Sunday lunches Martha and I would enjoy with the Sarluis in the early 1990s, with Eduardo stood in front of it on a kitchen chair declaiming as the King of France that he was repurchasing Louisiana, or acting out arriving breathless at the top floor of a Parisian apartment to be plied with raw eggs by Madame.

CHAPTER TWENTY-SIX

St Tropez Suntrap

CATHERINE
I don't want a relationship. I don't have time. But that
doesn't mean I don't fantasise about having one. So, yeah,
I envy what you have. But I don't want it. I mean, men are
okay... on holiday.

(*St Tropez Suntrap*, 1996)

I flew to L.A. The trip was memorable for a number of reasons. It was a little longer than the trip to see Joan Fontaine's agent. Not much. It was the last time I ate Rowntree's Fruit Pastilles. I used to eat a lot of Fruit Pastilles. Those boxes of them they used to sell at the Odeon Leicester Square. I got a reputation for offering one to my dentist when he asked if I ate a lot of sweets. I can still taste the delicious large oval blackcurrant one, although I haven't eaten one since. I came out in solidarity with my daughter as a vegetarian at this time. I remember offering one to Mr Sarlui. I was staying at his Beverly Hills mansion. He liked it.

The flight over was memorable. It was the worst in a series of traumatic airplane flights in the early 1990s that have put me off flying. One flight after another something unpleasant happened. I have done my best to forget them, but of course they continue to haunt my imagination. All were when Lockerbie was a fresh nightmare. In Houston we soared suddenly on landing because of 'an obstruction' on the runway. At LAX, just before Christmas, there was a telephoned bomb threat on the flight - they'd re-inspected all the luggage, believed it was a hoax and were going to fly anyway, but would allow anyone who wanted to stay behind to rebook. I found it remarkable that only one couple - and me - stood down. I was in the air - on an outbound flight to Canada - as the airline I was flying went bust. I had to take a plane from Boston that had had a real bomb plot foiled on its incoming flight...

I went for years without ever having a smooth flight. Whenever I was in the air I was being bumped around like an aerosol pea. This flight to L.A. in 1995, however, was the absolute worst. The plane hit an air pocket - I think they call it dead air - over the Rockies, and fell out of the sky. Well, it dropped a few thousand feet, suddenly - a rollercoaster dive - and when the pilot did at last get control of the aircraft, he came on the tannoy to say that in his 35 years of flying he had never experienced anything like that. I was starting to think Fate didn't want me in the air.

Before I had children, I didn't give much thought to being in a thin metal tube 36,000 feet in the sky. Children change you. Suddenly you think, if something bad happens up there, that's it. You would miss them. They would miss you.

I know the statistics. I know flying is statistically safer than playing hopscotch by a canal. I know airplanes work. I just don't like flying any more. I would rather drive. Or take the boat.

I will fly. If there is no boat. Or no bridge. Or no tunnel. If I have to. I will fly. I'll stare for hours at the Flight Information screen making sure we are pointing in the right direction, and repeating the mantra, "Bob Hope. Bob Hope. Bob Hope..."

This mantra comforts me, because Bob Hope flew most of the days of his working life, in any old ramshackled plane, around the world, through war zones, through storms, through everything... and lived to die in his bed aged 100. Planes do work. If Fate is on your side.

Safe in the Sarluis' Beverly Hills home, I found Eduardo questioning whether the French Government and Credit Lyonnais would want to spend even more tax-payers' money fighting endless lawsuits. The bank had made its own decisions. It was a bank. It could save face by changing a few faces. Eduardo knew his onions. But il avait tort about this. After 1994's *The Chase*, with Charlie Sheen, Eduardo did not get to make another movie. Well, he made one. But when this one was listed on IMDB, it did not list his name. Not even 'uncredited', as he's listed for 1988's *Killer Klowns From Outer Space*.

The IMDB listing for *St Tropez Suntrap* says 'Comedy'. As it should. But that's about as close to the truth as the listing gets. Almost everything about the entry - as I read it today - is wrong.

The true story of the first 'feature' film I made, is as follows.

With *The Maid* put on ice, and now no time or resources to put into the other five screenplays, Eduardo offered me a consolation. Having told him of the state-of-the-art video production kit that I had assembled, he asked me if, using this kit, I could make a film for $50,000? A 90 minute film?

Sure.

Deal.

I was given only two instructions. The film had to be sexy. And it had to have a blonde in it. With these two essential ingredients, it didn't matter what nonsense (he didn't use that word) I came up with, he'd be able to recoup his investment. Presumably in his cinemas in Guatamala. Oh, and could he have it by January?

This offer was made in Los Angeles at the beginning of September.

Clinging to my seat on the plane back to England, I set about figuring out how I could live up to this promise/opportunity. How to make $50,000 look like a whole lot more? *Red Shoe Diaries* episodes were 30 minutes, and had budgets ten times this.

Where to get my Production value? Knebworth House was the obvious answer. But at this point there was still the possibility that *The Maid* would resurface. I didn't want to play the Knebworth House card.

What did I think was sexy? Easy. The South of France. We'd rent the holiday home near St Tropez that I'd been to every summer as a kid - on a hillside overlooking the Mediterranean - put the cast and crew in it, and make the film there. At least it would be beautiful. But it was now September. I can't shoot a beach movie in November. We'd have to shoot in October. Better get a move on.

No time to write a script. But that was the easy bit. The bit I was trained for. I could leave that until I knew what elements I had.

The beautiful tiled terrace of La Maison Neuve above the Villa Dollfus on Boulevard Abel Favre on Gigaro beach, La Croix Valmer, France, with its stunning view over the Mediterranean. I spent bliss-ful holidays here every sum-mer of my childhood (that's me, left, sitting on the terrace). It belonged to the Rena fam-ily, close friends of my par-ents (left, top). My father had been holidaying here since his boyhood. The family holiday visits continued as we all grew up (left, with my siblings Pe-ter, Richard and Rosina, and Patti, our childhood nanny), and into the childhoods of my children (Morwenna, left, and Edward, left below). As the most beautiful place I knew where the sun was still shining in October, it was the obvious choice of a location for a sun-ny, sexy, low budget feature film. I could house the crew in the villa, shoot the film on the terrace and on the sandy beach below... and I could even bring Patti along, who knew it as well as I did, to ca-ter and look after us all.

I wanted as few actors as possible. I wanted a boy, a girl... and then someone to throw trouble into the mix. The basic formula of romantic drama. So, would it be a repressed couple and a carefree hod, like *Red Shoe Diaries?* Or a carefree couple and a repressed housewife, like *Lake Consequence?*...

I'd decide when I'd found the actors. And there was the challenge. How to find actors for a genre that didn't exist in the U.K., with no script, and very little money?

There was no such thing as an 'erotic' film in England in the 1990s. England had made 'sex' films in the 1970s - usually comedies - but by the 1990s the age of video had distilled this genre into either cheap tabloid glamour girl striptease vid-eos or imported pornography that the censors sliced senseless, and usually sexless. There was nothing like *Red Shoes Diaries* being made in England. *Red Shoe Diaries*, itself, was yet to be screened here. So there was no point of reference for the sort of film I was looking to make. That, and the fact I hadn't written a script, made this a difficult proposition with which to approach English actors.

Added to that, I had been out of the country since 1985. I didn't know any English actors. Well, I knew Helena Bonham Carter. Perhaps she'd like to follow her

BAFTA and Golden Globes nominations with a trip to the South of France to make a sex film? South of France - maybe yes. $50,000 Sex film - maybe no.

As an actor in England at that time you were either looking to do Shakespeare, or you were a model. There was no inbetween. In Los Angeles I could have just gone down the Sports Connection gym, smashed anyone's tail light and I'd have pulled over an actor who could both read lines and be happy to play hot. Not in England in 1995. The gyms were all still cinemas.

"Do you mean like *Basic Instinct*? That was a sexy film."

"Er, yes, kind of... but nobody gets stabbed fifty times in mine."

"Do you mean like *Fatal Attraction*? That was a sexy film."

"Yes... but again, nobody gets shot and drowned in a bathtub in my film."

"So where's the drama?"

"Well, it's in the everyday relationships."

"What, like *Coronation Street*?"

"No, not really like *Coronation Street*"...

Precious weeks of good weather were passing. In all other respects than casting preparations were going well. Mirroring the thinking behind *Red Shoe Diaries*, I felt it was essential to have a balance of female input in my 'sex' film. So I talked to La-

line Paull (left), who had recently left the Red Shoes Studio - like me, leaving Rafi Eisenman a screenplay to direct (her's called *Business For Pleasure*, 1997, with another Verhoeven alumni, Jeroen Krabbé). She agreed to co-write and co-direct the film with me. But she was in New York, and couldn't get back for a few more weeks.

I'd successfully rented a villa in the South of France. I'd assembled a great - albeit small - crew, people I'd been working with at All Digital. My friend Ronan Willson, who owned Elstree Light and Power, had generously contributed extra lights. We were all set to pile into my Toyota van and go to the Mediterranean... But I had no cast.

I needed a different approach to casting. It occurred to me that regional theatre was going on all around the country. My grandfather abolished stage censorship. There must surely be a penis waving around purposefully somewhere on an English stage. Who owns these penises? Can they do improv?...

A glimmer of light appeared. A young editor who had been working with my Avid partner Renée had a friend who lived in Camden Town who was, apparently, a good looking actor, who'd recently been on stage in Brighton... with, apparently, nothing on. That is, he had nothing on, workwise. And he'd been in a play with nothing on. Had we found our penis?

With my friend Jeremy Parkin - my Colonel Pickering from Pickering, gentleman enough to allow me to co-opt him, gratis, as co-producer - we went to meet Jay Simon (left & right) in a pub. I think the World's End. I was going to meet a guy in Camden Town to see if he was hot. Was this going to work?

Yes. But no. If only, if only, we'd had Laline with us. No question the guy was good looking. He was an actor. He relished the idea of improv. This had to be it. We hired him. £2,000 for eight days work, plus an ADR session in post. Nudity required. Alleluia. We had an actor.

If we'd been making *Confessions of a Lift Shaft Mechanic*, we'd have been right on the money. Jay could play cheeky chappy. He could play cute. But - as we were soon able to tell, even without female input - he was not... 'hot'. Not hod enough.

But, hey, we were a third of the way there. And there was better news still. Jay had been doing a play in Brighton with an actress who might be up for taking the female role. They'd hung out naked together (on stage). They'd done improv. They had 'a shorthand'. It sounded promising. The shoot was lightning short. If the two main actors knew each other it took an element of risk out of the project. At this stage, I was ready for that. What I was not thinking, was that familiarity does not necessarily lead to fizz.

Jeremy and I set off to Maidenhead Shopping Mall. Not a place I'd had cause to visit previously, or since. But this was where we were to find Lorna Elwyn Jones (below), selling hair ties. Lorna was the best possible find. I loved her line at the end

of our Food Court lunch, "So you two want me to go to the South of France with you for a week, get naked and kiss a girl. I can do that."

Hired. £2,000 for eight days work, plus an ADR session in post. Nudity required. And kissing a girl. We knew she'd be kissing both a boy and a girl now, because Lorna had dark hair. And Mr Sarlui, sir, had insisted that the film feature a blonde. And although our boy Jay was blonde, that was not going to cut it in Guatamala.

The plot was going to have to be the *Lake Consequence* dynamic, a man and two women. But Lorna herself had already evolved that dynamic. Lorna was bold. No nonsense. Her calm "I can do that" was not the repressed stay-at-home heroine of *Lake Consequence*. Clearly our film was not going to be the repressed housewife and the carefree couple. It was going to be the married couple and the black widow. That would work.

But we still needed our 'wife'. And it was at this point that I started to get concerned that we needed to spice things up. Two good-looking actors who knew each other, was a good start, but we needed to stir some danger into the mix. We needed some contrast beyond hair colour. So where were all these glamour girls that England had to offer? The ones that, at that time, were still featured daily on Page 3 of *The Sun* newspaper? - Or, more provocatively, in the pages of Richard Desmond's Northern & Shell magazines? Not that R.D.'s recent success, *Asian Babes,* was where we were going to find our 'blonde'.

An 'erotic' film. No script. Very little money. On set lodgings with the crew. No previous film credits that anybody in England recognised... London modelling agencies hung up before I'd rung them. I was becoming more and more grateful to have found the two actors I <u>had</u> found. Two years later I would have had no problem casting someone in this film to spice it up. Two years later - you will discover - I had cause to know exactly where to go to find talented people in what existed of England's erotica industries. But not in October 1995. And not having spent almost a decade in America.

There was one agency that would talk to me. A glamour agency in the Midlands town of Corby. It appeared to provide girls from the provinces for top shelf magazines. Magazines of girls showing off their nethers had just about survived into the age of video. Difficult to fit a VHS player into your lorry cab, or under your bedclothes at boarding school. There were no images of real sex in these magazines. Not like there was on the Continent, or across most of the rest of the Western World. There were minimal men, and no erections. No penises at a higher angle than Cornwall. Should an English person witness an erection that was not their own, clearly civilisation was at threat... but this paragraph belongs in a later chapter.

The Ruby Mear Agency suggested Jeremy and I might like to travel to Corby to meet a girl they thought could be perfect for the film. She would like to meet us in her home. What time could we be there? The scene that followed in Corby was straight out of Monty Python. Jeremy and I arrived at a terraced house to be met by an aggressive male teenager with a broken nose, angrily leaving,

"Yeah, what d'you want?!"

"We're here to see Shirley."

"What for?!"

"Is she in?" -

"Don't worry Darren, I'll deal with this." A brillcreamed 'Graham Chapman' in a cardigan, with tobacco pipe in hand, encourages the young man to move along. "Will you gentlemen please step into the lounge?"...

Jeremy and I squeeze our bottoms together onto a small flower-patterned sofa in front of a gas fire.

"Excuse my son, he got into a fight over his sister."

"That's gallant of him."

"Mmm... yes. He was not aware she'd had those photographs taken for that magazine. Came as a bit of a surprise. As it did to us all."

"Would you gentlemen like a cup of tea?" Hair-quaffed 'Terry Jones', in a frilly-edged flowery apron, has popped her head around the door...

A few minutes later - with still no sign of Shirley - Jeremy and I are balancing sugared Lincoln biscuits on our saucers from a little commemorative plate.

"So, you gentlemen want to take my daughter to the South of France to make a film?"

"Yes. It will be a lovely film, sir. Very beautiful."

"That's all very well, but I think I am correct when I say that you will want my daughter to appear naked in this film?"

"Er... yes sir. It is set at the beach. In the South of France."

"Now, don't get me wrong, boys," he lights his pipe, "I've seen a French film or two in my time. Very artistic, yes. Very nice, yes. But tell me this, just how naked will my daughter be in your film?"

"Er... she'll be very naked, sir."

"Indeed? Well, I appreciate your honesty, gentlemen. But I'm afraid that's not enough of an answer. Will we, for instance, be seeing her... breasts, when she is naked?"

"We will, sir."

"Both of them?"

"Yes, both of them, sir."

"I see. And what about her... her... the rest of her?"

"Yes, we will be seeing the rest of her too. We will be at the beach."

"Ah, but I think you will also be photographing her in bed too, won't you?" He is now pointing his pipe at us.

"Well, we haven't written the script yet, sir - but, yes, I suspect there will be a scene in the bedroom."

"So... in this scene in the bedroom. Tell me. Will my daughter have one leg one way... and the other, the other?"

"It is not a pornographic film, sir."

"So my daughter's legs will remain together?"

"Well, it's a moving picture, sir, so it is possible that they may not-"

At this point, the daughter bursts into the room - looking younger than in her photograph - "I'm making the film, Dad, You can't stop me!"

"Shirley! I told you to wait upstairs!" He is out of his chair. Mum has followed her into the room, looking alarmed.

"I didn't ask Darren to get his nose broken! It was just *Mayfair*! He reads *Mayfair*!"

"That's why it was a bit of a shock to him, dear..."

I notice Jeremy is now instinctively touching his own nose, feeling it nicely 'not broken'... Time to make our excuses. Shirley was - it was now clear - a little young to play a housewife. Well, not in Corby, maybe. And perhaps not in Guatemala... But certainly in our consciences.

I don't remember what our excuses were. I do remember on the A1 going home, getting the giggles. Childish, desperate, hopeless, giggles.

We were very close to our start date now. I think we had a week to go before we were booked to leave for the South of France. It was looking like we'd have to find our third performer on location. I don't know how that would've worked. What would we have done? Seduced somebody at a beach bar? If it was going to come to that, I was glad we had bachelor Jeremy Parkin on the team.

Then we got another call from Ruby Mear. A blonde girl from Doncaster called Mandy was going to meet us at King's Cross Station... How would she recognise us?

Fantastic. We'll be the two desperate film producers sharing a cup of tea.

"What experience does she have?"

"She's done a sex film before. One that couldn't be released in this country."

"Sounds promising." I remember the look on our actress Lorna's face.

So off Jeremy and I went to King's Cross. To meet a blonde called Mandy.

I'm sure this isn't how Merchant Ivory cast their films.

Mandy seemed nice enough. She wore red. She looked a little like Renée Soutendijk, with peroxide blonde curls. She didn't sound like Renée Soutendijk. She sounded like she was from Doncaster. But that didn't matter. We'd write around that. Hired. £2,000 for eight days work, plus an ADR session in post. Nudity required. And whatever else Mandy could throw into the mix to spice things up.

So we were off. Or at least we were if Mr Sarlui, sir, wired the money. I was starting to get that feeling in the pit of my stomach. I've been here before. No money. No film. But - at this 11th hour - Eduardo was good to his word.

$50,000 arrived in my account - as £35,000. I was already committed to about £28,000 of that. I knew I needed to save £5,000 to do the sound mix. So, we had about a couple of thousand pounds to drum up some fun and glamour for the cameras in the South of France. Should be possible.

We'd bought the actors flights, and were going to pick them up at Nice airport the next day. The crew were going to take my Toyota passenger van, with half the kit. Jeremy was going to take his E-type Jaguar (right, with him in it), which would add some easy glamour to the screen. He was going to drive down with Patti Razey, my childhood nanny, who was going to do the catering (in a villa kitchen she knew well from family holidays). I feel when one is off to make a sex film one should take  one's childhood nanny. Laline and I would drive with the other half of the kit in a run-around old Ford Escort, and write the script on the way. We were going to set off at night to catch the - cheaper - dawn ferry. In all three vehicles we could share the driving. But adrenaline was high. This was all too exciting to sleep.

Then, that evening, we got a call. It was the Ruby Mear Agency. Mandy's boyfriend had rung to say Mandy had glandular fever. Mandy was not coming.

Decide for yourself the truth about Mandy's glands. From our perspective, it didn't matter. We were off to St Tropez to make a drama with just two actors. Maybe *Waiting For Brigitte Godot*? Or *Rosencrantz and Guildenstein Are Dating?*... Fuck.

Remembering Lorna's brave but not-entirely-comfortable face when we'd told her she was going to have to kiss Peroxide Mandy who we'd met in Kings Cross station, I rang her with the news. Was there - please, please, please - any actress she knew who would consider coming to the South of France with us for a week? Tomorrow? Yes, I'd asked her this question before. But maybe if I asked her one more time it would make the difference. Otherwise we were off beach bar crawling. No such thing as Tinder in those days. Oh, and one more thing, Lorna... a blonde.

Maybe it was that word that triggered the thought. "She not an actress. But I do know a blonde that might come."

"Who is she?"

"My hairdresser."

"You think your hairdresser might fly to Nice with you tomorrow for a week of snogging and naked sunbathing?"

"She might."

Lorna called me back in ten minutes. "Well, she's already gone to bed, but I've woken her up and she's said yes."

"Yes?! Alleluia... What does she look like? Really? She'll definitely come? And she's definitely blonde?..."

"She's at her boyfriend's house, so she doesn't have a picture to hand, or a fax machine [Millennials, this is 1995]. But she's getting dressed and going back to hers, where there is a fax machine. You'll see a photo of her in 45 minutes."

45 minutes we can do. No one had envisaged much of a nap before departure. The whole crew was clustered round the fax machine as it started to whirr. It was a black and white headshot, top of the head first... the hair was fair. That was it. Hired. Before waiting to see the rest of the photograph I started to feed a contract back into the fax machine. £2,000 for eight days work, plus an ADR session in post. Nudity required. Leaving from Gatwick tomorrow. Booked name 'Mandy from Doncaster' to be changed to... Alison Walker, hairdresser from Horsham.

Everyone piled into their cars. We made the ferry.

I should have recognised, at this point - or perhaps in Corby - that the film we should have be shooting was not some fiction we'd dream up on the way to St Tropez, but our own 'making of' this film. It would likely be more entertaining than any fiction we could plan. But that had kind of been done before, in the last decent sex film the English had made, *Eskimo Nell*, in 1975. As it was, we set off into the night, and Laline and I started to build a story. We had six days to shoot in the South of France, followed by a day off (in my mind a contingency day), then there would be two contracted days left to shoot any wrap arounds in England. Could we get 90 minutes out of that? With two actors and a hairdresser? Sure we could.

Our secret weapon was going to be that Laline had lots of former boyfriends in the record label business. Music makes a movie. Laline had access to some truly great music from burgeoning record labels that were content to let their artists' music feature in our film for a peppercorn. With our dual state-of-the-art DigiBetacam cameras we could shoot lots of beautiful montage sequences in the beautiful South of France with our beautiful - well certainly very good-looking - cast, throwing the sequences into slow motion if we needed to pick up a few extra minutes... to hit the required 90.

But we still needed the basis of a story.

I turned again to L.A. Brazilian friend Monica. I remembered being impressed that when she was a foreign exchange dealer in L.A., she would get up at four in the morning and drive from Northridge to Downtown, so that she was in her office when the rest of the world east of Los Angeles were in theirs. She had talked of the empowering feeling of making thousands of dollars for your company before breakfast. The empowering feeling of being the only one awake in a city. High in a skyscraper. All alone. The intoxication of being astride your city. How this resolves into sexual desire... but how you are too much of a workaholic to have any time to satisfy this sexual intoxication.

The heroine of our film would be this woman. She would make a fortune overnight on a reckless foreign exchange deal, and her boss would force her that morning to take a vacation. He would give her the keys to his villa in the South of France for a week. But what good's a villa to this woman for a week when she has no one to share it with? The only person she ever meets in her work-ruled life is the skyscraper's leery - but 'hod' - night maintenance guy. So she follows 'maintenance guy' home, where she witnesses him have a fight with his - blonde - wife, and storm off down the street. So she cuts him off in her Jaguar E-type and challenges him to "Get in!"

He wakes up with her in the South of France, where she winds him up to a fever of sexual desire with sun, sea, sand and sex (poster byline), culminating in her tying him, blindfolded, to a bed head.

In the meantime she has phoned 'maintenance guy''s abandoned wife and persuaded her that she has won a supermarket competition for a free week in the South of France. She picks the wife up from Nice airport, and then does the same thing to her. She winds her up to a fever of sexual desire - with, for example, a blindfolded dinner of oysters, prawns, strawberries, etc... (c.f. *9 ½ Weeks*)... then she brings the blindfolded couple together... to make love, to the plaintively beautiful track *No More Tears* by Emperor's New Clothes.

Blindfolds are torn off, maintenance guy storms off at the deception... leaving the girls to continue having fun. But he returns, reconciled to the circumstances, with a fresh octopus that he proceeds to try to cook, with comical ineptitude, for the three of them. Cue food fight scene (c.f. *Summer Lovers*) and general good times... in the shower, on the beach, on a speedboat, at a party in a castle - where the husband and wife finally exclude our manipulative heroine in a scene of hyper romantic lovemaking in a white draped four-

poster to the even more beautiful *Her Lament* by Cleveland Lounge.

So our heroine leaves. Goes back to work alone in her skyscraper. Leaving the couple, who have refound their relationship, with the message: "The hardest thing in life is knowing that what you've got is what you want. And the best way of reminding yourself is, every once in a while, take a break."

I was quite pleased with it. Not bad for something cooked up between service stations on the A7 in the middle of the night. And in case you think that 11th hour screenwriting session wasn't seat-of-the-pants enough, while we were driving the Ford Escort was rear-ended in the fast lane by a businessman from Luxembourg. The only damage, thankfully, was to the rear of the car, but our boot-full of production gear now would only close with force, and - problematically for our equipment's insurance - no longer lock.

Six days later we were headed back up the same road in the middle of the night having shot our film, and - just to keep things interesting - I mistook a green pump for petrol and filled the Ford Escort up with diesel. Not content to sit in the hard shoulder a quarter of a mile on from the service station, I proceeded singlehandedly - with Laline steering - to push the kit-loaded car back up the hill into the service station. I have contemplated this since, and don't know how I had the strength to do that.

Certainly the adrenaline was still pumping after perhaps the most fun week I've ever had in my life. Certainly the most fun I've had in the absence of sex - just hanging out with people pretending to have it. No one - that I was aware of - was actually having sex while we made this sex film. I hope our characters looked like they were. But our eight person crew and three actors were all working 16 hour days (with 8 for eating & sleeping) to get 90 minutes of editable film with a vague story to it. After five days we felt we had it. So we did take the sixth day off. Eleven shattered naked vagrants asleep on Gigaro beach.

We did it by shooting with two cameras. Many of the big scenes were done in a single take. Since most of them were improvised there wasn't much point in trying to match them. As we'd hoped, Lorna and Jay were good at the improvisation. Indeed Lorna is good throughout the film.

Jay works okay. But I look back on two mistakes. One was casting him without a female opinion. And two was allowing him to play the role with an Irish accent. This was his request, to make the role more interesting for him. At the moment of the decision I was so relieved to have an actor - any actor - that I let him.

Jay plays the film for its comedy - which, again, I was too ready to let dominate the steaminess of the piece. I suppose this is in my nature, and echoes my preference for the comic episodes of *Red Shoe Diaries*. The ones Zalman wrote. But Zalman would not have accepted his actors simply looking good and playing funny. They had to be hot too. And Jay and his cod Irish accent was not hot.

Alison, the lovely hairdresser from Horsham, was... very lovely. She was blonde, and lovely and remains to this day a good friend. But, as we were all well aware, she had never acted in her life. She looks great in the film, Scandinavianly statuesque and white-skinned in contrast to the dark, tanned, mischief-maker Lorna. And Ali was brilliantly 'up for it'. She and Lorna were close mates, which made the unforgivingly short shoot possible.

Subsequently I have contemplated the potential nightmares we could have had if Mandy from Doncaster had not fit into this tightknit group. It might have made the film hotter, but also shorter. Much shorter.

Casting is all. And Alison was never going to be as convincing in her role as the two actors on set. And as much as Laline and I tried to use her unease for the character, and spread her dialogue scenes thick with overlayed (rather than underlayed) music, ultimately her unsure dialogue delivery distracts, and your film has a problem if your viewer is distracted, and suspended belief is grounded.

But much of the film works well. For our trials, Fate gifted us some serendipity. It turned out that the week we were shooting was also the week of the Cannes Television Market MIPCOM. The trade magazine *Screen International* was hosting an end-of-market party at

the beautiful sea-edge Château de la Napoule. Laline was friends with the magazine's acting publisher, Mike Downey. Mike allowed us not only to shoot our actors as though they were guests at this spectacular party (which alone will have cost more than our entire film), but also to use his lovely bedroom at the Château with its romantic white gauze curtained four poster bed for our big final love scene.

What is this decadence I have brought to the beautiful tiled terrace of La Maison Neuve? Perhaps the most successful simulated sex scene was one on the very edge of the terrace wall (right) - a wall I had sat on countless summers as a child (see p. 260). We set a hose spraying into the air below to create a mist of water - Lorna is hanging her knee over the precipice, looking as though, in the passion and movement of the moment, they both may go tumbling over. It worked well to keep one camera down below the wall, and the other at Lorna's head, catching the intensity of her breathing - not just because she was beautifully convincing... but because it was extremely unconvincing when the camera moved to a side view (which we didn't) and you could see Jay still wearing his shorts.

Looking back, there are a couple of clunky quasi-comic scenes on the beach that I would dispense with... but, for what it is, I think the narrative - that evolved as we went along - is pretty good for the genre. Yes, in retrospect, I would make it hotter and less of a comedy. But script-wise, I notice only one missing scene. There should be a final reckoning between our high-flying heroine and the maintenance guy at the big final party scene. There are some meaningful looks - we even had footage where the two of them encounter each other in the castle's lovely colonnade - but the thumping disco and the crazy whirl of the MIPCOM party was too much for us to get in any narrative-resolution dialogue. I cover it in the film with a little piece of voice over in an earlier sequence. "I don't want a relationship. I don't have time. But that doesn't mean I don't fantasise about having one. So, yeah, I envy what you have. But I don't want it. I mean, men are okay... on holiday."

I had to write up the script, after we'd made the film - so it could be subtitled/ dubbed in foreign-language territories - and I have often wondered how it would have turned out if we had actually shot it as a script. In fact, the whole experience was so much fun, I've considered shooting the same script all over again. Maybe every summer. I've also, over the years, considered building another film around the footage, using Lorna and her character twenty years on. I've also considered rotoscoping

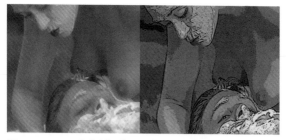

the film and turning it into an animation (left), and re-dubbing some of the dialogue.

When we got back to England, the drama was not over. I had my own Avid Film Composer editing system and Avid editor - Jeremy Shaw - to put the film together swiftly, but I needed to outsource the audio mix. I'd saved £5,000 of the £35,000 budget to do this, which I gave to Nigel Glynn-Davies and his audio post-production house, G.D.O. I liked Nigel, my age, friendly, a facilities owner and aspiring producer... and was sad and shocked to hear of his death in Cannes in May 2010 (whenever no reason is given for an early death, I don't know about you, but it makes my imagination run to what is probably much worse than what actually happened). But my experience at G.D.O. - and with the sound editor we were assigned - was not a happy one. In my naïvety, I was initially thrilled by the simply trick of boosting the loudness and sweetening my audio. Wow, that sounds amazing. I was less thrilled when we'd only made it 20 minutes into the film and I was told our £5,000 had been spent.

I was now hostage to G.D.O. £5,000 worth of work was useless unless I continued to throw money at the company. So I binned a seventh of the budget, and did what I should have done in the first place. I walked away, and spent another £5000 (now borrowed) on the equipment to do the mix myself. It was December. I had to deliver the film by January. I knew little about sound mixing, and the sophisticated software I was now presented with was alien to me. Fortunately there was Christmas inbetween. I could work over Christmas, and beyond 5pm, to teach myself the software, and audio mix my own movie. The software was called Soundscape and it was what you used for audio production in the mid-90s if you were PC-based (which most creatives were not, so Soundscape was subsequently crushed to death by its Mac equivalent, Pro-Tools, when that software was purchased by Avid - m.o.w.l.). Soundscape was a Welsh company, with again a lovely sales person, Carl Owen. He set the machine up for me, gave me a few pointers, and off I went. The atmos, the foley, the ADR... were all added. EQ. Compression. Loudness. By January the sound mix was done. Of course, if I'd done it a few years later, when I was running my own sound studio and was a practiced sound editor and audio producer, it would have been much better. But it wasn't half bad for Christmas.

Tormenting Mike Jones our lovely sound man

The big moment of delivering the film to Mr Sarlui, sir, I ducked. This sounds terrible, but my co-Producer Jeremy Parkin did have a trip to L.A. planned, so it did make sense for me to run and hide under a duvet and send my best mate instead. Eduardo had been encouraged by the teaser footage we'd sent him before Christmas. It was Lorna and Jay, fresh from the sea, pretending to have sex on the sheer wall above the beautiful blue Mediterranean, a lose hose spraying atmosphere into the air behind them (see p.271). Lovely. But, for delivery, we were obliged to add another 82 minutes to these 4. With some judicial extra slow-mo we'd managed to hit 86 minutes in total - again, a good result in 6+2 days.

Mr Sarlui, sir, hated the film. "It's not sexy! I asked you one thing! One thing! I asked you to make it sexy. It's not sexy! You have taken my money and gone on vacation!" Eduardo was not a man to make mad. And he was mad.

But he was not so mad that the friendship was lost. He did wash his hands of the film. He wanted his name taken off it. But I did not have the money to do that.

Resourcefully, Jeremy took the film to friends of his in L.A. - Mad Dog Productions (appropriate for a film by Englishmen called *Suntrap*) - and they managed to get it placed with a sales agent, Mustang Films. We'd done some good art work for the film (below) - with a young designer I had championed in Hitchin, Dean Harmer - and I was hopeful the artwork alone would sell it. The artwork is usually enough for this sort of film. Mustang sold the film in three territories - for... not enough to cover their fee.

The three territories were Albania, Taiwan & the Philippines. Bizarrely all three countries erupted into civil war shortly afterwards. I suspect the film was to blame. I imagine there is still a revolutionary cell in Albania where I am held as a folk hero. Lines from the film, I'm sure, are still quoted nightly in Philippine coffee shops. "St Tropez! Fuck me, St Tropez! I've always wanted to go to Spain!"

The film did get one other release. I took a dozen VHS copies with me to the Cannes Film Festival in 1996. But, as is depicted in the film, after the long drive down the A7 I stopped off for a swim in the sea before hitting the Croisette with

my debut masterpiece. While I was on the beach, my Toyota van was broken into. Although there were credit cards in my jacket in the van, only a plastic bag of *St Tropez Suntrap* videos and bunch of bananas were stolen. It was the best release *St Tropez Suntrap* ever got. 12 copies shifted! I picture the kids who stole the videos, sitting eating the bananas, scratching their heads how they were going to sell on this strange English contraband. I know how they felt. I had the same problem.

Back home, a nice lady called Tanya on the Channel 5 television show *X-Certificate* gave the film a thumbs up, calling it "erotic", "intriguing", with a "romantic quality". "I would buy it, definitely" she said. But the Channel 5's Controller of Acquisitions, Jeff Ford, was less ready to pull out his cheque book.

L!ve TV, a UK cable channel owned by the Mirror Group, rated it 9/10 - "Heartwarming... and really good fun film." But we couldn't get it on cable either.

In the U.S. Playboy TV also turned it down. Just not glossy enough.

St Tropez Suntrap (1997)

If only I was running my own video distribution company. Well, see Chapter 30. That's exactly what was round the corner. So the film did eventually get a U.K. video release in 1997. And made it into one or two Blockbuster stores.

Then sixteen years later, in 2013, the film was bootlegged on YouTube. By the time I noticed, after a couple of months, it had registered over 150,000 views. The comments were overwhelmingly positive - most of them, seemingly, from the Middle East. YouTube is clearly something that it's acceptable to be caught watching on your computer in the Middle East. This was all very flattering, but I did have the bootleg taken down. I contemplated posting a legitimate version, maybe dubbed in Arabic. But I couldn't find any actors who spoke Arabic who would agree to dub a 'sex' film. I'm still looking, if you know anyone. Unless you think these hundred and fifty thousand people were watching *Suntrap* to learn English?

I remain very fond of the film. It's a masterpiece for the money it cost. If only one could put in the titles at the beginning of a film how much it cost. 'The 39 Production Company presents... a feature film made with only £35,000'.

I was absolutely right to chose the South of France, which was sunny and hot every mid-October day we were there. Aside from the beautiful images, it absolutely does have one of the best soundtracks of any 1990s film, thanks to Laline. In fact, name me a '90s film that has a better soundtrack. Even my own little self-penned,

self-plucked, guitar piece over the 'kissing a girl' scene holds up. Although, ironically, every day since, when I look at the film's poster on my study wall I notice that
in our claim 'Hottest Indie Sountrack of the Year!' we somehow - can-you-believe-
it-having-stared-at-the-blessèd-thing-for-literally-weeks-and-weeks - managed to
spell 'Soundtrack' wrong (did you notice? p.273). But at least no one can now refute
the claim. I don't know about soundtrack, but *St Tropez Suntrap* certainly has the
hottest 'sountrack' of 1996.

I have listened to Mother Earth & Matt Deighton a lot since. If you haven't,
you should. I have even, as a fan, met Matt Deighton. Although - like Peter after
the Crucifixion - I did not mention my connection to the 'sex film' that, likely unbe-
knownst to him, has his music all over it.

In 2019, Mother Earth played a reunion concert at the 100 Club in London.

 Lorna and Alison joined me at the gig, walking into
the room just as the band
played *Freethinker*, our closing credit song. The 25 years
since I last saw the two of
them in a crowded room of
dancing people - in a moon-
lit chateau by the sea - dis-
solved in a moment of magic in the blue and purple light.

CHAPTER TWENTY-SEVEN

All Digital

NARRATOR
A thousand people a day are uttering those four little words
that will change the course of their lives forever...
"I think I'm pregnant."

[we were tempted - but the script actually read:]

NARRATOR
A thousand people a day are uttering those four little words
that will change the course of their lives forever...
"Will you marry me?"

(*The Brides Guide To A Traditional British Wedding*, 1995)

In the mid 1990s a small video distribution company started up in an Estate Office in North Hertfordshire. Its portfolio grew, championing brands such as *Tractor Tom* and *Peppa Pig*. By 2003 it had grown sufficiently to purchase another North Hertfordshire video distribution company, the UK's leading distributor of Jackie Chan martial arts films, "in a cash deal reputedly worth £8m." (*The Guardian*, 23/02/04). The report continues, "Together Contender and Medusa will reach total turnover of £24m and, because both companies were profitable, the newly combined Contender expects pre-tax profits of £4m to £5m by mid-2005." Contender's founder, Richard Bridgwood, 38, "found his solution at a dinner party, where he met David Hodgins, Medusa's co-founder. The two had their first formal discussion in October 2003 at MIPCOM, the TV programming market, and the deal was signed after an all-nighter last week." Three years later, on July 5th 2007, Contender Entertainment Group was acquired by the Canadian company Entertainment One in a deal worth - according to *Screen Daily* - $97 million.

Let's start this chapter again... In the mid 1990s a small video company started up in an Estate Office in North Hertfordshire. Its production kits grew, and it was soon making sell-through videos such as *Harry The Horny Hypnotist* and *Shape Up And Rave* for a North Hertfordshire video distribution company, Medusa Communications and Marketing Ltd. Within a couple of years All Digital Ltd. was wound up having over-extended on production kit that had become obsolete, and having been sued by its primary client Medusa.

So which of these two stories is mine?

Well... it was my dinner party in the first story.

For the first couple of years of being back in England, my new little business - renting state-of-the-art video equipment - was going well. I teamed up with my younger brother Richard and we formalised the company as All Digital Ltd.

ALL DIGITAL LIMITED

We were pleased to have snapped up this name. Aside from a fully digital video production flow, the challenge I saw for video technology at this time was to produce a desktop computer on which every aspect of video production could be completed. This was the grail. A single computer that could do it all - editing, audio, effects, grading & mastering. It was tantalisingly close. What was holding the dream back was that video and audio software was being written for Mac computers - and in some instances PC - but these desktop computers were not yet powerful enough to handle all there necessary software

Photo: Louise Bobbe

and memory for full video production. It seemed to me that the creators of this software should be building computers around their software rather than trying to shoehorn their software into existing office-standard Macs and PCs.

I was determined to be the first to put together this all singing, all dancing, video production desktop. There were more powerful computers being made at the time by a company called Silicon Graphics, which were focused on 3D imaging. Surely better to start at the top of the range, with a high performance computer like this, and then to make your video, audio and effects software for that computer?

I spotted a British company, Parallax Software, making video graphics software for a Silicon Graphics computer. The software was called Matador, and had been contributing to the Best Visual Effects Oscars won by *Death Become Her* (1992), *Jurassic Park* (1993) and *Forrest Gump* (1994). Until the perfect 'All Digital' video production computer could be born, a Matador system would at least complete my 1996 state-of-the-art video production desktop portfolio.

The systems cost £80,000. Could I mirror the success I'd had with the Avid Film Composer? Buy a state-of-the-art system for do-it-yourself graphics and rent it out to production companies to road test before they made a commitment to buy? Richard and I wrote a business plan and applied to the bank under a new 'Loan Guarantee Scheme' that the Government had just come up with to encourage new start-up businesses. We were successful. The bank lent us £80,000 and we bought a Matador graphics system.

The thinking was right. I know this. I know this because, when I bragged about the Matador purchase to the Avid company, and told them I'd found the missing link to the complete video production desktop, they agreed. They agreed by instantly buying the company, Parallax Software, trashing Matador, and coming out a little later with the prototype of the grail I'd been looking for, the Avid Symphony.

It felt good to be right. It did not feel good to left holding a worthless £80,000 Matador system.

All Digital was not sunk straight away. In bragging about my production set-up, I had attracted the interest of a local video distribution company, Medusa Communications and Marketing, operating from the site of the old Regal Cinema in Hitchin (see photo p.16). It is Medusa's liftshaft that 'maintenance guy' is maintaining when looking up Lorna Elwyn Jones' skirt at the beginning of *St Tropez Suntrap*. The company was owned by good cop & bad cop, Steve Rivers & David Hodgins. In David (right), a larger and louder than life Lancastrian, I had found an English Mr Sarlui, sir.

Medusa was batting above its weight as an independent in the UK distribution business, having secured U.K. video rights to a number of international brands that sold particularly well on home video - Jackie Chan, Playboy, the popular U.S. sitcom *Will & Grace*, etc. It was getting its product into the supermarkets which, in the days before Amazon, was key to making good money in home video distribution. And not easy. It saw an opportunity to use its distribution channels to sell a series of inexpensive self-produced sell-through home videos.

Having watched *Archery - Its History and Forms* and laughed at one or two of our jokes, Medusa commissioned All Digital to come up with ideas for sell-through home videos. My brother Rich and I got the lined yellow foolscap pad out. What are people who buy sell-through videos in to? Well, beyond Sports & Pastimes (such as Archery) lots of other 'S's... Self-help... Sex... Silliness... So:

The Teenager's Guide To:

- *First Dates*... all you need to know about drink, drugs, dancing & snogging

- *Boys*... what it's like to be born with a penis - for Girls

- *Girls*... what it's like to be born with a vulva - for Boys

- *Parents*... should I listen? The shit parents know.

The Parent's Guide To:

- *Teenagers...* yes, I've been out, so what?

- *Sex Talk...* beyond Mummy lies down and Daddy gets on top of her

Knobby Know-It-All's Guide To:

- *Sex Toys...* all the buzz

- *Seduction...* eye-liner & one-liners for come-to-bed eyes

- *STDs...* does it go away if I give it to somebody else?

The Lads Travel Guide To:

- [every European capital... and wherever else the team fancies a jolly]

Cooking For Sex... heat until warm throughout

How To Haggle... guide to getting something off

Tales From The Potting Shed... storytime with Stanley the gardener

Naked Football League... eyes on the ball, lads

Naked Rugby League... hands on the ball, lads

Stevenage Vigilante... Steve, who knows Britain's rumbling curry underbelly

Post Codes From The Edge... country talk from county corners

The Bride's Guide To:

- *A Traditional Wedding...* incl. vouchers worth more than the video's price

- *Setting Up Home-*

Stop a moment, what was that penultimate one? That might work.

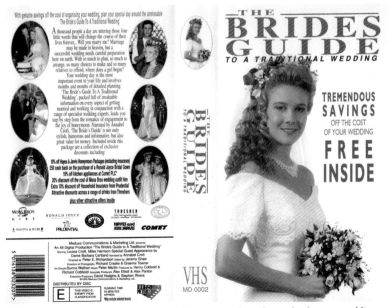

There's my daughter as a bridesmaid. She's now using this video to plan her own wedding

Cherrypicking from these musings, Medusa commissioned a series of £10,000 productions for different niche markets. Like Mr Sarlui sir, they knew that whatever 'nonsense' we came up with - with a good sleeve cover (courtesy of - we found him first - Dean Harmer) - they should be able, at least, to make that investment back.

The first idea they commissioned was *The Brides' Guide To A Traditional British Wedding*. The icing sugar in this plastic box was to be a fistful of money-off vouchers for wedding services - a Moss Bros suit, a Ronald Joyce gown, a Mappin & Webb ring, Threshers off-licence drinks, a Hayes and Jarvis honeymoon, etc. - which meant that by spending whatever the video cost - somewhere between £9.99 & £14.99 - you were, if you were getting married, getting a value of many hundreds of pounds. This video did well. Good start, All Digital.

As I had been inclined to do with Mr Sarlui sir's, screenplays, as soon as I had a good amount of work coming in, I immediately started giving it away. My wife accuses me of having a bad habit of doing this. Certainly I have given a lot more work to my friends over the years than they've given me. (But, hey, there's still time. You know where to find me.) My reasoning has always been, if times are good, pull in as much work as you can, and spread it around. It still has your mark on it, and you can get more done. It's the way Rembrandt worked. And Zalman King. But looking back now, at that stage of my career, it would have been better if I'd done the work myself, and more selectively.

I didn't write or direct any of the sell-through videos we made for Medusa. *The Bride's Guide* was directed by Peter E. Richardson (middle initial to distinguish him from *The Comic Strip*'s Peter Richardson), who as I write now is Head of Film at the University of Hertfordshire. To help produce it, we pulled in my sister's boyfriend, Alex (as in Alexander) Panton and - as ever, important not to be all boys making a mixed gender subject - my brother Richard's wife's friend, Alex (as in Alexandra) Elliot, who was brilliant in securing the many sponsorships.

I don't remember who wrote the script. That was not important enough to include in the sleeve credits. When was it ever? I recall all the good lines being written by my dear - previously mentioned - university friend Rosemarie Jarski. Rosemarie became a best-selling editor of quote compilation gift books for Ebury Press.

She dedicated one of the best of these, *Great British Wit (2005)*, to me, as 'a great British wit' - but she is hands downs and hands up the greatest British wit that I know. No returns. Although she may be Polish.

We shot *The Brides' Guide* using Knebworth House and St Mary's Church in Knebworth Park. We used our excellent cameraman from

And there's my Dad, playing 'Father of the Bride'. Oh dear, behind him I spot Richard Wells. The groom had better watch out.

Archery and *St Tropez Suntrap*, Graeme Towner, whose handheld work made us look foolish for buying a steadicam rig, and who I wish did not now live in Australia. We used Jeremy Shaw, our once £10-a-day picture-hanger, now fully qualified Avid editor. And everybody's friends and family appeared as extras in a mock wedding we staged to marry off Louisa Croft, sister of tennis star Annabel Croft who narrates the video. I have just re-watched the video for the first time in 20 years. It's better than I remember. This script hits all the salients, and is gently amusing, with lovely piano themes that do not date it. What does date it is the omission of any mention of a bachelor/stag or bachelorette/hen party. This illustrates that - like school proms and Halloween - American influence has made these rituals more ubiquitous only in the last 25 years.

My favourite section in the film is the 'successful marriage' advice of the then elderly, pink & powdered, Dame Barbara Cartland, who urges married couples to set aside time every year to go away and do what they did - "or should have done" - on their honeymoons. Being told to go and have sex by Barbara Cartland is, strangely, rather sexy.

My filmed interview with her for the programme, however, was terrifying. Early on she told me to sit on my hands. She would not say another word until I sat on my hands. I don't remember Michael Aspel having to sit on his hands. Like the Sundance Kid I'm better when I move, and I struggled with this instruction. My hands kept popping out from under my thighs to be expressive. And every time they did, the interview would come to a sharp halt,

From: Dame Barbara Cartland, D.B.E. D.St.J.

CAMFIELD PLACE,
HATFIELD,
HERTFORDSHIRE.
AL9 6JE

29th May 1996

Dear Henry,

Thank you so much for sending me the video which we enjoyed enormously.

I do think it is clever of you to think of something quite new. And I hope in future there will not be so many broken marriages as there are at the moment.

I loved doing this for you and hope you have a huge success with "The Brides Guide To A Traditional Wedding", which I am sure you will.

Thank you once again.

So much love to the family.

Barbara Cartland

"Sit on your hands!"

"But-"

"I said, sit on your hands!"

"Can I just sit on one hand?"

"No. Sit on your hands! Or I shan't continue."

It gave me a colourful picture in my head of Dame Barbara's own honeymoon.

Sitting on your hands featured in our next production. Or rather, putting your hand between your neighbour's thighs and seeing if, whilst under hypnosis, you could remove it. This was a thoroughly more 'downmarket' affair. About as far down the market, round-past-the-toilets-through-the-service-entrance-and-having-a-fag-behind-the-wheelie-bins-far as we could go.

It was called *Harry The Horny Hypnotist* and it sought to tap in on the only type of sex-related 'Adult' videos (apart from Glamour Girl profiles, such as Medusa released under the Playboy banner) that were being released in - and were acceptable in - the UK at this time. Adult comedy.

I have mentioned before that the best selling videos in the UK at this time - apart from the odd Hollywood blockbuster - featured the northern comedian Roy Chubby Brown: *Jingle Bollocks (1994)*, *Clitoris Allsorts (1995)*, *Saturday Night Beaver (1996)*, *Obscene and Not Heard (1997)*, *Chubby Goes Down Under and Other Sticky Regions (1998)*... you get the idea. These videos - I speak the honest truth - were No.1 in the home video charts through most of this period. Good on him. I've nothing against Roy Chubby Brown. Except ruining the pure three-chord genius that is the Smokie (Chinn/Chapman) song *Living Next Door To Alice*. His version *Who The Fuck Is Alice?* spent 27 weeks in the UK Singles Chart, reaching Number 3 in August 1995. This was 'adult entertainment' in the Britain we were living in in the 1990s. We may've now had a tunnel to the liberated Continent, but sex in the UK was still underground, only popping its little mole head up to be either funny or sleazy... m.o.w.l.

"It was not me, it was the other three" (Rik, *The Young Ones* 1983). *Harry The Horny Hypnotist* was -> my brother's idea. Hypnotism shows were popular in the UK at this time. Before another bloke called Brown (Derren rather than Roy Chubby) came along, there was a performer called Paul McKenna cleaning up in this curious corner of the market. All Digital should do 'hypnotism', we thought. But we should do what everybody actually fantasises they could use hypnosis for. Who, honestly, if they were able to hypnotise someone, would first think of making them act like a chicken?... You would?... So, its only me who, like Fred Astaire in *Carefree* (1938), would make Ginger Rogers want to dance with me? Clearly I'm depraved.

Harry The Horny Hypnotist was by far the most successful of our sell-through home videos for Medusa. I know this because it was the only one Medusa went on to re-release on DVD - when that new format stampede began a few years later, and which Medusa very successfully rode. It was also the worst.

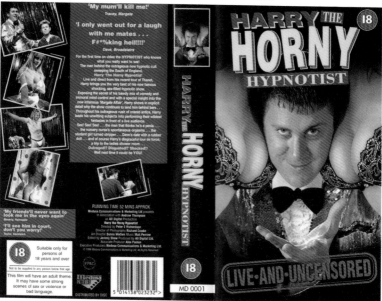

It was a very basic - very basic - comedy routine delivered in Knebworth Park's old Village Hall, in front of metallic tasselled curtains and a cajoled-by-alcohol audience of Goldsmith College students, with a handful of planted Glamour models (male & female) scattered amongst them. As I remember it, we conveniently got round the hypnotism bit with

THE PRODUCERS OF THIS VIDEO DO NOT ACCEPT RESPONSIBILITY FOR ANY UNNATURAL ACTS THAT MAY OCCUR DURING OR SUBSEQUENT TO THE VIEWING OF THIS PROGRAM

a title card saying we were not allowed to show this part of the show "in case people tried it at home". Because the '90s were the height of Nanny-State Britain, this was almost believable. However I've also just re-watched this video for the first time in 20 years, and the final edit seems to have replaced this title card with some nonsense about putting your hand between the thighs of your neighbour and seeing if you can then remove it.

For our hypnotist, we went to an improv actor called Andrew Thompson who was playing 'the Headmaster' at a London restaurant themed for hen & stag nights (which must have existed for some people), School Dinners. Andrew was naturally camp, and good when he was being camp - but the director became worried that this wouldn't play to the video's intended audience and asked him to 'butch' it up a bit. This was a mistake. 'Butch' did not come naturally to Andrew. The verbal abuse that he was great at dishing out for comic effect - when it moved away from camp... from 'phwoor' to 'fuck', from 'babe' to 'bitch', etc. - moved, inexcrementally (sic), from nonsense to nasty.

Awfully, the title *Harry The Horny Hypnotist* was mentioned in a court case in Hull in 2015, for having been found by the Police in the computer search directory of a man who was sent to jail for assault - according to *The Telegraph* (if you were ever in doubt that this paper has always been a tabloid) - "having convinced his victim she would feel orgasmic every time he said 'Kapow'". So, don't go looking this video up. It could be used against you in court. As the one Amazon review says, "I saw this on video in the 1990s and it was great fun but after 17ish years it has deteriorated very badly and is now more embarrassing than fun." Not just aged, but 'deteriorated'. This, remember, is the All Digital video that made the most money.

We were back in our old Village Hall for the next one. And on location on a rooftop beneath the Centre Point skyscraper in London. This was an exercise video. For ravers. Rave was all the rave in these early '90s years before Britpop. It seemed reasonable to us that ravers should have an exercise video too. Since *Jane Fonda's Workout* (1982) had become the highest selling home video of all time, every video company wanted an exercise video to release on December 26th. Every celebrity had done at least one. They'd done them in the air, under water, up mountains, down valleys, on the lawns of Stately Homes (Knebworth House's lawn featured in quite a good one from *Footballers' Wives'* Zoe Lucker in 2003), and of course in the nude... So Rave culture was pretty much all that was left, and it was the perfect theme for the group of performance actors we had met through fight-trainer Mike Loades (with whom I'd made *Archery - Its History and Forms*). The troupe was fronted by a sometime stilt walker called Bryony under the name Fairy Nuff, in hot

pick skin-tight lycra leggings that left little room for a Fairy Nuff. It was directed by Daniel Wilson, one of my Suntrap team (2nd camera) for whom I therefore had a special affection. Dan (right) died of a heart attack in 2010, aged 38.

In return for doing the video, I gave this troupe of actors the use of all of All Digital's production kit to film a version of a performance piece they'd staged at the Glastonbury Festival in 1994, *Peter Pandrogenous*. Still today I come across the footage of this on my hard drive. Although it looks freaky and fun, it continues to mystify me - it is sort of *Hair* without the sex and without the story. Which just leaves... the hair. Possibly hallucinogens also - and maybe that's why I don't get it. But I was not aware of any drugs in the making of *Peter Pandrogenous*, or *Shape Up And Rave*. Indeed *Shape Up And Rave*, as I understood it, was about health and happiness, and not needing drugs for these, only music and dance.

The fun for me of *Shape Up And Rave* was to put All Digital's blue screen backcloths to work. In those days the cloths were made of wool, and hung over scaffold poles. Our editor Jeremy Shaw created trippy psychedelic patterns to fill the screen behind the dance workouts (see video cover, above). I very much hope he used our £80,000 Matador. If he didn't, I can't think any other time we used it. Ouch.

Because this is when All Digital went bust. Avid's purchase of Matador completely wiped out the money we had borrowed on the Loan Guarantee Scheme. Thank goodness the money had been borrowed under this scheme, as that meant there was no comeback on Richard and I as directors, and the bank reclaimed most of its money off the Government. At least the money had gone into another enterprising British company, Parallax. Richard and I were, however, sued by Medusa.

The evening we were sued I'd been three-line-whipped into taking part in my first - and I hope last - Ceilidh. I was prancing around a barn dancefloor looking like a twat with all my village neighbours, pretending that Scottish dancing is fun... when who should I be in line to take the happy hand of, but - prancing towards me - the large and loud Lancastrian co-owner of Medusa, David Hodgins.

So I am holding hands, prancing, with the man who's just, that morning, sued me. Only in England... And perhaps Denmark. Certainly not Scotland. In any other country in the world, it would have been knives out in the car park.

As it was, a settlement was reached. We were to become Medusa's indentured servants. In other words, Medusa would continue to make our kit payments to the bank (minus the Matador, which was on a separate loan agreement, and written off) and in return, All Digital would continue to make programmes for Medusa. Forever. For nothing.

We were relieved at first. We were still in work. We could keep going. We would not let down our suppliers and friends. Richard went off to make - perhaps our best programme - *Bugmania: An A-Z of Creepy Crawlies*, also directed by Daniel Wilson; with Howie Watkins, the star of BBC 1's *Really Wild Show*; and Mr Sage and Mr Onion, the Leprechauns (aka Don Austen and John Ecclestone), puppet stars of the BBC's *Live and Kicking* and Channel 4's *The Big Breakfast*.

And I went off to make *The Love Chef* with ITV celebrity chef Rustie Lee (left). "Rustie, as the madcap 'Love Chef' dons her apron to bring the mysterious world of aphrodisiacs and romantic recipes to your dinner table. Let Rustie put the steam, the spice and the sauce back into your home cooking!"

The Love Chef is exactly the sort of programme that would've sold videos on the cover alone. And the cover photo was indeed excellent. I wish I had a copy of it. Bounteous and colourful Afro-Brummie Rustie Lee surrounded by bounteous and colourful cornucopias of aphrodisiac foods. I don't have a copy of it - in fact I only have an old VHS of rushes of our footage to show for *The Love Chef* - because Medusa cancelled the production. Despite the fact that we had shot 80% of it.

The 'we' was me and Laline Paull, reunited for a second attempt to shoot something 'sexy'. This time I'll challenge anyone to say it wasn't. I'd learnt my lesson on casting. This time Laline was with me to cast. Particularly successful was the New Zealand hod we used for the montage inserts. Our woman (who looked intriguingly like Barbara Stanwyck) returns from work to find him naked in her fridge. Out the Kiwi and all the food spills... onto the kitchen floor, for a much more down-and-dirty - milk, eggs, flour, sugar, fruit, chocolate sauce - sex session than you'll see ever see Kim Basinger slip-sliding in.

Barbara Stanwyck thought so too. As, when she and the Kiwi disappeared to the bathroom to shower off, it was audibly clear that they continued where they'd left off on the kitchen floor.

We also shot a beautiful romantic fireside love scene using Alison Walker from *St Tropez Suntrap* and her boyfriend Rick. Rick, who was a machine-gun armed policeman at Gatwick, had, I'm relieved to say, forgiven us for waking him up the previous autumn to

send Alison home to her fax machine. These two also genuinely had the hots for each other, and so no acting was required in this video.

On our Birmingham set, however, our celebrity chef Rustie Lee was so distracted by the two male models we used as her cooking assistants - naked, in aprons - that most of what Laline and I got was a lot of happy giggling & gags, and very little cooking in-

struction. My mistake, again, was thinking that comedy and raunch was what our audience would be buying this video for. Laline and I shot plenty of both. Medusa, however, for some reason was equally interested in the recipes - the premise of using everyday foods as aphrodisiacs - and, in particular, in Rustie giving detailed instruction. Having spent the first part of the morning of our one location day in Birmingham Wholesale Market asking traders what food they thought was erotic as Rustie collects ingredients, I felt it was more important in the limited time we had in 'Rustie's home in Birmingham' to

get the wide shots. The way to make this work on our time and budget, I thought, was to shoot the instructions as hand insets later in our studio at Knebworth, using Rustie's voice over. Medusa disagreed. The project was canned. Not even edited. The digital footage is now lost. Which is a shame, as I believe this one would have sold.

Yes, that's a gingerbreadman (left) - apparently they were originally used as part of fertility rituals. And yes, that's a man with bananas around his neck, kiwis on his chest and starfruit down his legs. I think purely for gratuitous reasons.

I think a breakdown in relations must have contributed to this cancellation. I, certainly, was beginning to rebel against the indentured servitude. I could see us endlessly struggling to turn out these programmes - the more lowbrow the more successful - on tiny budgets and the stretched good will of my friends and associates, and with no way of getting off the treadmill. I wanted to be making fiction. I wanted to make films that could afford scripts.

We had it out with David (Steve, remember, was good cop). There was torment (ours), tantrums (his), tears (mine). Richard and I wound up All Digital, selling off most of the gear to pay off the remaining loans.

This was a troubled time for me. My ancestors talk of the blue devils of depression that run through the Bulwer Lytton family. We've discussed already that cries and worries at work combined with the cries and worries of small children at home is a dangerous combination in a young marriage. I'd been through this at the end of our time in Los Angeles, and now back at Knebworth I was feeling the stress again. I was told by the lovely doctor at the Knebworth Surgery, Margaret Kalilani (who was a bit like Rustie Lee, but less giggly) that I was clinically depressed. I was offered the pills that go along with that. You will not be surprised to hear that I refused them. I did however end up in the back of an ambulance puking my way to Stevenage's Lister Hospital. But it wasn't Lithium. It was Lemsip.

One of the many reasons for my bitter dislike of an English winter, is that immediately the kids go back to school in September everybody - literally everybody - gets sick. Every year the cold weather heralds at least one Norovirus outbreak and about three or four cold viruses that we are all obliged to get. First you are given one by your children (that they've rubbed into their eyes at school). Then, come December, you're given one at the obligatory office and neighbourhood parties before Christmas, which will leave you feeling bloody awful throughout the holiday. Why not have the parties after Christmas, after the family time? No one listens to me.

My blue light and green vomit race to Stevenage's Lister Hospital was, thankfully, not at Christmas. But it was when all three of my family were throwing up with the Norovirus. When you're the next one in line for this treat, naturally you're not inclined to eat. I wasn't aware of it, but the only thing I was eating was grapes, and the only thing I was drinking was Paracetamol-laced Lemsips. Not surprisingly - in retrospect - my kidneys went on strike. I woke up in the early hours with my head spinning and my abdomen pierced with a crippling icicle-spike of pain. Margaret Kalilani was in my bedroom within a couple of hours (this was last century) and paramedics within three. I was stretchered down the stairs of Park Gate House, spewing left and right. Dr Kalilani needed to be sure it wasn't a ruptured appendix.

It wasn't. It was renal colic. A colic that - simultaneous to drinking a plastic cup of cool water in the Emergency Room - suddenly eased. They kept me in hospital for a couple of days for tests. And that worried them further. My bilirubin levels were off the scale, indicating liver damage or disease... or - alleluia, and all praise to the young doctor who must have just written his college thesis on the subject - Gilbert's Syndrome.

Now, I know you've just pronounced that in your head, Gilbert - as in Gilbert O'Sullivan - Syndrome. But you are wrong. I am here to tell you that this is a very sophisticated continental syndrome. No disrespect to Gilbert O'Sullivan. But this syndrome is not pronounced Gil-bert. It is pronounced Jill-bear - as in Joao Gilberto - after the clearly sophisticated moustachioed continental physician who identified it, Augustin Nicolas Gilbert (1858–1927) (right).

The 1st album I ever bought

Augustin Nicolas 'Gilbert's Syndrome' is genetic. Like bunions. Thanks Great-Uncle Quasimodo. It's a missing enzyme, an enzyme that helps break down bilirubin in your liver. Bilirubin - when he's not playing the Opry - is a toxic element produced when red blood cells are broken down. The liver detoxifies bilirubin - but has a harder time if you are a genetic freak missing this enzyme. Perhaps, therefore, my body knew all along, that - as a freak - I should not drink alcohol.

Jiiiiill-beaaaaar's Syndrome, therefore, is relatively simple to keep under control. And it has the best doctors' orders of all doctors' orders. Except perhaps, "Go to the South of France for the winter". It's "You need to eat. Eat regularly. Preferably every four hours. Otherwise you'll turn yellow." I don't mind being yellow. It tans better than being pink. And I don't mind eating. So win win.

But I haven't touched Paracetamol - or Lemsip - since that day.

Gilbert's Syndrome wasn't the last time I had doctors scratching their heads over me. A few years later my Mum and Dad were so depressed by the English winter that they prescribed themselves a February weekend in the South of France.

It's a dangerous drug that blue sky in February. It makes you do crazy things - like buy a villa in the hills above Cannes that you can't afford. They swore they hadn't intended to do it when they stepped onto the EasyJet. They'd had a lovely holiday farmhouse in the Dordogne (left) during the '80s and '90s. In a little village called Monsac. It was the childhood home of Juliet Gréco. But they'd sold it when my brother Peter was looking to purchase a villa in Spain that was big enough to summer holiday (my favourite verb) the whole extended family, including grandchildren.

Would I like to pay for their new home in France (right)? Then it could be mine one day. I could retire there, and save the Ibis bill when I went to the Cannes Film Festival. I want my Mum and Dad to be happy. So I agreed for the money to be borrowed against the only thing that I owned worth enough to cover it, Park Gate House, the house that Martha and I were living in. In order

La Bastide Longue
Le Rouret, South of France

Riviera Realty   Knight Frank

for me to buy the villa - by securing a loan from a French branch of Barclays - I had to give blood to a backstreet doctor in Nice. This white-coated Mengele scribbled in red ink on my results paper - 'presque diabétique' - 'borderline diabetic'

"No, no, no. I've got Jiiiiill-beaaaaar's Syndrome. You know, Jiiiiill-beaaaaar! Surely you studied him in French doctor school? Augustin Nicolas Jiiiiill-beaaaaar. He probably founded the college."

Despite my exotic medical condition, we got the loan. When I got to see the villa, I was able to agree that what I'd bought was indeed a beautiful place. It was not what I would have bought, but I could see it had the potential to make my Mum happy, while my Dad did the EasyJet commute back to Luton to earn enough money in the House of Lords to buy his lunch in the House of Lord's dining room.

A year later the villa was back on the market, my Dad conceding that we could not afford it. We lost £100,000, and some Winston Churchill letters to cover the amount. The place was called Le Rouret. Le Ruinée.

Meanwhile, was I diabetic? No, I had Gilbert Syndrome. But I had noticed - when driving myself to the sun - that I could no longer eat those deliciously sweet apple sauce kids cartons they sell in French service stations without my sigmoid colon becoming, less breezy French autoroute, more bumper-to-bumper blocked M25 on a grey Monday morning. In my advancing middle age, I was struggling to process sugar. A bottle of sweet peach Yop mixed with the adrenaline of driving for 11 hours at 80mph through the French countryside was - as the Chartres takeaway sandwich shop names itself - Instant Pain. Or, comme Les Anglais dit, constipation.

I realised that - rather like that day in my life (round about aged 30) when my skin went from being too greasy to being too dry - I had passed the day when my body had used up all its free sugar tokens. A childhood of boxes of bazooka  bubble gum in the kitchen cupboard and an entire youth of pints of Coca-Cola in place of any other drink - except perhaps Pschitt! when I was in France - had taken its péage, and from now on I would have to earn my sugar intake. I would have to exercise, eat (sugar-free) peanut butter for breakfast and not eat chocolate after 8pm... except on special occasions, when I could live with the fact that my bumhole would be shredded for a day or two. T.M.I.?... Sorry. At least I now don't need to explain it to you at the dinner table when I turn down your long-slaved-over tropical fruit compote.

Fructose is the worst. I discover sadly that I now cannot eat pineapple at all. That's a shame. I did like pineapple. And, goodness me, tomato ketchup. When I was a kid... that'll be up to about the age of 30... there was very little that I wouldn't improve with tomato ketchup. I accept now that I have consumed my lifetime's share of tomato ketchup. Mr Heinz's secret recipe is not so secret that we don't know it's 57 parts fructose. I now have to eat my chips with mayonnaise. Mais oui, eh?

Enough. Enough. Enough of my diet and the inside of my bottom. Time to talk about - the more aesthetically palatable - outside of my bottom.

No, this (below) isn't it. This is Barbara Stanwyck's.

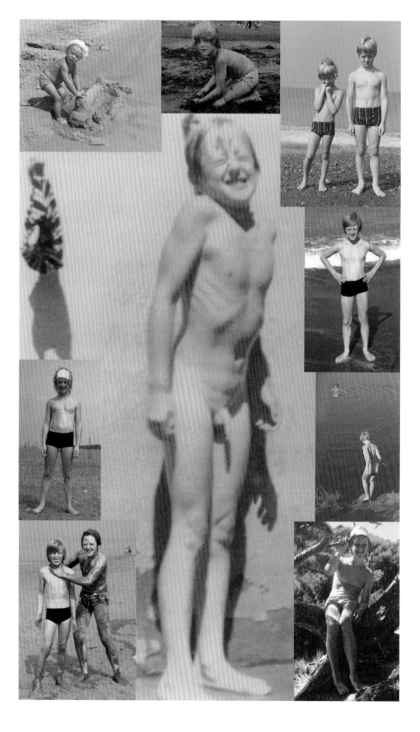

CHAPTER TWENTY-EIGHT

Cap D'Agde

I know people who have travelled to the source of the
Amazon, walked the flood planes of the mighty Zambezi,
trekked the Himalayas to the distant temples of Bhutan...
but I've never met anyone who's been to a nudist colony.

Henry Pettifer

Henry Pettifer now sells 19th Century paintings for Christies, but marvelled these words soon after sandaling & backpacking around the world with my brother Richard in the early 1990s. It is my favourite thing that anybody has ever said about me. I'd take it on my tombstone.

Even before my brief ownership of a villa above Cannes, I owned a little bit of France. Of actual French earth. It's a single tarmaced parking space in a car park near the beach in the south-western province of Languedoc. The perfect size of foreign field on which to erect a tombstone. It comes with a fourth floor studio flat

that I've owned now for almost twenty-five years. It is my favourite place in the world apart from Knebworth House. The perfect away-from-it-all holiday destination.

The flat is in the Cap D'Agde Quartier Na-turiste (right), a holiday resort for naked people.

I like naked people. They are not judge-mental. They are not aggressive. They are not

worried about unnecessary things. Naked people in the sun are less hot, and more chilled. In short, but not shorts, they are the perfect people to go on holiday with.

As a child, my summer holidays were all about the beach. My parents would find time for at least three different beaches. There would be rocky Hartland beach in Devon with my maternal grandparents, Dennis and Sheila (right). Then a spell on the sandy French cove at Gigaro at La

Croix Valmer (see p.256) - south of the coastal mamelon that is St Tropez - with family friends, the Renas. Then, at the end of August to coincide with the late summer birthdays of my pa-ternal grandparents Kim and Hermi-one (left), we would drive to Italy, and the endless sandy beach at Bolgheri - south of Livorno/Leghorn, west of Firenze/Florence (I do love that the English insisted on renaming Italy after sex and girls).

Italy was lovely. And to my taste it beat France on food. I've always preferred tomatos & basil to creamy sauces. A maternal goddess would appear every evening - appropriately called Dina (pronounced Deena, right) - to make large green glazed bowls of pasta. The beach house was across a train track. Another dark wispy matron would appear from a railway house to raise a pole to let us across. The walk to the beach was through a pine-needled wood that if I breathe deeply today I can still feel in my nostrils. The rough-sanded beach was long and deep and usually deserted,

with rustic wooden shelters, and between the toes one could catch funny hairy sand balls that I've never seen anywhere else in the world.

To most English people I know this is the perfect beach idyll. We had a Mediterranean coastline virtually to ourselves in late August, only acknowledging the existence of fellow holidaymakers and locals when we drove up into the hills for the evening passagiata, and where - having chosen a florescent ice cream from the Miko board - we'd watch a big fat evening sun sink, sated, into the sea's blue horizon... did you see a green flash? It was a magical time. Italy has been a special place to me ever since.

But, for a beach holiday, I do prefer France. France is where <u>this</u> Englishman would name the towns after sex and girls. But of course the French already have. Nice. Cannes. Frejus... Here is not, Bognor. Rottingdean. Ramsgate... But perhaps I'm being unfair, and 'Ramsgate' is sexy. Perhaps Portsmouth, Wha-hay-mouth & Broadstairs simply suggest the different sexual proclivities of the English?

But what this Englishman thinks is sexy is slipping from hot rocks into the crystal clear chill of the Cote D'Azur Mediterranean, and splashing in the surf of a long soft sandy Languedoc beach amongst carefree clothes-free holidaymakers.

As George Eliot expresses in *Mill On The Floss,* our joy in the world is born in the happy moments of our childhood. "We could never have loved the earth so well if we had had no childhood in it, if it were not the earth where the same flowers come up again every spring that we used to gather with our tiny fingers as we sat lisping to ourselves on the grass..." I feel the same about my tiny fingers in the warm sand of a French beach... amongst the coconut oil, flip flops, straw bags, straw floppy hats, and bronzed beautiful bodies of 1970s St Tropez. My joy in the world, my sensory pleasure principles, were born on Summer holidays in France spent laughing, game playing, dancing and singing to Peter Sarstedt (*Where Do You Go To*

My Lovely?) and Mary Hopkin (*Those Were The Days*) on the Rena family's terrace balcony overhanging a beautiful blue Mediterranean sea. These are the childhood joys that had the most permanent and deeply permeated effect on my psyche.

As a writer I spend most of the year alone in my study. On holiday I want to be with people. I don't need to be on holiday with people - unlike most, I am happy to be on holiday on my own (which I often am, as the summer sun clashes with Martha's busiest work time) - but I do like to be in the presence of people, specifically people on holiday. I love city breaks - but that is 'travel'. For me to be on 'holiday', I want to be surrounded by other people on holiday. Cannes is the best film festival in the world, because the whole town is swept up in the glamour and the love of film. Rio is the best carnival in the world, because the whole city sambas. Cap D'Agde Quartier Naturiste is a perfect holiday destination because everyone there, in this small town-by-the-sea, is on holiday. Not only that, they have - literally - shed the trappings of the world and everyday life.

At the moment I write this I am alone on my high white balcony at Cap D'Agde, but the sea breeze is filled with

the loud thumping beat of a foam disco party down below. Most grown ups I know would hate this. Every afternoon, 7 days a week, from 2pm to 6pm, the beachfront in this place becomes a party. I am alone. I am writing - working - but I am on holiday because I am amongst 40,000 happy naked people. They are all around me, dancing and pogo-ing in soap suds, playing happily in the cool surf fifty yards from me on the two kilometres of sandy beach, sipping coloured cocktails on high stools in thatched beach bars, sprawled reading in the warm soft sand, walking scuttling little pet dogs by jet-sprinkled lawns, shopping in the 'centre commercial' for supper and an evening outfit ('dress' is not the right word)... and, judging by animated gasps coming from a neighbour's balcony, having sex. Vicariously, by being amongst them - albeit on my own - I am also doing all of these things.

I am on holiday.

I love the routine I have here at my little holiday bolthole. Routine sets me up to write. It clears my mind of everything except what I really want to focus on. Routine is, for me, the route to relaxation. I know that is an anathema to most people, particularly on their holidays. But I love the routine of coming to the same place every year, and doing the same thing every day. Routine is the beat and rhythm of my summer holiday. I love all the parts of my Cap D'Agde day.

I wake at 9.30 to a patchwork of sunlight on my white walls through the perforated brown rollerblind, slip on my white flipflops and drape a blue kanga around my shoulders. Down four flights of steps and, within 30 yards, I am kicking off the flipflops and feeling the warm soft sand, and the chill of the clear calm Mediterranean. With the kanga still around my shoulders - to shield from the hot sun - I walk out into the shallows, soft sand all the way, to cool the blood. When I was younger the shock would come when the testicles dipped below the waterline, now I'm older it's when the belly does.

Once the chilled blood has been round the body a couple of times, I return to the beach, bundle the kanga, my glasses and flipflops in the sand, and head back out

into the sea. The first dive into the crystal clear water is magical - there are not many moments in the year when I am happier than I am at this moment. It is so beautiful below the surface, with the sunlight streaming through the water to the sandy sea bed below. I am Marine Boy again, my T.V. alter ego when I was six years old.

Back on my white balcony, I eat two slices of rye bread with smooth sugar-free peanut butter and glass of Evian. Then, cross-legged on my white bed, with a white pillow pressed against my lower back, I write...

From my bed, beyond the palm trees and fluttering flags and low white concrete of the Glamour sex club (which - honest - I've never been in) I can see the wide expanse of blue sea that I can still taste on my lips. On the horizon, a white ferry has just left the port of Sète, and heads for North Africa. On the flower-lined pedestrian walkways below, families return from the shops with baguettes and croissants for breakfast. The CD player - that I was told 20 years ago would not last one season in my rented property - spins on repeat a mix I have named *Beautiful Songs*.

Between 1 and 2pm I snap open a can of 'Thon à la Catalane'. The cupboard is piled high with these seductive red tins. Never let it be said that I ignore the speci-

My balcony is half the space of the apartment. I'd show you the reverse but it's just the bed I'm sitting on to take this photo

alities of the region. The tuna doused in the tomato sauce and chopped vegetables makes me feel I am getting both my protein and a start on my 5-a-day. If that doesn't do the trick, I have a packet of low salt Nairn Oat Cakes and a glass of Rose's lime cordial for dessert. Down below, young couples are heading towards the beach club as the beat of the foam disco begins.

A little more writing until the sun has burnt off its midday heat... then covering in Factor 30 those parts of my salt-flecked body that I can reach, it's back to the beach with a parasol and a little blue spade to dig a hole down to the wet sand to secure the parasol in. This coastline - flat from the hill of Sète to the Pyrénées - can be windy, so you need damp compacted sand to secure your parasol pole. When it is windy, this forest of willies (my grandmother's expression) becomes a windfarm of willies.

The Cap D'Agde Quartier Naturiste has two kilometres of sandy beach and each section of beach has a slightly different profile. In front of my apartment is a family section. Then, to the east, are the yellow deckchairs of a family section for those families that didn't get up early enough to reserve a place at the water's edge where they can keep an eye on their toddlers. Beyond this, is a large stretch serving the

camp site that runs for a kilometre to the east - holidaymakers without their own bathrooms make me a little wary of the sea water along this stretch of beach. Then there's the couples beach bar, which every evening turns into an Annette Funicello movie. With less clothes. Next, is the notorious 'swingers beach', which takes the car park and the layby out of dogging. This section of the beach merits its own pair of paragraphs.

The swingers beach at Cap D'Agde must be unique in the world as a lifeguard-supervised open-air orgy. Maybe 'Plage Surveillée' is in fact French for dogging. On those days when it is either too windy for a parasol, or - more rarely - when the weather is just not conducive to lying on

the beach, I tend to walk the whole length of the beach... and rain or shine, hail, or, for all I know, snow, the swingers beach is always populated, usually busy.

I have seen virtually every sex act imaginable on this beach, at all times of the day. And that's without looking for it. There are those who are there specifically to look at it. Groups of scopophilic sunflowers turn this way and that, in clusters, drawn to sexual activity. I am yet to understand the appeal of these clusters. Don't get me wrong, I enjoy watching people have sex as much as the next man, or woman, but a spectator sport? The crowd of (mainly) blokes waving their willies look to me like one of those bellowing choruses in a shouty musical about to sing *You'll Never Walk Alone*. I understand the heightened excitement of being part of a crowd. I've thrown my arms into the air as one of 125,000 people singing "And through it all!... She offers me protection". But these leering meerkats look more like they're trying to get on a Tokyo subway train. And as for being one of the athletes at play - well, I feel that's a job best left for professionals. The crazy golf course of sex presents so many pitfalls and pratfalls that only the most courageous and impulsive amateur would want an audience involved. And it's 2 o'clock in the afternoon.

The next section of the beach is the LGBT - mainly G - stretch. I have friends who, when I tell them I prefer to holiday at a nudist resort, ask if I didn't get enough of all that living in West Hollywood. This is a particularly odd response. It suggests the thinking, nudist = exhibitionist = gay. Or nudist = promiscuous = gay. Or nudist = pervert = gay. All bollocks. But indicative of how little naturists are understood. In every town of 40,000 people there is sizable gay contingent, and Cap D'Agde Quartier Naturiste is a normal town in this, if no other, respect.

I do note that the beach bar at the very French and hootingly heterosexual (except for scheduled minority nights) Le Glamour sex club has recently been renamed (in lower case) "l g b", and although this playful branding will not be lost on the Club's savvy owners, they would be loathe to restrict their haul of euros by these letters standing for anything other than 'Le Glamour Beach'.

The last section of beach - before the signs tell you are entering the 'textile' Marsaillan Plage - is either for the extremely anti-social, or for the extremely fit naturist who does not blink at carrying his beach bag two kilometres to find a pitch. Although there are always, amongst these naturists, one or two adventurous white-bummed tourists who having found themselves amongst the fluorescent lycra and uptight screaming kids of the 'textile' beach, have been happy to cross the border and lose their shorts for a more peaceful stretch of sand.

Then, invariably, there are one or two naturists who defiantly park themselves just the other side of the 'Fin de Plage Naturiste' sign. Liberté! Égalité! Fraternité!

To the west of my apartment, a more cosmetic, shop-front beach leads quickly to the cul-de-sac of the marina entrance. Again, my suspicious mind considers why the muscles grow so well on the rocks around this cul-de-sac of water.

So, my beach is the clear beautiful family stretch that is 100 paces from my balcony - and, naturist or not, it must be one of the most lovely beaches in Europe.

The same families return to this beach every July - I have never spoken a word to any of them, but I know them all well. Over 25 years I have witnessed children grow up and return with their own children. I have fallen in love - at a distance

- with beautiful supercilious French girls, forever tying up and unleashing silken pony tails. I love - and marvel at - how they continue to return on holiday with their parents well into middle age. I love the yummy Scandi mummies sat dunking their fat babies in the surf. I love parties of adventurous college-age students, who come down from the Cévennes hills to cast off their backpacks and their clothes to wonder why they've been sleeping on station platforms and trekking from dusty town to dusty town when they could have been here chilling on the beach.

I love all the residents of this lovely beach. But I would be discombobulated if a word ever passed between us. My French, Swedish, German, Dutch, Italian, Spanish is not strong enough for a conversation of any meaning. But, more importantly, I love the relaxation of anonymity. I have overheard that I am known as "L'Homme Avec Le Chapeau" - but since I've heard this I've set aside the straw panama, as it conjured for me some dreadful image of a pasty Graham Greene Englishman. I want to be as naked and continental as everybody else. I want to be melted by the sun into a pot of coffee-coloured people. I want to indistinguishable as anything but a European on holiday. A citizen of the sun.

"But it's much sexier to have something on." This revealing reaction is also common. People who say this, clearly go to the beach to be sexy. They must <u>wish</u> for a bonking section on their holiday beach. I suspect there isn't one. Of course it's sexier to drape cambric over your nipples, or - for some (please exclude me from this one) - to highlight your erogenous zones with fluorescent triangles. Unless you're a teenager living fulltime in your imagination - in which case, the novelty is <u>not</u> having to use it - most of us are turned on when we <u>are</u> made to use our imagination. Follow a pair of denim hotpants along a nudist beach and you will see this distinction immediately.

But when I'm at the beach, in 'relax' mode, the beautiful holds more interest to me than the sexual. Human bodies are beautiful. All human bodies are beautiful. You'll appreciate this if you spend time surrounded by happy naked people. If you feel beautiful, you are beautiful. I say this a lot. I say it every time my wife is made to have her photograph taken and, still, she can't get to grips with the concept.

But to me it is a truth self-evident. It doesn't matter what shape you are, what size you are, what colour you come in, whatever 'imperfections' may distinguish you from airbrushed norms... If you feel beautiful, you are beautiful.

And when you are on holiday, kissed by the sun, and surrounded by happy people who all look just like you and don't care. There is nothing more self-affirming. It's a beautiful thing. If only all the kids in the world were exposed to this kind of environment. How much happier a place the world would be.

The sad irony is that exposure to kids is what naturists are most often vilified for. Mothers, put your breasts away - you are not nurturing your children, you're turning them into perverts. Fathers, put your penises away - your babies will be traumatised into contemplating where they come from...

Doing thus, of course, you are achieving the opposite. But you don't need that essay here. Those that would benefit from it, I suspect, have not made it this far into this book. However if you want to read it, there's a version of it every month in *H&E* magazine. In continuous publication for more than a century, this glossy stalwart is easy to slip between the folds of your *Evening Standard* at the King's Cross W.H.Smith. Subscribe to it, and leave it on your coffee table. A Bas Les Bourgeois! Vive La Revolution!

But I was running through my Cap D'Agde day... I was enjoying three or four hours of late afternoon sun lying on a kanga under a fluttering parasol surrounded the sounds of a summer French beach... the lapping surf, children playing, the beat of the bar disco, the grunts and thuds of a game of volley-ball against the dunes, the distant roar of a jetski in the bay... Then comes the golden hour, when in the early evening light everything suddenly becomes even more beautiful... as the crowds thin, and the most chilled of the holidaying families are left, the children doing cartwheels in the sand, the parents

putting off until the very last moment the inevitable cleansing and catering chores that await back at the flat or in the tent...

Eventually, I pick up my glowing, sand-dusted and sun-braised limbs and head back to luxury of a desalinating, desanding bubble bath. I doubt many mini bathtubs like I have in my studio apartment have survived the post-Millennial pimping of these flats into the sexy love-lairs that the rental agencies now believe their discerning metro-wallets desire. My flat remains defiantly beach basic. A chilled West Indian from London called Gus plastered the artex walls and ceilings that I'd purchased in 1997 in flat white (until he ran out of English plaster and had to finish the loo walls in what we understood to be French for plaster, but was actually plaster of Paris (rather than plaster of France). It's all white. Except that it retains its '70s glazed brown kitchen tiles, its well-cooked omelette coloured floor tiles, and its large brown pin heads that I used to cover the screwheads under the lime-washed wall cupboards... but everything else - and there is very little else - is white. Breezy, simple, basic white. The complete opposite of my other home.

I have no furniture. There's a bed, covered with white pillows, and a set of white balcony chairs around a white balcony table. That's it. Perfect. Just disappointing not to have an excuse to text my WhatsApp groups about going into French furniture stores: "Looked in my Fly - nothing worth having in there" or "Look what I found in my But!" French furniture chain stores do have the best names. No 'Kingdom of Sofas' or 'Leather Furniture World' here, as the imperial English prefer.

I suppose two further things are not white. In the small hallway between the one room and the front door are two high-wall carpentered bunk beds. I have left these in their natural wood finish, because they were beautifully hewn by the bare hands of late friend Matt St Hill, the Stevenage (then Melbourne, now Heaven) fireman. And the light blue bathroom

tiles would be too big a job to replace. But all else is white. And I am particular - you say peculiar - that the sheets, blankets, cushion covers, bath mats, curtains (purely decorative, for blowing in the breeze), even the loo and kitchen rolls are plain white.

The white glazed ceramic mini bathtub is a prized relic from 20th Century. And I love it. I don't fit in it. My legs need to be up the wall to get the rest of me in. But it soaks away the sand and the salt every evening, and leaves me relaxed, clean and primed for taboulé orientale and carottes rapées on the balcony whilst surveying the mêlée of burgeoning parties, restaurant browsing and peacock passagiata below.

Then - like all the children peppered around the village - I park myself amongst the white cushions on my white bed and run my very own film festival - a film festival for one, until the early hours. I watch all the films I don't have the hours to watch at home. For instance, I will watch a 16-film Hitchcock boxset, in chronological sequence... and learn much. Or every Joan Fontaine film she made as an RKO contract girl in the 1930s, in chronological sequence... and yearn much. Or, this trip, I am watching all the TV shows I remember watching as a kid. I have a specific reason for doing this - to reawaken my childhood self for this book - but what fun! When else would one ever do this? Certainly not to entertain my own kids. Even my open-minded and beautifully interested children would struggle with more than one episode of these, usually black & white, 1960s *Watch With Mother* period pieces - *Champion The Wonder Horse, Belle and Sebastian, Skippy the Bush Kangaroo...*

Then - when, for the first time in 12 hours, all is quiet beyond the balcony except for a drunken leather-clad German foursome deciding whose apartment to sway home to - bleary-eyed and content I lift myself into a vertical position one last time to brush my teeth, lower the rollerblind to halfway, and collapse back into my white sheets.

That's a holiday.

Of course it's more fun in the company of my wife. And occasionally it is. Every once in a while Martha will shed the chains of her problem-laden desk and fly down for a few days. As mentioned it is problematic for her to do this in high sum-

mer - when the Knebworth House events she spends all year organising proliferate - but when she does it, she will usually admit it has been good for the soul.

Should I be staying at home in the high summer too? Yes, I could forgo a summer holiday. Plenty of people do. But I would not be happy. I would be miserable. Yes, my birthplace was America, the land where holidays are scattered Mondays, and retirement. Yes, I was born in the land where a three-month summer school recess is something to be endured for the humidity, or worked through to pay for the privilege of an education no one can afford. But I am not American. I am European. A spoilt Brit. To assuage my miserable Atlantic winters, I have been given the miraculous Mediterranean summer. Like A. E. Housman's cherry tree, it needs to be visited - for, take from seventy summers, fifty, it only leaves a score more... and since to look at the Med, a score of summers is little room, down the Autoroute I will go, to see the sun and naked buns.

The original purchase of my flat in Cap D'Agde was the result of the worst summer holiday ever. In the '90s, when both Martha and I were working jobs where the buck did not stop with us, we were both able to take ourselves and the kids on summer holidays. In the spring and summer of 1996 we had given lodgings to a descendant of Antoine de Saint-Exupéry (whose book *Vol De Nuit* was my O level French text). The young Frenchman was working in Stevenage for what was then Marconi and is now Airbus - and probably by the time you are reading this, wholly located in Toulouse, courtesy of the backward burghers of Brexit. His family home was a chateau and vineyard near Narbonne - 30 minutes from Cap D'Agde - and rather than taking rent from him, I innocently inquired if he might have somewhere we might stay for a couple of weeks in the school holidays?

He did. An old retainer had recently died leaving a free apartment - he was sure his parents wouldn't mind if we took it for a couple of weeks. Off we set in my Toyota Space Cruiser, loaded with provisions - I remember specifically trays of mini boxed apple juice for the kids - and, after a 16 hour drive, found this lovely old French chateau farm. The apartment, however was not lovely. His parents did look unnervingly surprised to be gifted nice house warming gifts - English tea, Knebworth House tea towels, etc. The dead retainer had been removed - along with his possessions - but not his collection of 50 years of dust and woodworm-infested furniture. We unloaded everything stalwartly from the Space Cruiser, bolstered by brave glances at one another. The dust literally swirled around us. Edward was only 4-years-old and it was difficult to find anywhere to put him down. Having unloaded, we examined the cast iron cot beds and pre-War mattresses. There were bugs crawling through the fabric of them.

We started swiftly reloading everything back into the van. Heads down. As quick as we could, so as not to face the embarrassment of being found leaving before we'd concocted an acceptable excuse. I remember in our haste I dropped one of the trays of apple juice and trod on it - so now my sticky shoe was collecting the dust and bugs. I found Maman, and explained that we felt we were just too far from the beach here, and that the kids were most looking forward to the beach. And we fled.

We drove to Cap D'Agde and to Tourist Information - we were told that the Quartier Naturiste was completely booked, as it always is in high season. So were the other Quartiers. The whole town was booked. We were put in touch with a letting agent, who spoke no English... but all that studying of *Vol de Nuit* and the inspiration of desperation allowed me to negotiate his one final remaining apartment for the two weeks, payment in advance.

It was at the very top of the plainest, dullest block in downtown Cap D'Agde. Despite the four floors that we then had to carry all the trays of apple juice up, it still managed to have no view but the side of the building next door. It had decent beds and linen, but the apartment had not been cleaned - still, we took it, and Day One of the vacation was spent cleaning the flat from top to toe. I mean literally top to toe, because I specifically remember scrubbing the slats of a high level extractor fan, that were thick with scum. I sometimes wonder whether this quest for cleanliness was excessive, but it was more than simply having small floor-wiping children, it was a determination to make a nice nest for my family for what was a particularly rare, special and - especially in Martha's case - deserved, summer break.

Having spent the whole day cleaning, we headed to the Quartier Naturiste for supper at the lovely beach front bar L'Horizon. I don't remember the meal - but my imagination colours in that, being the evening, our tired young children were not the preferred clientele. What is firmly etched in my memory, however, is the moment we left the restaurant, when Martha stumbled on the stone stairs in her sandals... Back on her feet, she could barely walk. So we skipped the planned evening stroll on the beach and headed back to the apartment.

Not only did 4-year-old Edward want carrying up the four flights of stairs, but now, so did Martha. Clearly this was not simply a sprain. The following day was spent at the Radiologist negotiating a lot of French vocabulary that is definitely not in *Vol de Nuit*. In our French school textbooks, 'Jacques et Françoise' had spent whole chapters 'À L'École' and 'En Vacances', even 'Au Zoo'... but never 'Au Radiologie'. Day Two of the vacation spent in this clinic determined that Martha had broken a bone in her foot and that it needed to be set in a - non-beach friendly and non-four-flights-of-stairs friendly - plastercast.

Martha didn't know what I was doing, but she was going home. First thing next morning she was being be wheeled across the tarmac of Carcassonne airport. For

the third time in a couple of days I reloaded the Space Cruiser, and the kids and I followed her home by road.

That was our Summer Holiday of 1996. I vowed that would never happen again.

The following Spring on my way to the Cannes Film Festival, I stopped off in Cap D'Agde. There was an 'À Vendre' sign on a top floor apartment of the beachside horseshoe-shaped building, Heliopolis, facing southeast to the sea. 'Agence Geneviève Naturisme' was on site, so I went and introduced myself to a Dutch lady named Petra. She explained that the flats were priced by floorspace. Since that upper floor flat had very little floorspace, it was the cheapest in the block. The best view of the ocean, no one above it... and the least expensive. 190,000 French Francs - roughly 19,000 English Pounds. It was this flat or a new car. I loved my ten-year-old Toyota van.

I rang Mr Carter, now the bank manager at Lloyds in Stevenage, and asked if he would lend me £25,000 (giving me some budget to plaster over the artex and paint it white), with a ten year payback. Without even illegally insisting that I take out Payment Protection Insurance, he said... "yes". (He did charge P.P.I. the following year on an equally good £25,000 investment - a replacement DigiBeta Video Mastering Deck, see p.237 - but Lloyds have recently repented and paid it back.) He did of course insist on a personal guarantee. For £75,000. Signed not only by me but also by my father. We may see the last century as the good old days of personal banking, but we shouldn't forget it had its own nonsenses. To be fair, I didn't really own anything realisable for £75,000 in the complex cat's cradle of trusts that is the Knebworth Estate. But it ought not to have been a difficult decision for Mr Carter. It was one of the best decisions I ever made.

Every year AGN sends me a few thousand Euros for renting out the apartment when I'm not there. One goes on taxes, one on utilities and the remainder pays for my summer holiday - for which I always have the best beach destination.

If I have Euros left over - which I usually do, because Thon à la Catalane is not

Twenty-five years of happy summer holidays at Cap D'Agde... and other lovely French Mediterranean beaches

expensive - I visit my French tailor. Gemo. 'Gemo of the Centre Commercial' is my 'Antonio of Rome' - a chain clothing store in every French town, that has clothed me - when I have to be clothed - for over 20 years. Each year I return home to spluttering admiration from my children at this year's Gemo Summer Collection.

I never buy clothes anywhere else. And I've never seen anyone in England wearing these distinctive summer classics. You are thinking, taking clothing tips from a naturist is like taking communion from an atheist. So why am I so often complimented in England for my natty cloth jackets and white collarless cotton shirts? I have for you one word. And always 30-50% off. My French tailor. Gemo.

Twenty years after this happy French apartment purchase - during which time the lower apartments have had their views of the ocean compromised by the development of Le Glamour Beach Club - my top floor studio (there is even now an elevator) is currently worth about 150,000 euros and climbing. The 'white against the blue' is the 'black against the red' in my personal finances.

And I still absolutely love it.

I know the French are just as petty as the English. I know in France you have neighbours and councils and nannying rules and regulations to make your everyday life just as difficult as it is in England. I know the grass isn't greener on the other side of La Manche. I know it still needs mowing and the dogs still crap on it. But the luxury of a summer holiday is that, for a few days, you can ignore all of that. You can live in a France that is warm, sunny, carefree and endlessly beautiful - and you can picture it always like that.

When I drive back, up into the Cévennes, over the stunning Millau bridge... my head is swimming with endorphins. Then, I feel the world is a magical place. I feel its endless possibilities. My creative energy is at its peak. I have so many stories to tell. I have so many plans to fulfil. I feel ready to meet the long English winter, ready for my desk, ready for work, ready for its frustrations and challenges.

France at 130 kph. The speed of the open road, the beauty of ancient sun-kissed landscapes, even the soft sweetness of the Thon Crudités garage sandwich... everything is on my side. I have a windscreen dongle that beeps me through the motorway pay stations, so I don't even have to contemplate that there's a price to use these magnificent roads. Even when I get pulled over for not noticing that my Aygo can go faster than France's very civilised speed limit, or for not coming to a complete stop at a Stop sign at a deserted junction, I feel have enjoyed munificent benefits well beyond the sting of any additional road tax.

I pass along la Route du Blé, beneath the wonder of the world that is Chartres Cathedral, and on to the hills and valleys of Normandy. Northern France I see, therefore, every year, in the golden hour of a summer evening. It is the same Northern France that was there on my drive down, but then my eye was fixed on my destination. Now the beauty of this land is overwhelming. As I speed through it, on mostly empty roads (why would anyone want to go towards Britain?), the evening summer sun throws a rich golden glow over meadows and farmland and little hamlets that seem undisturbed for centuries. This is peace. And then my mind - open for anything, in love with everything - is flooded with the thought of what this land looked like two generations ago. And the countless men who died here to create this peace. Am I the luckiest sack of skin, blood and bones that every lived?

In this moment, I must be.

CHAPTER TWENTY-NINE

Wearing A Smile

*From the comic book version of **Wearing A Smile** (2001)*
illustrated by Tim Major, watercoloured by my sister Rosina

VIRGINIA
I don't know why you're fussing, Mom. It's not like he's got
much to put on a postcard.

NICHOLAS
Classical sculpture idealised the small penis. A big penis
was considered bestial-

MR WHITE
We don't need a lecture on pornography, Nicholas

NICHOLAS
It's art, Dad.

MR WHITE
That doesn't stop it being pornography.

BARRIE
(Virginia's husband)
Chisel 'em off, I say. That's what they do in all the good
museums.

(*Wearing A Smile*, 1996)

There was clearly a screenplay to be written about nudity. There was not back then, and there has not been since, a mainstream movie about nudity. This will seem self-evident to those who equate nudity to sex, to shame, to the forbidden, and, at worse, to the perverse. To these people nudity is not a mainstream subject. This is plainly ridiculous. Every human being in the world is as much naked under their clothes as they have a heart beating under their left breast. How much more mainstream can you get? Nudity is the last absurd taboo.

Time to put nudity at the centre of a mainstream movie. So what's the most mainstream of genres? The RomCom. The Romantic Comedy. I determined to write a romantic comedy about nudity. A Romeo and Juliet love story where the conflict is nudity. Nothing sleazy about it, nothing knowing or cynical, nothing preachy, or arty, or dark - just a simple love story of two ordinary people whose cultures clash. No villains, just prejudice and closed minds, something that everybody recognises, that everybody has seen in their own families. And I will rub in Factor 30 Comedy, so that everybody can sit in it, and enjoy it. Comedy's a balm for the most blistering of subjects. Everybody is drawn to it, even if it's at their own expense. Comedy is the most mainstream, non-gender-specific genre of them all.

In a better world, our most mainstream genre would be Romance. Romance is the one ingredient that I don't think a successful story can be without (see Foreword). Sadly, in our age, Romance is still thought to be only for girls. So Hollywood studios - when they can be bothered to make movies for both sexes - add comedy to make it acceptable to boys. The same thinking applies in reverse to action movies, which are so expensive that, begrudgingly, they <u>have</u> to be made for both sexes. James Bond, for instance, adds comedy to reach the widest possible audience. For the current James Bond movie, it's not enough even to use funny writers like Rob Wade and Neal Purvis, they actually have to add to the credits a 'writer of comedy', like Phoebe Waller-Bridge

In my writing - and filmmaking - I set it as a primary goal to write for all sexes. Hence my search for female co-writers - Melanie Finn, Laline Paull, Rosemarie Jarski - when I doubt I can achieve this. Perhaps I should have looked for a female co-writer for my 'Romantic Comedy About Nudity'? Maybe I still will. When the film does eventually get made, it will need a re-write. The script is already twenty-five years old. And, as far as I can tell, it is still unique. There have been other films that have strayed onto nudist beaches and into naturist resorts, but these have either been short comic interludes - like *EuroTrip* (2004) - or dark - like *Les Textiles* (2004). There has still, to date, been no film like *Wearing A Smile*.

The spark for my Romeo and Juliet story came from lying on the beach at Cap D'Agde next to a French family that had clearly taken their daughter's boyfriend on holiday with them. The comic potential of this was immediately obvious. In fact, this young man was managing well. He was gamely acquiescing to the pestering of his girlfriend's young sister to play beachball with him. The parents were looking on, charmed. He looks like a keeper. The only specific thing I remember about this young man's unease - which he almost, but not quite, successfully hid - was that he had one of those penises that looks like it is permanently semi-erect. I saw how excruciatingly embarrassing this could have been for a lesser man in front of his girlfriend's extended family. It didn't feel right to use this type of penis in my script (that would have been an even trickier casting session than Brigitte Bako's bum). But I did use the embarrassment. Funnily enough, I have just seen a semi-erect penis used for comic effect in a mainstream movie - *Eurovision : The Story of Fire Saga* (2020), which parades semi-erect penises on statues of the actor Dan Stevens in our Banqueting Hall at Knebworth House (Dan suggests in our Visitors Book that we might like to keep them on display). But this is 2020. Then was 1996. Erections, like MI6, did not officially exist in Britain. And it was enough for me to have one taboo to bust with this screenplay.

So thanks to that family on the beach, I now have my French family. My Capulets. Ordinary. Happy. Carefree. Especially on their annual summer holiday, which they have always taken on the beach at Cap D'Agde's Quartier Naturiste. Over the years I have shared that beach with many families like this. Being naked in the company of others, to them, is as natural as natural can be.

So where to go for my Montagues? When I was later working to get the project financed, I was told by European sales agents that it would be less expensive and easier to put this film together as an Anglo-French co-production. Could I not make the boy British? What's funnier in the 1990s than a mumbling, floppy-haired, excruciatingly-embarrassed Hugh Grant? I like Hugh Grant as much as the next man. But this story is not for him. No. The British may not like the French, but they do understand them. I need an opposing family to whom this ordinary French family looks as alien as David Bowie in pupilless contact lenses.

I didn't have far to look. But let's get this straight. Or at lease semi-straight. My Alabama family are absolutely 100% not the family in the script. But... knowing them and loving them as I do, it was so easy to create an exaggerated version of a Bible-belt business-focused Southern United States family. Particularly during the time of a big marriage to an alien European family. I had petty well lived the third act of my intended script, where the extended French family attend their daughter's

wedding in the Deep South. My experience of being given my blood test by the family doctor is in the screenplay, so is the Pre-Nup that our parents had fun organising for us - but most relevant to my story, is the effect on a Southern town of a German company, Mercedes-Benz, building a massive factory on its outskirts, as had happened at Tuscaloosa.

When my son was two or three years old there had been consternation at a Florida beach house at him toddling around naked in front of his American relations. In Europe this would not have been noticed, let alone thought inappropriate. Drawing distinctions between these two cultures was going to be easy.

I knew what I wanted for the opening image of the film. The most famous and exposed penis in the world. The penis of Michelangelo's David in the Piazza Della Signoria in Florence. My workaholic American family are on a European vacation - not because they want to be, but because they feel they ought to see London, Paris, Vienna, Venice and Florence... in a week.

Nicholas (26), fresh out of business school, persuades his father that before joining the family steel business, he be allowed to stay on in Europe for a few weeks, to have some time to himself, to experience life first hand. Reluctantly, mother, father, power exec sister Virginia (32) and henpecked brother-in-law Barrie leave Nicholas behind.

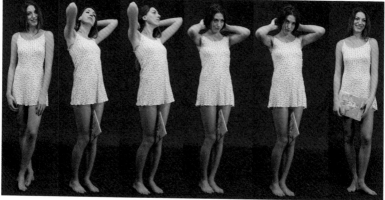

Two weeks later, blissful, backpacking through rural France, Nicholas is stampeded by a herd of pigs. Their herder is the most beautiful girl he has ever seen. Sylvie (24), a Parisian med student, is home for the summer vacation at her family's forest farm. She invites Nicholas to join her Grandpère's 75th birthday party, a glorious bucolic farmyard feast attended by the whole village.

The Riberac family are as carefree as the White family are uptight. Full of colour and character. Extended family includes maiden aunt Véronique, younger aunt Lou-Lou the dancer, her musician husband uncle Gui, grandchildren Martine and Eduard.. and mischievous old Grandpère. To Nicholas they are a revelation. As a laughter-filled summer romance develops with Sylvie, Nicholas becomes the happiest man alive...

I was given notes on the script subsequently that my naturist French family were much more likely to be metropolitan liberals than rural farmers. It's true, I could only guess where those families on the Cap D'Agde beach spend the rest of their year. I like to think they come from all over. All environments. All backgrounds. But as you've heard, I've never spoken a word to any them. I suppose that's not entirely true. I did speak to one father once, whose daughter had been building sand castles with my daughter. He was a air conditioning salesman from the Provence town of Brignoles. But what I did know, was that there was no better place

to have a dreamy summer romance in deepest France than amongst the sunflower fields of the Dordogne - Devon with sunshine - where my own parents owned a rural farmhouse in the 80s and 90s. There was a hilltop château near our farmhouse called Bridoire (right), now restored, but then an overgrown, crumbling Sleeping Beauty castle that we would climb through undergrowth into. It was abandoned, as though the family had just stood up from breakfast, and left. The windows and furniture were broken and scattered. There were books still on the dust-caked library shelves. It was now a home for the birds and the bats... and runaway lovers. It was breathlessly romantic. This is the place I

fantasised sharing an Orangina with a beautiful truffle farmer's daughter. So I gave that privilege to my protagonist. And my Capulets became farmers.

All good things must come to an end. The entire Riberac family are to depart on their July vacation to the beach. But Nicholas's misery is cut short when

Grandpère persuades the family to invite Nicholas along too. The family drive by night, in the farmyard van, to the Mediterranean.

The next morning, it is light of head and light of step that Nicholas appears in the kitchen for breakfast. So, when the family begin appearing at the breakfast table, each and everyone of them stark naked, he's convinced he's dreaming. The dream turns to terror when, from the balcony, he sees that every single person in the busy holiday resort is naked.

Sylvie doesn't know what Nicholas's problem is. The family

An early storyboard drawn by Dean Harmer

have been coming here since she was a child. But aspersions are cast - why didn't she tell him? There was nothing to tell. A row ensues. He would do anything for Sylvie - but not this! Cue lots of easy comedy surrounding his excruciating embarrassment and bourgeois insecurities... as he realises he is being ridiculous.

Promotional clips for the website
www.wearingasmile.com

Meanwhile in Florida, Mr White sends his power exec daughter Virginia on a business trip to Germany to persuade a major car company to build its U.S. plant in Florida next to the White family steel mills.

And while she's there, she can bring her little brother home too, before he gets too keen on this foreign girl.

Virginia, with husband Barrie in tow, arrives at the naturist resort. Under no circumstances is Barrie going in there. To Virginia it's business, and business is about compromise. Removing her bra beneath her blouse, she persuades the gatekeeper that she is not staying, only here to see her brother.

Becoming increasingly lost in the maze of shopping malls, supermarkets, restaurants of this naked resort town, Virginia loses her cool. A beautiful man who speaks English comes to her rescue. She can't keep her eyes off his suntanned, statuesque nakedness, and distracted, slips, straight into a sunken jacuzzi.

Nicholas, relaxed and having the time of his life, is dressed for dinner and heading out for the evening with the whole Riberac family when they come across the bedraggled Virginia in the arms of a beautiful stranger. Virginia joins them for dinner to hear Nicholas announce his engagement to Sylvie. Virginia chokes on her lobster - not at the news, but at Barrie desperately searching for her, stark naked except for his ankle socks and Hush Puppies.

On the beach the next day, firmly in her swimsuit - with her little brother enjoying her discomfort - Virginia strikes a deal with him. She'll sell Dad on the idea of his marriage to Sylvie, on the condition that the couple agree to have a big white wedding at the family mansion in Florida. Her plan is to use the event to entertain the German car execs, show them Florida's commitment to a union with Europe, and outdo stiff competition for the business from the State of Tennessee. The deal is almost done when Beach Patrol approaches and asks Virginia to remove her swimsuit or move to the textile beach, Protesting, she acquiesces gingerly, holding her suit over herself. But again the beautiful man approaches, holding out his hand

in greeting. She takes it without thinking. Standing there naked, mortified, she demands her brother get her out of this place.

The entire Riberac family are flown to Florida for the wedding, and put up in the White family beach house. Whilst in America, the good-natured family is determined to do as Americans do. For the beach, they have fun buying absurd bright florescent American swimsuits. Sylvie gets on less well. Finding her wedding has been wholly pre-organized for her, and Nicholas's parents disposed to dislike her, she becomes increasingly feisty and rebellious.

The day of the wedding is baking hot. The State Governor, local dignitaries, anybody-who-is-anybody is dressed to the nines in the flower gardens of the White Mansion. As guests take their places, Sylvie is still at the beach house, waiting while her mother fusses over last minute alterations to the wedding dress. Feeling nostalgic about the passing of her youth, Sylvie wanders out to take one last swim on the deserted beach.

Emerging naked from the surf, she is confronted by a Florida cop demanding to see her driver's licence. Riled by the absurdity of this request, Sylvie is tart, confrontational. For public indecency & resisting a police officer, she is promptly arrested, wrapped in a blanket and bundled into the back of a police car.

Virginia is concerned. The German car execs still haven't arrived. But more serious, where is the bride? News reaches the now sweltering guests that the bride has been arrested. Mr White, teeth gritted, uses his influence on the phone – minutes later, a police car, sirens blaring, comes screeching up onto the lawn.

Fired up and indignant, Sylvie jumps out of the car, tosses off the police blanket, grabs a posy from a pew and marches down the aisle... stark naked.

Chaos ensues. The congregation dominoes. Mrs White springs in Sylvie's path, declaring that this wedding will proceed only over her dead body. Nicholas confronts his mother, but it's no good - Sylvie now refuses to go ahead with the wedding. This match will not work. Sylvie can see that now. Retreating into the arms of her Grandpère, she leaves. The party disintegrates.

At this point, the Germans arrive.

To Virginia all is lost. But the triple whiskey was still a bad idea. Because the Chairman of Deutsche Auto is, of course - a RomCom is allowed one big conceit - the beautiful man from the French resort. Virginia falls, defeated, into his arms. The Chairman of Deutsche Auto is promptly punched in the nose by Barrie.

Desperate, Nicholas chases after Sylvie. He arrives at the beach house, but the Riberacs are gone. Devastated, he returns to the White Mansion to find the German Chairman alone in the pool, having had the very best of parties. He consoles Nicholas, telling him that events on the surface don't make your decisions for you, in life you must follow your gut instinct.

It's recriminations all round in the White drawing room, as Mr and Mrs White, Virginia and Barrie accuse each other of being responsible for the disaster. They are interrupted by Nicholas and the German Chairman, wet and naked from the swimming pool. Nicholas is resolute - he's going back to France to persuade Sylvie to change her mind. The German Chairman, meanwhile, has had a ball - he

thanks the Whites for the great party and says they must do it again - "lass uns das bald mal wiederholen!" - as soon as he's built his new factory, next to the White family's steel mills. Mrs White passes out.

Back in France, Nicholas finds Sylvie in the deserted chateau, her mind unchanged. Using all the charm he can muster, he persuades her that family obligations will never cease to be important, but that in their life, their love is more important. Besides, they should start a family simply so they can give their own kids as much grief.

With both families present, Nicholas and Sylvie are married on the beach at the French resort - everyone, wearing only a smile. The exceptions are a mellowed Mr and Mrs White – however Beach Patrol is headed their way.

There. Instant RomCom. Light. Silly. Fun. And not something that's been done before. Friday night fare. I was pleased with it. I particularly liked that I'd been able to run the nudity / body acceptance theme throughout all three acts.

I'd mentioned this idea for a feature film to David Hodgins and Steve Rivers at Medusa. I don't recall whether this was before or after they'd sued me - it may well have been after, as I am proud to say we all stayed friends through the trials of All Digital, just as I'd been determined to do with Eduardo Sarlui and his lovely family after the off-screen dramas of *St Tropez Suntrap*. Life's too short not to. Medusa commissioned me to write the screenplay.

Perfect. I could write off research trips to Cap D'Agde, the Dordogne, and to visit the in-laws!

David and Steve, who were veterans of the Film Markets, were well positioned to get *Wearing A Smile* made. They had started thinking about expanding their self-generated portfolio from sell-though videos (that All Digital had been making) into feature films. They had friends and associates from UK video distribution looking to do the same at that time. One was Graham King. He became Martin Scorsese's preferred producer, and in 2018 cleaned up around the world with *Bohemian Rhapsody*.

Lancastrian David Hodgins' style was more broad comedy. I recall he was interested in me writing an English version of the Italian film *Vediamoci Chiaro* (1984) about a cuckolded husband who doesn't let on that his blindness from an accident has been cured. Like *Wearing A Smile*, this was a broad comedy farce. Some would say both are one-joke films. I would say, plenty of one-joke films do very nicely thank you. *Big* (1988) with Tom Hanks comes to mind. And *The Full Monty* (1997). I liked David's popularist taste. It was rare in England. It remains rare amongst English producers.

I also like that when I delivered *Wearing A Smile* to Medusa, I only got two notes from David and Steve. Only two changes. That, I was not used to. One addition and one subtraction.

The addition I was content to add. They wanted more physical slapstick. I thought I was already stretching the pratfalls with Virginia's trip & slip into a jacuzzi. David felt there was more room for falling into water. Specifically they suggested that on his first morning at the resort, Nicholas should fall off the balcony into a swimming pool of full of naked people. Okay. I can make Nicholas's argument with Sylvie a little more physical, and have him take a feisty punch or slap - but was there ever a balcony that literally hangs over a swimming pool? I've been on balconies where you feel you are hanging over a swimming pool - our one in West Hollywood, for instance - but invariably there is quite a bit of concrete to fall on before you are anywhere near reaching the water. Who cares? It's the movies. Mel Gibson barely ruffles his hair jumping out of a skyscraper window into a swimming pool in *Lethal Weapon 2* (1989).

The second change, the subtraction, I made reluctantly. I couldn't understand David's objection. In the 1st Act, I had a scene when Nicholas on his first night staying in Sylvie's family farmhouse is looking for the bathroom and runs into Sylvie's mother walking naked across the landing from the bathroom to her bedroom. Nicholas is mortified, but Mrs Riberac is not remotely phased. I like this moment.

It's on theme, during an early sequence when the
building of the romance and relationships are more
the thrust of the narrative. And I found it believable.
David, interestingly, didn't. Maybe a moment from
his childhood? Maybe he's only ever had an en suite?
I took it out of the screenplay. But in recent years
I've returned it. I like it. It is one of the more subtle
scenes in a script where subtlety is not omnipresent.

Pleased with the second draft, David and Steve sent it to another friend and
associate from UK video who was thriving in the movie business. Stewart Till is
now head of United International Pictures, the biggest film distributor in the world.
Then, he was President of Polygram, and still glowing from the success of *Four Weddings And A Funeral* (1994). The response to *Wearing A Smile* came back, "Not
as good as *Four Weddings And A Funeral*". I agree. It's not as good as *Four Weddings And A Funeral*. But that doesn't mean it's not worth making. It doesn't mean
it doesn't have the potential to make money. And to entertain. *Bean: The Movie*
(1997) is not as good as *Four Weddings And A Funeral*. *Bean: The Movie*'s worldwide
box office was $251,212,670.

I got a better reaction touting the script myself. I cannot remember how, but
through Jeremy Saunders (the Executive Producer of *The Shooting Party*, who'd giv-
en me my first job) I'd had dinner in London with the Director Jean-Jacques Beineix.
Beineix was a hero of mine, having made the film *Betty Blue* (1986), France's equivalent of *9 1/2 Weeks* - beautiful music, beautiful images, beautiful doomed obsessive
sex, but with the great advantage of being set in France with beautiful French people.

I don't know that Jean-Jacques actually read it, but his wife read it, and loved it.
So Jean-Jacques said he was interested to do it. But he said he would like to spend
time developing the screenplay first. This set off red warning lights in my head. I
knew the French way. Spend years talking about it until you've talked it to death.
Wearing A Smile would not stand up to too much French philosophical scrutiny. It
was a simple - I'd say, effective - RomCom about nudity. I could see it very quickly
turning into something else. But again, who cares? This is Jean-Jacques Beineix.
How much fun would it be talking about your project with Jean-Jacques Beineix
for years on end? In retrospect I can't really believe I didn't take up this offer. But
at that time I was impatient. I felt the project was good enough to get picked up by
someone more likely to do it the way I saw it. And people were liking it.

Not only Jean-Jacques Beineix's wife liked it. Bob
Geldof's wife also liked it. Geldof was producing Channel 4's *The Big Breakfast* at that time. His girlfriend - now
wife - Jeanne Marine was pretty much an embodiment of
my character Sylvie. I imagined her coming from a very
similar family to my Riberac family - albeit that, in her
30s, she was a little old for the role. But she wanted to do
the film, and I recall an entertaining drink with her and
Bob, at which I reminded him of the tirade of amplified
swearing he'd let loose over Knebworth Park in September
1978 as frontman of The Boomtown Rats (left), supporting

Frank Zappa and The Tubes. He looked at me like I was taking the piss. He remembered the gig being "shit". I remembered it as an appropriate punk response to a festival billed as 'not another boring old Knebworth'.

I remain convinced that a lot of other people's wives would have liked *Wearing A Smile* had it been made. But it wasn't.

By the turn of the century, out of frustration that this idea was too good to remain on a black & white page, I got Medusa's permission to turn the script into a bande dessinée. A bande dessinée is a French comic that, then and still, tends to take the popular format in France of an A4 hardback. The phenomenon - and it is a phenomenon in France, where schoolkids stop off after school to sprawl over bookshop floors to read 'BDs' - only really made it to English shores in the form of *Tintin* and *Asterix* (m.o.w.l.).

I had spotted an illustrator in a publication called *The Erotic Review* - a monthly riposte to *The Literary Review* - called Tim Major (below), whose drawings I was instantly drawn to. Tim illustrated a regular strip for the magazine called *Harpinger* (left), a sort of erotic *Downton Abbey* before *Downton Abbey* had been invented. I asked the editor Rowan Pelling to put me in touch with him, and our meeting was the beginning of a beautiful working relationship. Tim has been my go-to illustrator ever since. He did the illustration for the cover of this book. Every year I am not working with Tim - and I haven't for a while - I consider a year wasted.

Tim Major is a textbook example of an under-appreciated artist. Much too good an artist to be much good at self-promotion, he nests in

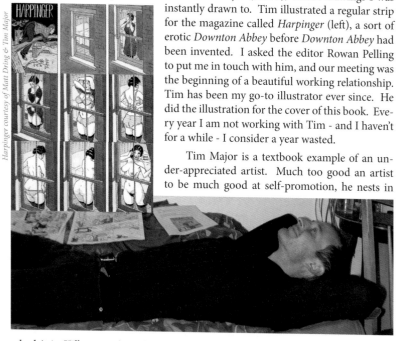

Harpinger courtesy of Matt Dring & Tim Major

a bedsit in Kilburn with nothing other than cigarette butts, pencils, and drawings of birds. Yes, both the Audubon and Aubade varieties. Except that he has a very English style. Perfect for *The Erotic Review,* a publication whose mailing list was peppered with old boys with 'Major' at the front of their names instead of at the end, retired to Rose Cottages in village lanes around the country.

I loved the process of working with Tim to create a comic book version of

The process from my scribbles, to Tim's drawings, to Rosina's colouring, to my dialogue insertion

Wearing A Smile. I was effectively directing my own movie. I would sketch out a storyboard, choose the angles and framing that best told the story, and Tim would respond a week or so later with fresh pages of beautiful comic strip. I not only love Tim's drafting, I also love his shading and muted colouring, which has a lovely nostalgic feel to it. But the workload was too great on a 48-page comic book for Tim to agree to do both, so I drafted in my sister Rosina to watercolour Tim's drawings. Rosina's colouring is more wholesome and colourful, and maybe that was better for the message of *Wearing a Smile.* Certainly she does a great job.

I published the book myself - as 'a 39 BD' - getting it printed in Belgium at a company called Proost (sadly no more) that specialised in bibles and bande dessinées, and had printed the Asterix books that I loved so much in my youth. Book dis-

"...addresses some of the stereotypes and false impressions many people have about naturism... a welcome addition in most naturist libraries." ~ N Spring 2003

tributors don't like a one-off, so despite a few meetings with comic distributors in the UK, I went on to sell the book myself, through ads in places where I knew the readership would appreciate it. *The Daily Telegraph* (before it became a comic itself in the Brexit years), *Private Eye*, and specifically naturist magazines across the world. America, Canada, New Zealand, Australia... all have their own naturist magazines, and of course Britain has the grand-

"HENRY COBBOLD'S MINI-MASTERPIECE... achieves a double first. It is the first nudist novel (or novella) and the first in graphic form." - H&E

"The comic book artistry is magnificent. We recommend it." - Naturally -

"It's like the missing link between Asterix and Milo Manara... Why aren't there more books like this?" - Borderline -

"God knows what would have happened if Tintin had got mixed up in all this, but Hergé is evidently an influence... a charming funny book." - The Erotic Review -

CHISEL IT OFF, I SAY... THAT'S WHAT THEY DO IN ALL THE GOOD MUSEUMS!

daddy of them all, *Health & Efficiency*. *H&E* wrote me a particularly nice review:

Like with the sell-though videos that we made, the rule was that if there's a magazine for it, there'll be people who want to buy it. This worked for Archery, it worked for Weddings, and now it worked for Naturism. It worked particularly well for Naturism, because naturists are a politically engaged and supportive tribe. So the book sold well. *Wearing A Smile* the bande dessinée comfortably paid for itself, and became a good pitch for the film.

I was hoping it would also sell in France. It had been a challenge during the drawing process to anticipate the space needed in the speech bubbles to allow for translating the lines into other languages for foreign editions. I had overlaid the English text (in Adobe Illustrator rather than today's InDesign) into generously spaced bubbles, so it would not have been difficult to overlay French text. I went to the French BD publisher Albin Michel in Paris and the artistry of the book was well received - but, again, it was "come back when you have half a dozen titles."

Instead, I found myself wanting to licence one of Albin Michel's bande dessinées for the English market - a period erotic romp set in the Indian Raj called *Les Perles de L'Amour*. We got to contract stage, but I lost my nerve. Unlike in other Western European countries, both comics and erotica were a difficult sell in the UK. At the time I thought I'd be better off concentrating on just one of those challenges.

When some years later, in early 2004, Medusa - the company that had commissioned the screenplay - was purchased by the Contender Entertainment Group (see p.276), partly as the result of my dinner party, Richard Bridgwood the CEO of Contender gifted me back the rights to my screenplay *Wearing A Smile*.

It, too, will cast off its manila envelope one day, and run around naked in the sun again.

CHAPTER THIRTY

Harold Mollin

PRICOLICI
It's primal, Alan. Tribal. It's "re-volting". It's "I won't do
what you tell me to do". "I will like what disgusts you".
It's pene-trating the pom-pous, pious, plati-tudes of your
parents!

CHAIRMAN
Are you all right, dear?.

FELICITY
Fine. Alan. Absolutely fine. Peach Melba anyone?

(*Pricolici's Circus of Screams* 2014)

When one lion cage door closes, another one opens. Avid had bought Matador. All Digital had collapsed. Mr Sarlui was no longer making films. I was living in rural Hertfordshire, taking the kids to school. Then along comes Jeremy Saunders again, "You <u>shall</u> go to the Ball!" Jeremy, you'll recall, is the one to whom I owed my first job, *The Shooting Party*; the "Jeremy who?" to whom I, circuitously, owed my introduction to Zalman King. 'Circus Ringmaster', 'Fairy Godmother' - I'm not painting the best visual picture for you of dear Jeremy... a blazered Englishman so English he of course now lives in France, Jeremy is better imagined as my Narrator in *The Rocky Horror Show*. "Fortune, it seems, had smiled on Henry Cobbold..."

One day in 1996, Jeremy Saunders (below, 2nd right) bought a man from Queens (like me, or Emilio Estevez if you chose to believe our parents) to lunch at Knebworth House. His name was Harold Mollin (below, behind the moustache). His father (below, right) I think was a dentist. Wasn't Zalman the son of a dentist too? I must go to the dentist. Harold was in insurance. High risk insurance. If the

hurricane was headed towards your house, his company would still insure you. It'd be expensive, but he'd step in when others wouldn't. High risk weather insurance.

Through this high risk pursuit he'd made a bob or two. He was New York resident, but when in London kept a suite at The Dorchester. He was in his 40s, not married. He'd been a tennis pro when he was younger. He might as well have wallpapered an airplane, as he spent most of his life in one. He'd been in Donald Trump's after a Donna Summer party at Mar-a-Lago. A 'high flyer' - but one who saw the sense in buying three adjacent seats in economy to sleep, rather than one in 1st Class. He loved being in England, and his taxi of choice was a chauffeur called Ray who carried him around in a Rolls Royce, and brought him to Knebworth that day.

Harold had accountants in London, who looked out for investment opportunities for him, and places for him to offset some tax. Through them he'd invested in a small independent video distribution company called Vision Replays Ltd., who had a small second floor office on the south-west corner of D'Arblay and Berwick Street in London's Soho. It was said that the founder and MD of this company was running it as a lifestyle rather than a business - Harold could be said to be have been doing the same - but the accountants also believed the MD was stealing from Vision Replays. As I recall, the accountants - and the primary 3rd Party investor - offered the founder/MD a way out if he surrendered his shares. Thus Harold Mollin found himself the proud owner of a video distribution company in Soho - with 100 odd titles - and no staff.

So Harold hired me to run the company. Straight Intta Soho. Together he and I hired a small skeleton staff to keep the show on the road. We then assessed the portfolio. 100 videos. Or rather the UK video distribution rights to 100 titles. There were some 'kids' titles - I recall a puppet film about Hanukkah; a number of documentaries - mostly about the Second World War, a little heavy on Nazis themes, as I recall, although as a Film Major I was impressed that we had Leni Riefenstahl's *Triumph of the Will* (1935) and *Olympia* (1936); and then there were what were called 'adult' titles... about 50% of the stock was themed for sexual interest.

Some of these were quasi documentaries. There was a film about John Wayne Bobbitt - having been de-penised by his wife Lorena - attempting to get into the 'adult' movie industry. There was a film about Divine Brown - having de-trousered Hugh Grant - attempting to get into the 'adult' movie industry... Typically '90s, not remotely erotic, extensions of tabloid fare.

There were a couple of inhouse produc-

I'm not sure I asked, but Mr Bobbitt has signed this one for me - "Henry, keep it safe slap on your stomach!"

tions. *The Statesman's Wife* (1996) was interesting because we had the original footage alongside the British release of the film - i.e. that had been granted an 18 certificate by the British Board of Film Classification. The original footage was actually quite sexy - a couple of good-looking English girls having their way with a reasonably good-looking male chauffeur (not Ray), etc. - but the sliced up British release of the film was pretty pointless. A mish-mash of shots of the furniture, the car, the Houses of Parliament... oh, and some close ups on the chauffeur's agonised face, intercut with the back of the girls' heads. Not good.

At least with *The A-Z of Lesbian Love* (this time not with Mr Sage & Mr Onion), the same two girls could be shown pretending to have sex with each other. This - as previously discussed - is because in their playtime there were no penises involved, and the British Board of Film Classification therefore felt that British people could be trusted to witness it. When, in 1984, the British Board of Film Classification changed its name from The British Board of Film Censors, it did so 16 years before it had any right to.

The rest of the portfolio - about 40% of the total - were themed for the sexual interest of the male 'Gay' market. Here the BBFC's malign scissor-work moved

from pointless & patronising to discriminatorily offensive. What was left after the faceless bureaucrats had snipped their way through these films was extreme long shots of men wrestling in plaid shirts on a woodpile, or in gym shots on a bench press-bench... intercut with extreme close ups of their furrowed agonised brows. Long shot. Close shot. Long shot. Close shot. Wholly ridiculous and insulting. Thirty years on from decriminalisation, Gay men were still being threatened with arrest for buying or importing video entertainment in which there was the remotest glimpse of a sexualised penis. Jack(boots) Straw, Home Secretary at the time, was quite content with this sexual inequality. Indeed it is hard to see that any British politician would ever have done anything to put this right had they not been required to by the European Human Rights Act of October 2000.

Jeff Stryker was the American square-jawed hunk behind most of the Vision Replays' 'Gay' catalogue. Titles such as *Powertool* (1986), *Stryker Force* (1987), *Powertool 2: Breaking Out* (1990), *Busted* (1991), *J.S. Big Time* (1995)... Stryker's 1993 classic *How to Enlarge Your Penis* had not, for obvious reasons, make it to these unenlightened shores.

So, what to do with this Vision Replays catalogue? Well, the first thing I did was to off-load

"...In The End Lies Madness" Indeed

the 40% of it that I felt would be better off in the hands of a specialist distributor. I'd have been happy to have kept a balance of mainstream 'Gay' titles, but then there was no such thing. Ever seeking balance, I wondered whether it wouldn't help to add a bisexual range. The tagline 'Buy Bi' sounded good. But it was time to consolidate, not conjugate.

We did keep *The A-Z of Lesbian Love*, which you could say was irrational logic, but the specialist distributor was not interested in this. And, as already discussed, 'lesbian love' had become mainstream by default, as the only truly acceptable love making in visual pornography in '70s, '80s & '90s Britain. Having decimated this half of Vision Replays' catalogue, it was then time to build it up again. And I knew exactly where to go. Medusa had the rights to Playboy's branded video. But Playboy had the rights to *Red Shoes Diaries*, and *Red Shoe Diaries* was not branded Playboy product. British TV had not yet quite had the courage to pick up *Red Shoe Diaries*, but Channels 4 & 5 were circling around it, particularly because David Duchovny was becoming increasingly high profile because of *The X Files*.

At Cannes, Harold and I took the Playboy sales people out to lunch. Harold ordered the 'Lapin à La Cocotte' - the rabbit stew - which I did not think was sensitive at a Playboy lunch. He was unsure how he would get on at Cannes. It was not his world, he told me. But emerging from the underground car park on the very first day we were almost run down by a posse of Hawaiian Tropic girls on roller skates. "Harold! What are you doing here?!" We'd been at the festival 5 minutes.

Clearly, however, I was the right person to package and distribute *Red Shoe Diaries* for the UK market. I'd been present at its inception and written the first three episodes. Playboy were happy to sign us the UK video rights. At 66 half hours that was over 30 video releases. We had instantly refilled the hole in our catalogue.

I then went after a neglected classic that I knew would be a tough negotiation. With ruthless business brilliance I beat the filmmaker down to virtually no fee. The film was called *St Tropez Suntrap*. That one will look good on the shelf next to Leni Riefenstahl's *Triumph of the Will*.

What next? Well, two types of people watch sell-though home videos. 'Adults' and 'Children'. I always liked that sales line. We'd got the grown-up fare sorted.

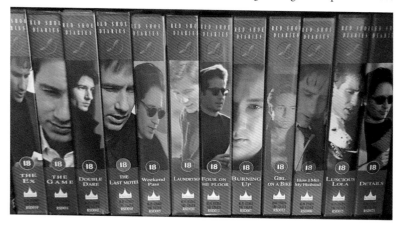

How about something for a younger audience to balance out the portfolio? Wandering through the Cannes Palais I knew instantly I'd found what I was looking for when I came across the French distribution company Dargaud. *Tintin* was not at that moment licenced for UK video. I think Dargaud felt that this high-profile continental product was destined for a UK broadcaster, or at least one of the Hollywood studio distributors. I managed to persuade the delightful Irish saleslady that, for expertise in 'Childrens' product she need look no further than Vision Replays, distributors of that much loved perennial childrens' classic, *Chanuka at Bubba's*. Okay, maybe she should not look at the Vision Replays catalogue. No, she shouldn't be bothered with our past, she should be dazzled by our bright and bounteous future. She should know that for something as important as *Tintin* this exciting young Soho

company would create a brand new video label, 'Mollin Video'. Mollin Video was where *Tintin* was going to receive the most love, care and attention in the UK market. A big fish in a small pond, rather than a big fish in a big pond... or something like that.

There was no pulling wool over those smiling eyes, but I had met lifelong friends in Julie Fox (above right) and her Cannes-born assistant Céline Carenco (above left, with Jeremy Saunders). They could see someone with a love, knowledge and enthusiasm for Bandes Dessinées, not common in England. The right person had come along at the right moment. I had secured for Harold the UK video rights for *Tintin*.

Would I like *Lucky Luke* too? Yes, I'd like *Lucky Luke* too. A tougher sell in the UK, a Belgian cowboy. But I personally had spent time travelling in the back of holiday cars in the '60s & '70s reading *Lucky Luke* comics. If I could love a Belgian cowboy, so could other English boys like me. English boys like me?... But I was on a roll. All we needed now for the mighty continental triumvirate of Bande Dessinée characters was the indomitable Gaul, who'd always been my favourite.

The various *Asterix* movies that existed at that time has been produced over time and without the quality control that *Tintin* enjoyed via the Hergé Foundation in Brussels. The English audio dubs for *Asterix* were poor. But the films were available, and in the hands of a UK-based sales agent named David Lamping. I envisaged sparkling re-dubs, using hip contemporary English comedians. However this time it was Harold that got carried away in negotiations. He'd made a handsome offer before we'd beaten David down with my suggestion, which would have increased the value of the films and been worth a lower price. We secured *Asterix* - but for the money we'd spent, we'd have to settle for releasing them in these dated versions. A shame.

But Mollin Video was looking good. We had *Tintin*, *Asterix* and *Lucky Luke*. We went to town on promoting *Lucky Luke*. A *Lucky Luke* rap (below left) was commissioned. A costume launch organised at a Belgian restaurant - Belgo, I think, which was suitably trendy having opened only a few years before. We certainly had fries & mayonnaise launches for *Tintin* at Belgo. As mentioned, the Hergé Foundation kept a tight rein on anything to do with *Tintin*. We were

Future distributor of Asterix

obliged to run every piece of artwork and every piece of marketing past their managing company Moulinsart. Harold and I went to Belgium to visit them. I don't remember if we were summoned, but it felt like it. We met Hergé's widow Fanny Rodwell and her new husband, who was then managing the company, Nick Rodwell. We were

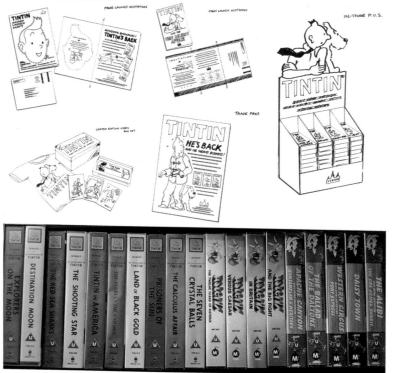

shown an entire room of unauthorised *Tintin* knock-offs from every corner of the world. It was an extraordinary sight. We could see why they needed a long and firm reach to protect their precious boy.

Suitably awed, Harold and I returned to our hotel in a central Brussels. Down in the square below was a long queue of everyday Belgian shoppers, everyday Belgian couples in everyday Belgian coats, with everyday Belgian shopping bags. They were waiting to get into an Exposition of Erotica. I marvelled at the ordinariness of this. Ordinary clientele. Ordinary Exhibition Centre. Ordinary central square in the middle of Brussels.

Harold asked who did Erotica Expos in the UK. I laughed. "We don't have 'Erotica' in the UK. We have Roy Chubby Brown and Page 3 of The Sun... There is a company called Ann Summers that has representatives going around organising housewife parties, like tupperware parties, for lingerie..." I was really struggling to come up with anything that represented an 'Erotica' industry in the UK. "Well let's go see what they are selling downstairs."

Yes, the Exposition was selling 'adult' videos that would have been banned in the UK. In Belgium they were content to acknowledge the existence of the erect penis. Yes, there was some eye-watering fetishwear... But also, yes, there was lingerie. Also, yes, there were general items associated with relaxation, health and wellbeing. Massage oils, scented candles, hot tubs... "Do you have these things in England?" "We do." "Then we should do this in England."

We determined to pursue this when we got home. But first, we noticed that an award ceremony was planned that evening for the 'adult' video industry. Aren't we in that? We were, after all, the proud UK distributors of *St Tropez Suntrap*. We weren't due back on the Eurostar until the next day. We bought tickets.

It was a night to remember. I was sat next to a very charming middle-aged Dutch lady who ran a fetish club in Den Haag. She was delightful, and pleased to introduce me to all manner of interesting people. Foremost, I remember the gracious and friendly greeting of the foremost Dutch 'adult' movie actress, Helen Duval, strikingly blonde and foremost. Here was what Mr Sarlui, sir, wanted in *St Tropez Suntrap*. She would have eaten my £35,000 budget, but I imagined how the film would have turned out if Helen Duval had been in it. Before catching the Eurostar the next day I bought one of her movies, risking arrest for smuggling corrupting images back into Nanny McBritain. It was called *Helen Presents Lea* (Lea being the Czech actress Lea Martini) and, as I recall, featured interesting views of Antwerp.

What, however, had Harold and I doubled up in tears of puerile laughter on the train ride home, were the actual 'Awards'. There were a lot of them. An award almost for every sexual position and predilection. A disarmingly sweet-looking young girl took the stage to accept an award for 'Best Anal' - "I'd like to thank my Mom, my Dad..." Then there was the big winner of the evening, the film *Paris Chic* (1997), which a succession of continental accents pronounced "Pile O'Shit". "Winner of Best Film - *Pile O'Shit!*" "Thank you! Oh My God! I'd like to thank all the people who helped me make *Pile O'Shit!* You know who you are. To all my *Pile O'Shit* team - I love you! You Are *Pile O'Shit*. Look out everyone! *Pile O'Shit 2* is coming!"

As each winner was announced, and the long sashay to the stage began, the speakers pumped out the bass riff of Queen's *Another One Bites The Dust*. This was effective the first time. By the twenty-sixth time we'd heard, Da-Da-Da Da Da, Da-Da-Da Da-Da-Da, I was wondering if this was the torture you could expect in the Den Haag fetish club. But in subsequent months I had fun Da-Da-Da-ing this riff every time Harold walked anywhere with purpose.

Which we did. To Olympia. When we got back to London. I was determined that if we were going to hold an Erotica Exposition in London, it needed to be done in the most mainstream exhibition hall in the country. This was about more than simply selling our *Red Shoe Diaries* videos. This was about dragging Britain into the 20th Century before we got to the 21st. This was about recognising that, beyond Belgium, sex is a normal and healthy human interest. That sex is not something to muffle under a tea-cosy, or laugh off. I was coming over all political. Harold was less bothered about any crusade, but was happy to humour me. He saw a potential introduction into every corner of whatever market existed for this sort of thing in the UK. If you build it, they will come.

To our surprise the management at Olympia were not only unfazed, but felt we were probably on to something, as they'd had another company approach them with exactly the same request last Tuesday. In this land where 'erotica' was something locked in a back room at the British Museum for gentlemen and academics only, where they threatened you with arrest for viewing it, two companies in one week had approached its most mainstream exhibition hall to host an Erotica Expo.

Harold and I arranged to meet this other company. We were invited to an office above Oxford Street. I was immediately suspicious. I'd been to this sort of place before. An office where the plaque on the door shows the wood-stain shapes of the plaques that have been there before it. We were met by a Romford nightclub owner and a man who had something to do with St Albans Van Hire.

We'd barely exchanged pleasantries about the weather before Harold pulled out his chequebook and handed over a cheque for half a million quid. "I want in." I knew Harold was crazy, but this struck me as about as crazy as he could get. How wrong I was. But how right he was he in this instance. It turned out the Romford nightclub owner, Savvas Christodoulou, and the man from St Albans Van Hire, Mike Deekes, were decent blokes. We were instantly in business, and Britain's first Erotica Expo was born. I was made Creative Director. We called the show... *Erotica*.

We negotiated our way to a licence off Fulham & Hammersmith Council for the end of November 1997. We conferred with the Metropolitan Vice Squad. An acceptable number of nipples were cleared for release as part of a big stage show devised by club promoters Alan Pelling and David Wood and their company *Torture Garden*. From all corners of the country exhibitors turned up with artwork, furniture, jewellery (I'll use the English spelling now), lingerie, dress-up, toys, food - my best friend from when I was six, Johnny, turned up with his chocolate penises - and, best of all, 30,000 adults turned up, to be turned on.

As much as I tried to talk it down, there was always a bigger fetish presence in the UK show than in its Continental forerunners. I fought hard to keep the event as mainstream as possible and with a balance of gender and sexual orientation that reflected the streets of Kensington outside. Maybe the British simply <u>are</u> kinky. I suppose that would explain why they were content to live in the Nanny State they

were living in at that time. Sad, though, that sex had to be naughty to be of interest.
I put it down to lack of sunlight. It is not this way in sunnier climes.

For the second year, I got to work with the photographer Bob Carlos Clarke for
the advertising campaign (see doormat below). I enjoyed witnessing a day of *Blow
Up* nonsense and creativity, and was sad to read of him throwing himself in front
of a train a few years later. His colleague posted an image of pills on his website the
day after. Again, I personally never witnessed any drug-taking during this period,
which I look back on now with some astonishment. Either I was remarkably naive,
or I am correct that sex industry folk are as ordinary and everyday as the folk in any
industry. If anything, they are more friendly and down-to-earth. This, I suspect, is

fostered by the camaraderie of enduring the endless slings and arrows of suspicion and prejudice that their profession, and often appearance, provokes. At Knebworth, we find this with heavy metal concert crowds, who are the least troublesome and - appearance aside - the most personable of all the demographics we host.

My job each year was to find a new way of expressing how mainstream we were. We asked former MP and Saturday night TV celebrities Neil and Christine

Hamilton (left) to open the show one year. I know, now, the Hamiltons are decidedly not mainstream, with Neil transgressing from the perfectly reasonable slipping on of fishnets for *The Rocky Horror Show* to the entirely unreasonable position of leader of UKIP. Then they were simply broad-minded Tories, and I liked them

and enjoyed their company. But I do remember giving them a hard time for their negativity towards Europe. I enjoyed the fact that the new house they had recently moved to in the country had a post code that ended in EU. In addressing their Christmas Card, I made sure to make these two letters annoyingly large. At a fund-raising dinner full of dodgy Tories that Savvas asked me to attend to sit next to Christine - and opposite Ian Duncan Smith (goodness, what I'd do for a wage) - I

delighted in offering only Euros for their raffle tickets. Christine promptly tore my 20 Euro note in half. Much more unforgivable is what they and their purple associates are now, as I write, doing this to this country, and to the precious hard-won peace of Europe.

Every year we won a little more freedom with the *Erotica* licence. I was particularly pleased when it was determined that there was no part of the human body that the English public had to be shielded from. This never

I thought sisters The Porcelain Twinz and their crazy string was close to the bone, but full nudity was more taboo

worried my colleagues, because - as previously discussed - it is easier to make something erotic if you teasingly cover it up. But, for me, there were important principles to be established. I was the one selling this on radio and television, and attempting to demystify it and to portray it as normal and natural and everyday and beautiful. While the show just got on with being rude and rubbery - and, frustrating to me, increasingly fetishistic. So I was particularly pleased when my Venn circle of 'natural' crossed everyone else's Venn circle of 'shocking', as it did with full-frontal nudity in 2004.

To front the full-frontal nudity we enlisted Alan Pelling's girlfriend of the time, the very wholesome and charming Lily Kwan, who was a newsreader on *Naked News*, a cable show out of Toronto. *Naked News* had the splendidly simple concept that what might make the daily news more palatable was if the newsreader was taking off their clothes as they read the stories of the day. Of course *The Sun* newspaper in the UK had done something similar for 30 years previously. Although *The Sun* would express an opinion alongside it. *"Zoe is certain Tony Blair was right to take Britain into the war with Iraq. She said, 'You don't need to be an International Diplomat to realise the world is better off without Saddam.'"* (*The Sun* 3/2/04). *Naked News* was much more serious. It offered impartiality, like a reputable News network. Remember them? Twenty years later Page 3 no longer exists, but I'm pleased to report that *Naked News* is still being made. Although disappointingly,

now only with female hosts, as the male version did not attract enough of a female audience. Women are clearly better able to concentrate on the News, even if delivered in a trouser suit.

So out Lily (left) strolls, stark naked, to open the 2004 show. She instantly has everybody's attention. She is joined by the, also very naked, Paulie Paul (left), a delightfully boisterous black dancer and regular Emcee of *Erotica*. And I become the one member of the show's creative team who is pleased to see how this becomes increasingly less interesting and less relevant as the show, and the weekend, goes on. Healthy politics and happy punters. The perfect combination, if it can be achieved.

Then there was the year they sent me out to open the show. No, not naked, but as conductor to orchestrate a mass snog. The challenge was to break the World Record for the most number of couples kissing in one place at one time. We had enough people in the audience to achieve this august goal and the proper adjudicator from the Guinness organisa-

tion. I led the countdown... and on "Go!" was unexpectedly backed over Paulie Paul's leg and given a big smackaroo on my own lips. Despite the flashing of cameras all around, I am pleased to say that they were all pointing at the record-breaking crowd, and I don't believe a photo exists of me being kissed by a large burly naked black man in a red floppy hat. Perhaps it will surface when I'm sworn in as Prime Minister.

Erotica ran for many years. There was a Manchester version. A New York version. Savvas (below) continued it into

the 2000s, after Harold was no longer involved, again asking me to front it. I did, for a couple more years, in 2004 & 2005, but it became increasingly difficult for me to represent *Erotica* alongside representing Knebworth House, which Martha and I had taken on the management of at the turn of the century. I pulled in others who I thought would be able to do a better job than me, like the dynamic Emma Sayle, a great spokesperson for equality in sexuality. Emma was busy creating *Killing Kittens*, the female-led upmarket orgy parties that are still going strong today, 15 years later. The Press were already obsessed by her because she'd been on the same rowing team as Kate Middleton.

That's not to say it wasn't problematic for me back in 1997. It was. Back then I was already a Trustee of the Knebworth House Education and Preservation Trust. This charity was working hard to appeal for public sympathy, public support and public funds. One of my fellow trustees had been asked by Stevenage Borough Council to sit on its Morals & Ethics Committee. He questioned whether, as the heir to Knebworth House, I really needed to appear in the media promoting sex shows?

I did point out that challenging the establishment, and activism to make the world a fairer, more inclusive and understanding place, was my Lytton genes. Whilst my great-aunt Constance Lytton, militant suffragette (right, disguised as a seamstress), was at the top of the 'Premier League', throwing stones and undergoing hunger strike in prison in the cause of female emancipation, I did, in my own very small 'Fourth Division' way, briefly and bizarrely, become a poster boy for anti-censorship and '90s sexual freedom. When in the early 1900s they discovered Constance was the daughter of an Earl and had a brother in the House of Lords, to her chagrin she was swiftly released out the back door of the prison, and had to disguise herself to rejoin her militant colleagues. When in the late 1900s they discovered I had a father in the House of Lords, they just laughed. I became *'The Blue Baron'* and *'The Heir on a G-String'.*

One particularly confrontational TV show stands out in the memory. It was an edition of *Thursday Night Live* with the journalists Jane Moore and Andrew Neil. This had the *Jerry Springer* format of pitting everybody against each other in loud and raucous debate with lots of heckling from the audience.

My colleague in the 'dangerous subversive' corner was Rowan Pelling (left), the beautifully articulate journalist and Editor of *The Erotic Review*. Pitted against us in the 'right and righteous' corner were two journalists from *The Daily Mail* and *The Daily Express*, Eve Pollard and Dorothy-Grace Elder. I enjoyed a good chat with Eve Pollard in the make-up room. But this was broken up. We were not meant to be getting along.

To stir proceedings up, the programme makers had set up on either side of the stage semi-naked mannequins wearing gimp masks. The one next to me and Rowan had an inbuilt black rubber penis protruding from its forehead and chains hanging off it leading to nipple clamps.

Trouser-suited Jane Moore began, "So Henry, what's a nice boy like you doing in a game like this?"

I bounced my way through my pitch - nervous energy makes me jiggle and gesticulate ("Sit on your hands!") - but, as I've said, like the Sundance Kid, I'm better when I move, "In Eng-

land our view of sex is either 'funny' or 'smutty'. Well, to me sex is normal. So if you can have exhibitions and expositions for caravans, for boats, dogs... no reason you shouldn't have one for sex. There are 46 million adults in this country and every single one of them is interested in sex. It's part of our genetic make-up. <u>We are interested in sex.</u> That's the way we are made. So, perfectly reasonable in my opinion to have a big exposition in the biggest exposition hall in the country - and the most prestigious."

Jane Moore then poses the counter-question, interestingly not as herself, "There are people here tonight who will probably say that it's just an excuse for you to parade weird sexual practices?"

"I think if it was that, we'd be doing it in a dungeon in Whetstone. We are doing it in Olympia to make a statement that this is part of the mainstream. We are doing it on the biggest shopping week of the year, the last week of November. It's even on the same Tube line as Oxford Circus-"

"Eve Pollard, Henry here says that everyone's doing it? Is it normal?"

"Well, call me old fashioned, but having edited a Sunday tabloid I think I know a bit about sex-" Laughter in the audience. "Is that my husband in the audience? ...and what people do at home is fine, but I think this is dragging slightly perverted sex-" Eve is drown out by the audience, half laughing, titillated that Eve Pollard has sex (as if daughter Claudia Winkleman wasn't proof enough) and half baying to have a go at me.

So Jane Moore walks over to the black rubber head mask, "Those who've led a sheltered life like me [note this second disassociative position from Jane Moore, having found herself presenting this particular edition of the show rather than the usual host Nicky Campbell] might think this is a unicorn. But actually this mask is appropriately called 'the dickhead'... and here we have nipple clamps that kind of bring tears to the eyes."

My round Harry Potter glasses bouncing on my nose, I respond, "Another reason for doing it in Olympia is that it is absolutely massive. There is room for all tastes. If what turns you on is shampoo and candles, well then there's room for shampoo and candles [not sure why I said 'shampoo'. I suspect I meant bath oil - but maybe luciente blue Head & Shoulders does do it for some people?]. Erotica is what you want to make it. What we want to buy, as people who are naturally interested in sex."

Jane can no longer hold back the baying church-people planted in the audience. First up, Dennis Wrigley, lower-thirded on screen as a 'Family Values Campaigner', but actually the Leader of the UK branch of the Maranatha Community, 'Christians united in prayer and action'. Pointing his accusatory finger at me, Dennis lets loose, "Let's face it, you are in it for money and nothing more." Waits for applause. He gets lots. More finger pointing. "You are the kind of person who is degrading human relationships, and you know it." More applause.

I parry with my riposte to the 'Family Values' chestnut, "You are absolutely right. Children exist. But because children exist is not a reason to prevent adults making their own decisions about what they buy and what they don't buy."

More aggressive finger pointing. "The issue is, that you are exploiting human relationships, and you are degrading them." More fervent applause.

I raise my voice above it, "And you are using children as an excuse-"

"Yes I am! I have counselled people with marriage problems and it's people like you [most determined finger point yet] who have destroyed marital relationships!"

The audience is stoked. A young woman with a gold crucifix at her neck gets her finger out and jabs it at 'the dickhead' and then at me, "The only person who should wear that, is the man doing this Erotica thing! That hat belongs to him!"... and so it goes on. Pariah am I.

At the end of the bait - sorry, debate - Andrew Neil reads out some of the calls the programme has been getting: "Tristan from Twickenham rang into the show, 'This exhibition is just filth. These people should be in Sodom and Gomorrah not W14.'" I rather suspected that was our MD Savvas making that call. "Angela from Wandsworth, 'Only sad and lonely people indulge in sex without love.'" Etc.

The British Press loved all this. I was asked to go on numerous television and radio shows. Erotica even hired Max Clifford to handle its PR. For those who only know Clifford as someone locked up for sexual impropriety with young girls, he was, back then, the king of tabloid publicists. He represented Simon Cowell for over ten years, made fortunes for anyone with an embarrassing story to tell, and offered damage control for those with an embarrassing story to hide. He was the go-to publicist for the big tabloid stories until he became one himself. I met him in his office above Bond Street with some trepidation, but was pleasantly surprised to find him, in my case, respectful to my sensitivity over Knebworth House, and my family not being used to sell my work or the companies I was working for.

I recall being on the radio with Johnny Walker, always a hero of mine (I recommend the very moving audiobook of his memoirs). I recall being on the radio with Lorraine Kelly, and the irony of being pressed on the suitability of fetishwear in Olympia when she herself was wearing the very tightest and shiniest pair of pvc trousers. Apparently I was on a TV show called *The Basement* alongside PJ & Duncan era Ant & Dec - I don't remember that one. But most fun of all was doing *The James Whale Show* on *Talk Radio*. I became a regular weekly guest on James's late night show, which meant heading back up to Oxford Street after supper at Knebworth for a 10pm start. James was a great supporter of the cause, and he and I got on well.

James grew to trust me to the extent that he would not be back from a bathroom break in time to pick up the show after the news. I found myself filling in for him, spouting his idents - "You are listening to James Whale on *Talk Radio*, 1053/1089 on AM radio - with us in the studio tonight is impressionist Jon Culshaw-" "Beautiful. Love 'im. Know whad I mean?" "Sorry - Frank Bruno." "Wickid! Who are you, my friend? Where's James?..." Most of the time it was hi-jinx and larking about at the edge of the envelope. James would promote self check-ups for testicular cancer by leading his audience through the motions of feeling their balls; his producer Ash would enter the studio with a tray of mugs asking, live on air, "Anyone Fuck-offey?"... there was always a positive anti-censorship or pro-body acceptance message behind all of the silliness.

James Whale and I have birthdays a day apart

One evening James held a phone in for people unhappy about their breast shapes and sizes. We interviewed the Queen's corsetiere, June Keaton of Rigby & Peller. A woman called in complaining her breasts were like spaniel's ears. My response was that there is very little in the world more pleasant to stroke and tickle than spaniel's ears. I continued to stress that as long as we were looking

after ourselves we should be proud of our unusual body shapes. I was promptly put in my place by a number of women informing me of the physical problems of especially large breasts. Running for the bus. Persistent back ache. Complex and elaborate scaffolding... The conversation was all in good humour, and genuinely informative. The last caller of the night was a woman in hospital awaiting surgery for a breast reduction in the morning. She said she had tears of laughter running down her cheeks, and wanted to thank us for cheering her up and making her feel so much better about herself, and ready to face her surgery.

I drove home after that show reflecting on how on earth I got to be in this position. What was it about my education and my career path that had led me to be on national radio discussing the Queen's breast size and offering pre-op counselling on breast reduction?

But my early morning drives back to Knebworth were not always moments of feelgood glory. One time I did the chivalrous thing and offered a lift home to a lovely young Glamour model from Hendon (please note: directly on my road home) who'd been on the show with me. She was wearing not a great deal more than some fruity exotic perfume and a lippy bag. It was this nighttime drive-home, of course, that the Police chose to pull me over. Believe it or not, for a broken taillight - I did not relish the idea of being tied up and seduced in a warehouse by this particular policeman. But that was not the issue. The conversation at my car window on the hard shoulder of the A41 at 2am went something like this:

"Is this your car, sir?"

"No officer, it's not. It's my wife's"

"I see. Is this your wife, sir?"

"No officer, it's not. It is... a friend. I mean someone I've been on air with."

"On air?"

"We've been doing a show together."

"Where are you headed?"

"To her place, here in Hendon."

"Her place?"

"I mean, I am dropping her home.."

"And your wife is aware you are driving her car?"...

I could not say anything that the Policeman was going to believe. But he let me drive on. Maybe he suspected I would get a more appropriate ticket in the morning, after the school run, explaining the fruity perfume on the seat belt.

This was a happy time. I enjoyed being on the radio, and the thought crossed my mind that this might have been something I'd have been good at. I imagined how my life would have been different if I had followed the DJ path I'd been on at University rather than the film path. The shared sense of humour with James and his producer Ash, and James's wife Melinda, who would often be at the studio, led to happy friendships. James and Melinda visited Knebworth on a number of occasions, bringing with them some of our all-time favourite house gifts, and often also their friends Chrissie and Jim Diamond, the Scottish singer/songwriter. This summons another bizarre memory of the large loud Lancastrian David Hodgins (p.278), who I'd skipped around a barn with holding hands the evening he'd sued me. Once upon a time, when Medusa and All Digital were looking for sell-through video projects, David and I had driven to somewhere odd, like Isleworth, to a leisure centre concert given by Jim Diamond. In a crowd of couples on 'date night', David and I had sat like Laurel and Hardy amongst them as Jim crooned *"I should have known better, to lie with one as beautiful as you"*. I was thinking, actually, this could be weirder. Shortly before, I'd been in a theatre in Leeds on a similar mission watching a muscled black dancer windmill his elephant trunk penis as we auditioned the Dreamboys dance troupe. In Isleworth, David was struggling to clap along in time to *Hi Ho Silver*. I don't think the gruff Lancastrian would have survived the elephant boy set.

And then they all started dying. James got cancer first. Kidney cancer. A miracle doctor took something the size of a football out of him. Born from this was *The James Whale Fund for Kidney Cancer*, now known as *Kidney Cancer UK*. As I write, over 20 years since I was on the radio with him, James is, somehow, not dead. In fact, brilliantly, he's back with Ash on an evening show at *Talk Radio*. But

the cancer has returned and is now spread to spine, lungs and brain. Lovely Melinda, his partner of 48 years, died of lung cancer on James's birthday in 2018. She was not a smoker. Jim Diamond died of a pulmonary edema in 2015. Before Jim died, he recorded a version of *Ae Fond Kiss* for me in my little recording studio at Knebworth House (m.o.w.l.). This beautiful Scottish ballad, with words by Robert Burns, is thought to take its melody from the work of the Scottish composer Sir James Oswald, who lived with widow Leonora Lytton at Knebworth House in the 1760s, and is buried in the churchyard in Knebworth Park. *"Fare-thee-weel, thou best and dearest!"*

Jim Diamond in my studio at Knebworth

The James Whale radio spot was not purely about the *Erotica* Expo. As well as fronting this I was running two video companies for Harold. Harold was having fun. He asked what else we should do? Buoyed by our auspicious trip to Belgium, I started to look at the idea of an adult award show. There was no point doing an adult video award show like we'd seen in Brussels. We didn't have that many sexual positions in England. We didn't have adult videos, except for smutty post-pub comedies featuring Roy Chubby Brown and Harry The Horny Hypnotist. So why not tackle that anomaly head on? Why not do an award show for all the people who were fighting censorship in Britain. We were the most censored country in the Western World, with the possible exception of Ireland. Why not celebrate the people pushing back against that?

And what better way to expand Harold's burgeoning little media operation in London, than to engage with professionals in every single media? If we give awards to people in film, television, magazines, newspapers, websites, books, etc. - those in each of these mediae most pushing the envelope - we would create introductions for our Mollin companies in all of these different marketplaces.

And what a party we'd have. With the most outrageous folk in the land.

CHAPTER THIRTY-ONE

The 18 Awards

There's a lot of people out there saying what's bad about adult entertainment -
we're here tonight to say what's good about it
Henry Cobbold, *The 1st Annual 18 Awards* 1997

I wish the British Public would admit it is much more fun
to look at bottoms than to see people punch each other.
Henry Cobbold, *News Of The World* March 14 1999

It's April 1997. With your best Pathé News voice, give this Voice Over a whirl:
A taste of fin-de-siècle decadence on the lips of London this week as The Savoy Hotel
played host to The 18 Awards, the first event ever to trumpet the very best of Brit-
ish adult media. Nude body-painted showgirls adorned the awning, lithe beautiful
men masquerading as wild animals ushered guests, and the paparazzi surged, as
celebrities - Tim Roth, Ruby Wax, Joanne Guest, Scorpio, cast members of EastEnd-
ers, Family Affairs - sailed through into the dramatic nightclub setting that was The
Savoy's transformed Lancaster Ballroom.

In the shadow of a revolving life-size version of the evening's provocative award
- a naked man and woman entwined together - guests were treated to the fiery
rhythm & blues of Snakehips Johnson & the Shuffling Hungarians. This was no or-
dinary awards ceremony. The house white flowed freely as the WAMBAM Dancers
took to the floor with a nerve-tingling routine of formation & gyration. Not only the

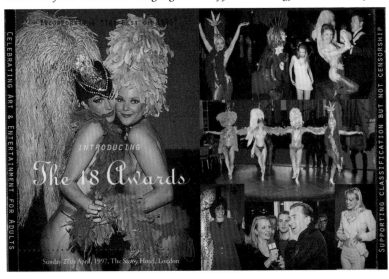

buffet was going to be hot tonight.

"*At last! An event solely for the 45 million adults in this country!*" proclaimed Web And Media's Henry Cobbold, kicking off formal proceedings. "*This is first and foremost a party. But it's also a party with a purpose. We have two missions - this year, next year, the year after and the year after that. Two missions. Firstly, most importantly, to celebrate art and entertainment produced and intended for adults - a concept all too frequently vilified in this country. And secondly, to focus attention on our extraordinarily discriminatory and outdated system of adult censorship.*"

I arrived at the evening without my trousers. Yup. No trousers. No, not intentional. I'd pulled my evening suit out of the cupboard at home not realising the trousers were not on the hanger. Changing in one of the rooms at The Savoy, I discovered I'd brought a fine even-

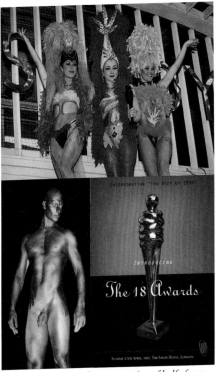

Not me - a physical representation of half of our golden 18 Award trophy designed by my sister Rosina

ing jacket, a formal shirt, even some shiny brogues... but no trousers.

I was nervous enough about Emcee-ing. If it hasn't come across, I am, in company, a shy, retiring, nervous creature at heart. For all my prowess misappropriating Lieutenant Uhura on stage at junior school, the reality was I'd hidden behind the balloon boobs. I'd spent very little time on stage before that moment. You'll recall even at my senior school's triumphant *Joseph and The Amazing Technicolour Dreamcoat*, all I'd done was to pull the rope that brought the cage down for *Close Every Door To Me*. When I'm nervous I shake. So I try to cover this by moving. But if I keep moving, I can't stand behind a lectern. So then I have to carry my notes. But if I carry my notes, when I hold them up to read they're shaking like a tasselled pompom. If I'm mic-ed up, I'm creating a rain sound effect.

So I'd brought a clipboard for my script this night. Very Denis Norden. A clip board I could jab against my ribs to hide the fact that I was shaking with nerves. But I hadn't bought my trousers.

Of course it was fairly unlikely anyone would be looking at me. Not only was the Lancaster Ballroom of The Savoy a Parthenon frieze of bodypainted naked models, but we'd enlisted as my co-presenter the future West End star, amazon blonde Hannah Waddingham. She had her legs out. Would it really matter if I had my legs out? It would be on theme. But the assembled celebrants - whose eyeline liter-

ally was my knees - were to be spared. This time. Fred Bari, a lawyer friend of Harold's from New York gamely gave up his trousers for the night. To the host.

Web and Media Ltd launched The 18 Awards at The Savoy Hotel in London on the evening of Sunday 27th April 1997. Web and Media Ltd. was the operating company Harold was using to expand his little media group beyond video distribution. Search words were important in those early days of the internet, but I pointed out that Web and Media Ltd. was particularly dull. So having created the Web And Media British Adult Media awards, I changed our name to the - much better - WAMBAM Ltd.

29 D'Arblay Street

London W1V 3FH

Telephone:

0171 434 3452

Facsimile:

0171 434 3518

Henry Cobbold
CREATIVE DIRECTOR

My own company, The 39, had recently been commissioned by the broadcaster Channel 5 to research adult award shows around the world. I'm not entirely sure why. I think I went to pitch to them as they were sniffing around *Red Shoe Diaries* for UK broadcast. Maybe I mentioned the Belgian Award Show? Maybe it was because they were picking up the UK rights to broadcast Miss World? Whatever, they chose not to make the documentary. But the research was an enlightening exercise. I found that each year in Europe and the United States, there were eight adult movie

1) *The AVN Awards Show* - Las Vegas - January

2) *XRCO Awards* - Los Angeles - February

3) *Hot D'Or* - Paris - February

4) *Foxe Fans Favorites Awards Show* - Los Angeles - February

5) *Awards Europeens Du X* - Brussels - March

6) *Barnasex* - Barcelona - September

7) *Impulse D'Oro* - Milan - September

8) *Gay Erotic Video Awards* - Los Angeles - December

award shows being hosted (left).

This was a thriving sector in the Western World in the age of sell-through video. But not in the UK. None of this would have meant anything in Nanny McBritain.

This made no sense to me. What was it about the Britain's fears and complexes that made these videos a threat to society? It was a criminal offence in Great Britain to sell or screen the films that were being honoured and showcased at these American and Continental events. Not only that. It was a criminal offence simply to own one of these films for one's own personal entertainment, or for that matter, information.

It was not just sell-through video. High profile feature films by world-renowned artists were being banned in Britain in the 1990s. David Cronenberg film-version of J. G. Ballard's 1973 novel *Crash*, featuring high-profile A-list actors including Oscar-winner Holly Hunter, was given a certificate for release by the BBFC, but after a campaign by *The Daily Mail* the film was banned by Westminster Council. This meant that it could not be shown in any cinema in the West End.

If there was no point having an award show in Britain for adult movies, there clearly was a point to having an award show in Britain to highlight the reason there was no point having an award show. If you see what I mean. Harold did. So we did.

We called it *The 18 Awards*. For two reasons. Firstly to highlight the basic human right, that when you are an adult, another adult should not tell you what you can or cannot read, see or hear. In Britain you are an adult at 18. And secondly, so we'd only have to play the bass riff of Queen's *Another One Bites The Dust* 18 times, by giving only 18 awards. We divided the 18 awards into two parts: People's Choice Awards - voted for by readers of the London lifestyle and listings magazine *Time Out*, and other entertainment publications; and Industry Awards - voted for by our Industry Jury, which in our first year, 1997, comprised: Mark Deitch (Head of Programming, Bravo TV, a cable channel specialising in cult programming), David McGilivray (Editor, *Scapegoat ~ The Anti-Censorship Magazine*), Kerri Sharp (Editor, *Black Lace* series, an erotica imprint of Virgin Publishing), Dominic Wells (Editor, *Time Out* magazine), and Chris Auty (Co-executive Producer of *Crash*) - although Chris stepped aside when *Crash* was unanimously voted two of the awards.

Our 1997 winners were:

1) **Favourite Adult Comedian** - Eddie Izzard (who stood out at this time as reactionary and devil-may-care)

2) **Favourite Publication For Adults** - Loaded (Editor James Brown, left, pauses partying momentarily to accept an award for moving sex down a couple of shelves at the newsagent, albeit unabashedly for lads)

3) **Favourite Programme For Adults** - Men Behaving Badly (also getting away with the lad zeitgeist, in a traditional sitcom watershed-edge environment)

4) **Favourite Book for Adults** - High Fidelity (Nick Hornby's novel beat out a reprint of The Joy of Sex. Accepting, the author, right with Gladiator Scorpio, expressed delight at have done something that 'that man with a beard' hasn't.)

5) **Favourite Movie for Adults** - Trainspotting (pumped with drug culture anti-heroes)

6) **Favourite Pin-Up** - Joanne Guest (home-grown Glamour model beating Brad Pitt & George Clooney. Clutching her award, Joanne, left, breathed into the mike, "I'd have never believed I'd get an award for getting my kit off.. but here it is!")

7) **Favourite Male Star** - Ewan McGregor (atypical amongst male movie stars, for being comfortable and egalitarian with full frontal nudity and sexuality)

8) **Favourite Female Star** - Sharon Stone (another A-lister at ease with sexuality)

9) **Best Selling Adult Video - Comedy** - Roy Chubby Brown (trouncing all and every one, both in bad taste, and persistently in the British home video retail charts)

10) **Best Selling Adult Video - Erotic** - Ben Dover (right, for his ten consecutive No.1 videos in the U.S.A. - not bad for a Brit, who could only release heavily censored versions of his films in his homeland.)

I was pleased to recognise Lindsay Honey (aka Ben Dover). I liked him and his wife, former Glamour Model, Linzi Drew. On the whole Lindsay/Steve/Simon - he used a number of akas - was refreshingly imaginative in how he shot his handheld camera seduction videos to allow for both a UK and a rest-of-the-world version. He was naturally supportive of the Awards, and a strong advocate of the cause. He gave one of the best speeches of the evening, "We were told many years

Lindsay Honey / Ben Dover

ago that we weren't living in a nanny state... but I tell you, you go into any living room in this country and you will see her there... white of hair, wrinkled of stocking, and fluffy of slipper, cup of cocoa in her hand... there's the nanny, standing in front of your television and video telling you what you can and cannot see. This is The 18 Awards, we're all grown-ups, we should be allowed to watch what we want to watch." I am pleased to see Lindsay and Linzi's son Tyger Drew-Honey doing well as an actor and presenter all these years later.

11) **Best Art Direction/Design - All Media** - Nigel Wingrove / Redemption Films (Nigel, right with Bravo TV's Mark Deitch, was a Soho vampire and video distributor who championed cult movies and released them lovingly in bespoke branded editions.)

I aspired for our little video company to be like Nigel Wingrove's Redemption Films and Salvation Films, and supported him later with establishing & garden shots of Knebworth House for his film Sacred Flesh (2000), in which his

then partner (in the biblical sense) Eileen Daly (left) featured as 'Repression'. Repression busting loose, then bleeding all over the place was a common theme in Nigel's work. Horny nuns, saints & martyrs were his speciality, and at that time he was being lauded by the anti-censorship community for taking his fight to lift the UK ban on his film Visions of Ecstasy (1989) for blasphemy, to the European court. It wasn't until 2008 that blasphemy laws were repealed in the UK, and the uncut Visions of Ecstasy didn't get a certificate until 2012.

12) **Best Photography - All Media** - Rankin (whose passion-fashion-magazine Dazed & Confused had been getting into trouble at retailers for printing above the barcode 'If you can't afford it, steal it.')

13) **Best Writer/Journalist** - Will Self (for unabashed and confrontational journalism - not, I assure you, for taking heroin on the P.M. John Major's jet, for which he'd recently been fired by The Observer.)

14) **Best Ad Campaign** - Bartle Bogle Hegarty - Levis (this was the year of the 'semi-naked mermaids trying to pull off a capsized hod's skinny jeans', continuing the provocative and award-winning tradition of their 1985 'hod getting undressed in the laundrette' to I Heard It Through The Grapevine.)

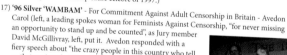

15) **Best Adult Web Page** - I honestly can't remember who won this. I hope it was the standout anti-censorship website www.melonfarmers.com, which we did honour at some point.

16) **International Star of Adult Media** - David Cronenberg (whose feature film Crash was becoming the censorship cause célèbre of 1997.)

17) **'96 Silver 'WAMBAM'** - For Commitment Against Adult Censorship in Britain - Avedon Carol (left, a leading spokes woman for Feminists Against Censorship, "for never missing an opportunity to stand up and be counted", as Jury member David McGillivray, left, put it. Avedon responded with a fiery speech about "the crazy people in this country who tell us that sex is evil. We can't wait for Europe to defend our rights here.. because Europe is catching our poison too!")

18) **'96 Golden 'WAMBAM'** - For Lifetime Achievement in British Adult Media - J.G. Ballard (left, right, and below, legendary literary provocateur and author of the novel Crash, about symphrophilia, sexual arousal in tragedy.)

It was a fine climax. Dominic Wells (above left), Editor of Time Out, introduced the elderly Ballard, as a man "who strides like colossus over other writers" Ballard got the largest ovation of the night and - not unexpectedly - gave a great speech, "Only two places in the world have banned David Cronenberg's film, this country and Singapore. Singapore, where if you drop a cigarette butt in the street you get arrested. As Harold Pearson [Singapore historian] said, Singapore is the land of the death penalty... we don't have the death penalty, we have Virginia Bottomley! Censorship in this country is political. If you allow the proles to use their imagination - what about sex? - What might they start thinking about next? It's been a great evening. I hope this campaign continues for many years."

But that was not the real drama of the evening. The real drama was going on behind the scenes. When we'd booked the Lancaster Ballroom at the Savoy Hotel, the banqueting manager - we were unaware - was leaving his job. I don't know whether he'd given in his notice or was being let go, but we didn't pick up on any particular mischief toward the hotel. But when, during the recce, I noticed the naked marble statues in ornamental niches around the hotel and suggested we echo this with real naked human statues, the banqueting manager seemed enthusiastic. If the models are body painted to look like marble statues surely they won't look any different? Great idea. Point well made.

I used this argument again when we were trying to get a licence for full nudity at the *Erotica* Expo in Manchester. I pointed out to the Licencing Officer that when you enter Manchester Art Gallery, the very first thing you see is a lifesize nude female statue (Francis Derwent Wood's *Atalanta*, right). She is even pointing at her two nipples, just in case you're not sure where to look. What makes this image acceptable for public display to all ages, and yet an image of the same thing, only real - and at an adults-only event - not? That Officer wasn't having any of it. More than his job's worth. The Savoy banqueting manager, however, had already said goodbye to his job. He thought naked human statues was a splendid idea.

The new Savoy banqueting manager - who we met for the first time on the evening of the Awards - did not. He clearly hadn't read the brief. Or his predecessor had left him with no briefs. First off, the new BM had moved the rooms we'd booked for the models to be painted in, to another part of the hotel. He had not appreciated that these rooms were booked next to the Lancaster Suite for a reason. Once the models were body painted, they couldn't put anything over their bodies without messing up the paintwork. So from early on in the evening naked men and women were having walk the full length of the Savoy Hotel corridors and stairwells trying to find their way to the Lancaster Suite. Unsurprisingly, a number of regular hotel guests questioned this. The new BM - on inspecting his ballroom, now lined on all four walls with naked human statues - was now looking more marble than they did. He attempted to put a stop to it, but of course this was the sort of battle that Harold Mollin relished. I don't think Harold saw much of the ceremony. He was having too much fun defending his event and the arrangements made with the former banqueting manager. I was on stage during all this, but I am told that Harold's New York tirade could be heard through the kitchen swing doors, "Close us down and I'll own this hotel by the morning!" New in his job, the BM felt the right thing to do was to phone the head of the Savoy Group, get him out of bed, and over to the hotel for a crisis meeting.

I heard about this, after the Awards had been presented, whilst my co-host Hannah Waddingham was distracting the room by strutting in the spotlight singing

Spank Me, Madonna's song from the movie *Dick Tracy (1990)*. I thought she's be better at that than me. I suggested to Harold that he might want to engineer it so that this 'crisis meeting' with the head of the Savoy Group took place in the manager's office around about midnight. I pointed out that, at midnight, we'd scheduled a transvestite nun to sing *Climb Every Mountain* out of his arse. Harold agreed this would be a good idea.

My father, brilliantly, left his table at this point to take my place at this 'crisis meeting'. I stayed to man the swing doors and keep out any Savoy management as the scheduled finale approached. I can't remember the act's name - the Alternative Miss World, I think - but it was splendidly outrageous. Reclining on his side, the Mother Superior turned his back to the audience and lifted his black nun's habit to present his arse to the Lancaster Suite. There were big red lipstick lips painted on either side of his bumhole, and so it contracted, released, contracted, released, singing "Climb Every Mountain! Ford Every Stream!..." It was the perfect end to our anti-censorship evening. A brilliant big pouting end.

As voices were raised down the hall in the manager's office, the arse bellowed away in the Savoy Ballroom. Oscar Wilde, I feel, would have approved. There were no chambermaids this time to stitch us up. As the head of the Savoy Group marched back to the party, ready to pull the plug, it was all over. The arse had left the building. It was just jolly dancing media folk. Slightly dumbstruck media folk. I'm not sure anyone in the audience was quite sure what they had just seen. But the party was left to stomp the night away. A report the following day concluded, *As Monday morning dawned on Waterloo bridge, the pink blush on the Savoy's cheeks spelt out the good time had by all.*

Needless to say, I have not been invited back to the Savoy.

Although I did slip quietly back into the Lancaster Suite once - disguised in a pair of trousers - to attend my younger brother's wedding. No one sang *Climb Every Mountain* out of their arse that day.

Well, that was fun. Let's do it all again next year.

So we did. In 1998. At Alexandra Palace.

Buoyed by the great time he'd had the year before, Harold threw even more resources at the The Second Annual 18 Awards. With a new team of trendy designers - slightly worryingly, I thought, named Titanic - he built a huge New Orleans set for a Mardi Gras theme. He hired celebrity presenters, Mark Lamarr and Ulrika Johnson (below). He flew in a dancers from a club in New York called Scores (m.o.w.l.) to perform on the truly spectacular two-

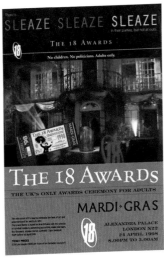

story stage and to host an upstairs 'bordello' lap dancing room. I say Harold 'did' all this. I was still the event's Creative Director. But for the second year of the 18 Awards, Harold - and the new team growing around him - focused their Creative Director's efforts and imagination on the awards themselves, and the politics. The stuff that was much less interesting to everyone else.

But I was involved again in what had been my idea the year before, the return of the naked body-

painted models. Casting naked models is an unusual work day. As we'd done the year before, we put an advert in *The Stage*, the theatrical journal, and the applications flooded in. It occurs to me we wouldn't get such a response nowadays. Nudity, in a 21st Century of self-consciousness and social media, has been put, like Baby, back in the corner. But in the repressed and cameraphone-free 1990s it was not difficult to find dancers and actors pleased to perform and present naked at a party in Alexandra Palace.

As I write this chapter, in 2019, the Director's Guild of Great Britain has just published *Directing nudity and simulated*

sex: Creating a safe environment for daring work. Guidance notes for screen directors.
It contains the following section:

Undressing

No full nudity in any audition or call back. If a performer's body needs to be seen, request bikinis or trunks.

No semi-nudity in first auditions. If semi-nudity is needed in recalls, give the performer notice so they can bring a chaperone with them who can stay in the room during the session... etc.

I understand that this guidance creates the conversation. I understand that this guidance empowers the employee. And, of course, I have nothing but disdain for the abuse it seeks to address. However, I also think that - in the craft of professional acting - it is ridiculous.

Where is the matching guidance that says:

Soul-baring

No soul-baring in any audition or call back. If a performer's inner truth needs to be seen, request crossed-fingers behind the back.

No true feelings in first auditions. If true feelings are needed in recalls, give the performer notice so they can bring a chaperone with them who can stay in the room during the session... etc.?

I summon Lee Strasberg. Have we not been taught, as actors, throughout the 20th Century, to 'act from the inside out', to 'communicate emotions that we really feel'? Do we not laud Hoffman, Pacino, Day Lewis? I will dazzle you with my tears, my pain, my anguish, the searing truth of my soul-baring performance... but I won't bare my skin. I won't reveal the outer me. Only the inner me.

All drama might as well only be on Radio.

This November 2019, Director's Guild Guidance is also published containing the following pearl of wisdom, *Nudity and simulated sex should only be in the script if they're essential to story.* Crickey. Directors clearly do need screenwriters after all.

NOTHING should be in the script that isn't essential to the story.

It is not necessary to treat professionals as children just because there will always be bad people in the world.

The Director's Guild goes on to suggest to all filmmakers *examples of alternatives to showing simulated sex.* These include: *a slow single finger trailing across a piece of inoffensive skin; straightening their collar or clothing; pressing up against someone fully clothed; two characters drinking from the same glass; dancing; preparing and serving food; a whisper in an ear; use of other objects / animals as metaphor; the closing bedroom door; use of audio over a black screen* (Radio again!); *juxtaposed image over intimate sounds...*

Has anybody noticed we've regressed to the 1930s? Always better if we get those pesky artists not to tell the truth.

It's starting to look, in the 2020s, like we need to stage The 18 Awards again. Indeed, as I write, our government looks set to withdraw us from the European Human Rights Act. It is only a matter of time before Britain is back in the bad old 20th

Century, and Henry Cobbold will have to return to the stage without his trousers...

Sorry, went off on one. As Joan Fontaine says to Tyrone Power in her record-breaking (for its uninterrupted length) speech in 1942's *This Above All*, "I'm sorry, Clive, it's just something I feel awfully strongly about."

I was telling you about auditions for naked bodypainted hosts at The 2nd Annual 18 Awards in 1998. Again our models would be on plinths around Alexandra Palace's West Hall, but since statues were less relevant to a giant exhibition space than a classical ballroom, and our theme this year was Mardi Gras, we contemplated our models not only being decoratively provocative, but actually vocative. In other words, presenting awards, alongside our celebrity presenters. Would society collapse if Mrs Henderson's Windmill Girls were seen not only to move, but to speak?

We therefore had two requirements of our girl and boy interviewees. Two essentials that it was reasonable to know before we committed to their handsomely-paid employment on our one-night-only, and not inexpensive, event. Firstly, would they be comfortable naked amongst strangers. And secondly, could they deliver a script. We could have ushered in our prospective candidates - with their chaperones - asked them if they could do these two things, accept their bright affirmative "yes", and said "Great, see you on Saturday!"... Or we could have auditioned them.

Please don't think I am belittling the need for respect in situations like this. Respect is the primary essential in the workplace, after turning up. I hope I have, will, and would always, treat colleagues and prospective colleagues with respect. But all jobs are not the same. Some jobs are not riveting ball bearings, or sitting at a screen. Some jobs require unusual levels of intimacy. Actors French kissing to tell a story. Models selling a message at an anti-censorship event. I am pleased there are people up for these jobs, and not judgemental of those who are not up for them. But please, if you want the job, be prepared to prove that you are fully up for it before the money is being spent and it's too late for Plan B.

Stanley Kubrick booked the Library at Knebworth House for a scene in his 1999 'erotic mystery psychological drama film' [*Wikipedia*] *Eyes Wide Shut*. By this stage in his much lauded career Kubrick was bankrolled sufficiently to be able to film his stories in time sequence, an unusual luxury that promotes truth in performance through actors being able to evolve as their characters. In this instance he was behind schedule, so our Library was kept ready for him, all made up as a Manhattan Library, the skyline of New York propped - as giant photo backcloths - outside the bay window. What was originally a one-or-two day booking turned into a four week booking for Knebworth House. The house sat unused, taking Warner Bros' money, whilst holding this Manhattan set for the Director's arrival.

Eventually, in week four, the Director and his crew turned up. Tom Cruise was with them. It was written in our contract that none of our staff should make eye-contact with Tom. Not a problem. We'll check out his butt instead.

Kubrick rehearsed with his actors all day, and around 6pm he felt ready to take the first shot. The actress was asked to remove her underwear. She refused. Removing her underwear was not in her contract. Production ground to a halt.

In the time it took to resolve this snafu the production lost both Harvey Keitel and Jennifer Jason Leigh, both of whom were scheduled to move onto other movies. The delay cost Warner Bros a bucketload more of its money - some of which continued to be paid to Knebworth House. In the end, not a single shot was taken in our Library. The scene was reset in a bathroom and shot at Pinewood Studios.

So, back to the job of casting naked presenters. No quibble that it's not an unusual one. But I do quibble that it is not a valid one. There I am in the main room of our second floor office at D'Arblay Street & Berwick. I'm with the man with the cheque book, Harold Mollin; our vicar's daughter show producer Anna Stokes; and our gentle gay casting director, Richard Meiklejohn. Up the stairs comes a parade of female and male performers and dancers. They turn up, strip off, speak a few lines of script, and, in most instances, get hired. One dancer standing with nothing on takes out her chewing gum, sticks it on her back, reads the lines, then pops the gum back in her mouth. Richard takes polaroids of them all - for reference, and for the body-paint artist - and sticks them into his casting book. Richard, very sadly, died a few years ago. And so did this type of casting book. Twenty years on, polaroids

Pritt-sticked into books are a thing of the past. The world is now a very different place.

But having done these auditions we can all now be comfortable that when it comes to the evening of Friday 24th April 1998, all our naked hosts in the West Hall at Alexandra Palace will look pleased to be there. And they did.

My message and I did notice that some of our body painted hosts were not as brazenly naked as they'd been the year before. It was like they'd raided *Mr Benn*'s backroom. I didn't want it to be like the second episode of a modern TV series - get the nudity and the audience ratings in the pilot, and from then on everyone has sex in their bras (to save editing the foreign versions). But Anna, our new show producer's, style was naturally going to be different from mine. And I did appreciate the some accessorising was necessary to stand out in this massive venue. But to do the award presenting we did highlight the ones who best expressed the message... that nudity is the last <u>absurd</u> taboo, and male glamour should be no different from female glamour.

Looking less pleased to be there, were our expensive celebrity hosts.

They had not been auditioned. Comedian Mark Lamarr did, sort of, get into the spirit of it. But Ulrika Johnson was a mistake. She put her glad rags on for the rehearsal, but then didn't bother for the show itself, spending the evening looking like she'd rather be somewhere else.

But our nominees and winners were enjoying themselves. And the celebrity quota was well up on the previous year. We were delighted Robbie Williams showed up. That gave The Scores Girls something to do in the lapdancing room. Accepting his 18 Award for 'Who's Hot - Male', Rob-

bie addressed the audience, "Being here is morally wrong. You can all redeem yourselves by joining with me in a chorus of.. 'Kum Ba Yah, My Lord, Kum Ba Yah... God bless you all."

The acceptance speech from 'Best Comedian' Paul Whitehouse is funnier now than it was to us as organisers on the day. He played up on the fact that the sound system was struggling in the cavernous hall. He mumbled on, purposely incomprehensible, even raising a smile from Johnson. Paul and Charlie Higson, were at the time riding high in *The Fast Show*, which won Best TV Comedy.

Paul: "Can I say how wonderful it is to be here on the night of a thousand titties."

Charlie: "I'll double that."

Anna and I kicked off business with a similar speech to my one of the year before about 'a party with a purpose', 'celebrating art and entertainment for adults

- something that nobody else does in this country' and 'focusing attention on our discriminatory and outdated system of adult censorship'. I had auto-cue (and trousers) this year - and no Barbara Cartland to tell me to sit on my hands - so I could happily Sundance around on stage, without having to grip notes to my

ribs, "Britain is the most censored country in the Western World [boos from the audience]... Why should one adult decide what another adult can see, read or hear? What makes them better able to make that choice? Classification is what's important. Informing people. Not making their choices for them. At 18 we are expected to be behave like adults. We should be treated like adults."

Anna - who I'm not sure even looked like she was 18 - explained that the awards were being given to artists and distributors "whose work showed quality and conviction, and was not watered down because there are children in the world."

Back to me, my Harry Potter glasses bouncing on my nose, "Of course children should be protected. But that doesn't mean stopping Mum and Dad from keeping a six pack of lager in the fridge, a medicine cabinet, or even an erotic video in the bedroom cupboard. It's about responsibility! Being responsible for our children. Being responsible! Different countries, different societies, have different ages when they expect their children to be responsible, to behave as adults. Usually when they expect them to leave school, go to war.. In

Ancient Greece it was 11. In modern Britain it's 18. So let's celebrate 18. Let's liberate 18... Ladies and Gentlemen, The 18 Awards!"

I won't Da-Da-Da Da Da, Da-Da-Da Da-Da-Da you through all the 1998 winners, but highlights for me were: Mike Champion, manager of Best Band, The Prodigy - this was the year of their track and video *Smack My Bitch Up* - "People have to push the limits, right, to get censorship laws broken down. Just a little bit. Bit by bit. All the people here tonight, you've turned up to talk about and do things that you pay money for, right? Fuck censorship. Just push it a bit more. Nice one to the band for having the balls to do that." And Helen Fielding for Best Book - *Bridget Jones's Diary* - which, when first published, was a refreshingly frank addition to sanitised mainstream so-called 'female' fiction, or worse 'chic lit'. "I am very grateful to have this firm, upstanding, young whippersnapper of a statuette... which I am sure will come in very useful."

My sister Rosina had designed and made the long thin statuettes. I wanted a couple entwined together. Rosina came up with that, but gave it the double look of a tall ice cream flute (like the Knickerbocker Glories served at Morelli's in Broadstairs) with whipped cream and a couple of cherries on top. I wonder where Robbie keeps his 18 Award? It remains, like Knebworth, something in his career that he attained that Gary Barlow didn't. I have since enjoyed the

*Previous year's 'Who's Hot - Female' Jo Guest (right) hands out awards to (below, left to right) Chris Auty & Jeremy Thomas (Best Film, **Crash**); Helen Fielding; Charlie Higson & Paul Whitehouse; Mike Champion, manager of The Prodigy; Robbie Williams; and David Sullivan*

thought that I performed in front of Robbie Williams before he performed in front of me.

The big debate amongst our judges in this second year

was who should win the evening's final prize, our Lifetime Achievement Award. The judges were: Dominic Wells (Editor, *Time Out*), Rachel Marlow (Journalist, *Tatler*), Steve Boxer (Journalist, *Telegraph/Esquire*), Moussa Clarke (Musician, The PF Project ~ *Trainspotting's Choose Life*), Rob Edwards (Senior Buyer, HMV - there you go, Harold, the upside to the politics), Richard Billingham (Artist), Edward Tudor-Pole (really? I'd forgotten that) (Musician & Presenter) and Joanne Guest (model). The judges deliberated that it should be the magazine *Private Eye*. One of the reasons this was a good choice was that it was intrinsic to the conviction of its publisher Ian Hislop that the magazine would never accept awards. I knew Harold wouldn't accept a no-show for the top award. So I over-ruled the judges on this one and we went with my nomination, the formally-imprisoned pioneer, promoter and publisher of British adult entertainment, David Sullivan. I saw Sullivan - now more in the news as an owner of West Ham United - as someone who had fought consistently throughout his career, through slings and arrows, against censorship. He was exactly the right person to give this award to. And he appreciated it.

"What Henry's done tonight is a marvellous thing for the Industry. We are fighting the British Board of Film Censors at this moment to try and get films passed that people want to see... because we believe in: CLASSIFICATION NOT CENSORSHIP!"

Yes! That was the show ending I wanted.

But there was still time for my co-host from the year before, Hannah Waddingham, to come on in a silver tasselled purple bra and sing *I'm Proud To Be A Vixen* (from the show *Saucy Jack and the Space Vixens*). Politics and Pom Poms. Perfect.

David Sullivan continued in an interview backstage for Sky TV, "It's madness that you can let a 12-year-old see a film with lots of violence... and adults can't watch sex films. There's tragedy and sadness here that we are in the sex industry and we are less acceptable than people in the arms business, less acceptable than people in the cigarette business, and a million other industries... and next to drugs, we are only the next stage up to most people. There are still people being sent to prison for publishing 'obscene' magazines."

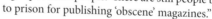

Hooray. Message delivered. High profile guests featured. Attention grabbed. We hadn't managed to get the show broadcast, but we had made it onto various TV magazine shows that were, at that time, sneaking titillating TV into the late night schedules on Sky and Channel 5. All good publicity for the Erotica Expo at Olympia that followed close behind. Harold was happy.

We were building a brand and we were making friends in the media. But I was becoming increasingly alarmed by the amount of money being spent. The final tally for the Alexandra Palace 18 Awards was half a million quid. The video companies and Erotica were doing well, but that was a shed load of money for a promo party.

Harold was employing me to come up with ideas. But was saying "yes" to all of them. All of them, that is, except for the one I was most interested in. Mollin Film.

I imagined what Mollin Film could have done with half a million quid.

As the Mollin Group grew, I became unsure of my continued role. Increasingly managers were needed, to see out these ideas, and grow the companies. I can do 'managing', but it's not the best use of my talents. I stayed on as Creative Director, but a new manager, Jane Garner, from the world of toy licensing, was put in charge. We'd moved to a new office on the opposite corner of D'Arblay and Berwick. We even got a new address registered, 7A D'Arblay Street, for the two floors above a corner Coffee Republic. And I continued to have ideas. But I wanted to be making films, and Harold kept promising that we would, but first 'did I have any other ideas?' Mollin Film was being used as the carrot on the stick.

I was given a couple of productions to keep me quiet. Not exactly the romantic epics I was looking for. While Harold was paying for The Scores Girls, the New York lapdancers, to be in London, why not make a couple of sell-through videos featuring them? So, under the banner of our adult video company, Vision Replays, we made *Scores Girls Go Cool Britannia* (1998) - the five girls each doing a striptease in a photo studio in Letchworth Industrial Area, intercut with shots of them having fun visiting the sights of London, e.g. teasing Buckingham Palace sentry guards and climbing on the lions in Trafalger Square; and *English Fantasies of Joy* (1998) - everyone's favourite Scores Girl, Joy Berman, a *Sports Illustrated* Swimsuit Edition alumni from Florida, touring an English Stately Home (I had access to one of those) and fanta-sising about various scenarios, such as teasing the butler during afternoon Tea in the library and being ravished by a ghost in a four-poster bed. Not exactly Merchant Ivory.

I felt I was not the right man to direct what were essentially stripteases. Present me with a belly dancer and I have no idea where to look. Can anybody tell me? Do you stare at the stom-ach? Do you stare the snapping fingers? It's all very confusing. Harold took me to a lapdancing club on one occasion. We were wooing a banker (the opposite of booing a wanker). I was a horrid disappointment to the third of the three lovely girls who sat at our table. I was pleased to chat, but I did not want her wiggling in front of me. I understand scopophilia, the love of looking. But I do not really understand one-on-one dancing, unless it's with someone I want to have sex with, or want to make laugh. To this day, I feel awkward 'attitude' dancing with anyone but my wife. Do I look at the bouncing breasts before me? Do I stare seductively into my dance partner's sparkling eyes? Am I bumping and grinding at them? Away from them? To me, dancing either needs to be a group thing or a narrative performance, otherwise I'd rather be with my wife. Admiring her breasts. And looking lustfully into her sparkling eyes.

So I enlisted a friend - who had been to both the London Film School and a lapdancing club - to direct this one. There I go again, giving my work away. Daniel Nyiri (who you may remember married our L.A. friend and Lamaze cohort Tina Tanen) won over the key Scores Girls with his gentle charm, and we shot some good-looking footage. Again I wanted to add a female perspective, and so on second camera I enlisted a Film Student from Central St Martins called Anna, who'd approached us during an Erotica Expo saying she wanted to direct Adult movies. She especially

with Daniel Nyiri and Joy Berman

wanted to do this as so few were being made with a female audience in mind. I strongly agreed with her on this. There were one or two foreign female Adult movie directors, but I don't recall there being any in the UK at that time. We went to see Anna's student film. It was, like all student films, black & white and grimy and made scant sense. But one shot suggested a possible future in the artistic possibilities of body fluids. A bloke pissing, played in reverse. Anna meant what she said, and said what she meant. She became the high profile Adult video director 'Anna Span'. I watched one or two of her movies. Artistically packaged, they were instantly more interesting than most UK fare, and easier to leave around the house. Inevitably though the films are let down by the English actors she was able to find to be in them. I know that problem. In the ones I saw the blokes in particular were pale and spotty and much less appetising to watch having sex in London council houses than tanned Californians in sunny condos in the Valley. But that's a taste thing. Her label Easy On The Eye appeared to be successful. And she became a great spokesperson for the business, and against censorship. Last I heard she was standing for Parliament as a Liberal Democrat. She's a reason I'd vote Liberal Democrat.

I had more direct creative involvement in the second of the two films. *English Fantasies of Joy* was a chance to experiment with some of the images I had in my mind for feature film screenplays. An opportunity to improve my showreel, with a particularly good looking star and a particularly good looking location. Damn Nearly (Dan Nyiri) and I even managed to slip in a tribute to Walerian Borowczyk's *La Bête* (1975) - a favourite from Scala Cinema days - in its nightdress and water bowl sequence (opposite, bottom right)... although he and I are probably the only two people in the world who'd ever recognise it. If only the brief had been to make more than a striptease video. If only we

could have shot a full 90-minute narrative. If only we could have used music that was not striptease music... for in the same way music makes a good movie a great movie, music also makes a good movie a striptease video. If only...

The revelation was working with someone who genuinely had the (can we still use the expression?) x-factor. Joy Berman could not have been more perfectly photogenic and delightful. What is it about American girls over English girls? I know I am biased, and as I've said above, it's a taste thing... but I couldn't help contemplating how *St Tropez Suntrap* would have turned out if I'd had access to Joy Berman when we were back visiting Corby to cast that. Casting is all, and this is the one film I've made where the casting - albeit of one - was aced.

The Third Annual 18 Awards on 1st July 1999 took place in a tent. A big temporary tent on a building site somewhere near Liverpool Street called Plannit 2000. It was not easy to find a venue in London of the size we needed, and for the content we were proposing. Plus we wanted to be somewhere unusual and interesting. We were supported again by James Whale on Talk Radio, and in our search for interesting places I found myself also looking for unusual places from where James could do outside broadcasts whilst we were promoting the show. We never did an outside broadcast - I recall a fiery "why are we doing this?" meeting with Kelvin Mackenzie who was about to turn Talk Radio into TalkSport and wasn't remotely interested in The 18 Awards - but I did, as a result of this location hunting, find myself somewhere I have never been before or since, but never forgotten. Up inside Marble Arch.

It is a unique feeling you get, standing alone in the peace and solitude of the Knebworth House rose garden when there are 125,000 people on the other side of the garden gate. An extraordinary sensation of calm in the eye of the storm. I got this same feeling inside Marble Arch. You are in the middle of one of the world's busiest roundabouts. The crossroads of London. Marble Arch used to be from where they would measure distances from London. Knebworth House was either 29.9 or 30 miles from Marble Arch depending on which side of the film production union rules you wanted to fall. Having climbed pokey stone stairs, you enter a long rectangular derelict and dusty stone space. Standing in the middle of this upper room, over the arch, as an Englishman, felt like standing at the centre of the world. So there you have it. The centre of world is a cold forgotten rectangular stone room. No beating heart here. No use for this hollow space except to pack it with hidden riot police when there's a contentious rally in Hyde Park. And that hasn't happened for a century. Of course the chill I got standing inside the upper space of the Arch may have been because I was standing elevated above Tyburn Tree, for 400 years the popular place of public execution for England's more high profile hangings. The kind that would pull a crowd. I was to write the 1st Act climax of my future screenplay *The Highwayman* set on this spot. It's a sequence I am proud of .

> EXT. OXFORD STREET, TYBURN FAIR - DAY
>
> As Tomlinson's cart approaches the end of the street, crowds pour - in advance of it - into the festivities of Tyburn Fair, and the most sensational "Hanging" for a generation..
>
>   CROWD (chants)
>   Gentleman George! Gentleman George!..
>
> London's finest GENTRY file into viewing stands towering high over the three-legged triangle that is the Hanging Tree.. whilst all around it, SOLDIERS struggle to contain the exuberance of the raucous PUBLIC CROWD..
>
> The cart appears, into the fair - Gentleman George roars a greeting to crowd,
>
>   GENTLEMAN GEORGE (roars)
>   GOOD DAY, LONDON!
>
> Followed by hearty, fearless, laughter. Behind him, Tomlinson winces, his hand strokes his blasted ear..

Of course London has another centre point. That's Centre Point. The tower block by Tottenham Court Tube, in the shadow of which we'd filmed some 'let loose' dancing for *Shape Up And Rave* (right). This tower block had been controversial for having been pugnaciously left empty by a property developer in some drawn-out battle with the Planning Authority. As a result a new homeless charity had been named 'Centrepoint'. For the Third 18 Awards we went looking to give our 'party with a purpose' the added credibility of having a charity attached. This, we hoped, would up the celebrity attendance and move us closer to the prize we'd been in touch of

reaching of last year - a TV broadcast deal. The Third Annual 18 Awards would benefit the charity Centrepoint, and although - frustratingly - it was still not broadcast by a free-to-air national broadcaster, Channel 5 did sponsor it.

It also wouldn't be called The Third 18 Awards. Our marketing department was complaining that they always had to explain the title '18'. I thought that was a good thing. Something to talk about. "Not explicit enough", said the Marketing Department. And they didn't

Creative Freedom Awards

1st July 1999
In Support of Centrepoint

Welcome to the Third Annual 18 Creative Freedom Awards

Tonight we are delighted to be rewarding the achievements of 1998 and in doing so supporting the valuable work of the charity Centrepoint - helping the homeless.

The 18 Creative Freedom Awards is the only event in this country to celebrate British artists, journalists, broadcasters and entertainers who make it their business to challenge us, tackle our prejudices, broaden our consciousness and thereby push us to a greater understanding of and compassion for the human condition.

Surely everybody in Great Britain today believes in creative freedom? Yet still there are rules and restrictions that we must duck and dodge on a daily basis. Careers and livelihoods are still being threatened by a will to inform and a will to question taboos.

In response to this we have the 18 Creative Freedom Awards. The people honoured here this evening are the heroes of our freedom of thought and expression and we must not take them for granted.

Join with me and all those throughout the UK who have voted for these awards, in celebrating those singled out this evening. May they continue to be innovative, thought provoking, uncompromising and ultimately entertaining!

Thanks,

Henry Cobbold

Henry Cobbold
Founder - The 18 Creative
Freedom Awards

mean what I meant when I said that at meetings.

So I suggested the 'Creative Freedom Awards'. Everyone liked that. Except me. So we compromised with The '18' Creative Freedom Awards.

Anna Stokes had moved on from Wambam, so Richard Meiklejohn was now producing the show. I was relieved that there was to be a paring down of the excesses and cost of the year before, but I did want the show to retain its edge. The outrageousness of the two previous years had given us a cult status in media circles, but we were still not making much impression on the national Press. There was disagreement on how best to achieve this. I favoured more outrageousness. Everyone else favoured more celebrities. It was felt the two were an uneasy mix. I lost the debate, and my title changed from 'Creative Director' to 'Founder'. Sex was replaced with execs. It was a shame, because in many respects the Awards truly found their feet this year. The winners were worthy. The presenters were on point. A good many high profile media execs - and celebrities - turned up. Our purpose was appreciated, but our party depreciated. There were still body painted hosts - boys and girls painted blue and tribal, like James Cameron *Avatar* prototypes - but with loin cloths and boob tubes. That felt pointless and silly to me. It felt like face-painting at a kids party. What next, magicians going round the tables? At least we still had Jo Guest, who along with bodypainting seemed to have become an informal trademark for the Awards.

Our presenter was Richard Bacon, who had recently been sacked as a *Blue Peter* presenter for admitting he'd taken cocaine. Apparently Richard wasn't the only one taking cocaine in the 90s - honestly, I never saw it - but he was forced to come clean by the *News Of The World*, and it was this hands up honesty that we thought made him a good host for our freedom of speech awards. I liked him and enjoyed bumping into him outside my bedroom a few years later during a junket for the first Harry Potter film.

Richard Bacon with, below, Bob Holness & John Diamond, Chris Eubank; then, Jo Guest & Caroline Aherne; and some dancers looking like they are advertising M&S underwear

"Welcome to the Creative Freedom Awards!..." Richard kicked off, "This event celebrates people who promote and exercise their creative freedom. The people honoured here tonight have been pushing at the edges. People who have said what they wanted to say, rather than [peering at the autocue] what.. they've.. been.. told.. to.. say.. and fought to be truthful rather than just popular. So tonight we say thank you, to all those in all parts of the media, who challenge us, make us think, outrage us, infuriate us, fascinate us, thrill us, and broaden our perspective."

My formula for the awards stayed intact and, as I say, I was pleased with the choices for this year's nominees and winners. Worthy recipients included John Diamond for his honest and taboo-busting book *C: Because Cowards Get Cancer Too*. He died soon after, with not much of a throat left, and when I hear his-then-wife Nigella Lawson's honeyed voice today I think of his very much less sexy rasp of "thank you" at our podium.

We split Television into 'Television - Issues' and 'Television - Comedy'. We honoured Channel 4's soap opera *Brookside* for the challenging storylines it was pushing pre-watershed - drug rape, incest, euthanasia - building on the positive effect of the first pre-watershed lesbian kiss it had featured in 1994. I read in Nicola Stephenson's *Wikipedia* entry that when director Danny Boyle used this 'lesbian kiss' clip at the 2012 London Olympics it was broadcast in 76 countries where homosexuality is still illegal.

For 'Television - Comedy' I'm happy we gave the award to someone who's also left us, before time, Caroline Aherne, for the originality of *The Royle Family*.

We gave 'Personality - Male' (what happened to 'Who's Hot - Male'? Hmm..) to Johnny Vaughan and thus got a hearty mention on Channel Four's *The Big Breakfast* the following morning (I loved the joyous anarchy of *The Big Breakfast*, and hang my head in despair comparing it to Breakfast TV options today), with Johnny Vaughan brandishing his golden Morelli's knickerbocker glory flute made-by-my-sister trophy. Johnny Vaughan was another who'd turned his life around post-cocaine, though in his case it

was, supposedly, selling the drug, It put him in prison soon after leaving the public school Uppingham, a place that had already seen Stephen Fry incarcerated for credit card fraud, and which must have been getting something of a complex in the 1980s.

But before you think that The 18 Awards was simply an apologist's club for co-caine-fiends, let me set you right... It was everything Richard Bacon says it was. Or rather I said it was, writing his speech. It was an important cause in the 1990s. And

I salute Harold for putting his money behind it. The Awards happened one further year, in 2000, after I had left the company, as simply The Creative Free-dom Awards. 15, not 18, awards were given out on 7th June 2000, at our old haunt, the Scala in King's Cross (great venue for it). I don't know why, but I was not there. Four months later, in October 2000, the UK signed *The Human Rights Act 1998*, incorpo-rating the rights set out in the European Convention of Human Rights, including Article 10: *"Everybody has the right to freedom of expression. This right shall include freedom to hold opinions and to receive and impart information and ideas without interference by public authority and regardless of frontiers."*

In addition to this, the Internet was running rings around Nanny. In less than a decade the revo-lution of 1s and 0s had unleashed all its good and its bads on the Western World. It was seen that the goods outweighed the bads. So the Government stepped back from censoring things, and worked harder at classifying things. The erection was un-leashed on the British public. There is was, the erect penis, all over the internet, doing its thing - and we were permitted to witness it. Not encouraged, but permitted. And, as a nation, over time we've become less pruriently obsessed by sex.

The 18 Awards, I hope, played its part. Mainly by pointing out the absurdity of its own existence.

If it made a dent in British hypocrisy, The 18 Awards certainly also made a dent in Harold's hip pocket. But then came an even bigger financial punt. Again, an idea of mine that Harold didn't have to say yes to.

The mid-90s was the Age of the 'Lad's Mag'. *FHM. Maxim. GQ. Esquire...* these magazines were all doing well featuring celebrities and beautiful people in very fine, but very few, clothes, interspersed with lifestyle articles. Doing particularly well were the magazines that forewent the clothes altogether and dolloped side-bars with bawdy humour. *Front*. *Loaded*. Since we were in business with Playboy Enterprises - distributing *Red Shoe Diaries* - the thought occurred to me that, during these boom years, the Granddaddy of these magazines (or perhaps the wicked Uncle - because *GQ* was already 22-year-old when Hugh Hefner gave birth in 1953), *Playboy* magazine was still languishing hidden on the top shelf, and only in a US edition. On a visit to France I saw that the French had their very own bespoke French edition of *Playboy*. Why did the land of lads and *Loaded* not have its own edition of the original girls, gags, and occasional gravitas, lifestyle magazine? If ever *Playboy* was going to make it onto the middle shelf in the UK - where I felt it belonged over *Front* and *Loaded* - the 90s was the time.

Harold agreed. We took Playboy Enterprises' licencing agent out to lunch. He said 'sure', he'd be pleased to licence *Playboy* magazine to the Mollin Group for a UK edition... but would we also like to consider UK editions of a range of fitness magazines put out by his other client, the Granddaddy of bodybuilding, Canadian Joe Weider?

Certainly, alongside lads, beer & Oasis, fitness was also a 90s thing. Gyms were springing up all over the country. But in retrospect I think Harold liked the Weider idea better than the Playboy idea because Joe Weider looked like his Dad, whereas Hugh Hefner looked like my Dad (the English one, not Martin Sheen). Honestly, I don't know why Harold liked this idea better. It didn't sound half as much fun to me. I think originally the idea was that we would publish both. But the business plans (yes, the irony is, we did a business plan for this) suggested that we would recoup Harold's money much quicker with fitness magazines. Something about 'less competition', and 'Playboy's image problem'. *Playboy* had the image that it was something your Dad would read ('eww, gross'). There was a feeling that it should have long been flushed down the '70s toilets it used to sit beside. I relished the idea of working on Playboy's image in the UK. If the French could make Playboy chic, why couldn't we? 'Playboy chic' not 'Paris chic'. To me *Playboy* magazine was not a shagpiled pine sauna of sideburns, brown flared suits and pubic hair... it was a bastion of liberal thought with a glittering anti-censorship legacy. It would add some class to the middle shelf of W.H.Smith sat alongside *Front* and *Loaded*.

But it was not to be. Playboy did become a commercially popular brand again, briefly, in the next decade, in the most bizarre form of accessories for young girls, its rabbit-head logo appearing on pencil-cases and lunchboxes. If anything was going to finish it off as being sleazy and inappropriate this was it.

Instead, via the Mollin Group, Britain got UK versions of *Men's Fitness* (previously *Muscles & Fitness*), *Shape* (Women's Fitness, but I guess someone else had that title) and *Jump* (Teenage Fitness - open to misinterpretation, so probably better as *Jump*). This was a hefty commitment. To publish three magazines we were not going to get away with a couple of D'Arblay Street rooms. New offices were sought. At first we looked across D'Arblay Street at a fine old four-story Soho townhouse from the 1740s that was competitively priced because it'd been empty for a few years - but for a mattress on each floor and a red light at the door. This would have been a great buy, and I sometime imagine an alternative universe where Harold doesn't bother with any of the businesses and just buys this. I'd have done my job for him then.

*My contribution was limited to recording the cover give-away. an inspirational audio pro-gramme **Secrets of Success**, at a new studio I was starting to build at Knebworth (m.o.w.l.)*

As I recall Harold was put off this Soho townhouse by a planning nonsense that I have oft recounted in decrying the nonsenses of this country. The top floor was two pokey rooms with a non-supporting woodworm-munched dividing wall between them. Health and Safety declared it a fire risk. Reason would have taken it down. But, as we know, Reason doesn't work for the Planning Authorities. What generations of woodworm had not passed through their guts to dust was original 18th Century wood. The wall must stay. But, as a fire risk, it must be completely covered on both sides with another fire-resistant wall. So, we must preserve a wall that nobody needs. That is a fire risk. And that nobody can see. For who? The woodworm. Maybe the Soho Planning Officer was a relation.

It could have been that Harold did not have the pocketbook for both a prem-ises purchase and a start-up publishing company. Or indeed for either. So that's probably the real reason that newly-formed 'Mollin Publishing' moved into rental accommodation above a fried chicken takeaway, I think at the bottom of Great Windmill Street. I can't remember because I went there, maybe, once. I was now convinced that it was time for me to move on, and stop giv-ing Harold ideas. Jane Garner was running Mollin Video, Vision Replays and Wam-bam in D'Arblay Street. Our Entertainment lawyer, John Woollcombe, fancied running 'Mollin Publishing'. Time for me to step back before Harold said "yes" to anything else. What's more, the biggest "yes" that he shouldn't have said was also now on the tip of his tongue. This idea I resolutely had nothing to do with.

Her name was Tiffany.

CHAPTER THIRTY-TWO

Mollin Film

ALISTAIR (V.O.)
Ritual. For some of us, it's the measure of our lives.
A way of telling one year from the next, one day from
another. Little coloured flags in the bunting of life.

(*Strawberries And Cream*, 2001)

I was impressed that Harold Mollin had made it to his late 40s unmarried. I think he was impressed too. As I recall, he wore it as something of a badge. A badge of resistance. Confirming this recollection is a recent discovery that he had in fact been once married. An article in *The New York Times* in 1992 talks of the 1970s and his 'then father-in-law'. But I did not know that. It was never mentioned. So clearly the unmarried status two decades later, in his forties, was a buttonhole to brandish.

What we saw was a wealthy and goodlooking man, a former tennis pro and successful businessman, with no partner ties. Nobody to tell him to paint his house magnolia. I suspect there'd been a few over the years who aspired to tell him this. But he'd successfully remained unshackled to their Farrow & Ball & Chain.

When I met him he was dating a very sensible and lovely media journalist, Debra Johnson. A Yorkshire girl indeed. I wonder how things would have turned out if it had stayed that way.

It didn't. At some point in the late 90s Harold met a Czech lingerie model called Tiffany, in London to take a course in International Business, working in The Sport's Bar on Haymarket. What have I just written! Just those facts read as horribly judgemental. Haymarket in the 1990s was not Haymarket in 1790s. Harold's praise of me regularly included that I was one of his rare non-judgemental friends.

So I'm here to say, I liked Tiffany. She was smiley, sexy and good fun. But of course I didn't know her. And neither

did Harold. But he decided almost instantly he wanted to marry her. After at least a couple of decades of foreswearing the institution. Most bizarre.

There were to be three weddings. One in New York. One at Knebworth. One in the Czech Republic. The one at Knebworth felt like half office party, half lingerie shoot. Tiffany appeared in a black nightdress, or rather through a black nightdress. No one at that celebration could have put their hand on a Bible and said they saw

underwear beneath it.

I don't remember how long the marriage lasted. But the wedding photographer was surprised that after some months nobody had picked up the wedding photographs.

Some things make you cry. Some things make you laugh. If I want to laugh, my go-to memory is being at Harold's Belgravia apartment around this time, and his leg catching the stereo button. Instantly the silence was broken by speakers blaring out the chorus of the Mousse T track:

"I'm Horny. Horny. Horny. Horny.
So Horny. I'm Horny. Horny. Horny..."

Harold reaches down to try and turn 'the damn thing' off. But the button he presses just makes it louder:

"I'm Horny. Horny. Horny. Horny.
So Horny. I'm Horny. Horny. Horny..."

He can't for the life of him turn it off...

"I'm Horny. Horny. Horny. Horny.
So Horny. I'm Horny. Horny. Horny...
tonight."*

It also makes me want to cry. Because, this is the very moment Harold's New York weather insurance business starts to get into trouble. Harold moves money into an account in Tiffany's name in the Czech Republic. Allegedly (I was not party to Harold's financial affairs), Harold has been leveraging his weather insurance reserves on his media business in London - especially on the early stages of launching a brand new publishing company.

Of course, as Tragedy dictates, you gamble with Mother Nature, she trumps at the most inopportune moment. Weather 'events' occur. Insurance claims are made. Harold cannot pay them. The F.B.I. turn up at his office in New York. Harold does not turn up at his arraignment. Harold does not return to America.

Harold asks Tiffany for that money he put in her Czech bank account.

"What money?" (allegedly - I was also not party to conversations with his wife.)

Being married to a man with his businesses crumbling around him, and not likely to return to America, was not what Tiffany signed up for. Tiffany disappears. Last heard of, living in Amsterdam with a Dutch architect.

At this time I am no longer working for the Mollin Group. It is poor John Woollcombe and Jane Garner who are left rudderless in this storm. Cashless. The fledgling Mollin Publishing company has no choice but to wind up fairly instantly. *Jump* dissolves. Felix Dennis's publishing company takes on *Men's Fitness* and *Shape*. Mollin Video limps on for a bit, but poor Jane - despite volunteering for the Samaritans in her own time - can only shoulder a suicidal owner with no cash for so long. The fine teams we had built up all dissolve. Everyone loses their job. The companies default on their licences. Tintin, Asterix, Lucky Luke, all pack their bags and head back East. And the giant bow-tied bunny bounces back West, where the sun puts hair on your chest, if you don't wax and oil it like Joe Weider.

I had moved on a year or so earlier. Partly because I felt Harold didn't need me. He had good managers in place. He needed the companies to do their thing. He didn't need any more product. He needed to consolidate. Mollin Video did licence one more series after I left. *Battle of the Planets.* I was not familiar with this animated series, but apparently in the '70s it was the first show to introduce Japanese anime to an English-language audience, so it seemed a good match for the Continental imports *Tintin* and *Asterix.* But, one moment please... wasn't my childhood alter ego *Marine Boy* Japanese anime? And my childhood was definitely in the 60s.

The other reason I had moved on from the Mollin Group was that my parents had finally set a date for their move out of Knebworth House. Despite calling us back from California in 1993, it took until the year 2000 for my father finally to pull his suitcase out of the attic. Mainly this seemed to be because - ever the king of the party - he was determined to host the Knebworth House Millennium Party.

My Dad greeting the year 2000 - an image he projected on the side of Knebworth House at an epic courtyard party chorus of Auld Lang Syne, preceded by Ken Follett and his band (left). I put The Carpenters' We've Only Just Begun on the turntable as the first sound of the new Millennium

In fact it was the following November before we actually moved in. After the University of London's Bulwer Lytton 2000 Conference (above right), an event my father also enjoyed hosting at Knebworth House, as EBL's great-great-grandson.

Martha had started working for the family catering business - Lytton Catering, at our Barns Conferencing and Banqueting Centre in Knebworth Park - about six months after we'd arrived from California in 1993. She'd run the arena bars at the 1996 Oasis concert, probably the most lucrative day in our company's history. The

beer supernova of the 90s, Oasis and an independent promoter coming together on the same weekend was only ever going to happen once.

It wasn't long before Martha was running Lytton Catering. But with a battering of new prescriptive food legislation entering the commercial kitchen, it was felt prudent to franchise out the catering arm of the family business to the international catering company, Sodexho. Sodexho, in origin, French, found its 'h' unspeakable - "'des 'erbs avec vos 'aricots 'uilés, 'enri?" - so became Sodexo.

Martha was needed to run the rest of the Knebworth show, which by the end of the century was not in great shape. Lots of reasons for this. I'll touch on them later. Originally my parents had thought that Martha and I would work - as they had - with an

Estate Manager. They had had a successful 14 years with a good one, John Hoy (right), just a little older than us. They felt we needed someone younger to work with - both for budgetary reasons and to give us a fresh start. John was sent off to become chief executive at Madame Tussauds, then Blenheim Palace, where the elder son was even more of a challenge.

The replacement was not a success, and short lived. He was a happy chap. A jovial Mr Toad, fairly fresh out of Cirencester. Enough charm to get away with calling his small two-seater sports car a "fat-bird filter". But his desk quickly became piles of unattended papers. He was burning bridges with clients, suppliers, neighbours, tenants... And if there is one lesson to learn about running a place like Knebworth House, it's that it's 50% politics. You can arm yourself with the rules of business, and the textbooks of Cirencester, but when your family business is 500 years set on its Hertfordshire hill and not going anywhere, relationships are more important. Particularly your relationships with your neighbours & local authorities.

Martha can do business and relationships. That's rare in a hired Estate Manager. Nobody runs a family business better than a member of the family who can do business.

I was to continue in my preferred - and much more suited (scruffy but suited) - role as 'Creative Director'. From Creative Director of the Mollin Group, to Creative Director of the Knebworth Group. Now, with a lot fewer 'yes'es.

I was to take on long term projects, planning & development, design, branding & website, and fronting our PR. Little Martha dislikes

Making Dickens' punch recipe with Jenny Agutter for a TV pilot. This was the sort of rigorous work I had to take on.

more than being on camera, so if there was an interview to do, or a TV or a radio appearance, in I stepped to gesticulate and look passionate. And make it look like everything was all my own work.

Parallel to that, I was to continue to try and make money doing what I was actually trained to do. Write screenplays. My commissions for Mr Sarlui and Mr Hodgins had come to an end, and clearly I was not going to be spending a lot of time in Los Angeles now. So it was time to find other producers to work for.

Working for Mollin - alongside visiting the TV markets in Cannes - I had started attending the Cannes Film Festival every May. A great way to stay in touch with friends from L.A, without going to L.A. To start with, I went to Cannes pretending that 'Mollin Film' was more than a promise. Jeremy Saunders, my veteran cohort, was the perfect companion. Those were the days when you didn't need accreditation to get into the Croisette's swanky hotel bars. You just needed to look like you were in the Film Business. Basically wear a baggy white suit.

Jeremy would settle himself at a bar table at the Hotel Majestic, and a procession of old friends and associates would pass by and say hello. I would collect fistfuls of business cards, and every once in a while encounter someone I knew. They could expect a call when I got back home. The great thing about the Cannes Film Festival is that it is open house on pestering business contacts. Everyone is there to be pestered, just for this few days ever year. Then they all go back to their impenetrable offices in Century City or Soho.

And of course Cannes is great for worldwide contacts. Execs from across the globe tip up for the 10-day cocktail party. At that time I was particularly zeroing in on French filmmakers. This was because my two most plausible projects were both set in France. *Wearing A Smile*, the romantic comedy about nudity, and *Strange Relations*, the Parisian apartment piece about being fed raw eggs by Madame Snow.

Strange Relations did generate interest at this time. Not en fin from a French producer, but a Luxembourg-based one. Tom Reeve (son of *The Shooting Party*'s

Geoff Reeve, and with whom I'd done the Marylebone / Beverley Hills apartment swap in 1986) had set himself up in Luxembourg for all sorts of good financing reasons. Jeremy and I went to visit Tom there to talk about *Strange Relations*. Tom was making back-to-back movies in a studio there, and when we visited was directing a childrens' film *Diggity's Treasure* (2001). He was shooting an earth tunnelling scene in the studio the day we turned up. The set for the earth tunnel stuck in my mind and sparked an idea a few years later when I adapted my great-great-great-grandfather's *The Last Days of Pompeii* (m.o.w.l.).

Tom was also co-producing, in the same studio, at the same time, a TV series called *Chromium Blue* (2002). This was not a childrens' film. This was a Zalman King project. There, in Luxembourg, was my former mentor, boss, and California dad, Zalman King. It was a joy to see him, and bizarre in this European studio environment. I wish I had good things to say about *Chromium Blue*. But I found it a difficult watch. It is a similar premise to *Red Shoe Diaries*. A damaged man being sent erotic stories by women - although this time a physically damaged man (motorbike accident). He's a Euro playboy, so not empathetic like David Duchovny's sweet betrayed architect. He's not wandering, lonely, the streets of L.A. with an adorable collie dog, he's holed up in a 'fuck-off' yacht in the Med with an English butler.

I'm all for watching rich people having a good time, but unless I'm watching a music video or pornography, I do, at some stage, need to care about somebody in the story. The *Chromium Blue* pilot is a mash up of three of the episodes. Problem is, the episodes themselves come across as mash ups. Zalman is working on much smaller budgets than on *Red Shoes Diaries*, so to pack production value on screen he is sewing in images from his extensive archive of old footage. Fireworks above a Mediterranean bay are in fact Rio carnival fireworks shot in the 80s at the time of *Wild Orchid* and already re-used in my *Red Shoe Diaries* episode *Night Of Abandon*.

These images and the collages are fun. And the music, of course - as always with Zalman - is great. But story is run off the road by style. I read a review that makes a comparison between this late career style of Zalman's to the late career style of Ken Russell - and I could add to that the late career style of Walerian Borowczyk. These early masters went even crazier late in their careers, with a determination to create, but less money and less time to do it with. Zalman, like Russell and Borowcyzk, was always going to get production value and fabulous images up on screen - and one day I'm sure *Chromium Blue* will look like a fascinating Frankenstein of worn-out turn of the century glamour. But it's not a monster one can care about.

But arriving in Luxembourg, it seemed an auspicious time, and there seemed to be money about. So I don't know why *Strange Relations* didn't happen. Jeremy came away with an Executive Producer credit on *Diggity's Treasure* for helping the production with some paperwork, and he and I were hooked up with an Italian Producer Silvio Muraglia, as mentioned (p.251), to move *Strange Relations* forward.

Wearing A Smile, as also mentioned previously (p.321) - and also through Jeremy Saunders - fell into the hands of Jean-Jacques Beineix before becoming my first 'bande dessinée' comic book. It was through Jean-Jacques Beineix that I was invited to be an advisor at a prestigious French Screenwriters' Symposium named Equinox. Possibly he himself had been asked, and at the last moment was unable to do it.

I took a train to some lovely chateau near Bordeaux, which apparently was very famous for its red wine. Lost on me, I'm afraid. There assembled were young screenwriters from all over Europe, who were to be given one-on-one time with a group of industry 'experts'. These were various producers, directors and screenwriters, one of whom was me. I was by far the youngest 'advisor', closer in age to most of the 'young screenwriters'. I don't remember all the advisors, but they were all suitably distinguished. Michael Radford, bicycling high from a good Academy Award showing for *Il Postino* (1994) a few years earlier, was, I think, advisor group leader. I had met him once before, through Chloe King, but he was the only one I knew personally.

Nicest, as I recall, was the late director Alastair Reid, who, in this seriously-French and Frenchly-serious surroundings, was unfashionably friendly. The 'advisors', I found, an intimidating bunch, and the group sessions with them were strangely difficult. I was well practiced at difficult rooms of combative filmmakers, but despite my Francophilia and international roots, I felt ideologically outnumbered and outvoiced.

I disagreed with pretty much everything said at the Symposium. Like a Film Studies class in 1980, everything was achingly over-intellectualised. To me, the two primary rules of cinema storytelling are 1) Romance 2) S.N.T. - Show-not-Tell. Around this French symposium table it was 1) Politics 2) S.A.T.T. - Sitting-At-Tables-Talking. Yes, all Cinema is politics (as my 1980 Film tutors would say) - but Cinema is more successful politics if told with some Hollywood thrill.

My contributions to 'advisor' discussions were invariably, slash the S.A.T.T. and SHOW people yearning, gerning & burning... fucking, fighting & falling... passion, pathos & purpose... Keep it moving. It's better when you move. It's a movie.

They all stared at me. Distracted I'm sure by my nervous agitation. 'Sex-ob-

sessed', I think they determined... and then they continued... sitting at tables talking, about people predominantly sitting at tables talking.

I made more of an impression on the 'young screenwriters'. The form was that each evening one of their screenplays would be read by all assembled, and the next day the young screenwriter would have a one-on-one session with each of the advisors, and I think a group session with their peers as well. I had a couple of the 'young screenwriters' come up and tell me that they had got the most from my session. Maybe they said that to all the 'advisors'? If so, they'll have since gone far in the business. But I believed them. If I'd have been one of them, I'd have been glad that I was there.

Best of all about this Médoc adventure, was that we were visited during the week by luminaries from the business. So I returned home having been kissed, at breakfast, by Jeanne Moreau. That, I tell you, is how to intoxicate a teetotaller in a temple of wine.

I was invited to one further event by the Equinox team, a couple of years later, a talk in Paris which was all in French and at which I knew no one. But here's the thing. Networking is hard. But in every room there is always a hook to latch onto. In this room was an ex-pat American director called Bob Swain. I could approach this stranger knowing that he could not deny knowing Geoff Reeve - as he'd directed Geoff Reeve's next project after *The Shooting Party*, a Paul Theroux novel, *Dr Slaughter*, released as *Half Moon Street* (1986). But I had an even better line to spark Bob Swain's interest. The title track to his breakout movie *La Balance* (1982) had been sung by my French cousin, Eleonore Lytton. "What did you say your name was again?"... There is always a hook. In every room of strangers.

My original Cannes cohort, Jeremy Saunders, was enfin to do what all self-respecting men should probably enfin do... retire into the French countryside into the arms of a loving sexy French woman. First off, dangling in a heavenly hilltop village amongst the plums of Agen, and later nestled cosily beneath Brest in Brittany. His fortunate find was the fabulous & French, Florence (right).

From my first film job on *The Shooting Party*... through *Green For A Season*... to the circuitous Los Angeles introduction to Pat and Zalman King... and the timely introduction back in the UK to Harold Mollin... through the countless introductions in the hotel bars of the Cannes Film Festival... to the so close, so far, might-of-beens of Mollin Film... Jeremy's influence on my career has been seismic. What fun we had. What gratitude I have.

If I get to go to The Cannes Film Festival nowadays, my Cannes cohort is former financial controller of Working Title Films, Shefali Ghosh. Shefali was a firm friend the moment she said she liked the Curiosity Killed The Cat album I was playing in my car. That's a first.

Having a car at Cannes is rare, and can increase your popularity when taxis are fiercely fought over and accommodation within walking distance only for the f.f.f. - the flashily financially fecund. I met Shefali at an annual first-Friday-of-the-Festival dinner held by another great Cannes friend Anne Sheehan. Over the years I have met countless friends and film folk through these first-Friday-of-the-Festival dinners, and therefore through Anne. What webs we weave!

Anne - also a film finance person - I first met at an Electric Portobello screening of a short film by Rosie Fellner, partner of my Los Angeles Red Shoes mate, Adrian Vitoria...

Therefore, if you trace it back, I met Anne through *Red Shoe Diaries*, therefore through Zalman King, therefore through... Jeremy Saunders. Jeremy is the wellspring of my career. The stream to so many beautiful friendships.

As the Croisette hotel bars have become harder to 'white suit' your way into, it becomes more important to be a 'plus one' on a party invite. It was great to be Shefali's 'plus one' the year *Victoria & Abdul* was being touted by Working Title and its various worldwide distributors.

The film had shot at Knebworth House and so I had plenty of hooks for small talk at a succession of glamorous beach-side cocktail parties. Yachts to the left, free bar to the right, beautiful people in the middle. It was *Chromium Blue* without the sex, bad dialogue & Brazilian fireworks.

Shefali had called her boss Eric Fellner (Rosie's uncle, another 6 degrees) in London on the morning of the Working Title party, so was surprised to bump into him at the beach bar that afternoon. He told me I'd just cost him a small fortune, as he'd had to CGI out a contemporary wood sculpture in the background of a scene for *Victoria & Abdul* shot in the garden of Knebworth House.

It is at moments like this - sipping someone else's ginger ale in the warm sunshine, by a glittering blue Mediterranean dotted with white boats, and surrounded by beautiful people in white suits talking film and finance and festival... that I feel that maybe I'm not so very far off that childhood dream. Almost a filmmaker.

My hot tip for anyone in search of a Cannes cohort is that you can't do better than a journalist. One Film Festival, Jeremy's old bedroom in our rented cliffside apartment in Théoule-sur-Mer went to Catherine Milner, then the Arts Correspondent of *The Sunday Telegraph*. *The Sunday Telegraph* was meant to be contributing to Catherine's rent, but when the paper subsequently became reluctant to do this, I was quite content to let it pass. Catherine, as a journalist, had been invited to every single festival premiere and party, and had included me - as her crucial 'ride home' - in every one of them. I'd not met Catherine before, and have only met her once since, but she was a brilliant Cannes cohort.

If I trace back how I met Catherine, again it goes back circuitously to *Red Shoes Diaries*, and ultimately to Jeremy Saunders. But this connection was via a different thread. Suzanne Barron, the Californian Playboy sales agent who'd sold us the video rights to *Red Shoe Diaries* had become a good friend, and offered to help with Mollin Film. At Cannes, she introduced me to her burstingly positive and fun (American) chum Mick Hawk, who was running the dominant Czech media group, Bonton. As part of his bursting positivity, Mick was supporting (English) entrepreneur Matthew Stillman in revitalising Prague's historic Barrandov Studios. Bear with me, we're going somewhere with this... Along with a stream of commercials and pop videos,

Stillking Productions was becoming a popular co-production partner for feature films. Studio and labour prices in Prague offered significant savings. Stillking had just made one about highwaymen called *Plunkett & Macleane* (1999) with Working Title, written by my old college mates Rob Wade and Neal Purvis.

At the merry dinner at which I met Mick, there was a very charming French-man whom Stillking had taken on to scout projects, called Thierry Morel. It was Thierry who hooked me up with Catherine Milner as a Cannes cohort... Phew. Was it worth it? Well, yes it was. Because it was also Thierry who initiated my next screen-play - *Strawberries and Cream* - which was to be a project for Stillking.

Above: Thierry Morel, Mick Hawk, John Woollcombe, Suzanne Barron & Rob Aft. Right: Mick and John insisting on licking my boules

But first. What happened to Harold Mollin?

The businesses had all collapsed. His wife had left him. I was told he'd made an attempt on his own life in a London hotel room. He never told me this. Next time I heard from him he is in Thailand (where there's no extradition treaty to the United States). His trusted Thai housekeeper in New York had a husband in Bang-kok... who was a General in the Thai airforce... who had a 'Mia Noi' (minor wife) called Pornthip... I know, I know, this can't be true, but do remember I am telling you about Harold Mollin.

The General and Pornthip were to help Harold start a new life. Harold had brought with him a final $500,000 he had managed to scrape together from a few scattered European assets he had not put in Tiffany's name. This $500,000 he trusted to the General and Pornthip to invest in various projects and real estate. This was done in the General's name, as - I think I'm right - a foreigner must have a Thai partner to do business in Thailand? Anyway, this money Harold never saw again.

Going after the General with no history in Thailand, no money, and not speak-ing the language, evolved into a Kafka-esque nightmare for Harold. But as we know - from midnight meetings at the Savoy - Mr Mollin is not one to shy away from con-frontation. For years, subsequently, I was copied in on emails spelling out his wors-ening struggles. This was because he was now pleading to be sent money. Reader, I did. This is a man who had employed me on a good wage through good times.

I was not in a position to send him very much. I was not earning money out-side of a Knebworth House subsistence now, and still was carrying large debts on my credit cards from All Digital days. But off I went to Western Union and drew £500 off my credit card. This, he told me, was a life-saver. Could I now send him more?

Clearly this was going to go on and on. I hoped he had other friends in the West like me, who had feasted on his dollar when times were good. He must have.

I know that Savvas sent him £1000. Harold needled Savvas with the memory of that cheque he had handed over in a makeshift office on Oxford Street at the birth of Erotica.

These pitiful and constant emails were difficult to read. It was hard to reconcile Harold's desperation with memories of the hay days of the Mollin Group. Harold was a man who used to live in an airplane - when he wasn't living at the Dorchester, or in the back of a Rolls Royce. Now he was destitute, begging in a Bangkok backstreet. Later - after more relentless and cliff-edge emails - I sent him another £100. Just £100 - but again, his gratitude suggested that I had pulled him bleeding from the gutter.

The reality was worse. His interpreter and friend Jongcharoen Chansrikesom was, literally, found bleeding to death in a gutter. Murdered by the 'Tahan Mafia', according to Harold, to intimidate him.

Horrible. Harold's life was becoming its own film. One of those miserable ones to be avoided around Awards season. Indeed a screenplay about Harold's tribulations has since been written, called - like rather too many other films - *Into The Void*. It's been written by a Brighton-based filmmaker Gaz Westman, at the behest of a banker associate of Harold's from old Vision Replays days, Roger Bassett.

So maybe one day there will be a Mollin Film after all.

Things did eventually settle down for Harold. He got work at Bangkok tennis clubs, coaching, and has built up his life again, producing books of tennis tips... and even a lovely daughter called Barrie. I like to think I'll get to Thailand one day, and I picture the two of us chewing over memories at some Pattaya beach bar.

In the meantime, I still hear from him every once in a while. His life continues Numquam Frigidus. Never Dull.

THE MOLLIN GROUP

Rescued from the wall of 7A D'Arblay Street... now a momento in my study

The motto we were going to carve above the door of the Mollin Group offices.

Here's a typical Harold update:

As I had mentioned prior, I live next door to the Hotel Alexander - but in a refurbished bar on adjacent to a parking lot. A major production company was filming a 'soap opera' that had a man dressed in a bear outfit. He was supposed to drive a van into the hotel, and then get out. Well, since he was wearing 'bear feet', his paws got stuck under the brake pedal and on the accelerator. Lo, and behold, he crashed right through the wall of my building, through the plate glass windows, and finally ended up next to my dining room table. The entire van was in the room!!

There's Mollin Life for you. Those emails now rarely end without the line, "I do miss laughing with you."

CHAPTER THIRTY-THREE

Knebworth House

Great houses and fine grounds require the presence of the proprietor
(Mrs Fairfax - *Jane Eyre*, Charlotte Brontë 1847)

Ah! Happy he, whose later home as man
Is made where Love first spoke, and Hope began,
Where haunted floors dear footsteps back can give
And in our Lares all our fathers live!
(*Constance; or The Portrait*, Edward Bulwer Lytton 1852)

Martha, Morwenna, Edward and I - and Meg our Great Dane - moved into Knebworth House in November 2000. I was bringing the beautiful family Martha and I had built to live in the beautiful family home that my ancestors had built. We were the 19th generation of the Lytton family to take on custodial duties of this ancient place. The 19th generation to take the baton, and look to fill every unforgiving minute with 60 seconds of distance run. To live in it, love it, and do our best to leave it better than we found it. The peripatetic journey was over. Now came the proprietorial journey.

On a personal level, I was excited to live out the fantasy I'd had since I left for boarding school, aged eight, of having all my things in one place. Now aged 38, I'd never lived in only one place. Either I was away at boarding school for half the year, or when living in other houses around the world, there had always been Knebworth House in the background, keeping safe the other half of me. The things that were mine - parts of me that I loved - were always scattered between these places.

When we lived in Knebworth village in the 1990s, I had been given an office in the Knebworth House Estate Offices. When this became needed, literally, as a granny flat - for my grandmother Hermione's 90s - I had been given my old childhood bedroom back on the top floor of Knebworth House to use as a study.

This wonderful large barrel-ceilinged 1880s room (below), had since I'd left it, been lined wall-to-wall in dark wood shelving units to take some of the house's overflowing book collections. It was used by my younger siblings as a snooker room, as it had stored a full-size billiards table for family friends the Pontes. But certain trappings of my childhood still remained. The red carpet and spacey red plastic lampshades. The cupboard basin with mirrored medicine cabinet containing an old box of henna, a jar of pomade and a torn open bag of pipe cleaners (to tie off my braid ends).

Converting the room into my study, I kept the red wallpaper - there was not much still visible above the wooden shelves. The basin cabinet I replaced completely with more shelves, more shelves, more shelves... I have never ever had enough shelves. The red 1970s carpet I replaced with forest green. Every carpet I have ever installed - where it has been my choice - has been forest green. Roy, the Knebworth village carpet man, tells me every time that old wives say that green carpets are bad luck. I don't understand this. If I'm not lucky enough to be gamboling out-on-the-meadows, on green grass and amongst brown wood, I want to be lucky enough to be gamboling in-on-the-meadows, amongst green carpet and brown wooden shelves.

And why would I want a flat floor? Are meadows flat? Not in Knebworth Park. So beneath my green carpet on one side of the room, I built a plinth. My desk sits on this plinth, raising me up above my dark wood book shelves - so the weight of their volumes does not oppress; and raising me up above the blue horizon outside - so I can see into its distant potential... plus it makes me feel like a Victorian governess.

Still today, this beautiful room is my study. And still, one or two things from my childhood bedroom are still in place. Unpulled in 40 years, the midnight blue roller blind is still set above the leaded fleur-de-lys mullioned windows. Inside those midnight blue rolls are still the fluorescent stars I stuck on it as a 10-year-old - Orion being the only constellation I've even known the shape of. And I've long forgotten

My study
(photos frankenmerged)

the far-off childhood day I tied an abseiling green toy soldier on the end of the pull cord - but he's still there today, clutching his rifle, clinging to the frayed nylon, silhouetted against the sky.

When I talk about my 'things', I mean objects acquired through my life that I've wanted to keep. Collections. Not the materials of life - clothes, furniture, family, friends. I mean the immaterial. The tchotchkes, the bric-à-brac, the curios of my curiosity. Most of these things mean nothing to most. They're the building blocks of my creativity. They are the things I love, often created by, or given to me by, people I love. Souvenirs. Memories. Writings. Images. Recordings. Things that inspire me.

Many of these things are related to projects. Not just past projects. But future projects. Projects I'll get to one day. Through my peripatetic life, this has been my fairly-pathetic fantasy. To have the sum of these material things in a single place. And in this wondrous room - my old childhood bedroom - at the age of 38, I was able to achieve that. My room. My study. My shed. The Beauchamp Room in Knebworth House.

Of course it only took a few years of staying in one place, for me to outgrow this huge room. My struggle since has been to keep my life edited. Curios keep collecting. Projects continue to evolve. I find myself saying my house is not big enough. I find myself getting no sympathy.

I know Knebworth House looks like castle, but it's actually only one wing of an old Tudor manor house with custard slapped on it to make it look like a castle. Half of Knebworth House is only five rooms. What's more, it's got nineteen generations of stuff stuffed into it. When we moved with our furniture and boxes, we found nothing but furniture and boxes from the previous millennium. Every cupboard was bulging, every drawer packed full, every shelf piled high.

Consider books. The Lyttons are a literary family. Yes, we are fortunate that one of these five rooms in the northern half of the house is a formal library. But the last five generations of the Lytton family all wrote and collected books. All had at least one library's worth of books. We could fill all five of those five rooms with libraries. We could fill half the house with libraries.

The thing is, as well as a home, Knebworth House is also a museum. It's a living museum of social history, and particularly fascinating as the home of one family reflecting that social history for over 500 years. What you find when you live in a mu-

seum, is that it's very difficult to bring yourself to throw anything out. Every piece of plastic, you know, will be absolutely fascinating in a hundred years time. You know that because it's the silly things from a hundred years ago that we treasure now. Like the discarded Vichy Water bottle found buried in the garden. The tongue scraper from Edward Bulwer Lytton's toiletries... My own Evian collapsible water bottle and my Gillette swivel head (and certainly my pipe cleaners) will be the fascinating treasures in 2150. By throwing these things out I'm depriving my descendants of

a rich legacy of toiletries.

Of course these things are only fascinating in 150 years' time because we <u>do</u> throw things out. We edit our homes. We distil our drawers, our cupboard & shelves. Making the one or two outtakes that slip through the floorboard precious rarities. William Morris says 'Have nothing in your house that you do not know to be useful, or believe to be beautiful.'... Except if you live in a museum. Then cram any old plastic into the attic.

I do try to live by Morris's maxim. I do my best to distinguish the 'useful', and the 'beautiful' from everything else. But in Knebworth House I find myself defaulting to a different filter. The story.

Does the object have a story? Simon Jenkins, in his 2001 book *England's Thousand Best Houses*, picks up on me describing Knebworth House as 'a treasure house of stories' (from an interview I did with Cassandra Jardine for *The Telegraph*). Certainly Knebworth House is not a 'treasure house' of the monetarily valuable. Anything worth any cash in Knebworth House has found its way to Christie's or Sotheby's over the years, to pay taxes or mend the roof. But every single thing in Knebworth House that escapes the black plastic sack flaps of oblivion, or the bring-out-your-dead tractor trailer to the earth pit, survives because there is a story attached to it. We are the story makers at Knebworth House, the scene of scenes and the dreamers of dreams - to twist the quote of Arthur O'Shaughnessy (1844-1881), who once was thought to be an illegitimate son of Edward Bulwer Lytton. But who was not. It's a good story though.

Knebworth House is a treasure house of stories. I love that it has five libraries, if not the five rooms to put them in. I love that it has an attic stuffed with trunks, stuffed with stuff. One trunk is actually stuffed with trunks - my Mum Chryssie's elephant collection. One day a great-great-great-grandchild will delight in discovering this.

Since my study started to overflow, I have been adding to the Knebworth House attic like the Marx brothers adding to that ship's cabin. It's one of the reasons I'm writing this book. To edit down the old me. To create room for new interests, new collections, new projects. As I've been writing, I've been going through my study tossing out bits of the old me, into the black plastic sack flaps of oblivion. Where my emotions have been piqued, I have distilled the memory into words on these pages - sometimes photographing or scanning - before tossing. But when I find a collection, or something unique, that I know somebody like me will want to discover in a hundred years time, my hand has passed over the black plastic sack flaps of oblivion... and opted instead for the white assembled cardboard of incarceration, and taped up a time capsule in a vampire coffin box for the recesses of the attic.

In the innocence of my youth, I received harsh words of admonishment for considering giving a piece of my Dad's childhood train set from the attic to my schoolfriend Guy Monson as a birthday present. Guy was obsessed with trains. The train set was in pieces, unloved, becoming increasingly scattered. Guy would have genuinely appreciated it. But I was told, "Never give away anything from the attic!"

I understand this admonishment now. The trunks in the attic are the flesh of a living museum. Or, a better analogy, they are the barrels of vintage balsamic vinegar, maturing into stories for future generations. Your own generation may think it absurd. You're storing vinegar? But the next generation will praise you for it.

Whenever I have - in desperation - had a space-creating purge of the attic, there is always - without fail - something that I subsequently regret throwing out. That piece of random flat board with a piece of right-angled metal screwed to it. What the hell is that? Surely we don't need that? Out it goes... Then, just when there's no hope of retrieving it, you hear, "Dad, I got that old photo developing kit out of the attic, but it is missing its board and arm. I can't use this great vintage kit without that piece."

My original Sony laptop from the 1980s. It was one of the first laptops ever made. It had two pop-up flaps above the keyboard - one for the 'A' drive, and one for the 'B' drive. Only a couple of years later nobody could remember why we all had 'C' drives and never a B drive. I can't believe I threw that laptop away! But it was bulky, heavy, and the attic needed the space.

The Currys electrical store delivery guys were understandably quizzical as to why they were carrying a freezer up three flights of narrow steps to a castle attic. To rid textiles of moth larvae of course... and for storing dead bodies.

This is Knebworth House telling me, "No! No! Don't do it!"

One cast off I am so horrified about, that I continue to hope that it's not true. There was a creepy piece of framed embroidery - it read like a angry curse - signed 'Lorina Bulwer'. There is no Lorina Bulwer in my line of the Bulwer family. It didn't make sense that we had this weird and troubling object in the attic.

Then I discover who Lorina Bulwer is. She was an extraordinary needleworker confined to a workhouse as a lunatic in Great Yarmouth in the late 19th Century, who made bizarre samplers that have now become treasured historical pieces. She was convinced of a family connection, and this rare piece of her work had found its way into the Knebworth House attic. Look her up on Wikipedia. I really really really hope I didn't throw that away. And if, thrash, thrash, I did - surely I took a photograph of it first? But I cannot, now, find either the needlepoint or a photograph.

"Don't do it. Just <u>don't</u> do it." It may mean nothing to you. You may desperately need the space. But let posterity judge what you don't understand, or don't have the time for.

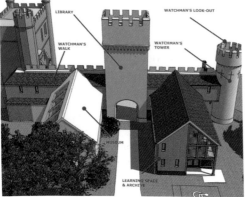

It is because of these traumas, and because of the delight I've experienced discovering stories in the attic, that I hope my eventual legacy at Knebworth House will be a proper archive and collections space. I have drawn up plans for one (left), extending beyond the southern screen wall of the house - for one day, when there is the money for it.

I fancy my new extension as Knebworth House's 'Literature and Learning Centre' - www.literatureandlearning.org. I like the idea of Edward Bulwer Lytton's house becoming not only a home of family and social history, but also it becoming some kind of national centre for literature. This would echo my great-great-great-grandfather's mid-19th Century reputation as the grand old man of literature. His most well-known phrases were almost written to be carved above the door. 'The pen is mightier than the sword', and 'Once upon a time...' - no, he didn't write that one, but he did write the second greatest opening to a story, 'It was a dark and stormy night...'

Not by design - but with some perseverance - I have, over the last 17 years, come to build a national network relating to English literature, which could perhaps one day be a cornerstone to Knebworth House's 'Literature and Learning Centre'. Since 2004 I have been the keeper, facilitator, organiser, person-who-does-the-

work... of The LitHouses Group. The Literary Homes and Museums of Great Britain.

Knebworth House was one of a number of writers' homes and museums in the U.K. to receive a letter in August 2002 from a former curator of The Wordsworth Trust, a Cumbrian literature professor named Terry McCormick. In the letter, Terry suggested a project where those responsible for the country's literary homes and museums form a group, wherein, together, they would prosper - his quote (this being a literary group), 'As bees doe in the sunne, all in a cluster' (Samuel Purchas).

Terry had recently attended a meeting in France of the 'Federation des Maisons d'Ecrivain et des Patrimoines Litteraires', and didn't understand why Britain didn't have something similar. Consequently, on 2nd April 2003, a group of British literary houses and museums - all the way from Burns Cottage in Scotland to Keats House in London - visited the Shakespeare Birthplace Trust in Stratford-upon-Avon for an exploratory meeting. The LitHouses Group was born.

Terry then mysteriously disappeared. I've never found out why. However, encouraged by the ideas generated, the group met again at Keats House on 19th January, 2004, and discussed how a formalised network might work. The group would 'celebrate the jewels in the crown of Britain's literary heritage'. It would meet twice a year: a smaller meeting in the summer, of core group members, to plan a second, larger, meeting in the autumn. At the larger meeting we would specifically tackle issues that relate to all literary houses and museums, in the form of a conference. At our LitHouses Annual Conference, we would welcome people from outside the group - and their expertise and ideas - and share our own knowledge and experience of the topic under discussion.

It seemed like a good idea. But who'd do all the work?... Oh, all right then. Since then, I have been the keeper of The LitHouses Group, and - with the assistance of the hosts - organised eighteen LitHouses Annual Conferences:

2004 - *The Role and Contribution of Literary Homes and Museums in Education* - at Knebworth House, home of Edward Bulwer Lytton.

2005 - *Making Literary Homes and Museums Relevant to a Modern Audience* - at the Roald Dahl Story Centre

2006 - *Interpreting Literary Houses and Their Collections* - at Newstead Abbey, home of Lord Byron

2007 - *Fund Raising for Literary Homes and Museums: Tales and Trails* - at Abbotsford House, home of Sir Walter Scott

2008 - *Texts and Tours: Developing the Potential of Literary Tourism* at the Centre for Tourism and Cultural Change at Leeds Metropolitan University

2009 - *Anniversaries and Audiences: Engaging an Audience with Modern Media and Marketing* at the Royal Institution

2010 - *Sustaining Museums, Sustaining Communities* at Dove Cottage, home of William Wordsworth

2011 - *Old Places, Narrative Spaces: Combining Conservation and Creativity* at the Freud Museum

2012 - *Writer As Brand* at the Robert Burns Birthplace Museum

2013 - *LitHouses In The Spotlight: 10th Anniversary Assessment of Achievements & Aspirations* at The Shakespeare Birthplace Trust

LitHouses 10th Anniversary Conference at Stratford-upon-Avon

2014 – *Net Working* at Elizabeth Gaskell's House

2015 – *Promoting Place Through Partnership* at the Dorchester Museum in Hardy Country

2016 - *Big Screen, Little Screen: Thrills, Ills and Tills* at the Brontë Parsonage

2017 - *Marketing: Mission Multifarious* at Penshurst Place, home of Sir Philip Sidney

2018 - *LitHouses and Learning: From Key Stage to Keyboard* at Knebworth House

2019 - *Celebrating Our Champions: Members, Friends & Literary Societies* at Brantwood, home of John Ruskin

2020 - *The Wit and Wisdom of the LitHouses Group* via Zoom, because a worldwide pandemic kept us from celebrating the 300th birthday of the naturalist Gilbert White at his home in Selborne

2021 - *Content: The Ugly, the Bad, and the Good*, at Gilbert White's House, celebrating his 301st

You'll notice, over the years, my main concern has been to come up with an alliterative title for each conference. Whether the title makes any sense, or its content is of any use... are secondary considerations. Happily, though, the feedback has been good. Most literary houses and museums in the country have attended these conferences at some point, and numbers continue strong. Wherever we are in the country it will be that exactly 40 people turn up. Never sure why that is.

LitHouses 15th Anniversary Conference at Knebworth House

There are about 60 literary homes or museums open to the public in Great Britain, and we've now added the homes and museums of musicians. All are de facto members of The LitHouses Group. The group is hosted by members, in rotation, so I have kept the annual membership fee minimal (the same £35 we started with back in 2004, to cover conference catering & the website) and I make sure meetings and conferences are held in every corner of the country. Consequently, whether you are a fabulously endowed cottage or an impoverished crumbling castle - and however remote you are - you have no excuse not to turn up at least once in a while.

The exchange of information and ideas, spending time at each other's museums, benchmarking, discussing best practice and legislation compliance, as well as sharing & comparing our problems & successes... all of these positives active members of the Group benefit from. Most important of all, when people spend time together, year after year, they develop a trust. From trust comes confidence. (Yes, I've cut-and-pasted my LitHouses speech. Picture me all dewy-eyed and passionate.) (Or skip to Chapter 36 if you're missing the saucy pictures.) The LitHouses Group gives us the confidence to stretch ourselves, to make our operations, and what we do, better; and to do justice the extraordinary heritage of which we are the privileged guardians and proud promoters. Yeah! The LitHouses Group! Yeah!

I am proud of this growing legacy.

And, over the years, I have loved every minute of being hosted in these lovely places by people who love them. The fact is, writers and musicians tend to live in beautiful places. Villages in Hampshire. Lakeside in Cumbria. Seaside towns in Suffolk...

And I've loved spending time with the lovely people who now run these lovely literary homes. Cue Rachel Weisz in 1999's *The Mummy* - before she collapses in a drunken stupor - "Look, I... I may not be an explorer, or an adventurer, or a treasure-seeker, or a gun-fighter, Mr O'Connell, but I am proud of what I am... I.. am a librarian."

A LitHouses Summer Meeting at Benjamin Britten's The Red House in Aldeburgh, with Lucy Walker, Ella Roberts, the late, lovely Sue Morgan of Shaw's Corner, and Elizabeth Nicholson of Handel Hendrix House

A fundamental challenge for all LitHouses is how to make documents sexy. The interpretation and presentation of bits of paper. A museum of scrawl will only sell so many ice creams. Particularly inspiring in its interpretation of its archive is the Roald Dahl Story Centre. In a converted stretch of Great Missenden High Street in Buckinghamshire, the Roald Dahl archive is visible behind glass at the centre of the building, with satellite rooms all around it in which Dahl's stories are interpreted - brilliantly - and used to inspire children to write their own stories. The archive is the beating heart of the building. This is how I'd like to see Knebworth House's Literature and Learning Centre. The Bulwer Lytton archive at the heart of an inspirational learning and storymaking space.

One the reasons I fell so easily into volunteering to run The LitHouses Group, was that in the preceding years, Martha and I had benefitted from - and enjoyed - being part of a similar networking group, that operated in a similar way. The Historic Houses Functions Group was formed by the Duke of Richmond at Goodwood House in 1991. It was similar set-up, for the more commercially-minded privately-run historic houses, all with well developed conference and banqueting operations.

The Historic Houses Functions Group ran for about ten years, and as part of this, on our return to the UK, Martha and I had been privileged to spend weekends at - and get to know the owners of - some of this country's most splendid fifty-ups fifty-downs. They were all magical places we would have been delighted to have bought tickets to visit, and ice creams at their cafes. But, as part of the Historic Houses Functions Group, we were being hosting by their owners, and fed sorbet in their dining rooms. Because the theme of the get-togethers was 'functions', we were consistently fine-functioned.

Highlights were overnight stays at Leeds Castle, Hever Castle, Ripley Castle, Castle Howard, Castle Ashby, Eastnor Castle... What, you ask, was plain old Knebworth 'House' doing amongst all these castles? Well, with the possible exception of the first two, this lot are all pretend castles too. Just more self-aggrandisingly so. Strike that. Don't want to blow my invite back.

But the fact is, Knebworth House has always punched above its weight. Partly because we were one of the first private historic houses in Britain to open commercially. Plenty of ancient homes, including Knebworth House, since the 1930s, had welcomed you for a cup of tea on the occasional Wednesday. But when, in 1971, we built our Adventure Playground in Knebworth Park, installed our Astroglide fibreglass slide, and moved two giant medieval barns to the edge of the garden to offer something more than a cup of tea... there weren't many who had gone before us. Beaulieu, Longleat, Woburn... had added classic cars, lions and deer parks in the 1960s. We were close behind, with our

giant inflatable whale (left, for Jonah-jumping in), bird garden and skateboard park. In those heady '70s days, before Sunday shopping, Knebworth Park was attracting 200,000 visitors each summer - and doubling that on a single weekend by hosting the biggest rock concerts in the country (as previously mentioned, see *Board Meetings In The Bath* by Chryssie Lytton Cobbold). Consequently, my father David had been one of the early founding members of the parent organisation to the Historic Houses Functions Group, the HHA, The Historic Houses Association (itself an off-shoot, of a sub-committee of the BTA, The British Tourist Authority). The HHA was formed in the 1970s as a support and lobbying group for historic houses and gardens. In 2020, it is now more catchily named Historic Houses, boasts 1650 members and my wife Martha as its first female President.

These support groups have been invaluable in learning the bell pulls of historic house custodianship. We go regularly to our HH meetings. "Hello, my name is Henry, and I have an historic house."

The doing-up of the buttons ceremony

It was during our time in the Historic Houses Functions Group, in the 1990s, that the digital age beeped into life. Websites suddenly became a marketing essential. The Group noticed that the words 'Functions' and 'Private' brought the wrong kind of search engine response. New titles for the Group were brainstormed... "Houses of Excellence"... "English Houses of Excellence"... "Historic Houses of Excellence"... "Private Homes of England"... We settled on "Historic Houses of England".

I, personally, had taken on the task of creating a website for the Group. For this I taught myself the ancient art of HTML. That's 'Hyper-Text Markup Language' for you Humanities students. For the first time in my life I saw a - very slight - value to those 'computing' classes that Eton College had tagged onto the Physics curriculum when only six people in the country knew what a computer was. (I exaggerate. I suspect 666 people knew.) With basic HTML, and a program called GoLive produced by

A new type of button - the basic beginnings of 'websites'

a burgeoning American company called Adobe (whose software should be, but for some reason still isn't, dominant in school curriculums), I created websites for Historic Houses of England, Knebworth House, The LitHouses Group, The Erotica Expo, The Knebworth Parish Plan, and - you may be surprised to hear - Blenheim Palace. One should always have at least one palace on one's books.

The 39 Production Company had enough work at that time for me to take on an assistant. I had a good one. An American. Amazingly some people leave California to come live in England of their own accord. She was the lovely, gothic-puppet making, *Phantom-of-the-Opera*-and-Tim-Burton-obsessed, Leigh Allen (left). The perfect person to come put my mind and study in order! As an American, Leigh knew what Adobe was. She was a blessèd find in the early days of keeping all these websites going. She allowed me the time to learn my ends of the Knebworth bell pulls, as Martha and I embarked on our early years of running Knebworth House.

Last heard of living in Wales (no 'h')

It was only in Year 3 of our custodianship that we hosted not only our biggest live event ever, but the biggest live event in British music history. The three days of Robbie Williams at Knebworth. This monster weekend coincided with the 30th anniversary of Knebworth Concerts, so I took it

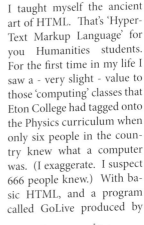

upon myself - and Leigh - to produce a scrapbook commemorating these 30 years. It was only with Leigh's help (she laid the groundwork of all the pages) that I was able to rush *Kneb-worth ~ 30 Years of the Greatest Rock Venue in The World!* (below) into pro-duction in time for sale at the concert. I did make the mistake of not putting Robbie Williams on the book's cover, and consequently sold only an handful of copies to the 370,000 Robbie fans who passed through that weekend. But the pro-moters of the concert did, handsomely, buy one for each member of the crew - and it was a sizable crew - so the book was paid for. Now almost 20 years out-of-date and still with its not-very-good (rushed) cover, the scrapbook continues to sell in our Gift Shop. However I am looking forward to the, not-so-rushed, *Knebworth ~ 50 Years of the Greatest Rock Venue in The World!* big shiny coffee table book. Like the one Michael & Emily Eavis have just done for Glastonbury.

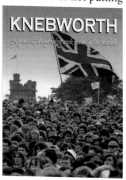

It made a big difference at that time for Knebworth House to be managing its own website. Most of our peers were not. They were spending a lot of money on something they did not understand. An early heffalump trap we fell into was to commission a computer diary system from a third party. The bespoke system that was built for us was a strange lumbering mystical beast that would only move to flick off a fly when you opened your wallet. We were consistently opening our wallet. With every small adjustment and update we moved further and further away from the developing mainstream of software evolution. Trapped. And at the mercy of an expensive maintenance agreement, and call out charges.

Ever since, I've done my best to avoid bespoke third party systems and main-tenance contracts. I felt this particularly about websites, which in those days were your day-to-day public face. Thus it made me anxious when, a few years later, my HTML knowledge was superseded by a newly evolved website language called

WordPress. So far I have not found the time to ac-quire this knowledge. I am, however, currently fortu-nate - and have been for over ten years - to have the part-time tech assistance of the lovely session bass ace & WordPresser Samer Sharawi (left).

Between HTML and WordPress, I took an even deeper lunge into website design. This involved a new company and working with actors again. But MOWL. There was a more challenging new skill I needed to acquire for Knebworth House.

Martha has never wanted to be on camera. She hates even having her photograph taken. Since these early years of Knebworth

House being our responsibility, she has always preferred for me to be its 'media face'. This has sometimes meant that I've received the credit for work that she has done. It wasn't me that spent a year and a half working with the promoters to plan the Robbie Williams concert - but it was me all over the television and radio that weekend in 2003 (see photo on p.76). Of course, on that occasion, much of what I was required to do was to defend Knebworth Park against ambulance-chasing BBC journalists seeking to make a story out of the heavy traffic. The 'news' journalists were relentless, poking their cameras into car windows wanting anger and outrage at the traffic queues... instead of exhilaration and marvel at a home-grown boy from Stoke pulling off such an unprecedented spectacle. The BBC press was so negative and targeted, I began to think they were bitter that Channel 4 got the broadcast rights.

My very first TV appearance was on Channel 4's The Tube back in the early '80s. I could show a close up of me being interviewed by Muriel Gray in our concert field, but this impressive pre-drone establishing shot and illuminating caption is more fun

"So Henry, how do you feel about Sally from Hoddesdon missing her father's funeral because of the traffic jam you've caused?" I had to learn, on camera, what politicians deal with every day, to be apologetic and sympathetic, but then to move the interview on to the positives of a truly remarkable and historic event. It's not easy if you've not done it before. I was live on air when I over-excitedly enthused about witnessing 125 people jump into the air in sheer delight at Mark Owen joining Robbie on stage. I meant, of course, 125,000 people. But that's not what came out of my mouth.

As mentioned, I like to move when I am both thinking and talking. I don't need to move if I'm doing only one of these things. But when I'm doing both, I'm better if I'm jigging around. Enthusing. There are interviews with me - which now are fixed for eternity on YouTube, two clicks from any phone or computer - where my children think I look like I am on cocaine. I tell them it's <u>passion</u>. Sell it with passion. Passion not plod. I draw the Sundance

Kid allusion again - you've got to move to hit the target. If it's worth airtime, it is worth being a little up in the air.

The journalists do keep coming back. So either I'm good for a line (of information) or I'm good for a laugh. Either way I'm happy. Besides, the only way to bury these digitally preserved-for-eternity interviews is to swamp them with new ones.

So, as Martha got the Knebworth House show back on the road, back making money, I was out front playing jester, town crier, media tart, keeping everyone distracted. The fact was - as I've alluded to before - there was a lot of getting back on track to do. The three Knebworth House entities - the property company Knebworth Estates; the heritage/leisure/venue company Lytton Enterprises; and the charity The Knebworth House Education and Preservation Trust - were all in a perilous state when we took over. All were losing money. It wasn't that my parents hadn't worked miracles over their 30 years to create and maintain these entities. They had. But, like at the Mollin Group, management had not yet caught up with the flurry of ideas.

The 'Knebworth Estate' had suffered an almost ruinous 20th Century. Three deaths in the wrong order in the 1930s and '40s had meant a big carve up for death duties. Then, after the Second World War, a large swathe of land was compulsorily purchased at agricultural rates to create Stevenage New Town Industrial Area. By my parents' time there was very little rental market, and repair & maintenance costs were having to be paid by selling off properties - at sale prices that would make Zeno the Stoic weep. Most of these Estate properties were older than Knebworth House itself, and in even worse shape. Many had wrinkled retainers (elderly former employees, not scrotums), or their spouses, in residence as a form of pension, with no maintenance contributions. The two small farms that survived, one to the north and one to the south of the Park, were both on fixed three-generation tenancies at an extremely basic rent level, which by now was less than was required to be spent by the landlord on their maintenance. The Estate was painfully and pitifully eating itself.

Knebworth Park and the leisure company - after an auspicious beginning in the heady leisure boom in the 1970s - also became an increasing struggle in the 1980s & '90s. Now not only was there the competition of all-weekend shopping and all-weekend sport, but the local authorities were ramping up red tape and looking to fill holes in their budgets as the Government privatised all the services. The big music events of the 1970s became fewer and further between, as the red tape and its expense made Knebworth Park viable only for hosting the huge crowd-pullers. Meanwhile the music industry was killing off the huge crowd-pullers, preferring a quick succession of pop sensations to nurturing acts to long term success. There was more money in teenage acts and dance, demographics that did not suit a large country field, and daylight. Even the older crowds from the '70s now wanted a proper seat for their denimed butt cheeks - and also for their de-denimed butt cheeks, when nature called. The empty glass bottle of Watney's they used to piss in, was now not

Water damage in Knebworth House's Banqueting Hall

even allowed in the arena. Mini plastic water bottles only, with the top removed. Have you tried fitting your penis in one of those? Or, even more of a challenge, aiming into one when you don't have a penis?

Watch documentaries and news clips from the 1980s (on our YouTube channel), and you will see how ragged Knebworth House looks. Turrets are missing, walls are badly crumbling on the outside and badly cracked on the inside, decora-

tive features are damaged or disintegrated. There was no money in the Estate or in the company to make any impression on this, or to halt the decline.

At this low point, when we were barely making payroll and my Mum and I were running the company and the park, a long five-year battle was finally won to create my parents' second great legacy for Knebworth, after its rock concerts. The Knebworth House Education and Preservation Trust. The Local Authorities were persuaded to grant planning permission in 'very special circumstances' on three small 'enabling developments' that the family had donated. £2 million was raised, and a charity to preserve Knebworth House was born.

The argument needed 'very special circumstances' because the restricted development zone 'Greenbelt' covers all of the Knebworth Estate. Greenbelt release is an emotive subject and there was much consternation and controversy surrounding the decision. I think now, however, most would agree that these developments have been positive for the local area - Old Knebworth Village Green, the 'Stevenage' Novotel, and the Woodstock development in New Knebworth village. I am not personally keen on the last, but the people who live in it are thankful for it.

This £2 million was skilfully invested over the subsequent 15 years by fine trustees, like my father's old B.P. colleague Alan Beale, to raise £5 million, which was spent on essential repairs to 40% of Knebworth House. However by 2000, that left only £1 million of investments, the annual return of which - even adding income the House generated itself - was not enough to cover the annual budget. The fund was getting smaller and smaller, and 60% of the House still needed urgent repair.

English Heritage was the only available grant body, and after a single - very welcome - contribution of £270,000 in the mid-90s had told us not to come back. We would receive no more. There was still £9 million to find, and that was just to stabilize the crumbling house, not make any improvements to access or facilities.

The National Lottery appeared around this time, so the charity spent the necessary £60,000 to put in an application - only to be told a year later that the rules had changed and it was no longer eligible as it was considered a 'private' charity. As the Lottery opened up different types of grants, we were turned down again and again. Our high profile, and our twice-a-decade rock concerts, gave the perception that we were successful, and therefore a less worthy recipient than other more backwater battlemented behemoths. Maybe that's true. But it doesn't banish the blasted bills.

My parents battled on, but determined not to let the responsibility consume them. What's the point of all the hard work if you can't build a life around it and have some fun? So the foreign holidays and the legendary weekend parties continued. My Dad (right) worked hard commuting to London every day for the wages to spend on these. But money also came from the Estate, and bits continued to be sold, including decaying cottages for their children to exchange for footholds on  the London property ladder. Considering my father spent a lifetime working in banks and company treasury departments, he never seemed, at Knebworth, to work to much of a budget. If we had the money we spent it. If we didn't have the money,

 we borrowed it, or we sold something to raise it, or we ignored the problem until it absolutely could not be ignored any longer.

My parents were devoted to Knebworth House, and are 100% the reason it survived. My mother (left) stitched every curtain, caned every chair, painted every wall, etc. etc... My father worked when he got home from work. Got up before he went to bed. They had board meetings in the bath (right). To-  gether they spent sleepless nights on all its problems. They put their lives into it. But they did not sacrifice their lives to it, and consequently the Estate diminished during these commercially difficult decades.

As the Second Millennium ended, half of which had been spent in Lytton family management, Knebworth House was caught deep in the 'more-going-out-than-coming-in' maelstrom. Oars were being sacrificed, on both sides of the galley - chattels and securities - to the monsters Charybdis and Scylla - that's Christies and Savills. My parents were surviving. But the plan was day-to-day. Not tomorrow.

Except of course that they'd brought their eldest son up to share the madness. The insane love and commitment to a pile of bricks. And I was tomorrow.

All I had to do was to find the right partner to take it on with. As my parents had demonstrated, Knebworth House is not a task for one. The galley in the whirlpool needs at least two oars, and preferably one on both sides of the boat. Finding the right partner was the one thing I had to get right. Reader, I got it right.

CHAPTER THIRTY-FOUR

The Village

LADY BROOKE-TEMPLE
This year's prize.. for best hat..
goes to.. Me!

(*Strawberries And Cream* 2001)

Martha and I were to do things differently from my parents. No surprise there. But always some getting used to to do. To do do. To do da.

Martha is the daughter of a successful businessman. Jim Boone ingrained in her the core principle. Spend less than you make. Stick to budget. Step one.

Step two. Get all your assets working for you. My father, as showman, had enjoyed certain patronages that descended from previous centuries, and a time when the Knebworth Estate had employed everyone in the Parish. The days when his Lordship would field a cricket team against the tenants. When her Ladyship, as the local pop star, would open the village fete and judge the obscene-shaped vegetable competition. When the Chairman of the Parish Council would begin the Annual General Meeting by welcoming the local landowners. When the Estate gifted a building rent-free to be the Village Nursery School. When his Lordship got to choose the vicar and got to sit in the front pew... etc.

Bafflingly all these ancient customs were still in place at the end of the 20th Century. My father played up to them. In the same way he enjoyed being Lord David of Knebworth at jousting tournaments, astride his puffing mare, draped in Cobbold colours, collecting ladies' favours on the end of his lance. If 'droit du seigneur' (the feudal right of his lordship to sleep the first night with any of his vassals' brides) had still been a thing, I suspect my father would have stepped up for that one too.

This was not me. I could face the media, and sell family stories - in that respect I was pleased to be showman - but I couldn't be doing with all the anachronistic Lord of the Manor stuff. We are a couple of centuries on from being the primary employer in the Parish. That's now Glaxo Smith Klein, or Airbus, or MBDA, or one of the other multi-nationals in Stevenage Industrial Area. These new neighbourhood employers should be the 21st Century patrons of the Village Nursery School if we want such a thing as patrons and patriarchy and all that nonsense. Local landowners have long since been taxed and regulated out of any local position of advantage. Our local family company is a local family company like any other local family company. We should go about our business in the same way, and deserve to be treated in the same way. We should be taxed, tolerated or treasured like any other local business.

But we're not. Because our business - 'land' - is not an acceptable way of making money. It is viewed disdainfully as inherited advantage. It is not seen as a bought, paid for, long-taxed and long-nurtured asset. People happily drive, cycle, ramble and empty their dogs on this land that we work, maintain and sustain. They do not consider someone doing the same to their garden, or to their workshop floor. If, for instance, we politely redirect someone back onto the public footpaths that criss-cross this land of ours, there's a likelihood - if we're not told to "fuck off" - that we'll be asked, "why does one family own so much land?" It is not enough to have purchased this land on 17th February 1490 for £800, and to have lovingly cared for it, and paid its dues across the centuries. To own land is thought unfair, and to earn money from land is, to many, an unacceptable business.

And so land continues, in this new century, to be taped in red. And more fool you if, over time, you've made your land beautiful, or imbued it with heritage. For in doing so, you've created a rock, like Sisyphus, to roll forever up the mountain. You have forfeited your freedom to do with your land as you please. Instead of making it your own, you have made it everybody else's.

In our evolved 21st Century the landowner remains inherently evil, remains ripe for pitchforking at the portcullis... but for some reason is still expected to provide a free cricket ground, a free nursery school, free tended parks and woods, etc.

So this was the second thing we had to deal with. End the anachronistic patronages. Get each one of the Estate's assets earning its keep. We began with Knebworth Park Cricket Club and the Old Knebworth Nursery School. And so unleashed a torrent of fury and abuse on House Cobbold.

"Cobbolds evict children." "Cobbolds destroy community cricket club." "We liked his father, but he's only interested in money."... What particularly galls in this reaction is that there's no thanks for the hundred years of providing the community facilities gratis in the first place. We are receiving abuse for levelling the economic playing field... literally, as we offer an alternative level playing field for the Cricket

Club opposite the village pub. Opposite the village pub is a field that we can afford to rent to the Club at a price the Club can afford, and where it has the opportunity to modernise its facilities. The gratis field we are reclaiming is Knebworth Park's prime show field, because it sits directly in front of our U.S.P., our long nurtured brand, Knebworth House.

The view of Knebworth House is what our event clients will pay a premium for. Without it, there are other parks in which to hold your special event.

Here we are over twenty years later and I have still not managed to relocate the Cricket Club. Planning permission now exists for the Club to move. But still, in 2022, the Club pays a peppercorn's rent for a field directly in front of Knebworth House. Patronage is an arse-biter. (Yes, I'm afraid this is 'the rant chapter'. It's only 14 pages. Just look at the pictures.)

The Nursery School we did successfully manage to move. Early on. Off the dangerous corner where a car had recently smashed into its front wall and into its childrens' urinals (right). The school moved into much more appropriate quarters within the grounds of Kneb-worth Primary School. The

Nursery School corner in 1900...   *...and in 2000*

Nursery School - despite rent-free premises - had fallen into bankruptcy. So the County took it on. Which is how it should be. Our first success. But also, in the first year of our custodianship, our first village meetings of being vilified and verbally abused.

I have grown more used to these public meetings now, but they are never pleasant. People don't like change in any form. No matter how clear the benefit. The landowner only ever has evil aforethought. The landowner, you can be sure, is hell-bent on destroying the community he has been a part of for 500 years. He has no thought for the value of my house, and my ability to sell up and comfortably retire to Norfolk.

It is difficult to write this without falling into the very same trap of bitterness. The fact is, suspicion of change, and suspicion of one's neighbours, is human nature. It's not going away. It has to be viewed as part of the challenge. Part of the job. If we've made our case. If we've imagined walking the mile in the other man's shoes. If we believe our cause is just. We just have to get on with it. And take the words, the sticks and the stones. Always, of course, only doing unto others what we would consider reasonable to have done unto ourselves.

Today, the 'Old Schoolhouse' is three well-loved residences (right) that - along with similar initiatives - raise the rent roll to a level where the Knebworth Estate is now sustainable. That is, can now pay its maintenance costs without having to take on debt or sell pieces of itself.

Twenty years on, we have reclaimed all but one residential property that the Estate is responsible for and yet receives no income for. There's still work to be done. There are still assets costing more to maintain than they earn. But, by slowly shedding the anachronisms of patronage, we are finally rescuing the Knebworth Estate from the curse of being a family business that is expected not to operate as a business.

The real difference between us and other local family businesses is that we'll only ever be a non-profit business. Because of a responsibility for historic buildings, gardens, woods and parkland, in the happy event of surplus, there is always an urgent repair or an overdue renewal to bring forward... and in the best case scenario, a family asset that was previously sold to pay maintenance or taxes, to buy back.

This progress we have made over 20 years has taken persistence, patience, perseverance, a Protestant-work-ethic... all of which my perfect partner (left) proffers, presents and provides, with panache, professionalism, and a sense of humour. Actually, Martha's less good at the patience. I'm better at that. But Martha is the one doing the work. She is one who should be writing on the workings of Knebworth House, its place in the community, and its business. But she is too busy doing the work. Brilliantly.

So you've got my take on it. Which I'll keep brief, in the hope that one day it will be written by her, and you'll get the truth of it. My take on the vicissitudes and the virtues - for despite what I find myself highlighting, there are of course plentiful virtues - of English village life, is probably best expressed in fiction and anecdote. I did write a screenplay about English village life - a comedy - around the time we moved into Knebworth House. It is perhaps the most autobiographical of my screenplays to date. It was commissioned originally for Stillking Films in Prague, but when Thierry Morel was let go from that company he took the project with him.

It was Thierry's original idea. *One Flew Over The Cuckoo's Nest* in an old peoples' home', I think, was his original pitch. As a Frenchman, he envisaged something especially English, with an ensemble cast of every single elderly English Shakespearian actor.

Thierry and I were working on the story together at Knebworth House the day airplanes flew into the World Trade Towers in New York. That I certainly remember.

The piece is called *Strawberries and Cream* - referencing the traditional nursery rhyme *Curly Locks*:

```
EXT. VILLAGE GREEN, LITTLEDUCK, ENGLAND - DAY - SUMMER 1960S

CLOSE ON:  A little boy overdressed and uncomfortable in a
blue doublet, ruff and white stockings - a 16th Century
French duke.  He holds a lighted stick to the wick of an
old black cannon.

BANG!  A puff of white smoke.  CHARGE!  The roar of an
army.

SLOW MOTION:  Emerging through the smoke, an army of middle-
aged ladies, holding their hats, balancing eggs on spoons,
charge down a course of festooned bunting..

                    ALISTAIR (V.O.)
          Ritual.  For some of us, it's the
          measure of our lives..

Flower necklaces bouncing on their bosoms, the village
ladies jostle for position, elbows out, jabbing,
competitive..

                    ALISTAIR (V.O.) (CONT'D)
          A way of telling one year from the
          next, one day from another..

A semicircle of picturesque cottages border a small grass
meadow.  At its head, the replica 16th Century cannon marks
the entrance to an old baronial Manor.  The little boy
crosses from the cannon to the finish line - too close -
the phalanx of large ladies charge into him, knocking him
off his feet.
```

The opening of the screenplay Strawberries And Cream

Thou shalt not wash dishes
Nor yet feed the swine,
But sit on a cushion
And sew a fine seam,
And feed upon strawberries,
Sugar and cream.

STRAWBERRIES AND CREAM

Inspired by the humour and resilience of a rebellious group of pensioners, selfish ex-pat Alistair returns to his roots and responsibilities in an old-world English village as it is trampled on by the 21st Century

A thunderous charge of elderly ladies fight for the finish line in an egg-and-spoon race, the climax of the Littleduck Green annual Village Fete. Their reward is Tea - more Pimms, more Earl Gray, cucumber sandwiches, fruit cake, strawberries and cream - followed by a village photo. At which point, every year, it starts to rain. England would be the best place in the world to live if it had a roof.

Playwright Alistair Brooke-Temple is son of the elderly village matriarch, Lady Brooke-Temple. He has abandoned cold parochial England – and a childhood sweetheart, Rosie - to pursue a tenuous career in New York. He returns only twice a year, for the Village Fete and Christmas Day – when, by tradition, he delivers a bottle of Christmas port to each of the cottages on the Village Green. Year on year, Alistair watches his mother's 'tribe' get older, madder and increasingly unable to look after themselves - the viagra-fuelled old chauffeur, the crabby blood-stained gamekeeper, the delusional dyed-haired vicar and his slave-wife, the weeping glass-eyed colonel, the fiercely socialist and closet-naturist councilor, the narcoleptic amnesic ex-schoolmistress and her abusive 100-year-old mother, the chain-smoking nymphomaniac mistress of his late father... Alistair's brother-in-law, oily real estate developer Tim Horn, has a solution. In return for planning permission for a housing development, he'll build a retirement home on the Village Green for them all to die in.

The grim institution is built. One-by-one the elderly villagers leave their cottages and cross the Green to die in their slippers. Fed on a diet of yellow eggs, yellow jelly and yellow cordial, their spirit is systematically broken by a white-coated gorgon – Matron – with a bottle of pills and a syringe. But Matron meets her match when tragedy strikes Littleduck Manor. Her ladyship's faithful housekeeper Clara has a mild heart-attack, and can no longer look after her ladyship. So the villagers are joined in their white-walled Purgatory by their chief, Lady Brooke-Temple. Her ladyship resists Matron's authority. However she has no defense against Matron's boss, her cold-hearted son-in-law, Tim, who exploits Alistair's absence – and playwright poverty – and puts the now empty Manor up for sale.

Maybe it is time to die. But a new 'guest' at the retirement home thinks otherwise. Tom Clark is a local boy recently returned from a lifetime in the Far East. He is irresponsible, irrepressible and irresistible. His charm transforms the dispirited Care Home residents. He moulds their fantasies, twists their delusions... towards positivity. Tom's soft spot is former housekeeper Clara. On Matron's night off, he organizes work-weary Clara the first party ever held in her honour alone – there's dancing, booze, sex, even a punch-up. It ends in tears when discovered by Matron, and ring-leader Tom is relocated to another home. This is the final straw, the catalyst for rebellion. Lady Brooke-Temple rouses the residents into a mass nighttime breakout from the retirement home.

Looking like the graveyard bust-out in *The Night of the Living Dead*, the line of refugees trail across the Green in their pajamas and dressing gowns, their belongings bundled under their arms. It doesn't matter that the night is dark. After years of trying to balance an egg on a spoon while racing across this meadow, every refugee know each clump of turf. The able-bodied assist those in wheel chairs, but the spirit of adventure is in all. Leading the flock, a cross between Moses and Ingrid Bergman, the redoubtable Lady Brooke-Temple.

It is the high-profile Estate Agent sales day for the Manor. The villagers barricade themselves in Lady Brooke-Temple's old home. There is nothing Tim Horn can do, but accept that his prospective buyers are shown the property by her ladyship and her mad mischievous household. Each leaves horrified. The day is won. Triumphant, returned to her own home and her own bed, Lady Brooke-Temple dies peacefully in the night.

After the funeral the 'Littleducks' are sent back to the retirement home with the news that the Manor has been sold. Worse still, without Lady Brooke-Temple, for the first time in its history Littleduck Green will have no Village Fete. But Alistair has returned from New York, and although he can do nothing about the Manor, the spirit of the Littleducks and a new-found responsibility at the loss of his mother, have caused him to rethink his horror of his childhood home and provincial English life. He will host the Village Fete if Rosie agrees that it shall be their wedding party.

Melancholy Clara, meanwhile, is packing up the last of her ladyship's belongings at the Manor, when she is surprised by Tom, and news that it is he who has bought the Manor – his business in Hong Kong has sold for a small fortune, his belongings have recently arrived, and he wants Clara to move in with him, and live in sin. But of course the Manor's too big for just the two of them, so he is hoping she won't mind if the rest of the Littleducks join them.

At that summer's Village Fete the charge to the finish line in the egg-and-spoon is no less thunderous, and no less vigorous. And all get their just deserts. Strawberries and cream. But most unbelievable of all, is - when it comes to the village photo - it doesn't rain.

I used the byline 'A Comedy About Living Before Dying'. That byline's probably been used since. Probably by my Eton College house contemporary Pete Czernin in one of his *Marigold Hotel* films. I know, I know, it's more fun to go to India than Newport Pagnell, but really he should have made this one as well.

Autobiographical? Well, I did used to do a Christmas Day 'port run' with my Grandfather in the 1960s. And the characters all have their genesis in village characters I have known. But a playwright with a tenuous career? No. Not me.

I wonder if I could write such a gentle comedy now? As this chapter reveals, 20 years on, I've become much more bitter and twisted about English country life. For reasons of balance, and to reflect how much of my time is now spent on the day-to-day workings of Knebworth House - despite my subsidiary role - I will now give you a little more taste of its frustrations.

Martha and I have a lot of fun as custodians of Knebworth House, and that I hope comes out in other chapters of this book. But my story would not be complete without giving you a little of the mundanity and frustrations of the 'day job' that currently puts food on my table, and takes up a good deal of my time. Again, I reiterate that I am extremely blessed to have a partner who is content to do the lion's share of it, but I do share in the responsibility (a hyena's share?), and it does take me away from writing, and from the career I trained for, and let's face it, am better suited for.

If you find my privileged bellyaching tiresome, and want to get back to the fun stuff, do skip to Chapter 35. I know the feeling. I feel the same urge at my desk every day, as I'm answering interminable pointless and bureaucratic emails from the real men in black hats, the policy-pushers, the jobsworths, the form compilers & filers, the monopolied utilities providers... etc.

For it's not only from friends and neighbours that those in the stewardship and business of land get grief in rural Great Britain. The Government is well in on the game too. I'll highlight for you just two examples. PRoWs and Planning. Both, I think all agree, important to our wellbeing, but both overplayed by Government. The former, Government over-insists on, the latter, Government over-resists on.

Public Rights of Way are an intrinsic freedom in a civilised society. They are immutable in the United Kingdom. 'Once a highway always a highway'. This is a noble edict. But for the landowner it also a nobbling edict. Footpaths can be opened, but not closed. Like eggs. One-way legislation frustrates rationalisation. Stewardship becomes compromised. Nobody wins.

In Britain the burden of the important freedom of footpaths is on the landowner. Again this harks back to patronage, and the politics of land. The landowner is responsible and liable for all Public Rights of Way on his/her land. Responsible for keeping them clear and maintained. Responsible for any accidents that happen on them, or indeed off them, should the footpath walker go 'prospecting'. We say 'prospecting' because 'trespassing' sounds like a crime. But it is not in this country.

One neighbouring landowner's response was to sell all the public footpaths on his land to a gentleman in Ghana. So when the Council calls to ask why he is not maintaining them, the officer is referred to said gentleman in Ghana. We seek a different relationship with our Local Authorities. And with our neighbours. We cherish footpaths, and accept that a positive network of them criss-cross our land, and are content that our stewardship of, and work on, the land is enjoyed by all. What we've always known we've had, we can manage.

At the beginning of the century, however, inspired by a Government initiative and a Government grant, an intrepid path prospector took it upon himself to spend months in local archives poring over ancient maps (which landowners had public-spiritedly deposited there for research purposes) to find forgotten footpaths. He found a doozy in Knebworth Park, straight through and along its commercial entrance. This medieval route swerved between the cars on the four-lane A1 motorway, trampled through the carpeted lobby of the Novotel hotel, barged through Knebworth Park's main gate, elbowed past its ticket booths, wandered salaciously around the kids playing in its Adventure Playground, and brazenly marched up the main entrance avenue, diverting only to muse a moment in the middle of the cricket pitch at the marvellous view of the magnificent, but maintenance-needing mansion.

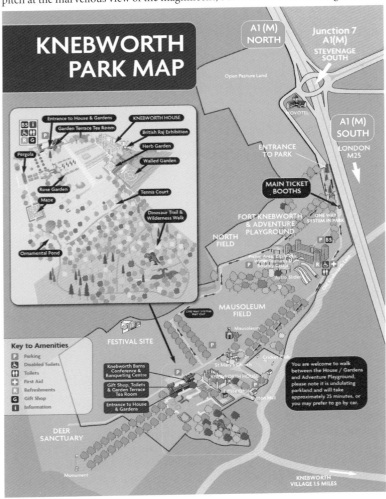

This 'Right of Way' had not been used or recognised since the early 19th Century. However, our path prospector argued, since it had never been formally closed up, it should be reopened - regardless of any impact that would have Knebworth Park's business, sustainability, or survival.

We spent over 10 years in meetings & tribunals and paying lawyers on this one. Even longer than the 8 years my great-grandfather Victor had spent in the 1930s negotiating around a similar initiative. In his time, this same forgotten path had also been spotted. Even back then it had been considered archaic and no longer of use. It was due to be formally closed as part of a 1930s rationalisation plan for all of the Right of Ways across Knebworth Park. This new arrangement was to be included in the then Local Plan, a general policy update that comes along every generation, and which - as with Greenbelt boundaries, m.o.w.l. - is the only vehicle (not the best word) to close up a public footpath apart from an Act of Parliament. This 1930s Local Plan made it all the way to an engrossed copy for signature. However... the Council meeting to sign it was scheduled for September 1939. Not a good month for focusing on archaic footpaths. The signing of the document was postponed. Five years later - after the War was over - this whole Local Plan was forgotten and passed over for more pressing issues. So, although many of the <u>new</u> Rights of Way in the 1930s arrangement started to be used, the old ones that were to be closed up as part of the deal were forgotten about... until, in 2000, the Government offered a grant to find them. Now, in the month this book goes to print, the Government has even scrapped its 25 year deadline for finding them. 21 years in.

Ultimately, this footpath battle has been one of the left-field time-&-money-eaters that Martha and I have managed to see through and conclude in our generation. Depressingly it is a rare example amongst many. It was important because it threatened our business. We had to fight it. But it took hundreds of hours of our working lives, fistfuls of funds that could've been spent on more positive things, lots of lining up with paid advisors at stressful and distressing Inquiries opposite hostile neighbours, even hostile tenants... However in the end we were able to negotiate for this ancient path not to be re-opened, in return for creating a brand new path that actually went somewhere useful... for the genuine Ramblers. Hooray, you say. It was all worthwhile. But in a better world, that rationalisation of lines on a map should have been possible with a handshake and back in time for Tea.

Then there are the knock on effects. For not everyone is a genuine Rambler. Not everyone is on their way to church - the original reason most Rights of Way were created. Footpaths are used not only to enjoy Knebworth Park free of contributing to its upkeep, they are also used as a primrose path of dalliance, to forage, poach, and cause mischief. Extra security. Extra fencing. Livestock issues. These collateral scars are not in the Government's sightline. Don't get me wrong. As I say, our public footpaths are the golden yellow brick roads of our countryside, the airways of our freedom, a pride of Britain. But credit the landowner for them. Don't cripple him/her with one-sided legislation, and ever-changing initiatives.

2001 - vandals break in and smash up Cupid & Psyche

That's rant number one. Here's rant number two. Then that's it. I promise. Well done for still reading this chapter. I'm impressed.

Nothing takes more time - and has filled more of my unforgiving minutes - than Planning & Development. Here, Government is less chasing new initiatives, more kicking of the can of decision-making down the decades. For planners and politicians, if there is no decision, it can't be the wrong decision. When the media talks of 'windfall profits' for landowners from development zoning and planning decisions, it should stop a moment and examine its prejudices. Generations of work can go into Planning & Development, and in my experience, for the landowner, usually does. Whole lifetimes of snakes and ladders, except with no ladders.

These protracted proceedings have been particularly problematic for the preservation of Knebworth House. For when the Quantity Surveyor's quotes came in at the end of the century for the remaining urgent structural repairs, they were eye-wateringly eight figures. Nothing - no concerts, no filming, no grants, no old master or furniture sales - is going to raise those sorts of numbers. So it is a blessing, long-earned, that Knebworth House still has (for so many historic houses do not) one or two parcels of land that are suitably well-serviced and sustainable to be appropriate for some generational re-zoning for residential development. Development income is the only realistic chance Knebworth House has to raise those sorts of numbers. But those big re-zoning planning decisions are only made every 20 years, as part of a Local Plan. Local Plans are so contentious and hard-fought that 20 years easily slips to 30 years (our current one is 30 years and counting). and as every year passes, the house continues to decay, and the quotes continue to runaway.

As mentioned, Knebworth House and its surrounding land sits deep within a no-development zone called Greenbelt. Knebworth Park hosted a Christian festival once called Greenbelt. As a planning zone, Greenbelt is even more dogmatic. It's lovely, and has done all sorts of good, just like Christianity. But as it gets older it has started to undermine itself, just like Christianity, with its own dogma. For whilst generational reassessments are fought over across the decades, day-to-day Greenbelt continues rigidly to preserve open spaces around towns and villages and, in doing so, starts instead to destroy open spaces within towns and villages. Councils are given annual residential building quotas by central Government to house a growing population, but if towns and villages are surrounded by immutable Greenbelt then the only way to fulfil these quotas is to clog up the towns and villages themselves. Residential targets are lobbed at, by splitting urban houses into flats, urban gardens into divided plots, etc.

This is particularly ironic in our country of Hertfordshire, which is the birthplace of the 'Garden City' movement - a much heralded philosophy of bringing the country into one's towns to make them more pleasant places to live. Letchworth Garden City, Welwyn Garden City... Knebworth itself, was designed in 1909 by my family to evolve into a 'Garden Village' (right). Stevenage New Town (paean on p.34) is a version of this vision,

The village of Knebworth is surrounded by beautiful fields, but they are not public open space. Because of the way the village has evolved, tightly bound in Greenbelt, its internal public open spaces (plentiful in its original 'Garden Village' design) have gradually been infilled and now the village has significantly less public open space than Stevenage - about 1 hectare for 5,000 residents

with its 8.5 hectares of open space designed in for every 1,000 residents. The good folk of Hertfordshire are rightly proud of this heritage, flocking to exhibitions and local history lectures, and applauding the legacy of Ebenezer Howard. But for some reason they then happily accept the dismantling of Howard's work when they get home to their own back yards. All in the name of protecting Greenbelt. Strange.

Nobody wants to build on open fields. Particularly not longterm residents of those fields. Especially not 500-year residents, who want to be residents of those fields for another 500 years, and beyond. But we need to examine the sort of selfishness that says that no one should come after us. The sort of selfishness that expects those that do come after us to be content squeezed into increasingly congested towns, either into divided houses or divided gardens, or onto so-called 'brownfield sites'. 'Brownfield sites' are otherwise failed or redundant sites, usually industrial. From our 'green sites' we want other people to live on 'brown sites'? The legacy of our beautifully designed 'Garden' communities is being eaten from the inside, by slavish intransigence over protecting their edges. The arrow of 'direction' has morphed into the boomerang of 'dogma'.

Precious Green Belt or Huge Secondary School
Your action will decide the fate of your village

A group called 'We need a school' (WNAS) are planning to build a huge 800 to 900 pupil secondary school on green belt farm land in our village. Please help to save and preserve our village for future generations.

...er, Secondary School, I'd say

But I would say that, wouldn't I? Development in Greenbelt is the only chance Knebworth House has of raising the funds to fix itself. "As always, we should not think that Henry Cobbold has the interest of Knebworth at heart." (Letter in *Knebworth Parish News,* July 2001). "The Lytton Cobbold family is only interested in money," snarls the convivial neighbour with whom I sing carols around the tree at Christmastime.

The argument goes on. It will forever. Each generation believing that it should be the last to have houses built for it. Thankfully somebody was prepared to become a pariah to fight for the houses these naysayers live in. Thankfully somebody will be prepared to become a pariah for the houses their children and grandchildren will live in.

STOCKENS GREEN.

The residential houses built on these precious green fields are now a precious village 'Conservation Area'

In my father's time, the big development that it was said our local Districts needed, and which might have come with the positive of halting the decline of Knebworth House, was a mythical Eldorado called 'West of Stevenage'. It was said that the town of Stevenage needed to break beyond its western border (the A1M motorway), and that when it did, it was likely that extension would include a slither of farmland at the northern edge of the Knebworth Estate.

Four decades later, they are still talking about 'West of Stevenage'.

Year after year after year has been spent arguing every blade of grass, every min-

CALL TO ACTION! Your submission of the enclosed North Herts Public Inquiry Form can help CASE fight Stevenage expansion!

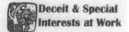**Deceit & Special Interests at Work**

The story of West of Stevenage is one of incompetence, political ambition and special pleading. Its origin lies in the insatiable ambition

etc...

"The expansion of Stevenage and loss of our Greenbelt will put an end to North Herts as we have known it."

ute mitigating minutia. Piles and piles and piles of paperwork have been generated. A mountain of paper that has already destroyed countless squirrel homes before a bulldozer's left the garage. They were arguing whether the increased population required a new lane on the existing community swimming pool. Each landowner - and there were many - spent long mornings signing and initialing every page of paper and every thrice-folded map. And then a change was made. So the entire mountain of paper had to be printed out and ribbon bound again, and another entire morning spent signing and initialing every page and map all over again.

The scheme sits dormant today because in the end only one clause in all this paperwork mattered. That there was a minimum price for the land. By the time all the lawyers, planners and politicians had spent decades arguing over it all - and the developers decades paying for the required consultants to make the required studies and surveys that every delay made out-of-date, and have to be done again - there was no longer any money left in the scheme. There was not enough money to pay the minimum price for the land. So the whole deal fell apart.

This is how planning works in England. And it seems to suit the English. No

existing resident wants anything built in their own back yard. And Planning Officers cannot conscience money being made out of their decisions. So this all goes on until there is no money left and the development is no longer affordable. Doesn't happen. Perfect. Everybody wins. Except, that is, the hard-working young family trying to afford a home, and - infinitely less important - the hard-working old family trying save a 500-year-old one.

A Great Crested Newt run - required in a new development because a single newt egg was found. The ecological surveys are the most useful paperwork for going out-of-date, because they can only be done when a particular amphibian or marsupial is not roosting or hibernating or laying its egg in a folded leaf - which is where, marvellously, Great Crested Newts like to lay them.

After West of Stevenage my father - in his quest for the holy grail of matching required local development with endowing the Knebworth House charity - turned his lance and its favours towards other Government dragons of acronym. The R.S.S. (Regional Spacial Strategy), the E.E.P. (East of England Plan) and, closest to home, the S.N.A.P. dragon. Or was it S.N.A.A.P.? Or S.N.H.A.A.P? I don't remember. All these legendary monsters are now long deceased. But they were all related, and the last of them, the magical, mythical, 'Stevenage and North Herts Area Action Plan', then chose our fields around Junction 7 of the A1M motorway as my father's field of combat, his field of the cloth of gold.

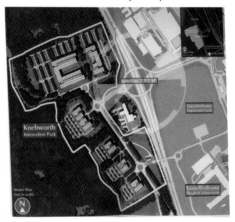

In order to build new residential homes, Councils have to create local employment areas to pretend that new residents won't simply commute to London. So S.N.A.A.P. determined that it would roll back Greenbelt to turn our woodland-bordered fields (that straddle both the Stevenage and North Herts districts) around Junction 7 of the A1(M) into a 'Science Park'. A 'Science Park' is a 'Business Park' that sounds better than a 'Business Park'. This Park's 'Science' credentials were certainly improved by being catty-corner to Stevenage Industrial Area's Glaxo Wellcome (now Smith Kline) Research Centre. Indeed at one point Glaxo also had an Option with my father to re-route its entrance off our Knebworth Park entrance, by building a bridge over the motorway. But Glaxo's entrance in the early 1990s was a Pollock canvas of militant animal rights protestors, so it became a relief when this option was let lapse. (Although Knebworth Park would still like a bridge to the Stevenage cycleway please.)

So it was a 'Science Park' that would save Knebworth House. Lots more signing and initialing to do on another Option Agreement. Again, this one took five long years for the lawyers to draw up. By which time it was 2002 and Martha and I had taken over. We saw the scheme as a disaster for Knebworth Park. The Robbie Williams concert was on the horizon, and it was very clear that if Knebworth Park lost these fields at its entrance it would lose its ability to host large events like these. This land is crucial access, crucial car parking space (right), and crucially free of third party interest to object. Lose these fields, Knebworth Park would lose its rock concerts. It would lose its U.S.P.

There were those who said, well, with the Science Park cash you wouldn't need rock concerts. The gold would be gained, the house would be saved. We knew they were wrong. Knebworth House and Park needs a sustainable business. 'A finite sum, out will run'. It may turn the hourglass over, but it doesn't stop the sand falling. Not only that, but a sustainable business is what gives purpose to, and the means for, the Lytton family to live and work in Knebworth House and Park, and, Gary - yes Alan - at the end of the day, no one is going to love it and look after it better than its own blood and bones and breath. So do not strangle it with a gooseneck of neighbours who only need to say "no" to cut its throat, and close it down.

Martha and I held that breath for ten, tortured, years, worried that the economy might pick up and the planners might actually want something built. Mercifully, neither of these, admittedly unlikely, things happened.

On the March night in 2012 when the Science Park Option Agreement expired, we stayed up to watch the hands of the wall clock pass midnight, and toasted the future of Knebworth Park.

But Knebworth House still needed £10 million.

And by now, it was accepted that it wouldn't make a great deal of sense only to restore Knebworth House to its exact Edwardian configuration. If one day we are to spend £10 million on it, wouldn't it be better also to put in some toilets, make it more accessible to the public, maybe add some facilities for school groups, some teaching space, put in a larger kitchen, a proper staff room, a proper archive, create some space to protect its collections...etc.

At this point, Knebworth House still needed £12 million.

15ᵗʰ November 2006

KNEBWORTH HOUSE

FEASIBILITY STUDY FOR FUTURE ALTERATIONS AND EXTENSIONS TO THE HOUSE TO SOLVE OPERATIONAL PROBLEMS AND TO ENHANCE THE VISITOR EXPERIENCE, TO BE EXECUTED AS PART OF THE RESTORATION OF THE SOUTHERN PART OF THE HOUSE.

for

The Trustees of the Knebworth House Education and Preservation Trust Ltd

2006 report by architect Matthew Seaborn (now Ed Sheeran's father-in-law).

Then, to protect the House's longterm future, for it to be sustainable, shouldn't the charity also have an endowment fund to invest, so that the House can feed itself in both good times and lean. An investment fund secures an annual budget, with contingency, to tackle the ongoing maintenance problems.

At this point Knebworth House still needed £15 million.

So Martha and I continued the previous generation's quest, and armoured ourselves to trail the grail. One acronym dragon still roamed after the demise of the R.S.S., E.E.P. & the S.N.A.A.P. The L.D.F. (Local Development Framework). A new Local Plan was due in North Herts in 2011, and the village of Knebworth - with its railway station, doctors' surgery, High Street, etc. - was thought to be an appropriate location for evolutionary expansion. The Estate owns land to the west of Knebworth village, between the new 20th Century settlement and the A1(M), a good defensible boundary that planners favour. So early in the L.D.F. process, at the beginning of the century, these fields became a possibility for Greenbelt rollback. And therefore development. And therefore a possible endowment for Knebworth House.

So, as Martha and I were taking over, the process began of village consultations to 'inform' the Local Plan. The first one was in the late 1990s, the 'Knebworth Village Appraisal'. I volunteered to be on the team of villagers working on the surveys, information gathering & report writing. So began 20 years of Wednesday evenings.

My father's community volunteer work had always focused more on our local town of Stevenage rather than our local village of Knebworth. He'd been involved in Stevenage's Bowes Lyon House youth centre (which in the 1960s hosted The Who and featured in the previously mentioned Stevenage sex comedy, *Here We Go Round The Mulberry Bush*, p.109) and, in 1990, he was one of the founders of the Stevenage Community Trust with Stevenage's first female mayor Hilda Lawrence, a much valued charity whose President, as I write, is Ken Follett. Speaking good French and staunchly pro-European, my father did also become President of the Knebworth Village Twinning Association, but there I feel his long presidency did also have a trace of the aforementioned 'Lord of the Manor' syndrome, illustrated by the Cobbold coat-of-arms that now greets you on the town sign as you enter the seaside community of Châtelaillon-Plage, Knebworth's twin community in France.

My Knebworth Wednesday evening volunteering was specifically a chance to get to know the village's inner workings. I'd been to school at Knebworth Primary for a year as a six year old, but since then I'd been off around the world. Although I'd put my signature on land conveyances and covenant releases from my condominium in West Hollywood, I had little idea of the daily life of Knebworth village.

I became a Governor of Knebworth Primary School for four years, I was on the Knebworth Village Fete committee for, I think, ten years (longer even than its knight in shining armour, Brian Worthington MBE). But the most useful string of Wednesday evenings - five years of them - were spent volunteering on the Knebworth Parish Plan team.

The Knebworth Parish Plan was the 2000s' village appraisal. The Local Plan commencement date - of 2011 - was approaching. The Knebworth Parish Plan's aim was *"to improve the social, economic and environmental wellbeing of the parish of Knebworth in line with the wishes of the community"* and to *"help guide its future development"*. As well as working on the surveys and the reports, I designed the finished booklet, created the artwork for it, including the cover image which I was quite proud of. This was an image of the façade of Knebworth Village Hall coloured and augmented in Photoshop.

I'd had to stand on the backseat of Martha's RAV4 to take the photo, and I like the way the car is reflected in the glass of the doors, whilst the tree behind me is reflected in the window above. Thus transport and the environment - two key considerations of the Plan - are reflected back by the village hall. This is the sort of completely inconsequential detail that gives me pleasure.

The Knebworth Parish Plan was a fine document. Well researched. Well reasoned. A

Your chance to help shape the future of our community...

Knebworth Parish Plan

Communication
Schools
Sport & Leisure
Heritage & History
Commerce
Health & Social Services
Crime & Policing
Housing
Countryside & Environment
Transport
Traffic & Parking
Planning & Development
Local Government

Local Business Forum
July 7th 6.30pm at the Lytton Arms.
Open to all Knebworth-based businesses.

Residents Survey
Arriving on your doorstep this September.
Open to all Knebworth residents.

Knebworth Parish Plan
The Knebworth Parish Plan Team
in association with the Parish Council
www.knebworthparishplan.org

pretty perfect snapshot of the feelings of the community of Knebworth at that time. After three and a half years work, in May 2007, I happened to be in the District Council Chamber (on another agenda item) when Knebworth Parish Chairman John Bantick formally presented the Plan. The District said thank you very much, put it in a drawer, and it has never been seen since.

And of course the District's Local Plan did not appear in 2011. It still hasn't appeared in 2022. Over the last five years the village has had to do yet another self-appraisal, a 2010s version, again "*to inform the Local Plan*". The Knebworth Neighbourhood Plan. Another three years of Wednesday evenings for a group of gallant volunteers. I was not on the team this third time. Now that Knebworth Estates fields were established in the Plan draft, perhaps it would not have been appropriate. Seeing myself as, first and foremost, a villager, I don't see that. But I do confess to a Sisyphean weariness. All that work we put in 15 years ago. And 25 years ago. Checked the box. Got forgot. I wonder if there'll have to be a fourth appraisal, in the 2020s, as we still today wait for the 2011 Local Plan?

Some good did come out of the 2007 Knebworth Parish Plan. The Knebworth Village Fete was reborn for a time. Knebworth House started an annual Parish Open Day, when all residents are invited to join us to celebrate the first Sunday of our Summer Season. I began a regular monthly column in the Knebworth Parish News. I have written over 17 years of this column now, never missing a month. I imagine it will be an interesting timepiece one day. All of it sits online on the Knebworth House website for the ponderings of posterity.

But most important, I got to know the inner workings of Knebworth village. My home. So, if those western fields do stay in the draft Local Plan, and if the draft Local Plan does ever become an actual Local Plan, I am much better informed on how their development could mitigate for their loss. How, with a bit of imagination and local support, the developments could not only satisfy a local need for housing, but also lead to some associated positives for the village and for all of our lives.

Since I've been writing this book, I've spent five more years of waiting for the Local Plan working on ideas for how best those western fields could be developed. How we could make something positive out of a perceived negative. I could fill another whole chapter - book even - with the absurdities and frustrations of the Planning System that I have encountered. But another time. Let's move on to other stories. Suffice to say, I have a lot of ideas, and still some energy.

Will I be listened to? Will I ever not be viewed with suspicion by my neighbours? I doubt it. But I imagine a few will turn up at my funeral. And I expect one day my son will hear the same, "His father was all right. But he's only interested in money."

And so the world goes round.

CHAPTER THIRTY-FIVE

Studio 39

*Genius does what it must
And talent does what it can*

(Robert Lytton)

Robert Lytton, my great-great-grandfather's definition of genius makes sense

to me. Although as a definition of genius, I want to run the two lines the other way around:

Talent does what is can.
Genius does what it <u>must</u>.

The lines make me think of the musician Prince. He had to create. Even if his record company wanted him to pace his output, give his current album time to make money before he put out another one.

But some people have to do what they have to do. They can't just plug it up. That, I think, is a good definition of 'genius'.

I keep Robert's quote on my writing desk - it is printed on the cover of my commonplace book - to remind myself daily that I am not a genius.

I can create. I love to create. I am good as creating. But do I <u>have</u> <u>to</u> create? I'm always pleased to take a break from it, and fill up the tank.

But as I get older, I do feel the unforgiving minute more acutely. I get antsy if I'm not doing something creative. If I'm spending my time doing stuff that any old fool could do just as well as me - or worse, better - steam starts to come out of my ears. I want to be doing what I know I do better than others.

So I do have restless 'talent'. I want 60 seconds of distance run in every minute. I keep a second quote in front of me on my writing desk. Charlotte Brontë's similar "I'm just going to write because I cannot help it." I do aspire to <u>having</u> <u>to</u> write *Jane Eyre*.

In those early days of living in, and getting to grips with, Knebworth

House, I could see that my writing was suffering. If I'm being paid to write, I can, with no problem, get up at 4 o'clock in the morning and do a good four or five hours before the Post Office opens. It's not that I need to go to the Post Office. It's just that when the Post Office is open, my brain fills with all the other things I could or should be doing. At 4am, there is nothing I need to do, or think about, other than writing. My brain can stay on track. I get a lot done.

If I am not being paid to write, I'd rather not get up at 4 in the morning. But writing for short bursts, in between dealing with general Knebworth House work - the 'day job' - I find particularly difficult on my creative brain. For instance, whilst writing this paragraph I've been interrupted to sign off on a new five year phone contract for Knebworth House's office & house phones. The beginning of this chapter will, I suspect, not be as splendidly written as the rest of the book because my mind has been wrestling with how many ported DDIs we need and how many PSDN lines we need to migrate. Returning to this paragraph now I have completely lost my train of thought. It takes me a good fifteen minutes to re-read what I have been writing, and regain my flow - just in time for a new telephone quotation to be sent, that seems to have gone up in price when it should have gone down...

I am very fortunate to have my 'day job', but it doesn't blend easily with my writing 'career'. Interruption is not good for creative writing. Soon after taking on Knebworth House - after writing *Strawberries and Cream* - I gave in to this reality. Knebworth House is constant interruption. At that time I had no writing commissions. I was not finding the will to get up at 4 in the morning to write spec scripts. So I chose to give up creative writing for a spell. But the creative brain does not stop.

The spell became audio work. Creative audio work, I discovered, not only weathers interruption, it thrives on it. Return to writing work after a short break, and you have lost your flow. Return to audio work after a short break, and you have fresh ears.

I turned to the Digital Audio Workstation that I'd bought back in 1995 to do the audio mix for *St Tropez Suntrap*. My 'Soundscape' P.C. I'd kept all the kit. Indeed I'd added to it over the years. A nice AKG Solitube large-diaphragm microphone. Some software 'plug in's to make whatever I recorded sound like it'd been crafted by a professional with years of experience. I'd even taken the plunge and ungraded to the new generation 'Soundscape', which in those days of primitive processing meant

also upgrading all the metal boxes that came with it. At some considerable expense. Soundscape was a sophisticated software programme and hardware rig that I knew how to use. It seemed a shame not to continue to use it. I'd even built a voice box for recording vocals in my study (right), lined with rubber carpet underlay for soundproofing. The only time in my entire life I remember being cross with my son was when, as a child, he started picking off the rubber bubbles of this green underlay on this inside of my makeshift sound booth. Aaaaaaagh!

I have already mentioned that during the video years, I composed and recorded the audio for animated video idents for Contender and Mollin Video. This work evolved into recording inspirational life coaching CDs, firstly for the Mollin publication Men's Fitness (see cover CD, p.365), and then, for some reason, for local hypnotherapists. I did a number for Life Practice UK in Hitchin (e.g. left). The challenge when recording hypnotherapists is to still be awake when they've finished. Twenty minutes of soothing vocal massage, telling me that I am feeling soooooo relaxed... "How was that take?... Henry?... Henry?!..."

Sometimes I was being asked to create actual soundscapes on my Soundscape. Sony came up with a software program called Acid, based on pre-cleared loops of sounds and beats, which made this a doddle. I could turn out endless background music for going to sleep to. It is so much easier to put people to sleep than to entertain them.

The service included creating the CDs. That's a Knebworth House floodlight in the upper image & the sea at Agde below

How am I doing with this book?

Commissions came in from Stevenage Museum to record audio for its exhibitions, and then a big one, to digitise and edit Stevenage's complete Oral Histories. This was a box of audio cassettes of recordings of local people recalling the history of the town, in particular the early days of Stevenage New Town. This was a gift commission for me, as I cannot think of anyone in the world who could have done this job and found it more fascinating than me. I was the perfect Venn diagram of audio producer and Hertfordshire local history professional. Listening, for instance, to every word of the motivations and intent of the original urban planners of Stevenage New Town gave me an in depth knowledge that has been invaluable in local planning meetings. I also found many of the more personal recordings - often of people long dead - very moving. I am someone you will often find weeping at work. Particularly affecting, for instance, were the recollections of original New Town residents who'd been displaced from London's Blitzed East End and how they adapted to early life in their newfound Hertfordshire utopia.

This drove home to me the importance of Oral Histories. I immediately enlisted my father to walk around Knebworth House with me and a microphone, to commit his memories and knowledge of the house and its contents to posterity. I am so pleased I did. My father now has dementia and that opportunity is no more. That recording evolved into an official Audio Tour of Knebworth House that we still use today. I particularly enjoyed researching and recording music associated with the

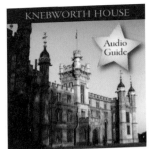

family and the house to score the tour. Placing my voice over Liszt's *Fantasy on Themes from Rienzi* makes me sound like Joan Fontaine in *Letter From An Unknown Woman*. I wish, when giving actual tours of Knebworth House, my two ears were two stereo speakers underscoring my spiel.

A particularly touching memory of my grandmother Hermione, is when we took her to the British Film Institute to see for the very first time a reel of silver nitrate

film that we'd discovered in the Knebworth House attic from the early 1930s. The film reel was unusual because it had sound on it. The early 1930s was the very beginnings of sound on film. It was a recording of her brother Antony (right) encouraging the viewer to attend a charity boxing match at the Royal Albert Hall. He died soon afterward, at the age of 29. I'd not seen my grandmother in tears before. It was not the <u>image</u> of her brother. She'd had that always, ever since his death. It was the sound of his voice. A treasured sound from her childhood that she had not heard in over half a century. There, at its rawest, was the emotional impact of sound.

My grandmother died in 2004, and the 'granny flat' she had been using in our old All Digital offices across the courtyard at Knebworth House was no longer needed. So I took the opportunity to build myself a dedicated recording studio. Some of the space I let to a local travel agency, Off Broadway Travel, to help pay the bills. Strike that. To help pay for more audio kit.

I bought a very fine Neumann U87, the gold standard of studio microphones, and four Genelec 2029 speakers, and built myself a better sound booth, this time with actual carpet on the walls instead of just underlay. In fact the whole studio I covered in thick green carpet, including the ceiling, which provided an appropriate challenge for Roy, the Knebworth carpet man. The concern was that the carpet

glue would not hold the weight of the carpet on the ceiling. So the night before the installation I was hurriedly painting wooden slats a matching forest green. To this day, I do not know if these slats made any difference, but they gave comfort (to Roy - I had faith), and nothing about that ceiling has shifted in over 15

Would've looked better if I'd taken the wind shield off the mic!

(Winter has come - the studio has turned blue - the actual green of the studio is as in the middle photo)

With Miles Winter Roberts in my all green studio

complete with cow bell, for when more is needed

and Crunchy Nut Cornflakes courtesy of Miles

years. It still looks as impressive as it did the day the carpet was installed on the ceiling, with Roy up a ladder muttering something that I'm sure was "What a brilliant idea this is!"

An early test recording was my friend Miles Winter Roberts' beautiful ballad *Head In My Cloud*. Miles, I had met in unusual circumstances. In 2004, the *Erotica* Expo team were hosting a post-show party in central Manchester. At the crush at the nightclub door, I was being persistently pestered by a bloke trying to get in, "I am friend of Howey's!" I was having none of it. A 'Howey' worked with us, but wasn't in Manchester. If the guy'd said he was a friend of Nick Valentine or of Emma Sayle - which he was, and both of whom were inside - of course I'd have let him in. It was much later when Nick came out and recognised Miles - and told me that he'd probably become my favourite musician ever - that we went on to spend the rest of the night, all together, partying in the hotel bar. It turns out, penniless troubadour Miles had won a competition for a supermarket sweep (where you can keep as much as you can put in your trolly in a set time) and a year's supply of Kellogg's Crunchy Nut Cornflakes. He'd had to borrow the money to get the train to Manchester for the supermarket sweep. Then, because of his night out, he overslept and missed it! He did however get a lorry-load delivery of Crunchy Nut Cornflakes - one box of which he bought to my studio and has been sitting prominently on top of my studio voice booth ever since. That's now about 15 years, so for health reasons I should probably bury it.

Now I had a formal recording studio, with a sweet jar for Glacier Mints and its own entrance, it was able to welcome a much wider client base. I started accepting bookings from local bands and singers. Singers mainly. The studio was not large, and more of a vocal studio than a band space. This was a time when advances in computers and software were making it possible for would-be musicians in their bedrooms to put together tracks that sounded like they'd been recorded in Abbey Road with top session musicians - indeed there were even 'Abbey Road plug-ins' that, literally, made your music sound like it had been put through the same studio desk as *Dark Side of the Moon*. But home recordings were still held back by the

quality of affordable microphones. My
Neumann U87 was worth booking my
studio for. And of course my superior
talent as a hip hop producer.

A regular client was a young Stevenage lad called Wayne (right), who already had a kid of his own but was still
living with his mum and making do
on warehouse jobs. He would turn up
regularly with a fist of crumpled sweaty
£5 notes and ask if I had any beats he
could set his hip hop lyrics to. His enthusiasm was infectious, and his lyrics
about love and ambition, rather than

I was pleased with this album cover for Wayne

gangstas and ganja. Most of his lyrics
were written for his baby daughter. I set him up with a computer to start writing his
own backing tracks. I spent time designing covers for his albums, and printing CDs
for him. I'd done this for other clients, but found myself subsidising Wayne with
more time than I gave to others. His self-belief was refreshing for someone with a
pretty basic start in life. Visits to his house to help him plug in a microphone, or set
up software, were revealing. The fence around his yard was smashed up with rotting
sofas and other broken furniture piled up around it. Credit to his mum for bringing
up a kid with a sweet heart in clearly difficult circumstances.

Audio production became a creative outlet for me that suited interruption and
worked well alongside the day job of Knebworth House projects. My studio I hoped

would also encourage my own kids' path to musical
eminence. We'd paid for early guitar lessons for our
daughter and early piano lessons for our son... for
what are children for if not for living out one's unfulfilled dreams vicariously? More importantly, we'd
placed a guitar by every chair in the house throughout their childhood, so there was no excuse for them
to sit down without picking one up.

My daughter now brings tears to my eyes (in a
good way) playing *Greensleeves*, but the real success
with this ruse was my son. As he grew up, Edward
went from wanting to be a policeman, like his American uncle, to wanting to be a musician, like... like
his father wanted to be. This led to him having to
become note perfect on Jimi Hendrix's *Little Wing*
in order to get into music college. I was delighted by
this choice of further education. Talk about living
vicariously. The college in question, BIMM (British
Institute of Modern Music) in Brighton was the sort
of place I'd absolutely loved to have gone to if it had
existed when I was 18. If I could have done film as

well. And that would have been the rub, because the ethos at BIMM - as they sold it to us at the time - was that you were not allowed to mix courses. You had to concentrate on a single discipline - guitar, keyboards, bass, drum or vocals - so that you were session standard when you left after three years. There was the option to do the wishywashy 'songwriting' - which is what I would have done - but we were

happy, as very sensible parents, to encourage the more job-oriented path of 'guitar'.

Within moments of arriving in Brighton, Ed found himself standing at the urinal with future life-friends and bandmates Josh Oliver and Lawrie Miller (with Ed above). Bands formed pretty instantly 'like bees in a clustre', based on haircut. Glass City Vice was an indie rock band, and over its five years of producing EPs and touring - including promoting its alma mater across Europe - hit a zenith support-

ing Metallica at the 2014 Knebworth Park Sonisphere (left). Glass City Vice were at the very bottom of the bill, and Metallica at the very top, but you only have to turn the poster upside down to reverse this.

GCV turned out some great music, and its members continue to do so in other incarnations. But Edward shows signs of having inherited his father's - and indeed his great-great-great-great-grandfather's - desire to do absolutely everything possible at the expense of anything single thing in particular. It was said of Edward Bulwer Lytton that had he concentrated on any one of his creative outlets, he would have been its greatest master of his day. But because he split himself across so many, he was overtaken... as a

novelist by Dickens, as a poet by Tennyson, as a politician by Disraeli, etc... It is said of Henry Lytton Cobbold that if he'd concentrated on screenwriting, he'd now be seven movies into a franchise like his peers Rob Wade and Neal Purvis... Where am I going with this? Oh yes... Edward has struggled with the BIMM ethos of sticking to one instrument, and now plays a myriad of instruments. He plays them all beautifully. But to date, like his forebears, remains an all-rounder, rather than a virtuoso.

I am envious of my son's musical talent and training. But through his youth I've managed to stay better than him at one thing. 'Beginnings, middles and ends'. Ed writes great music, but not very much of it, to date, has all three of the above. This is a screenwriting discipline. Three Acts. Beginning. Middle. End. What I write may not be 'great', it may not be 'genius', I may struggle with acts, but - until the day I keel over midflow - my creative work will always have a beginning, a middle, and an end.

Consequently, I have a clip file of songs with beginnings, middles and ends that I wrote as a teenager that it became my intention, on building a recording studio, to record... properly, as though through the Abbey Road desk. Of course, I am yet to get round to this. Because there are simply too many other interesting things to do.

The urge to write *Jane Eyre*, of course, did return before too long. The need to be doing what I know I do better than others. So I did, after a few years, leave behind the software plug ins that allowed me to pretend I was Alan Parsons, and went back to my study on the top floor of Knebworth House, and back to writing. I sublet my recording studio to Bill the saxophonist from Bennington. He uses it to do kids' 're-cording parties' and gives me a few hundred quid a month. But I will return to it one day. And I will record the soppy songs I wrote at seventeen with chords purloined from David Gates (who randomly, as I write this page, celebrates his 80 birthday.)

The other thing I'll do, is score my musical. I've only written one play. But I didn't hold back. I wrote a massive knobs & whistles production. A huge musical. That is, I wrote the 'book', and the 'lyrics', but left the music for Andrew Lloyd Webber. He hasn't had time yet. So I guess I'll have to do that myself when I get my studio back.

It wasn't out-of-the-question that Andrew Lloyd Webber would be interested in my play. Because I chose as my subject, his pet subject - apart from his actual pet subject, cats. The Lord has the largest collection of Pre-Raphaelite paintings outside of the Tate. He may also own most of the ones in the Tate. I do know that he, personally, has a penchant for the Pre-Raphaelites' religious subjects, as I've had the privilege of seeing the paintings he chooses to live with. My adored California mentor Pat King (Patricia Louisianna Knop) co-wrote the 'book' for the musical Andrew composed with Jim Steinman, *Whistle Down The Wind* (1996), and at that

Think what it is...
to see a poem lived!

PRE-RAPHAELITE
- The Musical -

time I had the treat of picking Pat up from his house in Eaton Square. I pointed out to the Lord that the paintings he had chosen to hang in his own house were all the religious ones. He asked me what Pre-Raphaelite paintings I liked, and without coming out directly with "I like the sexy ones", I did confess that my favourite is Sir Edward Poynter's - not Pre-Raphaelite at all - *The Cave of The Storm Nymphs*. "Ah yes," he replied, "I own that one. Never really liked it. I keep it in my 'record room'. I was thinking of giving it to Tim Rice."

"Did you know that Sir Edward Poynter was Sir Edward Burne-Jones's brother-in-law?" That was me. Not him. Because he did not know this. I'd struck a rich vein. "Yes," I continued, most sagely, "as well as being uncle to both Rudyard Kipling and Stanley Baldwin." Andrew was delighted by this trivia. He jumped up and immediately telephoned his Victorian Art dealer. He threw the question at him, "You know that painting in my 'record room', *The Cave of the Storm Nymphs*? Do you know who Edward Poynter's brother-in-law was?" The dealer did not. Andrew was even more delighted.

The following week I sent him a photocopy of the then out-of-print book *Victorian Sisters: The Remarkable Macdonald Women and the Great Men They Inspired*, and received a very nice thank you note in return. And so, many years later, when I determined to write a musical, I thought, why not write a Pre-Raphaelite musical? At least I know he'll read it.

I knew a lot about the Pre-Raphaelite Brotherhood - and had an extensive collection of books about the Pre-Raphaelites (above) - because, if truth be told, I'd always liked more than just the sexy ones. I had written many contrary essays about the PRB in all its guises both for A-Level and at University for tutors who believed all English Art stopped at Turner and didn't re-appear again until Hockney.

So I knew that the story of the doomed love affair between the Pre-Raphaelite Dante Gabriel Rossetti and his consumptive wife Lizzie Siddall was an opera-in-waiting. I'd always felt an affinity with Rossetti because we share a birthday. No logic to that, as I also share a birthday with Tony Blackburn, and I don't feel a special affinity to him. But Rossetti has always been my favourite Pre-Raphaelite Brother - no doubt because his pictures are the sexiest. The others are all a bit religious.

PRE-RAPHAELITE THE MUSICAL

"Think what it is... to see a poem lived!"
(Georgiana Burne-Jones)

The love story that gave birth to the cult of beauty amidst the grime and tragedy of industrialised London is told as a powerful new theatrical musical. "Pre-Raphaelite The Musical" brings to life the the story of the iconic model, artist and poet, Lizzie Siddal, and her tragic love affair with the Pre-Raphaelite artist and poet, Dante Gabriel Rossetti, the founding father of the aesthetic movement.

Blackfriars Bridge, the stone archway spanning the lifeblood of London - the River Thames - is the setting for one of London's greatest love stories, an epoch-defining tale of sex, drugs and poetry.

* * * * *

Dante Gabriel Rossetti is the most high-profile British artist of the Victorian age – he is the seam that runs from the revolutionary birth of the Pre-Raphaelite school to its commercial zenith in the Arts and Crafts movement of William Morris.

Elizabeth Eleanor Siddal is the original iconic model and red-headed beauty of the Pre-Raphaelite school – she is unique amongst the original school's models in also achieving her own success as a painter, and the admiration of the Victorian era's most influential critic, John Ruskin.

In an age when life-choices for woman are limited to marriage, service, or prostitution, ungovernable Lizzie breaks free of an impoverished childhood as one of seven children of a luckless ironmonger in industrial Southwark, south of the river, to become an accomplished artist and poet feted by the intelligentsia of the glittering City of London, north of the river.

Lizzie's childhood dreams are born on Blackfriars Bridge, spanning these two worlds. She crosses the bridge to inspire a generation of poets and painters, but in reality, only gets as far as the other side... Her love affair with Rossetti is played out overlooking Blackfriars Bridge from the northern bank, and – like the subject of the most famous of all Pre-Raphaelite paintings, for which she is the model, John Millais's "Death of Ophelia" – the river plays a part in her tragic young death.

Tortured by the troubled genius of her lover, her health wrecked by sickness, miscarriage and opiates, Lizzie succumbs to the miasma of industrial London, and takes her own life overlooking Blackfriars Bridge in 1862 - the same year that the old stone structure is demolished to make way for a new iron bridge, and a transformational sewage system along London's Embankment.

Rossetti's art flourishes, but his life spirals into grief and guilt as a new muse takes Lizzie's place in his heart, and his art – the beloved wife of his trusted friend and colleague William Morris...

* * * * *

Using the beautiful images of the best Victorian art and the beautiful lyrics of the best Victorian poetry, "Pre-Raphaelite The Musical" sweeps its audience, as it were the River Thames, from the miasma to the marvels of mid-19th Century London... from the Dickensian world of mudlarks and crossing sweepers to the beautiful art and poetry of the foremost aesthetes of the Victorian age.

* * * * *

Prologue: 1869. London. Distressed, dishevelled, drugged, artist Gabriel Rossetti (41) returns one morning to his fashionable riverside studio and – watched over by eerie ethereal images of his deceased wife, Lizzie – passionately embraces his dark beautiful model, Mrs Morris, and thrusts a mouldy collection of papers into her hands declaring that he has retrieved them for her, before collapsing at her feet...

Act 1: 1842. The corpse of a "fallen woman" is pulled from the River Thames, as high above on Blackfriars Bridge rebellious, copper-haired, ironmongers-daughter Lizzie Siddal (12) dreams of crossing from her industrial Southwark home to the excitements and opportunities of the towered City opposite. She is cold to her elder sister Annie (16) who has chosen a safe marriage; and a worry to her anxious debt-ridden parents who are struggling with seven children.

1849. Byronic painter Walter Deverell (22), excitedly informs his artist friends – the Pre-Raphaelite Brotherhood (PRB) – that he has discovered a "stunner". Using his mother to talk Lizzie's parents into permitting her to model for him, he spars with his enraptured colleagues – in particular the brilliant, obsessive Rossetti (21) – to feature Lizzie (now 19) in his paintings. Deverell's sudden death – and that of Lizzie's elder brother, Charles (21) – send Lizzie into a tailspin, leading Rossetti to rescue her from near death in a frozen bathtub during the painting of his colleague Millais's "The Death of Ophelia", a breakthrough painting for the Pre-Raphaelites and for Lizzie's own celebrity.

Act 2: 1852. A joyful Lizzie (22) crosses Blackfriars Bridge to live with Rossetti (24) overlooking the bridge and the river on the City bank. Her anxious parents are concerned that she has become his mistress, but Rossetti and Lizzie have a pact that their relationship will be strictly tutor/pupil. Impressed by Lizzie's painting, the influential critic John Ruskin helps to legitimise the relationship by becoming her patron and agent, leading to her success at the Pre-Raphaelite Fitzroy Street exhibition in 1857. Rossetti and Lizzie's passion for each other grows, but Rossetti will not break their vow, so Lizzie leaves him to go north, to take further art lessons in Sheffield, her father's home town.

Act 3: 1857. Rossetti (29) and a second incarnation of the PRB are painting murals in Oxford when they meet another "stunner", stableman's daughter, Jane Burden (18). Lizzie, missing Rossetti and hearing of the death of her bankrupt father, goes into another tailspin which brings Rossetti to her sickbed. The vow is finally broken. Jane, hearing that Rossetti is to marry Lizzie, marries his brilliant but awkward colleague William Morris.

A third incarnation of the PRB thrives, the artists now all married with children – but Lizzie, sickened by laudanum addiction and living over the polluted river, loses her baby. Rossetti tries to raise her spirits, but her addiction - and his persistent eye for other women - lead to her tragic suicide in 1862, just as Blackfriars Bridge is dismantled for a new river-side sewer. Rossetti is distraught, and buries Lizzie with a precious manuscript of poems written for her.

Act 4: 1867. Rossetti has moved to a fashionable riverside studio in Chelsea, where he is rich and famous for painting lush beautiful images of female models. He is not content - still tortured by the memory of Lizzie - his health is fading and he is also now addicted to painkilling drugs. Desperate to be recognised as a poet, and increasingly in love with his partner Morris's wife, Jane, he seeks Lizzie's approval - first at a séance, and then whilst contemplating suicide on the scaffold of New Blackfriars Bridge. Finally emboldened, Rossetti exhumes Lizzie's coffin to retrieve his poems (a collection of papers, now mouldy and worm-eaten) - but is terrorised by her startling copper-haired corpse. Returning to his studio (as in the Prologue), he collapses, traumatised, at Jane's feet.

Epilogue: 1870. Rossetti awakes in the earthly paradise of Morris's home, Kelmscott, by the Thames in Oxfordshire. True to his friend, Morris has chivalrously left Rossetti to recuperate with his wife and children. Jane hands Rossetti the mouldy collection of papers and, with the children's help, Rossetti sends them off on a little raft downstream. The poems float unnoticed under New Blackfriars Bridge as it is opened with a royal procession by Queen Victoria.

Writing prospective lyrics for this musical was a joy. Firstly, all the characters in this truer-than-you'd-imagine story wrote poetry, so the first point of call for lyrics was the characters' original poems. I snipped and sewed these into lyrics, which of course are only a basis for what the music will eventually fashion. But I also had fun creating the basis of lots of my own recitativo (sung dialogue). Here's an example:

RED LION MARY
AND WHO ARE THESE MODELS
I SEE IN YOUR ART?
IF YOU'RE BRINGING UP GIRLS
I DON'T WANT NO TARTS!
NO MODELS ALLOWED, EXCEPT
LADIES OF FASHION
AND NO GETTING UNDRESSED
NO PICTURES OF PASSION!

ROSSETTI
DEAR MISTRESS MARY
WHAT CAN YOU MEAN?
COULD IT BE EMILY PATMORE
YOU'VE SEEN?
COVENTRY'S WIFE IS
AN ANGEL, A SAINT
AND LOOK WHAT JAMES COLLINSON'S
CHOSEN TO PAINT -

THE RENUNCIATION OF
ELIZABETH OF HUNGARY
THERE'S NO FEMALE HERE WOULDN'T
THRIVE IN A NUNNERY
MY MODEL TODAY, MAYBE
YOU MISSED HER
MY VIRGIN MARY, MY SISTER
CHRISTINA

RED LION MARY
ALL RIGHT, I BELIEVE YOU
THOUGH NOT MANY WOULD
THERE'S NOT MANY ARTISTS
NOT UP TO NO GOOD
AND IF YOU ASK ME
THESE SUBJECTS YOU PICK
COULD BE A LITTLE LESS ROMAN
..AND LESS CATHOLIC.

Photo by Casey Gutteridge

Discussing the Lord with Tim Rice, at Mandy & Ricky Wilde's Wilde Winter Ball at Knebworth

I don't know if Andrew Lloyd Webber ever did read it. My friend, theatrical agent Alex Armitage was going to send it to him. A friend in Barbados who knew his maid was going to have it left at his holiday bedside! What I do know, is that Pat King wrote to him enthusing about it, and he replied that the Pre-Raphaelites was a subject that had come up in the past, but that he had sworn off doing it. I don't think he gave a reason.

Possibly it was a little too close to his religion.

All of this music and playwriting was diverting my film career even further off track. BAFTA - the British Academy of Film & Television Arts - did a membership review around this time and determined to take voting rights away from those who didn't have film or television credits from the previous five years. It was touch and go whether my 'Special Thanks' at the end of the *Robbie Williams Live At Knebworth* DVD was going to cut it for my continued membership. Fortunately I got a reprieve for being the director of a company that provided significant services to the industry. Knebworth House was - as it still is - used consistently for film location work.

I wasn't yet missing screenwriting, but I was missing production. Off Broadway, the travel agents who were renting the other half of my offices, decided that they would do better with a High Street presence and moved to Welwyn. So the opportunity arose to turn the offices' other main room into a video studio. This was at a time when the film/video process 'green screen' was taking an evolutionary leap. In 2004, an entire live-action feature film *Sky Captain and the World of Tomorrow* had been made in a studio against a 'green screen'. Then in 2006, an entire live-action feature-

film that-was-successful had been made in a studio against a 'green screen', called *300*. I was old school enough to know the process as 'blue screen'. You'll recall All Digital had invested in large rolls of woollen 'blue screen' in the mid 1990s, which we used for the video *Shape Up And Rave* (p.284). Now a grey reflective material was being marketed, that supposedly made 'green screen' even easier and more effective. You simply had a circle of green (or blue) lights around your lens and with the click of a button

on the computer the reflective material vanished from your image. You could then replace it with any other film/video background. So, switch on a wind machine and flick water in your performer's face and they'd not only be against the wall in your office, but also on the bow of the Titanic. This sort of thing could put a travel agency out of business. Good thing Off Broadway were upping their game to Welwyn High Street.

Animating a local witch to fly around websites on 31st October

Always a sucker for new video technology, I purchased this system for my new video studio and lined a split-level stage, three walls, ceiling & floor with this new miracle material. In theory I could now make *Sky Captain and the World of Tomorrow*. Although I'd struggle squeezing 300 Spartan warriors into the office.

In fact, this technology never worked that well. It is hard enough to correctly light green screen, but putting a green circle of lights in front of a performer made it hard to keep the performer from looking like a frog (or a witch). More seriously, it made it hard for the frog to read Autocue - and the advertising work we immediately started to get, required a good deal of Autocue. So I sold the reflective cloths and

instead painted the end of the office bright green. Before long the whole end of the room was bright green. Even the floor, which I covered with matching bright green linoleum. "You do know green carpet is bad luck, don't you?" With help from my friend Ronan Willson, who owned Elstree Light & Power, I installed a permanent lighting rig optimised for green screen. Et voila. A 'switch-on-and-go' green screen studio.

So, let's make a feature film... A guy - Guy Daniels - in the neighbouring village of Woolmer Green was putting together a feature film out of nothing. His *Love/Loss* (2010) was shooting in and around the villages of Knebworth & Woolmer Green with Virginia McKenna, Keith Michell and Len Goodman. I had no excuse.

Except that I needed to make some money to pay for this kit. And once more - as if I'd not learn my lesson - I got myself into a situation where I was trading work

for kit. I found myself making video after video for a local accountancy software company, WinWeb, who were not only providing me with kit but also subsidising my cameraman and editor Tom Skelton (above right). On top of this, to save my patron's money - and I suspect also for his amusement (Stefan Töpfer, above centre) - I was fronting these marketing videos myself. I'd purchased a couple of black t-shirts, and there I was, in front of camera, all Steve Jobs, reading Autocue, selling software.

Let me rewind a moment. Digital marketing was the new undiscovered territory in business at the turn of the Millennium. As well as teaching myself HTML, I had poured over the tips and techniques of North American internet gurus like Corey Rudl and Ralph Wilson, even spending $200 on the former's double ringbinders, *The Insiders Secrets To Marketing Your Business On The Internet*. "Your decision to purchase this course may be one of the smartest moves you've ever made!" As mentioned, I was responsible for the websites of various palaces and erotica expos, and the digital marketing of Knebworth House. I trawled the web for eye-catching ideas.

An early one I explored was called Ipix. This software stitched two 180 degree fisheye photographs together to create an entire 360 degree digital space. I purchased the licence and tripod attachment and set to work trying to produce digital recreations of the Knebworth House rooms. As with green/blue screen, it wasn't as straightforward as the manual suggested. Most rooms have windows, which unless you block them out (as most movies do) completely change the light of images captured in different directions and at different times. Even the finest Director of Photography isn't usually asked to shoot the ceiling above and the floor below at the

An unstitched Ipix of the State Drawing Room at Knebworth House.
Animals were harmed in the making of this picture. A very long time ago. Retain + Explain.

same time. Roger Deakins' extraordinary lighting work in the 'single shot' movie *1917* covers 360 degrees horizontally. An Ipix picture covers 360 degrees vertically as well. So the two images rarely stitched together well. Also problematic was the size of the digital files required to get decent resolution. They became too large to load onto the Internet in those days of dial-up connections. Nice idea. No cigar.

I came across a better idea. The basis of this one was 'green screen'. I've got one of those. I don't remember the actor's name, but he was a jobbing actor somewhere in never-hide-your-light-under-a-bushel-land who immediately started pitching me, in person, when I landed on his website. Open his website, he appeared. A full body length shot of him standing there, in his page, telling you about himself, and pointing you to the menus on his site. He was his own website presenter. Unlike an Ipix, he was a small digital file, so he popped up instantly, catching your attention.

I looked around the web to see if anyone was offering these 'website presenters'. It looked as though there were a couple of U.S. companies starting to. The sex industry was already there, of course. There was a site called VirtuaGirl, on which you could subscribe to full-body strippers standing in the bottom corner of your computer screen, slowly taking off their clothes. The point seemed to be that you could do something else (on screen) while this stripping was going on. As though the stripper was a pot plant or a ficus tree in the corner of the office. It is an odd product that works only by being not interesting enough for your full attention. For if you are giving it your full attention, you might as well have it full screen. Although, as I say, the beauty of these files was that they were very small, and appeared instantly even if you had a poor internet connection. I felt there were others better placed than me to compete in the stripper market. Yes, filming strippers is more fun than filming software commercials. But I'd been there before. Got the t-shirt. (The one cut just below the boobs, white & tight. But I don't wear it often).

So - after this brief distraction - I continued trawling the internet. Was anyone offering web presenters like this in the U.K.? No one that I could find. This idea, I thought, had potential. And I already owned all the right kit, and the studio. So I bought up a number of appropriate web domains - presentyoursite.com, mobilepresenters.com, cellspokesperson.com, webpresenters.org, celebritywebpresenters.com, animatedwebpresenters.com, nakedwebpresenters.com, etc. etc. (seriously, we stuck our flag in dozens of them)... and we started making Video Online Presenters (we had that one too, .com & .co.uk).

I say 'we'. My brother Peter also saw the potential of this idea, and suggested that we expand it into a company of its own, for which he'd do all the business stuff and I'd do all the creative stuff. Suddenly 'Cobbold-Together' was back in business, and in its old digs. Only with a different brother. And, again, with a better business name than 'Cobbold-Together'... Vopres.

There was no licenced software this time round. So in theory anyone with a production set-up could do this. If this was a good idea we would soon have competitors. We needed an angle other than owning the best domain names and being the first. Peter had the answer to this. His background was translation. He'd been working for his inlaws' international translation company in Dublin and Madrid. We would make foreign-language web presenters our speciality. Foreign-Language Online Presenters would offer companies the benefit of not needing to rebuild or translate their websites for foreign markets. F.L.O.P.!... We did not register that domain.

We set to work on some test examples for the Knebworth House website. First off, yours truly appeared, welcoming you to our 'hearth where rooted friendships grow'. I sat in my pin-stripped Nehru suit in one of Knebworth House's lovely high-back gothic chairs. But as you know, I'm better when I move, so then I did it standing up - and was much better.

French and German visitors were invited to go to the site's same English-language 'Visiting' pages - but there they were greeted by either Jasmine (left) in French, or Laura (right) in German, who would introduce them to the basics of that English page, and point to where they should click next. It was all very personable. And, I thought, rather brilliant. Laura Pradelska, our German guide, was shot first, still using the old grey reflective cloth (right, see the difference?), so it was harder to remove her shadows. Ironic. As she's since become Quaithe of the Shadow in *Game of Thrones* (2012).

Our key asset was going to be our roster of on-call presenters, particularly the foreign ones. We had the advantage of being close to London, and so had access to actors of every nationality. We found some great ones. I particularly liked Gustavo, our Brazilian. He could make the dullest of accountancy software sound as sexy as the Ipanema breeze. We created 'character' presenters for seasonal promotions, e.g. Father & Fräulein Christmas (below) and our flying Witch for Hallowe'en (p.420). Our Father Christmas was the honey-throated Tony Phillips, Paul and Jonathan Ross's step-father. I'd suggested him and the lovely Martha Ross for roles with Virginia McKenna in *Love/Loss*, so he owed me some nonsense.

What a curious world it is. At the very moment I place this picture

Akemi_Still.png   Alexia_Still.png   Borja_Still.png   Eiji_Still.png

Giacomo_Still.pn   Gustavo_Still.png   Hile_Still.png   Ines_Still.png
g

Janusz_Still.png   Jeremey_Still.png   Johanna_Still.png   Jonas_Still.png

Laura_Still.png   Mika_Still.png   Milli_Still.png   Nina_Still.png

of Tony as Santa into my book - a few days before Christmas 2020 - I get the call that Tony died this morning. I am literally looking at him as I hear the news. That wonderful smile (left),

that wonderful singing voice, those wonderful stories... All hail you, Tony. I can hear you and the lovely Martha laughing together in the East End of Heaven.

We also found two excellent young English language presenters. Our 'man' was Tony's friend and actor-collaborator Richard Mann, and our 'woman' was Sarah-Lou Buckle, star saleswoman of The Jewellery Channel and member of Polly Rae's Hurly Burly burlesque troupe - if you saw their show, you'll not have forgotten her grinding-

ly slow version of Olivia Newton-John's *Physical* performed with a large rubber exercise ball. These two were particularly fun to work

with - always upbeat and word perfect on autocue (which, across long drawn-out mornings, we found many of our presenters were not). I made a fun commercial for Vopres using Knebworth House with Richard and Sarah-Lou (right).

Feeling I hadn't put them through indignities enough, I purchased a full green screen body suit, which enabled invisible activity on screen - like sudden hair-raising or removal of body parts. The website for my new video studio featured Sarah-Lou stripping off this body suit (wearing a business suit beneath), appearing one limb at a time out of thin air... then putting it back on, and disappearing limb by limb. Our 'headless man' presenter, who carried his head under his arm, was in fact both Richard and Sarah-Lou.

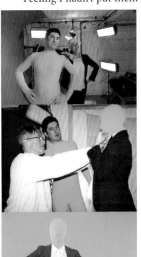

Vopres started to build clients and it was all going rather well. And then, once more, 'Cobbold Together' was slammed with C.B.O.C. - circumstances beyond our control. Or C.O.B.C. - the curse of my business career. This time an inter-company war between the two U.S. tech giants, Adobe and Apple. Our Vopres presenters were 'Adobe Flash' files. Apple computers stopped supporting Adobe Flash. Overnight, our presenters stopped appearing on half of the computers in the world. Pop-Ups became things that computers started to block, as more often than not - unless they were brilliant like ours - they irritated or infected.

It wasn't the same, having to click a link to make a presenter appear. It was like turning up to my house for dinner and having to tweak my nose to get me to talk to you. The magic was gone.

Peter did persist with Vopres for some time. But I was too old to be spending my unforgiving minutes making endless marketing videos. Having sublet the audio studio, I now also sublet the video studio, to Knebworth House's photographer caretaker, Rob Ryder. The kids' 'recording parties' became 'recording & video parties'. And I returned to the top floor of Knebworth House to do what I was trained to do, interruption or no interruption. I went back to my study to write. Because that what I was trained to do, by Master Po, by masters of the craft, not because Grasshopper could watch a YouTube video and wing it.

CHAPTER THIRTY-SIX

Bulwer Lyttons

My Grandmother Hermione died in October 2004. She was 99. Martha, Morwenna, Edward and I heard this news on a mobile phone in the Via delle Tombe - the Street of Tombs - in Pompeii. I sat on a stone outside the House of Diomed, the archeological discovery that had inspired her great-grandfather to begin his best-selling novel *The Last Days of Pompeii* (1834) "Ho Diomed, well met!", and considered all the stories that were passing with her. A hundred years of stories. Stories from a time when there were no motorcars in Knebworth village. Stories from the time when Peter Pan was a real boy. Stories from the Indian Raj in the 1920s. Fascist Italy in the 1930s. Wartime England in the 1940s. The Bank of England in the 1950s. The Royal household in the 1960s... Hermione had written a brief memoir of her childhood, for her family, *Memory Lane: Tales of Long Ago*, but nothing beyond this. Indeed she was inclined to burn letters and papers detailing her own life.

Alan Primett, father of Anita (the last person I'd walked the streets of Pompeii with, on InterRail aged 18. p.108/109) told me that when he and his wife Jacky were caretaking for Hermione at her later home Lake House, in Knebworth Park, she would have bonfires of old papers and mementos. When he could, he would rescue the occasional thing he was able to, things he guessed her descendants would prefer not destroyed. He gave me, for instance, the well-loved worn-cloth toy elephant that my grandfather kept from his childhood - and randomly, the service sheets from the

funerals Hermione attended as a young woman. Here is a great example of how the seemingly irrelevant can go on to provide a vital piece in a story jigsaw. Amongst the funeral service sheets was one for Alice Jennings. This was proof that Hermione remained friends with the Jennings daughters, whose father (Walter Jennings of the Standard Oil Company) had rented Knebworth House in the 1920s. The connection confirms that it is almost certainly her as a teenager (in the yellow dress) with her grandmother Edith (in dark blue), in the very early colour photograph (above left) discovered in the Jennings Collection at the Jekyll Island Archive in Georgia.

So many questions she could answer if she were here today. So many questions I wish I'd raised in the four decades I was fortunate that our lives intersected. The opportunities were ridiculously rife. In her final years, when she was our neighbour across the courtyard at Knebworth House I would pop over to visit her in the evening. She would be sitting alone playing Patience.

This is probably not as odd as I always thought it. Round and round in a circle with a pack of cards. I understand it keeps the brain sharp, but when I'm keeping my brain sharp - or if I'm relaxing - I want to be refuelling my brain with the creativity of others, or creating myself. Propagating stories. Not simply watching the endless mathematical circle of playing card patterns. But maybe Patience was simply what was going on on the surface. Maybe inside my grandmother's head there was a lifetime's whirl of

stories being made sense of. To do this she just had to move. Like the Sundance Kid.

Hermione took the great majority of her stories with her. Louisa May Alcott writes that "Love is the only thing we can carry with us when we go". It's an important proverb. One to live by. But incomplete. We also carry stories. My grandmother carried with her a long lifetime of love and a long lifetime of stories. She left us with more of the former.

The penultimate time I saw her, she was collapsed in a doorway in agony. Martha and I had hurried across the courtyard at the call of the alarm company. While Martha called an ambulance, I lay on the floor with her and held her long cold boney fingers. My hand was a sedative touch for her before the paramedics arrived and replaced it with morphine. As they loaded her into the back of the ambulance on a stretcher, she smiled at me. What a lovely smile. A smile that she was feeling, but her body was not. How unimportant the body eventually becomes to what we are. Until it is so unimportant, we can leave it behind, to live on in love and stories.

The town of Pompeii is a monument to this thought. It is the stories that are important, not the dust. This became the theme of my next screenplay, an adaptation of my great-great-great-grandfather's novel *The Last Days of Pompeii*. I surprise myself that it took twenty years of screenwriting before I tackled an Edward Bulwer Lytton book. My great-great-great-grandfather's novels are well-suited to screenplay adaptations. Strip away all the florid 19th Century wordplay and philosophical tangent that prevents them from being read nowadays and you invariably find 120 minutes of ripping yarn. Yarn laced with bright wit, for great dialogue. I've adapted two of his books now. I would like to do them all. I suspect my old bones will be dust before I'm able to achieve that. If I count them correctly, like Shakespeare's plays, there are 39 Bulwer Lytton books. Still, it is a fitting ambition.

1940s Comic Book Version

I adapted *The Last Days of Pompeii* on spec, but I was encouraged to do it by a big, bald - very lovely - man who lives on the Isle of Man. I met Dave Mousley through my old Harewood Avenue flat mate Gary Barker. Together they had been working to promote the work of Roger Dean, the psychedelic science fiction artist whose work is the basis of almost every Yes album cover, and whose work I loved as a teenager - not because I liked the music of Yes (I couldn't name you one track), but because I genuinely liked Roger Dean's work. The suspicion is that James Cameron does too, as the Avatar movie series looks very much inspired by it.

Having just recommended the stripping away of tangents, here's a quick one. I have enjoyed spending time with Roger. I've done well meeting my teenage heros. He would, I'm sure, dislike my description of him above. He seemed to me really to want his legacy to be as an architect. His quest has long been to find locations for his futuristic eco homes, that are all white curves and flower shapes, a little like the way we have since seen hobbit homes represented. So Knebworth came up frequently as a possible site. I would have loved this, but as previously mentioned, the little land we might have suitable for this kind of project is coloured & cross-hatched & lined & marked with every map key reference that means 'Don't Even Think About It'.

Visting a prototype of one of Roger Dean's eco-homes with the best Yorkshire builder in Hertfordshire, Andy Singleton

That, of course, was not going to put Roger, or Dave, off. Various investors have been brought up to Knebworth over the years, both for this project, and also for the idea of a futuristic Roger Dean hotel at Junction 7 of the A1(M). A little more interesting looking than the current Novotel. Exactly the thing needed to mark Stevenage's presence on the Great North Road. Stevenage is, after all, 'Space Town', home of Airbus and the Mars rovers. This would be an Angel of the North for the South. But one where you could actually get a kip and a kipper. The century is young. Who knows?

Dave Mousley in those days had a computer animation company in Manchester called Red Vision VFX. Red Vision had recreated in digital form, in precise historic detail, the city of Pompeii in AD79. This had been done for some documentary or video game, but Dave held the digital rights. So we started a company AD1 (left over from All Digital days, but appropriate for a 1st Century A.D. subject) to

develop *The Last Days of Pompeii* as a feature film. Each and every generation since the early days of silent movies has made a version of my great-great-great-grandfather's novel - except the CGI generation. The last version filmed was in the early 1980s by Paramount and RAI as a mini-series for television. Laurence Olivier was in it. And of course Brian Blessed. Some heavyweight actors. But not heavyweight scenery. The 1980s temple walls were all TV chipboard. The 1980s marble columns all bouncy polystyrene. It was time for the CGI generation to have its version of *The Last Days of Pompeii*. Mine goes like this:

THE LAST DAYS OF POMPEII

Trapped together in an earthquake subsidence, a passionate archaeologist tells a ruthless Italian developer a bittersweet tale of two lovers and a blind street-child escaping the cataclysmic destruction of Pompeii in AD79

The Bay of Naples. 2000 AD. Yellow smog clouds an industrial hinterland separated from the gray Mediterranean by a busy motorway, lined by heavy machinery for road widening... and towering above it, nature's awesome majesty, the black volcano, Vesuvius. An ominous plume of smoke rises from its summit.

A violent earthquake shakes the Bay, uncovering an underground cell beneath the road works. Ruthless local developer Roberto De Sica gives his most voracious opponent, British archaeologist Nydia Roberts, employed at the Pompeii Excavations, twenty-four hours to examine it before the bulldozers move back in.

The cell is a remarkable find. Symbols on the wall represent the first evidence that there were Christians in Pompeii before the volcanic eruption in AD79. They will bulldoze this over Nydia's dead body. Dismissive, amused, Roberto joins her in the cell – but as they are underground, there is a violent after-shock that destroys the cell, and traps the mismatched couple in a shaft of rocks and dirt... in each other's arms.

As Nydia's brash American colleague, Professor Edgar Lake, works to free them before they are crushed by another aftershock, Nydia, as distraction to their intimate, terrifying fate, Nydia recounts to Roberto the story of "The Last Days of Pompeii" and the four Greek teenagers, Glaucus, Ione, Apaecides... and Nydia, the feisty Pompeian street-child after she was named...

The Bay of Naples. 79 AD. Soft breezes from the beautiful blue Mediterranean; sun-kissed plains of olive groves and vines… and towering above it all, the black volcano, Vesuvius. An ominous plume of smoke rises from its summit.

The Romans are masters of the world. The palaces, villas, taverns, theatres, brothels, bathhouses and colosseums of the seaside resort of Pompeii are their playground. Fashionable, arrogant, decadent – their business is corruption and power, their pleasure is orgiastic parties and blood-thirsty duels in the gladiatorial ring

Sucked into the decadence of Pompeii society, a young Greek, Glaucus, becomes a beautiful prize to be won by the dissipated aristocrat, Julia. But Glaucus is distracted by the plight of blind, beautiful, child-of-the-street, Nydia. Nydia sees nothing, but knows everything – every wickedness, in every back alley of the city – and she knows that Glaucus is not like the men of Pompeii. She, too, would do anything to win him.

I did tests with Tim Major for a bande dessinée version - I love the results, and hope to complete this one day (indeed I'd like to do it for all of my screenplays… and all of Bulwer Lytton's novels) In this 'draft' Nydia begins too bosomy, looking like a glamour model, not an urchin, but the point becomes that the drug is sexualising her in Glaucus's eyes

But Glaucus is engaged to Ione, a fellow Greek, who lives with her wealthy brother Apaecides in the household of the corrupt Egyptian priest Arbaces. Arbaces wants Apaecides's money and Ione as his wife. He uses the gullible Julia to frame Glaucus for the murder of Apaecides. Glaucus is sentenced to death in the gladiatorial ring.

Only Nydia can prove Glaucus's innocence, but Nydia is imprisoned by Arbaces. In a race against time, Nydia must use her wiles to escape. Meanwhile, Glaucus survives duel after duel in front of a baying crowd. They still want blood. The lions are set on him... as the smoking volcano suddenly explodes, raining burning ash on the city.

Panic. Civilisation dissolves in a split second. All the basic instincts of man surface. Survival –as the weak are trampled under foot. Greed – as buildings blaze and collapse around families who refuse to be separated from their wealth. Lust – as looting and rape seem a better option than waiting to die.

In the thick black smoke and confusion, only one person knows where she is and where she needs to go. The blind girl, Nydia, finds Glaucus, drained, wounded. He persuades her to lead him to Ione. They find Ione in the clutches of Arbaces. Glaucus has one last duel to fight – but both men are distracted by a rampaging tiger that is loose from the Games. The tiger sinks its teeth in Ione's leg, crippling her – before the Egyptian is crushed by the Temple of Jupiter crashing around them.

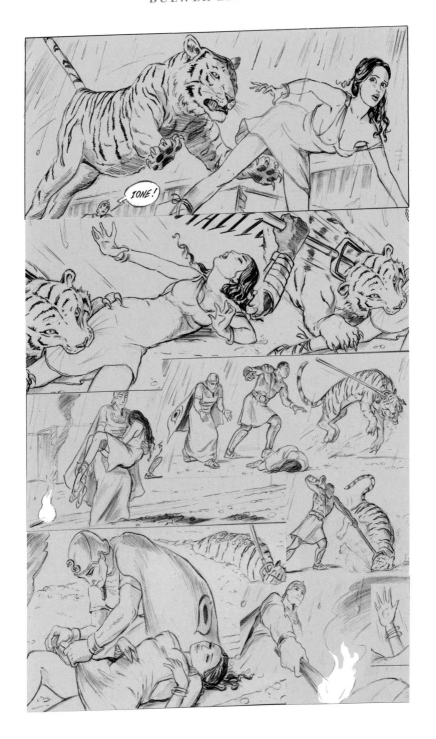

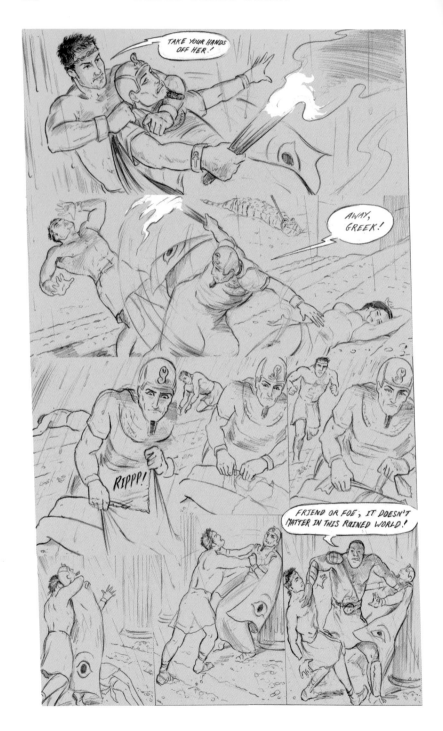

With the city falling around them, Nydia leads Glaucus – who insists on carrying Ione – through the burning black cloud. Stumbling through dunes of scalding ash, Ione begs them to leave her. Glaucus refuses to abandon her. Nydia, against her baser instincts, helps him. Choking in poisonous gases, blind but for the knowledge of the girl who cannot see, they reach the edge of the dying city...

At the port, it is the Christian dockworkers who rescue their Pompeian oppressors by manning the last of ships to set out to sea. They pull the three Greeks aboard. The water hisses, steams. Desperate people drown around them. The devastation they have left behind forms a panorama of death and destruction. Still they are not safe. The water lurches, lunges. Huge waves surge around them. The injured Ione would be swept overboard but for Nydia clinging to her, holding her safe, as Glaucus struggles to control the boat.

Dawn. Light. Everything is still. Everywhere a deathly beauty. But Nydia the blind girl cannot see it. Wrapped with her, on the deck of the battered boat are the sleeping figures of Glaucus and Ione. With her fingers, lightly, she traces the line of Glaucus's sleeping form – all the lines of his body lead to Ione.

The surface of the water is as still as glass, as Nydia's body slices through it, causing barely a ripple. Her torn garments billow around her, as she lies back her head and empties her lungs. The boat drifts away. The sun rises behind the distant volcano, spilling colour into the sleeping faces of the two lovers - but not on the city of Pompeii. The city has vanished.

Nydia Roberts finishes retelling the story just as she and Roberto are pulled free from the collapsed cavity. They are no longer the same two people. But their newfound intimacy is brought to a sharp end in the cold light of day. Roberto is married and Nydia has a job to do. Roberto vows greater co-operation with the archeologists. But Nydia too has changed. She now accepts that although Man is constantly and callously erasing Time, he is only following the lead of Nature. It is not the physical relic that is important, but the tale that is attached to it. It is the stories spun in the dust that enrich us, not the dust itself. As Nature reminds us, when...

Vesuvius, the black volcano looming above them, looming over the two million people in the Bay of Naples, shaken by the succession of earthquakes... begins to rumble.

In the lead up to Edward Bulwer Lytton's bicentenary in 2003, I recall a *Sunday Times* journalist muttering about "blue-rinsed devotees of the author of *The Last Days of Pompeii*" being shocked at the work of his great-great-great-grandson. I suspect the journalist meant 'blue-stockinged', but either way it is a ill-informed thing to say. Bulwer Lytton's early writing career was profoundly radical, and deeply shocking to its readership. There is no better example of this than the big 'villain speech' of the Egyptian priest Arbaces in *The Last Days of Pompeii*. This is ten years before Karl Marx called religion 'das Opium des Volkes', and many more years before that was published.

> *What in reality was Government, they named 'Religion'.*
> *True, they were also cheats, impostors if you will. But do you think, young man, that if they had not deceived their kind, they could have served them? They asked for belief - and returned the gift with civilization... The ignorant and the vulgar must be blinded for their own good. Do you think you that it is the Emperor of Rome - the man - that brings harmony to the vast and various tribes of earth, brings peace, order, law, the blessings of life? No, it is the pomp, the awe, the majesty that surround him. These are his impostures, his delusions...*

Of course the novel is buttered with the picturesques of its time. There is a witch making love potions, instead of drug dealers peddling narcotics. There are young 'flowergirls' in the Forum, rather than prostitutes peddling sex. But it took little more than my software's 'find and replace' button to update these. The sex and drugs are all present and provocative in the original 1834 novel.

The screenplay was reading well. It had all the structural elements of the most successful movie of all time (at that time) *Titanic* (1997). The modern story wrap-around, the star-crossed lovers, the cataclysmic backdrop - nature blindsiding human hubris. I sent it to James Cameron's company in Santa Monica, and was encouraged to receive one of those 'we have absolutely definitely 100% not looked at this project, we have shredded it and now don't believe we were ever sent it' letters. James Cameron was clearly interested in doing a Pompeii movie, and soon afterwards optioned the non-fiction book *Ghosts of Vesuvius*. Why a non-fiction book? Why not a proven classic?

Then the movie *300* (2006) was a huge hit. *Gladiator (2000)* hadn't been a one off. Sword & sandal movies were back, and ready for their close up, Mr DeMille. So I took *The Last Days of Pompeii* to Cannes in 2007... and the very first Press Release of the festival announced that Roman Polanski was financed to make a 100 million dollar production of Robert Harris's book *Pompeii*.

For my cover I used an image from Bulwer Lytton's study wall of a statue of Glaucus, Ione & Nydia by Charles Francis Fuller (1830-1875), which seems no longer to exist. Marble representations of Nydia, however, are often to be found in American museums. The Met's website calls Randolph Rogers' 1859 version "the most popular American sculpture of the nineteenth century. According to Rogers, it was replicated 167 times in two sizes"

Here again my 'very-nearly-but-not-quite' movie career kicks back in with more spectacular believe-it-or-not good-but-bad timing. As Cameron McCracken, head of Pathe-UK (and godfather to one of my Matovu nephews), wrote to me on the afternoon of my 45th birthday (which otherwise I recall as a lovely day) "that blows your project out of the water." I'd recently very much liked Cameron and Pathe's film of Patrick Süskind's novel *Perfume* (2006). But Cameron very much did not like my screenplay of *The Last Days of Pompeii*.

Polanski's film, he said, "will raise its funding and it will get made (Scarlett Johansson and Orlando Bloom are currently 'attached')." I accepted he was right that my screenplay needed more work, but I'd read Robert Harris's *Pompeii*. I knew there was no way he was going to be right about that. I'd found the novel about aqueducts interesting, as a novel, but you cannot make a 100 million dollar movie with no girls in it. Scarlett Johansson may be signed 'pay-or-play', but someone is going to have to write her a part. If Robert Harris had wanted romance in his story he'd have included it. Now some wretched screenwriter was going to have to angle-grind it in. It will end in tears. It always does. Robert Harris's novel is not a 100 million dollar tentpole movie unless it is completely rewritten. That movie will not happen.

I was right. But so was Cameron about blowing. The Cannes Press Release did blow my Pompeii project out of the water. So I'd have to sit on it for a bit. Spend some time improving it. I started toying with giving it the same treatment I'd given *Wearing A Smile*, and turning it into a bande dessinée comic book with Tim Major. We did some initial tests, which looked great, but I didn't have the money at that time. I did, however, do what I have never done before or since. I hired a group of local actors and recorded a read-through. This was exhilarating. I must do it more often. Importantly it gave me confidence that my revised script did work.

Four years later - 2011 - and still no Polanski film. I'm sure they could've made a couple of other movies with the money they'd spent talking about it. Robert Harris's *Pompeii* ended up being picked up by Ridley Scott's company as a miniseries, a much more appropriate format for that novel. But these were pre-Netflix days and volcanos remained an expensive proposition, and Scott's company had a queue of projects... It's now 2021. Netflix does exist. But a film version of Harris's *Pompeii* still doesn't.

Meanwhile Dave Mousley had found me an Italian director. Better than that, a Canadian Italian director. I say that because *300* had all been shot in a warehouse in Montreal. Sergio Navarretta had made award-winning independent movies in Canada, but his desire was to make a film in the Southern Italy of his roots. Sergio 'got' my Pompeii screenplay, and even better, so did his partner - also his partner - screenwriter, Alessandra Piccione. Together they gave me some of the best notes I've ever received on a screenplay. It was time to take the project back to Cannes,

We did. And would you believe it, the very first Press Release of the 2011 Cannes Film Festival announced that Paul W. S. Anderson was financed to make a 100 million dollar production of a movie about Pompeii.

Here we go again. This time, the director - of the successful *Resident Evil* series - was working from an original screenplay, so had room to include a love story amongst the pyrotechnics, to keep a bigger-budget audience emotionally involved. Not that he was particularly successful with this in the finished film. Despite Julian Fellowes's being one of a list of screenwriters (uncredited).

This film did appear. In 2014, as *Pompeii*. And it was entertaining. But it was not a better story that *The Last Days of Pompeii*.

Why did Paul W. S. Anderson, Roman Polanski, James Cameron... all resolutely turn their backs on Bulwer Lytton's classic novel, that had the pedigree and proven success? Odd.

But a Pompeii movie does come around every generation, and Vesuvius hasn't re-erupted yet... so no doubt the novel will be picked up again. And whoever does, let them know a solid adaptation exists by the author's great-great-great-grandson.

I felt I was on to something adapting Edward Bulwer Lytton. I recalled the mileage *Braveheart* (1995) got from its screenplay being written by a descendant of William Wallace. And surely at some point the boredcasters (sic) must pause from adapting Austen, Dickens & Brontë, and get to the best-selling author of the 1830s? For goodness sake they were even repeating Thackeray... even doing Trollope.

So I set to work on a second Bulwer Lytton adaptation. This was one my father had always told me he thought would make a great film. He'd even done a breakdown of the book for me. *Paul Clifford* (1830) was indeed an easy one to slice into a three-act screenplay. Wipe away the novel's surface of contemporary political satire and sophisticated wordplay, and underneath was, indeed, a splendid ripping yarn.

Paul Clifford is an interesting novel on so many levels. It is arguably the very first novel to feature an anti-hero. It preceded Harrison Ainsworth's *Rookwood* (1833), the novel which turned the Essex gangster Dick Turpin into a folk hero, and it was also much 'borrowed from' by Charles Dickens for *Oliver Twist* (1837).

It is also the novel for which Bulwer Lytton gets most publicity nowadays, for reasons that test the aphorism 'all news is good news'. For *Paul Clifford* is the novel that begins with the infamous 58-word sentence:

It was a dark and stormy night; the rain fell in torrents—except at occasional intervals, when it was checked by a violent gust of wind which swept up the streets (for it is in London that our scene lies), rattling along the housetops, and fiercely agitating the scanty flame of the lamps that struggled against the darkness.

In 1982 Professor Scott Rice at the University of San Jose foisted on the world an annual competition which, on the basis of this opening sentence, he named The Bulwer Lytton Fiction Contest. The competition challenges "man, woman, and (very precocious) child to write an atrocious opening sentence to a hypothetical bad novel. We're honored to receive thousands of odious entries from around the world each year. www.bulwer-lytton.com, where www means wretched writers welcome)"

This - it is supposed by people who should know better - implies that the opening sentence of the novel *Paul Clifford* is 'wretched writing'. Like so much criticism of the Arts, this is indolent and insouciant (as Bulwer Lytton himself, 'showing a casual lack of concern', might say). For, in common with the many wonderful annual entries to the Bulwer Lytton Contest, Bulwer Lytton's writing can only be 'atrocious' if it is not funny. For the original intention of this sentence was comic.

If you're in any doubt of this intent, you only have to read the novel - probably too much to expect of these critics - to see that this manner of speech - which inserts multiple and extended parentheses into the middle of sentences - is a running joke. It is the comic speech pattern of the heroine's father Sir Joseph Brandon.

You will notice I have given this subject of lazy criticism of my great-great-great-grandfather some consideration. In August 2008, I was invited to the town of Lytton in Western Canada as part of British Columbia's 150th birthday celebrations. Lytton is named after Edward Bulwer Lytton - indeed the only statue of him in the whole world is on British Columbia's State Capital Building in Victoria (left) - because, without him be-

The Banqueting Hall set

The Dastardly Villain

The Virginal Damsel

The Happy Resolve

The Hero, 8 year later, seen with a strange man off the Trans-Canada Highway

ing in the job of Colonial Secretary in the summer of 1858, these Pacific coast lands would almost certainly now be part of the U.S.A. It's is an interesting tale. Read the book *McGowan's War* by Donald Hauka.

Edward Bulwer Lytton's influence in Canada extends beyond keeping its western territories out of the hands of the Americans. He is also responsible for the happy union of Kate & Jonathan Love of Calgary, Alberta. Their romance began as University of Calgary students performing Bulwer Lytton's unpublished play *The Captives* in the Banqueting Hall of Knebworth House (left) as part of the *Bulwer Lytton 2000* conference. Kate & Jonathan were my warm, welcoming hosts that summer, as I stepped off the last ever flight of bankrupt Zoom Airlines (allowing the word 'Zoom', now, to mean the very opposite of getting on an airplane). I then made one of the most memorably beautiful drives of my life, early morning, through the Rockies, Bob Seger's *Greatest Hits* powering the car more than any gasoline. Arriving in the old wild frontier town of Lytton I was given a wonderfully rustic single-room cabin in the woods with a communal bathroom somewhere else in the woods, and have never felt more like Jeremiah Johnson.

A highlight of Lytton's anniversary celebrations was to pit its namesake's direct descendant against his nemesis, Professor Scott Rice of The Bulwer Lytton Contest. There would be a public debate - punch up, if needs be - in the town square on the subject of Bulwer Lytton's literary legacy. It was set up with a face-off - The Guardian picked up on the local newspaper coverage (19/08/08), *"I come to bury Lytton, not to praise him,"* said Rice. *"The evil that men do lives after them, in Lytton's case in 27 novels* [I know, I said 39 - 39 published works] *whose perfervid turgidity I intend to expose, denude, and generally make visible."*

"I'm off to defend his honour," Lytton Cobbold said. *"Bulwer-Lytton was a remarkable man and it's rather unfair...* etc." There was a procession down Main Street to a buntinged stage. I, the slighted Englishman, was, like Sydney Carton to the gallows, flanked by two Mounties in full uniform. Scott was to be the American villain. The Mayor said the town had had enough of Professor Rice making sport of its namesake. The crowd made clear who it expected to win. The crowd was to judge the winner of the debate. So the outcome looked promising. But, just in case, I leapt from the stage and made sure to bribe each and every one of the townsfolk with leather Bulwer Lyt-

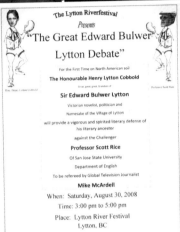

The Lytton Riverfestival

Presents

"The Great Edward Bulwer Lytton Debate"

For the First Time on North American soil

The Honourable Henry Lytton Cobbold

Great, great, great, Grandson of

Sir Edward Bulwer Lytton

Victorian novelist, politician and

Namesake of the Village of Lytton

will provide a vigorous and spirited literary defense of

his literary ancestor

against the Challenger

Professor Scott Rice

Of San Jose State University

Department of English

To be refereed by Global Television Journalist

Mike McArdell

When: Saturday, August 30, 2008

Time: 3:00 pm to 5:00 pm

Place: Lytton River Festival

Lytton, BC

"Literary Pugilism at it's Finest"

ton bookmarks bearing his most enduring sayings (right). It was a fun couple of hours to fly half round the world for. Scott Rice, before and since, has been the most genial of nemeses. When himself invited to Knebworth House's hearth "safe as altar e'en to foe" for Bulwer Lytton's Bicentenary, Scott gave one of the best - and certainly the funniest - of all the addresses.

Heartbreaking postscript: On 30th June 2021, the day after Lytton recorded 49.6 °C, the hottest ever Canadian temperature, the historic frontier town was 90% destroyed by wildfire

Paul Clifford is not, by any stretch of literary snobbism, a 'bad novel'. But its legacy is now overshadowed by its opening, "It was a dark and stormy night..." - storytelling's second most famous opening after "Once upon a time...". My feeling is that the book would be better remembered, not for its first words, but for its last, which quote the radical politician John Wilkes, "The very worst use you can put a man to, is to hang him." The challenge for me, in adapting it, was to include both of these great lines. Inspiration for how to do this came from a coda to the novel that Bulwer Lytton added to a later edition. This was instructions on *the popular*

THE HIGHWAYMAN

"The Genuine History of the Life of Paul Clifford, the Noted Highwayman"

The adventures of the original dandy pirate of the 18th Century highways – Captain Paul Clifford – as told by his friend and former accomplice, the very eminent Professor Augustus Tomlinson.

"The Highwayman" is a comic romp through the streets, inns, gambling dens, prisons, carriages, stately homes, brothels, bedrooms, ballrooms and backwaters of 18th Century England.

"The Highwayman" is based on the notorious novel "Paul Clifford" by Sir Edward Bulwer Lytton. Published in 1830, "Paul Clifford" shocked contemporary society as the first novel to feature an anti-hero. Today its notoriety is its opening line – the second most famous opening line of all time (after "Once Upon a Time...") – "It Was A Dark And Stormy Night..."

* * * * *

Captain Paul Clifford – formally Paul Lobb of the Mug Inn, Thames Court, London – is leader of a legendary band of gentlemen highwaymen, forever in the pursuit of fine silk and a reputation.

The gang are noted for the charm and good manners with which they rob the pompous and the proud, and the good humour and grace with which they accept their life on the run from the bitter and twisted Constable Nabbem.

Captain Clifford's primary accomplices are the endlessly bickering, back-stabbing and brilliantly bouffanted and behatted, Long Ned Pepper and Augustus Tomlinson, formally of the gang of the loud but late, Gentleman George.

Captain Clifford's primary distraction is the very beautiful Lucy Brandon, who represents a life of calm and comfort and the call of a courtyard clock... until she meets the Captain.

Captain Clifford's primary adversaries are the aforementioned Constable Nabbem of the Bow Street Runners, the absurd angular and arrogant aristocrat Lord Mauleverer, and Lucy's cold and calculating custodial creep of a guardian, Judge Brandon.

The allies of the Captain's youth are the pipe-smoking chatelaine of the Mug Inn, "Piggy" Lobb and the weasely rag-merchant Dummie Dunnaker, whom Charles Dickens stole seven years later to become Fagin.

"Dammee! What hunting is like the road?! How much more sport hunting a fop than a fox!"

The moral of the tale is "The very worst use to which you can put a man is to hang him".

* * * * *

The novel "Paul Clifford" has been adapted for the screen as "The Highwayman" by the great-great-great-grandson of the author, who currently resides in Bulwer Lytton's gothic mansion in rural England where every night is dark and stormy.

art of cheating, being an introduction to that noble science by which every man may become his own rogue by the ex-highwayman Augustus Tomlinson, now professor of moral philosophy at a German university. Anyone still believe this novel is not, at heart, a satire? It is even a rare 19th Century novel to contain a knob gag. When the same highwayman, Augustus Tomlinson, is parading as a dandy at a society

THE HIGHWAYMAN

A comedy adventure of dandy highwaymen - adapted from a novel by Edward Bulwer Lytton

In a gothic German University in the early 1800s, an 80-year-old professor in cracked make-up and dandy young clothes ambushes his students with loaded pistols, steals their belongings - "When you hear the life of a great man, you will perceive all the qualities given to him are the qualities necessary to a rogue". Whilst tormenting and enthralling his students, he tells them the story of his eminent friend and former accomplice, Captain Paul Clifford – "good... and in many ways... bad".

"It was a dark and stormy night..." (he writes on the blackboard) in the backstreets of London, mid 1700s. Brothel child Paul witnesses the death of his diseased prostitute mother. She makes the weasely rag-merchant, Dummie Dunnaker, swear he will never reveal Paul's origins. The boy is bought up in the rough underworld of The Mug pub, where he is seduced into debt by the dashing elder teenagers Long Ned Pepper and Augustus Tomlinson. All three are determined to rise above their origins, by educating themselves, dressing in high fashion, and behaving as gentlemen – but Paul chooses the honest path of a job as a clerk, whilst his friends become thieves.

Driven to poverty by his abusive employer, Paul is seduced back into fine society by Long Ned, who pick-pockets the ambitious lawyer William Brandon, whilst Paul is captivated by Brandon's beautiful niece Lucy. Paul is sent to Bridewell Prison for the crime, where he meets Tomlinson, who is to be hanged with the notorious highwayman Gentleman George and his gang. Paul escapes prison and rescues Tomlinson from the hanging, whilst Long Ned causes chaos in the crowd. But George and his gang are hung by the bitter Constable Nabbem.

Paul takes George's place as captain of the gentlemen highwaymen – and, with his friends, earns notoriety, only robbing ('taxing') the arrogantly wealthy – but Paul remains distracted by the lovely Lucy. He follows her to Bath, where she is being courted by the foppish aristocrat Lord Mauleverer. William Brandon is using his niece to win Lord Mauleverer's favour, but Lucy is not interested in the pompous elderly aristocrat. She is excited by the dashing Captain Clifford who, with his two bizarre comrades, becomes the talk of Bath society.

Paul, in love with Lucy, determines to leave behind his life of crime and leave the country – but Constable Nabbem is always one step behind, and captures Long Ned and Tomlinson. Meanwhile Judge Brandon, now Lord Brandon, wants an heir, so commissions the rag-merchant, Dummie, to find the son that was stolen from him two decades before.

Paul rescues Long Ned and Tomlinson from Constable Nabbem, but is himself caught and brought before Judge Brandon. Having seen Tomlinson off on a boat to Germany, Long Ned encounters Dummie and they learn of Paul's trial. Long Ned, disguised as Paul's defence barrister, calls Dummie as a witness - who reveals that Paul is Judge Brandon's son. The Judge goes ahead and passes the death sentence on Paul – but, tortured, dies of a stroke. Lucy offers to marry Lord Mauleverer if he will save Paul. Mauleverer accepts that he and Lucy will not make a happy couple – and in respect to her, agrees to commute Paul's to transportation to Australia.

The old professor – Tomlinson – finishes his story by returning the stolen items to his students and saying that, subsequently, Paul did the same, from exotic addresses all around the world. That was after, a year later - foiling Constable Nabbem one final time - he collects Lucy from a smuggler's beach and sails her off into the sunset.

ball in Bath Assembly Rooms, with a pistol stuck down the front of his trousers, *"after gazing for some moments on an envious rent in the right ruffle, (he) muttered some indistinct words, like 'the cock of that confounded pistol,' and then tucked up the mutilated ornament with a peculiarly nimble motion of the fingers of his left hand."*

"It's *Pirates of the Caribbean* with highwaymen" I tell producer David Heyman as I'm showing him around Knebworth House during auditions for the part of Young Dumbledore in *Fantastic Beasts* (2016), the *Harry Potter* (2001-2011) prequel. "Sounds interesting," he replies. "Expect to receive it at some point from Nick Saunders." "How do you know Nick Saunders?..."

Nick Saunders had turned up at one of

Captain Clifford, by Dave Flemons, in Knebworth House Gardens

my daughter's birthday parties dressed as a pilot. He'd spent time on the Warner Bros lot early in his career. I think he was Orlando Bloom's assistant around the time of *Pirates of the Caribbean* (2003). He loved the *Paul Clifford* script, saw it a Pirates of the Bath Road (Pirates of the A4?), and felt sure it would be something that Johnny Depp would be interested in. So off it went to Johnny Depp's production company as *The Highwayman*.

It languished there for long enough to suggest it was something of interest. Johnny Depp would indeed be a perfect Augustus Tomlinson. My suggestion for the highwaymen's nemesis Constable Nabbem was Adam Ant - you'll recall once lined up for *Green For A Season*, my very first screenplay. Constable Nabbem is the only character in *The Highwayman* who gets to cry "Stand and Deliver!".

Nick still has this screenplay out there. Recently he has been talking to director Alex-Henry Rubin (left, with partner Sarah Michler - now also his partner), Oscar-nominated for his documentary *Murderball*, whose recent feature *Semper Fi* (2019) I thought beat perfect.

I hope *Paul Clifford* gets made one day. The first story ever to begin "It was a dark and stormy night..." should be a motion picture.

CHAPTER THIRTY-SEVEN

Passion Projects

It's up to you and me
To change this world
We're livin' in

(Charles Pasi - *Up To Us*)

Whilst writing these screenplay adaptations of my great-great-great-grandfather's work, and working for the preservation and prosperity of his house, I also spent the first 17 years of this century (until I began this book) writing a book about his daughter, Emily.

Emily (right) was Edward Bulwer Lytton's eldest child. She was born in 1828 and died, aged 19, in 1848. 17 years to write a book about a 19-year-old? It was two books actually. Two books to write about a 19-year-old? Two volumes. Two volumes? Are you crazy? Who's going to read two volumes?

Not many people. No one in my immediate family has yet had time to read both volumes. The most pertinent - and impertinent - review of the book so far is my son's. "T.L.D.R." ("Too Long Didn't Read")

Of course I like my work to be read, but this project was a rare one where the lack of readership didn't greatly concern me. There's a little of Reverend Casaubon in me [George Eliot's *Middlemarch*, for those that haven't read it. I never finished it either. T.L.D.R.] In fact, literally - and literarily - in my blood, is my great-great-great-great-great-grandfather Richard Warburton Lytton, who authored plays in

Ancient Hebrew that very few of his contemporaries could read, let alone perform. I love Edward Bulwer Lytton's tribute to his grandfather:

> He [Richard Warburton Lytton, right] *loved learning for learning's sake. He disentangled himself from the world; from pleasure, from ambition, from all the usual aspirations of a man who unites knowledge & talent to wealth & station* [for 'station' now read 'the silver sugar spoon of privilege']. *The image of his life was like a statue, cold in its complete repose and shattered into fragments on his tomb. Nothing remains of it - nothing but a few notes and comments scattered here and there through remote regions and dim recesses of that silent world in which he lived unseen.*

> *Yet to me, his grandson, who with my poor acquirements, snatched from perturbed studies in the intervals of an active and unquiet life, have so boldly ventured out on the stormy sea of popular authorship, in search of that distant haven which so few of the ships of time (as books were called by Bacon) ever reach; -to me, amidst the hum and buzz that accompanies the feeblest fame, the most fleeting celebrity, - there is something unspeakably impressive in the oblivion to which this solitary scholar carried with him all the spoils and trophies of his vast research. I shrink back from it, startled and abashed. I feel that, had I been as wise as my grandfather, I had also been as silent. I feel that there is something infinitely nobler in this mute disdainful passage of the full river to the unknown deep, than in all the fretful noise with which we shallow streams go babbling over the pebbles that obstruct our course. It is greater to live for knowledge than by it.*

The Mausoleum in Knebworth Park - reserving my spot for eternity

I love that. What perfect therapy. I am inclined to end this book with that thought.

Don't get me wrong. It does bother me that good screenplays I have written sit on the shelf unread and unmade. The screenplays were written to be popular. In many cases they are time-sensitive, and as the years go by they start to lose their raisins - their raisons d'être.

The Emily book was written for the future. And for the past. It was written because my family wanted me to write it - not my contemporary family, but my forebears. A box of letters was left in the attic so that, someday, a descendant would write the book. I was chosen. I was chosen because I was the one who, in November 1999, broke into the family Mausoleum in Knebworth Park (which had been bricked up for 40 years) and found Emily's open coffin.

It was time. Enough time had passed. An immunity to the more acute sensitivities of the tragedy had built up through the generations. But the flailing nerve ends of the unanswered questions were still there. The needle to reattach them, and sew the ends of the story together, was, with time, disappearing deeper into the haystack. Another generation or two and the needle would have been lost.

I had a filial duty to write the book. My great-great-great-aunt wanted her story told. I also believe her father wanted his daughter's story told. But was he not the villain? Was it not Edward Bulwer Lytton who packed his poor unfortunate child off to the distant gothic German doctor to be strapped to a spine-stretching bed every day... then sidelined her as his secretary when she returned home to a house full of his mistresses... then left her abandoned in a Brompton boarding house to die in tortured agony aged nineteen?... You could say that. But he was also the one who left her letters in the attic to be found by a future generation. And there were plenty of letters from his life that he purposefully did not leave.

The most pleasing thing about the book I wrote, is that the few who have read it come away with different opinions of who the villain was. Or, if accepting there was no villain, what went wrong. This is why the book needed to be written by a member of the family. And five generations later. This book came with the keys to Knebworth House, as my destiny. Hoc Virtutis Opus [Lytton family motto] - 'by this virtuous work' - I did solve the mystery of how my great-great-great-aunt died.

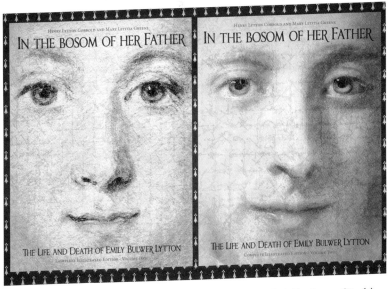

I am proud of my magnum opus. I particularly like the cover, which blends one of Emily's cross-written letters under an evocative close up of her face, with eyes that speak 10,000 lines.

I do wish someone had had time to proof-read the volumes though. That's 'though' not 'through'. On line 7, 'though' not 'through' is the first of many typos in the Complete Illustrated Edition of **In The Bosom Of Her Father** *that now torment me. Line 7! Line 7 of about 30,000. Was that a keyboard mishit in the final stages, or did I stare at this word for 17 years and never see it? T.T.T.T. - Typo Torment Th(r)ough Time! As you read, know that I am currently shivering in a corner, wretched, over the typos you've noticed in the printed version of this book.*

Forgive me for not going over it all again now (I see this book is already nearing half the length of that one). I do plan to publish an abridged paperback version of Emily's story for general readership. Maybe for her 200th birthday in 2028. The story does merit a mainstream telling. Whilst I was writing it I saw all manner of possible screenplays, novels... a stage play even, set in Pelham Street around the circumstances of her death...

But it was more important for me in the first instance to record the full story. To publish all of these letters from the attic (transcribed by Knebworth House's indefatigable then archivist Clare Fleck). And to solve in full forensic detail the long-hidden family mystery. Thus the 'Complete Illustrated Edition' of *In the Bosom Of Her Father: The Life and Death of Emily Bulwer Lytton,* in two beautiful, full-colour - and consequently rather expensive - hardback volumes.

I will, however reprint here the kind review on Amazon (where the book is still available) of the Bulwer Lytton scholar and enthusiast, the late John S. Moore:

The biography of a girl who died in 1848 at the age of nineteen may not sound promising, but this book transcends its subject. The core of the story concerns Emily's relation to her father, Edward Bulwer Lytton. His novels may not be much read in twenty-first century Britain, but as a leading Victorian celebrity, his life story gives striking insight into its era, its values and hypocrisies. A sensational tale is uncovered, one which Henry Lytton Cobbold with some justice compares to a novel by Charlotte Brontë. Arguably the correspondence between this Emily and her father is more psychologically revealing than any novel could be.

This well planned narrative is written with humour and insight and deserves to be far more popular than might be expected. It works on several different levels. Not least there is the memoir of seventeen years of dogged genealogical research, with some lucky breaks that seemed almost miraculous. The author is perfectly placed, living in his ancestral "treasure house of stories" with so many notable ancestors and connections to explore. This project involved the recovery and interpretation of barely legible manuscripts, the use of ancestry.com and much foreign travel to trace descendants of the actors in the drama, in search of writings and images from the past.

He credits as co-author Miss Mary Letitia Greene, Emily's childhood nurse and lifelong friend, including her own long emotional account of the girl's last few years. Then there are Emily's own letters, which took the Knebworth archivist much pain to decipher and transcribe, 'cross-written' as they were according to an obscure Victorian practice to save paper.

At the centre of the main narrative is a riveting mystery story. How and why did Emily die? The mystery is kept up throughout, enticing the reader to carry on, and continues to surprise right up to the end. If you've read any spoilers, don't believe them. The conclusion is complex.

Thanks John. Give Emily a hug from me.

A Knebworth House Garden rose in her hand and German wildflowers at her feet, a final farewell to Emily, before sealing her coffin on Monday 27th June 2016, her 188th birthday

Emily's was not the first biography I had written. Nor was it the first I felt obliged to write. I also found myself writing a biography of Cyril Frankel, the film director you'll recall from Chapter 14, who was to have directed my first screenplay, *Green For A Season*. Film lexicographer Leslie Halliwell had declared him dead at 50, but in fact Cyril lived on to the grand age of 95. He even outlived his young partner Steve, who died of cancer having devotedly cared for him through his Third Act.

I would pop in to see Cyril when I had meetings in London. The first floor Harley Street apartment was not large, but its cluttered surfaces and high walls gave clues to the remarkable 20th Century life he had lived - pots by Lucie Rie; paintings by

Martin Bloch; photos of the Maharishi, of Ava Gardner; VHS cassettes of television screenings of 1950s movies *Make Me An Offer!* and *It's Great To Be Young!*; shiny new DVD box sets of 1960s & 1970s TV series *The Baron* and *Randall and Hopkirk Deceased*; filing cabinets over-spilling with photos, clipping, letters...

As the new century began, Cyril's body was starting to 'Leslie Halliwell', but his mind stayed sharp. One of the last times I saw him on his feet was when I walked him to a performance of *The Boyfriend* at the Open Air Theatre in neighbouring Regents Park in 2006. He had given the musical's creator Sandy Wilson the part of Pierrot in the pantomime *L'Enfant Prodigue* at his second undergraduate spell at Oxford, the genesis of the Pierrot subplot of *The Boyfriend*.

A gift to Cyril from the Ugandan tribal chief in Man of Africa

A Lucie Rie, Cyril gifted to me

It was Cyril's second spell at university, because the first had been interrupted by having to be one of the first soldiers of the 5th Army into the streets of Naples. This was followed by time liberating concentration camp prisoners in northern Germany and becoming one of the youngest Majors in the British Army. It was only then, and

after he'd left Oxford a second time, that his distinguished film career began, working first for John Grierson at the Crown Film Unit, and then directing the first ever feature film with an all black African cast, *Man of Africa* (1953)... Again, you don't need all the details, you can read the book. The book you are currently reading is trying to make <u>my</u> pampered life sound interesting. My point is, I kept saying to Cyril, "Your story is too extraordinary. You need a memoir or a biography." I said it so often that I talked myself into doing it. Damn. How did I do that? There was no one else to do it, and it needed to be done.

There was someone who wanted to publish it. A Lou Grade / ATV series enthusiast - and local history book publisher

Eye to Eye

A MEMOIR

Cyril Frankel

- Dave Randle said he'd put it out on his imprint Bank House Books. So next time I visited Cyril I took my little Archos audio recorder (committed Francophile, I remained long loyal to this now obscure French tech company) and began collecting Cyril's oral history. To a background of whistling taxi cabs and clanking scaffold poles through the raised sash windows of 131 Harley Street, Cyril told me his remarkable story.

I typed it as prose, pretty well exactly as he told it to me. I kept Cyril's conversational style. I felt this best conveyed him. A mix of self-deprecation and what clearly had no business being depreciated. But unlike in the Emily book, I added nothing of me. Except a Foreword. Next to one by Alexandra Bastedo, sexy secret agent Sharron Macready in Cyril's TV series *The Champions* (1968). Happy to be between the covers next to Alexandra Bastedo.

Recording, transcribing, structuring, editing and laying out for posterity the remarkable stories of Cyril's very 20th Century life was a rich and life-affirming experience for me. It was also a great deal of work. Every once in a while I did stop and wonder why I was spending precious time in my prime, telling stories of someone's else's prime. Would Cyril be spending time on a project like this in his 40s? He was driven and ambitious to establish a career as a film director. I thought I was too. But I suppose there's another layer to my drive and ambition to tell stories. And that is not to leave behind ones that are in danger of being lost. Stories that should be told. Stories that would disappear if someone did not stop to tell them. *Hic Vivunt Vivere Digni* is the inscription above the Library mantelpiece at Knebworth House, *Here they live* [on these surrounding shelves] *that are worthy to live on!*

Cyril's book concludes: *And there we are - I am now in my eighties and I am enjoying life. It's been a rich life. Oh, it has.* Keeping Cyril's story simple - a K.I.S. to him - a straight chronology from birth to this lovely understated final comment, brought me a less positive Amazon review (anonymous): *Although the book itself might have benefited from a more experienced editor, I applaud Henry Cobbold's commitment to getting this life story into print. Cyril's unpretentious style is a journey through a remarkable life and an insight into a creative mind, which stretches beyond visual media into theatre and ballet, and modern ceramic art.*

I prefer Dave Randle's blurb: *Cyril's work and life are shot through with an underlying humour, a sense of humanity and a deep and unconventional spirituality - the honest and direct communication expressed in the title he chose for this book [**Eye to Eye**]. It was this intangible quality that attracted me to his work and to my first attempts to get his story told. It is an honour for Bank House Books finally to be able to bring him 'eye to eye' with the world at large.*

And it was an honour for me to be able to give something back to my friend, Cyril Frankel. I continued to visit him as his mind did eventually begin to go. Every time I went round,

Cyril was sure that he had worked at Knebworth once, but he couldn't remember when...

he was clutching the book on his lap. Apparently he would spend most of his day looking at it, long after he knew what the words meant. That made me feel good. I picture myself doing the same with this book. Possibly even before my mind goes.

What has shocked me since is that, when Cyril died in June 2017, there was not a single obituary for him in any newspaper. This was not because the obituary columns did not know about his death. Dave Randle informed them, offered to send them a precis of Cyril's life that he had written. Nothing appeared. The idea that a life as rich as Cyril Frankel's could pass unnoticed is a sobering thought.

As Shakespeare has Caesar say in *Antony and Cleopatra*, **The breaking of so great a thing should make a greater crack.**

In the summer of 2019 we held an exhibition in the Banqueting Hall of memorabilia from all the films and television shoots Knebworth House has hosted. Weaving between framed posters and typed memories of staff and family, we hung a washing line the length of the long hall and suspended (using inserted paper clips) the DVD covers (and some obscure VHS ones) of every fiction film and fiction TV show that has filmed with us. We came up with 78 of them. It was not completely exhaustive. I didn't hang the DVD cover of *Paul Raymond's Erotica* (1982). This curio had slipped in during the early 1980s with some 'bare' horseback riding in front of Knebworth House. It did have a vague story, but it was fiction with a small 'f', and would have attracted disproportionate attention. As it has in this paragraph.

78 is a lot of films. But this is stretched over 66 years. The first film was 1956's *Anastasia* with Ingrid Bergman and Yul Brunner. In this we are a single shot of Helen Hayes pulling up in front of a Danish castle. My grandparents would only countenance exterior filming. There was no interior filming at Knebworth House until the 1970s. My parents were more relaxed about the house being full of strangers. They let Michael Winner eat in their private dining room, during the making of *The Big Sleep* (1978). They gave *The Shooting Party* (1985) the run of the entire house. The first film to use the interior, I think, was the sex comedy, *Keep It Up Downstairs* (1976), a play on the popular TV series *Upstairs Downstairs* (1971-1975).

This did have a story. Jack Wild (aka *Oliver!*'s Artful Dodger) was more interested in his science experiments in the cellar than the shenanigans upstairs, until subplots converge with his invention of a rubber prophylactic. So I did hang that DVD cover.

What was most noticeable about the sequence of 76 films and series was that in the early ones Knebworth House tended to play run-down old ruins and forgotten gothic castles. In the more recent one the house has been playing home to royalty and oligarchs. As custodians of Knebworth House we must be doing something right. Our restoration program has clearly made progress. Specifically we've made hay as the interior of Balmoral, the royal family's Scottish retreat. Knebworth House has been Balmoral now in four separate projects. Why the Queen bothers to go all the way to Scotland for her holidays, I do not know. She might as well get off the train in Stevenage and stay with us.

At Knebworth/Balmoral with the Queen Mother, the Duke of Edinburgh, Diana Spencer, Princess Margaret, my sister Rosina Dorelli and Ruth Lady Fermoy, Diana's grandmother

One of the more high profile projects to feature us as Balmoral was the 2010 film *The King's Speech*. This shot for two days in February, which turned out to be more exciting than expected. A beast-from-the-east blizzard blew through, shutting down much of the country. A good many of the crew were staying in Knebworth Park at the Novotel. The actors, however were going to struggle to get home to London and then get back again in the morning. Playing the Queen Mum, was old chum Helena Bonham Carter. She asked if she and Colin Firth and Timothy Spall could spend the night.

Timothy ended up risking the storm. But Helena and Colin stayed. We had an amusing hatches-battened-down dinner, before showing them to the two most haunted bedrooms we could find. Colin confessed to having been at Knebworth in his youth. He jumped the fence into the 1979 Led Zeppelin concert. Immediately I demanded £7.50 off him. Sometime later I heard a rumour that he had joined a party of Repton schoolboys who had been driven to the concert by Jeremy Clarkson, who had borrowed his parents' Range Rover without asking. Please somebody tell me that this legend is true.

The following morning Colin made the most of not having to get up at 5am to negotiate the snowbound roads from London. He emerged from his haunted room at five to nine (his make up call time), but lost his way to the kitchen. He walked into Ken Holmes, our Head of Maintenance, who had no idea who he was,

"What are you doing here?"

"I'm an actor."

"You're not meant to be in here yet."

"I know, I am trying to find the door."

Ken showed him the door, briskly and brusquely, locking it firmly behind him. Colin was now standing in the front courtyard, snow falling all around him. The front courtyard was also locked. Colin could see his Unit Base in the distance on the other side of the balustrade. It was 9 o'clock. He was due in make up. He climbed the fence.

I told him that when he came back to make *St Trinian's 6*, I wouldn't bother to open up for him, he was so adept at climbing our fences. He lied that he wouldn't be doing *St Trinian's 6*. He did, however, come back a few years later to play crippled Colin's uncle, Archibald Craven, in *The Secret Garden* (2020). He was only here a day, and that was to burn the house down in a drunken stupor. I don't know, you invite a guy to supper...

I got my own back. Because of Colin Firth, I wrote what has become my favourite of all my screenplays. *The Apostasy of Francesco Terremoto.*

I am a fan of magazine and newspaper features where the interviewee is asked a set of random questions, which are often more revealing than tailored interview questions. I recall one - I think in *Smash Hits* - in which singer Terry Hall listed as his 'dream house', 'Knebworth Hall'.

I've done a couple of these over the years. I did one for The Cuckoo Club newsletter (left). The Cuckoo Club was a private members club on the site of the old Stork Club in Swallow Street. My friend Nick Valentine (from promoting the Erotica Expo days) had asked me to be a 'committee member'. I'd done this once before for a private members club on Shaftesbury Avenue called Teatro, set up by Lee Chapman and Leslie Ash. I recall sitting between designer Wayne Hemingway and comedian Rowland Rivron deciding who should be accepted as a member of a club that would have me - and them - as a member. It was very flattering to be asked, but let's face it, I was miscast in this role. I could count on one hand the number of times I have thought my evening would be best spent at a Private Members Club. In fact the only time I recall was once seeking some light relief after watching Tom Hiddleston bloodily knifed to death at the Donmar, Nick welcomed Rob Knepper and me at the Playboy Club, but I had to ask that we retire to a deserted antechamber as the main club room was too loud for any verbal communication. For me, the only reason to have a club membership in London is to have somewhere with a decent bathroom for when the rich food and sugar you'll be dining out on grips your guts. The London Library used to be good for this. Lovely old fashioned tiled space.

Where was I? Magazine interviews. The auctioneers Bonhams does a regular feature on the last page of its big glossy quarterly entitled 'My Favourite Room'. One day I found myself reading the Colin Firth edition of this feature. He chose the San Brizio Chapel in Orvieto Cathedral (right) as his favourite room in the world. He declared himself completely bowled over by its Luca Signorelli fresco, the *Apocalypse*, "it's pure theatre, it's Hollywood special effects."

After the second Cannes where *The Last Days of Pompeii* had been 'blown out of the water' by someone else's Pompeii project, I impulsively just got in my car and drove nine hours to Orvieto. I recalled this article, and wondered if there was a movie to be made about this room. If there was, I knew at least Colin would read it. Well, at least the pages about the cathedral.

If you've ever been to Orvieto Cathedral, you know that the San Brizio Chapel is indeed a magical place. Even the rampant atheist in me is cowed within these breathtaking stones. Like how the rampant atheist in me is subdued and soothed by Franco Zeffirelli's beautiful *Brother Sun Sister Moon* (1972). Or simply by Judi Bowker. Anyway, I'd never been to Assisi either. So early the next morning I set

off through seductive silver-misted Umbrian hills to find Assisi. On my stereo was an album I had discovered in FNAC in France, *Uncaged*, by half-Italian, half-French artist Charles Pasi. If you ever do an early morning drive from Orvieto to Assisi, I do recommend you listen to this album. The whole day became the closest I've ever come to a religious experience.

The drive takes you through the hill town of Todi, past its beautiful hillside cathedral.

In particular I became obsessed with *Uncaged*'s opening track, which to me was the perfect atheist anthem, *"Don't wait any longer for the holy prophet... He's on vacation now... He let us down... It's up to us, to grab another man's hand..."*

In Assisi I walked through the main part of the town, then diverted through backstreets to a hill path to the summit. There was no one else on this hill path... until I came to a junction with another quiet path, where a beautiful girl with flowing tresses and a flowing summer dress, barefoot, carrying her sandals, joined the path to the summit. We would have been walking up together if I had continued, so I held back and let her continue, as clearly she was having a moment. When I reached the top, she was

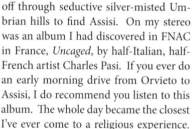

Assisi hill path

gone. But that was all I needed. I had my love scene. You'll remember the formula for how to write a screenplay (p.166). Dream up a love scene. How did the lovers get to this place is the first half of the screenplay, and how do they get out of it is the second half of the screenplay.

On that hilltop in Assisi, on a beautiful late Spring day, I could understand how people could have a Damascene moment. How, in the intense beauty of a moment, they could commit to anything. Anything.

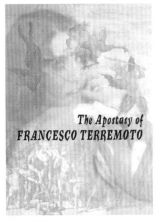

On my way down the hill I stopped at the St Francis Basilica (left, and above). In the Gift Shop, I watched on a little presentation screen the footage that a television crew had captured inside the cathedral on September 26th 1997, when, during an earthquake aftershock, the roof collapsed, killing four people in the nave below.

An earthquake. At the end of the century. I looked back over all the major earthquakes in Italy in the 20th Century. All the way back to the cataclysmic earthquake in the Sicilian port of Messina in December 1908. And I created a character who was present at every single one of them. Not God. But someone having to pick up the pieces that God leaves behind.

The Apostasy of
FRANCESCO TERREMOTO

But where was my part for Colin? My brother Peter provided the final piece of the puzzle. I wanted a lead role that someone like Colin Firth would be interested in playing. In other words I wanted an against-type role for a matinee idol. Peter told me about a very special Franciscan order of friars in Bradford who work with street kids. These holy men wear their hair shaved or bald, but grow long and bushy beards. Perfect.

And then I remembered the unusual earthquake that happened in the Midlands of England in the week of the collapse of the bank Northern Rock, that signalled the 2008 financial crash.

I had everything I needed.

The Apostasy of
FRANCESCO TERREMOTO

Original Screenplay by
Henry Cobbold

THE APOSTASY OF FRANCESCO TERREMOTO

An inner-city monk in northern England loses his faith, abandons his brotherhood, and walks to Italy on a pilgrimage through Europe and the beauties, tragedies and loves of his past.

Leeds, England - February 2008. Brother Francis (late 40s) lives in Hell. He has devoted his adult life to his Franciscan mission on the frontline of poverty, desolation and crime in a northern English city. One terrible night, his life collapses. A young mother dies of cancer making him promise to look after her teenage children and baby grandchild. Leaving the hospital in the middle of the night, Francis watches as one child is knifed in a gangland fight and the other leaves her baby to batter her brother's assailant. Francis's mental breakdown is complete when the violence is punctuated by a rare (for England) earthquake. He sees it as a sign.

Orvieto, Italy – August 1969. A minor earthquake rocks the beautiful cathedral. A Red Cross worker, Francesco (early 60s), finds an English boy, Antony (7), mesmerised by the frescos of Heaven and Hell in the evacuated San Brizio Chapel. The boy tells Francesco that he wants to be priest. Francesco warns the boy that priests live in Hell not in Heaven – he knows this because he once was a Franciscan monk. Francesco gives Antony a keepsake medal from an earthquake in Sicily and tells him that it is up to the two of them to make the world a better place. Heaven can look after itself.

Hull, England - February 2008. Brother Francis trudges through the rain-swept night, clutching the abandoned baby, towards Italy. He is picked up by a Polish truck driver, who offers to buy him passage on an immigrant-smuggler boat if he allows him to return the baby to safety. A salt-o'-the-sea female smuggler passes the troubled monk to a bohemian Dutch smuggler's boat, and the warmth of a beautiful Dutch girl, who offers all the comforts Brother Francis has spent a lifetime denying. Francis tells her he is walking to Italy to find a man from his past who is 100 years old. The Dutch girl says he must walk quickly. Francis knows the man will be there. He called for him - with an earthquake.

Messina, Italy – December 1908. An American Red Cross nurse finds an abandoned baby in the apocalyptic earthquake ruins. She adopts the child, christens him 'Francesco Terremoto'.

Leeds, England - February 2008. The Friars are visited by the Police, looking for Brother Francis and the baby. Brother Damian (40s) refuses to believe that the selfless Francis would have abandoned his bothers. An accountant arrives for an appointment with Francis, tells Damian and the Police that the Friary is bankrupt, due to the collapse of the Northern Rock bank.

Zoetermeer, Holland - February 2008. Brother Francis contemplates suicide, but the words and call of his mentor, Francesco, keep him going through the degradations and trials of his penniless journey by foot. He spends desolate nights in toilet cubicles, on park benches, whilst resisting the temptations of a drug den in Gouda and the sanctuary of Franciscan retreats along the Dutch canals.

Todi, Italy – September 1980. Antony and his friend Clem (both 18) seek out Francesco (now 70s) at the Red Cross district headquarters that he runs in an Umbrian hillside town. The lapsed monk remembers the boy, who still wants to become a priest. As the boys train with the Croce Rossa, during an idyllic Italian summer, the saintly but contrary Francesco continues to dissuade Antony from the priesthood and God. Playfully, he taunts Antony with his beautiful daughter, Anna (17) – and with horror stories of the senseless destruction caused by the many earthquakes he has witnessed throughout his life. Whenever there is an earthquake in Italy, as though by God's intervention, Francesco is always present. Antony reasons that it is God making sure Francesco is always where he is needed. Francesco insists it is proof there is no God.

Leeds, England - February 2008. The baby is left at the Friary door (by the Polish lorry driver), but Francis does not return. The Police use Francis's good name as bait to capture the baby's mother, the runaway teenage and avenger of her brother's knifing. Brother Damian hands the girl over to the Police, but he must still find Francis or the Friary will have to close. The only clues he has are a few relics from Francis's trips to Italy, as a teenager, including intimate photographs of a beautiful German girl in Assisi that he finds in a locked tin – the only lock in the whole Friary.

Castellucio, Italy – September 1980. From the retreat of an isolated derelict farmhouse in the most earthquake prone region of Italy, Francesco wages his own war against the injustices of the world and of God, through letter-writing and lending his support to international humanitarian charities. Antony continues to spar with Francesco, saying that it is people like him and Padre Pio and Mother Theresa that are proof of God's existence and of God's love – but Antony is becoming distracted by Anna, and must watch as the beautiful Italian girl and his best friend Clem fall into a hot teenage romance. Clem reminds Antony that, the year before, in Assisi, it was him that got the attention.

Assisi, Italy – September 1979. Antony spends a magical afternoon climbing to the top of this sacred town. On the hill path he meets a free-spirited German girl, Klara (18), who is contemplating returning to a life of duty at her family business, an apotheke (drug store) in the German town of Tubingen. Seduced by the beauty of the moment, and his companion, Antony is still not able to shake his principles, and his calling to be a priest. He remains awkward, arguing with the girl that virtue is the strength of will to fulfil your destiny. For the first time in his life, he is kissed by a girl – but he runs from it.

Tubingen, Germany – March 2008. Worn and ragged, his long hair and chest-length beard matted and wild, his feet bound to disintegrating sandals, Brother Francis continues his pilgrimage south, through the industrial towns of the Rhine. His strength failing him, on the verge of collapse, he finds himself at the hillside town of Tubingen. He shuffles from apotheke to apotheke, until he finds an old one in the town square, and the woman running it, Klara (now 40s) – but he loses his courage again, and flees, to the top of the town. Klara follows him. Not recognising him, she takes him in, cleans and bandages his infected worn feet. He asks her to shave off his thick chest-length monk's beard – as she does, and his face is revealed, she knows exactly who he is. He tells her that he now knows he was wrong about virtue and duty. Klara is divorced, lonely, and although that moment in Assisi has lived with them both, throughout their lives, she will not acquiesce to the temptation that he now wants to give into. She equips him to continue his journey, suggesting that, on his way back, he should look her up.

Sant'Angelo dei Lombardi, Italy – November 1980. Antony and Clem join Francesco and Anna on a trip to another hillside village, in Campania, to visit Anna's dying grandmother. Antony is taking communion in a convent for orphan girls when a massive earthquake hits. He manages to save two of the children before being buried in the rubble. Clem and Anna are almost killed in a collapsing bar where most of the village are crushed watching a football match on TV. Francesco survives the collapse of the hospital, and takes charge of the scene of devastation in his Croce Rossa Land Rover.

Orvieto, Italy – May 2008. Refreshed, and with a dawning comprehension of his place in the world, Francis crosses the Alps on foot and returns to Orvieto, and the frescos of Heaven and Hell. To his disbelief, he learns that Francesco died ten years before. Anna now runs the Croce Rossa headquarters in Todi. Francis revisits the happy scenes of his teenage years, and the Croce Rossa – but Anna is not there. Instead, he is met by Brother Damian.

Sant'Angelo dei Lombardi, Italy – November 1980. Francesco rescues Antony from the rubble of the collapsed convent. Together with Clem and Anna, they go searching for survivors in the ruins of the devastated village. Francesco is recognised by grief-stricken stragglers as the man who is always present at earthquakes, the man who causes earthquakes. Antony watches as Francesco is beaten by the superstitious locals to a bloody pulp. Clem intervenes, and is knifed – Anna intervenes, and her face is cruelly slashed. Antony is traumatised.

Erith, England – July 1986. Antony professes his vows and becomes Brother Francis. He spends a small inheritance from his deceased parents on creating the inner-city mission in Leeds and retreats from life to devote himself to the suffering of others.

Todi, Italy – May 2008. Francis tells Damian that he is no good to the order now – he hands back his monk's habit and suggests that Damian might as well hang him with its rope, and its three knots for the vows of poverty, chastity and obedience. Damian tells Francis that Anna was left a gift by Francesco on his death, which she does not want – the isolated derelict farmhouse in the most earthquake prone region of Italy. The lentil farm will produce a small income which will be enough for the mission in Leeds to survive.

Castellucio, Italy – May 2008. Francis returns to the derelict farmhouse on the distant hillside, where the view is now a glorious patchwork of lentil blossoms down in the valley. An image of Francesco appears to him, still berating him for believing in God, but crediting him for having the courage of his convictions, being always willing to test those convictions, and ultimately being happy, like him, to be wrong. As Francisco's image fades, Anna appears. She is real. Beneath a black eye patch and a long scar across her face, the bitterness of Clem's death has finally faded. She wants to know if Francis is the sort of person who can keep rebuilding a farmhouse that God/earthquakes keep knocking down? "We'll see". Together they walk down the hillside into the flowers of the valley. Anna tells Francis how Francesco died – in the earthquake of September 1997, that brought down the ceiling of the Basilica of St Francis in Assisi on top of him, in a cloud of dust...

I love so many things about this screenplay. I am tempted to print the whole thing in this book. Foremost, I love that it is all true. All the earthquakes are real. All the incidents associated with the earthquakes are real. All the places. Situations. Everything. Except, of course, for a man who was present at every one of them.

Unless of course you believe in God.

I enjoyed naming the kid who wakes Francis from the side of his bed Gabe, after the angel Gabriel. I enjoyed naming the Polish lorry driver Michal, after St Michael. I enjoyed naming the Brexiteer boat captain, Sharon, after Charon, the ferryman to Hades...

The submerged church at Reschensee, the entrance to Italy

And then there were the weird things that happened subsequently. Inner city kids knifing each other - which some thought extreme in my screenplay - evolved into a common and endemic problem in Britain after I'd written it. Particularly shocking, and waking up the media to the problem, was the knifing of a teacher in Harehills, the exact district in Leeds where I had set my fictional knifing. Bizarre. Then, there was a particularly destructive earthquake soon after in the Umbrian hills, close to Colin Firth's Italian home. He wrote to me, "We felt the earthquake quite violently, but our town was unaffected. Really devastating for the region obviously. Thousands

Reliefs on the exterior of Orvieto Cathedral

The steps of Orvieto Cathedral

of people without homes. It's going to be an ongoing crisis for many years to come."

Like with my Emily book, life seemed to collide with my work. As with the Emily book, this gave me a validatory feeling that I'd written something that was waiting, wanting to be written. Some divine affirmation that the project was worthwhile. Except I'd have to believe in God to believe that.

And so far God has not pulled the strings to get the project made. So I don't think he likes it. And Colin's with God on this one. The early signs were good. "I did tease myself with the first few pages - which were inspired. Always thought the San Brizio fresco was a movie. Looking forward to the read." Then it went to the partners in his production company, and I never heard another word about it.

I'm yet to find out why. In these situations - because you know there's a good film in your screenplay - you look for other reasons, aside from your screenplay. There is probably nothing to these musings. But they make you feel better. In this case I wondered if the role I had written was too much of a split role, jumping between young Antony and Brother Francis. Colin Firth had done a split role in *The Railwayman* (2013), where half the film was his younger self. Possibly the younger sections of my piece were too much of a Gap Year (urgh, p.93) paean, with too many cultural references to Supertramp and the Commodores? Maybe the unchecked cod Italian in the draft I sent him was simply too silly, and took him out of the narrative?... Maybe he gave it to his Italian wife to read and it quickly took her out of the

Apotheke in Tubingen

narrative?... You can sit wondering about these things, or you can polish up a new draft and go looking for others who might relate to it.

I did this, and got some encouraging responses from across Europe, pleasingly including Italy. The film travels from good tax scheme territory to good tax scheme territory - from Yorkshire, to the Netherlands, to Germany, to Italy... there's even a French tramp that Brother Francis meets along the way... all it needs is a Spanish director to be the perfect Euro-pudding of tax-credits and interminable screen pre-credits & animated logos. Call Julio Medem! But of course European directors don't make Original Screenplays that are not their own. And here in England, add to that the rule that it has to be a book first. It has to have someone else's pre-approval to be any good.

So maybe one day I'll write it as a book.

Coda. A couple of years later, I did the early morning drive from Orvieto to Todi again with my son Edward. At Todi we stopped at the Cathedral, and explored the arches below, where the teenagers punch it out in my story. We explored streets of tall marble tombs in the Cimitero Vecchio where I had buried Francesco's mother, Lillian, the Red Cross nurse. We passed between the photographs set in the tombstones -

mustachioed men in ties, Fedora hats... to a low wall overlooking a stunning view of the valley - the sun-softened Umbrian countryside, dotted with little frazioni farm buildings (far right, below).

The Cathedral at Todi, top right, and above, the Cimitero Vecchio

> FRANCESCO
> You see, Antony... In Italy, we build stronger houses for our dead than for our living. And yet, they all live in heaven. So why do they need these houses?

> ANT
> I think the point is, that <u>we</u> need them.

> FRANCESCO
> We need these palaces for our dust? And yet for ourselves we build with dust - with rubble stone and flour mortar, our wooden floors barely attached to the walls. We build marble houses for the dead and for God - and plasterdust tombs for the living!

Writing this story of travel and far away places from my study desk on the top floor of Knebworth House had been a very different experience to writing about Italy (in *Sirens*), and Spain (in *Madrid '37*) and France (in *Strange Relations*), from my study desk in Los Angeles in the 1980s. In those days I had relied on paper road maps and Green Michelin guides with a paragraph describing each village. Twenty-five years later I have Google Street View. On my large Eizo computer screen at Knebworth I can magically walk down the streets of Italian towns, explore the arches beneath the cathedral, look into the windows of the butcher's shops in Norcia, or peer through the gates of the Croce Rossa headquarters in Todi (right). Extraordinary.

But on my real life trip, with Edward, I brazenly drove myself through these gates, and up the drive of the Croce Rossa headquarters in Todi. There was no one about, just an open door into the main building (left). We walked in, and knocked on the glass of the door of a Reception Room. A surprised middle-aged lady looked up from an old grey 1990s computer, "Prego?".

I started to try and explain that I was a screenwriter, and that I had written a film in which the director of this branch of the Croce Rossa was the hero... I was talking in English, and it was me that was now talking cod. The lady had no idea what I was on about. But clearly I was a visitor with some passion, and no malice aforethought, so she stopped what she was doing and went to get Il Direttore. He appeared, a serious middle-aged Italian man, who spoke no English either. But there he was, standing before me, my 'Francesco Terremoto'.

I sat at the old 90s computer and pulled up Google Translate. I typed in my explanation for barging in on their day. For all I know, Google told them that my hippopotamus had piles. I don't think they would have looked any less bemused. But they were friendly, and said they would like to read the story. So I downloaded a pdf of the screenplay onto their desktop, and we all shook hands, and Edward and I stepped back out into the bright sunlight.

As we approached our car, what I can best describe as a hospital-gowned 'mental patient' came towards us, hairless, toothless-mouth open, addressing us with a wretched urgency. Clearly there was even less chance of communicating with him. So we smiled, warm, sympathetic, and manoeuvred around him to the car.

As we three-point turned, trying to avoid running over the distressed man, we glanced back at the building, and there was the Receptionist and Il Direttore standing in the doorway watching us go. I suppose there was nothing strange about this. My son and I were unquestionably the strange ones in this scenario. But I couldn't help all manner of gothic stories passing through my head - most obviously Edgar Allan Poe's *The Soothing System of Dr Tarr and Professor Feather* - goodness, the very first adaptation I ever attempted, as a dance piece for Presdales schoolgirls (I should have put that in Chapter 11) - in which the inmates have taken their carers captive and are now happily running the asylum themselves.

The primary musing this experience left with me, however, is that this place in these ancient Italian hills, which had grown so alive in my imagination, and from which I'd dreamt up my very favourite of all my stories, has a million stories of its own that are beyond my dreams... a myriad of stories that I will never know.

CHAPTER THIRTY-EIGHT

The Pool

*Nobody important really. Just a movie writer with a couple
of 'B' pictures to his credit.*

The poor dope. He always wanted a pool.

*Well, in the end he got himself a pool, but the price turned
out to be a little high.*

Sunset Boulevard (1950) Billy Wilder   Charles Brackett
D.M. Marshman Jr.

In December 2019, I made the most expensive purchase I've ever made. Excluding the long lost houses in Marylebone and West Hollywood; and the long lost Avid Film Composer... But three times as expensive as my current car, my 2015 Toyota Aygo. I bought an Exercise Pool. Note, Exercise Pool. Not Hot Tub,

My justification was, that unlike my car, I would use it every day. And so far

I have. Except for one morning when there was a hurricane, and another when I was in Norfolk. Since I turned 50, I have been conscious of the need to exercise or die.

This is a slight change of heart. As previously mentioned, my instinct has been to stand - or sit - with Peter O'Toole, "The only exercise I take is following the coffins of my friends who took exercise." I have friends and relations who have died, at a younger age than I am now, rowing, running... I recall what rowing as a teenager at school did to the skin of my poor blameless buttocks. Bouncing up and down the Knebworth House stairs five or six times a day tells me what taking up 'running' would do to my knees. Even - sitting down - using my Toyota Aygo's clutch pedal, now messes with my left knee. To lose the freedom of long drives in Europe because of this is a miserable thought. I could switch to an automatic transmission. But without that gearknob gripped in your hand where's the feeling of being in charge of your own destiny? Besides, I can't change my car. Because I've just bought an expensive Exercise Pool.

I hope my advancing age allows me a few more years of the freedom of the road. I'm prepared to exercise for 30 minutes every day to increase the chance of it. I do aspire to a few more years of incidents of interest in my life - who knows, maybe even enough to justify a Volume Two, *Happy Highways From Knebworth House*. But I'm also very aware of my own mortality. My father - who medical science suggests will be a Norwegian Blue fairly soon - has always resolutely refused to talk about his death. I don't get this. It makes it so much harder on love ones. So much harder for them to plan your wellbeing, happiness and finances in your dotage. So much harder for them to come to terms with your mortality. Surely that's not what you want?

I remain consistently conscious that I could drop down dead at any moment. Consistently unconscious. Instantly oblivious of all cares and worries and bills that I leave behind for my loved ones. I'd rather I'd been through it all with them, and talked about how I feel about it, and how they might feel about it. First.

My life will be measured in years - a short one, or a long one - but as I reasoned when I wrote about my great-great-great-aunt Emily, every life goes from A to Z. Some just get to Z quicker than others. There's still an 'L' in everyone's life, and an 'M'... and all the other letters. The measure of a life is not its length. It's what the letters spell.

We should not curse 'Z'. Only the uncertainty of the timing of its appearance.

Here I am writing the last chapter of this book (Chapter 39 I keep as my 'Angels' chapter, for 'thank you's), but I'm still worrying that Fate won't give me time to finish it. This is not as morbidly self-obsessed as it sounds. It's quite morbidly obsessed. But it's not as morbidly self-obsessed as it would have been a few months ago.

There is, as I write in May 2020, a killer virus sweeping the world. It kills you with greater ease if you are over 50, and like cheese. It nearly did for the Prime Minister, who is younger than me, because he likes cheese. And it doesn't give you much time to think about it. You get a cough, and if you've got sticky blood or have been pummelling your insulin production with ketchup, before you know it you're on a trolley in a hospital corridor with a tube in your throat and no chance of telling your family that you've changed your mind and you now don't want *We'll Meet Again* sung at your funeral. You would still quite like *I'll Be Seeing You*. And that song *Joy* by Janis Ian... But it matters not a jot, because your family won't be able to have a funeral for you. Because the whole country, by Government directive, is locked down.

Hundreds of thousands of humans, across the world, are hitting 'Z' before medical science would previously have called it. Horror stories abound, as we bind ourselves to our televisions and phones to understand it all. I consider, with awe, how that Director of the Todi Croce Rossa's last few months have been.

I am not a novice at lockdown. I've been under authoritarian curfew before. Quite often. At boarding school. During race riots in Los Angeles. In a chlorine chemical cloud in Old Knebworth when a neighbouring swimming pool supply warehouse burnt down. I have nurtured over many years an imagination to deal with being imprisoned. I can entertain myself quite happily under lock and key.

I do accept that my cages over the years have been particularly gilded ones. And I'll confess to you that if I do ever end up in prison I'd prefer it to be a Scandinavian one rather than a Central American one. But I will always be content to travel the mere paces from my bed to my desk, from my desk to my bed, from my bed to my desk... I understand the privilege in that. I understand the privilege of walking these 10 paces on a floor that somebody else carpentered and on a carpet that, usually, someone else hoovers. When I do get out the Henry hoover - as has been the Herculean extra burden of my huge historic house during the lockdowns of 2020 - I will find enjoyment doing this, semi-naked like Melanie Griffith in *Working Girl* (1988), listening on noise-cancelling headphones to self-improving podcasts that otherwise I would likely not find time for.

And while I'm fiddling with the hoover bag, the world is burning. Economies are crashing, people are dying alone and in pain, and the world, they say, will never be the same. Yes, I have no business enjoying this lockdown.

And if it goes on much longer I will have no business. For in 2020, like showbusiness, there's no business (*In A Lonely Place*, 1950). All the hard work that Martha has put into Knebworth House over the last 25 years could unravel if we continue not to be allowed to open for visitors. The contract with our catering company comes to an end in August. Finding a new catering company to take on our venue - and our catering staff - when there is no public catering going on anywhere in the country is not, you can imagine, proving easy. We started with 20 applications.

Now we have two. But I have faith that Knebworth House will get through it. It made it through the ravages of the 20th Century, and the love of a large family gives it as good a chance as any of making it through the ravages of the 21st.

How much more time have Martha and I got here? I don't know. We have a fine twenty-eight year old son who, if and when he finds the right partner, has enough of his father's passion and his mother's good sense to play a deft hand if he's dealt one. Once he finds that partner, we'll wind down our time at Knebworth House.

Of course, I will be back. If I expire in one piece I have requested in my Last Will and Testament (good track by Ed Harcourt, my Godmother's son) to be borne aloft to a shelf in the family Mausoleum in Knebworth Park. I'll note here, in case I don't have the time to tell you in my dying breath, that after all the sad songs and the tears (like Oliver Reed, "If I die I want everyone to come to my funeral and cry, and if they don't cry they're not allowed in" - quoted by his brother David in Robert Sellers' biography *What Fresh Lunacy Is This?*), I'd like to be carried out of the Banqueting Hall to the loud boisterous salsa of French artist Dany Brilliant's version of *My Way* - proof conclusive that there is a place for maracas at a funeral.

If I am not in one piece, I'm not so bothered. I don't want limbs hanging off me at those late night card games with my ancestors at the Mausoleum card table. The family accountant, Andrew Dagless, already knows that if I'm ashes, he's expected to set off, like Brother Francis from Leeds, all the way to the nudist beach in Cap D'Agde, and scatter me in the sand so I can stick to the bottoms of the beautiful sunny naturists of the world.

I do like the idea of being out in Knebworth Park for all eternity though. I like the idea of my bones vibrating to the Prodigys and Metallicas of the future at Knebworth Park concerts. I want to hear the happy howls of the harts of Hertfordshire rutting by night, and the happy howls of overexcited children rampaging to the

Adventure Playground by day. I want to hear the flap of rook wings, the low rumble of the A1(M), the Jurassic roar of the orange jets on their way to the Mediterranean. These are the things I want to hear to the end of time.

I like also the idea of being visited by my descendants and postbears. I make the observation in the Emily book, *In The Bosom Of Her Father*, that if one of my descendants visits me on my 188th birthday - as I visited Emily in the same Mausoleum on her 188th birthday - it will be the year 2150. Half way through the next century. If there are still Lyttons living in Knebworth House - as I very much hope there

are - I imagine them plucking a dusty copy of this book off the library shelf. I imagine them getting to know me as intimately as you now know me having made it - I'm impressed - to p.468. I imagine them then finding the long Mausoleum key and spending a moment contemplating my dust. Not that it's the dust that matters (cf *The Last Days of Pompeii*, right). But hopefully some stories are given resonance by the residue of me.

And some of the gags, in 2050, are still good for a laugh.

As Meryl Streep says as Karen Blixen in *Out of Africa* (1986), will Knebworth sing a song of me? Let's hope it's not *Would You Like To Suck My Thumb?* or anything by Toto. Let's hope my generation is remembered as the one that worked hard to set Knebworth House on a sure footing for the 21st Century (Martha). Let's hope it's remembered for preserving and evolving an internationally important archive of literature, film and family history (Henry). That would do me.

More likely of course, is that my L.D.O.B. - my life defining obituary byline - (should I, wrongly, be thought by the broadsheets to be more important than Cyril

Photo: Rob Ryder

Frankel, and get a newspaper obituary) will say *"wrote a couple of rude films, but married well"*. The guides and room wardens in Knebworth House will look a little flushed and sheepish and whisper, out of earshot of the children, that the first three decades of the 21st Century were the time of 'The Blue Baron'. The 'Heir On A G-String'. "We keep his papers in brown paper bags, locked away only for academics and aesthetes. Can I tell you about the next generation?..."

Hopefully the future card-carrying couple of Historic House enthusiasts will persist with difficult questions. "Is there anything of his on display in the tour?"

"I'm afraid that's impossible. He simply acquired too many things for anything to be put out on display. I mean, there's the Joan Fontaine Collection - the largest in the world beyond the Oscar-winning actress's papers at Boston University; the big plastic tubs of film director Cyril Frankel's Archive of film ephemera; the many shelves of late 20th Century film critic Barry Norman's film book library (wonderfully donated by his daughters Samantha and Emma)... along with his own extensive Film, Bande Dessinée, Pre-Raphaelite, Classical Civilisation and Anti-Censorship libraries; then there's a whole room of the exhaustive Cobbold Family History Trust,

Photo: Diana Owen

"War's annals will fade into night ere their story die" - at Thomas Hardy's Max Gate

documenting the full history and achievements of that illustrious East Anglian family, passed over to him in 2021 by its compiler, his distant cousin, Anthony Cobbold; not to mention the shelves and shelves of his extensive collection of late 20th Century music and films, which in those days came within physical objects called Records, Audio Cassettes, Compact Discs, Video Cassettes, DVDs-"

"Oh yes, we quite see... quite see the problem. That's quite a pool of paper and plastic. We'd like a cup of tea now, and a piece of cake."

"Certainly. Just down the corridor there, ask the guide in the 21st Century costume... oh, there is a portrait of The Blue Baron, and his wife, that you'll pass on the way out. Best not to let the children look him in the eyes."

Allow yourself a soft gasp - Henry turns 50 on 12th May
and requests the pleasure of your perfect presence at

"It's All About *Me!*"

Knebworth House, Hertfordshire - Saturday 12th May 2012 - 6pm-11pm

Featuring:

6:00pm Chocolate Al Fresco... expect jaffa cakes, chocolate fingers and lime cordial

7:00pm Bouncing Beach Tunes... expect live music from the Balearics & Brighton (Ed!)

8:30pm Sauces on the Side... expect ketchup and things to dip in it 😊

9:00pm Boogie Oogie Oogie... expect 7 & 12 inches from 1978-1987 excl.

11:00pm Aygos Dress: Sartorial-if-at-all (don't come as you, come as me!)

Directions: SG1 2AX ~ via House Iron Gates - Park Code: 5050*

RSVP: henry@knebworthhouse.com (at your earliest convenience)

carnivores eat before ~ imbibers pre-imbibe, although as a selfless gesture
to non-teetotal friends and family, a light naked pink wine from Cap D'Agde
Quartier Naturiste will be served alongside French water.

DEMOLITION BY
HENRY
Phoenix Rd, Lon NW1 01 387 2

My 50th Birthday Party is where I would finish this book if I was writing a screenplay. An upbeat finale to leave you grinning and spinning as you leave the theatre. Like the day of my birth, it fell on a Saturday. It was the right night for a party. The right night to string a circle of all the coloured bunting of my life around Knebworth House. To collect together all the people I have known and loved. To end up in the pool naked with the Chairman of Deutsche Auto telling me he's going to build his factory next to my steel mills... no, not that - that's *Wearing A Smile* - but I did end up naked... and in the newspapers (well, the tabloid, *The Telegraph*). Because I gave a speech in front of 250 of my friends and relations in my birthday suit.

At the suggestion of my family, the evening was entitled - in bold letters - **It's All About *Me!*** The Banqueting Hall and Garden Terrace of Knebworth House was the venue. The cake was made of Maltesers. The hor d'oeuvres were Jaffa Cakes and Chocolate Fingers. There was no alcohol except pink wine from Cap D'Agde. All the music was strictly from 1978-1987 (the decade of my youth), except for live sets by my friend Miles Winter Roberts (with Nick Valentine on cajón, above left) and my son Edward's band Glass City Vice (left). The band (who'd only recently met their guitarist's father) are all hiding behind the chandelier in the photo of me giving my speech (above left), rather than stare at my arse - but I wanted them ready to come on instantly, axing power chords, in case I died on my feet

My 50th Birthday Party - including, left, with Elena Bonham Carter and a 'Dorian Gray' portrait by my sister...

...that hasn't worked. Thus this caption covering a shirt that's too tight. Although I do notice I'm considerably less bald than my mates

and the party needed rescuing. I'm pleased to say there was not a deathly silence. In fact there was a loud collective gasp. I'll take that. My father's jaw was still dropped fifteen minutes later. It's an image I'll treasure from the man who taught me everything there is to know about parties.

To give the illusion of the old me, I asked Maree at Expressions hairdressers in Knebworth village to sew in my old braids that I had cut off before I got married. It did the trick. Although they were a different colour - I notice my hair becomes increasingly 'blonde' - at least I could reply to the questions, "yes, it is all my own hair."

Instead of a fee to Miles I bought 100 copies of his CD *Daymaker* (2006), and put one in each of the paper party bags, which also contained a copy of Glass City Vice's first EP, *Landslide* (2012), my *Wearing A Smile* comic book and a packet of Maltesers. Beautiful summer music, beautiful summer illustrations and chocolate. The perfect party bag. I had the paper bags custom printed with an image of me at 21 and the

...WHERE ARE YOUR TROUBLES NOW?

words (from *Cabaret*) *"..where are your troubles now?"*

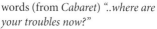

Ironically my two favourite tracks of this time - both by these artists - are not on these CDs. But they featured repeatedly through this magical weekend and now whenever I hear Glass City Vice's *Don't Change* or Miles's *Blue Sky Hotel* I feel a wash of happiness. Miles's recording of *Blue Sky Hotel* I keep permanently in the corner of my desktop screen to induce instant happiness whenever I need it - *summer's just a dream away...*

For my 45th birthday Miles gave me a single from 1962 (my birth year) on Ding-Dong records by Denise Bryer (the voice of Noddy). He said it was a 45 in honour of my 45th - but actually the single played at 33⅓ RPM - so I accepted it as a 7 inch in honour of my- I was telling you how much I love this beautiful beach bar bard from Ibiza. Miles and Nick are the source of so many of my favourite stories, including one from this night. Prior to the party, Nick rang me up to say his '+1' had changed. He then rang me again to say his '+1' had changed again. He then rang me a third time, to say his '+1' had changed again. The girl Nick did eventually turn up with promptly disappeared

Nick Valentine +2, but not his +1

off on the back of a younger guest's motorbike. Nick suspected the following morning that she was with Miles. He phoned a sleepy hungover Miles in bed, who couldn't make out what Nick was talking about. "Look next to you on the bed. Who's there?" "An empty bottle of wine?"

Richard Wells - also looking blonder - catches one of our old music videos.

The party was spread across the ground floor rooms of Knebworth House. The Malteaser tree and the Jaffa Cake & Chocolate Finger cake were in the Picture Gallery, as the chocolate chillout zone. The bar of lime cordial and pink wine was in the Library with a video compilation of favourite clips from films, and old home movies. The Terrace was for the veggie burger and fish & chip van. The Banqueting Hall was for dancing - to music from my years aged 18-25 - with a stage generously provided by Ronan Willson (whose much less important gig at that time was lighting Westminster Abbey for the Royal Wedding). I may not have looked like I did when I was 18, but my old Squire disco speakers were still sounding just as good as they did the day I bought them in a backstreet of Luton in 1980.

Planning the evening - which was spread out across a number of Knebworth House's rooms, and outside on its terrace - I was looking for a way to corral all the guests into the Banqueting Hall for my words of welcome. I asked Sarah-Lou Buckle to recommend two burlesque dancers who could lead a pied piper's march into the main room. The dancers rehearsed a choreographed march to Kid Creole and the Coconuts's *Don't Take My Coconuts*. Good track for it. Kid Creole is the only band I've ever marched from venue to venue for, when they were on tour back in 1982/3. It was either going to be *Don't Take My Coconuts* or Barbra Streisand's

Let's Hear It For Me! from *Funny Lady* (1975). The music came to a dramatic climax and the two dancers held out their jazz hands for my appearance from backstage...

I did not appear.

They had to shout for me, "Henry?!"

I shouted back, "Just trying to get my skinny jeans on!"

They made out that there wasn't time. So I came out anyway. Wearing a smile... and a red hat.

I did get dressed for my second speech of the night. Best to have your audience's concentration when you have something important to say. For this is the end of my lines, tracks and happy highways to Knebworth House. What do I find there? Of course, the companion who's been with me all along. My celestial soulmate. The one without whom the bunting of my life would flutter to the floor as triangles of old rags. My everything. My wife. Here is my sunset kiss. This is what I said on the night.

I looked up the word 'Boone' [Martha's maiden name]. *"'Boon. From the old Norse 'A Prayer'. From the old French 'bon' 'good'. From the Latin 'bonus'. And from the Middle English 'bone'...* [pause, shakes head] *Middle England. "Noun. A boon. 1) A benefit bestowed, especially in response to a request. 2) Something extremely useful, helpful, beneficial, an advantage, a godsend, a gift, something for which to be thankful!* [cheers from all around]

Martha Frances Boone Lytton Cobbold

...as in 'this battery booster is a boon for photographers'[?] *or 'the car was a boon to him'" - more relevant, for bringing back all that pink wine from France for the party (possible in Martha's RAV4, not my Aygo). "3) Archaic. A favour, request, a gift, a present, a grant, a benefaction, a donation, a gratuity, a hand out...*[?] *as in, 'he begged her to grant him one boon'"...*[?] *And 4) - perfectly appropriate - boon, "a desirable state... as in, 'a spanking breeze is a boon for sailors'...*[?]

Adjectives. Let's move on to "Adjective. Boon. 1) Convivial, jolly... as in 'a boon companion to all'. 2) Very close and convivial, special, or intimate... as in the phrase, 'a boon companion'."

Ladies and Gentlemen, will you please give a big hand to my wife... [cheers from all around]. *She's very difficult to buy presents for. Because she knows how thin my plastic is. And so, I'm going to... sing.* [groans, protestations...]

Okay, okay... I'll leave that to Frederick Tuxx [Paris-based Portland Oregon singer, whose album *All My Tomorrows* (2002) contains my favourite version of Alan Brandt & Bob Haymes's *That's All*]

- *Here's my spoken version...*
  "I can only give you love that lasts forever
  And a promise to be near each time you call
  And the only heart I own
  For you, and you alone

That's all. That's all."

I am 50-years-old. I have not achieved worldwide acclaim as the best selling author in the English-speaking world. I am not Viceroy of India or Governor of the Bank of England. But I have collected a few good stories for this old roof tree. And it has been great.

Great. Great. Great.

I used to think the meaning of life was apits. Not armpits. A. P. I. T. S.

'A Place In The Sun'.

A place in the sun, I long believed, was the human quest.

Now I have changed my mind.

Now I feel the meaning of life is:

'Stories'.

'Stories' are the human quest.

'Stories' are the meaning of life.

'Stories' are what we leave behind.

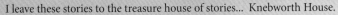

I leave these stories to the treasure house of stories... Knebworth House.

CHAPTER THIRTY-NINE

Angels

If you wonder who your heroes are
You never have to look too far

(*Confessions* - Bonneville)

Dad. I write this at a time when you can no longer get your words out. I lean close trying to decipher the whisper. But it is no use. You look so sad. I know this is the muscles of your face not working because of the Parkin-

son's. Your family is around you, but I know you are sad. It is a sunny summer scene you would have loved when you were... yourself. Now, you just want to get up and walk away. You don't want to be with us. It is too confusing. It is too sad.

This is not the you I will remember. The Dad in my heart is doing 'the dance of the fairies' in a French campsite after a boozy supper at a Michelin-starred restaurant. He is cajoling me out of bed for a midnight swim, or to be up at the top of the mountain to see the dawn, or face the challenge of the black ski run. He is side-stepping his skis back up the precipice and pulling his ski glove off with his teeth to reclip my frozen boots into my perpendicular skis. He is driving me in the hatchback boot wrapped in sleeping bags through Europe in the middle of the night so that we can squeeze every precious moment of sunshine and fun out of our beach or mountain adventure. He is suspending a Christmas stocking between two step ladders so its weight on my feet does not wake me. He is writing beautiful letters of love and support at all the important moments of my life. He is hurrying his Corn Flakes in a circular alphabet bowl and running for the train to a city job he tolerates so he can party like a prince all weekend. He is drinking whisky in the bath and reading me Hugh Lofting. He is coming down to supper in his evening kaftan, or his flashing Knebworth House jacket, Knebworth concert t-shirt and Brian May wig, and dancing inappropriately with every pretty girl. He is blasting *Dark Side of The*

Moon through the house the sleepy morning after. He is giving me more beautiful lifetime memories than a page can hold... *For all you mean to me.*

Mum. The retirement of travel, projects and companionship that you foresaw is not the one you are currently living. As you have always done, you are making a home for my father as his illness drifts him further from reality and deeper into reliance. I am so fortunate you started hummin' a song of me from 1962 and for all the sweet sweet summertimes you have given me. You are the one who is always sympathetic, the one who will always listen, who always has time for family and for me. The adventurer, always seeking a place in the sun, always with a Stucley story to tell. Maybe what the Stucley tells me, isn't altogther true, but I love every tale the Stucley tells me. I don't know any better ones. Do you?

For filling in my birth book (see inside front cover). For the love of movies and music and books and chocolate and ice cream and holidays and sunshine and sea. For the tears on the train platform and the school car park at the beginning of term. For the precious post cards from faraway places in the boarding school mail. For weekend treats in the West End. For walks on the Hartland cliffs, drives through the Arizona desert, and early morning sleeping bag runs to the concert field. For putting me on the train and meeting me from the plane. For playing me Wayne Fontana and Mindbenders and being happy to come with me to Supertramp concerts. Life has been so magical because of you.

Look at the family you have made.

It goes on...

...and on...

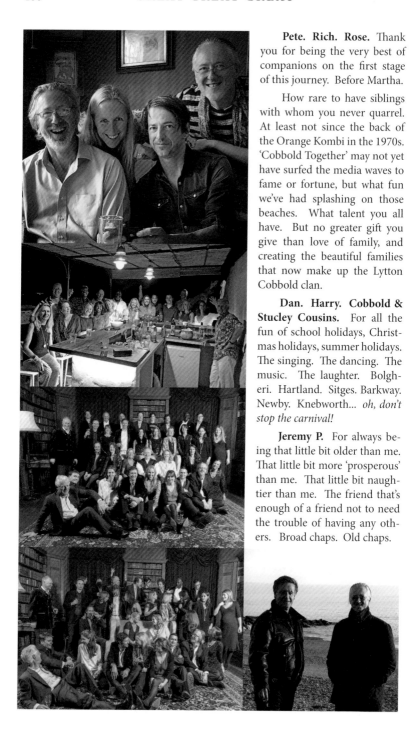

Pete. Rich. Rose. Thank you for being the very best of companions on the first stage of this journey. Before Martha.

How rare to have siblings with whom you never quarrel. At least not since the back of the Orange Kombi in the 1970s. 'Cobbold Together' may not yet have surfed the media waves to fame or fortune, but what fun we've had splashing on those beaches. What talent you all have. But no greater gift you give than love of family, and creating the beautiful families that now make up the Lytton Cobbold clan.

Dan. Harry. Cobbold & Stucley Cousins. For all the fun of school holidays, Christmas holidays, summer holidays. The singing. The dancing. The music. The laughter. Bolgheri. Hartland. Sitges. Barkway. Newby. Knebworth... *oh, don't stop the carnival!*

Jeremy P. For always being that little bit older than me. That little bit more 'prosperous' than me. That little bit naughtier than me. The friend that's enough of a friend not to need the trouble of having any others. Broad chaps. Old chaps.

Morwenna. Edward. The closing chapters of this book have been written in England's sunniest May on record, in the year 2020. Only in 1948 did England have anything close to as much sunshine. The irony is that we have also been living in the shadow of a worldwide pandemic. We have been at home at Knebworth House, as a family, for the whole month. We have been working, and work has continued with the extra challenge of an empty office. But, because of a nationwide curfew, there has not been the distraction of having to go anywhere, or see anyone, except a trip to the supermarket, or the post office. We have had the good fortune to stay healthy. And, the boon of all boons, we have had the privilege of the company of our two favourite people, our beautiful children. They, in turn, have had the company of their favourite people, Edward's Helena baking with rhubarb from the kitchen garden, Morwenna's Phil metal-detecting Elizabethan coins in the fields. Every evening we

have walked with the Great Danes in Knebworth House's lush oxygenated gardens, through breezes of white blossom from the snowdrop tree, bright purple rhododendrons, the scent of honeysuckle. It has been a month of Australian Christmases, without the stress of traditions and cocktail parties. What a moment in time. One I suspect we will not have again. It makes me think of Freddie Mercury vocal on *These Are The Days of Our Lives*. It makes me think of Bullshot's *"What will Heaven be like, Hugh?"*

How proud I am of my two children. There are no two happier, funnier, more personable people. Loyal, loving, hard-working and a credit to their family, their heritage and themselves. In their hands we can now comfortably and happily leave it all... and "run away!"

My great great great thanks to all whose images and words I've stitched with mine into this book - and extra especially if you are not referenced directly, which the passing of time annoyingly and embarrassingly frustrates. Please make me aware of omissions, so I can correct them in future editions.

Particular thanks to master illustrator Tim Major; to those who, for so long, have kept The 39 show on the road, Jocelyn and Sam; to Dean at Aitch Creative for stitching together the elements of the cover; to Daniel & Jamie at Jarrolds for the physical stitching of the book; and to the eye of the stitching needle that I camel dance my endless thread of nonsense through, my guardian and archangel, **Martha.**

You have this chapter because 39 is my lucky number.

APPENDIX

Portraits

One home there is, from which, how'er we stray,
True as a star, the smile pursues our way;
The home of thoughtful childhood's mystic tears,
Of earliest Sabbath bells on sinless ears,
Of noonday dreamings under summer trees,
And prayers first murmured at a mother's knees.
Ah! happy he, whose later home as man
Is made where Love first spoke, and Hope began,
Where haunted floors dear footsteps back can give,
And in our Lares all our fathers live.

Constance, or *The Portrait*, Edward Bulwer Lytton

Every pebble left behind to make a trail to us, and our generation, must in the waves of time eventually be tossed to sand, and washed away, or spread to the wind in the spray... or, let's face it, unceremoniously dustpanned with carpet fluff into the black plastic sack flaps of oblivion. It's the story that's important, not the dust.

But when the food in our larder, the sheets in our linen cupboard, the supermarket receipts at the back of our drawers, the hat and wellies at the back door... are all gone, what does tend to hang around in our descendants' everyday lives, and in their view, are - literally - the portraits.

The portraits are the Lares of a house. The household gods. ***In our Lares, all our fathers live***, my great-great-great-grandfather said in his poem *The Portrait*. I love being surrounded by my ancestors on the wall. They are family. My support group. They are keeping an eye on me. They are wanting the best for me. Willing me on. Willing me to succeed in my life and endeavours, and in preserving our home. But there are some whose names I forget. Some whose stories are less familiar to me than those who wrote down their stories. So while I'm writing down my stories, here's a little addendum to help future curators make up the information cards for the portraits that I leave behind in Knebworth House.

In May 2014, while I was away at the Film Festival in Cannes, a giant plywood Pushmi-Pullyu crate arrived at Knebworth House. Attached to it was a copy of Joan Fontaine's Last Will and Testament. It is significant that it was her 'last'. When I'd had the great treat of having Tea with Joan in her beautiful cliffside home in Carmel in 1994, a long paper roll was billowing out of her fax machine onto the carpet as I arrived. She told me she was re-doing her Will and that she'd like to leave me two of her paintings in it. She showed them to

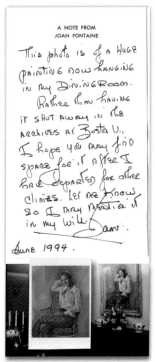

A NOTE FROM
JOAN FONTAINE

This photo is of a Huge painting now hanging in my Dining Room. Rather than having it shut away in the archives at Boston U., I hope you may find space for it after I have departed for other climes. Let me know so I may mention it in my will. Joan.

June 1994.

me. One was a large early 1970s portrait of her seated, wearing orange trousers and a white shirt (that my wife insists is see-through). Joan said I had a house that was big enough to hang it in.

The other was a small wistful close up of Joan at the time she was playing the teenage Lisa Brandt in *Letter From An Unknown Woman* (1948). There were not many 1940s Hollywood stars who could convincingly play both a dreamy teenager and a sophisticated married 30-year old (her true age) in the same movie. *Letter From An Unknown Woman* is not only my favourite film, it was Joan's too. This

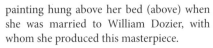

painting hung above her bed (above) when she was married to William Dozier, with whom she produced this masterpiece.

Needless to say, I was bewitched. By both paintings. But that day was too full of magical moments and memories for me to think too much of this princely promise. Joan was, after all, only 76. She was to live another 19 years.

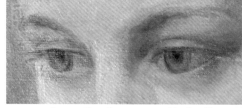

Reading her Will in 2014, I could see that she'd amended this Will with a codicil almost every one of those subsequent 19 years. By the time she died, she'd written out almost everybody previously in it. Joan left some money to her staff, and an entwined lock of her and her sister's childhood hair was to be sent to Olivia De Havilland in Paris. Otherwise everything was to be sold for the benefit of her dogs, and what her dogs did not need could go to the Dogs' Home in Carmel. Everything that is, except two paintings that were to be sent to Knebworth House in England.

That is where they now hang. In the Warburton Room bedroom. To puzzle the future.

Also from California, also arriving at Knebworth in a big plywood Pushmi-Pullyu crate, were a selection of paintings of my daughter Morwenna as Eve in the Garden of Eden by her god-mother Patricia Knop (Pat King). The first was gifted by Pat, and three more were gifted by Pat's daughters Chloe and Gillian after Pat died in 2019. One of these is a matching painting of Morwenna's boyfriend Phil Bush as the Serpent. Not all of these are likely to remain on the walls of

Knebworth House - as Morwenna should have her pick of them - but I am so pleased that there will always be something of my adored mentor and California mom in the house that she told me she found herself in so often in her dreams.

If there's a portrait of me spooking Kneb-worth House visitors in future centuries, I suspect it will be the 2019 one with Martha and the dogs (right), by my supremely talented sister Rosina (left). I hope that, by then, June Mendoza portraits will have become much too valuable not to be sold, and that the pain-fully awkward one of me as an 18-year-old standing on the stairs with my siblings will be long gone. I used to tell my-self that when I

Peter, Henry, Rosina & Richard
by June Mendoza (1980, detail)
All offers considered

was in charge I'd get rid of it. Or have my hair repainted long and straight, as June Mendoza promised to do when she was painting it - not the nasty pudding bowl she left me with for all eternity. Just as well, then, that I've never been in charge. Because June Mendoza may well become the Peter Lely of her day and, who knows, my bob could end up being worth a few bob.

Eighteen is not a good age to be painted. I've known that since, and yet still let my son be painted at that age. I like the Edward Cullen look my sister gave him (right), but Edward is now so far removed from looking like this beautiful pasty fashion-boy that I understand his unease at this being his representa-tion for eternity. I am also fond of the portrait Rosina did of my beautiful pasty fashion daughter, Morwen-

na, at this age (left), but this everyone agrees (except for me) is inappropriate to hang on the staircase, because she could be thought to be wearing a nightie. Where else do you wear a nightie if not the grand staircase of a gothic house?

I am still hoping that one day Martha Fiennes will create one her endlessly randomly responding video canvasses of me above the mantelpiece. Like the mov-ing paintings in Harry Potter. The technology is almost there. I fancy being an ever-present threat to my de-scendants' drawing room parties that I may suddenly take my clothes off and start doing the camel dance.

But I do especially like Rosina's very excellent 2019 portrait. Martha and I are all dressed up in Lutyens' Lytton Chamber. With us are Willow and Zak (Rescues. You know I wouldn't have called them Willow and Zak. I'd have called them Lovisalya Need and Bear... or, having got to know these too, Cleopatra and The Sultan.) Without them, Martha

would probably not have agreed to be in the portrait. It is hard enough to get her to sit down even when not asking her to pose. Putting a dog on the sofa for Martha is the equivalent of putting a biscuit on the cushion (which we also did).

Rosina brilliantly captured this staged moment. I particularly like the little tchotchkes we are surrounded with, each representing something special to us: the magnolia blossom, Martha's Southern United States heritage; the German figurine of a boy reading the newspaper once owned by Martha's grandparents, the Boone family's German and newspaper publishing heritage; the photo of us in our first year of marriage by Jim Cornfield, in a deco frame given to me by Rosemarie Jarski; a little wooden cross made by Edward in an early Design Technology class at the Leys School; the circular wooden table that had belonged to Martha's mother, Gray, and been in the home in Suffolk Virginia where Martha was born; also from Virginia, the Shirley pewter candle holder from Williamsburg; the embroidered pillow marking Morwenna's christening, made by Margaret who worked as a housekeeper at Hartland Abbey; the lanyards from the many events Martha oversaw at Knebworth, including Robbie Williams in 2003 and Sonisphere.

Alongside her wedding ring, Martha is wearing the engagement ring I bought for her with my option fee for my first screenplay *Green For A Season*; the bracelet was given to her on Morwenna's birth by her mother, Gray, and had been her grandmother's; the star-shaped brooch hanging from a necklace was also a gift from Gray; and the pearl earrings a gift from me at the first Christmas of our marriage.

On the dressing table are books and screenplays I have written, alongside DVDs of films that have a significance to me:

Dr Dolittle (1967). The favourite film of my childhood. See Chapter One.

Mildred Pierce (1945). *Stella Dallas* (1937). *Now Voyager* (1942). Hollywood melodramas I studied at university, whose influence is to be found in all my work.

The White Cliffs of Dover (1944). Another of these, but resonant as the story of the daughter of an American newspaper man marrying an English aristocrat. Thank heavens we've not suffered the trials they did, and none of the characters match, but the scene of the gossipy, dismissive West Country aunts will always make me laugh.

Letter From An Unknown Woman (1948). Another of these, but also the best of these. My favourite film, and the root of my Joan Fontaine story.

The novel of the Joan Fontaine film, *From This Day Forward* (1946), "marriage with its hair down and dander up!" Not the best Joan Fontaine film, but Joan is particularly lovely in it, as a young wife who works days, only fleetingly encountering her husband who works nights.

Rebecca (1940). Alfred Hitchcock's masterpiece about a tortured Estate owner with a woman called Rebecca in his past. *"Perfectly lovely. Perfectly perfectly lovely."* *"You thought I loved Rebecca? You thought that?"* The second best Fontaine film.

Walkabout (1971). Another epic influence. Directed by Nicholas Roeg. John Barry score. A.E. Housman poetry. Jenny Agutter. What's not to like?

Bullshot (1983). My favourite comedy. *"The secret formula to London bring."* Although this DVD case is now hidden behind the portrait's frame and not visible.

Red Shoe Diaries (1992-97) & *Lake Consequence* (1993). The TV series and film that have my name on them. Thank you Zalman King.

Un Homme et Une Femme (1966). Reminds me so much of my parents and my youth - not the story, but the style, the beauty, the romance, and above all, the music by Francis Lai.

Before Sunrise (1995). Although post-dating my youth, this film transports me straight back to it, and its fantasies. A stolen moment in time with a beautiful continental girl in a beautiful continental place.

Behind Convent Walls (1978). *The Beast* (1975). Yes, these will confuse future wanderers up the staircase of Knebworth House. Two films by the Polish *'genius who also happened to be a pornographer'* (Wikipedia) Walerian Borowczyk, that are

not my favourite films, or indeed great films. But they are important films to the development of me and of my work. Or at least *The Beast* is. I would have paired it with *Immoral Tales* (1973), but these were the two Borowczyk films that were on my dressing table! They were revelatory films to me in that they depicted sex in the way that my teenage brain saw it, and not how it was depicted in any other film. They counter-intuitively blended gothic sexual fantasy, the beauty and dullness of high art, and in-your-face hyper-realism (what's the deadline for my essay, Mr Brewster?). The censors hated them. So I loved them.

Summer Lovers (1982). Now we're talking. This is the film that Barry Norman called the worst film of 1982. But to me it's the ultimate fantasy movie. I would rather watch this film on a Friday night than any other. Glorious beautiful location. Glorious beautiful people. All at a Mediterranean beach with nothing on. Having a glorious good time. And all to the glorious disco anthem, the Pointer Sisters' *I'm So Excited*. I'm sorry, but that's worth the price of a movie ticket.

And lastly, *Walkabout* again! It's funny that for all the extraordinary care - over two or three years - that my sister took on this painting, she put in two of the same DVDs. In her defence, I do have two *Walkabout* DVDs. I have two copies of a number of my favourite DVDs, because often the better editions came out in America first, on the American standard NTSC (Never Twice the Same Colour). And then, much later, an even better transfer came out in Europe, on the European standard PAL (Pale in All Lights). Now we have Blu-Ray and High Definition, so it's time to buy a third DVD copy of *Walkabout,* which I've recently done. Instead the DVD in the picture should probably be *Out of Africa* (1985) or *Les Enfant Du Paradis* (1945), which vie to be my second favourite film. *Out of Africa* probably pips it. Directed by Sidney Pollack. John Barry score. A.E. Housman poetry. Jenny Agutter... okay not Jenny Agutter, but Meryl Streep. And the best movie 'voice over' since *Letter From An Unknown Woman*. And they don't make love until the third night on safari. In every other screenplay, ever, they would have made love on the second night.

Finally a couple of box sets. The Bob Hope & Bing Crosby *Road To* pictures and the Fred Astaire & Ginger Rogers Collection. These are the music movies for the dreamers of dreams that filled my childhood Christmas evenings - often spent with the portrait's artist, my sister - when the rest of the family were in the drawing room playing Nelson's Eye with the relations. *"Where we're going, why we're going, how can we be sure? I'll lay you 8 to 5 that we'll..."* be staying up for more.

Then, perched on top, are two of my collection of coloured bowler hats, although the ones that make the cut are the black & white ones. I like coloured bowler hats. They represent the Establishment subverted. The mundane made merry. The uniform undone. David Tomlinson in *Bedknobs and Broomsticks*. Marty Feldman in *Sherlock Holmes's Smarter Younger Brother*. Liza Minnelli in *Cabaret*. Henry Lytton Cobbold in his birthday suit at his 50th, asking, "Where are your troubles now?"

INDEX

I only ever talk about myself
even when I talk about other people.

(David Trueba - *Madrid '87* 2011)